PATTERN CLASSIFICATION AND SCENE ANALYSIS

PATTERN CLASSIFICATION AND SCENE ANALYSIS

RICHARD O. DUDA

PETER E. HART

Stanford Research Institute,
Menlo Park, California

A WILEY-INTERSCIENCE PUBLICATION

John Wiley & Sons

New York   London   Sydney   Toronto

Library of Congress Cataloging in Publication Data

Duda, Richard O.
  Pattern classification and scene analysis.

  "A Wiley-interscience publication."
  Includes bibliographical references.
  1. Perceptrons. 2. Statistical decision.
I. Hart, Peter E., joint author. II. Title.
Q327.D83   001.53′3   72-7008

ISBN 0-471-22361-1

Printed in the United States of America

10 9 8 7 6 5 4 3 2 1

to C. A. Rosen

PREFACE

Our purpose in writing this book has been to give a systematic account of major topics in pattern recognition, a field concerned with machine recognition of meaningful regularities in noisy or complex environments. Stimulated by the development of the digital computer, pattern recognition blossomed in the early 1960's and has enjoyed more than a decade of vigorous growth. Contributions to the growth have come from many disciplines, including statistics, communication theory, switching theory, control theory, operations research, biology, psychology, linguistics, and computer science. Readers who sample the literature will soon appreciate the color and vigor that this has lent the field.

This diversity also presents serious problems to anyone writing a book on the subject. No single theory of pattern recognition embraces all of the important topics because each domain of application has unique characteristics that mold and shape the appropriate approach. The most prominent domain-independent theory is classification theory, the subject of Part I of this book. Based on statistical decision theory, it provides formal mathematical procedures for classifying patterns once they have been represented abstractly as vectors.

Attempts to find domain-independent procedures for constructing these vector representations have not yielded generally useful results. Instead, every problem area has acquired a collection of procedures suited to its special characteristics. Of the many areas of interest, the pictorial domain has received by far the most attention. Furthermore, work in this area has progressed from picture classification to picture analysis and description. Part II of this book is devoted to a systematic presentation of these topics in visual scene analysis.

Since the theories and techniques of pattern recognition are largely mathematical in nature, we should say something about the level of mathematical rigor in our exposition. In a word, it is low. We have been far more concerned with providing insight and understanding than with establishing rigorous mathematical foundations. The presence of many illustrative examples, plausibility arguments, and discussions of the behavior of solutions reflects this concern. Concomitantly, we have avoided the use of measure theory, and we have tried to avoid preoccupation with such fine points as modes of convergence for sequences of random variables, justification for the use of delta functions, and possibilities of pathological cases. We do assume general knowledge of a number of basic topics in applied mathematics, including probability theory and linear algebra; an acquaintance with Fourier transforms would also be helpful in Chapter 8. The required mathematical maturity is that of a typical first-year graduate student in computer science, electrical engineering, or statistics.

Since pattern recognition appears to be a rather specialized topic, it is perhaps worthwhile to draw attention to the pedagogic flexibility of a course on the subject. Drawing as it does from several branches of mathematics as well as the other disciplines we mentioned, pattern recognition provides a nearly ideal vehicle for the presentation of a variety of topics within a single framework. Students with no long-term interest in pattern recognition per se are still likely to acquire knowledge and develop skills that will serve them well in other settings.

We have taught graduate courses based on the material in this book at the University of California, Berkeley, and at Stanford University. Each part of the book can be covered moderately well in independent, one-quarter, three-hour courses, and quite thoroughly in a one-semester course. For an abridged treatment, we recommend selecting a few topics from most of the chapters in preference to treating some chapters thoroughly and others not at all. As always, the interests of the instructor must dictate the final choice of material.

We also hope that this book will prove useful to the practicing professional, and to this end we have tried to make the material in it as accessible as possible. We have taken care to use standard notation whenever we could, and have included a comprehensive index. Each chapter concludes with bibliographical and historical remarks and a hopefully useful list of references. Although the lengths of these lists perhaps lend the book an air of scholarliness, the published literature is too extensive to allow us to be complete, and we make no claims in this regard.

While writing this book we benefitted from associations with many individuals and organizations. We would like first to thank the Information Systems Branch of the Office of Naval Research for its sponsorship under Contract N0014-68-C-0266. The Department of Electrical Engineering and Computer Sciences at Berkeley and the Computer Science Department at Stanford afforded us opportunities to test this material in the classroom. The Artificial Intelligence Center of Stanford Research Institute, under the enthusiastic leadership of Dr. Charles A. Rosen and Dr. Bertram Raphael, provided an ideal environment in which to work. Although we cannot mention everyone who has helped us with their comments, we would like especially to thank Dr. Nils J. Nilsson for his many suggestions for improving the manuscript. In addition, we feel indebted to Dr. Thomas O. Binford, Dr. Thomas M. Cover, Mr. Claude L. Fennema, Dr. Gabriel F. Groner, Mr. David J. Hall, Dr. Martin E. Hellman, Dr. Michael A. Kassler, and Dr. John H. Munson for their thoughtful comments. We want also to thank Dr. Richard C. Singleton for his work in producing the pictorial examples in Chapter 8. Finally, it is a pleasure to acknowledge the cheerful help of Katharine L. Spence in typing several drafts of the manuscript.

Menlo Park, California   RICHARD O. DUDA
                                            PETER E. HART

CONTENTS

Part I PATTERN CLASSIFICATION

1 INTRODUCTION   **1**

1.1 Machine Perception   1
1.2 An Example   2
1.3 The Classification Model   4
1.4 The Descriptive Approach   5
1.5 Summary of the Book by Chapters   6
1.6 Bibliographical Remarks   7

2 BAYES DECISION THEORY   **10**

2.1 Introduction   10
2.2 Bayes Decision Theory—The Continuous Case   13
2.3 Two-Category Classification   15
2.4 Minimum-Error-Rate Classification   16
2.5 Classifiers, Discriminant Functions and Decision Surfaces   17
    2.5.1 The Multicategory Case   17
    2.5.2 The Two-Category Case   20
2.6 Error Probabilities and Integrals   20
2.7 The Normal Density   22
    2.7.1 The Univariate Normal Density   22
    2.7.2 The Multivariate Normal Density   23
2.8 Discriminant Functions for the Normal Density   24
    2.8.1 Case 1: $\Sigma_i = \sigma^2 I$ 26
    2.8.2 Case 2: $\Sigma_i = \Sigma$ 27
    2.8.3 Case 3: Σ_i Arbitrary   30
2.9 Bayesian Decision Theory—The Discrete Case   31
2.10 Independent Binary Features   32
2.11 Compound Bayes Decision Theory and Context   34

2.12 Remarks   35
2.13 Bibliographical and Historical Remarks   36
     Problems   39

3 PARAMETER ESTIMATION AND SUPERVISED   44
     LEARNING

3.1 Parameter Estimation and Supervised Learning   44
3.2 Maximum Likelihood Estimation   45
     3.2.1 The General Principle   45
     3.2.2 The Multivariate Normal Case: Unknown Mean   47
     3.2.3 The General Multivariate Normal Case   48
3.3 The Bayes Classifier   49
     3.3.1 The Class-Conditional Densities   50
     3.3.2 The Parameter Distribution   51
3.4 Learning the Mean of a Normal Density   52
     3.4.1 The Univariate Case: $p(\mu \mid \mathcal{X})$ 52
     3.4.2 The Univariate Case: $p(x \mid \mathcal{X})$ 55
     3.4.3 The Multivariate Case   55
3.5 General Bayesian Learning   57
3.6 Sufficient Statistics   59
3.7 Sufficient Statistics and the Exponential Family   62
3.8 Problems of Dimensionality   66
     3.8.1 An Unexpected Problem   66
     3.8.2 Estimating a Covariance Matrix   67
     3.8.3 The Capacity of a Separating Plane   69
     3.8.4 The Problem-Average Error Rate   70
3.9 Estimating the Error Rate   73
3.10 Bibliographical and Historical Remarks   76
     Problems   80

4 NONPARAMETRIC TECHNIQUES   85

4.1 Introduction   85
4.2 Density Estimation   85
4.3 Parzen Windows   88
     4.3.1 General Discussion   88
     4.3.2 Convergence of the Mean   90
     4.3.3 Convergence of the Variance   91
     4.3.4 Two Examples   91
4.4 k-Nearest Neighbor Estimation   95

4.5   Estimation of A Posteriori Probabilities   97
4.6   The Nearest-Neighbor Rule   98
      4.6.1   General Considerations   98
      4.6.2   Convergence of the Nearest-Neighbor   99
      4.6.3   Error Rate for the Nearest-Neighbor Rule   100
      4.6.4   Error Bounds   101
4.7   The *k*-Nearest-Neighbor Rule   103
4.8   Approximations by Series Expansions   105
4.9   Approximations for the Binary Case   108
      4.9.1   The Rademacher-Walsh Expansion   108
      4.9.2   The Bahadur-Lazarsfeld Expansion   111
      4.9.3   The Chow Expansion   113
4.10 Fisher's Linear Discriminant   114
4.11 Multiple Discriminant Analysis   118
4.12 Bibliographical and Historical Remarks   121
      Problems   126

5   LINEAR DISCRIMINANT FUNCTIONS   130

5.1   Introduction   130
5.2   Linear Discriminant Functions and Decision Surfaces   131
      5.2.1   The Two-Category Case   131
      5.2.2   The Multicategory Case   132
5.3   Generalized Linear Discriminant Functions   134
5.4   The Two-Category Linearly-Separable Case   138
      5.4.1   Geometry and Terminology   138
      5.4.2   Gradient Descent Procedures   140
5.5   Minimizing the Perceptron Criterion Function   141
      5.5.1   The Perceptron Criterion Function   141
      5.5.2   Convergence Proof for Single-Sample Correction   142
      5.5.3   Some Direct Generalizations   146
5.6   Relaxation Procedures   147
      5.6.1   The Descent Algorithm   147
      5.6.2   Convergence Proof   148
5.7   Nonseparable Behavior   149
5.8   Minimum Squared Error Procedures   151
      5.8.1   Minimum Squared Error and the Pseudoinverse   151
      5.8.2   Relation to Fisher's Linear Discriminant   152
      5.8.3   Asymptotic Approximation to an Optimal Discriminant   154
      5.8.4   The Widrow-Hoff Procedure   155
      5.8.5   Stochastic Approximation Methods   156

5.9	The Ho-Kashyap Procedures	159
	5.9.1 The Descent Procedure	159
	5.9.2 Convergence Proof	161
	5.9.3 Nonseparable Behavior	163
	5.9.4 Some Related Procedures	163
5.10	Linear Programming Procedures	166
	5.10.1 Linear Programming	166
	5.10.2 The Linearly Separable Case	167
	5.10.3 Minimizing the Perceptron Criterion Function	168
	5.10.4 Remarks	169
5.11	The Method of Potential Functions	172
5.12	Multicategory Generalizations	174
	5.12.1 Kesler's Construction	174
	5.12.2 The Fixed-Increment Rule	176
	5.12.3 Generalization for MSE Procedures	177
5.13	Bibliographical and Historical Remarks	179
	Problems	186

6 UNSUPERVISED LEARNING AND CLUSTERING 189

6.1	Introduction	189
6.2	Mixture Densities and Identifiability	190
6.3	Maximum Likelihood Estimates	192
6.4	Application to Normal Mixtures	193
	6.4.1 Case 1: Unknown Mean Vectors	194
	6.4.2 An Example	195
	6.4.3 Case 2: All Parameters Unknown	198
	6.4.4 A Simple Approximate Procedure	201
6.5	Unsupervised Bayesian Learning	203
	6.5.1 The Bayes Classifier	203
	6.5.2 Learning the Parameter Vector	204
	6.5.3 An Example	207
	6.5.4 Decision-Directed Approximations	210
6.6	Data Description and Clustering	211
6.7	Similarity Measures	213
6.8	Criterion Functions for Clustering	217
	6.8.1 The Sum-of-Squared-Error Criterion	217
	6.8.2 Related Minimum Variance Criteria	219
	6.8.3 Scattering Criteria	221
	6.8.3.1 The Scatter Matrices	221

6.8.3.2   The Trace Criterion   222
6.8.3.3   The Determinant Criterion   222
6.8.3.4   Invariant Criteria   223
6.9 Iterative Optimization   225
6.10 Hierarchical Clustering   228
      6.10.1   Definitions   228
      6.10.2   Agglomerative Hierarchical Clustering   230
                6.10.2.1   The Nearest-Neighbor Algorithm   233
                6.10.2.2   The Furthest-Neighbor Algorithm   233
                6.10.2.3   Compromises   235
      6.10.3   Stepwise-Optimal Hierarchical Clustering   235
      6.10.4   Hierarchical Clustering and Induced Metrics   236
6.11 Graph Theoretic Methods   237
6.12 The Problem of Validity   239
6.13 Low-Dimensional Representations and Multidimensional Scaling 243
6.14 Clustering and Dimensionality Reduction   246
6.15 Bibliographical and Historical Remarks   248
      Problems   256

Part II SCENE ANALYSIS

7 REPRESENTATION AND INITIAL   263
   SIMPLIFICATIONS

7.1 Introduction   263
7.2 Representations   264
7.3 Spatial Differentiation   267
7.4 Spatial Smoothing   272
7.5 Template Matching   276
      7.5.1   Template Matching—Metric Interpretation   276
      7.5.2   Template Matching—Statistical Interpretation   282
7.6 Region Analysis   284
      7.6.1   Basic Concepts   284
      7.6.2   Extensions   288
7.7 Contour Following   290
7.8 Bibliographical and Historical Remarks   293
      Problems   297

8 THE SPATIAL FREQUENCY DOMAIN   298

8.1 Introduction   298
8.2 The Sampling Theorem   302
8.3 Template Matching and the Convolution Theorem   305
8.4 Spatial Filtering   308
8.5 Mean Square Estimation   318
8.6 Bibliographical and Historical Remarks   322
     Problems   325

9 DESCRIPTIONS OF LINE AND SHAPE   327

9.1 Introduction   327
9.2 Line Description   328
     9.2.1 Minimum-Squared-Error Line Fitting   328
     9.2.2 Eigenvector Line Fitting   332
     9.2.3 Line Fitting by Clustering   335
     9.2.4 Line Segmentation   337
     9.2.5 Chain Encoding   339
9.3 Shape Description   341
     9.3.1 Topological Properties   342
     9.3.2 Linear Properties   345
     9.3.3 Metric Properties   348
     9.3.4 Descriptions Based on Irregularities   352
     9.3.5 The Skeleton of a Figure   356
     9.3.6 Analytic Descriptions of Shape   362
     9.3.7 Integral Geometric Descriptions   367
9.4 Bibliographical and Historical Remarks   372
     Problems   377

10 PERSPECTIVE TRANSFORMATIONS   379

10.1 Introduction   379
10.2 Modelling Picture Taking   380
10.3 The Perspective Transformation in Homogeneous Coordinates 382
10.4 Perspective Transformations With Two Reference Frames   386
10.5 Illustrative Applications   392
      10.5.1 Camera Calibration   392
      10.5.2 Object Location   393
      10.5.3 Vertical Lines: Perspective Distortion   394
      10.5.4 Horizontal Lines and Vanishing Points   396

10.6 Stereoscopic Perception   398
10.7 Bibliographical and Historical Remarks   401
       Problems   404

11 PROJECTIVE INVARIANTS   405

11.1 Introduction   405
11.2 The Cross Ratio   407
11.3 Two-Dimensional Projective Coordinates   411
11.4 The Inter-Lens Line   414
11.5 An Orthogonal Projection Approximation   418
11.6 Object Reconstruction   421
11.7 Bibliographical and Historical Remarks   422
       Problems   424

12 DESCRIPTIVE METHODS IN SCENE ANALYSIS   425

12.1 Introduction   425
12.2 Descriptive Formalisms   426
     12.2.1 Syntactic Descriptions   426
     12.2.2 Relational Graphs   434
12.3 Three-Dimensional Models   436
12.4 The Analysis of Polyhedra   441
     12.4.1 Line Semantics   442
     12.4.2 Grouping Regions into Objects   449
     12.4.3 Monocular Determination of Three-Dimensional
             Structure   456
12.5 Bibliographical and Historical Remarks   462
       Problems   465

AUTHOR INDEX   467

SUBJECT INDEX   472

Part I

PATTERN CLASSIFICATION

Chapter 1

INTRODUCTION

1.1 MACHINE PERCEPTION

Since the advent of the digital computer there has been a constant effort to expand the domain of computer applications. Some of the motivation for this effort comes from important practical needs to find more efficient ways of doing things. Some of the motivation comes from the sheer challenge of building or programming a machine to do things that machines have never done before. Both of these motives are found in that area of artificial intelligence that we shall call machine perception.

At present, the ability of machines to perceive their environment is very limited. A variety of transducers are available for converting light, sound, temperature, etc., to electrical signals. When the environment is carefully controlled and the signals have a simple interpretation, as is the case with the standard computer input devices, the perceptual problems become trivial. But as we move beyond having a computer read punched cards or magnetic tapes to having it read hand-printed characters or analyze biomedical photographs, we move from problems of sensing the data to much more difficult problems of interpreting the data.

The apparent ease with which vertebrates and even insects perform perceptual tasks is at once encouraging and frustrating. Psychological and physiological studies have given us a great many interesting facts about animal perception, but no understanding sufficient for us to duplicate their performance with a computer. The problem area has a certain unique fascination to it because perception is something everyone experiences but no one really understands. Introspection has not proved as helpful in discovering the nature of perception as one might hope, apparently because most everyday perceptual processes are carried out below the conscious level. Paradoxically, we are all expert at perception, but none of us knows much about it.

The lack of a complete theory of perception has not prevented people from trying to solve more modest problems. Many of these involve pattern

1

classification—the assignment of a physical object or event to one of several prespecified categories. Extensive study of classification problems has led to an abstract mathematical model that provides the theoretical basis for classifier design. Of course, in any specific application one ultimately must come to grips with the special characteristics of the problem at hand. Of the various problem areas, the domain of pictorial problems has received by far the most attention. The purpose of this book is to give a systematic account of those principles of pattern classification and those techniques of pictorial scene analysis that seem to have the widest applicability and interest.

1.2   AN EXAMPLE

To illustrate some of the types of problems we shall address, let us consider the following imaginary and somewhat fanciful example. Suppose that a lumber mill producing assorted hardwoods wants to automate the process of sorting finished lumber according to species of tree. As a pilot project, it is decided to try first to distinguish birch lumber from ash lumber using optical sensing. A system to perform this very specific task might well have the form shown in Figure 1.1. The camera takes a picture of the lumber and passes the picture on to a *feature extractor*, whose purpose is to reduce the data by measuring certain "features" or "properties" that distinguish pictures of birch lumber from pictures of ash lumber. These features (or, more precisely, the values of these features) are then passed to a *classifier* that evaluates the evidence presented and makes a final decision about the lumber type.

   Let us consider how the feature extractor and classifier might be designed. Suppose somebody at the lumber mill tells us that birch is often lighter colored than ash. Then brightness becomes an obvious feature, and we might attempt to classify the lumber merely by seeing whether or not the average brightness x exceeds some critical value x_0. To choose x_0, we could obtain some samples of the different types of wood, make brightness measurements, and inspect the results. Suppose that we do this, and obtain the histograms

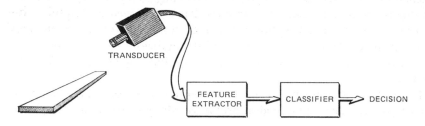

FIGURE 1.1.   A pattern classification system.

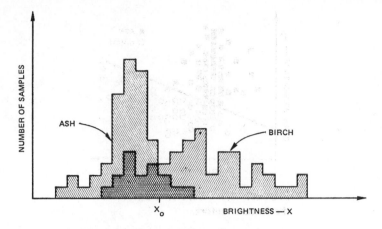

FIGURE 1.2. Histograms for the brightness feature.

shown in Figure 1.2. These histograms bear out the statement that birch is usually lighter than ash, but it is clear that this single criterion is not infallible. No matter how we choose x_0, we can not reliably separate birch from ash by brightness alone.

In our search for other features, we might try to capitalize on the observation that ash typically has a more prominent grain pattern than birch. This feature is much more difficult to measure than average brightness, but it is reasonable to assume that we can obtain a measure of grain prominence from the magnitude and frequency of occurrence of light-to-dark transitions in the picture. Now we have two features for classifying lumber, the brightness x_1 and the grain prominence x_2. The feature extractor has thus reduced each picture to a point or *feature vector* **x** in a two-dimensional feature space, where

$$\mathbf{x} = \begin{bmatrix} x_1 \\ x_2 \end{bmatrix}.$$

Our problem now is to partition the feature space into two regions, where all the points in one region correspond to birch, and all points in the other correspond to ash. Suppose that we measure the feature vectors for our samples and obtain the scattering of points shown in Figure 1.3. This plot suggests the following rule for classifying the data: Classify the lumber as ash if its feature vector falls above the line AB, and as birch otherwise.

While this rule appears to do a good job of separating our samples, we have no guarantee that it will perform as well on new samples. It would certainly be prudent to obtain some more samples and see how many are

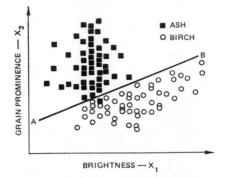

FIGURE 1.3. Scatter diagram for the feature vectors.

correctly classified. This suggests that our problem has a statistical component, and that perhaps we should look for a classification procedure that minimizes the probability of error.

Without forgetting this idea, we should remember that we chose a simple problem for a pilot project. A more realistic problem might involve sorting many different classes of lumber. To separate oak from birch and ash, we might well require less obvious features, such as "straightness-of-grain." With more categories and more features, the graphical approach to designing the classifier will probably have to be abandoned. To proceed further, we shall need whatever theoretical help we can get.

1.3 THE CLASSIFICATION MODEL

The preceding example contains many of the elements of the most commonly used abstract model for pattern recognition, the classification model. This model contains three parts: a transducer, a feature extractor, and a classifier The transducer senses the input and converts it into a form suitable for machine processing. The feature extractor (also called the receptor, property filter, attribute detector, or preprocessor) extracts presumably relevant information from the input data. The classifier uses this information to assign the input data to one of a finite number of categories.

A discussion of transducer specification or design lies outside the province of this book. However, we shall be concerned with both feature extraction and classification. From a theoretical viewpoint, the line between these topics is arbitrary. An ideal feature extractor would make the job of the classifier trivial, and an omnipotent classifier would not need the help of a feature extractor. The distinction is forced upon us for practical, not theoretical reasons, but the distinction is important nevertheless.

Generally speaking, the problem of feature extraction is much more problem dependent than the problem of classification. A good feature extractor for sorting lumber would probably be of little use for identifying fingerprints or classifying photomicrographs of blood cells. Nevertheless, a substantial body of techniques has been developed for extracting useful information from pictures. Part II of this book is devoted to an exposition of these techniques and their properties.

The problem of classification is basically one of partitioning the feature space into regions, one region for each category. Ideally, one would like to arrange this partitioning so that none of the decisions is ever wrong. When this cannot be done, one would like to minimize the probability of error, or, if some errors are more costly than others, the average cost of errors. In this case, the problem of classification becomes a problem in statistical decision theory, a subject that has many applications to pattern classification. Part I of this book is concerned with these and related topics in classification theory.

1.4   THE DESCRIPTIVE APPROACH

There are many problems in pattern recognition and machine perception for which the classification model is clearly inappropriate. For example, in analyzing a picture of bubble-chamber particle tracks, one wants a description, rather than just a classification, of the picture. Such a description should contain information about both the individual parts of the picture and about the relations among the parts. Ideally, it should directly reflect the structure present in the original scene.

Consider, for example, the simple scene shown in Figure 1.4. It is possible that a simple classification such as "office scene" or "telephone present" would be adequate for some purposes. A more complete analysis would include an identification of all the major objects present—the telephone, note pad, cup, pencils, eraser, etc. An even more complete analysis would indicate the relations between these objects, and might result in a description such as "(Two pencils on top of a pad) in front of (a cup to the left of (an eraser in front of a telephone))."

The problem of analyzing a visual scene and producing a structural description has proved to be quite difficult. A generally accepted formalization of the problem, analogous to the classification model, has yet to emerge from the work that has been done to date. Attempts have been made to borrow concepts from the theory of formal languages and to produce a linguistic model for scene analysis. Here the scene is viewed as a statement in a language whose grammar defines the allowed structural relations. With

FIGURE 1.4.   A simple scene.

this formulation, scene analysis is viewed as the process of using a picture grammar to parse the scene, producing a description of the scene as a composition of related subscenes.

The linguistic model does not exhaust the ways of using known structural relations among the elements of a picture to guide its analysis and produce a useful description. Some of the most interesting procedures that have been developed are ad hoc and heuristic; a unifying conceptual framework encompassing all of these methods has not yet been developed. The procedures themselves can be described, however, and this general topic of descriptive approaches to scene analysis concludes Part II.

1.5   SUMMARY OF THE BOOK BY CHAPTERS

The orientation of Part I of this book is primarily statistical. Chapter 2 states the classification problem in decision-theoretic terms, and derives the general form for an optimal classifier. This solution is obtained under the assumption that all of the probability distributions involved are known. The remainder of Part I is concerned with ways of proceeding when the probabilistic structure is not known.

In Chapter 3 we assume that everything is known except for some parameters of the distributions. Both maximum likelihood and Bayesian procedures for estimating parameters from samples are described. If none of the standard ways of parameterizing unknown distributions is suitable, one can resort to nonparametric techniques. These procedures, which are discussed in Chapter 4, exchange the need for knowledge of the forms of the distributions for the need for a large number of samples.

In Chapter 5 we parameterize the classifier and study ways of using samples to determine the classifier directly. These techniques have their origin in Fisher's linear discriminant, and include the well known perceptron and relaxation procedures, minimum-squared-error methods, stochastic approximation, the method of potential functions, and linear programming techniques. Chapter 6 concludes Part I with a discussion of various techniques for unsupervised learning and clustering.

Chapter 7 begins Part II with a discussion of procedures for representing pictures, and for performing such basic operations as sharpening, smoothing, template matching, and partitioning a picture into homogeneous regions. Chapter 8 develops the concept of spatial filtering, and interprets some of these operations in the frequency domain. Chapter 9 is concerned with a great variety of procedures for describing lines and shapes in pictures. Topological, linear, and metric properties of shape are described, together with a number of descriptive techniques based on these properties.

Chapters 10 and 11 present important mathematical background relevant to pictures of three-dimensional objects. Chapter 10 develops the equations for perspective transformation, and shows how they can be usefully employed in scene analysis. Chapter 11 treats the subject of projective invariants, quantities that are the same in different pictures of the same object. Finally, Chapter 12 discusses some of the more important contemporary approaches to the difficult problem of completely analyzing visual scenes.

1.6 BIBLIOGRAPHICAL REMARKS

The published literature on pattern classification and scene analysis has grown to the point where even specialized bibliographies can contain hundreds of references. The references that we give at the end of each chapter hopefully will provide the reader with some historical perspective and a good starting point for further study. Additional guidance can be obtained from other texts and from a number of valuable survey articles.

For a brief overview that treats pattern recognition as one topic in artificial intelligence, the influential article by Minsky (1961) is highly recommended. Nagy (1968) provides an excellent survey of work done using the classification model. The text by Nilsson (1965) provides an exceptionally clear treatment of classification procedures. A lucid and more recent survey of these procedures is given by Ho and Agrawala (1968). Levine (1969) gives a comprehensive survey of the techniques that have been used to extract features from pictures. The general subject of automatic picture processing is well surveyed by Hawkins (1970), and is systematically treated in the scholarly text by Rosenfeld (1969).

There are many interesting subject areas that are related to this book but beyond its scope. Readers interested in image enhancement and picture coding should be aware of the survey by Huang, Schreiber and Tretiak (1971). Those interested in the fascinating area of human and animal perception will find the surveys by Kolers (1968) and Gose (1969) most useful. Those interested in philosophical issues will find the books by Watanabe (1969) and Bongard (1970) thought provoking. Finally, those interested in the practical applications of all of this theory will find a wealth of references in the literature survey by Stevens (1970).

REFERENCES

1. Bongard, M., *Pattern Recognition* (Spartan Books, Washington, D.C., 1970).

2. Gose, E. E., "Introduction to biological and mechanical pattern recognition," in *Methodologies of Pattern Recognition*, pp. 203–252, S. Watanabe, ed. (Academic Press, New York, 1968).

3. Hawkins, J. K., "Image processing principles and techniques," in *Advances in Information Systems, Vol. 3*, pp. 113–214, J. T. Tou, ed. (Plenum Press, New York and London, 1970).

4. Ho, Y. C. and A. Agrawala, "On pattern classification algorithms: introduction and survey," *Proc. IEEE*, **56,** 2101–2114 (December 1968).

5. Huang, T. S., W. F. Schreiber, and O. J. Tretiak, "Image Processing," *Proc. IEEE*, **59,** 1586–1609 (November 1971).

6. Kolers, P. A., "Some psychological aspects of pattern recognition," in *Recognizing Patterns*, pp. 4–61, P. A. Kolers and M. Eden, eds. (MIT Press, Cambridge, Massachusetts, 1968).

7. Levine, M.D., "Feature extraction: a survey," *Proc. IEEE*, **57,** 1391–1407 (August 1969).

8. Minsky, M., "Steps toward artificial intelligence," *Proc. IRE*, **49,** 8–30 (January 1961); also in *Computers and Thought*, pp. 406–450, E. A. Feigenbaum and J. Feldman, eds. (McGraw-Hill, New York, 1963).

9. Nagy, G., "State of the art in pattern recognition," *Proc. IEEE*, **56**, 836–862 (May 1968).

10. Nilsson, N. J., *Learning Machines* (McGraw-Hill, New York, 1965).

11. Rosenfeld, A., *Picture Processing by Computer* (Academic Press, New York, 1969).

12. Stevens, M. E., "Research and development in the computer and information sciences. Volume 1. Information acquisition, sensing, and input—a selective literature review," National Bureau of Standards Monograph 113, Vol. 1 (March 1970).

13. Watanabe, M. S., *Knowing and Guessing* (John Wiley, New York, 1969).

Chapter 2

BAYES DECISION THEORY

2.1 INTRODUCTION

Bayes decision theory is a fundamental statistical approach to the problem of pattern classification. This approach is based on the assumption that the decision problem is posed in probabilistic terms, and that all of the relevant probability values are known. In this chapter we develop the fundamentals of this theory, and show how it can be viewed as being simply a formalization of common-sense procedures; in subsequent chapters we will consider the problems that arise when the probabilistic structure is not completely known.

While we will give a quite general, abstract development of Bayes decision theory in Section 2.2, we begin our discussion with a specific example. Let us reconsider the hypothetical problem posed in Chapter 1 of designing a classifier to separate two kinds of lumber, ash and birch. Suppose that an observer watching lumber emerge from the mill finds it so hard to predict what type will emerge next that the sequence of types of lumber appears to be random. Using decision-theoretic terminology, we say that as each piece of lumber emerges, nature is in one or the other of the two possible states: either the lumber is ash or the lumber is birch. We let ω denote the *state of nature*, with $\omega = \omega_1$ for ash and $\omega = \omega_2$ for birch. Because the state of nature is so unpredictable, we consider ω to be a random variable.

If the mill produced as much ash as birch, we would say that the next piece of lumber is equally likely to be ash or birch. More generally, we assume that there is some *a priori probability* $P(\omega_1)$ that the next piece is ash, and some a priori probability $P(\omega_2)$ that it is birch. These a priori probabilities reflect our prior knowledge of how likely we are to see ash or birch before

10

the lumber actually appears. It goes without saying that $P(\omega_1)$ and $P(\omega_2)$ are nonnegative and sum to one.*

Suppose for a moment that we were forced to make a decision about the type of lumber that will appear next without being allowed to see it. The only information we are allowed to use is the value of the a priori probabilities. If a decision must be made with so little information, it seems reasonable to use the following *decision rule:* Decide ω_1 if $P(\omega_1) > P(\omega_2)$; otherwise decide ω_2.

This may seem like a strange procedure, in that we always make the same decision even though we know that both types of lumber will appear. How well it works depends upon the values of the a priori probabilities. If $P(\omega_1)$ is very much greater than $P(\omega_2)$, our decision in favor of ω_1 will be right most of the time. If $P(\omega_1) = P(\omega_2)$, we have only a fifty-fifty chance of being right. In general, the probability of error is the smaller of $P(\omega_1)$ and $P(\omega_2)$, and we shall see later that under these conditions no other decision rule can yield a smaller probability of error.

In most circumstances, one is not asked to make decisions with so little evidence. In our example, we can use the brightness measurement x as evidence. Different samples of lumber will yield different brightness readings, and it is natural to express this variability in probabilistic terms; we consider x to be a continuous random variable whose distribution depends on the state of nature. Let $p(x \mid \omega_j)$ be the *state-conditional probability density function* for x, the probability density function for x given that the state of nature is ω_j. Then the difference between $p(x \mid \omega_1)$ and $p(x \mid \omega_2)$ describes the difference in brightness between ash and birch (see Figure 2.1).

Suppose that we know both the a priori probabilities $P(\omega_j)$ and the conditional densities $p(x \mid \omega_j)$. Suppose further that we measure the brightness of a piece of lumber and discover the value of x. How does this measurement influence our attitude concerning the true state of nature? The answer to this question is provided by *Bayes Rule:*

$$P(\omega_j \mid x) = \frac{p(x \mid \omega_j)P(\omega_j)}{p(x)}, \tag{1}$$

where

$$p(x) = \sum_{j=1}^{2} p(x \mid \omega_j)P(\omega_j). \tag{2}$$

Bayes rule shows how observing the value of x changes the a priori probability $P(\omega_j)$ to the *a posteriori* probability $P(\omega_j \mid x)$. The variation of $P(\omega_j \mid x)$ with x is illustrated in Figure 2.2 for the case $P(\omega_1) = 2/3$ and $P(\omega_2) = 1/3$.

---

* Regarding notation, we generally use an upper-case P to denote a probability mass function and a lower-case p to denote a probability density function. Probability density functions are nonnegative and integrate to one.

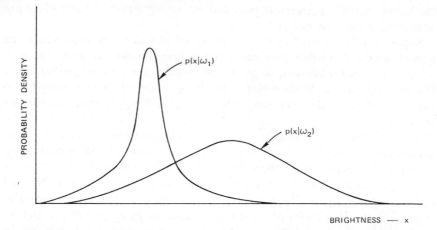

FIGURE 2.1.   Hypothetical class-conditional probability density functions.

If we have an observation x for which $P(\omega_1 \mid x)$ is greater than $P(\omega_2 \mid x)$, we would be naturally inclined to decide that the true state of nature is ω_1. Similarly, if $P(\omega_2 \mid x)$ is greater than $P(\omega_1 \mid x)$, we would be inclined to choose ω_2. To justify this procedure, let us calculate the probability of error whenever we make a decision. Whenever we observe a particular x,

$$P(\text{error} \mid x) = \begin{cases} P(\omega_1 \mid x) & \text{if we decide } \omega_2 \\ P(\omega_2 \mid x) & \text{if we decide } \omega_1. \end{cases}$$

Clearly, in every instance in which we observe the same value for x, we can minimize the probability of error by deciding ω_1 if $P(\omega_1 \mid x) > P(\omega_2 \mid x)$, and ω_2 if $P(\omega_2 \mid x) > P(\omega_1 \mid x)$. Of course, we may never observe exactly the same value of x twice. Will this rule minimize the average probability of

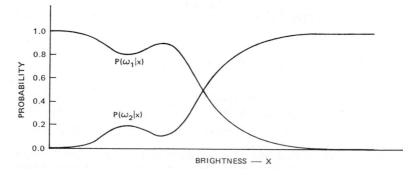

FIGURE 2.2.   A posteriori probabilities for $P(\omega_1) = \frac{2}{3}$, $P(\omega_2) = \frac{1}{3}$.

error? Yes, because the average probability of error is given by

$$P(\text{error}) = \int_{-\infty}^{\infty} P(\text{error, } x) \, dx$$

$$= \int_{-\infty}^{\infty} P(\text{error} \mid x) p(x) \, dx,$$

and if for every x, $P(\text{error} \mid x)$ is as small as possible, the integral must be as small as possible. Thus we have justified the following *Bayes decision rule* for minimizing the probability of error:

Decide ω_1 if $P(\omega_1 \mid x) > P(\omega_2 \mid x)$;   otherwise decide ω_2.

This form of the decision rule emphasizes the role of the a posteriori probabilities. By using Eq. (1), we can express the rule in terms of the conditional and a priori probabilities. Note that $p(x)$ in Eq. (1) is unimportant as far as making a decision is concerned. It is basically just a scale factor that assures us that $P(\omega_1 \mid x) + P(\omega_2 \mid x) = 1$. By eliminating this scale factor, we obtain the following completely equivalent decision rule:

Decide ω_1 if $p(x \mid \omega_1) P(\omega_1) > p(x \mid \omega_2) P(\omega_2)$;   otherwise decide ω_2.

Some additional insight can be obtained by considering a few special cases. If for some x, $p(x \mid \omega_1) = p(x \mid \omega_2)$, then that particular observation gives us no information about the state of nature; in this case, the decision hinges entirely on the a priori probabilities. On the other hand, if $P(\omega_1) = P(\omega_2)$, then the states of nature are equally likely a priori; in this case the decision is based entirely on $p(x \mid \omega_j)$, the *likelihood* of ω_j with respect to x. In general, both of these factors are important in making a decision, and the Bayes decision rule combines them to achieve the minimum probability of error.

2.2 BAYES DECISION THEORY— THE CONTINUOUS CASE

We shall now formalize the ideas just considered, and shall generalize them in four ways:

(1) We shall allow the use of more than one feature.
(2) We shall allow more than two states of nature.
(3) We shall allow actions other than deciding on the state of nature.
(4) We shall introduce a loss function more general than probability of error.

These generalizations and their attendant notational complexities should not be allowed to obscure the fact that things are basically much the same as they were in our simple example. Allowing the use of more than one feature merely requires replacing the scalar x by the *feature vector* $\mathbf{x}$. Allowing more than two states of nature provides us with a useful generalization for a small notational expense. Allowing actions other than classification primarily allows the possibility of rejection, i.e., of refusing to make a decision in close cases; this is a useful option if being indecisive is not too costly. The loss function states exactly how costly each action is. In theory, it also lets us treat situations in which some kinds of mistakes are more costly than others, although most of the nice analytical results are obtained for the case where all errors are equally costly. With this as a preamble, let us begin the formal treatment.

Let $\Omega = \{\omega_1, \ldots, \omega_s\}$ be the finite set of s states of nature and $A = \{\alpha_1, \ldots, \alpha_a\}$ be the finite set of a possible actions. Let $\lambda(\alpha_i \mid \omega_j)$ be the loss incurred for taking action α_i when the state of nature is ω_j. Let the feature vector $\mathbf{x}$ be a d-component vector-valued random variable, and let $p(\mathbf{x} \mid \omega_j)$ be the state-conditional probability density function for $\mathbf{x}$, the probability density function for $\mathbf{x}$ conditioned on ω_j being the state of nature. Finally, let $P(\omega_j)$ be the a priori probability that nature is in state ω_j. Then the a posteriori probability $P(\omega_j \mid \mathbf{x})$ can be computed from $p(\mathbf{x} \mid \omega_j)$ by Bayes rule:

$$P(\omega_j \mid \mathbf{x}) = \frac{p(\mathbf{x} \mid \omega_j)P(\omega_j)}{p(\mathbf{x})}, \tag{3}$$

where

$$p(\mathbf{x}) = \sum_{j=1}^{s} p(\mathbf{x} \mid \omega_j)P(\omega_j). \tag{4}$$

Suppose that we observe a particular $\mathbf{x}$ and that we contemplate taking action α_i. If the true state of nature is ω_j, we will incur the loss $\lambda(\alpha_i \mid \omega_j)$. Since $P(\omega_j \mid \mathbf{x})$ is the probability that the true state of nature is ω_j, the expected loss associated with taking action α_i is merely

$$R(\alpha_i \mid \mathbf{x}) = \sum_{j=1}^{s} \lambda(\alpha_i \mid \omega_j)P(\omega_j \mid \mathbf{x}). \tag{5}$$

In decision-theoretic terminology, an expected loss is called a *risk*, and $R(\alpha_i \mid \mathbf{x})$ is known as the *conditional risk*. Whenever we encounter a particular observation $\mathbf{x}$, we can minimize our expected loss by selecting the action that minimizes the conditional risk. We shall now show that this actually is the optimal Bayes decision procedure.

Stated formally, our problem is to find a Bayes decision rule against $P(\omega_j)$ that minimizes the overall risk. A *decision rule* is a function $\alpha(\mathbf{x})$ that tells us which action to take for every possible observation.* To be more specific, for every x the *decision function* $\alpha(\mathbf{x})$ assumes one of the a values $\alpha_1, \ldots, \alpha_a$. The overall risk R is the expected loss associated with a given decision rule. Since $R(\alpha_i \mid \mathbf{x})$ is the conditional risk associated with action α_i, and since the decision rule specifies the action, the overall risk is given by

$$R = \int R(\alpha(\mathbf{x}) \mid \mathbf{x})p(\mathbf{x}) \, d\mathbf{x}, \qquad (6)$$

where $d\mathbf{x}$ is our notation for a d-space volume element, and where the integral extends over the entire feature space. Clearly, if $\alpha(\mathbf{x})$ is chosen so that $R(\alpha(\mathbf{x}) \mid \mathbf{x})$ is as small as possible for every $\mathbf{x}$, then the overall risk will be minimized. This justifies the following statement of the *Bayes decision rule:* To minimize the overall risk, compute the conditional risk

$$R(\alpha_i \mid \mathbf{x}) = \sum_{j=1}^{s} \lambda(\alpha_i \mid \omega_j)P(\omega_j \mid \mathbf{x}) \qquad (5)$$

for $i = 1, \ldots, a$ and select the action α_i for which $R(\alpha_i \mid \mathbf{x})$ is minimum. (Note that if more than one action minimizes $R(\alpha_i \mid \mathbf{x})$, it does not matter which of these actions is taken, and any convenient tie-breaking rule can be used.) The resulting minimum overall risk is called the *Bayes risk* and is the best performance that can be achieved.

2.3 TWO-CATEGORY CLASSIFICATION

Let us specialize these results by considering the two-category classification problem. Here action α_1 corresponds to deciding that the true state of nature is ω_1, and action α_2 corresponds to deciding that it is ω_2. For notational simplicity, let $\lambda_{ij} = \lambda(\alpha_i \mid \omega_j)$, the loss incurred for deciding ω_i when the true state of nature is ω_j. If we write out the conditional risk given by Eq. (5), we obtain

$$R(\alpha_1 \mid \mathbf{x}) = \lambda_{11}P(\omega_1 \mid \mathbf{x}) + \lambda_{12}P(\omega_2 \mid \mathbf{x})$$
$$R(\alpha_2 \mid \mathbf{x}) = \lambda_{21}P(\omega_1 \mid \mathbf{x}) + \lambda_{22}P(\omega_2 \mid \mathbf{x}).$$

There are a variety of ways of expressing the minimum-risk decision rule each having its own minor advantages. The fundamental rule is to decide ω_1 if $R(\alpha_1 \mid \mathbf{x}) < R(\alpha_2 \mid \mathbf{x})$. In terms of the a posteriori probabilities, we decide, ω_1 if

$$(\lambda_{21} - \lambda_{11})P(\omega_1 \mid \mathbf{x}) > (\lambda_{12} - \lambda_{22})P(\omega_2 \mid \mathbf{x}).$$

* The reader familiar with game theory will recognize this as a deterministic decision rule. In game theory, nature is replaced by a malicious opponent who can take advantage of a deterministic strategy, and randomized decision rules are often advantageous. However, randomized decision rules offer no such advantage in our situation. Problem 8 leads the reader through a mathematical demonstration of this fact.

Ordinarily, the loss incurred for making an error is greater than the loss incurred for being correct, and both of the factors $\lambda_{21} - \lambda_{11}$ and $\lambda_{12} - \lambda_{22}$ are positive. Thus, our decision is basically determined by the more likely state of nature, although we must scale the a posteriori probabilities by the appropriate loss differences. By invoking Bayes rule, we can replace the a posteriori probabilities by the a priori probabilities and the conditional densities. This results in the equivalent rule to decide ω_1 if

$$(\lambda_{21} - \lambda_{11})p(\mathbf{x} \mid \omega_1)P(\omega_1) > (\lambda_{12} - \lambda_{22})p(\mathbf{x} \mid \omega_2)P(\omega_2).$$

Another alternative, which follows at once under the reasonable assumption that $\lambda_{21} > \lambda_{11}$, is to decide ω_1 if

$$\frac{p(\mathbf{x} \mid \omega_1)}{p(\mathbf{x} \mid \omega_2)} > \frac{\lambda_{12} - \lambda_{22}}{\lambda_{21} - \lambda_{11}} \frac{P(\omega_2)}{P(\omega_1)}.$$

This form of the decision rule focusses on the $\mathbf{x}$-dependence of the probability densities. Viewed as a function of ω_j, $p(\mathbf{x} \mid \omega_j)$ is called the *likelihood* of ω_j with respect to $\mathbf{x}$, and $p(\mathbf{x} \mid \omega_1)/p(\mathbf{x} \mid \omega_2)$ is called the *likelihood ratio*. Thus, the Bayes decision rule can be interpreted as calling for decision ω_1 if the likelihood ratio exceeds a threshold value that is independent of the observation $\mathbf{x}$.

2.4   MINIMUM-ERROR-RATE CLASSIFICATION

In classification problems, each state of nature is usually associated with a different one of the c classes, and the action α_i is usually interpreted as the decision that the true state of nature is ω_i.* If action α_i is taken and the true state of nature is ω_j, then the decision is correct if $i = j$, and in error if $i \neq j$. If errors are to be avoided, it is natural to seek a decision rule that minimizes the average probability of error, i.e., the *error rate*.

A loss function of particular interest for this case is the so-called *symmetrical* or *zero-one* loss function,

$$\lambda(\alpha_i \mid \omega_j) = \begin{cases} 0 & i = j \\ 1 & i \neq j \end{cases} \qquad i, j = 1, \ldots, c. \tag{7}$$

This loss function assigns no loss to a correct decision, and assigns a unit loss to any error. Thus, all errors are equally costly. The risk corresponding to this loss function is precisely the average probability of error, since the

---

* In this case $a = s = c$, the number of classes. Sometimes it is useful to define a reject action α_{c+1}; this case is the subject of Problems 6 and 7.

conditional risk is

$$R(\alpha_i \mid \mathbf{x}) = \sum_{j=1}^{c} \lambda(\alpha_i \mid \omega_j)P(\omega_j \mid \mathbf{x})$$

$$= \sum_{j \neq i} P(\omega_j \mid \mathbf{x})$$

$$= 1 - P(\omega_i \mid \mathbf{x}), \tag{8}$$

and $P(\omega_i \mid \mathbf{x})$ is the conditional probability that action α_i is correct. The Bayes decision rule to minimize risk calls for selecting the action that minimizes the conditional risk. Thus, to minimize the average probability of error, we should select the i that *maximizes* the a posteriori probability $P(\omega_i \mid \mathbf{x})$. In other words, for *minimum error rate:*

Decide ω_i if $P(\omega_i \mid \mathbf{x}) > P(\omega_j \mid \mathbf{x})$ for all $j \neq i$.

2.5 CLASSIFIERS, DISCRIMINANT FUNCTIONS, AND DECISION SURFACES

2.5.1 The Multicategory Case

There are many different ways to represent pattern classifiers. One way, which yields something like a canonical form for classifiers, is in terms of a set of *discriminant functions* $g_i(\mathbf{x})$, $i = 1, \ldots, c$. The classifier is said to assign a feature vector $\mathbf{x}$ to class ω_i if

$$g_i(\mathbf{x}) > g_j(\mathbf{x}) \qquad \text{for all } j \neq i. \tag{9}$$

Thus, the classifier is viewed as a machine that computes c discriminant functions and selects the category corresponding to the largest discriminant. This representation of a classifier is illustrated in block-diagram form in Figure 2.3.

A Bayes classifier is easily and naturally represented in this way. For the general case, we can let $g_i(\mathbf{x}) = -R(\alpha_i \mid \mathbf{x})$, since the maximum discriminant function will then correspond to the minimum conditional risk. For the minimum-error-rate case, we can simplify things further by taking $g_i(\mathbf{x}) = P(\omega_i \mid \mathbf{x})$, so that the maximum discriminant function corresponds to the maximum a posteriori probability.

Clearly, the choice of discriminant functions is not unique. We can always multiply the discriminant functions by a positive constant or bias them by an additive constant without influencing the decision. More generally, if we replace every $g_i(\mathbf{x})$ by $f(g_i(\mathbf{x}))$, where f is a monotonically increasing function,

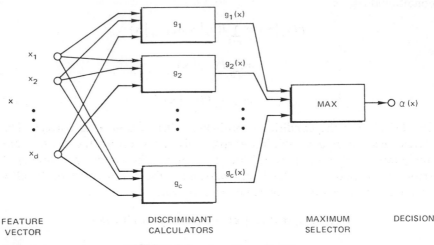

FIGURE 2.3.   A pattern classifier.

the resulting classification is unchanged. This observation can lead to significant analytical and computational simplifications. In particular, for minimum-
error-rate classification, any of the following choices gives identical
classification results, but some can be much simpler to understand or to
compute than others:

$$g_i(\mathbf{x}) = P(\omega_i \mid \mathbf{x}) \qquad (10)$$

$$g_i(\mathbf{x}) = \frac{p(\mathbf{x} \mid \omega_i)P(\omega_i)}{\sum\limits_{j=1}^{c} p(\mathbf{x} \mid \omega_j)P(\omega_j)} \qquad (11)$$

$$g_i(\mathbf{x}) = p(\mathbf{x} \mid \omega_i)P(\omega_i) \qquad (12)$$

$$g_i(\mathbf{x}) = \log p(\mathbf{x} \mid \omega_i) + \log P(\omega_i). \qquad (13)$$

Even though the discriminant functions can be written in a variety of
forms, the decision rules are equivalent. The effect of any decision rule is to
divide the feature space into c *decision regions*, $\mathscr{R}_1, \dots, \mathscr{R}_c$. If $g_i(\mathbf{x}) > g_j(\mathbf{x})$
for all $j \neq i$, then $\mathbf{x}$ is in $\mathscr{R}_i$, and the decision rule calls for us to assign $\mathbf{x}$ to
ω_i. The regions are separated by *decision boundaries*, surfaces in feature
space where ties occur among the largest discriminant functions (see Figure
2.4). If $\mathscr{R}_i$ and $\mathscr{R}_j$ are contiguous, the equation for the decision boundary
separating them is

$$g_i(\mathbf{x}) = g_j(\mathbf{x}). \qquad (14)$$

While this equation may appear to take different forms depending on the
forms chosen for the discriminant functions, the decision boundaries are, of

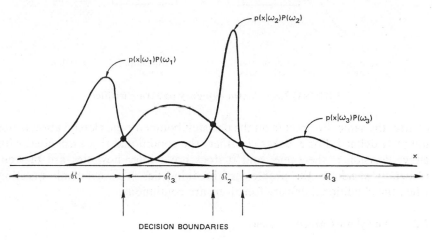

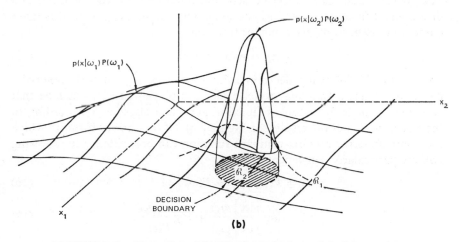

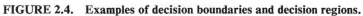

FIGURE 2.4. Examples of decision boundaries and decision regions.

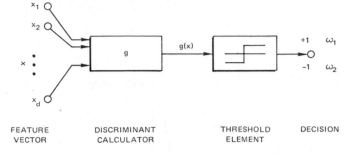

FIGURE 2.5.   A two-category pattern classifier.

course, the same. For points on the decision boundary the classification is not uniquely defined. For a Bayes classifier, the conditional risk associated with either decision is the same, and it does not matter how ties are broken. Generally speaking, the problem of breaking ties is an academic question when the conditional density functions are continuous.

2.5.2   The Two-Category Case

While the two-category case is just a special instance of the multicategory case, it has traditionally received separate treatment. Instead of using two discriminant functions g_1 and g_2 and assigning $\mathbf{x}$ to ω_1 if $g_1 > g_2$, it is more common to define one discriminant function

$$g(\mathbf{x}) = g_1(\mathbf{x}) - g_2(\mathbf{x}), \tag{15}$$

and to use the following decision rule: Decide ω_1 if $g(\mathbf{x}) > 0$; otherwise decide ω_2. Thus, a two-category classifier can be viewed as a machine that computes a single discriminant function $g(\mathbf{x})$, and classifies $\mathbf{x}$ according to the algebraic sign of the result (see Figure 2.5). Of the various forms in which the minimum-error-rate discriminant function can be written, the following two are particularly convenient:

$$g(\mathbf{x}) = P(\omega_1 \mid \mathbf{x}) - P(\omega_2 \mid \mathbf{x}) \tag{16}$$

$$g(\mathbf{x}) = \log \frac{p(\mathbf{x} \mid \omega_1)}{p(\mathbf{x} \mid \omega_2)} + \log \frac{P(\omega_1)}{P(\omega_2)} . \tag{17}$$

2.6   ERROR PROBABILITIES AND INTEGRALS

By thinking of a classifier as a device for partitioning feature space into decision regions, we can obtain additional insight into the operation of a Bayes classifier. Consider first the two-category case, and suppose that the classifier has divided the space into two regions, $\mathcal{R}_1$ and $\mathcal{R}_2$. There are two ways in which a classification error can occur; either an observation **x** falls in $\mathcal{R}_2$ and the true state of nature is ω_1, or **x** falls in $\mathcal{R}_1$ and the true state of nature is ω_2. Since these events are mutually exclusive and exhaustive,

$$
\begin{aligned}
P(\text{error}) &= P(\mathbf{x} \in \mathcal{R}_2, \omega_1) + P(\mathbf{x} \in \mathcal{R}_1, \omega_2) \\
&= P(\mathbf{x} \in \mathcal{R}_2 \mid \omega_1)P(\omega_1) + P(\mathbf{x} \in \mathcal{R}_1 \mid \omega_2)P(\omega_2) \\
&= \int_{\mathcal{R}_2} p(\mathbf{x} \mid \omega_1)P(\omega_1) \, dx + \int_{\mathcal{R}_1} p(\mathbf{x} \mid \omega_2)P(\omega_2) \, dx.
\end{aligned}
\tag{18}
$$

This result is illustrated in the one-dimensional case in Figure 2.6. The two terms in the sum are merely the areas in the tails of the functions $p(\mathbf{x} \mid \omega_i)P(\omega_i)$. Because the regions $\mathcal{R}_1$ and $\mathcal{R}_2$ were chosen arbitrarily, the probability of error is not as small as it might be. By moving the decision boundary to the left, it is clear that we can eliminate the dark "triangular" area and reduce the probability of error. In general, if $p(\mathbf{x} \mid \omega_1)P(\omega_1) > p(\mathbf{x} \mid \omega_2)P(\omega_2)$, it is advantageous to have **x** be in $\mathcal{R}_1$ so that the smaller quantity will contribute to the integral; this is exactly what the Bayes decision rule achieves.

In the multiclass case, there are more ways to be wrong than to be right, and it is simpler to compute the probability of being correct. Clearly

$$
\begin{aligned}
P(\text{correct}) &= \sum_{i=1}^{c} P(\mathbf{x} \in \mathcal{R}_i, \omega_i) \\
&= \sum_{i=1}^{c} P(\mathbf{x} \in \mathcal{R}_i \mid \omega_i)P(\omega_i) \\
&= \sum_{i=1}^{c} \int_{\mathcal{R}_i} p(\mathbf{x} \mid \omega_i)P(\omega_i) \, dx.
\end{aligned}
\tag{19}
$$

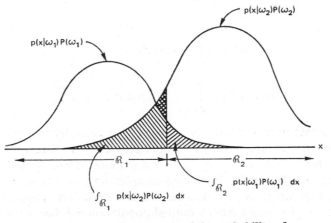

FIGURE 2.6.   **Components of the probability of error.**

This result is valid no matter how the feature space is partitioned into decision regions. The Bayes classifier maximizes this probability by choosing the regions so that the integrands are maximum; no other partitioning can yield a smaller probability of error.

2.7 THE NORMAL DENSITY

The structure of a Bayes classifier is determined primarily by the conditional densities $p(\mathbf{x} \mid \omega_i)$. Of the various density functions that have been investigated, none has received more attention than the multivariate normal density. It must be confessed that this attention is due largely to its analytical tractability. However, the multivariate normal density is also an appropriate model for an important situation, viz., the case where the feature vectors $\mathbf{x}$ for a given class ω_i are continuous valued, mildly corrupted versions of a single typical or prototype vector $\boldsymbol{\mu}_i$. This is what one would expect if the feature extractor were intentionally designed to extract features that were different for patterns in different classes but as similar as possible for patterns in the same class. In this section we provide a brief exposition of the properties of the multivariate normal density, focusing on the properties of greatest interest for classification problems.

2.7.1 The Univariate Normal Density

We begin with the univariate normal density

$$p(x) = \frac{1}{\sqrt{2\pi}\,\sigma} \exp\left[-\frac{1}{2}\left(\frac{x-\mu}{\sigma}\right)^2 \right] \tag{20}$$

for which

$$E[x] = \int_{-\infty}^{\infty} x p(x)\, dx = \mu \tag{21}$$

and

$$E[(x-\mu)^2] = \int_{-\infty}^{\infty} (x-\mu)^2 p(x)\, dx = \sigma^2. \tag{22}$$

The univariate normal density is completely specified by two parameters, the *mean* μ and the *variance* σ^2. For simplicity, we often abbreviate Eq. (20) by writing $p(x) \sim N(\mu, \sigma^2)$ to say that x is distributed normally with mean μ and variance σ^2. Normally distributed samples tend to cluster about the mean, with a spread proportional to the standard deviation σ; approximately 95% of the samples drawn from a normal population will fall in the interval $|x - \mu| \leq 2\sigma$.

2.7.2 The Multivariate Normal Density

The general multivariate normal density is written as

$$p(\mathbf{x}) = \frac{1}{(2\pi)^{d/2}|\Sigma|^{1/2}} \exp[-\tfrac{1}{2}(\mathbf{x} - \boldsymbol{\mu})^t \Sigma^{-1}(\mathbf{x} - \boldsymbol{\mu})] \qquad (23)$$

where $\mathbf{x}$ is a d-component column vector, $\boldsymbol{\mu}$ is the d-component *mean vector*, Σ is the d-by-d *covariance matrix*, $(\mathbf{x} - \boldsymbol{\mu})^t$ is the transpose of $\mathbf{x} - \boldsymbol{\mu}$, Σ^{-1} is the inverse of Σ, and $|\Sigma|$ is the determinant of Σ. For simplicity, we often abbreviate Eq. (23) as $p(\mathbf{x}) \sim N(\boldsymbol{\mu}, \Sigma)$. Formally,

$$\boldsymbol{\mu} = E[\mathbf{x}] \qquad (24)$$

and

$$\Sigma = E[(\mathbf{x} - \boldsymbol{\mu})(\mathbf{x} - \boldsymbol{\mu})^t], \qquad (25)$$

where the expected value of a vector or a matrix is found by taking the expected values of its components. To be more specific, if x_i is the ith component of $\mathbf{x}$, μ_i is the ith component of $\boldsymbol{\mu}$, and σ_{ij} is the i-jth component of Σ, then

$$\mu_i = E[x_i] \qquad (26)$$

and

$$\sigma_{ij} = E[(x_i - \mu_i)(x_j - \mu_j)]. \qquad (27)$$

The covariance matrix Σ is always symmetric and positive semidefinite. We shall restrict our attention to the case in which Σ is positive definite, so that the determinant of Σ is strictly positive.* The diagonal element σ_{ii} is the variance of x_i, and the off-diagonal element σ_{ij} is the covariance of x_i and x_j. If x_i and x_j are statistically independent, $\sigma_{ij} = 0$. If all of the off-diagonal elements are zero, $p(\mathbf{x})$ reduces to the product of the univariate normal densities for the components of $\mathbf{x}$.

It is not hard to show that the distribution of any linear combination of normally distributed random variables is again normal. In particular, if A is a d-by-n matrix and $\mathbf{y} = A^t\mathbf{x}$ is an n-component vector, then $p(\mathbf{y}) \sim N(A^t\boldsymbol{\mu}, A^t\Sigma A)$. In the special case where A is a unit-length vector $\mathbf{a}$, $y = \mathbf{a}^t\mathbf{x}$ is a scalar that represents the projection of $\mathbf{x}$ onto a line in the direction of $\mathbf{a}$. Thus, $\mathbf{a}^t\Sigma\mathbf{a}$ is the variance of the projection of $\mathbf{x}$ onto $\mathbf{a}$. In general, knowledge of the covariance matrix allows us to calculate the dispersion of the data in any direction.

The multivariate normal density is completely specified by $d + d(d + 1)/2$ parameters, the elements of the mean vector $\boldsymbol{\mu}$ and the independent elements

---

* If sample vectors drawn from a normal population are confined to a linear subspace, $|\Sigma| = 0$ and $p(\mathbf{x})$ is degenerate. This happens, for example, when one component of $\mathbf{x}$ has zero variance, or when two components are identical. We are specifically excluding such situations.

of the covariance matrix Σ. Samples drawn from a normal population tend to fall in a single cloud or cluster (see Figure 2.7). The center of the cluster is determined by the mean vector, and the shape of the cluster is determined by the covariance matrix. It follows from Eq. (23) that the loci of points of constant density are hyperellipsoids for which the quadratic form $(\mathbf{x} - \boldsymbol{\mu})^t \Sigma^{-1}(\mathbf{x} - \boldsymbol{\mu})$ is constant. The principal axes of these hyperellipsoids are given by the eigenvectors of Σ, the eigenvalues determining the lengths of these axes. The quantity

$$r^2 = (\mathbf{x} - \boldsymbol{\mu})^t \Sigma^{-1}(\mathbf{x} - \boldsymbol{\mu}) \tag{28}$$

is sometimes called the squared *Mahalanobis distance* from $\mathbf{x}$ to $\boldsymbol{\mu}$. Thus, the contours of constant density are hyperellipsoids of constant Mahalanobis distance to $\boldsymbol{\mu}$. The volume of these hyperellipsoids measures the scatter of the samples about the mean. It can be shown that the volume of the hyperellipsoid corresponding to a Mahalanobis distance r is given by

$$V = V_d |\Sigma|^{1/2} r^d, \tag{29}$$

where V_d is the volume of a d-dimensional unit hypersphere:

$$V_d = \begin{cases} \dfrac{\pi^{d/2}}{\left(\dfrac{d}{2}\right)!} & d \text{ even} \\[3ex] \dfrac{2^d \pi^{(d-1)/2} \left(\dfrac{d-1}{2}\right)!}{d!} & d \text{ odd.} \end{cases} \tag{30}$$

Thus, for a given dimensionality, the scatter of the samples varies directly with $|\Sigma|^{1/2}$.

2.8 DISCRIMINANT FUNCTIONS FOR THE NORMAL DENSITY

In Section 2.5 we saw that minimum-error-rate classification can be achieved by use of the discriminant functions

$$g_i(\mathbf{x}) = \log p(\mathbf{x} \mid \omega_i) + \log P(\omega_i). \tag{13}$$

This expression can be readily evaluated if the densities $p(\mathbf{x} \mid \omega_i)$ are multivariate normal. Let $p(\mathbf{x} \mid \omega_i) \sim N(\boldsymbol{\mu}_i, \Sigma_i)$. Then, from Eq. (23),

$$g_i(\mathbf{x}) = -\tfrac{1}{2}(\mathbf{x} - \boldsymbol{\mu}_i)^t \Sigma_i^{-1}(\mathbf{x} - \boldsymbol{\mu}_i) - \frac{d}{2}\log 2\pi - \tfrac{1}{2}\log|\Sigma_i| + \log P(\omega_i). \tag{31}$$

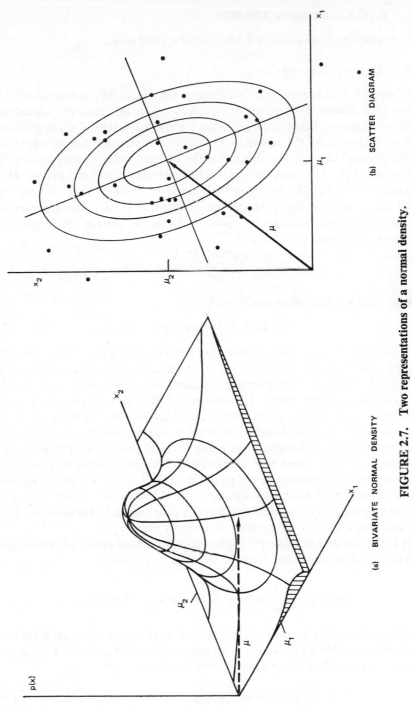

(b) SCATTER DIAGRAM

(a) BIVARIATE NORMAL DENSITY

FIGURE 2.7. Two representations of a normal density.

Let us examine this result for a number of special cases.

2.8.1   Case 1: $\Sigma_i = \sigma^2 I$

The simplest case occurs when the features are statistically independent, and when each feature has the same variance, σ^2. In this case the covariance matrix is diagonal, being merely σ^2 times the identity matrix, I. Geometrically, this corresponds to the situation in which the samples fall in equal-size hyperspherical clusters, the cluster for the ith class being centered about the mean vector μ_i. The computation of the determinant and the inverse of Σ_i is particularly easy: $|\Sigma_i| = \sigma^{2d}$ and $\Sigma_i^{-1} = (1/\sigma^2)I$. Since both $|\Sigma_i|$ and the $(d/2) \log 2\pi$ term in Eq. (31) are independent of i, they are unimportant additive constants that can be ignored. Thus, we obtain the simple discriminant functions

$$g_i(\mathbf{x}) = - \frac{\|\mathbf{x} - \mu_i\|^2}{2\sigma^2} + \log P(\omega_i), \tag{32}$$

where $\|\cdot\|$ is the Euclidean norm, with

$$\|\mathbf{x} - \mu_i\|^2 = (\mathbf{x} - \mu_i)^t(\mathbf{x} - \mu_i). \tag{33}$$

If the a priori probabilities $P(\omega_i)$ are the same for all c classes, then the $\log P(\omega_i)$ term becomes another unimportant additive constant that can be ignored. In this case, the optimum decision rule can be stated very simply: To classify a feature vector $\mathbf{x}$, measure the Euclidean distance $\|\mathbf{x} - \mu_i\|$ from $\mathbf{x}$ to each of the c mean vectors, and assign $\mathbf{x}$ to the category of the nearest mean. Such a classifier is called a *minimum-distance* classifier. If each mean vector is thought of as being an ideal prototype or template for patterns in its class, then this is essentially a *template-matching* procedure. If the a priori probabilities are not equal, then Eq. (32) shows that the squared distance $\|\mathbf{x} - \mu_i\|^2$ must be normalized by the variance σ^2 and biased by subtracting $\log P^2(\omega_i)$; thus, if $\mathbf{x}$ is equally near two different mean vectors, the decision will favor the a priori more likely category.

It is not actually necessary to compute distances in either of these cases. Expansion of the quadratic form $(\mathbf{x} - \mu_i)^t(\mathbf{x} - \mu_i)$ yields

$$g_i(\mathbf{x}) = - \frac{1}{2\sigma^2} [\mathbf{x}^t\mathbf{x} - 2\mu_i^t\mathbf{x} + \mu_i^t\mu_i] + \log P(\omega_i),$$

which appears to be a quadratic function of $\mathbf{x}$. However, the quadratic term $\mathbf{x}^t\mathbf{x}$ is the same for all i, making it an ignorable additive constant. Thus, we obtain the equivalent *linear* discriminant functions

$$g_i(\mathbf{x}) = \mathbf{w}_i^t\mathbf{x} + w_{i0}, \tag{34}$$

where*

$$\mathbf{w}_i = \frac{1}{\sigma^2} \boldsymbol{\mu}_i \qquad (35)$$

and

$$w_{i0} = -\frac{1}{2\sigma^2} \boldsymbol{\mu}_i^t \boldsymbol{\mu}_i + \log P(\omega_i). \qquad (36)$$

A classifier that uses linear discriminant functions is called a *linear machine*. This kind of classifier has many interesting theoretical properties, some of which will be discussed in detail in Chapter 5. At this point we merely note that the decision surfaces for a linear machine are pieces of hyperplanes defined by the linear equations $g_i(\mathbf{x}) = g_j(\mathbf{x})$. For our particular case, this equation can be written as

$$\mathbf{w}^t(\mathbf{x} - \mathbf{x}_0) = 0, \qquad (37)$$

where

$$\mathbf{w} = \boldsymbol{\mu}_i - \boldsymbol{\mu}_j \qquad (38)$$

and

$$\mathbf{x}_0 = \tfrac{1}{2}(\boldsymbol{\mu}_i + \boldsymbol{\mu}_j) - \frac{\sigma^2}{\|\boldsymbol{\mu}_i - \boldsymbol{\mu}_j\|^2} \log \frac{P(\omega_i)}{P(\omega_j)} (\boldsymbol{\mu}_i - \boldsymbol{\mu}_j). \qquad (39)$$

This equation defines a hyperplane through the point $\mathbf{x}_0$ and orthogonal to the vector $\mathbf{w}$. Since $\mathbf{w} = \boldsymbol{\mu}_i - \boldsymbol{\mu}_j$, the hyperplane separating $\mathcal{R}_i$ and $\mathcal{R}_j$ is orthogonal to the line between the means. If $P(\omega_i) = P(\omega_j)$, then the point $\mathbf{x}_0$ is halfway between the means, and the hyperplane is the perpendicular bisector of the line between the means (see Figure 2.8). This result could have been anticipated from the fact that the classifier for this case is a minimum-distance classifier. If $P(\omega_i) \neq P(\omega_j)$, the point $\mathbf{x}_0$ shifts away from the more likely mean. Note, however, that if the variance σ^2 is small relative to the squared distance $\|\boldsymbol{\mu}_i - \boldsymbol{\mu}_j\|^2$, then the position of the decision boundary is relatively insensitive to the exact values of the a priori probabilities.

2.8.2   Case 2: $\Sigma_i = \Sigma$

Another simple case arises when the covariance matrices for all of the classes are identical. Geometrically, this corresponds to the situation in which the samples fall in hyperellipsoidal clusters of equal size and shape, the cluster for the ith class being centered about the mean vector $\boldsymbol{\mu}_i$. Since both $|\Sigma_i|$ and the $(d/2) \log 2\pi$ term in Eq. (31) are independent of i, they can be ignored

---

* Readers familiar with signal detection theory will recognize this as a correlation detector. The discriminant $g_i(\mathbf{x})$ crosscorrelates the input $\mathbf{x}$ with the stored reference signal $\boldsymbol{\mu}_i$. The constant w_{i0} accounts for both the energy in the reference signal and its a priori probability of occurrence.

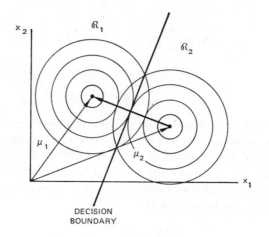

(a) TWO-CLASS PROBLEM

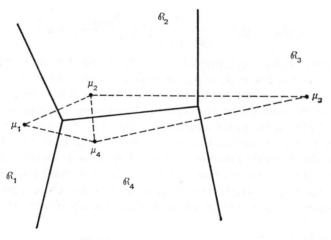

(b) FOUR-CLASS PROBLEM

FIGURE 2.8.   Decision boundaries for a minimum-distance classifier.

as superfluous additive constants. This results in the discriminant functions

$$g_i(\mathbf{x}) = -\tfrac{1}{2}(\mathbf{x} - \boldsymbol{\mu}_i)^t \Sigma^{-1}(\mathbf{x} - \boldsymbol{\mu}_i) + \log P(\omega_i). \tag{40}$$

If the a priori probabilities $P(\omega_i)$ are the same for all c classes, then the $\log P(\omega_i)$ term can be ignored. In this case, the optimal decision rule can once again be stated very simply: To classify a feature vector $\mathbf{x}$, measure the squared Mahalanobis distance $(\mathbf{x} - \boldsymbol{\mu}_i)^t \Sigma^{-1}(\mathbf{x} - \boldsymbol{\mu}_i)$ from $\mathbf{x}$ to each of the c

mean vectors, and assign x to the category of the nearest mean.* As before, unequal a priori probabilities bias the decision in favor of the a priori more likely category.

Expansion of the quadratic form $(\mathbf{x} - \boldsymbol{\mu}_i)^t \Sigma^{-1} (\mathbf{x} - \boldsymbol{\mu}_i)$ discloses that the quadratic term $\mathbf{x}^t \Sigma^{-1} \mathbf{x}$ is independent of i. If it is deleted, the resulting discriminant functions are again linear:

$$g_i(\mathbf{x}) = \mathbf{w}_i^t \mathbf{x} + w_{i0}, \tag{41}$$

where

$$\mathbf{w}_i = \Sigma^{-1} \boldsymbol{\mu}_i \tag{42}$$

and

$$w_{i0} = -\tfrac{1}{2} \boldsymbol{\mu}_i^t \Sigma^{-1} \boldsymbol{\mu}_i + \log P(\omega_i). \tag{43}$$

Since the discriminants are linear, the resulting decision boundaries are again hyperplanes (see Figure 2.9). If $\mathcal{R}_i$ and $\mathcal{R}_j$ are contiguous, the boundary between them has the equation

$$\mathbf{w}^t (\mathbf{x} - \mathbf{x}_0) = 0 \tag{44}$$

where

$$\mathbf{w} = \Sigma^{-1} (\boldsymbol{\mu}_i - \boldsymbol{\mu}_j) \tag{45}$$

and

$$\mathbf{x}_0 = \tfrac{1}{2}(\boldsymbol{\mu}_i + \boldsymbol{\mu}_j) - \frac{\log \dfrac{P(\omega_i)}{P(\omega_j)}}{(\boldsymbol{\mu}_i - \boldsymbol{\mu}_j)^t \Sigma^{-1}(\boldsymbol{\mu}_i - \boldsymbol{\mu}_j)} (\boldsymbol{\mu}_i - \boldsymbol{\mu}_j). \tag{46}$$

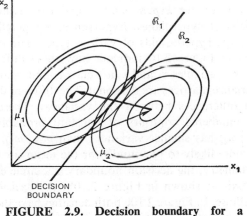

FIGURE 2.9. Decision boundary for a minimum-Mahalanobis-distance classifier.

* An alternative interpretation can be obtained by subjecting the feature coordinates to a linear transformation that rotates and scales the axes so that the hyperellipsoids of constant Mahalanobis distance become hyperspheres. This transformation reduces Case 2 to Case 1, and allows Mahalanobis distance to be interpreted as Euclidean distance in the transformed space.

Since $\mathbf{w} = \Sigma^{-1}(\boldsymbol{\mu}_i - \boldsymbol{\mu}_j)$ is generally not in the direction of $\boldsymbol{\mu}_i - \boldsymbol{\mu}_j$, the hyperplane separating $\mathscr{R}_i$ and $\mathscr{R}_j$ is generally not orthogonal to the line between the means. However, it does intersect that line at the point $\mathbf{x}_0$ which is halfway between the means if the a priori probabilities are equal. If the a priori probabilities are not equal, the boundary hyperplane is translated away from the more likely mean.

2.8.3   Case 3: Σ_i Arbitrary

In the general multivariate normal case, the covariance matrices are different for each category. The only term that can be dropped from Eq. (31) is the $(d/2) \log 2\pi$ term, and the resulting discriminant functions are inherently quadratic:

$$g_i(\mathbf{x}) = \mathbf{x}^t W_i \mathbf{x} + \mathbf{w}_i^t \mathbf{x} + w_{i0}, \tag{47}$$

where

$$W_i = -\tfrac{1}{2}\Sigma_i^{-1} \tag{48}$$

and

$$\mathbf{w}_i = \Sigma_i^{-1} \boldsymbol{\mu}_i \tag{49}$$

$$w_{i0} = -\tfrac{1}{2}\boldsymbol{\mu}_i^t \Sigma_i^{-1} \boldsymbol{\mu}_i - \tfrac{1}{2} \log |\Sigma_i| + \log P(\omega_i). \tag{50}$$

The decision surfaces are *hyperquadrics*, and can assume any of the general forms—pairs of hyperplanes, hyperspheres, hyperellipsoids, hyperparaboloids, and hyperhyperboloids of various types. The two-dimensional examples sketched in Figure 2.10 indicate how these different forms can arise. In all cases the variables x_1 and x_2 are class-conditionally independent, and thus the covariance matrices are diagonal. The different decision surfaces arise solely from differences between the variances. These variances are indicated by the numbered contours of constant probability density. In Figure 2.10a $p(\mathbf{x} \mid \omega_2)$ has smaller variances than $p(\mathbf{x} \mid \omega_1)$. Thus, samples from Class 2 are more likely to be found near the mean for that class, and, due to circular symmetry, the decision boundary is a circle enclosing $\boldsymbol{\mu}_2$. By stretching the x_2 axis as shown in Figure 2.10b, the decision boundary is stretched into an ellipse. In Figure 2.10c both densities have the same variance in the x_1 direction, but $p(\mathbf{x} \mid \omega_1)$ has more variance than $p(\mathbf{x} \mid \omega_2)$ in the x_2 direction. Thus, samples with large x_2 values are probably from Class 1, and the decision boundary is a parabola. By increasing the x_1 variance for $p(\mathbf{x} \mid \omega_2)$ as shown in Figure 2.10d, the boundary changes to a hyperbola. Finally, the special symmetry shown in Figure 2.10e causes the hyperbolic boundary to degenerate to a pair of straight lines.

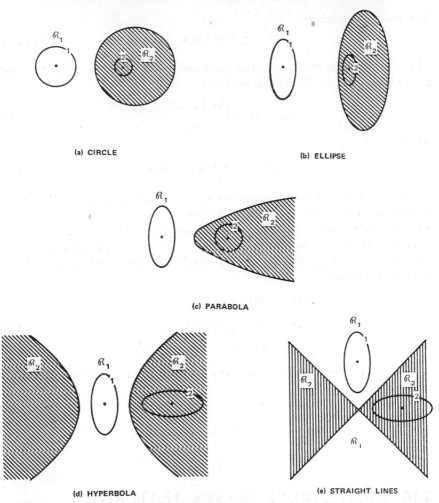

FIGURE 2.10.   Forms for decision boundaries for the general bivariate normal case.

2.9 BAYES DECISION THEORY— THE DISCRETE CASE

Until now we have assumed that the feature vector $\mathbf{x}$ could be any point $\mathbf{x}$ in Euclidean d-space. However, in many practical applications the components of $\mathbf{x}$ are binary-valued or ternary-valued variables, so that $\mathbf{x}$ can assume only one of m discrete values $\mathbf{v}_1, \ldots, \mathbf{v}_m$. In such cases, the probability density function $p(\mathbf{x} \mid \omega_j)$ becomes singular; integrals such as

$$\int p(\mathbf{x} \mid \omega_j) \, d\mathbf{x}$$

turn into sums such as

$$\sum_k P(\mathbf{v}_k \mid \omega_j),$$

where $P(\mathbf{v}_k \mid \omega_j)$ is the conditional probability that $\mathbf{x} = \mathbf{v}_k$, given that the state of nature is ω_j. Bayes rule becomes

$$P(\omega_j \mid \mathbf{x}) = \frac{P(\mathbf{x} \mid \omega_j)P(\omega_j)}{P(\mathbf{x})}, \tag{51}$$

where

$$P(\mathbf{x}) = \sum_{j=1}^s P(\mathbf{x} \mid \omega_j)P(\omega_j). \tag{52}$$

The definition of the conditional risk $R(\alpha_i \mid \mathbf{x})$ is unchanged, and the fundamental Bayes decision rule remains the same: To minimize the overall risk, select the action α_i for which $R(\alpha_i \mid \mathbf{x})$ is minimum. The basic rule to minimize the error-rate by maximizing the a posteriori probability is also unchanged; by using Bayes rule, we obtain the following equivalent discriminant functions:

$$g_i(\mathbf{x}) = P(\omega_i \mid \mathbf{x}) \tag{53}$$

$$g_i(\mathbf{x}) = P(\mathbf{x} \mid \omega_i)P(\omega_i) \tag{54}$$

$$g_i(\mathbf{x}) = \log P(\mathbf{x} \mid \omega_i) + \log P(\omega_i). \tag{55}$$

In the two-category case, the following discriminant functions are often convenient:

$$g(\mathbf{x}) = P(\omega_1 \mid \mathbf{x}) - P(\omega_2 \mid \mathbf{x}) \tag{56}$$

$$g(\mathbf{x}) = \log \frac{P(\mathbf{x} \mid \omega_1)}{P(\mathbf{x} \mid \omega_2)} + \log \frac{P(\omega_1)}{P(\omega_2)}. \tag{57}$$

2.10   INDEPENDENT BINARY FEATURES

As an example of a specific classification problem involving discrete features, consider the two-class case in which the components of the feature vector are binary valued and conditionally independent. To be more specific, let $\mathbf{x} = (x_1, \ldots, x_d)^t$, where the components x_i are either 1 or 0, with

$$p_i = \text{Prob}(x_i = 1 \mid \omega_1)$$

and

$$q_i = \text{Prob}(x_i = 1 \mid \omega_2).$$

This is a model of a classification problem in which each feature gives us a yes/no answer about the pattern. If $p_i > q_i$, we expect the ith feature to give a "yes" answer more frequently when the state of nature is ω_1 than when it is ω_2. By assuming conditional independence, we can write $P(\mathbf{x} \mid \omega_i)$ as the product of the probabilities for the components of $\mathbf{x}$. A particularly convenient way of writing this is as follows:

$$P(\mathbf{x} \mid \omega_1) = \prod_{i=1}^{d} p_i^{x_i}(1 - p_i)^{1-x_i}$$

$$P(\mathbf{x} \mid \omega_2) = \prod_{i=1}^{d} q_i^{x_i}(1 - q_i)^{1-x_i}.$$

Then the likelihood ratio is given by

$$\frac{P(\mathbf{x} \mid \omega_1)}{P(\mathbf{x} \mid \omega_2)} = \prod_{i=1}^{d} \left(\frac{p_i}{q_i}\right)^{x_i} \left(\frac{1 - p_i}{1 - q_i}\right)^{1-x_i},$$

and Eq. (57) yields the discriminant function

$$g(\mathbf{x}) = \sum_{i=1}^{d} \left[x_i \log \frac{p_i}{q_i} + (1 - x_i) \log \frac{1 - p_i}{1 - q_i} \right] + \log \frac{P(\omega_1)}{P(\omega_2)}.$$

Inspection of this equation shows that it is linear in the x_i. That is, we can write

$$g(\mathbf{x}) = \sum_{i=1}^{d} w_i x_i + w_0,$$

where

$$w_i = \log \frac{p_i(1 - q_i)}{q_i(1 - p_i)} \qquad i = 1, \ldots, d$$

and

$$w_0 = \sum_{i=1}^{d} \log \frac{1 - p_i}{1 - q_i} + \log \frac{P(\omega_1)}{P(\omega_2)}.$$

Let us examine these results to see what insight they can give. Recall first that we decide ω_1 if $g(\mathbf{x}) > 0$ and ω_2 if $g(\mathbf{x}) \leq 0$. We have seen that $g(\mathbf{x})$ is a weighted combination of the components of $\mathbf{x}$. The magnitude of the weight w_i measures the significance of a "yes" answer for x_i in determining the classification. If $p_i = q_i$, x_i gives us no information about the state of nature, and $w_i = 0$. If $p_i > q_i$, then $1 - p_i < 1 - q_i$ and w_i is positive. Thus, in this case a "yes" answer for x_i contributes w_i votes for ω_1. Furthermore, for any fixed $q_i < 1$, w_i gets larger as p_i gets larger. On the other hand, if $p_i < q_i$, w_i is negative, and a "yes" answer contributes $|w_i|$ votes for ω_2.

The a priori probabilities $P(\omega_i)$ appear in the discriminant only through the so-called threshold weight, w_0. Increasing $P(\omega_1)$ increases w_0 and biases the decision in favor of ω_1, while decreasing $P(\omega_1)$ has the opposite effect. Geometrically, the vectors $\mathbf{v}_k$ appear as the vertices of a d-dimensional hypercube. The decision surface defined by $g(\mathbf{x}) = 0$ is a hyperplane that separates

ω_1 vertices from ω_2 vertices. Clearly, in the discrete case one can perturb this hyperplane in many ways without crossing any vertices and changing the probability of error. Any one of these hyperplanes is an optimal separating surface, and all yield the optimal performance.

2.11 COMPOUND BAYES DECISION THEORY AND CONTEXT

Let us reconsider our introductory example of designing a classifier to sort two types of lumber, ash and birch. Our original assumption was that the sequence of types of lumber was so unpredictable that the state of nature looked like a random variable. Without abandoning this attitude, let us consider the possibility that the consecutive states of nature might not be statistically independent. For example, even though the a priori probabilities for ash and birch might be equal, it is possible that once a piece of lumber of one type emerges, it is much more likely that the next several pieces will be the same type than different types. In this case, the consecutive states of nature are dependent, and we should be able to exploit this dependence to gain improved performance. This is one example of the use of *context* to aid decision making.

The way in which we exploit such information is somewhat different when we can wait for n pieces of lumber to emerge and then make all n decisions jointly than when we must decide as each piece of lumber emerges. The first problem is a *compound decision problem*, and the second is a *sequential compound decision problem*. The former case is conceptually simpler, and is the only case we shall examine.

To state the general problem, let $\boldsymbol{\omega} = (\omega(1), \ldots, \omega(n))^t$ be a vector denoting the n states of nature, with $\omega(i)$ taking on one of the c values $\omega_1, \ldots, \omega_c$. Let $P(\boldsymbol{\omega})$ be the a priori probability for the n states of nature. Let $X = (\mathbf{x}_1, \ldots, \mathbf{x}_n)$ be a matrix giving the n observed feature vectors, with $\mathbf{x}_i$ being the feature vector obtained when the state of nature was $\omega(i)$. Finally, let $p(X | \boldsymbol{\omega})$ be the conditional probability density function for X, given the true set of states of nature $\boldsymbol{\omega}$. Then the a posteriori probability of $\boldsymbol{\omega}$ is given by

$$P(\boldsymbol{\omega} \mid X) = \frac{p(X \mid \boldsymbol{\omega})P(\boldsymbol{\omega})}{p(X)}, \tag{58}$$

where

$$p(X) = \sum_{\boldsymbol{\omega}} p(X \mid \boldsymbol{\omega})P(\boldsymbol{\omega}). \tag{59}$$

In general, one can define a loss matrix for the compound decision problem and seek a decision rule that minimizes the compound risk. The development of this theory parallels our development for the simple decision problem, and concludes that the optimal procedure is to minimize the compound conditional risk. In particular, if there is no loss for being correct, and if all errors are equally costly, then the procedure reduces to computing $P(\omega \mid X)$ for all ω and selecting the ω for which this a posteriori probability is maximum.

While this provides the theoretical solution, in practice the computation of $P(\omega \mid X)$ can easily prove to be an enormous task. If each component $\omega(i)$ can have one of c values, there are c^n possible values of ω to consider. Some simplification can be obtained if the distribution of the feature vector $\mathbf{x}_i$ depends only on the corresponding state of nature $\omega(i)$, not on the values of the other feature vectors or the other states of nature. In this case the joint density $p(X \mid \omega)$ is merely the product of the component densities $p(\mathbf{x}_i \mid \omega(i))$:

$$p(X \mid \omega) = \prod_{i=1}^{n} p(\mathbf{x}_i \mid \omega(i)). \tag{60}$$

While this simplifies the problem of computing $p(X \mid \omega)$, there is still the problem of computing the a priori probability $P(\omega)$. This joint probability is central to the compound Bayes decision problem, since it reflects the interdependence of the states of nature. Thus, it is unacceptable to simplify the problem of calculating $P(\omega)$ by assuming that the states of nature are independent. In addition, practical applications usually require some method of avoiding the computation of $P(\omega \mid X)$ for all c^n possible values of ω. We shall leave these problems as topics worth some pondering, and shall refer the interested reader to the literature for further details.

2.12 REMARKS

We have now completed an exposition of Bayes decision theory, with special emphasis on the solution for the multivariate normal case. The basic ideas are very simple. To minimize the overall risk, one should always choose the action that minimizes the conditional risk

$$R(\alpha_i \mid \mathbf{x}) = \sum_{j=1}^{c} \lambda(\alpha_i \mid \omega_j) P(\omega_j \mid \mathbf{x}).$$

In particular, to minimize the probability of error in a classification problem, one should always choose the state of nature that maximizes the a posteriori probability $P(\omega_j \mid \mathbf{x})$. Bayes rule allows us to calculate these probabilities from the a priori probabilities $P(\omega_j)$ and the conditional densities $p(\mathbf{x} \mid \omega_j)$.

For most pattern classification applications, the chief problem in applying these results is that the conditional densities $p(\mathbf{x} \mid \omega_j)$ are not known. In some cases we may know the form these densities assume, but may not know characterizing parameter values. The classic case occurs when the densities are known to be, or can be assumed to be multivariate normal, but the values of the mean vectors and the covariance matrices are not known. More commonly even less is known about the conditional densities, and procedures that are less sensitive to specific assumptions about the densities must be used. Most of the remainder of Part I of this book will be devoted to various procedures that have been developed to attack this problem.

2.13 BIBLIOGRAPHICAL AND HISTORICAL REMARKS

Decision theory is associated with the names of many well known statisticians, and there is a large body of literature on the topic. Among the standard textbooks on decision theory are those by Wald (1950), Blackwell and Girschick (1954), and the more elementary text by Chernoff and Moses (1959). We are also fond of the text by Ferguson (1967), who presents many topics in statistics from a decision theoretic viewpoint. Decision theory is also closely related to the theory of games, which is developed in the classic work by von Neumann and Morgenstern (1944), and the text by Luce and Raiffa (1957).

The pioneering decision theory work by Neyman and Pearson (1928, 1933) dealt with hypothesis testing, and used the probability of error as a criterion. Wald (1939) generalized this work by introducing the notions of loss and risk. Certain conceptual problems have always attended the use of loss functions and a priori probabilities. In fact, the Bayesian approach is avoided by many statisticians, partly because there are problems for which a decision is made only once (so that average loss is not meaningful), and partly because there may be no reasonable way to determine the a priori probabilities. Neither of these difficulties seems to present a serious problem in typical pattern recognition applications, and for simplicity we have taken a strictly Bayesian approach.

Chow (1957) was one of the first to apply Bayesian decision theory to pattern recognition. His analysis included a provision for rejection, and he later established a fundamental relation between error and reject rates (Chow 1970). The exact calculation of the probability of error is remarkably complicated, and most of the published results concern bounds on the error rate (Albrecht and Werner 1964; Chu and Chueh 1967; Lainiotis and Park 1971). The use of discriminant functions for classification problems was introduced by Fisher (1936), and we shall examine his approach to their use in Chapter 4. Our use of the term follows the pattern set by Nilsson (1965). Anderson (1958) treats the multivariate normal case in great detail, and derives the quadratic discriminant functions in a slightly different form. Marill and Green (1960) showed how this solution could be applied in a pattern classification context. Cooper (1964) has investigated other continuous distributions for which linear and quadratic discriminant functions are optimal.

Nilsson (1965) attributes the derivation of the linear discriminant functions for the binary independent (or multivariate Bernoulli) case to J. W. Jones, although the first published solution appears to be due to Minsky (1961), with other proofs being given by Winder (1963) and Chow (1965). Kazmierczak and Steinbuch (1963) derived quadratic optimal discriminant functions for the ternary independent case; it is easy to generalize this and derive nth degree polynomial discriminant functions that are optimal for the $(n + 1)$-ary independent case. If the independence assumption is relaxed, higher degree polynomials are needed even in the binary case. This will become more clear when we examine polynomial expansions of joint probabilities in Chapter 4.

Of course, high degree polynomials involving many variables are not computationally desirable. Thus, in those cases where the optimal discriminant function is not linear, it is tempting to seek the optimal linear discriminant. Unfortunately, it turns out to be surprisingly difficult to derive the minimum-risk linear discriminant function. Anderson and Bahadur (1962) have solved the general two-category multivariate normal case, but no other general solutions have been found. However, as we shall see in Chapter 5, many solutions can be found when criteria other than minimum risk are used.

General compound decision theory embraces a greater variety of problems than the simple Bayesian one that we described. Abend (1966) gives a clear introduction to compound decision theory, and a number of significant references to the statistical literature. Raviv (1967) and Abend (1968) derive optimal procedures when there is a Markov dependence between states of nature, and Raviv gives the results of applying such procedures to recognizing English legal text. Abend, Harley and Kanal (1965) show how the Markov dependence approach can be extended from one-dimensional to two-dimensional situations. A computationally efficient method of using context is described by Riseman and Ehrich (1971), who reference other papers on the use of context in character recognition.

Finally, it should be mentioned that throughout Part I we tacitly assume that all d components of the feature vector are measured before we contemplate making a decision. Another alternative is to use a decision tree, evaluating the features sequentially until a decision can be made. The statistical treatment of this approach requires considering the cost of measuring features as well as the cost of making errors, and is the subject of sequential decision theory (Wald 1947; Fu 1968). Slagle and Lee (1971) show

how techniques developed for searching game trees can be applied to such problems.

REFERENCES

1. Abend, K., T. J. Harley, and L. N. Kanal, "Classification of binary random patterns," *IEEE Trans. Info. Theory*, **IT-11**, 538–544 (October 1965).

2. Abend, K., "Compound decision procedures for pattern recognition," *Proc. NEC*, **22**, 777–780 (1966).

3. Abend, K., "Compound decision procedures for unknown distributions and for dependent states of nature," in *Pattern Recognition*, pp. 207–249, L. Kanal, ed. (Thompson Book Co., Washington, D.C., 1968).

4. Albrecht, R. and W. Werner, "Error analysis of a statistical decision method," *IEEE Trans. Info. Theory*, **IT-10**, 34–38 (January 1964).

5. Anderson, T. W., *An Introduction to Multivariate Statistical Analysis* (John Wiley, New York, 1958).

6. Anderson, T. W. and R. R. Bahadur, "Classification into two multivariate normal distributions with different covariance matrices," *Ann. Math. Stat.*, **33**, 422–431 (June 1962).

7. Blackwell, D. and M. A. Girshick, *Theory of Games and Statistical Decisions* (John Wiley, New York, 1954).

8. Chernoff, H. and L. E. Moses, *Elementary Decision Theory* (John Wiley, New York, 1959).

9. Chow, C. K., "An optimum character recognition system using decision functions," *IRE Trans. on Elec. Comp.*, **EC-6**, 247–254 (December 1957).

10. Chow, C. K., "Statistical independence and threshold functions," *IEEE Trans. on Comp.*, **EC-14**, 66–68 (February 1965).

11. Chow, C. K., "On optimum recognition error and reject tradeoff," *IEEE Trans. Info. Theory*, **IT-16**, 41–46 (January 1970).

12. Chu, J. T. and J. C. Chueh, "Error probability in decision functions for character recognition," *J. ACM*, **14**, 273–280 (April 1967).

13. Cooper, P. W., "Hyperplanes, hyperspheres, and hyperquadrics as decision boundaries," in *Computer and Information Sciences*, pp. 111–138, J. T. Tou and R. H. Wilcox, eds. (Spartan, Washington, D.C., 1964).

14. Ferguson, T. S., *Mathematical Statistics: A Decision Theoretic Approach* (Academic Press, New York, 1967).

15. Fisher, R. A., "The use of multiple measurements in taxonomic problems," *Ann. Eugenics*, **7**, Part II, 179–188 (1936); also in *Contributions to Mathematical Statistics* (John Wiley, New York, 1950).

16. Fu, K. S., *Sequential Methods in Pattern Recognition and Machine Learning* (Academic Press, New York, 1968).

17. Kazmierczak, H. and K. Steinbuch, "Adaptive systems in pattern recognition," *IEEE Trans. on Elec. Comp.*, **EC-12**, 822–835 (December 1963).

18. Lainiotis, D. G. and S. K. Park, "Probability of error bounds," *IEEE Trans. Sys. Man Cyb.*, **SMC-1**, 175–178 (April 1971).

19. Luce, R. D. and H. Raiffa, *Games and Decisions* (John Wiley, New York, 1957).

20. Marill, T. and D. M. Green, "Statistical recognition functions and the design of pattern recognizers," *IRE Trans. Elec. Comp.*, **EC-9**, 472–477 (December 1960).

21. Minsky, M., "Steps toward artificial intelligence," *Proc. IRE*, **49**, 8–30 (January 1961).

22. Neyman, J. and E. S. Pearson, "On the use and interpretation of certain test criteria for purposes of statistical inference," *Biometrica*, **20A**, 175–240 (1928).

23. Neyman, J. and E. S. Pearson, "On the problem of the most efficient tests of statistical hypotheses," *Phil. Trans. Royal Soc. London*, **231**, 289–337 (1933).

24. Nilsson, N. J., *Learning Machines* (McGraw-Hill, New York, 1965).

25. Raviv, J., "Decision making in Markov chains applied to the problem of pattern recognition," *IEEE Trans. Info. Theory*, **IT-13**, 536–551 (October 1967).

26. Riseman, E. M. and R. W. Ehrich, "Contextual word recognition using binary digrams," *IEEE Trans. Comp.*, **C-20**, 397–403 (April 1971).

27. Slagle, J. R. and R. C. T. Lee, "Applications of game tree searching techniques to sequential pattern recognition," *Comm. ACM*, **14**, 103–110 (February 1971).

28. von Neumann, J. and O. Morgenstern, *Theory of Games and Economic Behavior* (Princeton University Press, Princeton, N.J., First Edition, 1944).

29. Wald, A., "Contributions to the theory of statistical estimation and testing of hypotheses," *Ann. Math. Stat.*, **10**, 299–326 (1939).

30. Wald, A., *Sequential Analysis* (John Wiley, New York, 1947).

31. Wald, A., *Statistical Decision Functions* (John Wiley, New York, 1950).

32. Winder, R. O., "Threshold logic in artificial intelligence," *Artificial Intelligence*, IEEE Special Publication S-142, pp. 107–128 (January 1963).

PROBLEMS

1. Let the conditional densities for a two-category one-dimensional problem be given by the Cauchy distribution

$$p(x \mid \omega_i) = \frac{1}{\pi b} \cdot \frac{1}{1 + \left(\dfrac{x - a_i}{b}\right)^2}, \qquad i = 1, 2.$$

If $P(\omega_1) = P(\omega_2)$, show that $P(\omega_1 \mid x) = P(\omega_2 \mid x)$ if $x = (1/2)(a_1 + a_2)$. Sketch

$P(\omega_1 | x)$ for the case $a_1 = 3$, $a_2 = 5$, $b = 1$. How does $P(\omega_1 | x)$ behave as $x \to -\infty$? $+\infty$?

2. Using the conditional densities given in Problem 1, and assuming equal a priori probabilities, show that the minimum probability of error is given by

$$P(\text{error}) = \frac{1}{2} - \frac{1}{\pi} \tan^{-1} \left| \frac{a_2 - a_1}{2b} \right|.$$

Sketch this as a function of $|(a_2 - a_1)/b|$.

3. Consider the following decision rule for a two-category one-dimensional problem: Decide ω_1 if $x > \theta$; otherwise decide ω_2. Show that the probability of error for this rule is given by

$$P(\text{error}) = P(\omega_1) \int_{-\infty}^{\theta} p(x | \omega_1) \, dx + P(\omega_2) \int_{\theta}^{\infty} p(x | \omega_2) \, dx.$$

By differentiating, show that a necessary condition to minimize $P(\text{error})$ is that θ satisfy

$$p(\theta | \omega_1)P(\omega_1) = p(\theta | \omega_2)P(\omega_2).$$

Does this define θ uniquely? Give an example where a value of θ satisfying this equation actually maximizes the probability of error.

4. Let $\omega_{\max}(\mathbf{x})$ be the state of nature for which $P(\omega_{\max} | \mathbf{x}) \geq P(\omega_i | \mathbf{x})$ for all $i, i = 1, \ldots, c$. Show that $P(\omega_{\max} | \mathbf{x}) \geq 1/c$. In addition, show that for the minimum-error-rate decision rule the average probability of error is given by

$$P(\text{error}) = 1 - \int P(\omega_{\max} | \mathbf{x})p(\mathbf{x}) \, d\mathbf{x}.$$

Use these two results to show that $P(\text{error}) \leq (c - 1)/c$. Describe a situation for which $P(\text{error}) = (c - 1)/c$.

5. If a and b are nonnegative numbers, show that $\min(a, b) \leq \sqrt{ab}$. Use this to show that the error rate for a two-category Bayes classifier must satisfy

$$P(\text{error}) \leq \sqrt{P(\omega_1)P(\omega_2)} \ \rho \leq \tfrac{1}{2}\rho,$$

where ρ is the so-called *Bhattacharrya coefficient*

$$\rho = \int [p(\mathbf{x} | \omega_1)p(\mathbf{x} | \omega_2)]^{1/2} \, d\mathbf{x}.$$

6. In many pattern classification problems one has the option either to assign the pattern to one of c classes, or to *reject* it as being unrecognizable. If the cost for rejects is not too high, rejection may be a desirable action. Let

$$\lambda(\alpha_i | \omega_j) = \begin{cases} 0 & i = j \ \ i, j = 1, \ldots, c \\ \lambda_r & i = c + 1 \\ \lambda_s & \text{otherwise,} \end{cases}$$

where λ_r is the loss incurred for choosing the $(c + 1)$th action of rejection, and λ_s is the loss incurred for making a substitution error. Show that the minimum risk is obtained if we decide ω_i if $P(\omega_i \mid \mathbf{x}) \geq P(\omega_j \mid \mathbf{x})$ for all j and if $P(\omega_i \mid \mathbf{x}) \geq 1 - \lambda_r/\lambda_s$, and reject otherwise. What happens if $\lambda_r = 0$? What happens if $\lambda_r > \lambda_s$?

7. Using the results of Problem 6, show that the following discriminant functions are optimal:

$$g_i(\mathbf{x}) = \begin{cases} p(\mathbf{x} \mid \omega_i)P(\omega_i) & i = 1, \ldots, c \\ \dfrac{\lambda_s - \lambda_r}{\lambda_s} \displaystyle\sum_{j=1}^{c} p(\mathbf{x} \mid \omega_j)P(\omega_j) & i = c + 1. \end{cases}$$

Sketch these discriminant functions and the decision regions for the two-category one-dimensional case with $p(x \mid \omega_1) \sim N(1, 1)$, $p(x \mid \omega_2) \sim N(-1, 1)$, $P(\omega_1) = P(\omega_2) = 1/2$, and $\lambda_r/\lambda_s = 1/4$. Describe qualitatively what happens as λ_r/λ_s is increased from 0 to 1.

8. Suppose that we replace the deterministic decision function $\alpha(\mathbf{x})$ with a *randomized rule*, viz., the probability $P(\alpha_i \mid \mathbf{x})$ of taking action α_i upon observing $\mathbf{x}$. Show that the resulting risk is given by

$$R = \int \left[\sum_{i=1}^{a} R(\alpha_i \mid \mathbf{x})P(\alpha_i \mid \mathbf{x}) \right] p(\mathbf{x}) \, d\mathbf{x}.$$

In addition, show that R is minimized by choosing $P(\alpha_i \mid \mathbf{x}) = 1$ for the action α_i associated with the minimum conditional risk $R(\alpha_i \mid \mathbf{x})$, thereby showing that no benefit can be gained from randomizing.

9. Consider the multivariate normal density for which $\sigma_{ij} = 0$ and $\sigma_{ii} = \sigma_i^2$. Show that

$$p(\mathbf{x}) = \frac{1}{\displaystyle\prod_{i=1}^{d} \sqrt{2\pi}\,\sigma_i} \exp\left[-\frac{1}{2} \sum_{i=1}^{d} \left(\frac{x_i - \mu_i}{\sigma_i} \right)^2 \right].$$

Describe the contours of constant density, and write an expression for the Mahalanobis distance from $\mathbf{x}$ to $\boldsymbol{\mu}$.

10. Let $p(x \mid \omega_i) \sim N(\mu_i, \sigma^2)$ for a two-category one-dimensional problem with $P(\omega_1) = P(\omega_2) = 1/2$. Show that the minimum probability of error is given by

$$P_e = \frac{1}{\sqrt{2\pi}} \int_a^\infty e^{-(1/2)u^2} \, du,$$

where $a = |\mu_2 - \mu_1|/2\sigma$. Use the inequality

$$\frac{1}{\sqrt{2\pi}} \int_a^\infty e^{-(1/2)t^2} \, dt \leq \frac{1}{\sqrt{2\pi}\,a} e^{-(1/2)a^2}$$

to show that P_e goes to zero as $|\mu_2 - \mu_1|/\sigma$ goes to infinity.

11. Let $p(\mathbf{x} \mid \omega_i) \sim N(\boldsymbol{\mu}_i, \sigma^2 I)$ for a two-category d-dimensional problem with $P(\omega_1) = P(\omega_2) = 1/2$. Show that the minimum probability of error is given by

$$P_e = \frac{1}{\sqrt{2\pi}} \int_a^\infty e^{-(1/2)u^2} \, du,$$

where $a = \|\boldsymbol{\mu}_2 - \boldsymbol{\mu}_1\|/2\sigma$. Let $\boldsymbol{\mu}_1 = 0$ and $\boldsymbol{\mu}_2 = (\mu, \ldots, \mu)^t$. Use the inequality of Problem 10 to show that P_e approaches zero as d approaches infinity. Express the meaning of this result in words.

12. Let $p(\mathbf{x} \mid \omega_i) \sim N(\boldsymbol{\mu}_i, \Sigma)$ for a two-category d-dimensional problem with arbitrary a priori probabilities, and consider the Mahalanobis distance

$$r_i^2 = (\mathbf{x} - \boldsymbol{\mu}_i)^t \Sigma^{-1} (\mathbf{x} - \boldsymbol{\mu}_i).$$

(a) Show that the gradient of r_i^2 is given by

$$\nabla r_i^2 = 2\Sigma^{-1}(\mathbf{x} - \boldsymbol{\mu}_i).$$

(b) Show that ∇r_i^2 points in the same direction along any line through $\boldsymbol{\mu}_i$.
(c) Show that ∇r_1^2 and ∇r_2^2 point in opposite directions along the line from $\boldsymbol{\mu}_1$ to $\boldsymbol{\mu}_2$.
(d) Show that the optimal separating hyperplane in tangent to the constant probability density hyperellipsoids at the point that the separating hyperplane cuts the line from $\boldsymbol{\mu}_1$ to $\boldsymbol{\mu}_2$.

13. Under the assumption that $\lambda_{21} > \lambda_{11}$ and $\lambda_{12} > \lambda_{22}$, show that the general minimum risk discriminant function for the independent binary case described in Section 2.10 is given by $g(\mathbf{x}) = \mathbf{w}^t \mathbf{x} + w_0$, where $\mathbf{w}$ is unchanged, and

$$w_0 = \sum_{i=1}^{d} \log \frac{1 - p_i}{1 - q_i} + \log \frac{P(\omega_1)}{P(\omega_2)} + \log \frac{\lambda_{21} - \lambda_{11}}{\lambda_{12} - \lambda_{22}}.$$

14. Let the components of the vector $\mathbf{x} = (x_1, \ldots, x_d)^t$ be binary valued (1 or 0). Let $P(\omega_j)$ be the a priori probability for the state of nature ω_j $(j = 1, \ldots, c)$, and let

$$p_{ij} = \mathrm{Prob}(x_i = 1 \mid \omega_j) \qquad \begin{aligned} i &= 1, \ldots, d \\ j &= 1, \ldots, c \end{aligned}$$

with the components x_i being statistically independent for all $\mathbf{x}$ in ω_j. Show that the minimum probability of error is achieved by the following decision rule:
    Decide ω_k if $g_k(\mathbf{x}) \geq g_j(\mathbf{x})$ for all j, where

$$g_j(\mathbf{x}) = \sum_{i=1}^{d} x_i \log \frac{p_{ij}}{1 - p_{ij}} + \sum_{i=1}^{d} \log(1 - p_{ij}) + \log P(\omega_j).$$

15. Let the components of the vector $\mathbf{x} = (x_1, \ldots, x_d)^t$ be ternary valued $(1, 0$ or $-1)$, with

$$p_{ij} = \mathrm{Prob}(x_i = 1 \mid \omega_j)$$

$$q_{ij} = \mathrm{Prob}(x_i = 0 \mid \omega_j)$$

$$r_{ij} = \mathrm{Prob}(x_i = -1 \mid \omega_j)$$

and with the components x_i being statistically independent for all $\mathbf{x}$ in ω_j. Show that a minimum probability of error decision rule can be derived that involves discriminant functions $g_j(\mathbf{x})$ that are quadratic functions of the components x_i. Suggest a generalization of the results of Problems 14 and 15.

16. Let **x** be distributed as in Problem 14 with $c = 2$, d odd, and

$$p_{i1} = p > \tfrac{1}{2} \qquad i = 1, \ldots, d$$
$$p_{i2} = 1 - p \qquad i = 1, \ldots, d$$

and

$$P(\omega_1) = P(\omega_2) = \tfrac{1}{2}.$$

(a) Show that the minimum-error-rate decision rule becomes:

$$\text{Decide } \omega_1 \text{ if } \sum_{i=1}^{d} x_i > \frac{d}{2}.$$

(b) Show that the minimum probability of error is given by

$$P_e(d, p) = \sum_{k=0}^{(d-1)/2} \binom{d}{k} p^k (1 - p)^{d-k}.$$

(c) What is the limiting value of $P_e(d, p)$ as $p \to 1/2$?

(d) Show that $P_e(d, p)$ approaches zero as $d \to \infty$. (This is difficult to do without invoking the Law of Large Numbers. It is worthwhile to understand why it is true, however, and those who are curious but short on time should see pp. 139–142 of W. Feller, *An Introduction to Probability Theory and Its Applications* (John Wiley, New York, Volume I, Second Edition, 1959).)

Chapter 3

PARAMETER ESTIMATION AND SUPERVISED LEARNING

3.1 PARAMETER ESTIMATION AND SUPERVISED LEARNING

In Chapter 2 we saw how we could design an optimal classifier if we knew the a priori probabilities $P(\omega_j)$ and the class-conditional densities $p(\mathbf{x} \mid \omega_j)$. Unfortunately, in pattern recognition applications we rarely if ever have this kind of complete knowledge about the probabilistic structure of the problem. In a typical case we merely have some vague, general knowledge about the situation, together with a number of *design samples*—particular representatives of the patterns we want to classify.* The problem, then, is to find some way to use this information to design the classifier.

One approach to this problem is to use the samples to estimate the unknown probabilities and probability densities, and to use the resulting estimates as if they were the true values. In typical pattern classification problems, the estimation of the a priori probabilities presents no serious difficulties. However, estimation of the class-conditional densities is quite another matter. The number of available samples always seems too small, and serious problems arise when the dimensionality of the feature vector $\mathbf{x}$ is large. If our general knowledge about the problem permits us to parameterize the

---

* In the statistical literature, a sample of size n is a set of n such representatives. In calling each representative a sample, we are following the practice of the engineering literature. Statisticians should consider each of our samples as a sample of size one.

conditional densities, the severity of these problems can be reduced significantly. Suppose, for example, that we can reasonably assume that $p(\mathbf{x} \mid \omega_j)$ is normally distributed with mean $\boldsymbol{\mu}_j$ and covariance matrix Σ_j, although we do not know the exact values of these quantities. This simplifies the problem from one of estimating a *function* $p(\mathbf{x} \mid \omega_j)$ to one of estimating the *parameters* $\boldsymbol{\mu}_j$ and Σ_j.

The problem of parameter estimation is a classical problem in statistics, and it can be approached in several ways. We shall consider two common and reasonable procedures, *maximum likelihood* estimation and *Bayesian* estimation. Although the results obtained by these two procedures are frequently nearly identical, the approaches are conceptually quite different. Maximum likelihood methods view the parameters as quantities whose values are fixed but unknown. The best estimate is defined to be the one that maximizes the probability of obtaining the samples actually observed. Bayesian methods view the parameters as random variables having some known a priori distribution. Observation of the samples converts this to an a posteriori density, thereby revising our opinion about the true values of the parameters.

In the Bayesian case, we shall see that a typical effect of observing additional samples is to sharpen the a posteriori density function, causing it to peak near the true values of the parameters. This phenomenon is known as *Bayesian learning*. It is important to distinguish between *supervised learning* and *unsupervised learning*. In both cases, samples $\mathbf{x}$ are assumed to be obtained by selecting a state of nature ω_j with probability $P(\omega_j)$, and then independently selecting $\mathbf{x}$ according to the probability law $p(\mathbf{x} \mid \omega_j)$. The distinction is that with supervised learning we know the state of nature (class label) for each sample, whereas with unsupervised learning we do not. As one would expect, the problem of unsupervised learning is the more difficult one. In this chapter we shall consider only the supervised case, deferring consideration of unsupervised learning to Chapter 6.

3.2   MAXIMUM LIKELIHOOD ESTIMATION

3.2.1   The General Principle

Suppose that we separate a set of samples according to class, so that we have c sets of samples $\mathcal{X}_1, \ldots, \mathcal{X}_c$, with the samples in $\mathcal{X}_j$ having been drawn independently according to the probability law $p(\mathbf{x} \mid \omega_j)$. We assume that $p(\mathbf{x} \mid \omega_j)$ has a known parametric form, and is therefore determined uniquely by the value of a parameter vector $\boldsymbol{\theta}_j$. For example, we might have $p(\mathbf{x} \mid \omega_j) \sim N(\boldsymbol{\mu}_j, \Sigma_j)$, where the components of $\boldsymbol{\theta}_j$ include the components of both $\boldsymbol{\mu}_j$ and Σ_j. To show the dependence of $p(\mathbf{x} \mid \omega_j)$ on $\boldsymbol{\theta}_j$ explicitly, we write

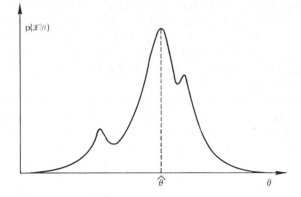

FIGURE 3.1.   The maximum likelihood estimate for a parameter θ.

$p(\mathbf{x} \mid \omega_j)$ as* $p(\mathbf{x} \mid \omega_j, \boldsymbol{\theta}_j)$. Our problem is to use the information provided by the samples to obtain good estimates for the unknown parameter vectors $\boldsymbol{\theta}_1, \ldots, \boldsymbol{\theta}_c$.

To simplify treatment of this problem, we shall assume that samples in $\mathscr{X}_i$ give no information about $\boldsymbol{\theta}_j$ if $i \neq j$. That is, we shall assume that the parameters for the different classes are functionally independent.† This permits us to work with each class separately, and to simplify our notation by deleting indications of class distinctions. Thus, with this assumption we have c separate problems of the following form: Use a set $\mathscr{X}$ of samples drawn independently according to the probability law $p(\mathbf{x} \mid \boldsymbol{\theta})$ to estimate the unknown parameter vector $\boldsymbol{\theta}$.

Suppose that $\mathscr{X}$ contains n samples, $\mathscr{X} = \{\mathbf{x}_1, \ldots, \mathbf{x}_n\}$. Then, since the samples were drawn independently,

$$p(\mathscr{X} \mid \boldsymbol{\theta}) = \prod_{k=1}^{n} p(\mathbf{x}_k \mid \boldsymbol{\theta}). \tag{1}$$

Viewed as a function of $\boldsymbol{\theta}$, $p(\mathscr{X} \mid \boldsymbol{\theta})$ is called the *likelihood* of $\boldsymbol{\theta}$ with respect to the set of samples. The *maximum likelihood estimate* of $\boldsymbol{\theta}$ is, by definition, that value $\hat{\boldsymbol{\theta}}$ that maximizes $p(\mathscr{X} \mid \boldsymbol{\theta})$ (see Figure 3.1). Intuitively, it corresponds to the value of $\boldsymbol{\theta}$ that in some sense best agrees with the actually observed samples.

---

* Some authors prefer to write $p(\mathbf{x} \mid \omega_j; \boldsymbol{\theta}_j)$, since, strictly speaking, the notation $p(\mathbf{x} \mid \omega_j, \boldsymbol{\theta}_j)$ implies that $\boldsymbol{\theta}_j$ is a random variable. We shall forgo this notational distinction, treating $\boldsymbol{\theta}_j$ as an ordinary parameter for maximum likelihood analysis and as a random variable for Bayesian analysis.

† Sometimes this is not the case, as, for example, when all of the samples share the same covariance matrix. The way to treat such cases is indicated in Problem 6.

For analytical purposes, it is usually easier to work with the logarithm of the likelihood than with the likelihood itself. Since the logarithm is monotonically increasing, the $\hat{\boldsymbol{\theta}}$ that maximizes the log-likelihood also maximizes the likelihood. If $p(\mathscr{X} \mid \boldsymbol{\theta})$ is a well behaved, differentiable function of $\boldsymbol{\theta}$, $\hat{\boldsymbol{\theta}}$ can be found by the standard methods of differential calculus. Let $\boldsymbol{\theta}$ be the p-component vector $\boldsymbol{\theta} = (\theta_1, \ldots, \theta_p)^t$, let $\boldsymbol{\nabla}_{\boldsymbol{\theta}}$ be the gradient operator

$$\boldsymbol{\nabla}_{\boldsymbol{\theta}} = \begin{bmatrix} \dfrac{\partial}{\partial \theta_1} \\ \cdot \\ \cdot \\ \cdot \\ \dfrac{\partial}{\partial \theta_p} \end{bmatrix}, \tag{2}$$

and let $l(\boldsymbol{\theta})$ be the log-likelihood function

$$l(\boldsymbol{\theta}) = \log p(\mathscr{X} \mid \boldsymbol{\theta}). \tag{3}$$

Then

$$l(\boldsymbol{\theta}) = \sum_{k=1}^{n} \log p(\mathbf{x}_k \mid \boldsymbol{\theta}) \tag{4}$$

and

$$\boldsymbol{\nabla}_{\boldsymbol{\theta}} l = \sum_{k=1}^{n} \boldsymbol{\nabla}_{\boldsymbol{\theta}} \log p(\mathbf{x}_k \mid \boldsymbol{\theta}). \tag{5}$$

Thus, a set of necessary conditions for the maximum likelihood estimate for $\boldsymbol{\theta}$ can be obtained from the set of p equations $\boldsymbol{\nabla}_{\boldsymbol{\theta}} l = 0$.

3.2.2 The Multivariate Normal Case: Unknown Mean

To see how these results apply to a specific case, suppose that the samples are drawn from a normal population with mean $\boldsymbol{\mu}$ and covariance matrix Σ. For simplicity, consider first the case where only the mean is unknown. Then

$$\log p(\mathbf{x}_k \mid \boldsymbol{\mu}) = -\tfrac{1}{2} \log\{(2\pi)^d \mid \Sigma \mid\} - \tfrac{1}{2}(\mathbf{x}_k - \boldsymbol{\mu})^t \Sigma^{-1}(\mathbf{x}_k - \boldsymbol{\mu})$$

and

$$\boldsymbol{\nabla}_{\boldsymbol{\mu}} \log p(\mathbf{x}_k \mid \boldsymbol{\mu}) = \Sigma^{-1}(\mathbf{x}_k - \boldsymbol{\mu}).$$

Identifying $\boldsymbol{\theta}$ with $\boldsymbol{\mu}$, we see from Eq. (5) that the maximum likelihood estimate for $\boldsymbol{\mu}$ must satisfy

$$\sum_{k=1}^{n} \Sigma^{-1}(\mathbf{x}_k - \hat{\boldsymbol{\mu}}) = 0.$$

Multiplying by Σ and rearranging, we obtain

$$\hat{\mu} = \frac{1}{n} \sum_{k=1}^{n} \mathbf{x}_k. \tag{6}$$

   This is a very satisfying result. It says that the maximum likelihood estimate for the unknown population mean is just the arithmetic average of the samples—the *sample mean*. Geometrically, if we think of the n samples as a cloud of points, the sample mean is the centroid of the cloud. The sample mean has a number of desirable statistical properties as well, and one would be inclined to use this rather obvious estimate even without knowing that it is the maximum likelihood solution.

3.2.3   The General Multivariate Normal Case

In the general (and more typical) multivariate normal case, neither the mean $\mathbf{\mu}$ nor the covariance matrix Σ is known. Thus, these unknown parameters constitute the components of the parameter vector $\mathbf{\theta}$. Consider the univariate case with $\theta_1 = \mu$ and $\theta_2 = \sigma^2$. Here

$$\log p(x_k \mid \mathbf{\theta}) = -\tfrac{1}{2} \log 2\pi\theta_2 - \frac{1}{2\theta_2}(x_k - \theta_1)^2$$

and

$$\nabla_{\mathbf{\theta}} \log p(x_k \mid \mathbf{\theta}) = \begin{bmatrix} \dfrac{1}{\theta_2}(x_k - \theta_1) \\[2ex] -\dfrac{1}{2\theta_2} + \dfrac{(x_k - \theta_1)^2}{2\theta_2^2} \end{bmatrix}.$$

Then, Eq. (5) leads to the conditions

$$\sum_{k=1}^{n} \frac{1}{\hat{\theta}_2}(x_k - \hat{\theta}_1) = 0$$

and

$$-\sum_{k=1}^{n} \frac{1}{\hat{\theta}_2} + \sum_{k=1}^{n} \frac{(x_k - \hat{\theta}_1)^2}{\hat{\theta}_2^2} = 0,$$

where $\hat{\theta}_1$ and $\hat{\theta}_2$ are the maximum likelihood estimates for θ_1 and θ_2, respectively. By substituting $\hat{\mu} = \hat{\theta}_1$, $\hat{\sigma}_1^2 = \hat{\theta}_2$ and doing a little rearranging, we obtain the following maximum likelihood estimates for μ and σ^2:

$$\hat{\mu} = \frac{1}{n} \sum_{k=1}^{n} x_k \tag{7}$$

$$\hat{\sigma}^2 = \frac{1}{n} \sum_{k=1}^{n} (x_k - \hat{\mu})^2. \tag{8}$$

While the analysis of the multivariate case is basically very similar, considerably more manipulation is involved. The well known* result is that the maximum likelihood estimates for $\boldsymbol{\mu}$ and $\varSigma$ are given by

$$\hat{\boldsymbol{\mu}} = \frac{1}{n} \sum_{k=1}^{n} \mathbf{x}_k \tag{9}$$

and

$$\hat{\varSigma} = \frac{1}{n} \sum_{k=1}^{n} (\mathbf{x}_k - \hat{\boldsymbol{\mu}})(\mathbf{x}_k - \hat{\boldsymbol{\mu}})^t. \tag{10}$$

Thus, once again we find that the maximum likelihood estimate for the mean vector is the sample mean. The maximum likelihood estimate for the covariance matrix is the arithmetic average of the n matrices $(\mathbf{x}_k - \hat{\boldsymbol{\mu}}) \times (\mathbf{x}_k - \hat{\boldsymbol{\mu}})^t$. Since the true covariance matrix is the expected value of the matrix $(\mathbf{x} - \boldsymbol{\mu})(\mathbf{x} - \boldsymbol{\mu})^t$, this is also a very satisfying result.

3.3 THE BAYES CLASSIFIER

Readers familiar with statistics know that the maximum likelihood estimate for a covariance matrix is biased; that is, the expected value of $\hat{\varSigma}$ is not equal to $\varSigma$. An unbiased estimate for $\varSigma$ is supplied by the *sample covariance matrix*

$$C = \frac{1}{n-1} \sum_{k=1}^{n} (\mathbf{x}_k - \hat{\boldsymbol{\mu}})(\mathbf{x}_k - \hat{\boldsymbol{\mu}})^t. \tag{11}$$

Clearly, $\hat{\varSigma} = [(n-1)/n]C$, and these two estimates are essentially identical when n is large. However, the existence of two similar but nevertheless distinct estimates for the covariance matrix is disconcerting to many students, and it is natural to ask which one is "correct." Of course, the answer is that these estimates are neither right nor wrong, they are just different. What the existence of two different estimates actually shows is that no single estimate possesses all of the properties one might desire. For our purposes, the most desirable property is rather complex—we want the estimate that leads to the best classification performance. While it is usually both reasonable and sound to design a classifier by substituting the maximum likelihood estimates for the unknown parameters, one might well wonder if other estimates might not lead to better performance. In this section we address this question from a Bayesian viewpoint.

* Cf., T. W. Anderson, *An Introduction to Multivariate Statistical Analysis*, Chap. 3 (John Wiley, New York, 1958).

3.3.1   The Class-Conditional Densities

The computation of the a posteriori probabilities $P(\omega_i \mid \mathbf{x})$ lies at the heart of Bayesian classification. Bayes rule allows us to compute these probabilities from the a priori probabilities $P(\omega_i)$ and the class-conditional densities $p(\mathbf{x} \mid \omega_i)$, but how can we proceed when these quantities are unknown? The general answer to this question is that the best we can do is to compute $P(\omega_i \mid \mathbf{x})$ using all of the information at our disposal. Part of this information might be a priori knowledge, such as knowledge of the functional forms for unknown densities and ranges for the values of unknown parameters. Part of this information might reside in a set of samples. If we let $\mathscr{X}$ denote the set of samples, then we can emphasize the role of the samples by saying that our goal is to compute the a posteriori probabilities $P(\omega_i \mid \mathbf{x}, \mathscr{X})$. From these probabilities we can obtain the Bayes classifier.

By Bayes rule,*

$$P(\omega_i \mid \mathbf{x}, \mathscr{X}) = \frac{p(\mathbf{x} \mid \omega_i, \mathscr{X})P(\omega_i \mid \mathscr{X})}{\displaystyle\sum_{j=1}^{c} p(\mathbf{x} \mid \omega_j, \mathscr{X})P(\omega_j \mid \mathscr{X})}. \tag{12}$$

As this equation suggests, we can use the information provided by the samples to help determine both the class-conditional densities and the a priori probabilities.

Although we could maintain this generality, we shall henceforth assume that the true values of the a priori probabilities are known, so that $P(\omega_i \mid \mathscr{X}) = P(\omega_i)$. Furthermore, since we are treating the supervised case, we can separate the samples by class into c subsets $\mathscr{X}_1, \ldots, \mathscr{X}_c$, with the samples in $\mathscr{X}_i$ belonging to ω_i. In many cases of interest, and in all of the cases we shall treat, the samples in $\mathscr{X}_j$ have no influence on $p(\mathbf{x} \mid \omega_i, \mathscr{X})$ if $i \neq j$. This has two simplifying consequences. First, it allows us to work with each class separately, using only the samples in $\mathscr{X}_i$ to determine $p(\mathbf{x} \mid \omega_i, \mathscr{X})$. Used in conjunction with our assumption that the a priori probabilities are known, this allows us to write Eq. (12) as

$$P(\omega_i \mid \mathbf{x}, \mathscr{X}) = \frac{p(\mathbf{x} \mid \omega_i, \mathscr{X}_i)P(\omega_i)}{\displaystyle\sum_{j=1}^{c} p(\mathbf{x} \mid \omega_j, \mathscr{X}_j)P(\omega_j)}. \tag{13}$$

Second, because each class can be treated independently, we can dispense with needless class distinctions and simplify our notation. In essence, we have c

---

* Note that every probability and probability density function in this equation is conditioned by the set of samples. The fact that this equation is merely Bayes rule becomes more clear when common conditioning quantities are ignored. The reader may find this device helpful in interpreting similar equations elsewhere in this chapter.

separate problems of the following form: Use a set $\mathscr{X}$ of samples drawn independently according to the fixed but unknown probability law $p(\mathbf{x})$ to determine $p(\mathbf{x} \mid \mathscr{X})$. This is the central problem of Bayesian learning.

3.3.2   The Parameter Distribution

Although the desired probability density $p(\mathbf{x})$ is unknown, we assume that it has a known parametric form. The only thing assumed unknown is the value of a parameter vector $\boldsymbol{\theta}$. We shall express the fact that $p(\mathbf{x})$ is unknown but has known parametric form by saying that the function $p(\mathbf{x} \mid \boldsymbol{\theta})$ is completely known. The Bayesian approach assumes that the unknown parameter vector is a random variable. Any information we might have about $\boldsymbol{\theta}$ prior to observing the samples is assumed to be contained in a *known* a priori density $p(\boldsymbol{\theta})$. Observation of the samples converts this to an a posteriori density $p(\boldsymbol{\theta} \mid \mathscr{X})$, which, hopefully, is sharply peaked about the true value of $\boldsymbol{\theta}$.

Our basic goal is to compute $p(\mathbf{x} \mid \mathscr{X})$, which is as close as we can come to obtaining the unknown $p(\mathbf{x})$. We do this by integrating the joint density $p(\mathbf{x}, \boldsymbol{\theta} \mid \mathscr{X})$ over $\boldsymbol{\theta}$. That is,

$$p(\mathbf{x} \mid \mathscr{X}) = \int p(\mathbf{x}, \boldsymbol{\theta} \mid \mathscr{X})\, d\boldsymbol{\theta},$$

where the integration extends over the entire parameter space.* Now we can always write $p(\mathbf{x}, \boldsymbol{\theta} \mid \mathscr{X})$ as the product $p(\mathbf{x} \mid \boldsymbol{\theta}, \mathscr{X})p(\boldsymbol{\theta} \mid \mathscr{X})$. Since the selection of $\mathbf{x}$ and of the samples in $\mathscr{X}$ is done independently, the first factor is merely $p(\mathbf{x} \mid \boldsymbol{\theta})$. That is, the distribution of $\mathbf{x}$ is known completely once we know the value of the parameter vector. Thus,

$$p(\mathbf{x} \mid \mathscr{X}) = \int p(\mathbf{x} \mid \boldsymbol{\theta})p(\boldsymbol{\theta} \mid \mathscr{X})\, d\boldsymbol{\theta}. \tag{14}$$

This key equation links the desired "class-conditional" density $p(\mathbf{x} \mid \mathscr{X})$ to the a posteriori density $p(\boldsymbol{\theta} \mid \mathscr{X})$ for the unknown parameter vector. If $p(\boldsymbol{\theta} \mid \mathscr{X})$ peaks very sharply about some value $\hat{\boldsymbol{\theta}}$, we obtain $p(\mathbf{x} \mid \mathscr{X}) \approx p(\mathbf{x} \mid \hat{\boldsymbol{\theta}})$, i.e., the result we would obtain by substituting the estimate $\hat{\boldsymbol{\theta}}$ for the true parameter vector. In general, if we are less certain about the exact value of $\boldsymbol{\theta}$, this equation directs us to average $p(\mathbf{x} \mid \boldsymbol{\theta})$ over the possible values of $\boldsymbol{\theta}$. Thus, when the unknown densities have a known parametric form, the samples exert their influence on $p(\mathbf{x} \mid \mathscr{X})$ through the a posteriori density $p(\boldsymbol{\theta} \mid \mathscr{X})$.

---

* Throughout this chapter we shall take the domain of integration for all integrals to be the entire space involved.

3.4 LEARNING THE MEAN OF A NORMAL DENSITY

3.4.1 The Univariate Case: $p(\mu \mid \mathscr{X})$

In this section we calculate the a posteriori density $p(\theta \mid \mathscr{X})$ and the desired probability density $p(\mathbf{x} \mid \mathscr{X})$ for the case where $p(\mathbf{x} \mid \boldsymbol{\mu}) \sim N(\boldsymbol{\mu}, \Sigma)$, the mean vector $\boldsymbol{\mu}$ being the unknown parameter vector. For simplicity, we begin with the univariate case, so that

$$p(x \mid \mu) \sim N(\mu, \sigma^2), \tag{15}$$

where the only unknown quantity is the mean μ. We assume that whatever prior knowledge we might have about μ can be expressed by a *known* a priori density $p(\mu)$. In the sequel, we shall make the further assumption that

$$p(\mu) \sim N(\mu_0, \sigma_0^2), \tag{16}$$

where both μ_0 and σ_0^2 are known. Roughly speaking, μ_0 represents our best a priori guess for μ, and σ_0^2 measures our uncertainty about this guess. The assumption that the a priori distribution for μ is normal will simplify the subsequent mathematics. However, the crucial assumption is not so much that the a priori distribution for μ is normal, but that it exists and is known.

Having selected the a priori density for μ, we can view the situation as follows. Imagine that a value is drawn for μ from a population governed by the probability law $p(\mu)$. Once this value is drawn, it becomes the true value of μ and completely determines the density for x. Suppose now that n samples $x_1, \ldots, x_n$ are independently drawn from the resulting population. Letting $\mathscr{X} = \{x_1, \ldots, x_n\}$, we use Bayes rule to obtain

$$p(\mu \mid \mathscr{X}) = \frac{p(\mathscr{X} \mid \mu)p(\mu)}{\displaystyle\int p(\mathscr{X} \mid \mu)p(\mu)\, d\mu}$$

$$= \alpha \prod_{k=1}^{n} p(x_k \mid \mu)p(\mu), \tag{17}$$

where α is a scale factor that depends on $\mathscr{X}$ but is independent of μ. This equation shows how the observation of a set of samples affects our ideas about the true value of μ, changing the a priori density $p(\mu)$ into an a posteriori density $p(\mu \mid \mathscr{X})$. Since $p(x_k \mid \mu) \sim N(\mu, \sigma^2)$ and $p(\mu) \sim N(\mu_0, \sigma_0^2)$,

$$
\begin{aligned}
p(\mu \mid \mathscr{X}) &= \alpha \prod_{k=1}^{n} \frac{1}{\sqrt{2\pi}\,\sigma} \exp\left[-\frac{1}{2}\left(\frac{x_k - \mu}{\sigma}\right)^2\right] \frac{1}{\sqrt{2\pi}\,\sigma_0} \exp\left[-\frac{1}{2}\left(\frac{\mu - \mu_0}{\sigma_0}\right)^2\right] \\
&= \alpha' \exp\left[-\frac{1}{2}\left\{\sum_{k=1}^{n}\left(\frac{\mu - x_k}{\sigma}\right)^2 + \left(\frac{\mu - \mu_0}{\sigma_0}\right)^2\right\}\right] \\
&= \alpha'' \exp\left[-\frac{1}{2}\left\{\left(\frac{n}{\sigma^2} + \frac{1}{\sigma_0^2}\right)\mu^2 - 2\left(\frac{1}{\sigma^2}\sum_{k=1}^{n}x_k + \frac{\mu_0}{\sigma_0^2}\right)\mu\right\}\right],
\end{aligned}
\tag{18}
$$

where factors that do not depend on μ have been absorbed in the constants α' and α''. Thus, $p(\mu \mid \mathscr{X})$ is an exponential function of a quadratic function of μ, i.e., is again a normal density. Since this is true for any number of samples, $p(\mu \mid \mathscr{X})$ remains normal as the number n of samples is increased, and $p(\mu \mid \mathscr{X})$ is said to be a *reproducing density*. If we write $p(\mu \mid \mathscr{X}) \sim N(\mu_n, \sigma_n^2)$, then μ_n and σ_n^2 can be found by equating coefficients in Eq. (18) with corresponding coefficients in

$$
p(\mu \mid \mathscr{X}) = \frac{1}{\sqrt{2\pi}\,\sigma_n} \exp\left[-\frac{1}{2}\left(\frac{\mu - \mu_n}{\sigma_n}\right)^2\right].
\tag{19}
$$

This yields

$$
\frac{1}{\sigma_n^2} = \frac{n}{\sigma^2} + \frac{1}{\sigma_0^2}
\tag{20}
$$

and

$$
\frac{\mu_n}{\sigma_n^2} = \frac{n}{\sigma^2}\,m_n + \frac{\mu_0}{\sigma_0^2},
\tag{21}
$$

where m_n is the *sample mean*

$$
m_n = \frac{1}{n}\sum_{k=1}^{n} x_k.
\tag{22}
$$

Solving explicitly for μ_n and σ_n^2, we obtain

$$
\mu_n = \frac{n\sigma_0^2}{n\sigma_0^2 + \sigma^2}\,m_n + \frac{\sigma^2}{n\sigma_0^2 + \sigma^2}\,\mu_0
\tag{23}
$$

and

$$
\sigma_n^2 = \frac{\sigma_0^2 \sigma^2}{n\sigma_0^2 + \sigma^2}.
\tag{24}
$$

These equations show how the a priori information is combined with the empirical information in the samples to obtain the a posteriori density $p(\mu \mid \mathscr{X})$. Roughly speaking, μ_n represents our best guess for μ after observing

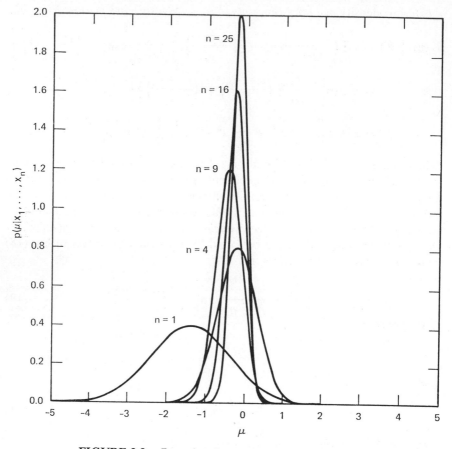

FIGURE 3.2.   Learning the mean of a normal density.

n samples, and σ_n^2 measures our uncertainty about this guess. Since σ_n^2 decreases monotonically with n, approaching σ^2/n as n approaches infinity, each additional observation decreases our uncertainty about the true value of μ. As n increases, $p(\mu \mid \mathcal{X})$ becomes more and more sharply peaked, approaching a Dirac delta function as n approaches infinity. This behavior is commonly known as *Bayesian learning* (see Figure 3.2).

In general, μ_n is a linear combination of m_n and μ_0, with coefficients that are nonnegative and sum to one. Thus, μ_n always lies somewhere between m_n and μ_0. If $\sigma_0 \neq 0$, μ_n approaches the sample mean as n approaches infinity. If $\sigma_0 = 0$, we have a degenerate case in which our a priori certainty that $\mu = \mu_0$ is so strong that no number of observations can change our opinion. At the other extreme, if $\sigma_0 \gg \sigma$, we are so uncertain about our a priori guess that we take $\mu_n = m_n$, using only the samples to estimate μ. In general, the relative balance between prior knowledge and empirical data is set by the ratio of σ^2 to σ_0^2, which is sometimes called the *dogmatism*. If the dogmatism is not infinite, after enough samples are taken the exact values assumed for μ_0 and σ_0^2 will be unimportant, and μ_n will converge to the sample mean.

3.4.2 The Univariate Case: $p(x \mid \mathcal{X})$

Having obtained the a posteriori density $p(\mu \mid \mathcal{X})$, all that remains is to obtain the "class-conditional" density $p(x \mid \mathcal{X})$.* From Eqs. (14), (15), and (19),

$$p(x \mid \mathcal{X}) = \int p(x \mid \mu)p(\mu \mid \mathcal{X}) \, d\mu$$

$$- \int \frac{1}{\sqrt{2\pi}\,\sigma} \exp\left[-\frac{1}{2}\left(\frac{x-\mu}{\sigma}\right)^2\right] \frac{1}{\sqrt{2\pi}\,\sigma_n} \exp\left[-\frac{1}{2}\left(\frac{\mu-\mu_n}{\sigma_n}\right)^2\right] d\mu$$

$$= \frac{1}{2\pi\sigma\sigma_n} \exp\left[-\frac{1}{2}\frac{(x-\mu)_n{}^2}{\sigma^2 + \sigma_n^2}\right] f(\sigma, \sigma_n),$$

where

$$f(\sigma, \sigma_n) = \int \exp\left[-\frac{1}{2}\frac{\sigma^2+\sigma_n^2}{\sigma^2\sigma_n^2}\left(\mu - \frac{\sigma_n^2 x + \sigma^2\mu_n}{\sigma^2+\sigma_n^2}\right)^2\right] d\mu.$$

That is, as a function of x, $p(x \mid \mathcal{X})$ is proportional to $\exp[-(1/2)(x-\mu_n)^2/(\sigma^2+\sigma_n^2)]$, and hence $p(x \mid \mathcal{X})$ is normally distributed with mean μ_n and variance $\sigma^2 + \sigma_n^2$:

$$p(x \mid \mathcal{X}) \sim N(\mu_n, \sigma^2 + \sigma_n^2). \tag{25}$$

In other words, to obtain the "class-conditional" density $p(x \mid \mathcal{X})$, whose parametric form is known to be $p(x \mid \mu) \sim N(\mu, \sigma^2)$, we merely replace μ by μ_n and σ^2 by $\sigma^2 + \sigma_n^2$. In effect, the conditional mean μ_n is treated as if it were the true mean, and the known variance is increased to account for the additional uncertainty in x resulting from our lack of exact knowledge of the mean μ. This, then, is our final result; the density $p(x \mid \mathcal{X})$ is the desired class-conditional density $p(x \mid \omega_j, \mathcal{X}_j)$, and together with the a priori probabilities $P(\omega_j)$ it gives us the probabilistic information needed to design the Bayes classifier.

3.4.3 The Multivariate Case

The treatment of the multivariate case is a direct generalization of the univariate case. Thus, we shall only sketch the proof briefly. As before, we

---

* Recall that we dropped class distinctions for simplicity, but that all the samples come from the same class, say ω_j, and $p(x \mid \mathcal{X})$ is really $p(x \mid \omega_j, \mathcal{X}_j)$.

assume that

$$p(\mathbf{x} \mid \boldsymbol{\mu}) \sim N(\boldsymbol{\mu}, \Sigma) \tag{26}$$

and

$$p(\boldsymbol{\mu}) \sim N(\boldsymbol{\mu}_0, \Sigma_0), \tag{27}$$

where Σ, Σ_0, and $\boldsymbol{\mu}_0$ are assumed to be known. After observing a set $\mathcal{X}$ of n independent samples $\mathbf{x}_1, \ldots, \mathbf{x}_n$, we use Bayes rule to obtain

$$p(\boldsymbol{\mu} \mid \mathcal{X}) = \alpha \prod_{k=1}^{n} p(\mathbf{x}_k \mid \boldsymbol{\mu}) p(\boldsymbol{\mu})$$

$$= \alpha'' \exp\left[-\tfrac{1}{2}\left\{ \boldsymbol{\mu}^t (n\Sigma^{-1} + \Sigma_0^{-1})\boldsymbol{\mu} - 2\boldsymbol{\mu}^t \left(\Sigma^{-1} \sum_{k=1}^{n} \mathbf{x}_k + \Sigma_0^{-1}\boldsymbol{\mu}_0 \right) \right\} \right],$$

which has the form

$$p(\boldsymbol{\mu} \mid \mathcal{X}) = \alpha''' \exp[-\tfrac{1}{2}(\boldsymbol{\mu} - \boldsymbol{\mu}_n)^t \Sigma_n^{-1}(\boldsymbol{\mu} - \boldsymbol{\mu}_n)].$$

Thus, $p(\boldsymbol{\mu} \mid \mathcal{X}) \sim N(\boldsymbol{\mu}_n, \Sigma_n)$, and once again we have a reproducing density. Equating coefficients, we obtain the analogs of Eqs. (20) and (21),

$$\Sigma_n^{-1} = n\Sigma^{-1} + \Sigma_0^{-1} \tag{28}$$

and

$$\Sigma_n^{-1}\boldsymbol{\mu}_n = n\Sigma^{-1}\mathbf{m}_n + \Sigma_0^{-1}\boldsymbol{\mu}_0, \tag{29}$$

where $\mathbf{m}_n$ is the sample mean

$$\mathbf{m}_n = \frac{1}{n} \sum_{k=1}^{n} \mathbf{x}_k. \tag{30}$$

The solution of these equations for $\boldsymbol{\mu}_n$ and Σ_n is simplified by knowledge of the matrix identity

$$(A^{-1} + B^{-1})^{-1} = A(A + B)^{-1}B = B(A + B)^{-1}A,$$

which is valid for any pair of nonsingular, d-by-d matrices A and B. After a little manipulation, we obtain the final results

$$\boldsymbol{\mu}_n = \Sigma_0\left(\Sigma_0 + \frac{1}{n}\Sigma\right)^{-1}\mathbf{m}_n + \frac{1}{n}\Sigma\left(\Sigma_0 + \frac{1}{n}\Sigma\right)^{-1}\boldsymbol{\mu}_0 \tag{31}$$

and

$$\Sigma_n = \Sigma_0\left(\Sigma_0 + \frac{1}{n}\Sigma\right)^{-1}\frac{1}{n}\Sigma. \tag{32}$$

The proof that $p(\mathbf{x} \mid \mathcal{X}) \sim N(\boldsymbol{\mu}_n, \Sigma + \Sigma_n)$ can be obtained as before by performing the integration

$$p(\mathbf{x} \mid \mathcal{X}) = \int p(\mathbf{x} \mid \boldsymbol{\mu}) p(\boldsymbol{\mu} \mid \mathcal{X})\, d\boldsymbol{\mu}.$$

However, this result can be obtained with less effort by observing that $\mathbf{x}$ can be viewed as the sum of two random variables, a random vector $\boldsymbol{\mu}$ with $p(\boldsymbol{\mu} \mid \mathscr{X}) \sim N(\boldsymbol{\mu}_n, \Sigma_n)$ and an independent random vector $\mathbf{y}$ with $p(\mathbf{y}) \sim N(\mathbf{0}, \Sigma)$. Since the sum of two independent, normally distributed vectors is again a normally distributed vector whose mean is the sum of the means and whose covariance matrix is the sum of the covariance matrices, we have

$$p(\mathbf{x} \mid \mathscr{X}) \sim N(\boldsymbol{\mu}_n, \Sigma + \Sigma_n), \tag{33}$$

and the generalization is complete.

3.5 GENERAL BAYESIAN LEARNING

We have just seen how the Bayesian approach can be used to obtain the desired density $p(\mathbf{x} \mid \mathscr{X})$ in a special, multivariate normal case. This approach can be generalized to apply to any situation in which the unknown density can be parameterized. The basic assumptions are summarized as follows:

(1) The form of the density $p(\mathbf{x} \mid \boldsymbol{\theta})$ is assumed to be known, but the value of the parameter vector $\boldsymbol{\theta}$ is not known exactly.
(2) Our initial knowledge about $\boldsymbol{\theta}$ is assumed to be contained in a known a priori density $p(\boldsymbol{\theta})$.
(3) The rest of our knowledge about $\boldsymbol{\theta}$ is contained in a set $\mathscr{X}$ of n samples $\mathbf{x}_1, \ldots, \mathbf{x}_n$ drawn independently according to the unknown probability law $p(\mathbf{x})$.

The basic problem is to compute the a posteriori density $p(\boldsymbol{\theta} \mid \mathscr{X})$, since from this we can use Eq. (14) to compute $p(\mathbf{x} \mid \mathscr{X})$:

$$p(\mathbf{x} \mid \mathscr{X}) = \int p(\mathbf{x} \mid \boldsymbol{\theta}) p(\boldsymbol{\theta} \mid \mathscr{X}) \, d\boldsymbol{\theta}. \tag{14}$$

By Bayes rule,

$$p(\boldsymbol{\theta} \mid \mathscr{X}) = \frac{p(\mathscr{X} \mid \boldsymbol{\theta}) p(\boldsymbol{\theta})}{\int p(\mathscr{X} \mid \boldsymbol{\theta}) p(\boldsymbol{\theta}) \, d\boldsymbol{\theta}}, \tag{34}$$

and by the independence assumption

$$p(\mathscr{X} \mid \boldsymbol{\theta}) = \prod_{k=1}^{n} p(\mathbf{x}_k \mid \boldsymbol{\theta}). \tag{35}$$

This constitutes the formal solution to the problem. Eqs. (14) and (34) illuminate its relation to the maximum likelihood solution. Suppose that $p(\mathscr{X} \mid \boldsymbol{\theta})$ reaches a sharp peak at $\boldsymbol{\theta} = \hat{\boldsymbol{\theta}}$. If the a priori density $p(\boldsymbol{\theta})$ is not zero at $\boldsymbol{\theta} = \hat{\boldsymbol{\theta}}$ and does not change much in the surrounding neighborhood, then

$p(\theta \mid \mathcal{X})$ also peaks at that point. Thus, Eq. (14) shows that $p(\mathbf{x} \mid \mathcal{X})$ will be approximately $p(\mathbf{x} \mid \hat{\theta})$, the result one would obtain by using the maximum likelihood estimate as if it were the true value. If the peak of $p(\mathcal{X} \mid \theta)$ is not so sharp that the influence of a priori information or the uncertainty in the true value of θ can be ignored, then the Bayesian solution tells us how to use the available information to compute the desired density $p(\mathbf{x} \mid \mathcal{X})$.

While we have obtained the formal Bayesian solution to the problem, a number of interesting questions remain. One concerns the difficulty of carrying out these computations. Another concerns the convergence of $p(\mathbf{x} \mid \mathcal{X})$ to $p(\mathbf{x})$. We shall discuss the matter of convergence briefly, and shall then turn to the computational question.

To indicate explicitly the number of samples in a set, we shall write $\mathcal{X}^n = \{\mathbf{x}_1, \ldots, \mathbf{x}_n\}$. Then from Eq. (35), if $n > 1$

$$p(\mathcal{X}^n \mid \theta) = p(\mathbf{x}_n \mid \theta) p(\mathcal{X}^{n-1} \mid \theta).$$

Substituting this in Eq. (34) and using Bayes rule, we see that the a posteriori density satisfies the recursion relation

$$p(\theta \mid \mathcal{X}^n) = \frac{p(\mathbf{x}_n \mid \theta) p(\theta \mid \mathcal{X}^{n-1})}{\displaystyle\int p(\mathbf{x}_n \mid \theta) p(\theta \mid \mathcal{X}^{n-1}) \, d\theta} \tag{36}$$

With the understanding that $p(\theta \mid \mathcal{X}^0) = p(\theta)$, repeated use of this equation produces the sequence of densities $p(\theta)$, $p(\theta \mid \mathbf{x}_1)$, $p(\theta \mid \mathbf{x}_1, \mathbf{x}_2)$, and so forth. This is called the *recursive Bayes* approach to parameter estimation. When this sequence of densities converges to a Dirac delta function centered about the true parameter value, the resulting behavior is frequently called *Bayesian learning*.

For most of the typically encountered probability densities $p(\mathbf{x} \mid \theta)$, the sequence of a posteriori densities does converge to a delta function. Roughly speaking, this implies that with a large number of samples there is only one value for θ that causes $p(\mathbf{x} \mid \theta)$ to fit the data, i.e., that θ can be determined uniquely from $p(\mathbf{x} \mid \theta)$. When this is the case, $p(\mathbf{x} \mid \theta)$ is said to be *identifiable*. A rigorous proof of convergence under these conditions requires a precise statement of the properties required of $p(\mathbf{x} \mid \theta)$ and $p(\theta)$ and considerable care, but presents no serious problems.

There are occasions, however, when more than one value of θ may yield the same value for $p(\mathbf{x} \mid \theta)$. In such cases, θ can not be determined uniquely from $p(\mathbf{x} \mid \theta)$, and $p(\theta \mid \mathcal{X}^n)$ will peak near all of the values of θ that explain the data. Fortunately, this ambiguity is erased by the integration in Eq. (14), since $p(\mathbf{x} \mid \theta)$ is the same for all of these values of θ. Thus, $p(\mathbf{x} \mid \mathcal{X}^n)$ will typically converge to $p(\mathbf{x})$ whether or not $p(\mathbf{x} \mid \theta)$ is identifiable. While this might make the problem of identifiability appear to be something of a straw man, we shall see in Chapter 6 that identifiability presents a genuine problem in the case of unsupervised learning.

3.6 SUFFICIENT STATISTICS

From a practical viewpoint, the formal solution provided by Eqs. (14), (34), and (35) is not computationally attractive. In pattern classification applications it is not unusual to have dozens or hundreds of unknown parameters and thousands of samples, which makes the direct computation and tabulation of $p(\mathscr{X} \mid \theta)$ or $p(\theta \mid \mathscr{X})$ quite out of the question. The only hope for a computationally feasible solution lies in being able to find a parametric form for $p(\mathbf{x} \mid \theta)$ that on the one hand matches the characteristics of the problem and on the other hand allows a reasonable analytical solution.

Consider the simplification that occurred in the problem of learning the mean of a multivariate normal density. Assuming that the a priori density $p(\mu)$ was normal, we found that the a posteriori density $p(\mu \mid \mathscr{X})$ was also normal. Equally important, Eqs. (31) and (32) show that the basic data processing required was merely the computation of the sample mean $\mathbf{m}_n$. This easily computed and easily updated statistic contained all the information in the samples relevant to estimating the unknown population mean. One might suspect that this simplicity is just one more happy property of the normal distribution, and that such good fortune is not likely to occur in other cases. While this is largely true, there is a family of distributions for which computationally feasible solutions can be obtained, and the key to their simplicity lies in the notion of a *sufficient statistic*.

To begin with, any function of the samples is a statistic. Roughly speaking, a sufficient statistic $\mathbf{s}$ is a function* of the samples $\mathscr{X}$ that contains all of the information relevant to estimating some parameter θ. Intuitively, one might expect the definition of a sufficient statistic to involve the requirement that $p(\theta \mid \mathbf{s}, \mathscr{X}) = p(\theta \mid \mathbf{s})$. However, this would require treating θ as a random variable, limiting the definition to a Bayesian domain. Thus, the conventional definition is as follows: A statistic $\mathbf{s}$ is said to be *sufficient* for θ if $p(\mathscr{X} \mid \mathbf{s}, \theta)$ is independent of θ. If we think of θ as a random variable, we can write

$$p(\theta \mid \mathbf{s}, \mathscr{X}) = \frac{p(\mathscr{X} \mid \mathbf{s}, \theta)p(\theta \mid \mathbf{s})}{p(\mathscr{X} \mid \mathbf{s})},$$

whereupon it becomes evident that $p(\theta \mid \mathbf{s}, \mathscr{X}) = p(\theta \mid \mathbf{s})$ if $\mathbf{s}$ is sufficient for θ. Conversely, if $\mathbf{s}$ is a statistic for which $p(\theta \mid \mathbf{s}, \mathscr{X}) = p(\theta \mid \mathbf{s})$, and if $p(\theta \mid \mathbf{s}) \neq 0$, it is easy to show that $p(\mathscr{X} \mid \mathbf{s}, \theta)$ is independent of θ. Thus, the intuitive and the conventional definitions are basically equivalent.

---

* When we must distinguish between the function and its value, we shall write $\mathbf{s} = \varphi(\mathscr{X})$.

A fundamental theorem concerning sufficient statistics is the *factorization theorem*, which states that **s** is sufficient for $\boldsymbol{\theta}$ if and only if $p(\mathcal{X} \mid \boldsymbol{\theta})$ can be factored into the product of two functions, one depending only on **s** and $\boldsymbol{\theta}$, and the other depending only on the samples. The virtue of the factorization theorem is that it allows us to shift our attention from the rather complicated density $p(\mathcal{X} \mid \mathbf{s}, \boldsymbol{\theta})$ used to define a sufficient statistic to the simpler function

$$p(\mathcal{X} \mid \boldsymbol{\theta}) = \prod_{k=1}^{n} p(\mathbf{x}_k \mid \boldsymbol{\theta}).$$

In addition, the factorization theorem makes it clear that the characteristics of a sufficient statistic are completely determined by the density $p(\mathbf{x} \mid \boldsymbol{\theta})$, and have nothing to do with a felicitous choice for an a priori density $p(\boldsymbol{\theta})$. A proof of the factorization theorem in the continuous case is slightly sticky because degenerate situations are involved. Since the proof has some intrinsic interest, however, we include a proof for the simpler discrete case.

The Factorization Theorem: A statistic **s** is sufficient for $\boldsymbol{\theta}$ if and only if the probability $P(\mathcal{X} \mid \boldsymbol{\theta})$ can be written as the product

$$P(\mathcal{X} \mid \boldsymbol{\theta}) = g(\mathbf{s}, \boldsymbol{\theta})h(\mathcal{X}). \tag{37}$$

Proof: *(a)* Suppose first that **s** is sufficient for $\boldsymbol{\theta}$, so that $P(\mathcal{X} \mid \mathbf{s}, \boldsymbol{\theta})$ is independent of $\boldsymbol{\theta}$. Since we want to show that $P(\mathcal{X} \mid \boldsymbol{\theta})$ can be factored, our attention is directed toward computing $P(\mathcal{X} \mid \boldsymbol{\theta})$ in terms of $P(\mathcal{X} \mid \mathbf{s}, \boldsymbol{\theta})$. We do this by summing the joint probability $P(\mathcal{X}, \mathbf{s} \mid \boldsymbol{\theta})$ over all values of **s**:

$$P(\mathcal{X} \mid \boldsymbol{\theta}) = \sum_{\mathbf{s}} P(\mathcal{X}, \mathbf{s} \mid \boldsymbol{\theta})$$

$$= \sum_{\mathbf{s}} P(\mathcal{X} \mid \mathbf{s}, \boldsymbol{\theta})P(\mathbf{s} \mid \boldsymbol{\theta}).$$

But since $\mathbf{s} = \boldsymbol{\varphi}(\mathcal{X})$, there is only one possible value for **s**, and thus

$$P(\mathcal{X} \mid \boldsymbol{\theta}) = P(\mathcal{X} \mid \mathbf{s}, \boldsymbol{\theta})P(\mathbf{s} \mid \boldsymbol{\theta}).$$

Moreover, since by hypothesis $P(\mathbf{x} \mid \mathbf{s}, \boldsymbol{\theta})$ is independent of $\boldsymbol{\theta}$, the first factor depends only on $\mathcal{X}$. Identifying $P(\mathbf{s} \mid \boldsymbol{\theta})$ with $g(\mathbf{s}, \boldsymbol{\theta})$, we see that $P(\mathcal{X} \mid \boldsymbol{\theta})$ factors as desired.

(b) To show that the ability to factor $P(\mathcal{X} \mid \boldsymbol{\theta})$ as the product $g(\mathbf{s}, \boldsymbol{\theta})h(\mathcal{X})$ implies that **s** is sufficient for $\boldsymbol{\theta}$, we must show that such a factoring implies that the conditional probability $P(\mathcal{X} \mid \mathbf{s}, \boldsymbol{\theta})$ is independent of $\boldsymbol{\theta}$. Because $\mathbf{s} = \boldsymbol{\varphi}(\mathcal{X})$, specifying a value for **s** constrains the possible sets of samples to some set $\overline{\mathcal{X}}$. Formally, $\overline{\mathcal{X}} = \{\mathcal{X} \mid \boldsymbol{\varphi}(\mathcal{X}) = \mathbf{s}\}$. If $\overline{\mathcal{X}}$ is empty, no assignment of values to the samples can yield that value of **s**, and $P(\mathbf{s} \mid \boldsymbol{\theta}) = 0$. Excluding

such cases, i.e., considering only values of **s** that can arise, we have

$$P(\mathcal{X} \mid \mathbf{s}, \mathbf{\theta}) = \frac{P(\mathcal{X}, \mathbf{s} \mid \mathbf{\theta})}{P(\mathbf{s} \mid \mathbf{\theta})}.$$

The denominator can be computed by summing the numerator over all values of $\mathcal{X}$. Since the numerator will be zero if $\mathcal{X} \notin \overline{\mathcal{X}}$, we can restrict the summation to $\mathcal{X} \in \overline{\mathcal{X}}$. That is,

$$P(\mathcal{X} \mid \mathbf{s}, \mathbf{\theta}) = \frac{P(\mathcal{X}, \mathbf{s} \mid \mathbf{\theta})}{\sum\limits_{\mathcal{X} \in \overline{\mathcal{X}}} P(\mathcal{X}, \mathbf{s} \mid \mathbf{\theta})}.$$

But by the same argument used before, since $\mathbf{s} = \mathbf{\varphi}(\mathcal{X})$, $P(\mathcal{X}, \mathbf{s} \mid \mathbf{\theta}) = P(\mathcal{X} \mid \mathbf{\theta})$. Furthermore, by hypothesis $P(\mathcal{X} \mid \mathbf{\theta}) = g(\mathbf{s}, \mathbf{\theta})h(\mathcal{X})$. Thus,

$$P(\mathcal{X} \mid \mathbf{s}, \mathbf{\theta}) = \frac{g(\mathbf{s}, \mathbf{\theta})h(\mathcal{X})}{\sum\limits_{\mathcal{X} \in \overline{\mathcal{X}}} g(\mathbf{s}, \mathbf{\theta})h(\mathcal{X})} = \frac{h(\mathcal{X})}{\sum\limits_{\mathcal{X} \in \overline{\mathcal{X}}} h(\mathcal{X})},$$

which is independent of $\mathbf{\theta}$. Thus, by definition, **s** is sufficient for $\mathbf{\theta}$.

It should be pointed out that there are trivial ways of constructing sufficient statistics. For example, one can define **s** to be a vector whose components are the n samples $\mathbf{x}_1, \ldots, \mathbf{x}_n$, so that $g(\mathbf{s}, \mathbf{\theta}) = p(\mathcal{X} \mid \mathbf{\theta})$ and $h(\mathcal{X}) = 1$. One can even produce a scalar sufficient statistic by the trick of interleaving the digits in the decimal expansions of the components of the n samples. Sufficient statistics such as these are of little interest, since they do not provide us with simpler results. The ability to factor $p(\mathcal{X} \mid \mathbf{\theta})$ into a product $g(\mathbf{s}, \mathbf{\theta})h(\mathcal{X})$ is interesting only when the function g and the sufficient statistic **s** are simple.*

It should also be mentioned that the factoring of $p(\mathcal{X} \mid \mathbf{\theta})$ into $g(\mathbf{s}, \mathbf{\theta})h(\mathcal{X})$ is obviously not unique. If $f(\mathbf{s})$ is any function of **s**, then $g'(\mathbf{s}, \mathbf{\theta}) = f(\mathbf{s})g(\mathbf{s}, \mathbf{\theta})$ and $h'(\mathcal{X}) = h(\mathcal{X})/f(\mathbf{s})$ are equivalent factors. This kind of ambiguity can be eliminated by defining the *kernel density*

$$\bar{g}(\mathbf{s}, \mathbf{\theta}) = \frac{g(\mathbf{s}, \mathbf{\theta})}{\displaystyle\int g(\mathbf{s}, \mathbf{\theta}) \, d\mathbf{\theta}} \tag{38}$$

which is invariant to this kind of scaling.

What is the importance of sufficient statistics and kernel densities for parameter estimation? The general answer is that the only practical applications of classical parameter estimation to pattern classification involve density

---

* In statistics, the concept of a minimal sufficient statistic is related to what we want. However, even a minimal sufficient statistic is of little interest if it does not simplify the computational problem.

functions that possess simple sufficient statistics and simple kernel densities. In the case of maximum likelihood estimation, when searching for a value of $\boldsymbol{\theta}$ that maximizes $p(\mathcal{X} \mid \boldsymbol{\theta}) = g(\mathbf{s}, \boldsymbol{\theta})h(\mathcal{X})$, we can restrict our attention to $g(\mathbf{s}, \boldsymbol{\theta})$. In this case, the normalization provided by Eq. (38) is of no particular value unless $\bar{g}(\mathbf{s}, \boldsymbol{\theta})$ is simpler than $g(\mathbf{s}, \boldsymbol{\theta})$. The significance of the kernel density is revealed in the Bayesian case. If we substitute $p(\mathcal{X} \mid \boldsymbol{\theta}) = g(\mathbf{s}, \boldsymbol{\theta})h(\mathcal{X})$ in Eq. (34), we obtain

$$p(\boldsymbol{\theta} \mid \mathcal{X}) = \frac{g(\mathbf{s}, \boldsymbol{\theta})p(\boldsymbol{\theta})}{\displaystyle\int g(\mathbf{s}, \boldsymbol{\theta})p(\boldsymbol{\theta}) \, d\boldsymbol{\theta}}. \tag{39}$$

If our a priori knowledge of $\boldsymbol{\theta}$ is very vague, $p(\boldsymbol{\theta})$ will tend to be uniform, changing very slowly with $\boldsymbol{\theta}$. If $p(\boldsymbol{\theta})$ is essentially uniform, $p(\boldsymbol{\theta} \mid \mathcal{X})$ is approximately the same as the kernel density. Roughly speaking, the kernel density is the a posteriori distribution of the parameter vector when the a priori distribution is uniform.* Even when the a priori distribution is far from uniform, the kernel density typically gives the asymptotic distribution of the parameter vector. In particular, when $p(\mathbf{x} \mid \boldsymbol{\theta})$ is indentifiable and when the number of samples is large, $g(\mathbf{s}, \boldsymbol{\theta})$ usually peaks sharply at some value $\boldsymbol{\theta} = \hat{\boldsymbol{\theta}}$. If the a priori density $p(\boldsymbol{\theta})$ is continuous at $\boldsymbol{\theta} = \hat{\boldsymbol{\theta}}$ and if $p(\hat{\boldsymbol{\theta}})$ is not zero, $p(\boldsymbol{\theta} \mid \mathcal{X})$ will approach the kernel density $\bar{g}(\mathbf{s}, \boldsymbol{\theta})$.

3.7   SUFFICIENT STATISTICS AND THE EXPONENTIAL FAMILY

To see how the Factorization Theorem can be used to obtain sufficient statistics, consider once again the familiar multivariate normal case with $p(\mathbf{x} \mid \boldsymbol{\theta}) \sim N(\boldsymbol{\theta}, \Sigma)$. Here

$$
\begin{aligned}
p(\mathcal{X} \mid \boldsymbol{\theta}) &= \prod_{k=1}^{n} \frac{1}{(2\pi)^{d/2}|\Sigma|^{1/2}} \exp[-\tfrac{1}{2}(\mathbf{x}_k - \boldsymbol{\theta})^t \Sigma^{-1}(\mathbf{x}_k - \boldsymbol{\theta})] \\
&= \frac{1}{(2\pi)^{nd/2}|\Sigma|^{n/2}} \exp\left[-\tfrac{1}{2}\sum_{k=1}^{n}(\boldsymbol{\theta}^t \Sigma^{-1}\boldsymbol{\theta} - 2\boldsymbol{\theta}^t \Sigma^{-1}\mathbf{x}_k + \mathbf{x}_k^t \Sigma^{-1}\mathbf{x}_k)\right] \\
&= \exp\left[-\frac{n}{2}\boldsymbol{\theta}^t \Sigma^{-1}\boldsymbol{\theta} + \boldsymbol{\theta}^t \Sigma^{-1}\left(\sum_{k=1}^{n}\mathbf{x}_k\right)\right] \\
&\quad \times \frac{1}{(2\pi)^{nd/2}|\Sigma|^{n/2}} \exp\left[-\tfrac{1}{2}\sum_{k=1}^{n}\mathbf{x}_k^t \Sigma^{-1}\mathbf{x}_k\right].
\end{aligned}
$$

---

* If the parameter space is finite, we can actually let $p(\boldsymbol{\theta})$ be a uniform distribution. While it is not possible to have a uniform distribution over a parameter space of infinite extent, this situation can often be approximated arbitrarily well.

This factoring isolates the $\boldsymbol{\theta}$ dependence of $p(\mathscr{X} \mid \boldsymbol{\theta})$ in the first factor, and from the factorization theorem we see that $\sum_{k=1}^{n} \mathbf{x}_k$ is sufficient for $\boldsymbol{\theta}$. Of course, any one-to-one function of this statistic is also sufficient for $\boldsymbol{\theta}$; in particular, the sample mean

$$\mathbf{m}_n = \frac{1}{n} \sum_{k=1}^{n} \mathbf{x}_k$$

is also sufficient for $\boldsymbol{\theta}$. Using this statistic, we can write

$$g(\mathbf{m}_n, \boldsymbol{\theta}) = \exp\left[-\frac{n}{2}(\boldsymbol{\theta}^t \Sigma^{-1}\boldsymbol{\theta} - 2\boldsymbol{\theta}^t \Sigma^{-1}\mathbf{m}_n) \right].$$

By using Eq. (38), or by completing the square, we obtain the kernel density

$$\bar{g}(\mathbf{m}_n, \boldsymbol{\theta}) = \frac{1}{(2\pi)^{d/2} \left|\frac{1}{n}\Sigma\right|^{1/2}} \exp\left[-\tfrac{1}{2}(\boldsymbol{\theta} - \mathbf{m}_n)^t \frac{1}{n}\Sigma^{-1}(\boldsymbol{\theta} - \mathbf{m}_n) \right].$$

From this it is immediately clear that $\mathbf{m}_n$ is the maximum likelihood estimate for $\boldsymbol{\theta}$. The Bayesian a posteriori density can be obtained from $\bar{g}(\mathbf{m}_n, \boldsymbol{\theta})$ by performing the integration indicated in Eq. (39). If the a priori density is essentially uniform, $p(\boldsymbol{\theta} \mid \mathscr{X}) = \bar{g}(\mathbf{m}_n, \boldsymbol{\theta})$.

This same general approach can be used to find sufficient statistics for other density functions. In particular, it applies to any member of the *exponential family*, a group of probability and probability density functions that possess simple sufficient statistics. Members of the exponential family include the normal, exponential, Rayleigh, Poisson, and many other familiar distributions. They can all be written in the form

$$p(\mathbf{x} \mid \boldsymbol{\theta}) = \alpha(\mathbf{x}) \exp[a(\boldsymbol{\theta}) + b(\boldsymbol{\theta})^t c(\mathbf{x})]. \tag{40}$$

Thus,

$$p(\mathscr{X} \mid \boldsymbol{\theta}) = \exp\left[na(\boldsymbol{\theta}) + b(\boldsymbol{\theta})^t \sum_{k=1}^{n} c(\mathbf{x}_k) \right] \prod_{k=1}^{n} \alpha(\mathbf{x}_k) = g(\mathbf{s}, \boldsymbol{\theta})h(\mathscr{X}), \tag{41}$$

where we can take

$$\mathbf{s} = \frac{1}{n} \sum_{k=1}^{n} c(\mathbf{x}_k), \tag{42}$$

$$g(\mathbf{s}, \boldsymbol{\theta}) = \exp[n\{a(\boldsymbol{\theta}) + b(\boldsymbol{\theta})^t \mathbf{s}\}], \tag{43}$$

and

$$h(\mathscr{X}) = \prod_{k=1}^{n} \alpha(\mathbf{x}_k). \tag{44}$$

The distributions, sufficient statistics, and unnormalized kernels for a number of commonly encountered members of the exponential family are given in Table 3-1. It is a fairly routine matter to derive maximum likelihood

TABLE 3-1. Common Distributions from the Exponential Family

Name	Distribution	Domain	s	$[g(s, \theta)]^{1/n}$
Univariate Normal	$p(x \mid \boldsymbol{\theta}) = \sqrt{\dfrac{\theta_2}{2\pi}}\, e^{-(1/2)\theta_2(x-\theta_1)^2}$	$\theta_2 > 0$	$\begin{bmatrix} \dfrac{1}{n}\displaystyle\sum_{k=1}^n x_k \\[2ex] \dfrac{1}{n}\displaystyle\sum_{k=1}^n x_k^2 \end{bmatrix}$	$\theta_2^{1/2} e^{-(1/2)\theta_2(s_2 - 2\theta_1 s_1 + \theta_1^2)}$
Multivariate Normal	$p(\mathbf{x} \mid \boldsymbol{\theta}) = \dfrac{|\Theta_2|^{1/2}}{(2\pi)^{d/2}}\, e^{-(1/2)(\mathbf{x}-\theta_1)^t \Theta_2 (\mathbf{x}-\theta_1)}$	Θ_2 positive definite	$\begin{bmatrix} \dfrac{1}{n}\displaystyle\sum_{k=1}^n \mathbf{x}_k \\[2ex] \dfrac{1}{n}\displaystyle\sum_{k=1}^n \mathbf{x}_k \mathbf{x}_k^t \end{bmatrix}$	$|\Theta_2|^{1/2} e^{-(1/2)(\operatorname{tr}\Theta_2 S_2 - 2\theta_1^t \Theta_2 s_1 + \theta_1^t \Theta_2 \theta_1)}$
Exponential	$p(x \mid \theta) = \begin{cases} \theta e^{-\theta x}, \\ 0 \end{cases} \quad \begin{matrix} x \geq 0 \\ \text{otherwise} \end{matrix}$	$\theta > 0$	$\dfrac{1}{n}\displaystyle\sum_{k=1}^n x_k$	$\theta e^{-\theta s}$
Rayleigh	$p(x \mid \theta) = \begin{cases} 2\theta x e^{-\theta x^2}, \\ 0 \end{cases} \quad \begin{matrix} x \geq 0 \\ \text{otherwise} \end{matrix}$	$\theta > 0$	$\dfrac{1}{n}\displaystyle\sum_{k=1}^n x_k^2$	$\theta e^{-\theta s}$
Maxwell	$p(x \mid \theta) = \begin{cases} \dfrac{4}{\sqrt{\pi}}\,\theta^{3/2} x^2 e^{-\theta x^2}, \\ 0 \end{cases} \quad \begin{matrix} x \geq 0 \\ \text{otherwise} \end{matrix}$	$\theta > 0$	$\dfrac{1}{n}\displaystyle\sum_{k=1}^n x_k^2$	$\theta^{3/2} e^{-\theta s}$

Distribution	$p(x\mid\boldsymbol{\theta})$	Range	Parameter constraints	Sufficient statistics	Reproducing density
Gamma	$p(x\mid\boldsymbol{\theta})=\begin{cases}\dfrac{\theta_2^{\theta_1+1}}{\Gamma(\theta_1+1)}x^{\theta_1}e^{-\theta_2 x}, & x\geq 0\\[2mm] 0 & \text{otherwise}\end{cases}$		$\theta_1>-1$ $\theta_2>0$	$\left[\left(\displaystyle\prod_{k=1}^{n}x_k\right)^{1/n}\right.$ $\left.\dfrac{1}{n}\displaystyle\sum_{k=1}^{n}x_k\right]$	$\dfrac{\theta_2^{\theta_1+1}}{\Gamma(\theta_1+1)}s_1^{\theta_1}e^{-\theta_2 s_2}$
Beta	$p(x\mid\boldsymbol{\theta})=\begin{cases}\dfrac{\Gamma(\theta_1+\theta_2+2)}{\Gamma(\theta_1+1)\Gamma(\theta_2+1)}x^{\theta_1}(1-x)^{\theta_2}, & 0\leq x\leq 1\\[2mm] 0 & \text{otherwise}\end{cases}$		$\theta_1>-1$ $\theta_2>-1$	$\left(\displaystyle\prod_{k=1}^{n}x_k\right)^{1/n}$ $\left(\displaystyle\prod_{k=1}^{n}(1-x_k)\right)^{1/n}$	$\dfrac{\Gamma(\theta_1+\theta_2+2)}{\Gamma(\theta_1+1)\Gamma(\theta_2+1)}s_1^{\theta_1}s_2^{\theta_2}$
Poisson	$P(x\mid\theta)=\dfrac{\theta^x}{x!}\,e^{-\theta},$	$x=0,1,2,\ldots$	$\theta>0$	$\dfrac{1}{n}\displaystyle\sum_{k=1}^{n}x_k$	$\theta^s e^{-\theta}$
Bernoulli	$P(x\mid\theta)=\theta^x(1-\theta)^{1-x},$	$x=0,1$	$0<\theta<1$	$\dfrac{1}{n}\displaystyle\sum_{k=1}^{n}x_k$	$\theta^s(1-\theta)^{1-s}$
Binomial	$P(x\mid\theta)=\dfrac{m!}{x!(m-x)!}\,\theta^x(1-\theta)^{m-x},$	$x=0,1,\ldots,m$	$0<\theta<1$	$\dfrac{1}{n}\displaystyle\sum_{k=1}^{n}x_k$	$\theta^s(1-\theta)^{m-s}$
Multinomial	$P(\mathbf{x}\mid\boldsymbol{\theta})=\dfrac{m!}{\displaystyle\prod_{i=1}^{d}x_i!}\prod_{i=1}^{d}\theta_i^{x_i},$	$x_i=0,1,\ldots,m$ $\displaystyle\sum_{i}^{d}x_i=m$	$0<\theta_i<1$ $\displaystyle\sum_{i=1}^{d}\theta_i=1$	$\dfrac{1}{n}\displaystyle\sum_{k=1}^{n}\mathbf{x}_k$	$\displaystyle\prod_{i=1}^{d}\theta_i^{s_i}$

estimates and Bayesian a posteriori distributions from these solutions. With two exceptions, the solutions given are for univariate cases, though they can be used in multivariate situations if statistical independence can be assumed.*

It would be pleasant to conclude that this collection of results solves most problems in pattern classification. Unfortunately this is not the case. In many applications, these members of the exponential family with their smooth variations and unimodal shapes do not give good approximations to the densities actually encountered. The simplifying assumption of statistical independence, though frequently made, is rarely valid. Even when a member of the exponential family gives a good approximation to the unknown density, there are usually many unknown parameters to estimate but only a limited number of available samples. As we shall see, this can cause optimal estimates to give less than satisfactory results, and can even lead to situations where "optimal" systems do not perform as well as "suboptimal" ones.

3.8 PROBLEMS OF DIMENSIONALITY

3.8.1 An Unexpected Problem

In practical multicategory applications, it is not at all unusual to encounter problems involving fifty or a hundred features, particularly if the features are binary valued. The designer usually believes that each feature is useful for at least some of the discriminations. While he may doubt that each feature provides independent information, he has not intentionally included superfluous features.

If the features are statistically independent, there are some theoretical results that suggest the possibility of excellent performance. For example, consider the two-class multivariate normal case where $p(\mathbf{x} \mid \omega_j) \sim N(\boldsymbol{\mu}_j, \Sigma)$, $j = 1, 2$. If the a priori probabilities are equal, then it is not hard to show that the Bayes error rate is given by

$$P(e) = \frac{1}{\sqrt{2\pi}} \int_{r/2}^{\infty} \exp[-\tfrac{1}{2}u^2] \, du, \tag{45}$$

where r^2 is the squared Mahalanobis distance

$$r^2 = (\boldsymbol{\mu}_1 - \boldsymbol{\mu}_2)^t \Sigma^{-1} (\boldsymbol{\mu}_1 - \boldsymbol{\mu}_2). \tag{46}$$

* To be more precise, the necessary assumption is that $p(\mathbf{x} \mid \omega_j, \boldsymbol{\theta}_j) = \prod_{i=1}^{d} p(x_i \mid \omega_j, \boldsymbol{\theta}_{ij})$ In the literature, when one encounters the statement that "the features are assumed to be statistically independent," what is almost always meant is that they are assumed class-conditionally independent.

Thus, the probability of error decreases as r increases, approaching zero as r approaches infinity. In the independent case, $\Sigma = \mathrm{diag}(\sigma_1^2, \ldots, \sigma_d^2)$, and

$$r^2 = \sum_{i=1}^{d} \left(\frac{\mu_{i1} - \mu_{i2}}{\sigma_i} \right)^2. \tag{47}$$

This shows how each feature contributes to reducing the probability of error. The most useful features are the ones for which the difference between the means is large relative to the standard deviations. However, no feature is useless if its means for the two classes differ. An obvious way to reduce the error rate further is to introduce new, independent features. Each new feature need not add much, but if r can be increased without limit, the probability of error can be made arbitrarily small.

In general, if the performance obtained with a given set of features is inadequate, it is natural to consider adding new features, particularly ones that will help separate the class pairs most frequently confused. Although increasing the number of features increases the cost and complexity of both the feature extractor and the classifier, it is reasonable to believe that the performance will improve. After all, if the probabilistic structure of the problem were completely known, the Bayes risk could not possibly be increased by adding new features; at worst, the Bayes classifier would ignore the new features, and if the new features provide any additional information, the performance must improve.

Unfortunately, it has frequently been observed in practice that, beyond a certain point, the inclusion of additional features leads to worse rather than better performance. This apparent paradox presents a genuine and serious problem for classifier design. The basic source of the problem can always be traced to the fact that the number of design samples is finite. However, analysis of the problem is both difficult and subtle. Simple cases do not exhibit the experimentally observed phenomena, and more realistic cases are difficult to analyze. In an attempt to provide some insight, we shall discuss several topics related to problems of dimensionality and sample size. While most of the analytical results will be presented without proof, the interested reader will find pertinent references in the Bibliographical and Historical Remarks.

3.8.2 Estimating a Covariance Matrix

We begin by considering the problem of estimating a covariance matrix. This requires the estimation of $d(d + 1)/2$ parameters, the d diagonal elements and $d(d - 1)/2$ independent off-diagonal elements. We observe first that the appealing maximum likelihood estimate

$$\hat{\Sigma} = \frac{1}{n} \sum_{k=1}^{n} (\mathbf{x}_k - \mathbf{m}_n)(\mathbf{x}_k - \mathbf{m}_n)^t$$

is the sum of $n - 1$ independent d-by-d matrices of rank one, and thus is guaranteed to be singular if $n \leq d$. Since we must invert $\hat{\Sigma}$ to obtain the discriminant functions, we have an algebraic requirement for at least $d + 1$ samples. To smooth out statistical fluctuations and obtain a really good estimate, it would not be surprising if several times that number of samples were needed.

It frequently happens that the number of available samples is inadequate, and the question of how to proceed arises. One possibility is to reduce the dimensionality, either by redesigning the feature extractor, by selecting an appropriate subset of the existing features, or by combining the existing features in some way.* Another possibility is to assume that all c classes share the same covariance matrix, and to pool the available data. Yet another alternative is to look for a better estimate for Σ. If any reasonable a priori estimate Σ_0 is available, a Bayesian or pseudo-Bayesian estimate of the form $\lambda\Sigma_0 + (1 - \lambda)\hat{\Sigma}$ might be employed. If Σ_0 is diagonal, this diminishes the troublesome effects of "accidental" correlations. Alternatively, one can remove chance correlations heuristically by thresholding the sample covariance matrix. For example, one might assume that all covariances for which the magnitude of the correlation coefficient is not near unity are actually zero. An extreme of this approach is to assume statistical independence, thereby making all the off-diagonal elements be zero, regardless of empirical evidence to the contrary. Even though such assumptions are almost surely incorrect, the resulting heuristic estimates often provide better performance than the maximum likelihood estimate.

Here we have another apparent paradox. The classifier that results from assuming independence is almost certainly suboptimal. It is understandable that it will perform better if it happens that the features actually are independent, but how can it provide better performance when this assumption is untrue?

The answer again involves the problem of insufficient data, and some insight into its nature can be gained from considering an analogous problem in curve fitting. Figure 3.3 shows a set of five data points and several candidate curves for fitting them. The data points were obtained by adding zero-mean, independent noise to a parabola. Thus, of all the possible polynomials, a parabola should give the best fit, assuming that we are interested

---

* We shall have more to say about dimensionality reduction in Chapters 4 and 6.

**FIGURE 3.3.   Fitting curves to a set of
data points.**

in fitting data obtained in the future as well as the points at hand. The straight
line shown fits the given data fairly well. The parabola provides a better fit,
but one might wonder whether the data are adequate to fix the curve. The
best parabola for a larger data set might be quite different, and over the
interval shown the straight line could easily be superior. The tenth-degree
polynomial fits the given data perfectly. However, no one would expect such
an under-determined solution to fit new data well. Indeed, many more
samples would be needed to get a good fit with a tenth-degree polynomial
than with a second-degree polynomial, despite the fact that the latter is a
special case of the former. In general, reliable interpolation or extrapolation
can not be obtained unless the solution is overdetermined.

3.8.3   The Capacity of a Separating Plane

The importance of having an overdetermined solution is as significant for
classification as it is for estimation. For a relatively simple example, consider the partitioning of a d-dimensional feature space by a hyperplane
$\mathbf{w}^t\mathbf{x} + w_0 = 0$. Suppose that we are given n sample points in general position,*
each point being labelled either ω_1 or ω_2. Of the 2^n possible dichotomies of n
points in d dimensions, a certain fraction $f(n, d)$ are said to be linear dichotomies. These are the labellings for which there exists a hyperplane

---

* Points in d-space are in general position if no subset of $d + 1$ points falls in a $(d - 1)$-
dimensional subspace.

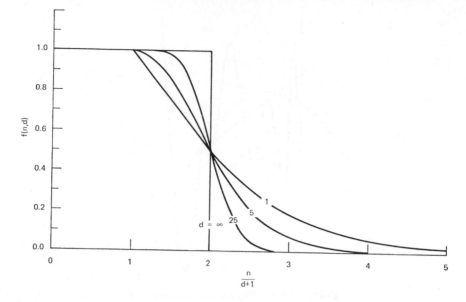

FIGURE 3.4. The fraction of dichotomies of n points in d dimensions that are linear.

separating the points labelled ω_1 from the points labelled ω_2. It can be shown that this fraction is given by

$$f(n, d) = \begin{cases} 1 & n \le d + 1 \\ \dfrac{2}{2^n} \displaystyle\sum_{i=0}^{d} \binom{n-1}{i} & n > d + 1. \end{cases} \tag{48}$$

This function is plotted in Figure 3.4 for several values of d. Note that all dichotomies of $d + 1$ or fewer points are linear. That means that a hyperplane is not overconstrained by the requirement of correctly classifying $d + 1$ or fewer points. In fact, if d is large it is not until n is a sizeable fraction of $2(d + 1)$ that the problem begins to become difficult. At $n = 2(d + 1)$, which is sometimes called the *capacity* of a hyperplane, half of the possible dichotomies are still linear. Thus, a linear discriminant is not effectively overdetermined until the number of samples is several times as large as the dimensionality.

3.8.4 The Problem-Average Error Rate

The examples we have given thus far suggest that the problem with having only a small number of samples is that the resulting classifier will not perform well on new data. Thus, we expect the error rate to be a function of the number

n of samples, typically decreasing to some minimum value as n approaches infinity. To investigate this analytically, we must carry out the following steps:

(1) Estimate the unknown parameters from samples.
(2) Use these estimates to determine the classifier.
(3) Calculate the error rate for the resulting classifier.

In general, this analysis is very complicated. The answer depends on everything—on the particular samples obtained, on the way they are used to determine the classifier, and on the unknown, underlying probability structure. However, by using histogram approximations to the unknown probability densities and averaging appropriately, it is possible to draw some interesting conclusions.

Consider the two-class case in which the two classes are equally likely a priori. Suppose that we partition the feature space into some number m of disjoint cells $\mathscr{C}_1, \ldots, \mathscr{C}_m$. If the conditional densities $p(\mathbf{x} \mid \omega_1)$ and $p(\mathbf{x} \mid \omega_2)$ do not vary appreciably within any cell, then instead of needing to know the exact value of $\mathbf{x}$, we need only know into which cell $\mathbf{x}$ falls. This reduces the problem to the discrete case. Let $p_i = P(\mathbf{x} \in \mathscr{C}_i \mid \omega_1)$ and $q_i = P(\mathbf{x} \in \mathscr{C}_i \mid \omega_2)$. Then, since we have assumed that $P(\omega_1) = P(\omega_2) = 1/2$, the vectors $\mathbf{p} = (p_1, \ldots, p_m)^t$ and $\mathbf{q} = (q_1, \ldots, q_m)^t$ determine the probability structure of the problem. If $\mathbf{x}$ falls in $\mathscr{C}_i$, the Bayes decision rule is to decide ω_i if $p_i > q_i$. The resulting Bayes error rate is given by

$$P(e \mid \mathbf{p}, \mathbf{q}) = \frac{1}{2} \sum_{i=1}^{m} \min[p_i, q_i].$$

When the parameters $\mathbf{p}$ and $\mathbf{q}$ are unknown and must be estimated from a set of samples, the resulting error rate will be larger than the Bayes rate. The exact answer will depend on the set of samples and the way in which they are used to obtain the classifier. Suppose that half of the samples are labelled ω_1 and half are labelled ω_2, with n_{ij} being the number that fall in $\mathscr{C}_i$ and are labelled ω_j. Suppose further that we design the classifier by using the maximum likelihood estimates $\hat{p}_i = 2n_{i1}/n$ and $\hat{q}_i = 2n_{i2}/n$ as if they were the true values. Then a new feature vector falling in $\mathscr{C}_i$ will be assigned to ω_1 if $n_{i1} > n_{i2}$. With all of these assumptions, it follows that the probability of error for the resulting classifier is given by

$$P(e \mid \mathbf{p}, \mathbf{q}, \mathscr{X}) = \frac{1}{2} \sum_{n_{i1} > n_{i2}} q_i + \frac{1}{2} \sum_{n_{i1} \leq n_{i2}} p_i.$$

To evaluate this probability of error, we need to know the true conditional probabilities $\mathbf{p}$ and $\mathbf{q}$, and the set of samples, or at least the numbers n_{ij}. Different sets of n random samples will yield different values for $P(e \mid \mathbf{p}, \mathbf{q}, \mathscr{X})$. We can use the fact that the numbers n_{ij} have a multinomial distribution to

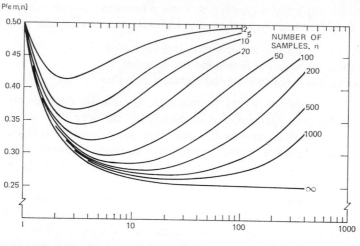

FIGURE 3.5.   The problem-average error rate (Adapted from G. F. Hughes, 1968).

average over all of the possible sets of n random samples and obtain an average probability of error $P(e \mid \mathbf{p}, \mathbf{q}, n)$. Roughly speaking, this is the typical error rate one should expect for n samples. However, evaluation of this average error rate still requires knowing the underlying problem, i.e., the values for $\mathbf{p}$ and $\mathbf{q}$. If $\mathbf{p}$ and $\mathbf{q}$ are quite different, the average error rate will be near zero, while if $\mathbf{p}$ and $\mathbf{q}$ are quite similar it will be near one-half.

A sweeping way to eliminate this dependence of the answer on the problem is to average the answer over all possible problems! That is, we assume some a priori distribution for the unknown parameters $\mathbf{p}$ and $\mathbf{q}$, and average $P(e \mid \mathbf{p}, \mathbf{q}, n)$ with respect to $\mathbf{p}$ and $\mathbf{q}$. The resulting *problem-average probability of error* $\bar{P}(e \mid m, n)$ will depend only on the number m of cells, the number n of samples, and the a priori distribution.

Of course, choosing the a priori distribution is a delicate matter. By favoring easy problems, we can make $\bar{P}$ approach zero, and by favoring hard problems we can make $\bar{P}$ approach one-half. We would like to choose an a priori distribution corresponding to the class of problems we typically encounter, but there is no obvious way to do that. A bold approach is merely to assume that problems are "uniformly distributed," i.e., that the vectors $\mathbf{p}$ and $\mathbf{q}$ are distributed uniformly over the simplexes $p_i \geq 0$, $\sum_{i=1}^{m} p_i = 1$, $q_i \geq 0$, $\sum_{i=1}^{m} q_i = 1$. G. F. Hughes, who suggested this approach, actually carried out the required computations and obtained the results shown graphically in Figure 3.5. Let us consider some of the implications of these results.

Note first that the curves show $\bar{P}$ as a function of the number of cells for a fixed number of samples. With an infinite number of samples, the maximum likelihood estimates are perfect, and $\bar{P}$ is the average of the Bayes error rate over all problems. The corresponding curve for $\bar{P}(e \mid m, \infty)$ decreases rapidly from 0.5 at $m = 1$ to the asymptotic value of 0.25 as m approaches infinity. The fact that $\bar{P} = 0.5$ if $m = 1$ is not surprising, since if there is only one cell the decision must be based solely on the a priori probabilities. The fact that $\bar{P}$ approaches 0.25 as m approaches infinity is aesthetically pleasing, since it it halfway between the extremes of 0.0 and 0.5. The fact that the problem-average error rate is so high merely shows that many hopelessly difficult classification problems are included in this average. Clearly, it would be rash indeed to conclude that the "average" pattern recognition problem will have this error rate.

However, the most interesting feature of these curves is that for every curve involving a finite number of samples there is an optimum number of cells. This is directly related to the fact that with a finite number of samples the performance will worsen if too many features are used. In this case it is clear why this occurs. At first, increasing the number of cells makes it easier to distinguish between $p(\mathbf{x} \mid \omega_1)$ and $p(\mathbf{x} \mid \omega_2)$ (as represented by the vectors $\mathbf{p}$ and $\mathbf{q}$), thereby allowing improved performance. However, if the number of cells becomes too large, there will not be enough samples to fill them. Eventually, the number of samples in most cells will be zero, and we must return to using just the ineffective a priori probabilities for classification. Thus, for any finite n, $\bar{P}(e \mid m, n)$ must approach 0.5 as m approaches infinity.

The value of m for which $\bar{P}(e \mid m, n)$ is minimum is remarkably small. For $n = 500$ samples, it is somewhere around $m = 20$ cells. Suppose that we were to form the cells by dividing each feature axis into l intervals. Then with d features we would have $m = l^d$ cells. If $l = 2$, which is extremely crude quantization, this implies that using more than four or five binary features will lead to worse rather than better performance. This is a very pessimistic result, but then so is the statement that the average error rate is 0.25. These numerical values are a consequence of the a priori distribution chosen for the problems, and are of no significance when one is facing a particular problem. The main thing to be learned from this analysis is that the performance of a classifier certainly does depend on the number of design samples, and that if this number is fixed, increasing the number of features beyond a certain point is likely to be counterproductive.

3.9   ESTIMATING THE ERROR RATE

There are at least two reasons for wanting to know the error rate of a classifier. One is to see if the classifier performs well enough to be useful. Another is to compare its performance with a competing design.

One approach to estimating the error rate is to compute it from the assumed parametric model. For example, in the two-class multivariate normal case, one might compute $P(e)$ from Eqs. (45) and (46), substituting estimates of the means and the covariance matrix for the unknown parameters. However, there are three problems with this approach. First, such an estimate for $P(e)$ is almost always overoptimistic; characteristics that make the design samples peculiar or unrepresentative will not be revealed. Second, one should always suspect the validity of an assumed parametric model; a performance evaluation based on the same model can not be believed unless the evaluation is unfavorable. Finally, in more general situations it is very difficult to compute the error rate exactly, even if the probabilistic structure is completely known.

An empirical approach that avoids these problems is to test the classifier experimentally. In practice, this is frequently done by running the classifier on a set of *test samples*, using the fraction of the samples that are misclassified as an estimate of the error rate. Needless to say, the test samples should be different from the design samples or the estimated error rate will definitely be optimistic.* If the true but unknown error rate of the classifier is p, and if k of the n independent, randomly drawn test samples are misclassified, then k has the binomial distribution†

$$P(k) = \binom{n}{k} p^k (1 - p)^{n-k}. \tag{49}$$

Thus, the fraction of test samples misclassified is exactly the maximum likelihood estimate for p: .

$$\hat{p} = \frac{k}{n}. \tag{50}$$

The properties of this estimate for the parameter p of a binomial distribution are well known. In particular, Figure 3.6 shows 95 percent confidence intervals as a function of $\hat{p}$ and n. For a given value of $\hat{p}$, the probability is 0.95 that the true value of p lies in the interval between the lower and upper

---

* In the early work on pattern recognition, when experiments were often done with very small numbers of samples, the same data were often used for designing and testing the classifier. This mistake is frequently referred to as "testing on the training data." A related but less obvious problem arises when a classifier undergoes a long series of refinements guided by the results of repeated testing on the same test data. This form of "training on the testing data" often escapes attention until new test samples are obtained.

† For this assumption to be satisfied, the selection of the states of nature must be done randomly. In multiclass problems, this can result in some classes not being represented at all. To circumvent this obvious small-sample defect, it is common practice to make the number of test samples in each class correspond, at least roughly, to the a priori probabilities. This improves the estimate of the error rate, but complicates an exact analysis.

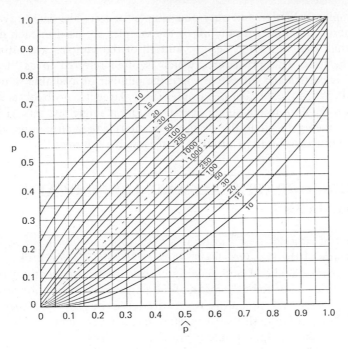

FIGURE 3.6. Confidence intervals for error-rate estimates (From Highleyman, 1962. Copyright 1962, American Telephone and Telegraph Company (reprinted by permission.).)

curves for the number n of test samples. These curves show that unless n is fairly large the maximum likelihood estimate must be interpreted with caution. For example, if no errors are made on 50 test samples, with probability 0.95 the true error rate is between zero and eight percent. The classifier would have to make no errors on more than 250 test samples to be reasonably sure that the true error rate is below two percent.

The need for data to design the classifier and additional data to evaluate it presents the designer with a dilemma. If he reserves most of his data for the design, he can not have confidence in the test. If he reserves most of his data for the test, he will not obtain a good design. The question of how best to partition a set of samples into a design set and a test set has received some analysis, and considerable discussion, but no definitive answer.

In fact, there are more options available than just partitioning the data, designing the classifier once, and testing it. For example, one might repeat this process several times, using a different partition each time, and average the resulting error-rate estimates. If computation costs are of no concern, there are strong arguments in favor of doing this n times, each time using

$n - 1$ samples for design and only one sample for test. The basic advantage of this approach is that virtually all of the samples are used in each design, which should lead to a good design, and all of the samples are ultimately used in the tests. This procedure, which is often referred to as "leaving-one-out," is particularly attractive when the number of available samples is quite small. When the number of samples is very large it is probably sufficient to partition the data into a single design set and a single test set. Although there is no theory to guide the designer in intermediate situations, it is at least pleasant to have a large number of reasonable options.

3.10   BIBLIOGRAPHICAL AND HISTORICAL REMARKS

The subject of parameter estimation is a basic topic in statistics, and is well treated in any of the standard texts, such as Hoel (1971) or Wilks (1962). Both maximum likelihood and Bayesian estimates are frequently used, the latter often being taken to be the mean of the a posteriori distribution $p(\theta \mid \mathcal{X})$. Maximum likelihood estimation was introduced by R. A. Fisher, who pointed out many of its desirable properties. In particular, it avoids the thorny matter of choosing an appropriate a priori density $p(\theta)$.

The thoughtless use of Laplace's principle of insufficient reason to justify assuming uniform prior distributions, and the practice of assuming that a parameter is random when it is merely unknown were criticized so severely by Fisher and Neyman that Bayesian estimation fell into a period of philosophical disrepute. In recent years, Bayesian methods have regained some of their lost respectability, due in part to the ease with which they can incorporate known constraints on the unknown parameters. With the introduction of new principles, such as the principle of maximum entropy, some of the old paradoxes have been resolved (Jaynes 1968). More controversial, but nevertheless revitalizing support has come from the "subjectivist" or "personalist" school of statisticians, who view the a priori distributions as a statement of belief about the possible values of the unknown parameters (Savage 1962). Since under ordinary circumstances Bayesian and maximum likelihood estimates yield nearly identical results when the sample size is large enough to be useful, these philosophical differences rarely have serious practical consequences.

The Bayesian approach to learning in pattern recognition was initiated by the suggestion that the proper way to use samples when the conditional densities are unknown is in the calculation of $P(\omega_i \mid \mathbf{x}, \mathcal{X})$ (Braverman 1962). Abramson and Braverman (1962) obtained the recursive Bayes solution for learning the mean of a normal density, and Keehn (1965) extended this to the case where both the mean vector and the covariance matrix are unknown. Bayesian learning in some nonnormal and nonstationary cases has been investigated by Beisner (1968) and Chen (1969). As part of a very general treatment of Bayesian learning, Lainiotis (1970) related the multivariate normal solution to results well known in two other fields, viz., to Kalman filtering in control theory and to correlator-estimator detection in communications theory. Chien and Fu (1967) investigated convergence of the estimates by relating Bayesian learning to stochastic approximation. A good, brief treatment of convergence questions is given by Aoki (1965).

The derivation of a simple expression for the a posteriori density $p(\theta \mid \mathcal{X})$ usually requires a careful choice for the a priori density $p(\theta)$, the so-called "natural conjugate" density. Spragins (1965) pointed out that the essential simplification provided by reproducing densities was due not to any special property of the a priori density, but to the existence of a simple sufficient statistic for $p(x \mid \theta)$. The introduction of sufficient statistics is another of the contributions of R. A. Fisher. A rigorous treatment of the factorization theorem is given by Lehmann (1959), and an analysis of forms of densities admitting simple sufficient statistics is given by Dynkin (1961).

The problems raised by high dimensionality are lucidly treated in an article by Kanal and Chandrasekaran (1968), which influenced our treatment of the topic. These problems are not restricted to parametric methods; if anything, they are more severe for the nonparametric methods we shall present in Chapters 4 and 5. Although these problems plagued many experimental projects, they received little attention in the early published literature, probably because they were so difficult to analyze. However, symptoms of the problems can be discerned in frequent remarks about the possible inadequacy or nonrepresentative character of the available data. Kanal and Randall (1964) described the problem of estimating covariance matrices, and gave an ad hoc estimate suggested by T. J. Harley that they found useful. The capacity results for linear separation and their extention to other separating surfaces were given by Cover (1965), who pointed out their implications for generalizing from design samples. Allais (1966) analyzed an estimation problem in which the variables were normally distributed and maximum likelihood estimates of the unknown parameters were used. His analysis disclosed conditions under which increasing the number of variables would increase the expected squared error, and he suggested that similar mechanisms might be at work in classification problems. Unfortunately, this phenomenon does not arise in simple cases. The results of Chandrasekaran (1971) suggest that if the features are statistically independent this effect will never appear. This relegates the phenomenon to dependent cases that are hard to analyze.

The problem-average results of Hughes (1968) cut this Gordian knot by mixing together all kinds of classification problems—problems with complete dependence, complete independence, and every intermediate degree of dependence. Since the problem-average error rate decreases to some minimum and then increases as the number of features increases, one can conclude that this is rather typical behavior when the number of samples is limited. We gave results for the case where the two classes are equally likely a priori. Hughes also gave the error rates for arbitrary a priori probabilities, but these results were rather hard to understand, the performance sometimes being worse than that obtained on the basis of the a priori probabilities alone. Abend and Harley (1969) traced this behavior to the fact that maximum likelihood rather than Bayesian estimates were used, and Chandrasekaran and Harley (1969) derived and investigated the problem-average error rate for the Bayesian case. In the case of equal a priori probabilities and equal numbers of samples in each class, the maximum likelihood and Bayesian answers turn out to be the same.

The matter of estimating performance and comparing different classifiers was another source of controversy in the early pattern recognition literature. Some of this can be appreciated from the exchange of letters on handprinted character recognition that appeared in the June 1960 and March 1961 *IRE Transactions on Electronic Computers*. The common procedure of using some of the samples for design and reserving the rest for test is frequently called the *holdout* or *H* method. An analysis by Highleyman (1962) indicated the need for a surprisingly large number of test samples, but Kanal and Chandrasekaran (1968) pointed out that this analysis was essentially for the large-sample case. A Monte Carlo study by Lachenbruch and Mickey (1968) gave evidence for the superiority of the method of leaving one out, which they called the *U* method. Although this method requires the classifier to be designed *n* times, they point out that in the normal case, at least, the labor of repeatedly inverting covariance matrices can be greatly reduced through the use of Bartlett's identity (see Problem 10). Simple, explicit formulas derived by Fukunaga and Kessell (1971) show that very little extra computation is needed in this case.

REFERENCES

1. Abend, K. and T. J. Harley, Jr., "Comments 'On the mean accuracy of statistical pattern recognizers'," *IEEE Trans. Info. Theory*, **IT-15,** 420–421 (May 1969).

2. Abramson, N. and D. Braverman, "Learning to recognize patterns in a random environment," *IRE Trans. Info. Theory*, **IT-8,** S58–S63 (September 1962).

3. Allais, D. C., "The problem of too many measurements in pattern recognition and prediction," *IEEE Int. Con. Rec.*, Part 7, 124–130 (March 1966).

4. Aoki, M., "On some convergence questions in Bayesian optimization problems," *IEEE Trans. Auto. Control*, **AC-10**, 180–182 (April 1965).

5. Beisner, H. M., "A recursive Bayesian approach to pattern recognition," *Pattern Recognition*, **1**, 13–31 (July 1968).

6. Braverman, D., "Learning filters for optimum pattern recognition," *IRE Trans. Info. Theory*, **IT-8**, 280–285 (July 1962).

7. Chandrasekaran, B. and T. J. Harley, Jr., "Comments 'On the mean accuracy of statistical pattern recognizers'," *IEEE Trans. Info. Theory*, **IT-15**, 421–423 (May 1969).

8. Chandrasekaran, B., "Independence of measurements and the mean recognition accuracy," *IEEE Trans. Info. Theory*, **IT-17**, 452–456 (July 1971).

9. Chen, C. H., "A theory of Bayesian learning systems," *IEEE Trans. Sys. Sci. Cyb.*, **SSC-5**, 30–37 (January 1969).

10. Chien, Y. T. and K. S. Fu, "On Bayesian learning and stochastic approximation," *IEEE Trans. Sys. Sci. Cyb.*, **SSC-3**, 28–38 (June 1967).

11. Cover, T. M., "Geometrical and statistical properties of systems of linear inequalities with applications in pattern recognition," *IEEE Trans. Elec. Comp.*, **EC-14**, 326–334 (June 1965).

12. Dynkin, E. B., "Necessary and sufficient statistics for a family of probability distributions," in *Selected Translations in Mathematical Statistics and Probability*, **1**, 17–40 (1961).

13. Fukunaga, K. and D. L. Kessell, "Estimation of classification error," *IEEE Trans. Comp.*, **C-20**, 1521–1527 (December 1971).

14. Highleyman, W. H., "The design and analysis of pattern recognition experiments," *Bell System Technical Journal*, **41**, 723–744 (March 1962).

15. Hoel, P. G., *Introduction to Mathematical Statistics* (Fourth Edition, John Wiley, New York, 1971).

16. Hughes, G. F., "On the mean accuracy of statistical pattern recognizers," *IEEE Trans. Info. Theory*, **IT-14**, 55–63 (January 1968).

17. Jaynes, E. T., "Prior probabilities," *IEEE Trans. Sys. Sci. Cyb.*, **SSC-4**, 227–241 (September 1968).

18. Kanal, L. N. and N. C. Randall, "Recognition system design by statistical analysis," *ACM, Proc. 19th Nat. Conf.*, pp. D2.5-1–D2.5-10 (August 1964).

19. Kanal, L. N. and B. Chandrasekaran, "On dimensionality and sample size in statistical pattern classification," *Proc. NEC*, **24**, 2–7 (1968); also in *Pattern Recognition*, **3**, 225–234 (October 1971).

20. Keehn, D. G., "A note on learning for gaussian properties," *IEEE Trans. Info. Theory*, **IT-11**, 126–132 (January 1965).

21. Lachenbruch, P. A. and M. R. Mickey, "Estimation of error rates in discriminant analysis," *Technometrics*, **10**, 1–11 (February 1968).

22. Lainiotis, D. G., "Sequential structure and parameter-adaptive pattern recognition—part I: supervised learning," *IEEE Trans. Info. Theory*, **IT-16**, 548–556 (September 1970).

23. Lehmann, E. L., *Testing Statistical Hypotheses* (John Wiley, New York, 1959).

24. Savage, L. J., *The Foundations of Statistical Inference* (Methuen, London, 1962).

25. Spragins, J., "A note on the iterative application of Bayes' rule," *IEEE Trans. Info. Theory*, **IT-11**, 544–549 (October 1965).

26. Wilks, S. S., *Mathematical Statistics* (John Wiley, New York, 1962).

PROBLEMS

1. Let x have an exponential distribution

$$p(x \mid \theta) = \begin{cases} \theta e^{-\theta x} & x \geq 0 \\ 0 & \text{otherwise.} \end{cases}$$

(a) Sketch $p(x \mid \theta)$ versus x for a fixed value of the parameter θ.
(b) Sketch $p(x \mid \theta)$ versus θ, $\theta > 0$, for a fixed value of x.
(c) Suppose that n samples $x_1, \ldots, x_n$ are drawn independently according to $p(x \mid \theta)$. Show that the maximum likelihood estimate for θ is given by

$$\hat{\theta} = \frac{1}{\dfrac{1}{n} \sum\limits_{k=1}^{n} x_k}.$$

2. Let x have a uniform distribution

$$p(x \mid \theta) = \begin{cases} \dfrac{1}{\theta} & 0 \leq x \leq \theta \\ 0 & \text{otherwise.} \end{cases}$$

(a) Sketch $p(x_1 \mid \theta)$ versus θ for some arbitrary value of x_1.
(b) Suppose that n samples $x_1, \ldots, x_n$ are drawn independently according to $p(x \mid \theta)$. Show that the maximum likelihood estimate for θ is $\max_k x_k$.

3. Let samples be drawn by successive, independent selections of a state of nature ω_i with unknown probability $P(\omega_i)$. Let $z_{ik} = 1$ if the state of nature for the kth sample is ω_i and $z_{ik} = 0$ otherwise. Show that

$$P(z_{i1}, \ldots, z_{in} \mid P(\omega_i)) = \prod_{k=1}^{n} P(\omega_i)^{z_{ik}} (1 - P(\omega_i))^{1 - z_{ik}}$$

and that the maximum likelihood estimate for $P(\omega_i)$ is

$$\hat{P}(\omega_i) = \frac{1}{n} \sum_{k=1}^{n} z_{ik}.$$

4. Let $\mathbf{x}$ be a binary $(0, 1)$ vector with a multivariate Bernoulli distribution

$$P(\mathbf{x} \mid \boldsymbol{\theta}) = \prod_{i=1}^{d} \theta_i^{x_i}(1 - \theta_i)^{1-x_i},$$

where $\boldsymbol{\theta} = (\theta_1, \ldots, \theta_d)^t$ is an unknown parameter vector, θ_i being the probability that $x_i = 1$. Show that the maximum likelihood estimate for $\boldsymbol{\theta}$ is

$$\hat{\boldsymbol{\theta}} = \frac{1}{n} \sum_{k=1}^{n} \mathbf{x}_k.$$

5. Let $p(\mathbf{x} \mid \Sigma) \sim N(\boldsymbol{\mu}, \Sigma)$ where $\boldsymbol{\mu}$ is known and Σ is unknown. Show that the maximum likelihood estimate for Σ is given by

$$\hat{\Sigma} = \frac{1}{n} \sum_{k=1}^{n} (\mathbf{x}_k - \boldsymbol{\mu})(\mathbf{x}_k - \boldsymbol{\mu})^t$$

by carrying out the steps in the following argument:
(a) Prove the matrix identity $\mathbf{a}^t A \mathbf{a} = \text{tr}\{A\mathbf{a}\mathbf{a}^t\}$, where the trace, tr A, is the sum of the diagonal elements of A.
(b) Show that the likelihood function can be written in the form

$$p(\mathbf{x}_1, \ldots, \mathbf{x}_n \mid \Sigma) = \frac{1}{(2\pi)^{nd/2}} |\Sigma^{-1}|^{n/2} \exp\left[-\tfrac{1}{2} \text{tr}\, \Sigma \sum_{k=1}^{n} (\mathbf{x}_k - \boldsymbol{\mu})(\mathbf{x}_k - \boldsymbol{\mu})^t \right].$$

(c) Letting $A = \Sigma^{-1}\hat{\Sigma}$ and $\lambda_1, \ldots, \lambda_d$ be the eigenvalues of A, show that this leads to

$$p(\mathbf{x}_1, \ldots, \mathbf{x}_n \mid \Sigma) = \frac{1}{(2\pi)^{nd/2} |\hat{\Sigma}|^{n/2}} (\lambda_1 \cdots \lambda_d)^{n/2} \exp\left[-\frac{n}{2} (\lambda_1 + \cdots + \lambda_d) \right].$$

(d) Complete the proof by showing that the likelihood is maximized by the choice $\lambda_1 = \cdots = \lambda_d = 1$.

6. Suppose that $p(\mathbf{x} \mid \boldsymbol{\mu}_i, \Sigma, \omega_i) \sim N(\boldsymbol{\mu}_i, \Sigma)$, where Σ is a common covariance matrix for all c classes. Let n samples $\mathbf{x}_1, \ldots, \mathbf{x}_n$ be drawn as usual, and let $l_1, \ldots, l_n$ be their labels, so that $l_k = i$ if the state of nature for $\mathbf{x}_k$ was ω_i.
(a) Show that

$$p(\mathbf{x}_1, \ldots, \mathbf{x}_n, l_1, \ldots, l_n \mid \boldsymbol{\mu}_1, \ldots, \boldsymbol{\mu}_c, \Sigma) = \frac{\prod_{k=1}^{n} P(\omega_{l_k})}{(2\pi)^{nd/2} |\Sigma|^{n/2}}$$

$$\times \exp\left[-\tfrac{1}{2} \sum_{k=1}^{n} (\mathbf{x}_k - \boldsymbol{\mu}_{l_k})^t \Sigma^{-1} (\mathbf{x}_k - \boldsymbol{\mu}_{l_k}) \right].$$

(b) Using the results for samples drawn from a single normal population, show that the maximum likelihood estimates for $\boldsymbol{\mu}_i$ and Σ are given by

$$\hat{\boldsymbol{\mu}}_i = \frac{\displaystyle\sum_{l_k=i} \mathbf{x}_k}{\displaystyle\sum_{l_k=i} 1}$$

and

$$\hat{\Sigma} = \frac{1}{n} \sum_{k=1}^{n} (\mathbf{x}_k - \hat{\mu}_{l_k})(\mathbf{x}_k - \hat{\mu}_{l_k})^t.$$

7. Consider the problem of learning the mean of a univariate normal distribution. Let $n_0 = \sigma^2/\sigma_0^2$ be the dogmatism, and imagine that μ_0 is formed by averaging n_0 fictitious samples x_k, $k = -n_0 + 1, \ldots, 0$. Show that Eqs. (23) and (24) for μ_n and σ_n^2 yield

$$\mu_n = \frac{1}{n + n_0} \sum_{k=-n_0+1}^{n} x_k$$

and

$$\sigma_n^2 = \frac{\sigma^2}{n + n_0}.$$

Use this result to give an interpretation of the a priori density $p(\mu) \sim N(\mu_0, \sigma_0^2)$.

8. Prove the matrix identity

$$(A^{-1} + B^{-1})^{-1} = A(A + B)^{-1}B = B(A + B)^{-1}A,$$

where A and B are nonsingular matrices of the same order. Use this result in showing that Eqs. (31) and (32) do indeed follow from Eqs. (28) and (29).

9. Let the sample mean $\mathbf{m}_n$ and the sample covariance matrix C_n for a set of n samples $\mathbf{x}_1, \ldots, \mathbf{x}_n$ be defined by

$$\mathbf{m}_n = \frac{1}{n} \sum_{k=1}^{n} \mathbf{x}_k$$

and

$$C_n = \frac{1}{n-1} \sum_{k=1}^{n} (\mathbf{x}_k - \mathbf{m}_n)(\mathbf{x}_k - \mathbf{m}_n)^t.$$

Show that the effect of adding a new sample $\mathbf{x}_{n+1}$ can be computed by the recursion relations

$$\mathbf{m}_{n+1} = \mathbf{m}_n + \frac{1}{n+1}(\mathbf{x}_{n+1} - \mathbf{m}_n)$$

and

$$C_{n+1} = \frac{n-1}{n} C_n + \frac{1}{n+1}(\mathbf{x}_{n+1} - \mathbf{m}_n)(\mathbf{x}_{n+1} - \mathbf{m}_n)^t.$$

10. The relations given in Problem 9 make it easy to update estimates for the covariance matrix. However, one is often interested in the inverse covariance matrix, and matrix inversion is time consuming. By proving the matrix identity

$$(A + \mathbf{x}\mathbf{x}^t)^{-1} = A^{-1} - \frac{A^{-1}\mathbf{x}\mathbf{x}^t A^{-1}}{1 + \mathbf{x}^t A^{-1}\mathbf{x}}$$

and using the results of Problem 9, show that

$$C_{n+1}^{-1} = \frac{n}{n-1}\left[C_n^{-1} - \frac{C_n^{-1}(\mathbf{x}_{n+1} - \mathbf{m}_n)(\mathbf{x}_{n+1} - \mathbf{m}_n)^t C_n^{-1}}{\dfrac{n^2-1}{n} + (\mathbf{x}_{n+1} - \mathbf{m}_n)^t C_n^{-1}(\mathbf{x}_{n+1} - \mathbf{m}_n)} \right].$$

11. The purpose of this problem is to derive the Bayesian classifier for the multi-variate Bernoulli case. As usual, we work with each class separately, interpreting $P(\mathbf{x} \mid \mathcal{X})$ to mean $P(\mathbf{x} \mid \mathcal{X}_i, \omega_i)$. Let the conditional probability for a given class be given by

$$P(\mathbf{x} \mid \boldsymbol{\theta}) = \prod_{i=1}^{d} \theta_i^{x_i}(1 - \theta_i)^{1-x_i},$$

and let $\mathcal{X}$ be a set of n samples $\mathbf{x}_1, \ldots, \mathbf{x}_n$ independently drawn according to this probability law.

(a) If $\mathbf{s} = (s_1, \ldots, s_d)^t$ is the sum of the n samples, show that

$$P(\mathcal{X} \mid \boldsymbol{\theta}) = \prod_{i=1}^{d} \theta_i^{s_i}(1 - \theta_i)^{1-s_i}.$$

(b) Assuming a uniform a priori distribution for $\boldsymbol{\theta}$ and using the identity

$$\int_0^1 \theta^m (1 - \theta)^n \, d\theta = \frac{m! \, n!}{(m + n + 1)!},$$

show that

$$p(\boldsymbol{\theta} \mid)\mathcal{X} = \prod_{i=1}^{d} \frac{(n + 1)!}{s_i! \, (n - s_i)!} \theta_i^{s_i}(1 - \theta_i)^{n-s_i}.$$

Sketch this density for the case $d = 1$, $n = 1$, and for the two resulting possibilities for s_1.

(c) Integrate the product $P(\mathbf{x} \mid \boldsymbol{\theta})p(\boldsymbol{\theta} \mid \mathcal{X})$ over $\boldsymbol{\theta}$ to obtain the desired conditional probability

$$P(\mathbf{x} \mid \mathcal{X}) = \prod_{i=1}^{d} \left(\frac{s_i + 1}{n + 2}\right)^{x_i} \left(1 - \frac{s_i + 1}{n + 2}\right)^{1-x_i}.$$

If we think of obtaining $P(\mathbf{x} \mid \mathcal{X})$ by substituting an estimate $\hat{\boldsymbol{\theta}}$ for $\boldsymbol{\theta}$ in $P(\mathbf{x} \mid \boldsymbol{\theta})$, what is the effective Bayesian estimate for $\boldsymbol{\theta}$?

12. Using the results given in Table 3-1, show that the maximum likelihood estimate for the parameter θ of a Rayleigh distribution is given by

$$\hat{\theta} = \frac{1}{\dfrac{1}{n} \displaystyle\sum_{k=1}^{n} x_k^2}.$$

13. Using the results given in Table 3-1, show that the maximum likelihood estimate for the parameter θ of a Maxwell distribution is given by

$$\hat{\theta} = \frac{3/2}{\dfrac{1}{n} \displaystyle\sum_{k=1}^{n} x_k^2}.$$

14. Using the results given in Table 3-1, show that the maximum likelihood estimate for the parameter θ of a multinomial distribution is given by

$$\theta_i = \frac{s_i}{\displaystyle\sum_{j=1}^{d} s_j},$$

where the vector $\mathbf{s} = (s_1, \ldots, s_d)^t$ is the average of the n samples $\mathbf{x}_1, \ldots, \mathbf{x}_n$.

15. Consider the two-class problem described in Problem 16 of Chapter 2, in which the probability of error is known to approach zero as the dimensionality d approaches infinity.

(a) Suppose that a single sample $\mathbf{x} = (x_1, \ldots, x_d)^t$ is drawn from Class 1. Show that the maximum likelihood estimate for p is given by

$$\hat{p} = \frac{1}{d} \sum_{i=1}^{d} x_i.$$

(b) Describe the behavior of $\hat{p}$ as d approaches infinity. Indicate why this means that by letting the number of features increase without limit we can obtain an error-free classifier even though we have only one sample from only one class.

Chapter 4

NONPARAMETRIC TECHNIQUES

4.1 INTRODUCTION

In the last chapter we treated supervised learning under the assumption that the forms for the underlying density functions were known. In most pattern recognition applications this assumption is suspect. The common parametric forms rarely fit the densities actually encountered in practice. In particular, all of the classical parametric densities are unimodal (have a single local maximum), whereas many practical problems involve multimodal densities. In this chapter we shall examine *nonparametric* procedures that can be used without assuming that the forms of the underlying densities are known.

There are several different types of nonparametric methods of interest to pattern recognition. One consists of procedures for estimating the density functions $p(\mathbf{x} \mid \omega_j)$ from sample patterns. If these estimates are satisfactory, they can be substituted for the true densities in designing the optimal classifier. Another consists of procedures for directly estimating the a posteriori probabilities $P(\omega_j \mid \mathbf{x})$. This is closely related to nonparametric decision procedures, such as the nearest-neighbor rule, which bypass probability estimation and go directly to decision functions. Finally, there are nonparametric procedures for transforming the feature space in the hope that it may be possible to employ parametric methods in the transformed space. These discriminant analysis techniques include the well-known Fisher linear discriminant method, which provides an important link between the parametric techniques of Chapter 3 and the adaptive techniques of Chapter 5.

4.2 DENSITY ESTIMATION

The basic ideas behind many of the methods of estimating an unknown probability density function are very simple, although rigorous demonstrations that the estimates converge require considerable care. The most fundamental techniques rely on the fact that the probability P that a vector $\mathbf{x}$ will fall in a region $\mathcal{R}$ is given by

$$P = \int_{\mathcal{R}} p(\mathbf{x}') \, d\mathbf{x}'. \tag{1}$$

Thus P is a smoothed or averaged version of the density function $p(\mathbf{x})$, and we can estimate this smoothed value of p by estimating the probability P. Suppose that n samples $\mathbf{x}_1, \ldots, \mathbf{x}_n$ are independently drawn according to the probability law $p(\mathbf{x})$. Clearly, the probability that k of these n fall in $\mathcal{R}$ is given by the binomial law

$$P_k = \binom{n}{k} P^k (1 - P)^{n-k},$$

and the expected value for k is

$$E[k] = nP. \tag{2}$$

Moreover, this binomial distribution for k peaks very sharply about the mean, so that we expect that the ratio k/n will be a very good estimate for the probability P, and hence for the smoothed density function. If we now assume that $p(\mathbf{x})$ is continuous and that the region $\mathcal{R}$ is so small that p does not vary appreciably within it, we can write

$$\int_{\mathcal{R}} p(\mathbf{x}') \, d\mathbf{x}' \approx p(\mathbf{x})V, \tag{3}$$

where $\mathbf{x}$ is a point within $\mathcal{R}$ and V is the volume enclosed by $\mathcal{R}$. Combining (1), (2), and (3), we arrive at the following obvious estimate for $p(\mathbf{x})$:

$$p(\mathbf{x}) \approx \frac{k/n}{V}. \tag{4}$$

There are several problems that remain, some practical and some theoretical. If we fix the volume V and take more and more samples, the ratio k/n will converge (in probability) as desired, but we have only obtained an estimate of the space-average value of $p(\mathbf{x})$,

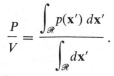

$$\frac{P}{V} = \frac{\int_{\mathcal{R}} p(\mathbf{x}') \, d\mathbf{x}'}{\int_{\mathcal{R}} d\mathbf{x}'}.$$

If we want to obtain $p(\mathbf{x})$ rather than an averaged version of $p(\mathbf{x})$, we must be prepared to let V approach zero. However, if we fix the number n of samples and let V approach zero, the region will eventually become so small that it will enclose no samples, and our estimate $p(\mathbf{x}) \approx 0$ will be useless.*

---

* If by chance one or more samples coincide at $\mathbf{x}$, the estimate diverges to infinity, which is equally useless.

From a practical standpoint, the number of samples is always limited. Thus, the volume V can not be allowed to become arbitrarily small. If this kind of estimate is to be used, one will have to accept a certain amount of variance in the ratio k/n and a certain amount of averaging of the density $p(\mathbf{x})$.

From a theoretical standpoint, it is interesting to ask how these limitations can be circumvented if an unlimited number of samples is available. Suppose we use the following procedure. To estimate the density at $\mathbf{x}$, we form a sequence of regions $\mathcal{R}_1, \mathcal{R}_2, \ldots$, containing $\mathbf{x}$, the first region to be used with one sample, the second with two, and so on. Let V_n be the volume of $\mathcal{R}_n$, k_n be the number of samples falling in $\mathcal{R}_n$, and $p_n(\mathbf{x})$ be the nth estimate for $p(\mathbf{x})$:

$$p_n(\mathbf{x}) = \frac{k_n/n}{V_n}. \tag{5}$$

If $p_n(\mathbf{x})$ is to converge to $p(\mathbf{x})$, three conditions appear to be required:

(1) $\lim_{n \to \infty} V_n = 0$

(2) $\lim_{n \to \infty} k_n = \infty$

(3) $\lim_{n \to \infty} k_n/n = 0.$

The first condition assures us that the space average P/V will converge to $p(\mathbf{x})$, provided that the regions shrink uniformly and that p is continuous at $\mathbf{x}$. The second condition, which only makes sense if $p(\mathbf{x}) \neq 0$, assures us that the frequency ratio will converge (in probability) to the probability P. The third condition is clearly necessary if $p_n(\mathbf{x})$ given by Eq. (5) is to converge at all. It also says that although a huge number of samples will eventually fall within the small region $\mathcal{R}_n$, they will form a negligibly small fraction of the total number of samples.

There are two common ways of obtaining sequences of regions that satisfy these conditions. One is to shrink an initial region by specifying the volume V_n as some function of n, such as $V_n = 1/\sqrt{n}$. It then must be shown that the random variables k_n and k_n/n behave properly, or, more to the point, that $p_n(\mathbf{x})$ converges to $p(\mathbf{x})$. This is basically the Parzen-window method that will be examined in the next section. The second method is to specify k_n as some function of n, such as $k_n = \sqrt{n}$. Here the volume V_n is grown until it encloses k_n neighbors of $\mathbf{x}$. This is the k_n-nearest-neighbor estimation method. Both of these methods do in fact converge, although it is difficult to make meaningful statements about their finite-sample behavior.

4.3   PARZEN WINDOWS

4.3.1   General Discussion

The Parzen-window approach to estimating densities can be introduced by temporarily assuming that the region $\mathscr{R}_n$ is a d-dimensional hypercube. If h_n is the length of an edge of that hypercube, then its volume is given by

$$V_n = h_n^d. \tag{6}$$

We can obtain an analytic expression for k_n, the number of samples falling in the hypercube, by defining the following *window function:*

$$\varphi(\mathbf{u}) = \begin{cases} 1 & |u_j| \le 1/2 \quad j = 1, \dots, d \\ 0 & \text{otherwise.} \end{cases} \tag{7}$$

Thus, $\varphi(\mathbf{u})$ defines a unit hypercube centered at the origin. It follows that $\varphi((\mathbf{x} - \mathbf{x}_i)/h_n)$ is equal to unity if $\mathbf{x}_i$ falls within the hypercube of volume V_n centered at $\mathbf{x}$, and is zero otherwise. Hence the number of samples in this hypercube is given by

$$k_n = \sum_{i=1}^{n} \varphi\left(\frac{\mathbf{x} - \mathbf{x}_i}{h_n}\right),$$

and when we substitute this in Eq. (5) we obtain the estimate

$$p_n(\mathbf{x}) = \frac{1}{n} \sum_{k=1}^{n} \frac{1}{V_n} \varphi\left(\frac{\mathbf{x} - \mathbf{x}_i}{h_n}\right). \tag{8}$$

This equation suggests a more general approach to estimating density functions. Rather than limiting ourselves to the hypercube window function of Eq. (7), suppose we allow a more general class of window functions. Then Eq. (8) expresses our estimate for $p(\mathbf{x})$ as an average of functions of $\mathbf{x}$ and the samples $\mathbf{x}_i$. In essence, the window function is being used for *interpolation*, each sample contributing to the estimate in accordance with its distance from $\mathbf{x}$.

It is natural to ask that the estimate $p_n(\mathbf{x})$ be a legitimate density function, i.e., that it be nonnegative and integrate to one. This can be assured by requiring the window function to be a legitimate density function. To be more precise, if we require that

$$\varphi(\mathbf{u}) \ge 0 \tag{9}$$

and

$$\int \varphi(\mathbf{u}) \, d\mathbf{u} = 1, \tag{10}$$

and if we maintain the relation $V_n = h_n^d$, then it follows at once that $p_n(\mathbf{x})$ also satisfies these conditions.

Let us examine the effect that the *window width* h_n has on $p_n(\mathbf{x})$. If we define the function $\delta_n(\mathbf{x})$ by

$$\delta_n(\mathbf{x}) = \frac{1}{V_n}\, \varphi\left(\frac{\mathbf{x}}{h_n}\right), \tag{11}$$

then we can write $p_n(\mathbf{x})$ as the average

$$p_n(\mathbf{x}) = \frac{1}{n} \sum_{i=1}^{n} \delta_n(\mathbf{x} - \mathbf{x}_i). \tag{12}$$

Since $V_n = h_n^d$, h_n affects both the amplitude and the width of $\delta_n(\mathbf{x})$. If h_n is very large, the amplitude of δ_n is small, and $\mathbf{x}$ must be far from $\mathbf{x}_i$ before $\delta_n(\mathbf{x} - \mathbf{x}_i)$ changes much from $\delta_n(\mathbf{0})$. In this case, $p_n(\mathbf{x})$ is the superposition of n broad, slowly changing functions, and is a very smooth, "out-of-focus" estimate for $p(\mathbf{x})$. On the other hand, if h_n is very small, the peak value of $\delta_n(\mathbf{x} - \mathbf{x}_i)$ is large and occurs near $\mathbf{x} = \mathbf{x}_i$. In this case, $p_n(\mathbf{x})$ is the superposition of n sharp pulses centered at the samples, and is an erratic, "noisy" estimate of $p(\mathbf{x})$. For any value of h_n

$$\int \delta_n(\mathbf{x} - \mathbf{x}_i)\, d\mathbf{x} = \int \frac{1}{V_n}\, \varphi\left(\frac{\mathbf{x} - \mathbf{x}_i}{h_n}\right) d\mathbf{x} = \int \varphi(\mathbf{u})\, d\mathbf{u} = 1. \tag{13}$$

Thus, as h_n approaches zero, $\delta_n(\mathbf{x} - \mathbf{x}_i)$ approaches a Dirac delta function centered at $\mathbf{x}_i$, and $p_n(\mathbf{x})$ approaches a superposition of delta functions centered at the samples.

Clearly, the choice of h_n (or V_n) has a major effect on $p_n(\mathbf{x})$. If V_n is too large, the estimate will suffer from too little resolution. If V_n is too small, the estimate will suffer from too much statistical variability. With a limited number of samples, the best one can do is to seek some acceptable compromise. However, with an unlimited number of samples, it is possible to let V_n slowly approach zero as n increases and have $p_n(\mathbf{x})$ converge to the unknown density $p(\mathbf{x})$.

In talking about convergence, we must recognize that we are talking about the convergence of a sequence of random variables, since for any fixed $\mathbf{x}$ the value of $p_n(\mathbf{x})$ depends on the values of the random samples $\mathbf{x}_1, \ldots, \mathbf{x}_n$. Thus, $p_n(\mathbf{x})$ has some mean $\bar{p}_n(\mathbf{x})$ and some variance $\sigma_n^2(\mathbf{x})$. We shall say that the estimate $p_n(\mathbf{x})$ converges to $p(\mathbf{x})$ if*

$$\lim_{n \to \infty} \bar{p}_n(\mathbf{x}) = p(\mathbf{x}) \tag{14}$$

---

* This type of convergence is called *convergence in mean square*. For a discussion of the modes of convergence of a sequence of random variables, see E. Parzen, *Modern Probability Theory and its Applications*, Chapter 10 (John Wiley, New York, 1960).

and

$$\lim_{n \to \infty} \sigma_n^2(\mathbf{x}) = 0. \tag{15}$$

To prove convergence we must place conditions on the unknown density $p(\mathbf{x})$, on the window function $\varphi(\mathbf{u})$, and on the window width h_n. In general, continuity of p at $\mathbf{x}$ is required, and the conditions imposed by Eqs. (9) and (10) are customarily invoked. With care, it can be shown that the following additional conditions assure convergence:

$$\sup_{\mathbf{u}} \varphi(\mathbf{u}) < \infty \tag{16}$$

$$\lim_{\|\mathbf{u}\| \to \infty} \varphi(\mathbf{u}) \prod_{i=1}^{d} u_i = 0 \tag{17}$$

$$\lim_{n \to \infty} V_n = 0 \tag{18}$$

and

$$\lim_{n \to \infty} n V_n = \infty. \tag{19}$$

Equations (16) and (17) keep φ well behaved, and are satisfied by most density functions that one might think of using for window functions. Equations (18) and (19) state that the volume V_n must approach zero, but at a rate slower than $1/n$. We shall now see why these are the basic conditions for convergence.

4.3.2 Convergence of the Mean

Consider first $\bar{p}_n(\mathbf{x})$, the mean of $p_n(\mathbf{x})$. Since the samples $\mathbf{x}_i$ are identically distributed according to the (unknown) density $p(\mathbf{x})$,

$$\bar{p}_n(\mathbf{x}) = E[p_n(\mathbf{x})]$$

$$= \frac{1}{n} \sum_{i=1}^{n} E\left[\frac{1}{V_n} \varphi\left(\frac{\mathbf{x} - \mathbf{x}_i}{h_n} \right) \right]$$

$$= \int \frac{1}{V_n} \varphi\left(\frac{\mathbf{x} - \mathbf{v}}{h_n} \right) p(\mathbf{v}) \, d\mathbf{v}$$

$$= \int \delta_n(\mathbf{x} - \mathbf{v}) p(\mathbf{v}) \, d\mathbf{v}. \tag{20}$$

This equation shows that the expected value of the estimate is an averaged value of the unknown density, a *convolution* of the unknown density and the window function. Thus, $\bar{p}_n(\mathbf{x})$ is a blurred version of $p(\mathbf{x})$ as seen through the averaging window. But as V_n approaches zero, $\delta_n(\mathbf{x} - \mathbf{v})$ approaches a delta function centered at **x**. Thus, if p is continuous at **x**, Eq. (18) ensures that $\bar{p}_n(\mathbf{x})$ will approach $p(\mathbf{x})$ as n approaches infinity.*

4.3.3 Convergence of the Variance

Equation (20) shows that there is no need for an infinite number of samples to make $\bar{p}_n(\mathbf{x})$ approach $p(\mathbf{x})$; one can achieve this for any n merely by letting V_n approach zero. Of course, for a particular set of n samples, the resulting "spiky" estimate is useless, and this observation emphasizes the need for considering the variance of the estimate. Since $p_n(\mathbf{x})$ is the sum of functions of statistically independent random variables, its variance is the sum of the variances of the separate terms, and hence

$$\sigma_n^2(\mathbf{x}) = \sum_{i=1}^{n} E\left[\left\{\frac{1}{nV_n}\, \varphi\left(\frac{\mathbf{x}-\mathbf{x}_i}{h_n}\right) - \frac{1}{n}\,\bar{p}_n(\mathbf{x})\right\}^2\right]$$

$$= nE\left[\frac{1}{n^2 V_n^2}\, \varphi^2\left(\frac{\mathbf{x}-\mathbf{x}_i}{h_n}\right)\right] - \frac{1}{n}\,\bar{p}_n^2(\mathbf{x})$$

$$= \frac{1}{nV_n}\int \frac{1}{V_n}\, \varphi^2\left(\frac{\mathbf{x}-\mathbf{v}}{h_n}\right) p(\mathbf{v})\, d\mathbf{v} - \frac{1}{n}\,\bar{p}_n^2(\mathbf{x}). \qquad (21)$$

By dropping the second term, bounding φ, and using Eq. (20), we obtain

$$\sigma_n^2(\mathbf{x}) \le \frac{\sup(\varphi)\bar{p}_n(\mathbf{x})}{nV_n}. \qquad (22)$$

Clearly, to obtain a small variance we want a large value for V_n, not a small one. However, since the numerator stays finite as n approaches infinity, we can let V_n approach zero and still obtain zero variance, provided that nV_n approaches infinity. For example, we can let $V_n = V_1/\sqrt{n}$ or $V_1/\log n$ or any other function satisfying Eqs. (18) and (19).

This is the principal theoretical result. Unfortunately, it does not tell us how to choose φ and V_n to obtain good results in the finite sample case. Indeed, unless we have more knowledge about $p(\mathbf{x})$ than the mere fact that it is continuous, we have no basis for optimizing finite sample results.

4.3.4 Two Examples

It is interesting to see how the Parzen window method behaves on some simple examples. Consider first the case where $p(\mathbf{x})$ is a zero-mean, unit-variance, univariate normal density. Let the window function be of the same

---

* This argument is not rigorous but is intuitively clear and basically sound. More careful analysis discloses a problem if the unknown density is not bounded, as happens when $p(\mathbf{x})$ contains delta functions. The added condition of Eq. (17) eliminates this problem.

form:

$$\varphi(u) = \frac{1}{\sqrt{2\pi}} \exp[-\tfrac{1}{2}u^2].$$

Finally, let $h_n = h_1/\sqrt{n}$, where h_1 is a parameter at our disposal. Thus $p_n(x)$ is an average of normal densities centered at the samples:

$$p_n(x) = \frac{1}{n} \sum_{i=1}^{n} \frac{1}{h_n}\, \varphi\left(\frac{x - x_i}{h_n}\right).$$

While it is not hard to evaluate Eqs. (20) and (21) to find the mean and variance of $p_n(x)$, it is even more interesting to see numerical results. When a particular set of normally distributed random samples was generated and used to compute $p_n(x)$, the results shown in Figure 4.1 were obtained. These results depend both on n and h_1. For $n = 1$, $p_n(x)$ is merely a single gaussian hill centered about the first sample. For $n = 16$ and $h_1 = 1/4$ the contributions of the individual samples are clearly discernible; this is not the case for $h_1 = 1$ and $h_1 = 4$. As n gets larger, the ability of p_n to resolve variations in p increases. Concomitantly, p_n appears to be more sensitive to local sampling irregularities when n is large, although we are assured that p_n will converge to the smooth normal curve as n goes to infinity. While one should not judge on visual appearance alone, it is clear that many samples are required to obtain an accurate estimate.

For the second example, we let $\varphi(u)$ and h_n be the same as before, but let the unknown density be a mixture of two uniform densities:

$$p(x) = \begin{cases} 1 & -2.5 < x < -2 \\ 0.25 & 0 < x < 2 \\ 0 & \text{elsewhere.} \end{cases}$$

Figure 4.2 shows the behavior of Parzen window estimates for this density. As before, the case $n = 1$ tells more about the window function than it tells about the unknown density. For $n = 16$, none of the estimates is particularly good, but the results for $n = 256$ and $h_1 = 1$ are beginning to appear acceptable.

These examples illustrate some of the power and some of the limitations of nonparametric methods. Their power resides in their generality. Exactly the same procedure was used for the unimodal normal case and the bimodal mixture case. With enough samples, we are essentially assured of convergence to an arbitrarily complicated unknown density. On the other hand, the number of samples needed may be very large indeed, much greater than the number that would be required if we knew the form of the unknown density. Little or nothing in the way of data reduction is provided, which leads to severe

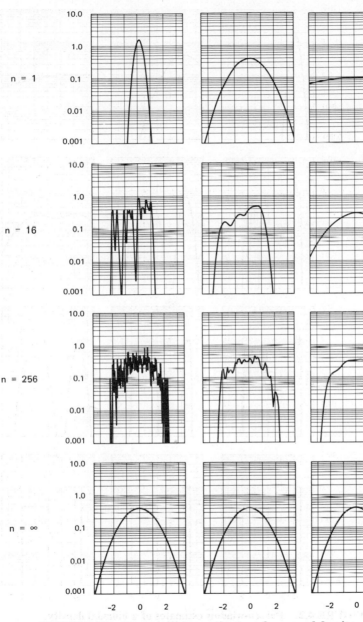

FIGURE 4.1. Parzen-window estimates of a normal density.

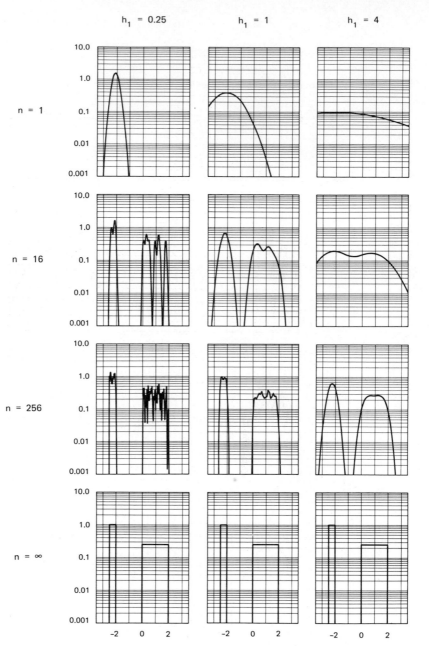

FIGURE 4.2.   Parzen-window estimates of a bimodal density.

requirements for computation time and storage. Moreover, the demand for a large number of samples grows exponentially with the dimensionality of the feature space. This limitation is related to what Bellman calls "the curse of dimensionality," and severely restricts the practical application of such nonparametric procedures.

4.4 k_n-NEAREST-NEIGHBOR ESTIMATION

One of the problems encountered in the Parzen-window approach concerns the choice of the sequence of cell volumes $V_1, V_2, \ldots$. For example, if we take $V_n = V_1/\sqrt{n}$, the results for any finite n will be very sensitive to the choice for the initial volume V_1. If V_1 is too small, most of the volumes will be empty, and the estimate $p_n(\mathbf{x})$ will be very erratic. On the other hand, if V_1 is too large, important spatial variations in $p(\mathbf{x})$ may be lost due to averaging over the cell volume. Furthermore, it may well be the case that a cell volume appropriate for one value of $\mathbf{x}$ might be entirely unsuitable elsewhere.

One potential remedy for these problems is to let the cell volume be a function of the data, rather than some arbitrary function of the number of samples. For example, to estimate $p(\mathbf{x})$ from n samples, one can center a cell about $\mathbf{x}$ and let it grow until it captures k_n samples, where k_n is some specified function of n. These samples are the k_n nearest neighbors of $\mathbf{x}$. If the density is high near $\mathbf{x}$, the cell will be relatively small, which leads to good resolution. If the density is low, it is true that the cell will grow large, but it will stop soon after it enters regions of higher density. In either case, if we take

$$p_n(\mathbf{x}) = \frac{k_n/n}{V_n} \tag{5}$$

we want k_n to go to infinity as n goes to infinity, since this assures us that k_n/n will be a good estimate of the probability that a point will fall in the cell of volume V_n. However, we also want k_n to grow sufficiently slowly that the size of the cell needed to capture k_n samples will shrink to zero. Thus, it is clear from Eq. (5) that the ratio k_n/n must go to zero. Although we shall not supply a proof, it can be shown that the conditions $\lim_{n\to\infty} k_n = \infty$ and $\lim_{n\to\infty} k_n/n = 0$ are necessary and sufficient for $p_n(\mathbf{x})$ to converge to $p(\mathbf{x})$ in probability at all points where p is continuous. If we take $k_n = \sqrt{n}$ and assume that $p_n(\mathbf{x})$ is a reasonably good approximation to $p(\mathbf{x})$, we see from Eq. (5) that $V_n \approx 1/(\sqrt{n}p(\mathbf{x}))$. Thus, V_n again has the form $V_1/\sqrt{n}$, but the initial volume V_1 is determined by the nature of the data rather than by some arbitrary choice on our part.

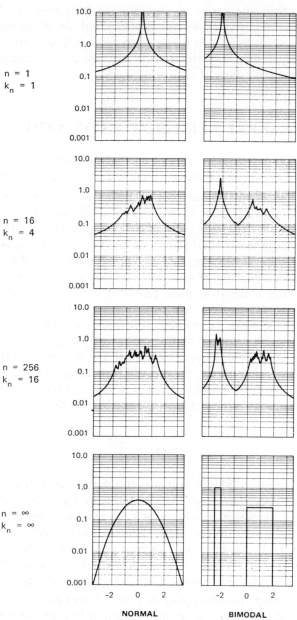

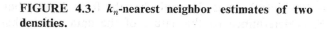

FIGURE 4.3. k_n-nearest neighbor estimates of two densities.

It is instructive to compare the performance of this method with that of the Parzen-window method on the data used in the previous examples. With $n = 1$ and $k_n = \sqrt{n} = 1$, the estimate becomes

$$p_n(x) = \frac{1}{2 |x - x_1|}.$$

This is clearly a poor estimate of $p(x)$, with its integral embarrassing us by diverging to infinity. As shown in Figure 4.3, the estimate becomes considerably better as n gets larger, even though the integral of the estimate always remains infinite. This unfortunate fact is compensated by the fact that $p_n(x)$ never plunges to zero just because no samples fall within some arbitrary cell or window. While this might seem to be a meager compensation, it can be of considerable value in higher-dimensional spaces.

As with the Parzen-window approach, we could obtain a family of estimates by taking $k_n = k_1 \sqrt{n}$ and choosing different values for k_1. However, in the absence of any additional information, one choice is as good as another, and we can be confident only that the results will be asymptotically correct.

4.5 ESTIMATION OF A POSTERIORI PROBABILITIES

The techniques discussed in the previous sections can be used to estimate the a posteriori probabilities $P(\omega_i \mid \mathbf{x})$ from a set of n labelled samples by using the samples to estimate the densities involved. Suppose that we place a cell of volume V around $\mathbf{x}$ and capture k samples, k_i of which turn out to be labelled ω_i. Then the obvious estimate for the joint probability $p(\mathbf{x}, \omega_i)$ is

$$p_n(\mathbf{x}, \omega_i) = \frac{k_i/n}{V}.$$

Thus, a reasonable estimate for $P(\omega_i \mid \mathbf{x})$ is

$$P_n(\omega_i \mid \mathbf{x}) = \frac{p_n(\mathbf{x}, \omega_i)}{\sum_{j=1}^{c} p_n(\mathbf{x}, \omega_j)} = \frac{k_i}{k}.$$

That is, the estimate of the a posteriori probability that ω_i is the state of nature is merely the fraction of the samples within the cell that are labelled ω_i. For minimum error rate, we select the category most frequently represented within the cell. If there are enough samples and if the cell is sufficiently small, it can be shown that this will yield performance approaching the best possible.

When it comes to choosing the size of the cell, it is clear that we can use either the Parzen-window approach or the k_n-nearest-neighbor approach. In the first case, V_n would be some specified function of n, such as $V_n = 1/\sqrt{n}$. In the second case, V_n would be expanded until some specified number of samples were captured, such as $k = \sqrt{n}$. In either case, as n goes to infinity an infinite number of samples will fall within the infinitely small cell. The fact that the cell volume can become arbitrarily small and yet contain an arbitrarily large number of samples allows us to learn the unknown probabilities with virtual certainty and thus eventually obtain optimum performance. Interestingly enough, we shall now see that we can obtain comparable performance if we base our decision solely on the label of the single nearest neighbor of $\mathbf{x}$.

4.6   THE NEAREST-NEIGHBOR RULE

4.6.1   General Considerations

Let $\mathcal{X}^n = \{\mathbf{x}_1, \ldots, \mathbf{x}_n\}$ be a set of n labelled samples, and let $\mathbf{x}'_n \in \mathcal{X}^n$ be the sample nearest to $\mathbf{x}$. Then the *nearest-neighbor rule* for classifying $\mathbf{x}$ is to assign it the label associated with $\mathbf{x}'_n$. The nearest-neighbor rule is a suboptimal procedure; its use will usually lead to an error rate greater than the minimum possible, the Bayes rate. We shall see, however, that with an unlimited number of samples the error rate is never worse than twice the Bayes rate.

Before we get immersed in details, let us try to gain a heuristic understanding of why the nearest-neighbor rule should work so well. To begin with, note that the label θ'_n associated with the nearest neighbor is a random variable, and the probability that $\theta'_n = \omega_i$ is merely the a posteriori probability $P(\omega_i \mid \mathbf{x}'_n)$. When the number of samples is very large, it is reasonable to assume that $\mathbf{x}'_n$ is sufficiently close to $\mathbf{x}$ that $P(\omega_i \mid \mathbf{x}'_n) \approx P(\omega_i \mid \mathbf{x})$. In that case, we can view the nearest-neighbor rule as a randomized decision rule that classifies $\mathbf{x}$ by selecting the category ω_i with probability $P(\omega_i \mid \mathbf{x})$. Since this is exactly the probability that nature will be in state ω_i, the nearest-neighbor rule is effectively matching probabilities with nature.

If we define $\omega_m(\mathbf{x})$ by

$$P(\omega_m \mid \mathbf{x}) = \max_i P(\omega_i \mid \mathbf{x}), \qquad (23)$$

then the Bayes decision rule always selects ω_m. When $P(\omega_m \mid \mathbf{x})$ is close to unity, the nearest-neighbor selection is almost always the same as the Bayes selection. That is, when the minimum probability of error is small, the nearest-neighbor probability of error is also small. When $P(\omega_m \mid \mathbf{x})$ is close to $1/c$, so that all classes are essentially equally likely, the selections made by the nearest-neighbor rule and the Bayes decision rule are rarely the same, but the probability of error is approximately $1 - 1/c$ for both. While more careful analysis is clearly necessary, these observations should make the good performance of the nearest-neighbor rule less surprising.

Our analysis of the behavior of the nearest-neighbor rule will be directed at obtaining the large-sample conditional average probability of error $P(e \mid \mathbf{x})$, where the averaging is with respect to the samples. The unconditional average probability of error will then be found by averaging $P(e \mid \mathbf{x})$ over all $\mathbf{x}$:

$$P(e) = \int P(e \mid \mathbf{x}) p(\mathbf{x}) \, dx. \tag{24}$$

We note in passing that the Bayes decision rule minimizes $P(e)$ by minimizing $P(e \mid \mathbf{x})$ for every $\mathbf{x}$. If we let $P^*(e \mid \mathbf{x})$ be the minimum possible value of $P(e \mid \mathbf{x})$, and P^* be the minimum possible value of $P(e)$, then

$$P^*(e \mid \mathbf{x}) = 1 - P(\omega_m \mid \mathbf{x}) \tag{25}$$

and

$$P^* = \int P^*(e \mid \mathbf{x}) p(\mathbf{x}) \, dx. \tag{26}$$

4.6.2   Convergence of the Nearest Neighbor

We now wish to evaluate the average probability of error for the nearest-neighbor rule. In particular, if $P_n(e)$ is the n-sample error rate, and if

$$P = \lim_{n \to \infty} P_n(e), \tag{27}$$

then we want to show that

$$P^* \leq P \leq P^* \left(2 - \frac{c}{c-1} P^* \right). \tag{28}$$

We begin by observing that when the nearest-neighbor rule is used with a particular set of n samples, the resulting error rate will depend on the accidental characteristics of the samples. In particular, if different sets of n samples are used to classify $\mathbf{x}$, different vectors $\mathbf{x}'_n$ will be obtained for the nearest neighbor of $\mathbf{x}$. Since the decision rule depends on this nearest neighbor, we have a conditional probability of error $P_n(e \mid \mathbf{x}, \mathbf{x}'_n)$ that depends on both $\mathbf{x}$ and $\mathbf{x}'_n$. By averaging over $\mathbf{x}'_n$, we obtain

$$P_n(e \mid \mathbf{x}) = \int P_n(e \mid \mathbf{x}, \mathbf{x}'_n) p(\mathbf{x}'_n \mid \mathbf{x}) \, dx'_n. \tag{29}$$

It is usually very difficult to obtain an exact expression for the conditional density $p(\mathbf{x}'_n \mid \mathbf{x})$. However, since $\mathbf{x}'_n$ is by definition the nearest neighbor of

$\mathbf{x}$, we expect this density to be very peaked in the immediate vicinity of $\mathbf{x}$, and very small elsewhere. Furthermore, as n goes to infinity we expect $p(\mathbf{x}'_n \mid \mathbf{x})$ to approach a delta function centered at $\mathbf{x}$, making the evaluation of Eq. (29) trivial. To show that this is indeed the case, we must assume that at the given $\mathbf{x}$, p is continuous and not equal to zero. Under these conditions, the probability that any sample falls within a hypersphere S centered about $\mathbf{x}$ is some positive number P_s:

$$P_s = \int_{\mathbf{x}' \in S} p(\mathbf{x}')\, d\mathbf{x}'.$$

Thus, the probability that all n of the independently drawn samples fall outside this hypersphere is $(1 - P_s)^n$, which approaches zero as n goes to infinity. Thus $\mathbf{x}'_n$ converges to $\mathbf{x}$ in probability, and $p(\mathbf{x}'_n \mid \mathbf{x})$ approaches a delta function, as expected. In fact, by using measure theoretic methods one can make even stronger (as well as more rigorous) statements about the convergence of $\mathbf{x}'_n$ to $\mathbf{x}$, but this result is sufficient for our purposes.

4.6.3   Error Rate for the Nearest Neighbor Rule

We now turn to the calculation of the conditional probability of error $P_n(e \mid \mathbf{x}, \mathbf{x}'_n)$. To avoid a potential source of confusion, we must state the problem with somewhat greater care than has been exercised so far. When we say that we have n independently drawn labelled samples, we are talking about n pairs of random variables $(\mathbf{x}_1, \theta_1), (\mathbf{x}_2, \theta_2), \ldots, (\mathbf{x}_n, \theta_n)$, where θ_i may be any of the c states of nature $\omega_1, \ldots, \omega_c$. We assume that these pairs were generated by selecting a state of nature ω_j for θ_i with probability $P(\omega_j)$ and then selecting an $\mathbf{x}_i$ according to the probability law $p(\mathbf{x} \mid \omega_j)$, with each pair being selected independently. Suppose now that nature selects a pair $(\mathbf{x}, \theta)$, and that $\mathbf{x}'_n$, labelled θ'_n, is the sample nearest $\mathbf{x}$. Since the state of nature when $\mathbf{x}'_n$ was drawn is independent of the state of nature when $\mathbf{x}$ is drawn,

$$P(\theta, \theta'_n \mid \mathbf{x}, \mathbf{x}'_n) = P(\theta \mid \mathbf{x})P(\theta'_n \mid \mathbf{x}'_n). \tag{30}$$

Now if we use the nearest-neighbor decision rule, we commit an error whenever $\theta \neq \theta'_n$. Thus, the conditional probability of error $P_n(e \mid \mathbf{x}, \mathbf{x}'_n)$ is given by

$$P_n(e \mid \mathbf{x}, \mathbf{x}'_n) = 1 - \sum_{i=1}^{c} P(\theta = \omega_i, \theta'_n = \omega_i \mid \mathbf{x}, \mathbf{x}'_n)$$

$$= 1 - \sum_{i=1}^{c} P(\omega_i \mid \mathbf{x})P(\omega_i \mid \mathbf{x}'_n). \tag{31}$$

To obtain $P_n(e)$ we must substitute this expression in Eq. (29) for $P_n(e \mid \mathbf{x})$ and then average the result over $\mathbf{x}$. This is very difficult in general, but, as we remarked earlier, the integration called for in Eq. (29) becomes trivial as n goes to infinity and $p(\mathbf{x}'_n \mid \mathbf{x})$ approaches a delta function. If $P(\omega_i \mid \mathbf{x})$ is continuous at $\mathbf{x}$, we obtain

$$\lim_{n \to \infty} P_n(e \mid \mathbf{x}) = \int \left[1 - \sum_{i=1}^{c} P(\omega_i \mid \mathbf{x}) P(\omega_i \mid \mathbf{x}'_n) \right] \delta(\mathbf{x}'_n - \mathbf{x}) \, d\mathbf{x}'_n$$

$$= 1 - \sum_{i=1}^{c} P^2(\omega_i \mid \mathbf{x}). \tag{32}$$

Thus, provided we can exchange some limits and integrals,† the asymptotic nearest-neighbor error rate is given by

$$P = \lim_{n \to \infty} P_n(e)$$

$$= \lim_{n \to \infty} \int P_n(e \mid \mathbf{x}) p(\mathbf{x}) \, d\mathbf{x}$$

$$= \int \left[1 - \sum_{i=1}^{c} P^2(\omega_i \mid \mathbf{x}) \right] p(\mathbf{x}) \, d\mathbf{x}. \tag{33}$$

4.6.4   Error Bounds

While Eq. (33) presents an exact result, it is more illuminating to obtain bounds on P in terms of the Bayes rate P^*. An obvious lower bound on P is P^* itself. Furthermore, it can be shown that for any P^* there is a set of conditional and prior probabilities for which the bound is achieved, so that in this sense it is a tight lower bound.

The problem of establishing a tight upper bound is more interesting. The basis for hoping for a low upper bound comes from observing that if the Bayes rate is low, $P(\omega_i \mid \mathbf{x})$ is near one for some i, say $i = m$. Thus the integrand in Eq. (33) is approximately $1 - P^2(\omega_m \mid \mathbf{x}) \approx 2(1 - P(\omega_m \mid \mathbf{x}))$, and since

$$P^*(e \mid \mathbf{x}) = 1 - P(\omega_m \mid \mathbf{x}), \tag{34}$$

integration over $\mathbf{x}$ might yield about twice the Bayes rate, which is still low. To obtain an exact upper bound, we must find out how large the nearest-neighbor error rate P can become for a given Bayes rate P^*. Thus, Eq. (33) leads us to ask how small $\sum_{i=1}^{c} P^2(\omega_i \mid \mathbf{x})$ can be for a given $P(\omega_m \mid \mathbf{x})$. Writing

$$\sum_{i=1}^{c} P^2(\omega_i \mid \mathbf{x}) = P^2(\omega_m \mid \mathbf{x}) + \sum_{i \neq m} P^2(\omega_i \mid \mathbf{x})$$

† Readers familiar with measure theory will recognize that the dominated convergence theorem permits us to make this interchange. If there are regions where $p(\mathbf{x})$ is identically zero, Eq. (32) is not valid for those values of $\mathbf{x}$. (Why?) However, such regions can be excluded from the integration in Eq. (33).

we can bound this sum by minimizing the second term subject to the following constraints:

(1) $P(\omega_i \mid \mathbf{x}) \geq 0$

(2) $\sum\limits_{i \neq m} P(\omega_i \mid \mathbf{x}) = 1 - P(\omega_m \mid \mathbf{x}) = P^*(e \mid \mathbf{x})$.

With a little thought we see that $\sum_{i=1}^{c} P^2(\omega_i \mid \mathbf{x})$ is minimized if all of the a posteriori probabilities except the mth are equal, and the second constraint yields

$$P(\omega_i \mid \mathbf{x}) = \begin{cases} \dfrac{P^*(e \mid \mathbf{x})}{c - 1} & i \neq m \\ 1 - P^*(e \mid \mathbf{x}) & i = m. \end{cases} \tag{35}$$

Thus

$$\sum_{i=1}^{c} P^2(\omega_i \mid \mathbf{x}) \geq (1 - P^*(e \mid \mathbf{x}))^2 + \frac{P^{*2}(e \mid \mathbf{x})}{c - 1}$$

and

$$1 - \sum_{i=1}^{c} P^2(\omega_i \mid \mathbf{x}) \leq 2P^*(e \mid \mathbf{x}) - \frac{c}{c - 1} P^{*2}(e \mid \mathbf{x}). \tag{36}$$

This immediately shows that $P \leq 2P^*$, since we can substitute this result in Eq. (33) and merely drop the second term. However, a tighter bound can be obtained by observing that

$$\mathrm{Var}[P^*(e \mid \mathbf{x})] = \int [P^*(e \mid \mathbf{x}) - P^*]^2 p(\mathbf{x}) \, d\mathbf{x}$$

$$= \int P^{*2}(e \mid \mathbf{x}) p(\mathbf{x}) \, d\mathbf{x} - P^{*2} \geq 0,$$

so that

$$\int P^{*2}(e \mid \mathbf{x}) p(\mathbf{x}) \, d\mathbf{x} \geq P^{*2},$$

with equality holding if and only if the variance of $P^*(e \mid \mathbf{x})$ is zero. Using this result and substituting Eq. (36) in Eq. (33), we obtain the desired bounds

$$P^* \leq P \leq P^* \left(2 - \frac{c}{c - 1} P^* \right). \tag{28}$$

It is easy to show that this upper bound is achieved in the so-called zero-information case in which the densities $p(\mathbf{x} \mid \omega_i)$ are identical, so that $P(\omega_i \mid \mathbf{x}) = P(\omega_i)$ and $P^*(e \mid \mathbf{x})$ is independent of $\mathbf{x}$. Thus the bounds given by Eq. (28) are as tight as possible, in the sense that for any P^* there exist conditional and a priori probabilities for which they are achieved. Figure 4.4 illustrates the nature of the bounds graphically. The Bayes rate P^* can be

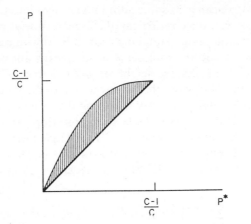

FIGURE 4.4. Bounds on the nearest-neighbor error rate.

anywhere between 0 and $(c - 1)/c$. The bounds meet at these two extreme points. When the Bayes rate is small, the upper bound is approximately twice the Bayes rate. In general, the nearest-neighbor error rate must fall in the shaded area shown.

Since P is always less than or equal to $2P^*$, if one had an infinite collection of data and used an arbitrarily complicated decision rule, one could at most cut the error rate in half. In this sense, at least half of the classification information in an infinite data set resides in the nearest neighbor.

It is natural to ask how well the nearest-neighbor rule works in the finite-sample case, and how rapidly the performance converges to the asymptotic value. Unfortunately, the only statements that can be made in the general case are negative. It can be shown that convergence can be arbitrarily slow, and the error rate $P_n(e)$ need not even decrease monotonically with n. As with other nonparametric methods, it is difficult to obtain anything other than asymptotic results without making further assumptions about the underlying probability structure.

4.7   THE *k*-NEAREST-NEIGHBOR RULE

An obvious extension of the nearest-neighbor rule is the *k-nearest-neighbor rule*. As one would expect from the name, this rule classifies **x** by assigning it the label most frequently represented among the k nearest samples; in other words, a decision is made by examining the labels on the k nearest neighbors and taking a vote. We shall not go into a thorough analysis of the *k*-nearest-neighbor rule. However, by considering the two-class case with k

odd (to avoid ties), we can gain some additional insight into these procedures.

The basic motivation for considering the k-nearest-neighbor rule rests on our earlier observation about matching probabilities with nature. We notice first that if k is fixed and the number n of samples is allowed to approach infinity, then all of the k nearest neighbors will converge to $\mathbf{x}$. Hence, as in the single-nearest-neighbor case, the labels on each of the k-nearest-neighbors are random variables, independently assuming the value ω_i with probability $P(\omega_i \mid \mathbf{x})$, $i = 1, 2$. If $P(\omega_m \mid \mathbf{x})$ is the larger a posteriori probability, then the Bayes decision rule always selects ω_m. The single-nearest-neighbor rule selects ω_m with probability $P(\omega_m \mid \mathbf{x})$. The k-nearest-neighbor rule selects ω_m if a majority of the k nearest neighbors are labeled ω_m, an event of probability

$$\sum_{i=(k+1)/2}^{k} \binom{k}{i} P(\omega_m \mid \mathbf{x})^i [1 - P(\omega_m \mid \mathbf{x})]^{k-i}.$$

In general, the larger the value of k, the greater the probability that ω_m will be selected.

We could analyze the k-nearest-neighbor rule in much the same way that we analyzed the single-nearest-neighbor rule. However, since the arguments become more involved and supply little additional insight, we shall content ourselves with stating the results. It can be shown that if k is odd, the large-sample two-class error rate for the k-nearest-neighbor rule is bounded above by the function $C_k(P^*)$, where C_k is defined to be the smallest concave function of P^* greater than

$$\sum_{i=0}^{(k-1)/2} \binom{k}{i} [(P^*)^{i+1}(1 - P^*)^{k-i} + (P^*)^{k-i}(1 - P^*)^{i+1}].$$

Now it is perfectly clear that very little insight can be gained by staring at the above function, except perhaps to note the family resemblance to the binomial distribution. Fortunately, it is easy to compute $C_k(P^*)$ and inspect the results. Figure 4.5 shows the bounds on the k-nearest-neighbor error rates for several values of k. The case $k = 1$ corresponds to the two-class instance of Figure 4.4. As k increases, the upper bounds get progressively closer to the lower bound, the Bayes rate. In the limit as k goes to infinity, the two bounds meet and the k-nearest-neighbor rule becomes optimal.

At the risk of sounding repetitive, we conclude by commenting once again on the finite-sample situation encountered in practice. The k-nearest-neighbor rule can be viewed as another attempt to estimate the a posteriori probabilities $P(\omega_i \mid \mathbf{x})$ from samples. We want to use a large value of k to obtain a reliable estimate. On the other hand, we want all of the k nearest neighbors $\mathbf{x}'$ to be very near $\mathbf{x}$ to be sure that $P(\omega_i \mid \mathbf{x}')$ is approximately the same as $P(\omega_i \mid \mathbf{x})$. This forces us to choose a compromise k that is a small

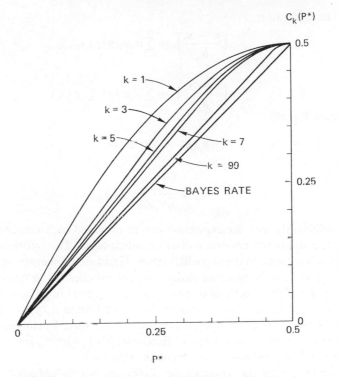

FIGURE 4.5. Bounds on the error-rate for the *k*-nearest-neighbor rule.

fraction of the number of samples. It is only in the limit as *n* goes to infinity that we can be assured of the nearly optimal behavior of the *k*-nearest-neighbor rule.

4.8 APPROXIMATIONS BY SERIES EXPANSIONS

All of the nonparametric methods described thus far suffer from the requirement that all of the samples must be stored. Since a large number of samples is needed to obtain good estimates, the memory requirements can be severe. In addition, considerable computation time may be required each time one of the methods is used to estimate $p(\mathbf{x})$ or classify a new $\mathbf{x}$. In certain circumstances the Parzen-window procedure can be modified to reduce these problems considerably. The basic idea is to approximate the window function by a finite series expansion that is acceptably accurate in the region of interest. If we are fortunate and can find two sets of functions $\psi_j(\mathbf{x})$ and $\chi_j(\mathbf{x})$ that allow the expansion

$$\varphi\left(\frac{\mathbf{x} - \mathbf{x}_i}{h_n}\right) = \sum_{j=1}^{m} a_j \psi_j(\mathbf{x}) \chi_j(\mathbf{x}_i), \tag{37}$$

then

$$\sum_{i=1}^{n} \varphi\left(\frac{\mathbf{x} - \mathbf{x}_i}{h_n}\right) = \sum_{j=1}^{m} a_j \psi_j(\mathbf{x}) \sum_{i=1}^{n} \chi_j(\mathbf{x}_i)$$

and, from Eq. (8),

$$p_n(\mathbf{x}) = \sum_{j=1}^{m} b_j \psi_j(\mathbf{x}), \tag{38}$$

where

$$b_j = \frac{a_j}{nV_n} \sum_{i=1}^{n} \chi_j(\mathbf{x}_i). \tag{39}$$

If a sufficiently accurate expansion can be obtained with a reasonable value for m, this approach has some obvious advantages. The information in the n samples is reduced to the m coefficients b_j. If additional samples are obtained, Eq. (39) for b_j can be updated easily, and the number of coefficients remains unchanged.* If the functions ψ_j and χ_j are polynomial functions of the components of $\mathbf{x}$ and $\mathbf{x}_i$, the expression for the estimate $p_n(\mathbf{x})$ is also a polynomial, which can be computed relatively efficiently. Furthermore, use of this estimate to obtain discriminant functions $p(\mathbf{x} \mid \omega_i)P(\omega_i)$ leads to a simple way of obtaining *polynomial discriminant functions*.

Before becoming too enthusiastic, however, we should note one of the problems with this approach. A key property of a useful window function is its tendency to peak at the origin and fade away elsewhere. Thus $\varphi((\mathbf{x} - \mathbf{x}_i)/h_n)$ should peak sharply at $\mathbf{x} = \mathbf{x}_i$, and contribute little to the approximation of $p_n(\mathbf{x})$ for $\mathbf{x}$ far from $\mathbf{x}_i$. Unfortunately, polynomials have the annoying property of becoming unbounded. Thus, a polynomial expansion might find the terms associated with an $\mathbf{x}_i$ far from $\mathbf{x}$ contributing most rather than least to the expansion. Hence, it is quite important to be sure that the expansion of each window function is in fact accurate in the region of interest, and this may well require a large number of terms.

There are many types of series expansions one might consider. Readers familiar with integral equations will naturally interpret Eq. (37) as an expansion of the kernel $\varphi(\mathbf{x}, \mathbf{x}_i)$ in a series of eigenfunctions. Rather than computing eigenfunctions, one might choose any reasonable set of functions orthogonal over the region of interest and obtain a least-squares fit to the window function. We shall take an even more straightforward approach and

---

* It should be pointed out, however, that if h_n is reduced when new samples are added, φ will more nearly approach an impulse, and more terms may in fact be required for an accurate approximation.

expand the window function in a Taylor's series. For simplicity, we confine our attention to a one-dimensional example using a gaussian window function:

$$\sqrt{\pi}\,\varphi(u) = e^{-u^2}$$

$$\approx \sum_{j=0}^{m-1} (-1)^j \frac{u^{2j}}{j!}.$$

This expansion is most accurate near $u = 0$, and is in error by less than $u^{2m}/m!$. If we substitute

$$u = \frac{x - x_i}{h}$$

we obtain a polynomial of degree $2(m - 1)$ in x and x_i. For example, if $m = 2$

$$\sqrt{\pi}\,\varphi\!\left(\frac{x - x_i}{h}\right) \approx 1 - \left(\frac{x - x_i}{h}\right)^2$$

$$\approx 1 + \frac{2}{h^2}\,xx_i - \frac{1}{h^2}\,x^2 - \frac{1}{h^2}\,x_i^2$$

and thus

$$\sqrt{\pi}\,p_n(x) = \frac{1}{nh}\sum_{i=1}^{n}\sqrt{\pi}\,\varphi\!\left(\frac{x - x_i}{h}\right) \approx b_0 + b_1 x + b_2 x^2$$

where

$$b_0 = \frac{1}{h} - \frac{1}{h^3}\frac{1}{n}\sum_{i=1}^{n} x_i^2$$

$$b_1 = \frac{2}{h^3}\frac{1}{n}\sum_{i=1}^{n} x_i$$

$$b_2 = -\frac{1}{h^3}.$$

This simple expansion condenses the information in n samples into 3 coefficients, b_0, b_1, and b_2. It is accurate if the largest value of $|x - x_i|$ is not greater than h. Unfortunately, this restricts us to a very wide window that is not capable of much resolution. By taking more terms we can use a narrower window. If we let r be the largest value of $|x - x_i|$, use the fact that the error in the m-term expansion of $\sqrt{\pi}\,\varphi[(x - x_i)/h]$ is less than $(r/h)^{2m}m!$, and use Stirling's approximation for $m!$, we find that the error in approximating $p_n(x)$ is less than

$$\frac{1}{\sqrt{\pi}\,h}\frac{\left(\frac{r}{h}\right)^{2m}}{m!} \approx \frac{1}{\sqrt{\pi}\,h\sqrt{2\pi m}}\left[\left(\frac{e}{m}\right)\left(\frac{r}{h}\right)^2\right]^m.$$

Thus, the error becomes small only when $m > e(r/h)^2$. This implies the need for many terms if the window size h is small relative to the distance r from x to the most distant sample. Although this example is rudimentary, similar considerations arise in the multidimensional case even when more sophisticated expansions are used, and the procedure is most attractive when the window size is relatively large.

4.9   APPROXIMATIONS FOR THE BINARY CASE

4.9.1   The Rademacher-Walsh Expansion

When the components of the vector $\mathbf{x}$ are discrete, the problem of estimating a density becomes the problem of estimating the probability $P(\mathbf{x} = \mathbf{v}_k)$. Conceptually, the problem is even simpler—one need only count the number of times that $\mathbf{x}$ is observed to have the value $\mathbf{v}_k$ and rely on the law of large numbers. However, consider the case in which the d components of $\mathbf{x}$ are binary valued (0 or 1). Since there are 2^d possible vectors $\mathbf{v}_k$, we must estimate 2^d probabilities, which is an enormous task for the large values of d frequently encountered in pattern recognition work.

If the components of $\mathbf{x}$ are statistically independent, the problem is greatly simplified. In this case we can write

$$P(\mathbf{x}) = \prod_{i=1}^{d} P(x_i) = \prod_{i=1}^{d} p_i^{x_i}(1 - p_i)^{1-x_i} \tag{40}$$

where

$$p_i = P(x_i = 1) \tag{41}$$

and

$$1 - p_i = P(x_i = 0). \tag{42}$$

Thus, in this special case the estimation of $P(\mathbf{x})$ reduces to the estimation of d probabilities p_i. Moreover, if we consider the logarithm of $P(\mathbf{x})$ we see that it is a linear function of $\mathbf{x}$, which simplifies both its storage and its computation:

$$\log P(\mathbf{x}) = \sum_{i=1}^{d} w_i x_i + w_0 \tag{43}$$

where

$$w_i = \begin{cases} \log \dfrac{p_i}{1 - p_i} & i = 1, \ldots, d \\ \displaystyle\sum_{i=1}^{d} \log(1 - p_i) & i = 0. \end{cases} \tag{44}$$

It is natural to ask whether or not there are any compromise positions between being completely accurate, which requires estimating 2^d probabilities, and being forced to assume statistical independence, which reduces the problem to one of estimating only d probabilities. One answer is provided by finding an expansion for $P(\mathbf{x})$ and approximating $P(\mathbf{x})$ by a partial sum. When binary variables are involved, it is natural to use the *Rademacher-Walsh polynomials* as basis functions. This set of 2^d polynomials can be obtained by systematically forming products of the distinct factors $2x_i - 1$ taken none at a time, one at a time, two at a time, etc. Thus

$$\varphi_i(\mathbf{x}) = \begin{cases} 1 & i = 0 \\ 2x_1 - 1 & i = 1 \\ \vdots & \vdots \\ 2x_d - 1 & i = d \\ (2x_1 - 1)(2x_2 - 1) & i = d + 1 \\ \vdots & \vdots \\ (2x_{d-1} - 1)(2x_d - 1) & i = d + 1 + d(d-1)/2 \\ (2x_1 - 1)(2x_2 - 1)(2x_3 - 1) & i = d + 2 + d(d-1)/2 \\ \vdots & \vdots \\ (2x_1 - 1) \cdots (2x_d - 1) & i = 2^d - 1. \end{cases} \tag{45}$$

It is not hard to see that these polynomials satisfy the orthogonality relation

$$\sum_{\mathbf{x}} \varphi_i(\mathbf{x})\varphi_j(\mathbf{x}) = \begin{cases} 2^d & i = j \\ 0 & i \neq j, \end{cases} \tag{46}$$

where the summation extends over the 2^d possible values of $\mathbf{x}$. Thus, any function $P(\mathbf{x})$ defined on the unit d-cube can be expanded as

$$P(\mathbf{x}) = \sum_{i=0}^{2^d-1} a_i \varphi_i(\mathbf{x}), \tag{47}$$

where

$$a_i = \frac{1}{2^d} \sum_{\mathbf{x}} \varphi_i(\mathbf{x})P(\mathbf{x}). \tag{48}$$

Viewing $P(\mathbf{x})$ as a probability function, we see that

$$a_i = \frac{1}{2^d} E[\varphi_i(\mathbf{x})]. \tag{49}$$

Since the Rademacher-Walsh functions $\varphi_i(\mathbf{x})$ are polynomials, we see that the coefficients a_i are essentially moments. Thus, if $P(\mathbf{x})$ is unknown, but if n

samples $\mathbf{x}_1, \ldots, \mathbf{x}_n$ are available, the coefficients can be estimated by computing sample moments:

$$a_i \approx \frac{1}{n} \sum_{j=1}^{n} \frac{1}{2^d} \varphi_i(\mathbf{x}_j). \tag{50}$$

In the limit as n goes to infinity, the law of large numbers assures us that this estimate will converge (in probability) to the true value for a_i.

Now Eq. (47) gives us an exact expansion of $P(\mathbf{x})$, and, as such, it does not reduce our computational problem. Instead of estimating 2^d joint probabilities, we must estimate 2^d moments, the coefficients a_i. However, we can approximate $P(\mathbf{x})$ by truncating the expansion and computing just the lower order moments. A first-order approximation obtained by taking the first $1 + d$ terms is linear in $\mathbf{x}$. A second-order approximation containing the first $1 + d + d(d - 1)/2$ terms is quadratic in $\mathbf{x}$.* In general, Eq. (47) shows that an approximation involving kth degree Rademacher-Walsh polynomials requires the evaluation of moments of order k and lower. These moments can be estimated from data or computed directly from $P(\mathbf{x})$. In this latter case, the fact that one can sum first over variables not involved in the polynomial shows that one need only know marginal probabilities of order k. For example, a first-order expansion is determined by the probabilities $p_i = P(x_i = 1)$:

$$P_1(\mathbf{x}) = a_0 + \sum_{i=1}^{d} a_i(2x_i - 1)$$

where

$$a_i = \begin{cases} 2^{-d} & i = 0 \\ 2^{-d}(2p_i - 1) & i = 1, \ldots, d. \end{cases}$$

It is natural to ask how well such a truncated expansion approximates the actual probability $P(\mathbf{x})$. In general, if we approximate $P(\mathbf{x})$ by a series involving a subset of the Rademacher-Walsh polynomials, such as

$$\tilde{P}(\mathbf{x}) = \sum_{i \in I} b_i \varphi_i(\mathbf{x}),$$

then the orthogonality relations can be used to show that the sum of squared error $\sum (P(\mathbf{x}) - \tilde{P}(\mathbf{x}))^2$ is minimized by the choice $b_i = a_i$. Thus, a truncated expansion is optimal in this mean-squared sense. Furthermore, as long as the constant polynomial φ_0 is included in the approximation, it is easy to show that $\sum \tilde{P}(\mathbf{x}) = 1$, as desired. However, nothing prevents $\tilde{P}(\mathbf{x})$ from becoming negative for some $\mathbf{x}$. Indeed, if φ_0 is not included, $\sum \tilde{P}(\mathbf{x}) = 0$, and

---

* Because the components of $\mathbf{x}$ are binary, products such as $x_i x_j$ are especially easy to compute and can be implemented in hardware by AND gates.

at least one of the probabilities must be negative. This annoying result can be avoided by expanding $\log P(\mathbf{x})$ rather than $P(\mathbf{x})$, although then we are no longer assured that the resulting approximation for $P(\mathbf{x})$ will sum to one.

4.9.2 The Bahadur-Lazarsfeld Expansion

An interesting alternative expansion is obtained by introducing the normalized variables

$$y_i = \frac{x_i - p_i}{\sqrt{p_i(1 - p_i)}}, \tag{51}$$

assuming of course that p_i is neither zero nor one. These normalized variables have zero mean and unit variance. A set of polynomials much like the Rademacher-Walsh polynomials can be obtained by systematically forming distinct products of the y_i taken none at a time, one at a time, two at a time, etc. Thus

$$\psi_i(\mathbf{x}) = \begin{cases} 1 & i = 0 \\ y_1 & i = 1 \\ \cdot & \cdot \\ \cdot & \cdot \\ \cdot & \cdot \\ y_d & i = d \\ y_1 y_2 & i = d + 1 \\ \cdot & \cdot \\ \cdot & \cdot \\ \cdot & \cdot \\ y_{d-1} y_d & i = d + 1 + d(d-1)/2 \\ y_1 y_2 y_3 & i = d + 2 + d(d-1)/2 \\ \cdot & \cdot \\ \cdot & \cdot \\ \cdot & \cdot \\ y_1 y_2 \cdots y_d & i = 2^d - 1 \end{cases} \tag{52}$$

These polynomials are not orthogonal in themselves, but they are orthogonal with respect to the weighting function

$$P_1(\mathbf{x}) = \prod_{i=1}^{d} p_i^{x_i}(1 - p_i)^{1-x_i}. \tag{53}$$

That is,

$$\sum_{\mathbf{x}} \psi_i(\mathbf{x})\psi_j(\mathbf{x})P_1(\mathbf{x}) = \begin{cases} 1 & i = j \\ 0 & i \neq j. \end{cases} \tag{54}$$

This should be clear from the observation that $P_1(\mathbf{x})$ is the distribution for the independent case, and that in this case the moments $E[\psi_i(\mathbf{x})\psi_j(\mathbf{x})]$ are either zero or one. It follows that any function defined on the unit d-cube can be expanded as

$$F(\mathbf{x}) = \sum_{i=0}^{2^d-1} a_i \psi_i(\mathbf{x}),$$

where

$$a_i = \sum_{\mathbf{x}} \psi_i(\mathbf{x}) P_1(\mathbf{x}) F(\mathbf{x}).$$

In particular, the function $P(\mathbf{x})/P_1(\mathbf{x})$ has the expansion

$$P(\mathbf{x}) = P_1(\mathbf{x}) \sum_{i=0}^{2^d-1} a_i \psi_i(\mathbf{x}) \tag{55}$$

where

$$a_i = \sum_{\mathbf{x}} \psi_i(\mathbf{x}) P(\mathbf{x}) = E[\psi_i(\mathbf{x})]. \tag{56}$$

Recalling that $\psi_i(\mathbf{x})$ is a product of the normalized variables $y_i = (x_i - p_i)/\sqrt{p_i(1-p_i)}$, we see that the a_i are correlation coefficients. Clearly, $a_0 = 1$ and $a_1 = \cdots = a_d = 0$. If we define

$$\left. \begin{aligned} \rho_{ij} &= \sum_{\mathbf{x}} y_i y_j P(\mathbf{x}) \\ \rho_{ijk} &= \sum_{\mathbf{x}} y_i y_j y_k P(\mathbf{x}) \\ &\quad . \\ &\quad . \\ &\quad . \\ \rho_{12:..d} &= \sum_{\mathbf{x}} y_1 y_2 \cdots y_d P(\mathbf{x}), \end{aligned} \right\} \tag{57}$$

then we can write the expansion of Eq. (55) as

$$P(\mathbf{x}) = P_1(\mathbf{x}) \left[1 + \sum_{i<j} \rho_{ij} y_i y_j + \sum_{i<j<k} \rho_{ijk} y_i y_j y_k + \cdots + \rho_{12\cdots d} y_1 y_2 \cdots y_d \right]. \tag{58}$$

This is known as the *Badahur-Lazarsfeld expansion* of $P(\mathbf{x})$. It contains $2^d - 1$ coefficients, the d first order probabilities p_i, the $\binom{d}{2}$ second-order correlation coefficients ρ_{ij}, the $\binom{d}{3}$ third-order correlation coefficients ρ_{ijk}, and so on. A natural way to approximate $P(\mathbf{x})$ is to ignore all correlations above a certain order. Thus,

$$P_1(\mathbf{x}) = \prod_{i=1}^{d} p_i^{x_i} (1 - p_i)^{1-x_i}$$

is a first-order approximation to $P(\mathbf{x})$,

$$P_2(\mathbf{x}) = P_1(\mathbf{x}) \left[1 + \sum_{i<j} \rho_{ij} y_i y_j \right]$$

is a second-order approximation, and so on. If the higher-order correlation coefficients are small and we use the approximation $\log(1 + x) \approx x$, we see that $\log P_1(\mathbf{x})$ is linear in x, $\log P_2(\mathbf{x})$ adds a quadratic correction term, and so on. Thus the logarithm of the Bahadur-Lazarsfeld expansion provides an interesting sequence of approximations. The first is equivalent to assuming independence, and is linear in $\mathbf{x}$. The second accounts for second-order correlations, and is approximately quadratic in $\mathbf{x}$. Each successive approximation accounts for correlations of one higher order, but of course requires the computation of more terms.

4.9.3 The Chow Expansion

Another interesting class of approximations to a joint probability distribution $P(\mathbf{x})$ is based on the identity

$$P(\mathbf{x}) = P(x_1, \ldots, x_d) = P(x_1)P(x_2 \mid x_1)P(x_3 \mid x_2, x_1) \cdots P(x_d \mid x_{d-1}, \ldots, x_1). \tag{59}$$

If the variables are statistically independent, this reduces to the product of the individual probabilities $P(x_i)$. Suppose that the variables are not independent, but that $P(x_i \mid x_{i-1}, \ldots, x_1)$ depends only on the immediately preceding variable x_{i-1}. Then we have a first-order Markov chain, and

$$P(\mathbf{x}) = P(x_1)P(x_2 \mid x_1)P(x_3 \mid x_2) \cdots P(x_d \mid x_{d-1}). \tag{60}$$

We shall see that each factor $P(x_i \mid x_{i-1})$ can be determined by two coefficients; thus, $P(\mathbf{x})$ can be determined by $2d - 1$ coefficients, which is less of an increase in complexity than if we had allowed for all $\binom{d}{2}$ second-order correlations. Similar higher-order Markov approximations can be obtained if we assume that x_i depends only on the k immediately preceding variables.

While an assumption that a given variable x_i depends only upon certain preceding variables is reasonable if we are dealing with a temporal process, it is a rather strange assumption in more general circumstances. However, it is reasonable to expect that a given variable x_i may be primarily dependent upon only a few other variables. Suppose that we can number the variables so that $P(x_i \mid x_{i-1}, \ldots, x_1)$ is solely dependent on some preceding variable, $x_{j(i)}$. For example, suppose that

$$P(x_4 \mid x_3, x_2, x_1) = P(x_4 \mid x_2) \qquad \text{and} \qquad P(x_3 \mid x_2, x_1) = P(x_3 \mid x_1).$$

Then it follows from Eq. (59) that $P(x_1, x_2, x_3, x_4)$ can be written as $P(x_1)P(x_2 \mid x_1)P(x_3 \mid x_1)P(x_4 \mid x_2)$. In general, we obtain the product expansion

$$P(\mathbf{x}) = P(x_1)P(x_2 \mid x_{j(2)}) \cdots P(x_d \mid x_{j(d)}). \tag{61}$$

By substituting 0 or 1 for x_i and $x_{j(i)}$, the reader can verify that

$$P(x_i \mid x_{j(i)}) = [p_i^{x_i}(1 - p_i)^{1-x_i}]^{x_{j(i)}}[q_i^{x_i}(1 - q_i)^{1-x_i}]^{1-x_{j(i)}} \quad (62)$$

where

$$p_i = P(x_i = 1 \mid x_{j(i)} = 1) \quad (63)$$

and

$$q_i = P(x_i = 1 \mid x_{j(i)} = 0). \quad (64)$$

By letting $q_i = P(x_i = 1)$, substituting Eq. (62) in Eq. (61), taking the logarithm, and collecting terms, we obtain the *Chow expansion:*

$$\log P(x) = \sum_{i=1}^{d} \log(1 - q_i) + \sum_{i=1}^{d} x_i \log \frac{q_i}{1 - q_i}$$

$$+ \sum_{i=2}^{d} x_{j(i)} \log \frac{1 - p_i}{1 - q_i} + \sum_{i=2}^{d} x_i x_{j(i)} \log \frac{p_i(1 - q_i)}{(1 - p_i)q_i}. \quad (65)$$

Similar results for higher-order dependence can be obtained in an obvious way.

A few observations about these results are in order. First, we note that if the variables are indeed independent, $p_i = q_i$ and the last two sums in the expansion disappear, leaving the familiar expansion for the independent case. When dependence exists, we obtain additional linear and quadratic terms. Of course, the linear terms can be combined, so that the expansion effectively contains a constant, d linear terms, and $d - 1$ quadratic terms.

Comparing this with the second-order Rademacher-Walsh or Bahadur-Lazarsfeld expansions, either of which requires $d(d - 1)/2$ quadratic terms, we see that the savings can be appreciable. Of course, the savings can only be realized if we know the *dependence tree*, the function $j(i)$ which exhibits the limited dependence of one variable on preceding variables. If the dependence tree cannot be inferred from the physical significance of the variables, it may be necessary to compute all of the correlation coefficients merely to find the significant ones. However, even in this case it should be pointed out that one might prefer to use the Chow expansion because the resulting approximate probabilities are always nonnegative and sum to one.

4.10   FISHER'S LINEAR DISCRIMINANT

One of the recurring problems encountered in applying statistical techniques to pattern recognition problems is what Bellman calls the curse of dimensionality. Procedures that are analytically or computationally manageable in low-dimensional spaces can become completely impractical in a space of 50 or 100 dimensions. Thus, various techniques have been developed for

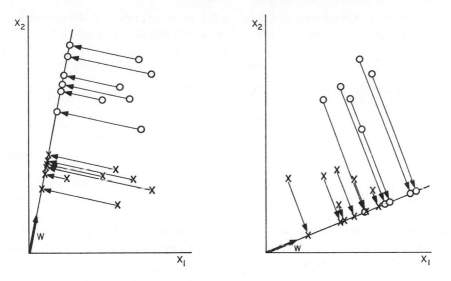

FIGURE 4.6.   Projection of samples onto a line.

reducing the dimensionality of the feature space in the hope of obtaining a more manageable problem.

We can reduce the dimensionality from d dimensions to one dimension if we merely project the d-dimensional data onto a line. Of course, even if the samples formed well-separated, compact clusters in d-space, projection on an arbitrary line will usually produce a confused mixture of samples from all of the classes. However, by moving the line around, we might be able to find an orientation for which the projected samples are well separated. This is exactly the goal of classical discriminant analysis.

Suppose that we have a set of n d-dimensional samples $x_1, \ldots, x_n$, n_1 in the subset $\mathcal{X}_1$ labelled ω_1 and n_2 in the subset $\mathcal{X}_2$ labelled ω_2. If we form a linear combination of the components of x, we obtain the scalar

$$y = w^t x \tag{66}$$

and a corresponding set of n samples $y_1, \ldots, y_n$ divided into the subsets $\mathcal{Y}_1$ and $\mathcal{Y}_2$. Geometrically, if $\|w\| = 1$, each y_i is the projection of the corresponding x_i onto a line in the direction of w. Actually, the magnitude of w is of no real significance, since it merely scales y. The direction of w is important, however. If we imagine that the samples labelled ω_1 fall more or less in one cluster while those labelled ω_2 fall in another, we want the projections falling on the line to be well separated, not thoroughly intermingled. Figure 4.6 illustrates the effect of choosing two different values for w for a two-dimensional example.

A measure of the separation between the projected points is the difference of the sample means. If $\mathbf{m}_i$ is the d-dimensional sample mean given by

$$\mathbf{m}_i = \frac{1}{n_i} \sum_{\mathbf{x} \in \mathcal{X}_i} \mathbf{x}, \tag{67}$$

then the sample mean for the projected points is given by

$$\tilde{m}_i = \frac{1}{n_i} \sum_{y \in \mathcal{Y}_i} y$$

$$= \frac{1}{n_i} \sum_{\mathbf{x} \in \mathcal{X}_i} \mathbf{w}^t \mathbf{x} = \mathbf{w}^t \mathbf{m}_i. \tag{68}$$

It follows that $|\tilde{m}_1 - \tilde{m}_2| = |\mathbf{w}^t(\mathbf{m}_1 - \mathbf{m}_2)|$, and that we can make this difference as large as we wish merely by scaling $\mathbf{w}$. Of course, to obtain good separation of the projected data we really want the difference between the means to be large relative to some measure of the standard deviations for each class. Rather than forming sample variances, we define the *scatter* for projected samples labelled ω_i by

$$\tilde{s}_i^2 = \sum_{y \in \mathcal{Y}_i} (y - \tilde{m}_i)^2. \tag{69}$$

Thus, $(1/n)(\tilde{s}_1^2 + \tilde{s}_2^2)$ is an estimate of the variance of the pooled data, and $\tilde{s}_1^2 + \tilde{s}_2^2$ is called the total *within-class scatter* of the projected samples. The *Fisher linear discriminant* is then defined as that linear function* $\mathbf{w}^t\mathbf{x}$ for which the *criterion function*

$$J(\mathbf{w}) = \frac{|\tilde{m}_1 - \tilde{m}_2|^2}{\tilde{s}_1^2 + \tilde{s}_2^2} \tag{70}$$

is maximum.

To obtain J as an explicit function of $\mathbf{w}$, we define the *scatter matrices* S_i and S_W by

$$S_i = \sum_{\mathbf{x} \in \mathcal{X}_i} (\mathbf{x} - \mathbf{m}_i)(\mathbf{x} - \mathbf{m}_i)^t \tag{71}$$

and

$$S_W = S_1 + S_2. \tag{72}$$

Then

$$\tilde{s}_i^2 = \sum_{\mathbf{x} \in \mathcal{X}_i} (\mathbf{w}^t \mathbf{x} - \mathbf{w}^t \mathbf{m}_i)^2$$

$$= \sum_{\mathbf{x} \in \mathcal{X}_i} \mathbf{w}^t (\mathbf{x} - \mathbf{m}_i)(\mathbf{x} - \mathbf{m}_i)^t \mathbf{w}$$

$$= \mathbf{w}^t S_i \mathbf{w}, \tag{73}$$

* It should be noted that we are now using the term "discriminant function" to mean any function of $\mathbf{x}$ that is helpful in solving the decision problem; we do not insist that the resulting discriminant function be used directly to define the classifier. Because $y = \mathbf{w}^t\mathbf{x}$ is a sum of random variables, it is common to make reference to the central limit theorem and to assume that $p(y \mid \omega_i)$ is a normal density, thereby simplifying the problem of obtaining a classifier. When this assumption is not justified, one can still afford to use fairly elaborate methods to estimate $p(y \mid \omega_i)$ and derive an "optimal" classifier.

so that

$$\tilde{s}_1^2 + \tilde{s}_2^2 = \mathbf{w}^t S_W \mathbf{w}. \tag{74}$$

Similarly,

$$(\tilde{m}_1 - \tilde{m}_2)^2 = (\mathbf{w}^t \mathbf{m}_1 - \mathbf{w}^t \mathbf{m}_2)^2$$

$$= \mathbf{w}^t (\mathbf{m}_1 - \mathbf{m}_2)(\mathbf{m}_1 - \mathbf{m}_2)^t \mathbf{w}$$

$$= \mathbf{w}^t S_B \mathbf{w}, \tag{75}$$

where

$$S_B = (\mathbf{m}_1 - \mathbf{m}_2)(\mathbf{m}_1 - \mathbf{m}_2)^t. \tag{76}$$

The matrix S_W is called the *within-class scatter matrix*. It is proportional to the sample covariance matrix for the pooled d-dimensional data. It is symmetric and positive semidefinite, and is usually nonsingular if $n > d$. S_B is called the *between-class scatter matrix*. It is also symmetric and positive semidefinite, but because it is the outer product of two vectors, its rank is at most one. In particular, for any $\mathbf{w}$, $S_B \mathbf{w}$ is in the direction of $\mathbf{m}_1 - \mathbf{m}_2$, and S_B is quite singular.

In terms of S_B and S_W, the criterion function J can be written as

$$J(\mathbf{w}) = \frac{\mathbf{w}^t S_B \mathbf{w}}{\mathbf{w}^t S_W \mathbf{w}}. \tag{77}$$

This expression is well known in mathematical physics as the generalized Rayleigh quotient. It is easy to show that a vector $\mathbf{w}$ that maximizes J must satisfy

$$S_B \mathbf{w} = \lambda S_W \mathbf{w} \tag{78}$$

which is a generalized eigenvalue problem. If S_W is nonsingular we can obtain a conventional eigenvalue problem by writing

$$S_W^{-1} S_B \mathbf{w} = \lambda \mathbf{w}. \tag{79}$$

In our particular case, it is unnecessary to solve for the eigenvalues and eigenvectors of $S_W^{-1} S_B$ due to the fact that $S_B \mathbf{w}$ is always in the direction of $\mathbf{m}_1 - \mathbf{m}_2$. Since the scale factor for $\mathbf{w}$ is immaterial, we can immediately write the solution

$$\mathbf{w} = S_W^{-1}(\mathbf{m}_1 - \mathbf{m}_2). \tag{80}$$

Thus, we have obtained Fisher's linear discriminant, the linear function with the maximum ratio of between-class scatter to within-class scatter. The problem has been converted from a d-dimensional problem to a hopefully more manageable one-dimensional problem. This mapping is many-to-one, and in theory can not possibly reduce the minimum achievable error rate. In general, one is willing to sacrifice some of the theoretically attainable performance for the advantages of working in one dimension. When the conditional densities $p(\mathbf{x} \mid \omega_i)$ are multivariate normal with equal covariance matrices Σ, one need not even sacrifice any performance. In that case we recall that the optimal decision boundary has the equation

$$\mathbf{w}^t\mathbf{x} + w_0 = 0$$

where

$$\mathbf{w} = \Sigma^{-1}(\boldsymbol{\mu}_1 - \boldsymbol{\mu}_2),$$

and where w_0 is a constant involving $\mathbf{w}$ and the prior probabilities. If we use sample means and the sample covariance matrix to estimate $\boldsymbol{\mu}_i$ and Σ, we obtain a vector in the same direction as the $\mathbf{w}$ of Eq. (80) that maximizes J. Thus, for the normal, equal-covariance case, the optimal decision rule is merely to decide ω_1 if Fisher's linear discriminant exceeds some threshold, and to decide ω_2 otherwise.

4.11   MULTIPLE DISCRIMINANT ANALYSIS

For the c-class problem, the natural generalization of Fisher's linear discriminant involves $c - 1$ discriminant functions. Thus, the projection is from a d-dimensional space to a $(c - 1)$-dimensional space, and it is tacitly assumed that $d \geq c$. The generalization for the within-class scatter matrix is obvious:

$$S_W = \sum_{i=1}^{c} S_i \tag{81}$$

where, as before,

$$S_i = \sum_{\mathbf{x} \in \mathscr{X}_i} (\mathbf{x} - \mathbf{m}_i)(\mathbf{x} - \mathbf{m}_i)^t \tag{82}$$

and

$$\mathbf{m}_i = \frac{1}{n_i} \sum_{\mathbf{x} \in \mathscr{X}_i} \mathbf{x}. \tag{83}$$

The proper generalization for S_B is not quite so obvious. Suppose that we define a *total mean vector* $\mathbf{m}$ and a *total scatter matrix* S_T by

$$\mathbf{m} = \frac{1}{n} \sum_{\mathbf{x}} \mathbf{x} = \frac{1}{n} \sum_{i=1}^{c} n_i \mathbf{m}_i \tag{84}$$

and

$$S_T = \sum_{\mathbf{x}} (\mathbf{x} - \mathbf{m})(\mathbf{x} - \mathbf{m})^t. \tag{85}$$

Then it follows that

$$S_T = \sum_{i=1}^{c} \sum_{\mathbf{x} \in \mathcal{X}_i} (\mathbf{x} - \mathbf{m}_i + \mathbf{m}_i - \mathbf{m})(\mathbf{x} - \mathbf{m}_i + \mathbf{m}_i - \mathbf{m})^t,$$

$$= \sum_{i=1}^{c} \sum_{\mathbf{x} \in \mathcal{X}_i} (\mathbf{x} - \mathbf{m}_i)(\mathbf{x} - \mathbf{m}_i)^t + \sum_{i=1}^{c} \sum_{\mathbf{x} \in \mathcal{X}_i} (\mathbf{m}_i - \mathbf{m})(\mathbf{m}_i - \mathbf{m})^t$$

$$= S_W + \sum_{i=1}^{c} n_i (\mathbf{m}_i - \mathbf{m})(\mathbf{m}_i - \mathbf{m})^t.$$

It is natural to define this second term as the between-class scatter matrix, so that the total scatter is the sum of the within-class scatter and the between-class scatter:

$$S_B = \sum_{i=1}^{c} n_i (\mathbf{m}_i - \mathbf{m})(\mathbf{m}_i - \mathbf{m})^t \tag{86}$$

and

$$S_T = S_W + S_B. \tag{87}$$

If we check the two-class case, we find that the resulting between-class scatter matrix is $n_1 n_2 / n$ times our previous definition. We could redefine S_B for the two-class case to obtain complete consistency, but we shall recall Emerson's remark that a foolish consistency is the hobgoblin of little minds and proceed.

The projection from a d-dimensional space to a $(c - 1)$-dimensional space is accomplished by $c - 1$ discriminant functions

$$y_i = \mathbf{w}_i^t \mathbf{x} \qquad i = 1, \ldots, c - 1. \tag{88}$$

If the y_i are viewed as components of a vector $\mathbf{y}$ and the weight vectors $\mathbf{w}_i$ are viewed as the columns of a d-by-$(c - 1)$ matrix W, then the projection can be written as a single matrix equation

$$\mathbf{y} = W^t \mathbf{x}. \tag{89}$$

The samples $\mathbf{x}_1, \ldots, \mathbf{x}_n$ project to a corresponding set of samples $\mathbf{y}_1, \ldots, \mathbf{y}_n$ which can be described by their own mean vectors and scatter matrices. Thus, if we define

$$\tilde{\mathbf{m}}_i = \frac{1}{n_i} \sum_{\mathbf{y} \in \mathcal{Y}_i} \mathbf{y} \tag{90}$$

$$\tilde{\mathbf{m}} = \frac{1}{n} \sum_{i=1}^{c} n_i \tilde{\mathbf{m}}_i \tag{91}$$

$$\tilde{S}_W = \sum_{i=1}^{c} \sum_{\mathbf{y} \in \mathcal{Y}_i} (\mathbf{y} - \tilde{\mathbf{m}}_i)(\mathbf{y} - \tilde{\mathbf{m}}_i)^t \tag{92}$$

and

$$\tilde{S}_B = \sum_{i=1}^{c} n_i (\tilde{\mathbf{m}}_i - \tilde{\mathbf{m}})(\tilde{\mathbf{m}}_i - \tilde{\mathbf{m}})^t \tag{93}$$

it is a straightforward matter to show that

$$\tilde{S}_W = W^t S_W W \tag{94}$$

and

$$\tilde{S}_B = W^t S_B W. \tag{95}$$

These equations show how the within-class and between-class scatter matrices are transformed by the projection to the lower dimensional space. What we seek is a transformation matrix W that in some sense maximizes the ratio of the between-class scatter to the within-class scatter. A simple scalar measure of scatter is the determinant of the scatter matrix. The determinant is the product of the eigenvalues, and hence is the product of the "variances" in the principal directions, thereby measuring the square of the hyper-ellipsoidal scattering volume. Using this measure, we obtain the criterion function

$$J(W) = \frac{|\tilde{S}_B|}{|\tilde{S}_W|} = \frac{|W^t S_B W|}{|W^t S_W W|}. \tag{96}$$

The problem of finding a rectangular matrix W that maximizes J is not an easy one. Fortunately, it turns out that the solution is relatively simple.* The columns of an optimal W are the generalized eigenvectors that correspond to the largest eigenvalues in

$$S_B \mathbf{w}_i = \lambda_i S_W \mathbf{w}_i. \tag{97}$$

A few observations about this solution are in order. First, if S_W is nonsingular, this can be converted to a conventional eigenvalue problem as before. However, this is actually undesirable, since it requires an unnecessary computation of the inverse of S_W. Instead, one can find the eigenvalues as the roots of the characteristic polynomial

$$|S_B - \lambda_i S_W| = 0$$

and then solve

$$(S_B - \lambda_i S_W)\mathbf{w}_i = 0$$

directly for the eigenvectors $\mathbf{w}_i$. Because S_B is the sum of c matrices of rank one or less, and because only $c - 1$ of these are independent, S_B is of rank $c - 1$ or less. Thus, no more than $c - 1$ of the eigenvalues are nonzero, and the desired weight vectors correspond to these nonzero eigenvalues. If the within-class scatter is isotropic, the eigenvectors are merely the eigenvectors of S_B, and the eigenvectors with nonzero eigenvalues span the space spanned by the vectors $\mathbf{m}_i - \mathbf{m}$. In this special case the columns of W can be found simply by applying the Gram-Schmidt orthonormalization procedure to the

---

* A derivation of the solution can be found in S. Wilks, *Mathematical Statistics*, pp. 577–578 (John Wiley, New York, 1962).

$c - 1$ vectors $\mathbf{m}_i - \mathbf{m}$, $i = 1, \ldots, c - 1$. Finally, we observe that in general the solution for W is not unique. The allowable transformations include rotating and scaling the axes in various ways. These are all linear transformations from a $(c - 1)$-dimensional space to a $(c - 1)$-dimensional space, however, and do not change things in any significant way. In particular, they leave the criterion function $J(W)$ invariant.

As in the two-class case, multiple discriminant analysis primarily provides a reasonable way of reducing the dimensionality of the problem. Parametric or nonparametric techniques that might not have been feasible in the original space may work well in the lower-dimensional space. In particular, it may be possible to estimate separate covariance matrices for each class and use the general multivariate normal assumption after the transformation where this could not be done with the original data. In general, the transformation causes some unnecessary overlapping of the data and increases the theoretically achievable error rate, and the problem of classifying the data still remains. There are other ways to reduce the dimensionality of data, and we shall encounter this subject again in Chapter 6. There are also other methods of discriminant analysis, some of which are given in the references for this chapter. Of all of these, Fisher's method remains one of the most fundamental and most widely used techniques.

4.12   BIBLIOGRAPHICAL AND HISTORICAL REMARKS

In this chapter we have examined some fundamental nonparametric techniques that have played a significant role in statistical pattern classification. Many other topics in nonparametric statistics have gone unmentioned, and the interested reader may want to consult Gibbons (1971) or Thomas (1970) for an introduction to this literature. The classical tradition in statistics is to derive estimates of density functions from empirical distribution functions (Fisz, 1963), but this is clumsy in the multivariate case. A frequently referenced but rather inaccessible report by Fix and Hodges (1951) developed the implications of density estimation for classification theory and set the stage for most of the subsequent work on density estimation.

Our treatment of the Parzen-window method is a slight generalization of the univariate formulation by M. Rosenblatt (1956). Rosenblatt's work actually preceded that of Parzen (1962), but Parzen had previously employed similar methods for the estimation of spectra, and the phrase "Parzen-window" is now well established. In addition to demonstrating pointwise convergence, Parzen showed that the estimate of the density is asymptotically normal, and established conditions under which the resulting sample mode converges to the true mode. The relation between the estimation of densities and the estimation of spectra suggests that by working with characteristic functions one can obtain interesting results in the frequency domain. Watson and Leadbetter (1963) took this approach and showed how the window functions could be optimized in the finite-sample case if constraints could be placed on the spectrum of the unknown density. Undoubtedly, this approach could be used to transfer many of the results in filtering theory to the problem of estimating densities. Except for Fix and Hodges, all of these results were stated for the univariate case. The basic generalizations to the multivariate case were given by Murthy (1965, 1966) and Cacoullos (1966).

A rigorous demonstration that the k_n-nearest-neighbor method yields a consistent estimate of a multivariate density was given by Loftsgaarden and Quesenberry (1965). The surprising nearest-neighbor classification results are due to Cover and Hart (1967), who also found bounds on the performance of the k-nearest-neighbor rule. Wagner (1971) extended these results by showing that the probability of error conditioned on the n samples converges to the average probability of error $P_n(e)$ with probability one. Hellman (1970) showed how the nearest-neighbor rule can be extended to allow rejects. The important topic of rates of convergence is examined by Cover (1968). Since the nearest-neighbor error rate bounds the Bayes rate, it can be used to measure the inherent difficulty of a pattern classification problem. Cover (1969) conjectures that even in the small-sample case the results will tell how well any nonparametric procedure using the same samples will perform. Fralick and Scott (1971) give an experimental comparison of Parzen-window and nearest-neighbor rules used to estimate the Bayes rate.

One problem with all of these methods is that the complete set of samples must be stored, and must be searched each time a new feature vector is to be classified. Many suggestions have been offered for reducing this problem, but few possess any known statistical properties. Barus (1966) gave an interesting approximation to the Fix and Hodges procedure, and Hart (1968) proposed a condensed nearest-neighbor rule. The problem of finding an effective, small reference set is essentially a problem in clustering. Moreover, certain clustering procedures, such as those by Sebestyen (1962) and Sebestyen and Edie (1966), can be interpreted as heuristic methods for approximating probability density functions. Tarter, Holcomb and Kronmal (1967) suggested the use of orthogonal series expansions for density estimation. The idea of obtaining polynomial discriminant functions by approximating the Parzen-window estimate by a Taylor's series was introduced by Specht (1967). Meisel (1969) pointed out that such expansions can require many terms for convergence, and related the Parzen-window approach to the method of potential functions (Arkedev and Braverman, 1966). The method of potential functions is in turn related to the adaptive techniques and the stochastic approximation techniques discussed in Chapter 5. Most of these techniques are concerned with obtaining a posteriori probabilities. However, Tsypkin (1966) and Kashyap and Blaydon (1968) have shown that in theory they can also be used to estimate density functions.

The prevalence of binary measurements in many practical pattern recognition systems makes the estimation of the joint probability of binary variables of more than academic significance. The Rademacher-Walsh expansion occurs frequently in switching theory, and is closely related to the Bahadur-Lazarsfeld expansion. Bahadur (1961) gives an extension of this latter expansion from the binary case to the general discrete case. Where orthogonal-function expansions minimize mean-square error, Brown (1959) and Lewis (1959) have shown that under certain conditions product approximations maximize entropy. Ito (1969) presents bounds on the error rate that results from truncating series expansions. The idea of simplifying the approximations by limiting the nature of the dependence has been explored by Chow (1962) and by Abend, Harley and Kanal (1965), who were particularly interested in the natural spatial dependencies in binary pictures. The interesting idea of tree dependence was introduced by Chow (1966), and methods for finding the dependence tree were reported by Chow and Liu (1966, 1968). A significant extension of this concept to the multivariate normal case was reported by Chow in 1970.

The subject of discriminant analysis has its origins in the classic paper by R. A. Fisher (1936). The literature on this subject is fairly extensive, and is well surveyed in the paper by Tatsuoka and Tiedeman (1954). The generalization of Fisher's linear discriminant to the multiclass case is due to Bryan (1951). By using criteria other than the ratio of between-class scatter to within-class scatter, other types of linear discriminant functions can be obtained. Kullback (1959) suggests other criteria and investigates their properties, and Peterson and Mattson (1966) develop a general procedure for finding the optimal discriminant function for a fairly broad class of criterion functions. As we remarked before, the goal of all of these techniques is the reduction of the dimensionality of the feature space, and the resulting discriminant functions do not in themselves solve the classification problem. The discriminant functions discussed in the next chapter are designed to solve the classification problem directly.

REFERENCES

1. Abend, K., T. J. Harley, and L. N. Kanal, "Classification of binary random patterns," *IEEE Trans. Info. Theory*, **IT-11,** 538–544 (October 1965).

2. Arkedev, A. G. and E. M. Braverman, *Computers and Pattern Recognition* (Thompson, Washington, D.C., 1966).

3. Bahadur, R. R., "A representation of the joint distribution of responses to n dichotomous items," in *Studies in Item Analysis and Prediction*, pp. 158–168, H. Solomon, ed. (Stanford University Press, Stanford, Calif., 1961).

4. Barus, C., "An easily mechanized scheme for an adaptive pattern recognizer," *IEEE Trans. Elec. Comp.*, **EC-15**, 385–387 (June 1966).

5. Brown, D. T., "A note on approximations to discrete probability distributions," *Info. and Control*, **2**, 386–392 (December 1959).

6. Bryan, J. G., "The generalized discriminant function: mathematical foundation and computational routine," *Harvard Educ. Rev.*, **21**, 90–95 (Spring 1951).

7. Cacoullos, T., "Estimation of a multivariate density," *Annals of the Institute of Statistical Mathematics*, **18**, 179–189 (1966).

8. Chow, C. K., "A recognition method using neighbor dependence," *IRE Trans. Elec. Comp.*, **EC-11**, 683–690 (October 1962).

9. Chow, C. K., "A class of nonlinear recognition procedures," *IEEE Trans. Sys. Sci. Cyb.*, **SSC-2**, 101–109 (December 1966).

10. Chow, C. K. and C. N. Liu, "An approach to structure adaptation in pattern recognition," *IEEE Trans. Sys. Sci. Cyb.*, **SSC-2**, 73–80 (December 1966).

11. Chow, C. K. and C. N. Liu, "Approximating discrete probability distributions with dependence trees," *IEEE Trans. Info. Theory*, **IT-14**, 462–467 (May 1968).

12. Chow, C. K., "Tree dependence in normal distributions," presented at the *1970 International Symposium on Information Theory*, Noordwijk, The Netherlands (June 1970).

13. Cover, T. M. and P. E. Hart, "Nearest neighbor pattern classification," *IEEE Trans. Info. Theory*, **IT-13**, 21–27 (January 1967).

14. Cover T. M., "Rates of convergence of nearest neighbor decision procedures," *Proc. First Annual Hawaii Conference on Systems Theory*, pp. 413–415 (January 1968).

15. Cover, T. M., "Learning in pattern recognition," in *Methodologies of Pattern Recognition*, pp. 111–132, S. Watanabe, ed. (Academic Press, New York, 1969).

16. Fisher, R. A., "The use of multiple measurements in taxonomic problems," *Ann. Eugenics*, **7**, Part II, 179–188 (1936); also in *Contributions to Mathematical Statistics* (John Wiley, New York, 1950).

17. Fisz, M., *Probability Theory and Mathematical Statistics* (John Wiley, New York, 1963).

18. Fix, E. and J. L. Hodges, Jr., "Discriminatory analysis: nonparametric discrimination: consistency properties." Report No. 4, USAF School of Aviation Medicine, Randolph Field, Texas (February 1951).

19. Fralick, S. C. and R. W. Scott, "Nonparametric Bayes risk estimation," *IEEE Trans. Info. Theory*, **IT-17**, 440–444 (July 1971).

20. Gibbons, J. D., *Nonparametric Statistical Inference* (McGraw-Hill, New York, 1971).

21. Hart, P. E., "The condensed nearest neighbor rule," *IEEE Trans. Info. Theory*, **IT-14**, 515–516 (May 1968).

22. Hellman, M. E., "The nearest neighbor classification rule with a reject option," *IEEE Trans. Sys. Sci. Cyb.*, **SSC-6**, 179–185 (July 1970).

23. Ito, T., "Note on a class of statistical recognition functions," *IEEE Trans. Computers*, **C-18**, 76–79 (January 1969).

24. Kashyap, R. L. and C. C. Blaydon, "Estimation of probability density and distribution functions," *IEEE Trans. Info. Theory*, **IT-14**, 549–556 (July 1968).

25. Kullback, S., *Information Theory and Statistics* (John Wiley, New York, 1959).

26. Lewis, P. M., II, "Approximating probability distributions to reduce storage requirements," *Info. and Control*, **2**, 214–225 (1959).

27. Loftsgaarden, D. O. and C. P. Quesenberry, "A nonparametric estimate of a multivariate density function," *Ann. Math. Stat.*, **36**, 1049–1051 (June 1965).

28. Meisel, W. S., "Potential functions in mathematical pattern recognition," *IEEE Trans. Computers*, **C-18**, 911–918 (October 1969).

29. Murthy, V. K., "Estimation of probability density," *Ann. Math. Stat.*, **36**, 1027–1031 (June 1965).

30. Murthy, V. K., "Nonparametric estimation of multivariate densities with applications," in *Multivariate Analysis*, pp. 43–56, P. R. Krishnaiah, ed. (Academic Press, New York, 1966).

31. Parzen, E., "On estimation of a probability density function and mode," *Ann. Math. Stat.*, **33**, 1065–1076 (September 1962).

32. Peterson, D. W. and R. L. Mattson, "A method of finding linear discriminant functions for a class of performance criteria," *IEEE Trans. Info. Theory*, **IT-12**, 380–387 (July 1966).

33. Rosenblatt, M., "Remarks on some nonparametric estimates of a density function," *Ann. Math. Stat.*, **27**, 832–837 (1956).

34. Sebestyen, G. S., "Pattern recognition by an adaptive process of sample set construction," *IRE Trans. Info. Theory*, **IT-8**, S82–S91 (September 1962).

35. Sebestyen, G. S. and J. L. Edie, "An algorithm for nonparametric pattern recognition," *IEEE Trans. Elec. Comp.*, **EC-15**, 908–915 (December 1966).

36. Specht, D. F., "Generation of polynomial discriminant functions for pattern recognition," *IEEE Trans. Elec. Comp.*, **EC-16**, 308–319 (June 1967).

37. Tarter, M. E., R. L. Holcomb, and R. A. Kronmal, "After the histogram what? A description of new computer methods for estimating the population density," *ACM, Proc. 22nd Nat. Conf.*, pp. 511–519 (Thompson Book Co., Washington, D.C., 1967).

38. Tatsuoka, M. M. and D. V. Tiedeman, "Discriminant analysis," *Rev. Educ. Res.*, **24**, 402–420 (1954).

39. Thomas, J. B., "Nonparametric detection," *Proc. IEEE*, **58**, 623–631 (May 1970).

40. Tsypkin, Ya. Z., "Use of the stochastic approximation method in estimating unknown distribution densities from observations," *Automation and Remote Control*, **27**, 432–434 (March 1966).

41. Wagner, T. J., "Convergence of the nearest neighbor rule," *IEEE Trans. Info. Theory*, **IT-17**, 566–571 (September 1971).

42. Watson, G. S. and M. R. Leadbetter, "On the estimation of a probability density, I," *Ann. Math. Stat.*, **34**, 480–491 (June 1963).

PROBLEMS

1. Let $p(x) \sim N(\mu, \sigma^2)$ and $\varphi(x) \sim N(0, 1)$. Show that the Parzen-window estimate

$$p_n(x) = \frac{1}{nh_n} \sum_{i=1}^{n} \varphi\left(\frac{x - x_i}{h_n}\right)$$

has the following properties:

(a) $\bar{p}_n(x) \sim N(\mu, \sigma^2 + h_n^2)$

(b) $\mathrm{Var}[p_n(x)] \approx \dfrac{1}{nh_n 2\sqrt{\pi}} p(x)$

(c) $p(x) - \bar{p}_n(x) \approx \dfrac{1}{2}\left(\dfrac{h_n}{\sigma}\right)^2 \left[1 - \left(\dfrac{x - \mu}{\sigma}\right)^2\right] p(x)$

for small h_n. (Note: if $h_n = h_1/\sqrt{n}$, this shows that the error due to bias goes to zero as $1/n$, whereas the standard deviation of the noise only goes to zero as $1/n^{0.25}$.)

2. Let $p(x)$ be uniform from 0 to a, and let $\varphi(x) = e^{-x}$ for $x > 0$ and 0 for $x \leq 0$. Show that the mean of the Parzen-window estimate is given by

$$\bar{p}_n(x) = \begin{cases} 0 & x < 0 \\[2mm] \dfrac{1}{a}(1 - e^{-x/h_n}) & 0 \leq x \leq a \\[2mm] \dfrac{1}{a}(e^{a/h_n} - 1)e^{-x/h_n} & a < x \end{cases}$$

Sketch $\bar{p}_n(x)$ versus x for $h_n = a$, $a/4$, and $a/16$. How small does h_n have to be to have less than one percent bias over 99 percent of the range $0 < x < a$?

3. Let $\mathcal{X} = \{x_1, \ldots, x_n\}$ be a set of n independent labelled samples and let $\mathcal{X}_k(x) = \{x_1', \ldots, x_k'\}$ be the k nearest neighbors of x. The k-nearest neighbor rule for classifying x is to give x the label most frequently represented in $\mathcal{X}_k(x)$. Consider a two-category problem with $P(\omega_1) = P(\omega_2) = 1/2$. Assume further that the conditional densities $p(x \mid \omega_i)$ are uniform within unit hyperspheres a distance of ten units apart.

(a) Show that if k is odd the average probability of error is given by

$$P_n(e) = \frac{1}{2^n} \sum_{j=0}^{(k-1)/2} \binom{n}{j}.$$

(b) Show that for this case the single-nearest-neighbor rule has a lower error rate than the k-nearest-neighbor error rate, $k > 1$.

(c) (Optional) If k is allowed to increase with n but is restricted by $k < a\sqrt{u}$, show that $P_n(e) \to 0$ as $n \to \infty$.

4. It is easy to see that the nearest-neighbor error rate P can equal the Bayes rate P^* if $P^* = 0$ (the best possibility) or if $P^* = (c - 1)/c$ (the worst possibility). One might ask whether or not there are problems for which $P = P^*$ when P^* is between these extremes.

(a) Show that the Bayes rate for the one-dimensional case where $P(\omega_i) = 1/c$ and

$$p(x \mid \omega_i) = \begin{cases} 1 & 0 \leq x \leq \dfrac{cr}{c-1} \\[2ex] 1 & i \leq x \leq i + 1 - \dfrac{cr}{c-1} \\[2ex] 0 & \text{elsewhere} \end{cases}$$

is $P^* = r$.

(b) Show that for this case $P = P^*$.

5. Consider the following set of seven two-dimensional vectors: $\mathbf{x}_1^t = (1\ 0)$, $\mathbf{x}_2^t = (0\ 1)$, $\mathbf{x}_3^t = (0\ -1)$, $\mathbf{x}_4^t = (0\ 0)$, $\mathbf{x}_5^t = (0\ 2)$, $\mathbf{x}_6^t = (0\ -2)$, $\mathbf{x}_7^t = (-2\ 0)$. Suppose that the first three are labelled ω_1 and the other four are labelled ω_2

(a) Sketch the decision boundary resulting from the nearest-neighbor rule. (It should be composed of nine straight line segments.)

(b) Find the sample means $\mathbf{m}_1$ and $\mathbf{m}_2$ and sketch the decision boundary corresponding to classifying $\mathbf{x}$ by assigning it to the category of the nearest sample mean.

6. Let $\varphi(x) \sim N(0, 1)$ and let

$$p_n(x) = \frac{1}{nh_n} \sum_{i=1}^{n} \varphi\left(\frac{x - x_1}{h_n}\right).$$

Approximate this estimate by factoring the window function and expanding the factor e^{xx_i/h_n^2} in a Taylor's series about the origin.

(a) Show that in terms of the normalized variable $u = x/h_n$ the m-term approximation is given by

$$p_{nm}(x) = \frac{1}{\sqrt{2\pi}\,h_n} e^{-(1/2)u^2} \sum_{j=0}^{m-1} b_j u^j$$

where

$$b_j = \frac{1}{n} \sum_{i=1}^{n} \frac{1}{j!} u_i^j e^{-(1/2)u_i^2}.$$

(b) Suppose that the n samples happen to be extremely tightly clustered about $u = u_0$. Show that the two-term approximation peaks at the two points where $u^2 + u/u_0 - 1 = 0$. Show that one peak occurs approximately at $u = u_0$, as desired, if $u_0 \ll 1$, but that it moves only to $u = 1$ for $u_0 \gg 1$. Sketch p_{n2} versus u for $u_0 = 0.1$, 1, and 10.

7.   Let $p_x(\mathbf{x} \mid \omega_i)$ be an arbitrary density with mean $\boldsymbol{\mu}_i$ and covariance matrix Σ_i, $i = 1, 2$. Let $y = \mathbf{w}^t\mathbf{x}$, and let the induced density $p_y(y \mid \omega_i)$ have mean μ and variance σ_i^2.

(a) Show that the criterion function

$$J_1(\mathbf{w}) = \frac{(\mu_1 - \mu_2)^2}{\sigma_1^2 + \sigma_2^2}$$

is minimized by

$$\mathbf{w} = (\Sigma_1 + \Sigma_2)^{-1}(\boldsymbol{\mu}_1 - \boldsymbol{\mu}_2).$$

(b) If $P(\omega_i)$ is the prior probability for ω_i, show that

$$J_2(\mathbf{w}) = \frac{(\mu_1 - \mu_2)^2}{P(\omega_1)\sigma_1^2 + P(\omega_2)\sigma_2^2}$$

is minimized by

$$\mathbf{w} = (P(\omega_1)\Sigma_1 + P(\omega_2)\Sigma_2)^{-1}(\boldsymbol{\mu}_1 - \boldsymbol{\mu}_2).$$

(c) To which of these criterion functions is the $J(\mathbf{w})$ of Eq. (70) more closely related?

8.   The expression

$$J_1 = \frac{1}{n_1 n_2} \sum_{\mathbf{v}_i \in \mathscr{Y}_1} \sum_{\mathbf{v}_j \in \mathscr{Y}_2} (y_i - y_j)^2$$

clearly measures the between-group scatter of two sets of samples, one containing n_1 samples labelled ω_1 and the other containing n_2 labelled ω_2. Similarly,

$$J_2 = \frac{1}{n_1^2} \sum_{\mathbf{v}_i \in \mathscr{Y}_1} \sum_{\mathbf{v}_j \in \mathscr{Y}_1} (y_i - y_j)^2 + \frac{1}{n_2^2} \sum_{\mathbf{v}_i \in \mathscr{Y}_2} \sum_{\mathbf{v}_j \in \mathscr{Y}_2} (y_i - y_j)^2$$

clearly measures the total within-group scatter.

(a) Show that

$$J_1 = (m_1 - m_2)^2 + \frac{1}{n_1} s_1^2 + \frac{1}{n_2} s_2^2$$

and

$$J_2 = \frac{1}{n_1} s_1^2 + \frac{1}{n_2} s_2^2.$$

(b) If $y = \mathbf{w}^t\mathbf{x}$, show that the $\mathbf{w}$ minimizing J_1 subject to the constraint that $J_2 = 1$ is given by

$$\mathbf{w} = \lambda \left(\frac{1}{n_1} S_1 + \frac{1}{n_2} S_2 \right)^{-1} (\mathbf{m}_1 - \mathbf{m}_2)$$

where

$$\lambda = (m_1 - m_2)^t \left(\frac{1}{n_1} S_1 + \frac{1}{n_2} S_2 \right)^{-1} (m_1 - m_2)$$

$$m_i = \frac{1}{n_i} \sum_{x \in \mathcal{X}_i} x$$

and

$$S_i = \sum_{x \in \mathcal{X}_i} (x - m_i)(x - m_i)^t.$$

9. Using the multiclass definition of the between-group scatter matrix

$$S_B = \sum_{i=1}^{c} n_i (m_i - m)(m_i - m)^t,$$

show that $S_B = [(n_1 n_2)/n](m_1 - m_2)(m_1 - m_2)^t$ if $c = 2$.

10. If S_B and S_W are any two real, symmetric, d-by-d matrices, it is well known that there exists a set of n eigenvalues $\lambda_1, \ldots, \lambda_n$ satisfying $|S_B - \lambda_i S_W| = 0$, and a corresponding set of n eigenvectors $e_1, \ldots, e_n$ satisfying $S_B e_i = \lambda_i S_W e_i$. Furthermore, if S_W is positive definite, the eigenvectors can always be normalized so that

$$e_i^t S_W e_j = \delta_{ij}$$

and

$$e_i^t S_B e_j = \lambda_i \delta_{ij}.$$

Let $\tilde{S}_W = W^t S_W W$ and $\tilde{S}_B = W^t S_B W$, where W is a d-by-n matrix whose columns correspond to n distinct eignvectors.

(a) Show that $\tilde{S}_W$ is the n-by-n identity matrix, and that $\tilde{S}_B$ is a diagonal matrix whose elements are the corresponding eigenvalues.*

(b) What is the value of $J = |\tilde{S}_B|/|\tilde{S}_W|$?

(c) Let $y = W^t x$ be transformed by scaling the axes with a nonsingular n-by-n diagonal matrix D and by rotating this result with an orthogonal matrix Q: $y' = QDy$. Show that J is invariant to this transformation.

* This shows that the discriminant functions in multiple discriminant analysis are uncorrelated.

Chapter 5

LINEAR DISCRIMINANT FUNCTIONS

5.1 INTRODUCTION

In Chapter 3 we assumed that the forms for the underlying probability distributions were known, and used the samples to estimate the values of their parameters. In this chapter we shall assume that the forms for the *discriminant functions* are known, and shall use the samples to estimate the values of parameters of the classifier. We shall examine various procedures for determining discriminant functions, some of which are statistical and some of which are not. However, none of them requires knowledge of the forms of underlying probability distributions, and in this sense all of them can be said to be nonparametric.

Throughout this chapter we shall be concerned with discriminant functions that are either linear in the components of **x** or linear in some given set of functions of **x**. Linear discriminant functions have a variety of pleasant properties from an analytical point of view. As we have seen in Chapter 2, they can be optimal if the underlying distributions are cooperative. Even when they are not optimal, one might be willing to sacrifice some performance to gain the advantage of simplicity. Linear discriminant functions are relatively easy to compute, and a classifier of fixed structure is an attractive candidate for implementation as a special-purpose computer.

The Fisher linear discriminant provides a model for the approach we shall adopt. The problem of finding a linear discriminant function will be formulated as a problem of minimizing a criterion function. The obvious criterion function for classification purposes is the *sample risk*, the average loss incurred in classifying the set of design samples. However, because it is so difficult to derive the minimum-risk linear discriminant, we shall investigate several related criterion functions that are analytically more tractable. Most of our attention will be devoted to studying the convergence properties

130

of various gradient descent procedures for minimizing these criterion functions. The similarities between many of the procedures sometimes makes it difficult to keep the differences between them clear. For this reason we have included a summary of the principal results at the end of Section 5.10 in Table 5-1, which can be consulted as needed.

5.2 LINEAR DISCRIMINANT FUNCTIONS AND DECISION SURFACES

5.2.1 The Two-Category Case

A discriminant function that is a linear combination of the components of $\mathbf{x}$ can be written as

$$g(\mathbf{x}) = \mathbf{w}^t\mathbf{x} + w_0, \tag{1}$$

where $\mathbf{w}$ is called the *weight vector* and w_0 the *threshold weight*. A two-category linear classifier implements the following decision rule: Decide ω_1 if $g(\mathbf{x}) > 0$ and ω_2 if $g(\mathbf{x}) < 0$. Thus, $\mathbf{x}$ is assigned to ω_1 if the inner product $\mathbf{w}^t\mathbf{x}$ exceeds the threshold $-w_0$. If $g(\mathbf{x}) = 0$, $\mathbf{x}$ can ordinarily be assigned to either class, but in this chapter we shall leave the assignment undefined.

The equation $g(\mathbf{x}) = 0$ defines the decision surface that separates points assigned to ω_1 from points assigned to ω_2. When $g(\mathbf{x})$ is linear, this decision surface is a *hyperplane*. If $\mathbf{x}_1$ and $\mathbf{x}_2$ are both on the decision surface, then

$$\mathbf{w}^t\mathbf{x}_1 + w_0 = \mathbf{w}^t\mathbf{x}_2 + w_0$$

or

$$\mathbf{w}^t(\mathbf{x}_1 - \mathbf{x}_2) = 0,$$

so that $\mathbf{w}$ is normal to any vector lying in the hyperplane. In general, the hyperplane H divides the feature space into two halfspaces, the decision region $\mathcal{R}_1$ for ω_1 and the decision region $\mathcal{R}_2$ for ω_2. Since $g(\mathbf{x}) > 0$ if $\mathbf{x}$ is in $\mathcal{R}_1$, it follows that the normal vector $\mathbf{w}$ points into $\mathcal{R}_1$. It is sometimes said that any $\mathbf{x}$ in $\mathcal{R}_1$ is on the positive side of H, and any $\mathbf{x}$ in $\mathcal{R}_2$ is on the negative side.

The discriminant function $g(\mathbf{x})$ gives an algebraic measure of the distance from $\mathbf{x}$ to the hyperplane. Perhaps the easiest way to see this is to express $\mathbf{x}$ as

$$\mathbf{x} = \mathbf{x}_p + r\frac{\mathbf{w}}{\|\mathbf{w}\|},$$

where $\mathbf{x}_p$ is the normal projection of $\mathbf{x}$ onto H, and r is the desired algebraic distance, positive if $\mathbf{x}$ is on the positive side and negative if $\mathbf{x}$ is on the negative side. Then, since $g(\mathbf{x}_p) = 0$,

$$g(\mathbf{x}) = \mathbf{w}^t\mathbf{x} + w_0 = r\|\mathbf{w}\|,$$

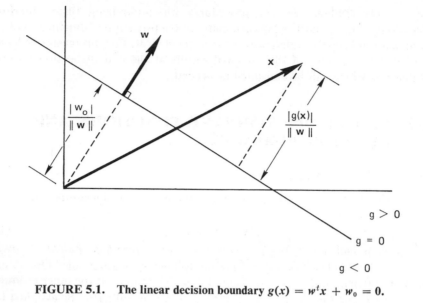

FIGURE 5.1.   The linear decision boundary $g(x) = w^t x + w_0 = 0$.

or

$$r = \frac{g(\mathbf{x})}{\|\mathbf{w}\|} .$$

In particular, the distance from the origin to H is given by $w_0/\|\mathbf{w}\|$. If $w_0 > 0$ the origin is on the positive side of H, and if $w_0 < 0$ it is on the negative side. If $w_0 = 0$, then $g(\mathbf{x})$ has the homogeneous form $\mathbf{w}^t\mathbf{x}$, and the hyperplane passes through the origin. A geometric illustration of these algebraic results is given in Figure 5.1.

To summarize, a linear discriminant function divides the feature space by a hyperplane decision surface. The orientation of the surface is determined by the normal vector $\mathbf{w}$, and the location of the surface is determined by the threshold weight w_0. The discriminant function $g(\mathbf{x})$ is proportional to the signed distance from $\mathbf{x}$ to the hyperplane, with $g(\mathbf{x}) > 0$ when $\mathbf{x}$ is on the positive side, and $g(\mathbf{x}) < 0$ when $\mathbf{x}$ is on the negative side.

5.2.2   The Multicategory Case

There is more than one way to devise multicategory classifiers employing linear discriminant functions. For example, one might reduce the problem to $c - 1$ two-class problems, where the ith problem is solved by a linear discriminant function that separates points assigned to ω_i from those not assigned to ω_i. A more extravagant approach would be to use $c(c - 1)/2$

linear discriminants, one for every pair of classes. As illustrated in Figure 5.2, both of these approaches can lead to regions such as the shaded areas in which the classification is undefined. We shall avoid this problem by adopting the approach taken in Chapter 2, defining c linear discriminant functions

$$g_i(\mathbf{x}) = \mathbf{w}_i^t \mathbf{x} + w_{i0} \qquad i = 1, \ldots, c, \tag{2}$$

and assigning $\mathbf{x}$ to ω_i if $g_i(\mathbf{x}) > g_j(\mathbf{x})$ for all $j \neq i$; in case of ties, the classification is left undefined. The resulting classifier is called a *linear machine*. A linear machine divides the feature space into c decision regions, with $g_i(\mathbf{x})$ being the largest discriminant if $\mathbf{x}$ is in region $\mathcal{R}_i$. If $\mathcal{R}_i$ and $\mathcal{R}_j$ are contiguous, the boundary between them is a portion of the hyperplane H_{ij} defined by

$$g_i(\mathbf{x}) = g_j(\mathbf{x})$$

or

$$(\mathbf{w}_i - \mathbf{w}_j)^t \mathbf{x} + (w_{i0} - w_{j0}) = 0.$$

It follows at once that $\mathbf{w}_i - \mathbf{w}_j$ is normal to H_{ij}, and the signed distance from $\mathbf{x}$ to H_{ij} is given by $(g_i - g_j)/\|\mathbf{w}_i - \mathbf{w}_j\|$. Thus, with the linear machine it is not the weight vectors themselves but their *differences* that are important. While there are $c(c-1)/2$ pairs of regions, they need not all be contiguous, and the total number of hyperplane segments appearing in the decision surfaces is often fewer than $c(c-1)/2$. Two-dimensional examples of these surfaces are shown in Figure 5.3.

It is easy to show that the decision regions for a linear machine are convex. This restriction definitely limits the flexibility of the classifier. In particular, every decision region must be singly connected, which tends to make the

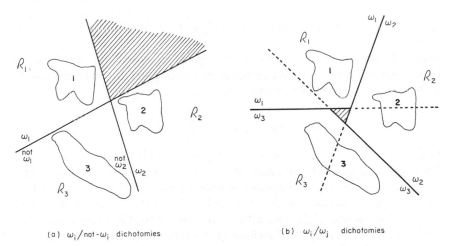

(a) $\omega_i / \text{not-}\omega_i$ dichotomies   (b) ω_i / ω_j dichotomies

FIGURE 5.2. Linear decision boundaries for a three-class problem.

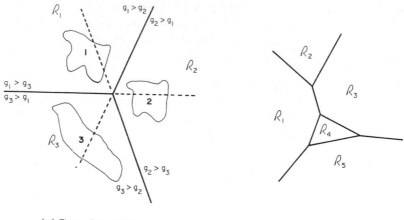

(a) Three-class problem   (b) Five-class problem

FIGURE 5.3.   Decision boundaries produced by a linear machine.

linear machine most suitable for problems for which the conditional densities $p(\mathbf{x} \mid \omega_i)$ are unimodal. Within these limitations, the linear machine offers a fair amount of flexibility and the virtue of analytical simplicity.

5.3   GENERALIZED LINEAR DISCRIMINANT FUNCTIONS

The linear discriminant function $g(\mathbf{x})$ can be written as

$$g(\mathbf{x}) = w_0 + \sum_{i=1}^{d} w_i x_i, \tag{3}$$

where the coefficients w_i are the components of the weight vector $\mathbf{w}$. By adding additional terms involving the products of pairs of components of $\mathbf{x}$, we obtain the *quadratic discriminant function*

$$g(\mathbf{x}) = w_0 + \sum_{i=1}^{d} w_i x_i + \sum_{i=1}^{d} \sum_{j=1}^{d} w_{ij} x_i x_j.$$

Since $x_i x_j = x_j x_i$, we can assume that $w_{ij} = w_{ji}$ with no loss in generality. Thus, the quadratic discriminant function has an additional $d(d + 1)/2$ coefficients at its disposal with which to produce more complicated separating surfaces. The separating surface defined by $g(\mathbf{x}) = 0$ is a second-degree or *hyperquadric* surface. If the symmetric matrix $W = [w_{ij}]$ is nonsingular, then the linear terms in $g(\mathbf{x})$ can be eliminated by translating the axes, and the basic character of the separating surface can be described in terms of the scaled matrix $\overline{W} = W/(\mathbf{w}^t W^{-1}\mathbf{w} - 4w_0)$. If $\overline{W}$ is a positive multiple of the identity matrix, the separating surface is a *hypersphere*. If $\overline{W}$ is positive definite, the separating surface is a *hyperellipsoid*. If some of the eigenvalues of $\overline{W}$ are positive and others are negative, the surface is one of a variety of types of *hyperhyperboloids*. As we observed in Chapter 2, these are the kinds of separating surfaces that arise in the general multivariate normal case.

By continuing to add terms such as $w_{ijk}x_ix_jx_k$ we can obtain the class of *polynomial discriminant functions*. These can be thought of as truncated series expansions of some arbitrary $g(\mathbf{x})$, and this in turn suggests the *generalized linear discriminant function*

$$g(\mathbf{x}) = \sum_{i=1}^{\hat{d}} a_iy_i(\mathbf{x}) \tag{4}$$

or

$$g(\mathbf{x}) = \mathbf{a}^t\mathbf{y}, \tag{5}$$

where $\mathbf{a}$ is an $\hat{d}$-dimensional weight vector, and where the $\hat{d}$ functions $y_i(\mathbf{x})$ (sometimes called φ functions) can be arbitrary functions of $\mathbf{x}$. By selecting these functions judiciously and letting $\hat{d}$ be sufficiently large, one can approximate any desired discriminant function by such a series expansion. The resulting discriminant function is not linear in $\mathbf{x}$, but it is linear in $\mathbf{y}$. The $\hat{d}$ functions $y_i(\mathbf{x})$ merely map points in d-dimensional $\mathbf{x}$-space to points in $\hat{d}$-dimensional $\mathbf{y}$-space. The homogeneous discriminant $\mathbf{a}^t\mathbf{y}$ separates points in this transformed space by a hyperplane passing through the origin. Thus, the mapping from $\mathbf{x}$ to $\mathbf{y}$ reduces the problem to one of finding a homogeneous linear discriminant function.

Some of the advantages and disadvantages of this approach can be clarified by considering a simple example. Let $g(x)$ be the quadratic discriminant function

$$g(x) = a_1 + a_2x + a_3x^2,$$

so that the three-dimensional vector $\mathbf{y}$ is given by

$$\mathbf{y} = \begin{bmatrix} 1 \\ x \\ x^2 \end{bmatrix}.$$

The mapping from x to $\mathbf{y}$ is illustrated in Figure 5.4. The data remain inherently one dimensional, since varying x causes $\mathbf{y}$ to trace out a curve in three-space. Thus, one thing to notice immediately is that if x is governed by a probability law $p(x)$, the induced density $\hat{p}(\mathbf{y})$ will be degenerate, being zero everywhere except on the curve, where it is infinite. This is a common problem whenever $\hat{d} > d$, and the mapping takes points from a lower-dimensional space to a higher-dimensional space.

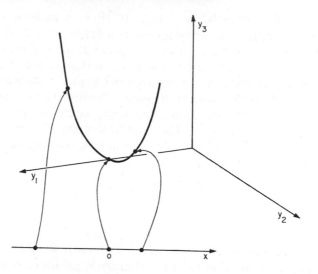

FIGURE 5.4.   The mapping $y = (1\ x\ x^2)^t$.

The plane $\hat{H}$ defined by $\mathbf{a}^t\mathbf{y} = 0$ divides the y-space into two decision regions $\mathscr{R}_1$ and $\mathscr{R}_2$. Figure 5.5 shows the separating plane corresponding to $\mathbf{a} = (-1\ 1\ 2)^t$, and the corresponding decision regions $\mathscr{R}_1$ and $\mathscr{R}_2$ in x-space. The quadratic discriminant function $g(x) = -1 + x + 2x^2$ is positive if $x < -1$ or if $x > 0.5$, so that $\mathscr{R}_1$ is multiply connected. Thus, although the decision regions in y-space are convex, this is by no means the case in x-space. Even with relatively simple functions $y_i(\mathbf{x})$, the decision surfaces induced in x-space can be fairly complex.

Unfortunately, the curse of dimensionality makes it hard to capitalize on this flexibility in practice. A complete quadratic discriminant function involves $\hat{d} = (d + 1)(d + 2)/2$ terms. If d is modestly large, say $d = 50$, this requires the computation of a great many terms. Inclusion of cubic and higher order terms leads to even larger values for $\hat{d}$. Furthermore, the $\hat{d}$ components of the weight vector $\mathbf{a}$ must be determined from samples. If we think of $\hat{d}$ as specifying the number of degrees of freedom for the discriminant function, it is natural to require that the number of samples be not less than the number of degrees of freedom. Clearly, a general series expansion of $g(\mathbf{x})$ can easily lead to completely unrealistic requirements for computation and data.

While it may be hard to realize the potential benefits of a generalized linear discriminant function, we can at least exploit the convenience of being able to write $g(\mathbf{x})$ in the homogeneous form $\mathbf{a}^t\mathbf{y}$. In the particular case of the linear discriminant function

$$g(\mathbf{x}) = w_0 + \sum_{i=1}^{d} w_i x_i \qquad (3)$$

we can write

$$y = \begin{bmatrix} 1 \\ x_1 \\ \cdot \\ \cdot \\ \cdot \\ x_d \end{bmatrix} = \begin{bmatrix} 1 \\ \mathbf{x} \end{bmatrix} \tag{6}$$

and

$$\mathbf{a} = \begin{bmatrix} w_0 \\ w_1 \\ \cdot \\ \cdot \\ \cdot \\ w_d \end{bmatrix} = \begin{bmatrix} w_0 \\ \mathbf{w} \end{bmatrix}. \tag{7}$$

This mapping from d-dimensional $\mathbf{x}$-space to $(d + 1)$-dimensional $\mathbf{y}$-space is mathematically trivial but nonetheless convenient. The addition of a constant component to $\mathbf{x}$ preserves all distance relationships among samples. The resulting $\mathbf{y}$ vectors all lie in a d-dimensional subspace, which is the $\mathbf{x}$-space itself. The hyperplane decision surface $\hat{H}$ defined by $\mathbf{a}^t\mathbf{y} = 0$ always passes through the origin in $\mathbf{y}$-space, even though the corresponding hyperplane H can be in any position in $\mathbf{x}$-space. The distance from $\mathbf{y}$ to $\hat{H}$ is given by $|\mathbf{a}^t\mathbf{y}|/\|\mathbf{a}\|$, or $|g(\mathbf{x})|/\|\mathbf{a}\|$. Since $\|\mathbf{a}\| > \|\mathbf{w}\|$, this distance is less than, or at

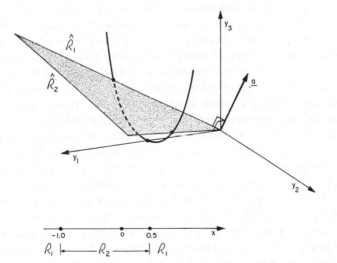

FIGURE 5.5.   Decision regions in x-space and y-space.

most equal to the distance from $\mathbf{x}$ to H. By using this mapping we reduce the problem of finding a weight vector $\mathbf{w}$ and a threshold weight w_0 to the problem of finding a single weight vector $\mathbf{a}$.

5.4   THE TWO-CATEGORY LINEARLY-SEPARABLE CASE

5.4.1   Geometry and Terminology

Suppose now that we have a set of n samples $\mathbf{y}_1, \ldots, \mathbf{y}_n$, some labelled ω_1 and some labelled ω_2. We want to use these samples to determine the weights in a linear discriminant function $g(\mathbf{x}) = \mathbf{a}^t\mathbf{y}$. Suppose we have reason to believe that there exists a solution for which the probability of error is very, very low. Then a reasonable approach is to look for a weight vector that classifies all of the samples correctly. If such a weight vector exists, the samples are said to be *linearly separable*.

A sample $\mathbf{y}_i$ is classified correctly if $\mathbf{a}^t\mathbf{y}_i > 0$ and $\mathbf{y}_i$ is labelled ω_1, or if $\mathbf{a}^t\mathbf{y}_i < 0$ and $\mathbf{y}_i$ is labelled ω_2. In the latter case, we observe that $\mathbf{y}_i$ is classified correctly if $\mathbf{a}^t(-\mathbf{y}_i) > 0$. This suggests a normalization that simplifies the treatment of the two-category case, viz., the replacement of all samples labelled ω_2 by their negatives. With this normalization we can forget the labels and look for a weight vector $\mathbf{a}$ such that $\mathbf{a}^t\mathbf{y}_i > 0$ for all of the samples. Such a weight vector is called a *separating vector* or a *solution vector*.

The weight vector $\mathbf{a}$ can be thought of as specifying a point in *weight space*. Each sample $\mathbf{y}_i$ places a constraint on the possible location of a solution vector. The equation $\mathbf{a}^t\mathbf{y}_i = 0$ defines a hyperplane through the origin of weight space having $\mathbf{y}_i$ as a normal vector. The solution vector, if it exists, must be on the positive side of every hyperplane. Thus, the solution vector must lie in the intersection of n half-spaces, and any vector in this region is a solution vector. The corresponding region is called the *solution region*. A two-dimensional example illustrating the solution region for both the normalized and the unnormalized case is shown in Figure 5.6.

From this discussion, it should be clear that the solution vector, if it exists, is not unique. There are several ways to impose additional requirements to constrain the solution vector further. One possibility is to seek a unit-length weight vector that maximizes the minimum distance from the samples to the separating plane. Another possibility is to seek the minimum-length weight vector satisfying $\mathbf{a}^t\mathbf{y}_i \geq b$ for all i, where b is a positive constant called the *margin*. Sometimes it is convenient to require merely that $\mathbf{a}^t\mathbf{y}_i \geq b$. As shown in Figure 5.7, the solution region resulting from the intersections of the halfspaces for which $\mathbf{a}^t\mathbf{y}_i \geq b > 0$ lies within the previous solution region, being insulated from the old boundaries by the distance $b/\|\mathbf{y}_i\|$.

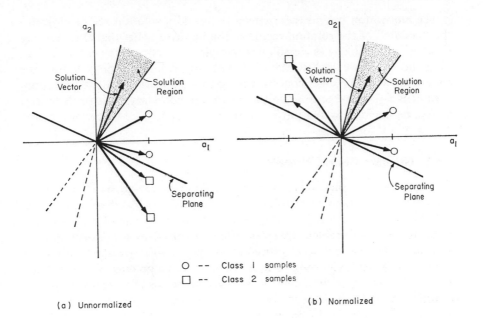

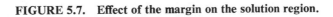

O   --   Class   1   samples
□   --   Class   2   samples

(a)   Unnormalized   (b)   Normalized

FIGURE 5.6.   Linearly separable samples and the solution region in weight space.

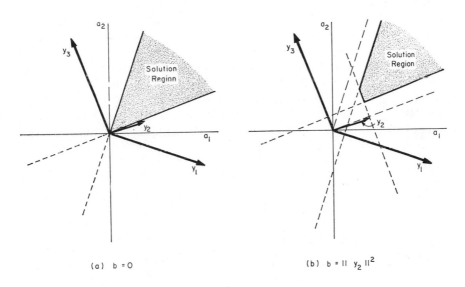

(a) $b = 0$ (b) $b = \| y_2 \|^2$

FIGURE 5.7.   Effect of the margin on the solution region.

The motivation behind these attempts to find a solution vector closer to the "middle" of the solution region is the intuitive belief that the resulting solution is more likely to classify new samples correctly. In the cases we shall treat, however, we shall be satisfied with any solution strictly within the solution region. Our chief concern will be to see that any iterative procedure used does not converge to a limit point on the boundary. This problem can always be avoided by the introduction of a margin, i.e., by requiring that $\mathbf{a}^t \mathbf{y}_i \geq b > 0$ for all i.

5.4.2   Gradient Descent Procedures

The approach we shall take to finding a solution to the set of linear inequalities $\mathbf{a}^t \mathbf{y}_i > 0$ will be to define a criterion function $J(\mathbf{a})$ that is minimized if $\mathbf{a}$ is a solution vector. This reduces our problem to one of minimizing a scalar function, a problem that can often be solved by a gradient descent procedure. The basic descent procedure is very simple. We start with some arbitrarily chosen weight vector $\mathbf{a}_1$ and compute the gradient vector $\nabla J(\mathbf{a}_1)$. The next value $\mathbf{a}_2$ is obtained by moving some distance from $\mathbf{a}_1$ in the direction of steepest descent, i.e., along the negative of the gradient. In general, $\mathbf{a}_{k+1}$ is obtained from $\mathbf{a}_k$ by the algorithm

$$\mathbf{a}_{k+1} = \mathbf{a}_k - \rho_k \nabla J(\mathbf{a}_k), \tag{8}$$

where ρ_k is a positive scale factor that sets the step size. Hopefully, such a sequence of weight vectors will converge to a solution minimizing $J(\mathbf{a})$.

The many problems associated with gradient descent procedures are well known. Fortunately, we shall be constructing the functions we want to minimize, and shall be able to avoid the most serious of these problems. One that will confront us repeatedly, however, is the choice of the scale factor ρ_k. If ρ_k is too small, convergence is needlessly slow, whereas if ρ_k is too large, the correction process will overshoot and can even diverge. Suppose that the criterion function can be well approximated by the second-order expansion

$$J(\mathbf{a}) \approx J(\mathbf{a}_k) + \nabla J^t(\mathbf{a} - \mathbf{a}_k) + \tfrac{1}{2}(\mathbf{a} - \mathbf{a}_k)^t D(\mathbf{a} - \mathbf{a}_k), \tag{9}$$

where D is the matrix of second partial derivatives $\partial^2 J / \partial a_i \, \partial a_j$ evaluated at $\mathbf{a} = \mathbf{a}_k$. Then, using $\mathbf{a}_{k+1}$ from Eq. (8) in Eq. (9),

$$J(\mathbf{a}_{k+1}) \approx J(\mathbf{a}_k) - \rho_k \|\nabla J\|^2 + \tfrac{1}{2}\rho_k^2 \, \nabla J^t D \, \nabla J,$$

and it follows that $J(\mathbf{a}_{k+1})$ can be minimized by the choice

$$\rho_k = \frac{\|\nabla J\|^2}{\nabla J^t D \, \nabla J}. \tag{10}$$

An alternative descent procedure can be obtained by ignoring Eq. (8) and by choosing $\mathbf{a}_{k+1}$ to minimize the second-order expansion. This leads to *Newton's algorithm*,

$$\mathbf{a}_{k+1} = \mathbf{a}_k - D^{-1}\nabla J. \tag{11}$$

Generally speaking, Newton's algorithm will usually give a greater improvement *per step* than the simple gradient descent algorithm, even with the optimal value of ρ_k. However, Newton's algorithm is not applicable if the matrix D is singular. Furthermore, even when D is nonsingular, the time required for matrix inversion can easily offset this advantage. In fact, it often takes less time to set ρ_k to a constant ρ that is smaller than necessary and make a few more corrections than to compute the optimal ρ_k at each step. At different times we shall have recourse to all of these solutions.

5.5 MINIMIZING THE PERCEPTRON CRITERION FUNCTION

5.5.1 The Perceptron Criterion Function

Consider now the problem of constructing a criterion function for solving the linear inequalities $\mathbf{a}^t\mathbf{y}_i > 0$. The most obvious choice is to let $J(\mathbf{a}; \mathbf{y}_1, \dots, \mathbf{y}_n)$ be the number of samples misclassified by $\mathbf{a}$. However, because this function is piecewise constant, it is obviously a poor candidate for a gradient search. A better choice is the *perceptron criterion function*

$$J_p(\mathbf{a}) = \sum_{\mathbf{y} \in \mathscr{Y}} (-\mathbf{a}^t\mathbf{y}), \tag{12}$$

where $\mathscr{Y}(\mathbf{a})$ is the set of samples *misclassified* by $\mathbf{a}$. (If no samples are misclassified, we define J_p to be zero.) Since $\mathbf{a}^t\mathbf{y} \leq 0$ if $\mathbf{y}$ is misclassified, $J_p(\mathbf{a})$ is never negative, being zero only if $\mathbf{a}$ is a solution vector, or if $\mathbf{a}$ is on the decision boundary. Geometrically, $J_p(\mathbf{a})$ is proportional to the sum of the distances from the misclassified samples to the decision boundary. Figure 5.8 illustrates J_p for a simple two-dimensional example.

Since the jth component of the gradient of J_p is $\partial J_p/\partial a_j$, we see from Eq. (12) that

$$\nabla J_p = \sum_{\mathbf{y} \in \mathscr{Y}} (-\mathbf{y}),$$

and hence the basic gradient descent algorithm (8) becomes

$$\mathbf{a}_{k+1} = \mathbf{a}_k + \rho_k \sum_{\mathbf{y} \in \mathscr{Y}_k} \mathbf{y}, \tag{13}$$

where $\mathscr{Y}_k$ is the set of samples misclassified by $\mathbf{a}_k$. Thus, the descent procedure for finding a solution vector can be stated very simply: the next

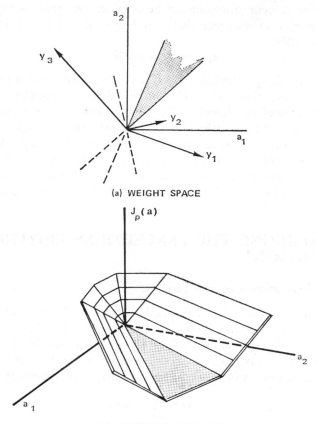

(a) WEIGHT SPACE

(b) CRITERION FUNCTION

FIGURE 5.8. **The perceptron criterion function.**

weight vector is obtained by adding some multiple of the sum of the mis-classified samples to the present weight vector. Figure 5.9 shows how this algorithm yields a solution vector for a simple two-dimensional example with $\mathbf{a}_1 = \mathbf{0}$, and $\rho_k = 1$. We shall now show that it will yield a solution for any linearly separable problem.

5.5.2 Convergence Proof for Single-Sample Correction

We shall begin our examination of convergence properties of the descent algorithm with a variant that is easier to analyze. Rather than testing $\mathbf{a}_k$ on all of the samples and basing our correction of the set $\mathcal{Y}_k$ of misclassified samples, we shall consider the samples in a sequence and shall modify the weight vector whenever it misclassifies a sample. For the purposes of the convergence proof, the detailed nature of the sequence is unimportant as long as every sample appears in the sequence infinitely often. The simplest way to assure this is to repeat the samples cyclically.

Two further simplifications help to clarify the exposition. First, we shall temporarily restrict our attention to the case in which ρ_k is constant. This is the so-called *fixed-increment* case. It is clear from Eq. (13) that if ρ_k is constant it merely serves to scale the samples. Thus, in the fixed-increment case we can take $\rho_k = 1$ with no loss in generality. The second simplification merely involves notation. When the samples are considered sequentially, some will be misclassified. Since we shall only change the weight vector when there is an error, we really need only pay attention to the misclassified samples. Thus, we shall denote the sequence of samples by $\mathbf{y}^1, \mathbf{y}^2, \dots, \mathbf{y}^k, \dots$, where each $\mathbf{y}^k$ is one of the n samples $\mathbf{y}_1, \dots, \mathbf{y}_n$, and where each $\mathbf{y}^k$ is misclassified. For example, if the samples $\mathbf{y}_1$, $\mathbf{y}_2$, and $\mathbf{y}_3$ are considered cyclically, and if the marked samples

$$\overset{\vee}{\mathbf{y}_1}, \mathbf{y}_2, \overset{\vee}{\mathbf{y}_3}, \overset{\vee}{\mathbf{y}_1}, \overset{\vee}{\mathbf{y}_2}, \mathbf{y}_3, \mathbf{y}_1, \overset{\vee}{\mathbf{y}_2}, \dots$$

are misclassified, then the sequence $\mathbf{y}^1, \mathbf{y}^2, \mathbf{y}^3, \mathbf{y}^4, \mathbf{y}^5, \dots$ denotes the sequence $\mathbf{y}_1, \mathbf{y}_3, \mathbf{y}_1, \mathbf{y}_2, \mathbf{y}_2, \dots$. With this understanding, the *fixed-increment rule* for generating a sequence of weight vectors can be written as

$$\left. \begin{aligned} \mathbf{a}_1 \quad & \text{arbitrary} \\ \mathbf{a}_{k+1} = \mathbf{a}_k + \mathbf{y}^k \quad & k \geq 1, \end{aligned} \right\} \tag{14}$$

where $\mathbf{a}_k^t \mathbf{y}^k \leq 0$ for all k.

The fixed-increment rule is the simplest of many algorithms that have been proposed for solving systems of linear inequalities. Historically, it first

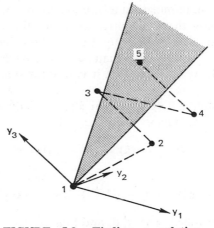

FIGURE 5.9. Finding a solution region by a gradient search.

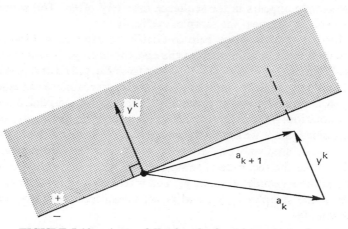

FIGURE 5.10.   A step following the fixed-increment rule.

appeared in a reinforcement learning scheme proposed by Frank Rosenblatt for his *perceptron* brain model, and the proof of its convergence is known as the *Perceptron Convergence Theorem*. Geometrically, its interpretation in weight space is particularly clear. Since $\mathbf{a}_k$ misclassifies $\mathbf{y}^k$, $\mathbf{a}_k$ is not on the positive side of the $\mathbf{y}^k$ hyperplane $\mathbf{a}^t\mathbf{y}^k = 0$. The addition of $\mathbf{y}^k$ to $\mathbf{a}_k$ moves the weight vector directly toward and perhaps across this hyperplane (see Figure 5.10). Whether the hyperplane is crossed or not, the new inner product $\mathbf{a}_{k+1}^t\mathbf{y}^k$ is larger than the old inner product $\mathbf{a}_k^t\mathbf{y}^k$ by the amount $\|\mathbf{y}^k\|^2$, and the correction is clearly moving the weight vector in a good direction.

We shall now show that if the samples are linearly separable the sequence of weight vectors will terminate at a solution vector. In seeking a proof, it is natural to try to show that each correction brings the weight vector closer to the solution region. That is, one might try to show that if $\hat{\mathbf{a}}$ is any solution vector, then $\|\mathbf{a}_{k+1} - \hat{\mathbf{a}}\|$ is smaller than $\|\mathbf{a}_k - \hat{\mathbf{a}}\|$. While this turns out not to be true in general, we shall see that it is true for solution vectors that are sufficient long.

Let $\hat{\mathbf{a}}$ be any solution vector, so that $\hat{\mathbf{a}}^t\mathbf{y}_i$ is strictly positive for all i, and let α be a positive scale factor. From Eq. (14),

$$(\mathbf{a}_{k+1} - \alpha\hat{\mathbf{a}}) = (\mathbf{a}_k - \alpha\hat{\mathbf{a}}) + \mathbf{y}^k$$

and hence

$$\|\mathbf{a}_{k+1} - \alpha\hat{\mathbf{a}}\|^2 = \|\mathbf{a}_k - \alpha\hat{\mathbf{a}}\|^2 + 2(\mathbf{a}_k - \alpha\hat{\mathbf{a}})^t\mathbf{y}^k + \|\mathbf{y}^k\|^2.$$

Since $\mathbf{y}^k$ was misclassified, $\mathbf{a}_k^t\mathbf{y}^k \leq 0$, and thus

$$\|\mathbf{a}_{k+1} - \alpha\hat{\mathbf{a}}\|^2 \leq \|\mathbf{a}_k - \alpha\hat{\mathbf{a}}\|^2 - 2\alpha\hat{\mathbf{a}}^t\mathbf{y}^k + \|\mathbf{y}^k\|^2.$$

Since $\hat{\mathbf{a}}^t \mathbf{y}^k$ is strictly positive, the second term will dominate the third if α is sufficiently large. In particular, if we let

$$\beta^2 = \max_i \|\mathbf{y}_i\|^2 \tag{15}$$

and

$$\gamma = \min_i \hat{\mathbf{a}}^t \mathbf{y}_i > 0, \tag{16}$$

then

$$\|\mathbf{a}_{k+1} - \alpha\hat{\mathbf{a}}\|^2 \leq \|\mathbf{a}_k - \alpha\hat{\mathbf{a}}\|^2 - 2\alpha\gamma + \beta^2,$$

and with the choice

$$\alpha = \frac{\beta^2}{\gamma} \tag{17}$$

we obtain

$$\|\mathbf{a}_{k+1} - \alpha\hat{\mathbf{a}}\|^2 \leq \|\mathbf{a}_k - \alpha\hat{\mathbf{a}}\|^2 - \beta^2.$$

Thus, the squared distance from $\mathbf{a}_k$ to $\alpha\hat{\mathbf{a}}$ is reduced by at least β^2 at each correction, and after k corrections

$$\|\mathbf{a}_{k+1} - \alpha\hat{\mathbf{a}}\|^2 \leq \|\mathbf{a}_1 - \alpha\hat{\mathbf{a}}\|^2 - k\beta^2.$$

Since the squared distance can not become negative, it follows that the sequence of corrections must terminate after no more than k_0 corrections, where

$$k_0 = \frac{\|\mathbf{a}_1 - \alpha\hat{\mathbf{a}}\|^2}{\beta^2}. \tag{18}$$

Since a correction occurs whenever a sample is misclassified, and since each sample appears infinitely often in the sequence, it follows that when corrections cease the resulting weight vector must classify all of the samples correctly.

The number k_0 gives us a bound on the number of corrections. If $\mathbf{a}_1 = \mathbf{0}$, we get the following particularly simple expression for k_0:

$$k_0 = \frac{\alpha^2 \|\hat{\mathbf{a}}\|^2}{\beta^2} = \frac{\beta^2 \|\hat{\mathbf{a}}\|^2}{\gamma^2} = \frac{\max_i \|\mathbf{y}_i\|^2 \|\hat{\mathbf{a}}\|^2}{\min_i [\mathbf{y}_i^t \hat{\mathbf{a}}]^2}. \tag{19}$$

This shows that the difficulty of the problem is essentially determined by the samples most nearly orthogonal to the solution vector. Unfortunately, it provides no help when we face an unsolved problem, since the bound is expressed in terms of an unknown solution vector. In general, it is clear that linearly-separable problems can be made arbitrarily difficult to solve by making the samples be almost coplanar. Nevertheless, if the samples are linearly separable, the fixed-increment rule will yield a solution after a finite number of corrections.

5.5.3   Some Direct Generalizations

The fixed increment rule can be generalized to provide a variety of related algorithms. We shall briefly consider two variants of particular interest. The first variant introduces a *variable increment* ρ_k and a margin b, and calls for a correction whenever $\mathbf{a}_k^t \mathbf{y}^k$ fails to exceed the margin. The algorithm is given by

$$\left.\begin{array}{ll} \mathbf{a}_1 & \text{arbitrary} \\ \mathbf{a}_{k+1} = \mathbf{a}_k + \rho_k \mathbf{y}^k & k \geq 1 \end{array}\right\}, \tag{20}$$

where now $\mathbf{a}_k^t \mathbf{y}^k \leq b$ for all k. It can be shown that if the samples are linearly separable and if

$$\rho_k \geq 0, \tag{21}$$

$$\lim_{m \to \infty} \sum_{k=1}^{m} \rho_k = \infty \tag{22}$$

and

$$\lim_{m \to \infty} \frac{\displaystyle\sum_{k=1}^{m} \rho_k^2}{\left(\displaystyle\sum_{k=1}^{m} \rho_k\right)^2} = 0, \tag{23}$$

then $\mathbf{a}_k$ converges to a solution vector $\mathbf{a}$ satisfying $\mathbf{a}^t \mathbf{y}_i > b$ for all i. In particular, these conditions on ρ_k are satisfied if ρ_k is a positive constant, or if it decreases like $1/k$.

Another variant of interest is our original gradient descent algorithm for J_p,

$$\left.\begin{array}{ll} \mathbf{a}_1 & \text{arbitrary} \\ \mathbf{a}_{k+1} = \mathbf{a}_k + \rho_k \displaystyle\sum_{\mathbf{y} \in \mathscr{Y}_k} \mathbf{y}, \end{array}\right\} \tag{24}$$

where $\mathscr{Y}_k$ is the set of samples misclassified by $\mathbf{a}_k$. It is easy to see that this algorithm will also yield a solution once one recognizes that if $\hat{\mathbf{a}}$ is a solution vector for $\mathbf{y}_1, \ldots, \mathbf{y}_n$, then it correctly classifies the correction vector

$$\mathbf{y}^k = \sum_{\mathbf{y} \in \mathscr{Y}_k} \mathbf{y}.$$

Thus, if the samples are linearly separable, all of the possible correction vectors form a linearly separable set, and if ρ_k satisfies Eqs. (21)–(23), the sequence of weight vectors produced by the gradient descent algorithm for J_p will always converge to a solution vector.

It is interesting to note that the conditions on ρ_k are satisfied if ρ_k is a positive constant, if it decreases like $1/k$, or even if it increases like k. Generally speaking, one would prefer to have ρ_k become smaller as time goes on. This is particularly true if there is reason to believe that the set of samples is not linearly separable, since it reduces the disruptive effects of a few "bad" samples. However, in the separable case it is a curious fact that one can allow ρ_k to become larger and still obtain a solution.

This observation brings out one of the differences between theoretical and practical attitudes. From a theoretical viewpoint, it is interesting that we can obtain a solution in a finite number of steps for any finite set of separable samples, for any initial weight vector $\mathbf{a}_1$, for any nonnegative margin b, and for any scale factor ρ_k satisfying Eqs. (21)–(23). From a practical viewpoint, we want to make wise choices for these quantities. Consider the margin b, for example. If b is much smaller than $\rho_k \, \|\mathbf{y}^k\|^2$, the amount by which a correction increases $\mathbf{a}_k^t \mathbf{y}^k$, it is clear that it will have little effect at all. If it is much larger than $\rho_k \, \|\mathbf{y}^k\|^2$, many corrections will be needed to satisfy the condition $\mathbf{a}_k^t \mathbf{y}^k > b$. A value close to $\rho_k \, \|\mathbf{y}^k\|^2$ is often a useful compromise. In addition to these choices for ρ_k and b, the scaling of the components of $\mathbf{y}^k$ can also have a great effect on the results. The possession of a convergence theorem does not remove the need for thought in applying these techniques.

5.6   RELAXATION PROCEDURES

5.6.1   The Descent Algorithm

The criterion function $J_p(\mathbf{a})$ is by no means the only function we can construct that is minimized when $\mathbf{a}$ is a solution vector. A close but distinct relative is

$$J_q(\mathbf{a}) = \sum_{\mathbf{y} \in \mathscr{Y}} (\mathbf{a}^t \mathbf{y})^2, \tag{25}$$

where $\mathscr{Y}(\mathbf{a})$ again denotes the set of samples misclassified by $\mathbf{a}$. Like J_p, J_q focuses attention on the misclassified samples. Its chief difference is that its gradient is continuous, whereas the gradient of J_p is not. Thus, J_q presents a smoother surface to search. Unfortunately, J_q is so smooth near the boundary of the solution region that the sequence of weight vectors can converge to a point on the boundary. It is particularly embarrassing to spend some time following the gradient merely to reach the boundary point $\mathbf{a} = \mathbf{0}$. Another problem with J_q is that its value can be dominated by the longest sample vectors. Both of these problems are avoided by the criterion function*

$$J_r(\mathbf{a}) = \tfrac{1}{2} \sum_{\mathbf{y} \in \mathscr{Y}} \frac{(\mathbf{a}^t \mathbf{y} - b)^2}{\|\mathbf{y}\|^2}, \tag{26}$$

where now $\mathscr{Y}(\mathbf{a})$ is the set of samples for which $\mathbf{a}^t \mathbf{y} \leq b$. (If $\mathscr{Y}(\mathbf{a})$ is empty, we define J_r to be zero.) Thus, $J_r(\mathbf{a})$ is never negative, and is zero if and only

---

* The normalization by $\|\mathbf{y}\|^2$ simplifies the choice for ρ_k. In effect, it makes the choice $\rho_k = 1$ correspond to the optimal choice of Eq. (10). This matter is explored further in Problem 13.

if $\mathbf{a}^t\mathbf{y} \geq b$ for all of the samples. The gradient of J_r is given by

$$\nabla J_r = \sum_{y \in \mathcal{Y}} \frac{\mathbf{a}^t\mathbf{y} - b}{\|\mathbf{y}\|^2}\,\mathbf{y},$$

so that the basic descent algorithm becomes

$$\left.\begin{array}{l} \mathbf{a}_1 \qquad \text{arbitrary} \\[2mm] \mathbf{a}_{k+1} = \mathbf{a}_k + \rho_k \sum_{y \in \mathcal{Y}_k} \dfrac{b - \mathbf{a}^t\mathbf{y}}{\|\mathbf{y}\|^2}\,\mathbf{y} \end{array}\right\}. \tag{27}$$

As before, we find it easier to prove convergence when the samples are considered one at a time rather than jointly. We also limit our attention to the case $\rho_k = \rho$. Thus, we are again led to consider a sequence $\mathbf{y}^1, \mathbf{y}^2, \ldots$ formed from those samples that call for the weight vector to be corrected. The single-sample correction rule analogous to Eq. (27) is

$$\left.\begin{array}{l} \mathbf{a}_1 \qquad \text{arbitrary} \\[2mm] \mathbf{a}_{k+1} = \mathbf{a}_k + \rho\,\dfrac{b - \mathbf{a}_k^t\mathbf{y}^k}{\|\mathbf{y}^k\|^2}\,\mathbf{y}^k \end{array}\right\}, \tag{28}$$

where $\mathbf{a}_k^t\mathbf{y}^k \leq b$ for all k.

This algorithm is known as the *relaxation rule*, and it has a simple geometrical interpretation. The quantity

$$r_k = \frac{b - \mathbf{a}_k^t\mathbf{y}^k}{\|\mathbf{y}^k\|}$$

is the distance from $\mathbf{a}_k$ to the hyperplane $\mathbf{a}^t\mathbf{y}^k = b$. Since $\mathbf{y}^k/\|\mathbf{y}^k\|$ is the unit normal vector for that hyperplane, Eq. (28) calls for $\mathbf{a}_k$ to be moved a certain fraction ρ of the distance from $\mathbf{a}_k$ to the hyperplane. If $\rho = 1$, $\mathbf{a}_k$ is moved exactly to the hyperplane, so that the "tension" created by the inequality $\mathbf{a}_k^t\mathbf{y}^k \leq b$, is "relaxed." From Eq. (28), after a correction,

$$(\mathbf{a}_{k+1}^t\mathbf{y}^k - b) = (1 - \rho)(\mathbf{a}_k^t\mathbf{y}^k - b).$$

If $\rho < 1$, $\mathbf{a}_{k+1}^t\mathbf{y}^k$ is still less than b, while if $\rho > 1$, $\mathbf{a}_{k+1}^t\mathbf{y}^k$ is greater than b. These conditions are referred to as *underrelaxation* and *overrelaxation*, respectively. In general, we shall restrict ρ to the range $0 < \rho < 2$.

5.6.2 Convergence Proof

When the relaxation rule is applied to a set of linearly separable samples, the number of corrections may or may not be finite. If it is finite, then of course we have obtained a solution vector. If it is not finite, we shall see that $\mathbf{a}_k$ converges to a limit vector on the boundary of the solution region. Since the region in which $\mathbf{a}^t\mathbf{y} \geq b$ is contained in a larger region where $\mathbf{a}^t\mathbf{y} > 0$ if $b > 0$, this implies that $\mathbf{a}_k$ will enter this larger region at least once, eventually remaining there for all k greater than some finite k_0.

The proof depends upon the fact that if $\hat{\mathbf{a}}$ is *any* vector in the solution region, i.e., any vector satisfying $\hat{\mathbf{a}}^t\mathbf{y}_i > b$ for all i, then at each step $\mathbf{a}_k$ gets closer to $\hat{\mathbf{a}}$. This fact follows at once from Eq. (28), since

$$\|\mathbf{a}_{k+1} - \hat{\mathbf{a}}\|^2 = \|\mathbf{a}_k - \hat{\mathbf{a}}\|^2 - 2\rho \frac{(b - \mathbf{a}_k^t\mathbf{y}^k)}{\|\mathbf{y}^k\|^2}(\hat{\mathbf{a}} - \mathbf{a}_k)^t\mathbf{y}^k + \rho^2 \frac{(b - \mathbf{a}_k^t\mathbf{y}^k)^2}{\|\mathbf{y}^k\|^2}$$

and

$$(\hat{\mathbf{a}} - \mathbf{a}_k)^t\mathbf{y}^k > b - \mathbf{a}_k^t\mathbf{y}^k \geq 0,$$

so that

$$\|\mathbf{a}_{k+1} - \hat{\mathbf{a}}\|^2 \leq \|\mathbf{a}_k - \hat{\mathbf{a}}\|^2 - \rho(2 - \rho)\frac{(b - \mathbf{a}_k^t\mathbf{y}^k)^2}{\|\mathbf{y}^k\|^2}.$$

Since we restrict ρ to the range $0 < \rho < 2$, it follows that $\|\mathbf{a}_{k+1} - \hat{\mathbf{a}}\| \leq \|\mathbf{a}_k - \hat{\mathbf{a}}\|$. Thus, the vectors in the sequence $\mathbf{a}_1, \mathbf{a}_2, \ldots$ get closer and closer to $\hat{\mathbf{a}}$, and in the limit as k goes to infinity the distance $\|\mathbf{a}_k - \hat{\mathbf{a}}\|$ approaches some limiting distance $r(\hat{\mathbf{a}})$. This means that as k goes to infinity $\mathbf{a}_k$ is confined to the surface of a hypersphere with center $\hat{\mathbf{a}}$ and radius $r(\hat{\mathbf{a}})$. Since this is true for any $\hat{\mathbf{a}}$ in the solution region, the limiting $\mathbf{a}_k$ is confined to the intersection of the hyperspheres centered about all of the possible solution vectors.

Let us show that the common intersection of these hyperspheres is a single point on the boundary of the solution region. Suppose first that there are at least two points $\mathbf{a}'$ and $\mathbf{a}''$ on the common intersection. Then $\|\mathbf{a}' - \hat{\mathbf{a}}\| = \|\mathbf{a}'' - \hat{\mathbf{a}}\|$ for every $\hat{\mathbf{a}}$ in the solution region. But this implies that the solution region is contained in the $(\hat{d} - 1)$-dimensional hyperplane of points equidistant from $\mathbf{a}'$ to $\mathbf{a}''$, whereas we know that the solution region is $\hat{d}$-dimensional. (Stated formally, if $\hat{\mathbf{a}}^t\mathbf{y}_i > 0$ for $i = 1, \ldots, n$, then for any $\hat{d}$-dimensional vector $\mathbf{v}$, $(\hat{\mathbf{a}} + \epsilon\mathbf{v})^t\mathbf{y}_i > 0$ for $i = 1, \ldots, n$ if ϵ is sufficiently small.) Thus, $\mathbf{a}_k$ converges to a single point $\mathbf{a}$. This point is certainly not inside the solution region, for then the sequence would be finite. It is not outside either, since each correction causes the weight vector to move ρ times its distance from the boundary plane, thereby preventing the vector from being bounded away from the boundary forever. Hence the limit point must be on the boundary.

5.7   NONSEPARABLE BEHAVIOR

The fixed-increment and relaxation procedures give us a number of simple methods for finding a separating vector when the samples are linearly separable. All of these methods are called *error-correction procedures*, because they call for a modification of the weight vector when and only when an error is encountered. Their success on separable problems is largely due to this relentless search for an error-free solution. In practice, one would only consider the use of these methods if there was reason to believe that the error rate for the optimal linear discriminant function is low.

Of course, even if a separating vector is found for the design samples, it does not follow that the resulting classifier will perform well on independent test data. In Chapter 3 we pointed out that *any* set of fewer than $2\hat{d}$ samples is likely to be linearly separable. Thus, one should use several times that many design samples to overdetermine the classifier, thereby ensuring that the performance on design and test data will be similar. Unfortunately, sufficiently large design sets are almost certainly not linearly separable. This makes it important to know how the error-correction procedures will behave when the samples are nonseparable.

Since no weight vector can correctly classify every sample in a nonseparable set, it is clear that the corrections in an error-correction procedure can never cease. Each algorithm produces an infinite sequence of weight vectors, any member of which may or may not yield a useful solution. The exact non-separable behavior of these rules has been studied thoroughly in only a few special cases. It is known, for example, that the length of the weight vectors produced by the fixed-increment rule is bounded. Empirical rules for terminating the correction procedure are often based on this tendency for the length of the weight vector to fluctuate near some limiting value. From a theoretical viewpoint, if the components of the samples are integer-valued, the fixed-increment procedure produces a finite-state process. If the correction process is terminated at some arbitrary point, the weight vector may or may not be in a good state. By averaging the weight vectors produced by the correction rule, one can reduce the risk of obtaining a bad solution by accidentally choosing an unfortunate termination time.

A number of similar heuristic modifications to the error-correction rules have been suggested and studied empirically. The goal of these modifications is to obtain acceptable performance on nonseparable problems while preserving the ability to find a separating vector on separable problems. A common suggestion is the use of a variable increment ρ_k, with ρ_k approaching zero as k approaches infinity. The rate at which ρ_k approaches zero is quite important. If it is too slow, the results will still be sensitive to those samples that render the set nonseparable. If it is too fast, the weight vector may converge prematurely with less than optimal results. One way to choose ρ_k is to make it a function of recent performance, decreasing it as performance improves. Another way is to program ρ_k by a choice such as $\rho_k = \rho_1/k$. When we examine stochastic approximation techniques, we shall see that this latter choice is the theoretical solution to an analogous problem. Before we take up this topic, however, we shall consider an approach that sacrifices the ability to obtain a separating vector for good compromise performance on both separable and nonseparable problems.

5.8 MINIMUM SQUARED ERROR PROCEDURES

5.8.1 Minimum Squared Error and the Pseudoinverse

The criterion functions we have considered thus far have focussed their attention on the misclassified samples. We shall now consider a criterion function that involves all of the samples. Where previously we have sought a weight vector $\mathbf{a}$ making all of the inner products $\mathbf{a}^t\mathbf{y}_i$ positive, now we shall try to make $\mathbf{a}^t\mathbf{y}_i = b_i$, where the b_i are some arbitrarily specified positive constants. Thus, we have replaced the problem of finding the solution to a set of linear inequalities with the more stringent but better understood problem of finding the solution to a set of linear equations.

The treatment of simultaneous linear equations is simplified by introducing matrix notation. Let Y be the n-by-$\hat{d}$ matrix whose ith row is the vector $\mathbf{y}_i^t$, and let $\mathbf{b}$ be the column vector $\mathbf{b} = (b_1, \ldots, b_n)^t$. Then our problem is to find a weight vector $\mathbf{a}$ satisfying

$$Y\mathbf{a} = \mathbf{b}. \tag{29}$$

If Y were nonsingular, we could write $\mathbf{a} = Y^{-1}\mathbf{b}$ and obtain a formal solution at once. However, Y is rectangular, usually with more rows than columns. When there are more equations than unknowns, $\mathbf{a}$ is overdetermined, and ordinarily no exact solution exists. However, we can seek a weight vector $\mathbf{a}$ that minimizes some function of the error between $Y\mathbf{a}$ and $\mathbf{b}$. If we define the error vector $\mathbf{e}$ by

$$\mathbf{e} = Y\mathbf{a} - \mathbf{b}, \tag{30}$$

then one approach is to try to minimize the squared length of the error vector. This is equivalent to minimizing the sum-of-squared-error criterion function

$$J_s(\mathbf{a}) = \|Y\mathbf{a} - \mathbf{b}\|^2 = \sum_{i=1}^{n} (\mathbf{a}^t\mathbf{y}_i - b_i)^2. \tag{31}$$

The problem of minimizing the sum of squared errors is a classical one. It can be solved by a gradient search procedure, as we shall see in Section 5.8.4. A simple closed-form solution can also be found by forming the gradient

$$\nabla J_s = \sum_{i=1}^{n} 2(\mathbf{a}^t\mathbf{y}_i - b_i)\mathbf{y}_i = 2Y^t(Y\mathbf{a} - \mathbf{b})$$

and setting it equal to zero. This yields the necessary condition

$$Y^t Y \mathbf{a} = Y^t \mathbf{b}, \tag{32}$$

and we have converted the problem of solving $Y\mathbf{a} = \mathbf{b}$ to that of solving $Y^t Y\mathbf{a} = Y^t\mathbf{b}$. This celebrated equation has the great advantage that the $\hat{d}$-by-$\hat{d}$ matrix $Y^t Y$ is square and often nonsingular. If it is nonsingular, we can solve for $\mathbf{a}$ uniquely as

$$\mathbf{a} = (Y^t Y)^{-1} Y^t \mathbf{b}$$

$$= Y^\dagger \mathbf{b}, \tag{33}$$

where the $\hat{d}$-by-n matrix

$$Y^\dagger = (Y^t Y)^{-1} Y^t \tag{34}$$

is called the *pseudoinverse* of Y. Note that if Y is square and nonsingular, the pseudoinverse coincides with the regular inverse. Note also that $Y^\dagger Y = I$, but $YY^\dagger \neq I$ in general. If $Y^t Y$ is singular, the solution to Eq. (32) is not unique. However, a minimum-squared-error (MSE) solution always exists. In particular, if $Y^\dagger$ is defined more generally by

$$Y^\dagger = \lim_{\epsilon \to 0} (Y^t Y + \epsilon I)^{-1} Y^t, \tag{35}$$

it can be shown that this limit always exists, and that $\mathbf{a} = Y^\dagger \mathbf{b}$ is a MSE solution to $Y\mathbf{a} = \mathbf{b}$. These and other interesting properties of the pseudo-inverse are well treated in the literature.

The MSE solution depends on the margin vector $\mathbf{b}$, and we shall see that different choices for $\mathbf{b}$ give the solution different properties. If $\mathbf{b}$ is fixed arbitrarily, there is no reason to believe that the MSE solution yields a separating vector in the linearly separable case. However, it is reasonable to hope that by minimizing the squared-error criterion function we might obtain a useful discriminant function in both the separable and the nonseparable cases. We shall now examine two properties of the solution that support this hope.

5.8.2 Relation to Fisher's Linear Discriminant

In this section we shall show that with the proper choice of the vector $\mathbf{b}$, the MSE discriminant function $\mathbf{a}^t \mathbf{y}$ is directly related to Fisher's linear discriminant. To do this, we must return to the use of linear rather than generalized linear discriminant functions. We assume that we have a set of n d-dimensional samples $\mathbf{x}_1, \ldots, \mathbf{x}_n$, n_1 of which are in the subset $\mathscr{X}_1$ labelled ω_1, and n_2 of which are in the subset $\mathscr{X}_2$ labelled ω_2. Further, we assume that a sample $\mathbf{y}_i$ is formed from $\mathbf{x}_i$ by adding a threshold component of unity, and by multiplying the resulting vector by -1 if the sample is labelled ω_2. With no loss in generality, we can assume that the first n_1 samples are labelled ω_1 and the second n_2 are labelled ω_2. Then the matrix Y can be partitioned as follows:

$$Y = \begin{bmatrix} \mathbf{u}_1 & X_1 \\ -\mathbf{u}_2 & -X_2 \end{bmatrix},$$

where $\mathbf{u}_i$ is a column vector of n_i ones, and X_i is a n_i-by-d matrix whose rows are the samples labelled ω_i. We partition $\mathbf{a}$ and $\mathbf{b}$ correspondingly, with

$$\mathbf{a} = \begin{bmatrix} w_0 \\ \mathbf{w} \end{bmatrix}$$

and with

$$\mathbf{b} = \begin{bmatrix} \dfrac{n}{n_1}\mathbf{u}_1 \\[2ex] \dfrac{n}{n_2}\mathbf{u}_2 \end{bmatrix}.$$

We shall see that this special choice for $\mathbf{b}$ links the MSE solution to Fisher's linear discriminant.

We begin by writing Eq. (32) for $\mathbf{a}$ in terms of the partitioned matrices:

$$\begin{bmatrix} \mathbf{u}_1^t & -\mathbf{u}_2^t \\ X_1^t & -X_2^t \end{bmatrix}\begin{bmatrix} \mathbf{u}_1 & X_1 \\ -\mathbf{u}_2 & -X_2 \end{bmatrix}\begin{bmatrix} w_0 \\ \mathbf{w} \end{bmatrix} = \begin{bmatrix} \mathbf{u}_1^t & -\mathbf{u}_2^t \\ X_1^t & -X_2^t \end{bmatrix}\begin{bmatrix} \dfrac{n}{n_1}\mathbf{u}_1 \\[2ex] \dfrac{n}{n_2}\mathbf{u}_2 \end{bmatrix}. \qquad (36)$$

By defining the sample means $\mathbf{m}_i$ and the pooled sample scatter matrix S_W as

$$\mathbf{m}_i = \frac{1}{n_i}\sum_{\mathbf{x}\in\mathcal{X}_i}\mathbf{x} \qquad i = 1, 2 \qquad (37)$$

and

$$S_W = \sum_{i=1}^{2}\sum_{\mathbf{x}\in\mathcal{X}_i}(\mathbf{x} - \mathbf{m}_i)(\mathbf{x} - \mathbf{m}_i)^t, \qquad (38)$$

we can multiply the matrices in Eq. (36) and obtain

$$\begin{bmatrix} n & (n_1\mathbf{m}_1 + n_2\mathbf{m}_2)^t \\ (n_1\mathbf{m}_1 + n_2\mathbf{m}_2) & S_W + n_1\mathbf{m}_1\mathbf{m}_1^t + n_2\mathbf{m}_2\mathbf{m}_2^t \end{bmatrix}\begin{bmatrix} w_0 \\ \mathbf{w} \end{bmatrix} = \begin{bmatrix} 0 \\ n(\mathbf{m}_1 - \mathbf{m}_2) \end{bmatrix}.$$

This can be viewed as a pair of equations, the first of which can be solved for w_0 in terms of $\mathbf{w}$:

$$w_0 = -\mathbf{m}^t\mathbf{w}, \qquad (39)$$

where $\mathbf{m}$ is the mean of all of the samples. Substituting this in the second equation and performing a few algebraic manipulations, we obtain

$$\left[\frac{1}{n} S_W + \frac{n_1 n_2}{n^2} (\mathbf{m}_1 - \mathbf{m}_2)(\mathbf{m}_1 - \mathbf{m}_2)^t\right] \mathbf{w} = \mathbf{m}_1 - \mathbf{m}_2. \tag{40}$$

Since the vector $(\mathbf{m}_1 - \mathbf{m}_2)(\mathbf{m}_1 - \mathbf{m}_2)^t \mathbf{w}$ is in the direction of $\mathbf{m}_1 - \mathbf{m}_2$ for any value of $\mathbf{w}$, we can write

$$\frac{n_1 n_2}{n^2} (\mathbf{m}_1 - \mathbf{m}_2)(\mathbf{m}_1 - \mathbf{m}_2)^t \mathbf{w} = (1 - \alpha)(\mathbf{m}_1 - \mathbf{m}_2),$$

where α is some scalar. Then Eq. (40) yields

$$\mathbf{w} = \alpha n S_W^{-1}(\mathbf{m}_1 - \mathbf{m}_2), \tag{41}$$

which, except for an unimportant scale factor, is identical to the solution for Fisher's linear discriminant. In addition, we obtain the threshold weight w_0 and the following decision rule: Decide ω_1 if $\mathbf{w}^t(\mathbf{x} - \mathbf{m}) > 0$; otherwise decide ω_2.

5.8.3 Asymptotic Approximation to an Optimal Discriminant

Another property of the MSE solution that recommends its use is that if $\mathbf{b} = \mathbf{u}_n$ it approaches a minimum mean-squared-error approximation to the Bayes discriminant function

$$g_0(\mathbf{x}) = P(\omega_1 \mid \mathbf{x}) - P(\omega_2 \mid \mathbf{x}) \tag{42}$$

in the limit as the number of samples approaches infinity. To demonstrate this fact, we must assume that the samples are drawn independently according to the probability law

$$p(\mathbf{x}) = p(\mathbf{x} \mid \omega_1)P(\omega_1) + p(\mathbf{x} \mid \omega_2)P(\omega_2). \tag{43}$$

In terms of the augmented vector $\mathbf{y}$, the MSE solution yields the series expansion $g(\mathbf{x}) = \mathbf{a}^t \mathbf{y}$, where $\mathbf{y} = \mathbf{y}(\mathbf{x})$. If we define the mean-squared approximation error by

$$\epsilon^2 = \int [\mathbf{a}^t \mathbf{y} - g_0(\mathbf{x})]^2 p(\mathbf{x}) \, d\mathbf{x}, \tag{44}$$

then our goal is to show that ϵ^2 is minimized by the solution $\mathbf{a} = Y^\dagger \mathbf{u}_n$.

The proof is simplified if we preserve the distinction between Class 1 and Class 2 samples. In terms of the unnormalized data, the criterion function J_s becomes

$$J_s(\mathbf{a}) = \sum_{\mathbf{y} \in \mathcal{Y}_1} (\mathbf{a}^t \mathbf{y} - 1)^2 + \sum_{\mathbf{y} \in \mathcal{Y}_2} (\mathbf{a}^t \mathbf{y} + 1)^2$$

$$= n\left[\frac{n_1}{n} \cdot \frac{1}{n_1} \sum_{\mathbf{y} \in \mathcal{Y}_1} (\mathbf{a}^t \mathbf{y} - 1)^2 + \frac{n_2}{n} \cdot \frac{1}{n_2} \sum_{\mathbf{y} \in \mathcal{Y}_2} (\mathbf{a}^t \mathbf{y} + 1)^2\right].$$

Thus, by the law of large numbers, as n approaches infinity $(1/n)J_s(\mathbf{a})$ approaches

$$\bar{J}(\mathbf{a}) = P(\omega_1)E_1[(\mathbf{a}^t\mathbf{y} - 1)^2] + P(\omega_2)E_2[(\mathbf{a}^t\mathbf{y} + 1)^2], \qquad (45)$$

with probability one, where

$$E_1[(\mathbf{a}^t\mathbf{y} - 1)^2] = \int (\mathbf{a}^t\mathbf{y} - 1)^2 p(\mathbf{x} \mid \omega_1)\, d\mathbf{x}$$

and

$$E_2[(\mathbf{a}^t\mathbf{y} + 1)^2] = \int (\mathbf{a}^t\mathbf{y} + 1)^2 p(\mathbf{x} \mid \omega_2)\, d\mathbf{x}.$$

Now, if we recognize from Eq. (42) that

$$g_0(\mathbf{x}) = \frac{p(\mathbf{x}, \omega_1) - p(\mathbf{x}, \omega_2)}{p(\mathbf{x})}$$

we see that

$$\bar{J}(\mathbf{a}) = \int (\mathbf{a}^t\mathbf{y} - 1)^2 p(\mathbf{x}, \omega_1)\, d\mathbf{x} + \int (\mathbf{a}^t\mathbf{y} + 1)^2 p(\mathbf{x}, \omega_2)\, d\mathbf{x}$$

$$= \int (\mathbf{a}^t\mathbf{y})^2 p(\mathbf{x})\, d\mathbf{x} - 2 \int \mathbf{a}^t\mathbf{y} g_0(\mathbf{x}) p(\mathbf{x})\, d\mathbf{x} + 1$$

$$= \int [\mathbf{a}^t\mathbf{y} - g_0(\mathbf{x})]^2 p(\mathbf{x})\, d\mathbf{x} + \left[1 - \int g_0^2(\mathbf{x}) p(\mathbf{x})\, d\mathbf{x} \right]. \qquad (46)$$

The second term in this sum is independent of the weight vector $\mathbf{a}$. Hence, the $\mathbf{a}$ that minimizes $\bar{J}_s$ also minimizes ϵ^2, the mean-squared-error between $\mathbf{a}^t\mathbf{y}$ and $g_0(\mathbf{x})$.

This result gives considerable insight into the MSE procedure. By approximating $g_0(\mathbf{x})$, the discriminant function $\mathbf{a}^t\mathbf{y}$ gives direct information about the a posteriori probabilities $P(\omega_1 \mid \mathbf{x}) = 1/2(1 + g_0)$ and $P(\omega_2 \mid \mathbf{x}) = 1/2(1 - g_0)$. The quality of the approximation depends on the functions $y_i(\mathbf{x})$ and the number of terms in the expansion $\mathbf{a}^t\mathbf{y}$. Unfortunately, the mean-square-error criterion places emphasis on points where $p(\mathbf{x})$ is large, rather than on points near the decision surface $g_0(\mathbf{x}) = 0$. Thus, the discriminant function that "best" approximates the Bayes discriminant does not necessarily minimize the probability of error. Despite this defect, the MSE solution has interesting properties, and has received considerable attention in the literature. We shall encounter the mean-square approximation of $g_0(\mathbf{x})$ again when we consider stochastic approximation methods.

5.8.4   The Widrow-Hoff Procedure

We remarked earlier that $J_s(\mathbf{a}) = \| Y\mathbf{a} - \mathbf{b}\|^2$ could be minimized by a gradient descent procedure. Such an approach has two advantages over merely computing the pseudoinverse: (1) it avoids the problems that arise when $Y^t Y$ is singular, and (2) it avoids the need for working with large matrices. In addition, the computation involved is effectively a feedback scheme which automatically copes with some of the computational problems due to roundoff or truncation. Since $\nabla J_s = 2Y^t(Y\mathbf{a} - \mathbf{b})$, the obvious descent algorithm is

$$\left.\begin{aligned} \mathbf{a}_1 \quad & \text{arbitrary} \\ \mathbf{a}_{k+1} = \mathbf{a}_k &- \rho_k Y^t(Y\mathbf{a}_k - \mathbf{b}) \end{aligned}\right\}.$$

It is a good exercise to show that if

$$\rho_k = \rho_1/k,$$

where ρ_1 is any positive constant, then this rule generates a sequence of weight vectors that converges to a limiting vector $\mathbf{a}$ satisfying

$$Y^t(Y\mathbf{a} - \mathbf{b}) = 0.$$

Thus, the descent algorithm always yields a solution regardless of whether or not $Y^t Y$ is singular.

While the $\hat{d}$-by-$\hat{d}$ matrix $Y^t Y$ is usually smaller than the $\hat{d}$-by-n matrix Y^t, the storage requirements can be reduced still further by considering the samples sequentially and using the *Widrow-Hoff* or *LMS rule*

$$\left.\begin{aligned} \mathbf{a}_1 \quad & \text{arbitrary} \\ \mathbf{a}_{k+1} = \mathbf{a}_k &+ \rho_k(b_k - \mathbf{a}_k^t \mathbf{y}^k)\mathbf{y}^k \end{aligned}\right\}. \tag{47}$$

At first glance this descent algorithm appears to be essentially the same as the relaxation rule. The primary difference is that the relaxation rule is an error-correction rule, so that $\mathbf{a}_k^t \mathbf{y}^k$ is always less than b_k, whereas the Widrow-Hoff rule "corrects" $\mathbf{a}_k$ whenever $\mathbf{a}_k^t \mathbf{y}^k$ does not equal b_k. In most cases of interest, it is impossible to satisfy all of the equations $\mathbf{a}^t \mathbf{y}^k = b_k$, so that corrections never cease. Thus, ρ_k must decrease with k to obtain convergence, the choice $\rho_k = \rho_1/k$ being common. Exact analysis of the behavior of the Widrow-Hoff rule in the deterministic case is rather complicated, and merely indicates that the sequence of weight vectors tends to converge to the desired solution. Instead of pursuing this topic further, we shall turn to a very similar rule that arises from a stochastic descent procedure.

5.8.5   Stochastic Approximation Methods

All of the iterative descent procedures we have considered thus far have been described in deterministic terms. We are given a particular set of samples, and we generate a particular sequence of weight vectors. In this section we digress briefly to consider a MSE procedure in which the samples are drawn randomly, resulting in a random sequence of weight vectors. A complete analysis would require use of the theory of stochastic approximation, and will not be attempted. However, the main ideas, which will be presented without proof, are simple.

Suppose that samples are drawn independently by selecting a state of nature with probability $P(\omega_i)$ and then selecting an $\mathbf{x}$ according to the probability law $p(\mathbf{x} \mid \omega_i)$. For each $\mathbf{x}$ we let z be its *label*, with $z = +1$ if $\mathbf{x}$ is labelled ω_1 and $z = -1$ if $\mathbf{x}$ is labelled ω_2. Then the data consist of an infinite sequence of independent pairs $(\mathbf{x}_1, z_1), (\mathbf{x}_2, z_2), \ldots, (\mathbf{x}_k, z_k), \ldots$.

Even though the label variable z is binary-valued, it can be thought of as a noisy version of the Bayes discriminant function $g_0(\mathbf{x})$. This follows from the observation that

$$P(z = 1 \mid \mathbf{x}) = P(\omega_1 \mid \mathbf{x}),$$

and

$$P(z = -1 \mid \mathbf{x}) = P(\omega_2 \mid \mathbf{x}),$$

so that the conditional mean of z is given by

$$E_{z|x}[z] = \sum_z zP(z \mid \mathbf{x}) = P(\omega_1 \mid \mathbf{x}) - P(\omega_2 \mid \mathbf{x}) = g_0(\mathbf{x}). \tag{48}$$

Suppose that we wish to approximate $g_0(\mathbf{x})$ by the finite series expansion

$$g(\mathbf{x}) = \mathbf{a}^t \mathbf{y} = \sum_{i=1}^{\hat{d}} a_i y_i(\mathbf{x}),$$

where both the basis functions $y_i(\mathbf{x})$ and the number of terms $\hat{d}$ are known. Then we can seek a weight vector $\hat{\mathbf{a}}$ that minimizes the mean-squared approximation error

$$\epsilon^2 = E[(\mathbf{a}^t \mathbf{y} - g_0(\mathbf{x}))^2]. \tag{49}$$

Minimization of ϵ^2 would appear to require knowledge of the Bayes discriminant $g_0(\mathbf{x})$. However, as one might have guessed from the analogous situation in Section 5.8.3, it can be shown that the weight vector $\hat{\mathbf{a}}$ that minimizes ϵ^2 also minimizes the criterion function

$$J_m(\mathbf{a}) = E[(\mathbf{a}^t \mathbf{y} - z)^2]. \tag{50}$$

This should also be plausible from the fact that z is essentially a noisy version of $g_0(\mathbf{x})$ (see Figure 5.11). Since

$$\nabla J_m = 2E[(\mathbf{a}^t \mathbf{y} - z)\mathbf{y}],$$

we can obtain the closed-form solution

$$\hat{\mathbf{a}} = E[\mathbf{y}\mathbf{y}^t]^{-1}E[z\mathbf{y}]. \tag{51}$$

Thus, one way to use the samples is to estimate $E[\mathbf{y}\mathbf{y}^t]$ and $E[z\mathbf{y}]$, and use Eq. (51) to obtain the MSE optimum linear discriminant. An alternative is to

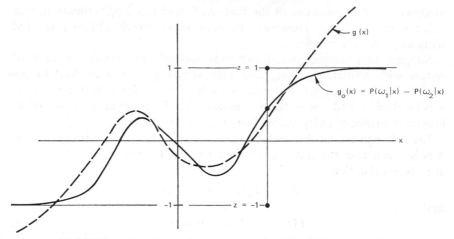

FIGURE 5.11.   Approximating the Bayes discriminant function.

minimize $J_m(\mathbf{a})$ by a gradient descent procedure. Suppose that in place of the true gradient we substitute the noisy version $2(\mathbf{a}^t \mathbf{y}_k - z_k)\mathbf{y}_k$. This leads to the descent algorithm

$$\mathbf{a}_{k+1} = \mathbf{a}_k + \rho_k (z_k - \mathbf{a}_k^t \mathbf{y}_k)\mathbf{y}_k, \tag{52}$$

which is basically just the Widrow-Hoff rule. It can be shown that if $E[\mathbf{yy}^t]$ is nonsingular and if the coefficients ρ_k satisfy

$$\lim_{m \to \infty} \sum_{k=1}^{m} \rho_k = +\infty \tag{53}$$

and

$$\lim_{m \to \infty} \sum_{k=1}^{m} \rho_k^2 < \infty, \tag{54}$$

then $\mathbf{a}_k$ converges to $\hat{\mathbf{a}}$ in mean square:

$$\lim_{k \to \infty} E[\|\mathbf{a}_k - \hat{\mathbf{a}}\|^2] = 0. \tag{55}$$

The reasons we need these conditions on ρ_k are simple. The first condition keeps the weight vector from converging so fast that a systematic error will remain forever uncorrected. The second condition ensures that random fluctuations are eventually suppressed. Both conditions are satisfied by the conventional choice $\rho_k = 1/k$. Unfortunately, this kind of programmed decrease of ρ_k, independent of the problem at hand, often leads to very slow convergence.

Of course, this is neither the only nor the best descent algorithm for minimizing J_m. For example, if we note that the matrix of second partial derivatives for J_m is given by

$$D = 2E[\mathbf{yy}^t],$$

we see that Newton's algorithm for minimizing J_m (Eq. (11)) is

$$\mathbf{a}_{k+1} = \mathbf{a}_k + E[\mathbf{y}\mathbf{y}^t]^{-1}E[(z - \mathbf{a}^t\mathbf{y})\mathbf{y}].$$

A stochastic analog of this algorithm is

$$\mathbf{a}_{k+1} = \mathbf{a}_k + R_{k+1}(z_k - \mathbf{a}_k^t\mathbf{y}_k)\mathbf{y}_k \qquad (56)$$

with

$$R_{k+1}^{-1} = R_k^{-1} + \mathbf{y}_k\mathbf{y}_k^t, \qquad (57)$$

or, equivalently,*

$$R_{k+1} = R_k - \frac{R_k\mathbf{y}_k(R_k\mathbf{y}_k)^t}{1 + \mathbf{y}_k^t R_k\mathbf{y}_k}. \qquad (58)$$

This algorithm also produces a sequence of weight vectors that converges to the optimal solution in mean square. Its convergence is faster, but it requires more computation per step.

These gradient procedures can be viewed as methods for minimizing a criterion function, or finding the zero of its gradient, in the presence of noise. In the statistical literature, functions such as J_m and ∇J_m that have the form $E[f(\mathbf{a}, \mathbf{x})]$ are called *regression functions*, and the iterative algorithms are called *stochastic approximation procedures*. The best known of these are the Kiefer-Wolfowitz procedure for minimizing a regression function, and the Robbins-Monro procedure for finding a root of a regression function. Often the easiest way to obtain a convergence proof for a particular descent or approximation procedure is to show that it satisfies the convergence conditions for these more general procedures. Unfortunately, an exposition of these methods in their full generality would lead us rather far afield, and we must close this digression by referring the interested reader to the literature.

5.9 THE HO-KASHYAP PROCEDURES

5.9.1 The Descent Procedure

The procedures we have considered thus far differ in several ways. The perceptron and relaxation procedures find separating vectors if the samples are linearly separable, but do not converge on nonseparable problems. The MSE procedures yield a weight vector whether the samples are linearly separable or not, but there is no guarantee that this vector is a separating vector in the separable case. If the margin vector $\mathbf{b}$ is chosen arbitrarily, all we can say is that the MSE procedures minimize $\|Y\mathbf{a} - \mathbf{b}\|^2$. Now if the

---

* This recursive formula for computing R_k, which is roughly $(1/k)E[\mathbf{y}\mathbf{y}^t]^{-1}$, can not be used if R_k is singular. The equivalence of Eq. (57) and Eq. (58) follows from Problem 10 of Chapter 3.

samples happen to be linearly separable, then there exists an $\hat{\mathbf{a}}$ and a $\hat{\mathbf{b}}$ such that

$$Y\hat{\mathbf{a}} = \hat{\mathbf{b}} > 0,$$

where by $\hat{\mathbf{b}} > 0$, we mean that every component of $\hat{\mathbf{b}}$ is positive. Clearly, were we to take $\mathbf{b} = \hat{\mathbf{b}}$ and apply the MSE procedure, we would obtain a separating vector. Of course, we usually do not know $\hat{\mathbf{b}}$ beforehand. However, we shall now see how the MSE procedure can be modified to obtain both a separating vector $\mathbf{a}$ and a margin vector $\mathbf{b}$. The underlying idea comes from the observation that if the samples are separable, and if both $\mathbf{a}$ and $\mathbf{b}$ in the criterion function

$$J_s(\mathbf{a}, \mathbf{b}) = \| Y\mathbf{a} - \mathbf{b} \|^2$$

are allowed to vary (subject to the constraint $\mathbf{b} > 0$), then the minimum value of J_s is zero, and the $\mathbf{a}$ that achieves that minimum is a separating vector.

To minimize J_s, we shall use a modified gradient descent procedure. The gradient of J_s with respect to $\mathbf{a}$ is given by

$$\nabla_{\mathbf{a}}J_s = 2 Y^t(Y\mathbf{a} - \mathbf{b}), \tag{59}$$

and the gradient of J_s with respect to $\mathbf{b}$ is given by

$$\nabla_{\mathbf{b}}J_s = -2(Y\mathbf{a} - \mathbf{b}). \tag{60}$$

For any value of $\mathbf{b}$, we can always take

$$\mathbf{a} = Y^\dagger \mathbf{b}, \tag{61}$$

thereby obtaining $\nabla_{\mathbf{a}}J_s = 0$ and minimizing J_s with respect to $\mathbf{a}$ in one step. We are not so free to modify $\mathbf{b}$, however, since we must respect the constraint $\mathbf{b} > 0$, and we must avoid a descent procedure that converges to $\mathbf{b} = 0$. One way to prevent $\mathbf{b}$ from converging to zero is to start with $\mathbf{b} > 0$ and to refuse to reduce any of its components. We can do this and still try to follow the negative gradient if we first set all positive components of $\nabla_{\mathbf{b}}J_s$ to zero. Thus, if we let $|\mathbf{v}|$ denote the vector whose components are the magnitudes of the corresponding components of $\mathbf{v}$, we are led to consider a descent procedure of the form

$$\mathbf{b}_{k+1} = \mathbf{b}_k - \rho\tfrac{1}{2}[\nabla_{\mathbf{b}}J_s - |\nabla_{\mathbf{b}}J_s|].$$

Using Eqs. (60) and (61), and being a bit more specific, we obtain the *Ho-Kashyap algorithm* for minimizing $J_s(\mathbf{a}, \mathbf{b})$:

$$\left.\begin{array}{l} \mathbf{b}_1 > 0 \text{ but otherwise arbitrary} \\[4pt] \mathbf{b}_{k+1} = \mathbf{b}_k + 2\rho\mathbf{e}_k^+ \end{array}\right\} \tag{62}$$

where $\mathbf{e}_k$ is the error vector

$$\mathbf{e}_k = Y\mathbf{a}_k - \mathbf{b}_k, \tag{63}$$

$\mathbf{e}_k^+$ is the positive part of the error vector

$$\mathbf{e}_k^+ = \tfrac{1}{2}(\mathbf{e}_k + |\mathbf{e}_k|), \qquad (64)$$

and

$$\mathbf{a}_k = Y^\dagger \mathbf{b}_k, \qquad k = 1, 2, \ldots . \qquad (65)$$

Since the weight vector $\mathbf{a}_k$ is completely determined by the margin vector $\mathbf{b}_k$, this is basically an algorithm for producing a sequence of margin vectors. The initial vector $\mathbf{b}_1$ is positive to begin with, and if $\rho > 0$, all subsequent vectors $\mathbf{b}_k$ are positive. We might worry that if none of the components of $\mathbf{e}_k$ is positive, so that $\mathbf{b}_k$ stops changing, we might fail to find a solution. However, we shall see that in that case either $\mathbf{e}_k = 0$ and we have a solution, or $\mathbf{e}_k \leq 0$ and we have proof that the samples are not linearly separable.

5.9.2 Convergence Proof

We shall now show that if the samples are linearly separable, and if $0 < \rho < 1$, then the Ho–Kashyap procedure will yield a solution vector in a finite number of steps. To make the algorithm terminate, we should add a terminating condition stating that corrections cease once a solution vector is obtained. However, it is mathematically more convenient to let the corrections continue and show that the error vector $\mathbf{e}_k$ either becomes zero for some finite k, or converges to zero as k goes to infinity.

It is clear that either $\mathbf{e}_k = 0$ for some k, say k_0, or there are no zero vectors in the sequence $\mathbf{e}_1, \mathbf{e}_2, \ldots .$ In the first case, once a zero vector is obtained, no further changes occur to $\mathbf{a}_k$, $\mathbf{b}_k$, or $\mathbf{e}_k$, and $Y\mathbf{a}_k = \mathbf{b}_k > 0$ for all $k \geq k_0$. Thus, if we happen to obtain a zero error vector, the algorithm automatically terminates with a solution vector.

Suppose now that $\mathbf{e}_k$ is never zero for finite k. To see that $\mathbf{e}_k$ must nevertheless converge to zero, we begin by asking whether or not we might possibly obtain an $\mathbf{e}_k$ with no positive components. This would be most unfortunate, since we would have $Y\mathbf{a}_k \leq \mathbf{b}_k$, and since $\mathbf{e}_k^+$ would be zero, we would obtain no further changes in $\mathbf{a}_k$, $\mathbf{b}_k$, or $\mathbf{e}_k$. Fortunately, this can never happen if the samples are linearly separable. A proof is simple, and is based on the fact that if $Y^t Y\mathbf{a}_k = Y^t\mathbf{b}_k$, then $Y^t\mathbf{e}_k = 0$. But if the samples are linearly separable, there exists an $\hat{\mathbf{a}}$ and a $\hat{\mathbf{b}} > 0$ such that

$$Y\hat{\mathbf{a}} = \hat{\mathbf{b}}.$$

Thus,

$$\mathbf{e}_k^t Y\hat{\mathbf{a}} = 0 = \mathbf{e}_k^t \hat{\mathbf{b}},$$

and since all the components of $\hat{\mathbf{b}}$ are positive, either $\mathbf{e}_k = 0$ or at least one of the components of $\mathbf{e}_k$ must be positive. Since we have excluded the case $\mathbf{e}_k = 0$, it follows that $\mathbf{e}_k^+$ can not be zero for finite k.

The proof that the error vector always converges to zero exploits the fact that the matrix $YY^\dagger$ is symmetric, positive semidefinite, and satisfies

$$(YY^\dagger)^t(YY^\dagger) = YY^\dagger. \tag{66}$$

Although these results are true in general, for simplicity we demonstrate them only for the case where Y^tY is nonsingular. In this case $YY^\dagger = Y(Y^tY)^{-1}Y^t$, and the symmetry is evident. Since Y^tY is positive definite, so is $(Y^tY)^{-1}$; thus, $\mathbf{b}^t Y(Y^tY)^{-1}Y^t\mathbf{b} \geq 0$ for any $\mathbf{b}$, and $YY^\dagger$ is at least positive semidefinite. Finally, Eq. (66) follows from

$$(YY^\dagger)^t(YY^\dagger) = [Y(Y^tY)^{-1}Y^t][Y(Y^tY)^{-1}Y^t].$$

To see that $\mathbf{e}_k$ must converge to zero, we eliminate $\mathbf{a}_k$ between Eqs. (63) and (65) and obtain

$$\mathbf{e}_k = (YY^\dagger - I)\mathbf{b}_k.$$

Then, using Eq. (62), we obtain the recursion relation

$$\mathbf{e}_{k+1} = (YY^\dagger - I)(\mathbf{b}_k + 2\rho\mathbf{e}_k^+)$$
$$= \mathbf{e}_k + 2\rho(YY^\dagger - I)\mathbf{e}_k^+, \tag{67}$$

so that

$$\tfrac{1}{4}\|\mathbf{e}_{k+1}\|^2 = \tfrac{1}{4}\|\mathbf{e}_k\|^2 + \rho\mathbf{e}_k^t(YY^\dagger - I)\mathbf{e}_k^+ + \|\rho(YY^\dagger - I)\mathbf{e}_k^+\|^2.$$

Both the second and the third terms simplify considerably. Since $\mathbf{e}_k^t Y = 0$, the second term becomes

$$\rho\mathbf{e}_k^t(YY^\dagger - I)\mathbf{e}_k^+ = -\rho\mathbf{e}_k^t\mathbf{e}_k^+ = -\rho\|\mathbf{e}_k^+\|^2,$$

the nonzero components of $\mathbf{e}_k^+$ being the positive components of $\mathbf{e}_k$. Since $YY^\dagger$ is symmetric and is equal to $(YY^\dagger)^t(YY^\dagger)$, the third term simplifies to

$$\|\rho(YY^\dagger - I)\mathbf{e}_k^+\|^2 = \rho^2\mathbf{e}_k^{+t}(YY^\dagger - I)^t(YY^\dagger - I)\mathbf{e}_k^+$$
$$= \rho^2\|\mathbf{e}_k^+\|^2 - \rho^2\mathbf{e}_k^{+t}YY^\dagger\mathbf{e}_{k,}^+.$$

Thus

$$\tfrac{1}{4}(\|\mathbf{e}_k\|^2 - \|\mathbf{e}_{k+1}\|^2) = \rho(1 - \rho)\|\mathbf{e}_k^+\|^2 + \rho^2\mathbf{e}_k^{+t}YY^\dagger\mathbf{e}_k^+. \tag{68}$$

Since $\mathbf{e}_k^+$ is nonzero by assumption, and since $YY^\dagger$ is positive semidefinite, $\|\mathbf{e}_k\|^2 > \|\mathbf{e}_{k+1}\|^2$ if $0 < \rho < 1$. Thus, the sequence $\|\mathbf{e}_1\|^2, \|\mathbf{e}_2\|^2, \ldots$ is monotonically decreasing and must converge to some limiting value $\|\mathbf{e}\|^2$. But for convergence to take place, $\mathbf{e}_k^+$ must converge to zero, so that all of the positive components of $\mathbf{e}_k$ must converge to zero. And since $\mathbf{e}_k^t\mathbf{b} = 0$ for all k, it follows that all of the components of $\mathbf{e}_k$ must converge to zero. Thus, if $0 < \rho < 1$ and if the samples are linearly separable, $\mathbf{a}_k$ will converge to a solution vector as k goes to infinity.

If we test the signs of the components of $Y\mathbf{a}_k$ at each step and terminate the algorithm when they are all positive, we will in fact obtain a separating vector in a finite number of steps. This follows from the fact that $Y\mathbf{a}_k = \mathbf{b}_k + \mathbf{e}_k$, and that the components of $\mathbf{b}_k$ never decrease. Thus, if $\mathbf{b}_{\min}$ is the smallest component of $\mathbf{b}_1$ and if $\mathbf{e}_k$ converges to zero, $\mathbf{e}_k$ must enter the hypersphere $\|\mathbf{e}_k\| = b_{\min}$ after a finite number of steps, at which point $Y\mathbf{a}_k > 0$. Although we ignored terminating conditions to simplify the proof, such a terminating condition would always be used in practice.

5.9.3 Nonseparable Behavior

If the convergence proof just given is examined to see how the assumption of separability was employed, it will be seen that it was needed twice. First, the fact that $\mathbf{e}_k^t\mathbf{b} = 0$ was used to show that either $\mathbf{e}_k = 0$ for some finite k, or $\mathbf{e}_k^+$ is never zero and corrections go on forever. Second, this same constraint was used to show that if $\mathbf{e}_k^+$ converges to zero, $\mathbf{e}_k$ must converge to zero.

If the samples are not linearly separable, it no longer follows that if $\mathbf{e}_k^+$ is zero then $\mathbf{e}_k$ must be zero. Indeed, on a nonseparable problem one may well obtain a nonzero error vector having no positive components. If this occurs, the algorithm automatically terminates and we have proof that the samples are not separable.

What happens if the patterns are not separable, but $\mathbf{e}_k^+$ is never zero? In this case it still follows that

$$\mathbf{e}_{k+1} = \mathbf{e}_k + 2\rho(YY^\dagger - I)\mathbf{e}_k^+ \tag{67}$$

and

$$\tfrac{1}{4}(\|\mathbf{e}_k\|^2 - \|\mathbf{e}_{k+1}\|^2) = \rho(1-\rho)\|\mathbf{e}_k^+\|^2 + \rho^2\mathbf{e}_k^{+t}YY^\dagger\mathbf{e}_k^+. \tag{68}$$

Thus, the sequence $\|\mathbf{e}_1\|^2, \|\mathbf{e}_2\|^2, \ldots$ must still converge, though the limiting value $\|\mathbf{e}\|^2$ can not be zero. Since convergence requires that $\mathbf{e}_k^+$ converge to zero, in the nonseparable case we conclude that either $\mathbf{e}_k^+ = 0$ for some finite k, or $\mathbf{e}_k^+$ converges to zero while $\|\mathbf{e}_k\|$ is bounded away from zero. Thus, the Ho–Kashyap algorithm provides us with a separating vector in the separable case, and with evidence of nonseparability in the nonseparable case. However, there is no bound on the number of steps needed to disclose nonseparability.

5.9.4 Some Related Procedures

If we write $Y^\dagger = (Y^tY)^{-1}Y^t$ and make use of the fact that $Y^t\mathbf{e}_k = 0$, we can rewrite the Ho–Kashyap algorithm as

$$\left.\begin{aligned}
&\mathbf{b}_1 > 0 \text{ but otherwise arbitrary} \\
&\mathbf{a}_1 = Y^\dagger\mathbf{b}_1 \\
&\mathbf{b}_{k+1} = \mathbf{b}_k + \rho(\mathbf{e}_k + |\mathbf{e}_k|) \\
&\mathbf{a}_{k+1} = \mathbf{a}_k + \rho Y^\dagger|\mathbf{e}_k|
\end{aligned}\right\}, \tag{69}$$

where, as usual,

$$\mathbf{e}_k = Y\mathbf{a}_k - \mathbf{b}_k. \tag{70}$$

This algorithm differs from the perceptron and relaxation algorithms for solving linear inequalities in at least three ways: (1) it varies both the weight vector $\mathbf{a}$ and the margin vector $\mathbf{b}$, (2) it provides evidence of nonseparability, but (3) it requires the computation of the pseudoinverse of Y. Even though this last computation need be done only once, it can be time consuming, and it requires special treatment if Y^tY is singular. An interesting alternative algorithm that resembles Eq. (69) but avoids the need for computing $Y^\dagger$ is

$$\left.\begin{array}{ll} \mathbf{b}_1 > 0 & \text{but otherwise arbitrary} \\[6pt] \mathbf{a}_1 & \text{arbitrary} \\[6pt] \mathbf{b}_{k+1} = \mathbf{b}_k + (\mathbf{e}_k + |\mathbf{e}_k|) \\[6pt] \mathbf{a}_{k+1} = \mathbf{a}_k + \rho R\,Y^t\,|\mathbf{e}_k| \end{array}\right\}, \tag{71}$$

where R is an arbitrary, constant, positive-definite $\hat{d}$-by-$\hat{d}$ matrix. We shall show that if ρ is properly chosen, this algorithm also yields a solution vector in a finite number of steps, provided that a solution exists. Furthermore, if no solution exists the vector $Y^t\,|\mathbf{e}_k|$ either vanishes, exposing the nonseparability, or converges to zero.

The proof is fairly straightforward. Whether the samples are linearly separable or not, Eqs. (70) and (71) show that

$$\begin{aligned} \mathbf{e}_{k+1} &= Y\mathbf{a}_{k+1} - \mathbf{b}_{k+1} \\ &= (\rho\,YRY^t - I)\,|\mathbf{e}_k|. \end{aligned}$$

Thus,

$$\|\mathbf{e}_{k+1}\|^2 = |\mathbf{e}_k|^t\,(\rho^2\,YRY^tYRY - 2\rho\,YRY^t + I)\,|\mathbf{e}_k|$$

and

$$\|\mathbf{e}_k\|^2 - \|\mathbf{e}_{k+1}\|^2 = (Y^t\,|\mathbf{e}_k|)^t A(\,Y^t\,|\mathbf{e}_k|), \tag{72}$$

where

$$A = 2\rho R - \rho^2 RY^tR. \tag{73}$$

Clearly, if ρ is positive but sufficiently small, A will be approximately $2\rho R$ and hence positive definite. Thus, if $Y^t\,|\mathbf{e}_k| \neq 0$ we will have $\|\mathbf{e}_k\|^2 > \|\mathbf{e}_{k+1}\|^2$.

At this point we must distinguish between the separable and the nonseparable case. In the separable case there exists an $\hat{\mathbf{a}}$ and a $\hat{\mathbf{b}} > 0$ satisfying $Y\hat{\mathbf{a}} = \hat{\mathbf{b}}$. Thus, if $|\mathbf{e}_k| \neq 0$,

$$|\mathbf{e}_k|^t\,Y\hat{\mathbf{a}} = |\mathbf{e}_k|^t\hat{\mathbf{b}} > 0,$$

so that $Y^t |\mathbf{e}_k|$ can not be zero unless $\mathbf{e}_k$ is zero. Thus, the sequence $\|\mathbf{e}_1\|^2$, $\|\mathbf{e}_2\|^2$, ... is monotonically decreasing and must converge* to some limiting value $\|\mathbf{e}\|^2$. But for convergence to take place, $Y^t |\mathbf{e}_k|$ must converge to zero, which implies that $|\mathbf{e}_k|$ and hence $\mathbf{e}_k$ must converge to zero. Since $\mathbf{e}_k$ starts out positive and never decreases, it follows that $\mathbf{a}_k$ must converge to a separating vector. Moreover, by the same argument used before, a solution must actually be obtained after a finite number of steps.

In the nonseparable case, $\mathbf{e}_k$ can neither be zero nor converge to zero. It may happen that $Y^t |\mathbf{e}_k| = 0$ at some step, which would provide proof of nonseparability. However, it is also possible for the sequence of corrections to go on forever. In this case, it again follows that the sequence $\|\mathbf{e}_1\|^2$, $\|\mathbf{e}_2\|^2$, ... must converge to a limiting value $\|\mathbf{e}\|^2 \neq 0$, and that $Y^t |\mathbf{e}_k|$ must converge to zero. Thus, we again obtain evidence of nonseparability in the nonseparable case.

Before closing this discussion, let us look briefly at the question of choosing ρ and R. The simplest choice for R is the identity matrix, in which case $A = 2\rho I - \rho^2 Y^t Y$. This matrix will be positive definite, thereby assuring convergence, if $0 < \rho < 2/\lambda_{\max}$, where $\lambda_{\max}$ is the largest eigenvalue of $Y^t Y$. Since the trace of $Y^t Y$ is both the sum of the eigenvalues of $Y^t Y$ and the sum of the squares of the elements of Y, one can use the pessimistic bound $\partial \lambda_{\max} \leq \sum \|\mathbf{y}_i\|^2$ in selecting a value for ρ.

A more interesting approach is to change ρ at each step, selecting that value that maximizes $\|\mathbf{e}_k\|^2 - \|\mathbf{e}_{k+1}\|^2$. Eqs. (72) and (73) give

$$\|\mathbf{e}_k\|^2 - \|\mathbf{e}_{k+1}\|^2 = |\mathbf{e}_k|^t\, Y(2\rho R - \rho^2 R Y^t Y R) Y^t |\mathbf{e}_k|. \qquad (74)$$

By differentiating with respect to ρ, we obtain the optimal value

$$\rho_k = \frac{|\mathbf{e}_k|^t\, Y R Y^t |\mathbf{e}_k|}{|\mathbf{e}_k|^t\, Y R Y^t Y R Y^t |\mathbf{e}_k|}, \qquad (75)$$

which, for $R = I$, simplifies to

$$\rho_k = \frac{\|\, Y^t |\mathbf{e}_k|\, \|^2}{\|\, Y Y^t |\mathbf{e}_k|\, \|^2}. \qquad (76)$$

This same approach can also be used to select the matrix R. By replacing R in Eq. (74) by the symmetric matrix $R + \delta R$ and neglecting second-order terms, we obtain

$$\delta(\|\mathbf{e}_k\|^2 - \|\mathbf{e}_{k+1}\|^2) = |\mathbf{e}_k|\, Y[\delta R^t(I - \rho Y^t Y R) + (I - \rho R Y^t Y)\, \delta R] Y^t |\mathbf{e}_k|.$$

---

* It is possible, of course, that at some step we obtain $\mathbf{e}_k = 0$, in which case convergence occurs at that point.

Thus, the decrease in the squared error vector is maximized by the choice

$$R = \frac{1}{\rho}(Y^tY)^{-1} \qquad (77)$$

and since $\rho R Y^t = Y^\dagger$, the descent algorithm becomes virtually identical with the original Ho–Kashyap algorithm.

5.10 LINEAR PROGRAMMING PROCEDURES

5.10.1 Linear Programming

The perceptron, relaxation, and Ho–Kashyap procedures are basically gradient descent procedures for solving simultaneous linear inequalities. Linear programming techniques are procedures for maximizing or minimizing linear functions subject to linear equality or inequality constraints. This at once suggests that one might be able to solve linear inequalities by using them as the constraints in a suitable linear programming problem. In this section we shall consider two of several ways that this can be done. The reader need have no knowledge of linear programming to understand these formulations, though such knowledge would certainly be useful in applying the techniques.

A classical linear programming problem can be stated as follows: Find a vector $\mathbf{u} = (u_1, \ldots, u_m)^t$ that minimizes the linear *objective function*

$$z = \boldsymbol{\alpha}^t \mathbf{u} \qquad (78)$$

subject to the constraint

$$A\mathbf{u} \geq \boldsymbol{\beta}, \qquad (79)$$

where $\boldsymbol{\alpha}$ is an m-by-1 *cost vector*, $\boldsymbol{\beta}$ is an l-by-1 vector, and A is an l-by-m matrix. The *simplex algorithm*, described in any text on linear programming, is the classical iterative procedure for solving this problem. For technical reasons, it requires the imposition of one more constraint, viz.,

$$\mathbf{u} \geq 0. \qquad (80)$$

If we think of $\mathbf{u}$ as being the weight vector $\mathbf{a}$, this constraint is unacceptable, since in most cases the solution vector will have both positive and negative components. However, suppose that we write

$$\mathbf{a} = \mathbf{a}^+ - \mathbf{a}^-, \qquad (81)$$

where

$$\mathbf{a}^+ = \tfrac{1}{2}(|\mathbf{a}| + \mathbf{a}) \qquad (82)$$

and

$$\mathbf{a}^- = \tfrac{1}{2}(|\mathbf{a}| - \mathbf{a}). \qquad (83)$$

Then both $\mathbf{a}^+$ and $\mathbf{a}^-$ are nonnegative, and by identifying the components of $\mathbf{u}$ with the components of $\mathbf{a}^+$ and $\mathbf{a}^-$, for example, we can accept the constraint $\mathbf{u} \geq 0$.

5.10.2 The Linearly Separable Case

Suppose that we have a set of n samples $\mathbf{y}_1, \ldots, \mathbf{y}_n$ and we want a weight vector $\mathbf{a}$ that satisfies $\mathbf{a}^t \mathbf{y}_i \geq b_i > 0$ for all i. How can we formulate this as a linear programming problem? One approach is to introduce what is called an *artificial variable* t by writing

$$\mathbf{a}^t \mathbf{y}_i + t \geq b_i$$

and

$$t \geq 0.$$

If t is sufficiently large, there is no problem in satisfying these constraints; for example, they are satisfied if $\mathbf{a} = 0$ and $t = \max_i b_i$.* However, this hardly solves our original problem. What we want is a solution with $t = 0$, which is the smallest value t can have and still satisfy $t \geq 0$. Thus, we are led to consider the following problem: Minimize t over all values of t and $\mathbf{a}$ that satisfy the conditions $\mathbf{a}^t \mathbf{y}_i + t \geq b_i$ and $t \geq 0$. If the answer is zero, the samples are linearly separable, and we have a solution. If the answer is positive, there is no separating vector, but we have proof that the samples are nonseparable.

Formally, our problem is to find a vector $\mathbf{u}$ that minimizes the objective function $z = \boldsymbol{\alpha}^t \mathbf{u}$ subject to the constraints $A\mathbf{u} \geq \boldsymbol{\beta}$ and $\mathbf{u} \geq 0$, where

$$A = \begin{bmatrix} \mathbf{y}_1^t & -\mathbf{y}_1^t & 1 \\ \mathbf{y}_2^t & -\mathbf{y}_2^t & 1 \\ \cdot & \cdot & \cdot \\ \cdot & \cdot & \cdot \\ \cdot & \cdot & \cdot \\ \mathbf{y}_n^t & -\mathbf{y}_n^t & 1 \end{bmatrix}, \quad \mathbf{u} = \begin{bmatrix} \mathbf{a}^+ \\ \mathbf{a}^- \\ t \end{bmatrix}, \quad \boldsymbol{\alpha} = \begin{bmatrix} 0 \\ 0 \\ 1 \end{bmatrix}, \quad \boldsymbol{\beta} = \begin{bmatrix} b_1 \\ b_2 \\ \cdot \\ \cdot \\ \cdot \\ b_n \end{bmatrix}.$$

Thus, the linear programming problem involves $m = 2\hat{d} + 1$ variables and $l = n$ constraints, plus the simplex algorithm constraints $\mathbf{u} \geq 0$. The simplex

---

* In linear programming terminology, any solution satisfying the constraints is called a *feasible solution*. A feasible solution for which the number of nonzero variables does not exceed the number of constraints (not counting the simplex requirement for nonnegative variables) is called a *basic feasible solution*. Thus, the solution $\mathbf{a} = 0$ and $t = \max_i b_i$ is a basic feasible solution. Possession of such a solution simplifies the application of the simplex algorithm.

algorithm will find the minimum value of the objective function $z = \boldsymbol{\alpha}^t \mathbf{u} = t$ in a finite number of steps, and will exhibit a vector $\hat{\mathbf{u}}$ yielding that value. If the samples are linearly separable, the minimum value of t will be zero, and a solution vector $\hat{\mathbf{a}}$ can be obtained from $\hat{\mathbf{u}}$. If the samples are not separable, the minimum value of t will be positive. The resulting $\hat{\mathbf{u}}$ is usually not very useful as an approximate solution, but at least one obtains proof of non-separability.

5.10.3 Minimizing the Perceptron Criterion Function

In most pattern classification applications one cannot assume that the samples are linearly separable. In particular, when the patterns are not separable, one still wants to obtain a weight vector that classifies as many samples correctly as possible. Unfortunately, the number of errors is not a linear function of the components of the weight vector, and its minimization is not a linear programming problem. However, it turns out that the problem of minimizing the perceptron criterion function can be posed as a problem in linear programming. Since minimization of this criterion function yields a separating vector in the separable case and a reasonable solution in the non-separable case, this approach is quite attractive.

The basic perceptron criterion function is given by

$$J_p(\mathbf{a}) = \sum_{\mathbf{y} \in \mathcal{Y}} (-\mathbf{a}^t \mathbf{y}), \tag{12}$$

where $\mathcal{Y}(\mathbf{a})$ is the set of samples misclassified by $\mathbf{a}$. To avoid the useless solution $\mathbf{a} = 0$, we introduce a positive margin vector $\mathbf{b}$ and write

$$J_p'(\mathbf{a}) = \sum_{\mathbf{y}_i \in \mathcal{Y}'} (b_i - \mathbf{a}^t \mathbf{y}_i), \tag{84}$$

where $\mathbf{y}_i \in \mathcal{Y}'$ if $\mathbf{a}^t \mathbf{y}_i \leq b_i$. Clearly, J_p' is a piecewise-linear function of $\mathbf{a}$, not a linear function, and linear programming techniques are not immediately applicable. However, by introducing n artificial variables and their constraints we can construct an equivalent linear objective function. Consider the problem of finding vectors $\mathbf{a}$ and $\mathbf{t}$ that minimize the linear function

$$z = \sum_{i=1}^{n} t_i$$

subject to the constraints

$$t_i \geq 0$$

and

$$t_i \geq b_i - \mathbf{a}^t \mathbf{y}_i.$$

Clearly, for any fixed value of $\mathbf{a}$, the minimum value of z is exactly equal to $J_p'(\mathbf{a})$, since under these constraints the best we can do is to take $t_i = \max(0, b_i - \mathbf{a}^t\mathbf{y}_i)$. If we minimize z over $\mathbf{t}$ *and* $\mathbf{a}$, we shall obtain the minimum possible value of $J_p'(\mathbf{a})$. Thus, we have converted the problem of minimizing $J_p'(\mathbf{a})$ to one of minimizing a linear function z subject to linear inequality constraints. Letting $\mathbf{u}_n$ denote an n-dimensional unit vector, we obtain the following problem with $m = 2\hat{d} + n$ variables and $l = n$ constraints: Minimize $\boldsymbol{\alpha}^t\mathbf{u}$ subject to $A\mathbf{u} \geq \boldsymbol{\beta}$ and $\mathbf{u} \geq 0$, where

$$
A = \begin{bmatrix}
\mathbf{y}_1^t & -\mathbf{y}_1^t & 1 & 0 & \cdots & 0 \\
\mathbf{y}_2^t & -\mathbf{y}_2^t & 0 & 1 & \cdots & 0 \\
\cdot & \cdot & \cdot & \cdot & & \cdot \\
\cdot & \cdot & \cdot & \cdot & & \cdot \\
\cdot & \cdot & \cdot & \cdot & & \cdot \\
\mathbf{y}_n^t & -\mathbf{y}_n^t & 0 & 0 & \cdots & 1
\end{bmatrix}, \quad
\mathbf{u} = \begin{bmatrix} \mathbf{a}^+ \\ \mathbf{a}^- \\ \mathbf{t} \end{bmatrix}, \quad
\boldsymbol{\alpha} = \begin{bmatrix} 0 \\ 0 \\ \mathbf{u}_n \end{bmatrix}, \quad
\boldsymbol{\beta} = \begin{bmatrix} b_1 \\ b_2 \\ \cdot \\ \cdot \\ \cdot \\ b_n \end{bmatrix}.
$$

The choice $\mathbf{a} = 0$ and $t_i = b_i$ provides a basic feasible solution to start the simplex algorithm, and the simplex algorithm will provide an $\hat{\mathbf{a}}$ minimizing $J_p'(\mathbf{a})$ in a finite number of steps.

5.10.4 Remarks

We have shown two ways to formulate the problem of finding a linear discriminant function as a problem in linear programming. There are other possible formulations, the ones involving the so-called *dual problem* being of particular interest from a computational standpoint. Generally speaking, methods such as the simplex method are merely sophisticated gradient descent methods for extremizing linear functions subject to linear constraints. The coding of a linear programming algorithm is usually more complicated than the coding of the simpler descent procedures we described earlier. However, general purpose linear programming packages can often be used directly or modified appropriately with relatively little effort. When this can be done, one can secure the advantage of guaranteed convergence on both separable and nonseparable problems.

The various algorithms for finding linear discriminant functions presented in this chapter are summarized in Table 5-1. It is natural to ask which one is best, but none uniformly dominates or is uniformly dominated by all others. The choice depends upon such considerations as desired characteristics, ease of programming, the number of samples, and the dimensionality of the samples. If a linear discriminant function can yield a low error rate, any of these procedures, intelligently applied, can provide good performance.

TABLE 5-1. Summary of Descent Procedures for Obtaining Linear Discriminant Functions

Name	Criterion Function	Descent Algorithm	Conditions	Remarks
Fixed Increment	$J_p = \sum\limits_{\mathbf{a}^t\mathbf{y}\le 0}(-\mathbf{a}^t\mathbf{y})$	$\mathbf{a}_{k+1} = \mathbf{a}_k + \mathbf{y}^k \qquad (\mathbf{a}_k^t\mathbf{y}^k \le 0)$	—	Finite convergence if linearly separable to solution with $\mathbf{a}^t\mathbf{y} > 0$; $\mathbf{a}_k$ always bounded.
Variable Increment	$J_p' = \sum\limits_{\mathbf{a}^t\mathbf{y}\le b}-(\mathbf{a}^t\mathbf{y}-b)$	$\mathbf{a}_{k+1} = \mathbf{a}_k + \rho_k\mathbf{y}^k \qquad (\mathbf{a}_k^t\mathbf{y}^k \le b)$	$\rho_k \ge 0,\ \Sigma\rho_k \to \infty,\ \dfrac{\Sigma\rho_k^2}{(\Sigma\rho_k)^2}\to 0$	Convergence if linearly separable to solution with $\mathbf{a}^t\mathbf{y} > b$. Finite convergence if $0 < \alpha \le \rho_k \le \beta < \infty$.
Relaxation	$J_r = \tfrac{1}{2}\sum\limits_{\mathbf{a}^t\mathbf{y}\le b}\dfrac{(\mathbf{a}^t\mathbf{y}-b)^2}{\|\mathbf{y}\|^2}$	$\mathbf{a}_{k+1} = \mathbf{a}_k + \rho\,\dfrac{b-\mathbf{a}_k^t\mathbf{y}^k}{\|\mathbf{y}^k\|^2}\,\mathbf{y}^k$ $(\mathbf{a}_k^t\mathbf{y}^k \le b)$	$0 < \rho < 2$	Convergence if linearly separable to solution with $\mathbf{a}^t\mathbf{y} \ge b$. If $b > 0$, finite convergence to solution with $\mathbf{a}^t\mathbf{y} > 0$.
Widrow-Hoff	$\tfrac{1}{2}J_s = \tfrac{1}{2}\sum(\mathbf{a}^t\mathbf{y}_i - b_i)^2$	$\mathbf{a}_{k+1} = \mathbf{a}_k + \rho_k(b_k - \mathbf{a}_k^t\mathbf{y}^k)\mathbf{y}^k$	$\rho_k > 0,\ \rho_k \to 0$	Tends toward solution minimizing J_s.
Stochastic Approximation	$J_m = E[(\mathbf{a}^t\mathbf{y} - z)^2]$	$\mathbf{a}_{k+1} = \mathbf{a}_k + \rho_k(z_k - \mathbf{a}_k^t\mathbf{y}_k)\mathbf{y}_k$	$\Sigma\rho_k \to \infty,\ \Sigma\rho_k^2 \to L < \infty$	Involves an infinite number of randomly drawn samples; converges in mean square to a solution minimizing J_m; also provides a MSE approximation to Bayes discriminant.
		$\mathbf{a}_{k+1} = \mathbf{a}_k + R_k(z_k - \mathbf{a}_k^t\mathbf{y}_k)\mathbf{y}_k$	$R_{k+1}^{-1} = R_k^{-1} + \mathbf{y}_k\mathbf{y}_k^t$	

	Criterion function	Algorithm	Conditions	Properties
Pseudoinverse	$J_s = \|Ya - b\|^2$	$a = Y^\dagger b$		Classical MSE solution; special choices for **b** yield Fisher's linear discriminant and MSE approximation to Bayes discriminant.
Ho-Kashyap	$J_s = \|Ya - b\|^2$	$b_{k+1} = b_k + \rho(e_k + |e_k|)$ $e_k = Ya_k - b_k$ $a_k = Y^\dagger b_k$	$0 < \rho < 1,\ b_1 > 0$	a_k is MSE solution for each b_k; finite convergence if linearly separable; if $e_k \leq 0$ but $e_k \neq 0$, the samples are nonseparable.
		$b_{k+1} = b_k + (e_k + |e_k|)$ $a_{k+1} = a_k + \rho_k R Y^t |e_k|$	$\rho_k = \dfrac{|e_k|^t Y R Y^t |e_k|}{|e_k|^t Y R Y^t Y R Y^t |e_k|}$ is optimum; R symmetric, positive definite; $b_1 > 0$	Finite convergence if linearly separable; if $Y^t|e_k| = 0$ but $e_k \neq 0$, the samples are nonseparable.
Linear Programming	$t = \max_{a^t y_i \leq b_i} [-(a^t y_i - b_i)]$	Simplex algorithm	$a^t y_i + t \geq b_i,\ t \geq 0$	Finite convergence in both separable and nonseparable cases; useful solution only if separable.
	$J'_p = \sum_{i=1}^{n} t_i = \sum_{a^t y_i \leq b_i} -(a^t y_i - b_i)$	Simplex algorithm	$a^t y_i + t_i \geq b_i,\ t_i \geq 0$	Finite convergence to solution minimizing perceptron criterion function whether separable or not.

5.11   THE METHOD OF POTENTIAL FUNCTIONS

A discussion of methods for determining linear discriminant functions would not be complete without mentioning the method of potential functions. This approach is related to several of the techniques we have discussed, including Parzen-window estimates, the perceptron procedure, and stochastic approximation. The method originally developed from the idea that if the samples x_i were thought of as points in space, and if electrical charges q_i were placed at these points, positive if x_i were labelled ω_1 and negative if x_i were labelled ω_2, then perhaps the resulting electrostatic potential would serve as a useful discriminant function (see Figure 5.12). If the potential at a point x due to a unit charge at a point x_i is $K(x, x_i)$, then the potential due to n charges is given by

$$g(x) = \sum_{i=1}^{n} q_i K(x, x_i). \tag{85}$$

The *potential function* $K(x, x_i)$ of classical physics varies inversely with $\|x - x_i\|$, but many other functions are equally suitable. There is a clear analogy between $K(x, x_i)$ and the Parzen-window function $\varphi[(x - x_i)/h]$, and the behavior of the discriminant function $g(x)$ is generally similar to the behavior of the difference of the Parzen-window estimates of two densities. However, since we are interested only in constructing a useful discriminant function, we are much less constrained in choosing a potential function than

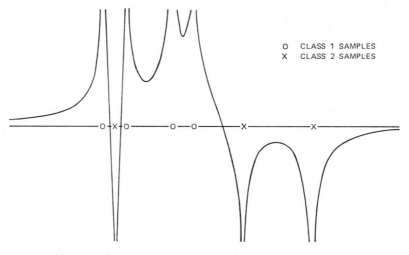

O   CLASS 1 SAMPLES
X   CLASS 2 SAMPLES

FIGURE 5.12.   The potential field as a discriminant function.

we are in choosing a window function. The most frequently suggested potential functions are maximum when $\mathbf{x} = \mathbf{x}_i$ and decrease monotonically to zero as $\|\mathbf{x} - \mathbf{x}_i\|$ approaches infinity. However, even these constraints can be ignored if it is convenient to do so.

Suppose that we have a set of n samples and we construct a discriminant function according to Eq. (85). Suppose further that we check one of the samples, say $\mathbf{x}_k$, and discover that it is misclassified by $g(\mathbf{x})$. Then it is natural to think of changing q_k slightly in an attempt to correct the error.* Suppose that we either add a unit charge to q_k if $\mathbf{x}_k$ is labelled ω_1 or subtract a unit charge if $\mathbf{x}_k$ is labelled ω_2. If we let $g'(\mathbf{x})$ denote the discriminant function after the correction, we see that this leads to the following algorithm for constructing a discriminant function:

$$g'(\mathbf{x}) = \begin{cases} g(\mathbf{x}) + K(\mathbf{x}, \mathbf{x}_k) & \text{if } \mathbf{x}_k \text{ is labelled } \omega_1 \quad \text{and } g(\mathbf{x}_k) \le 0 \\ g(\mathbf{x}) - K(\mathbf{x}, \mathbf{x}_k) & \text{if } \mathbf{x}_k \text{ is labelled } \omega_2 \quad \text{and } g(\mathbf{x}_k) \ge 0 \quad (86) \\ g(\mathbf{x}) & \text{otherwise.} \end{cases}$$

This error-correction rule bears a close resemblance to the fixed-increment rule. The exact nature of this relation becomes clear if it is possible to represent $K(\mathbf{x}, \mathbf{x}_k)$ by the symmetric, finite expansion

$$K(\mathbf{x}, \mathbf{x}_k) = \sum_{j=1}^{\hat{d}} y_j(\mathbf{x}) y_j(\mathbf{x}_k) = \mathbf{y}_k^t \mathbf{y}. \quad (87)$$

where $\mathbf{y} = \mathbf{y}(\mathbf{x})$ and $\mathbf{y}_k = \mathbf{y}(\mathbf{x}_k)$. Substituting this in Eq. (85), we obtain

$$g(\mathbf{x}) = \mathbf{a}^t \mathbf{y},$$

where

$$\mathbf{a} = \sum_{i=1}^{n} q_i \mathbf{y}_i.$$

Furthermore, the algorithm for changing $g(\mathbf{x})$ to $g'(\mathbf{x})$ is merely the unnormalized fixed-increment rule,

$$\mathbf{a}' = \begin{cases} \mathbf{a} + \mathbf{y}_k & \text{if } \mathbf{y}_k \text{ is labelled } \omega_1 \quad \text{and } \mathbf{a}^t \mathbf{y}_k \le 0 \\ \mathbf{a} - \mathbf{y}_k & \text{if } \mathbf{y}_k \text{ is labelled } \omega_2 \quad \text{and } \mathbf{a}^t \mathbf{y}_k \ge 0 \\ \mathbf{a} & \text{otherwise.} \end{cases}$$

Thus, when $K(\mathbf{x}, \mathbf{x}_k)$ has the form of Eq. (87), we can prove convergence by the same techniques we used for the fixed-increment rule. Moreover, it is

---

* If the potential function peaks sufficiently sharply relative to the distance between samples, it is clear that we can always adjust the charges so that all of the samples are correctly classified. However, if the potential function is relatively spread out, this may not be the case.

clear that we can take the other procedures, such as the relaxation, MSE, and stochastic approximation procedures, and immediately obtain parallel procedures and convergence proofs involving potential functions.

The method of potential functions is not restricted to potential functions having finite expansions, however. Any convenient function, such as

$$K(\mathbf{x}, \mathbf{x}_k) = \frac{\sigma^2}{\sigma^2 + \|\mathbf{x} - \mathbf{x}_k\|^2}$$

or

$$K(\mathbf{x}, \mathbf{x}_k) = \exp\left[-\frac{1}{2\sigma^2} \|\mathbf{x} - \mathbf{x}_k\|^2 \right],$$

can be selected for a potential function,* and a discriminant function can be obtained by considering the samples in a sequence $\mathbf{x}^1, \mathbf{x}^2, \ldots, \mathbf{x}^k, \ldots$, and using iterative rules such as

$$g_{k+1}(\mathbf{x}) = g_k(\mathbf{x}) + r_k(\mathbf{x}, \mathbf{x}^k)K(\mathbf{x}, \mathbf{x}^k),$$

where r_k is some function of the error.

From a practical standpoint, this use of the method of potential functions encounters many of the same problems encountered with the use of Parzen-window estimates. The potential function must be carefully chosen to obtain good interpolation between sample points. If the number of samples is large, the computational problems are severe. This procedure is most attractive when either the number of samples is small, or the dimensionality of $\mathbf{x}$ is sufficiently small to allow $g(\mathbf{x})$ to be stored as a table for discrete values of $\mathbf{x}$.

5.12 MULTICATEGORY GENERALIZATIONS

5.12.1 Kesler's Construction

There is no uniform way to extend all of the two-category procedures we have discussed to the multicategory case. In Section 5.2.2 we defined a multicategory classifier called a linear machine which classifies a pattern by computing c linear discriminant functions

$$g_i(\mathbf{x}) = \mathbf{w}_i^t \mathbf{x} + w_{i0} \qquad i = 1, \ldots, c,$$

* Those familiar with integral equations will see the similarity between $K(\mathbf{x}, \mathbf{x}_k)$ and the kernel $K(s, t)$. Under certain conditions, symmetric kernels possess infinite series expansions of the form $\sum \varphi_i(s)\varphi_i(t)/\lambda_i$, where the φ_i and λ_i are the eigenfunctions and eigenvalues of K, respectively (see Courant and Hilbert, Chapter Three, 1953). The familiar orthogonal functions of mathematical physics are eigenfunctions of symmetric kernels, and their use is often suggested for the construction of potential functions. However, these suggestions are more appealing for their mathematical beauty than their practical usefulness.

and assigning $\mathbf{x}$ to the category corresponding to the largest discriminant. This is a natural generalization for the multiclass case, particularly in view of the results of Chapter 2 for the multivariate normal problem. It can obviously be extended to generalized linear discriminant functions by letting $\mathbf{y}(\mathbf{x})$ be a $\hat{d}$-dimensional vector of functions of $\mathbf{x}$, and by writing

$$g_i(\mathbf{x}) = \mathbf{a}_i^t \mathbf{y} \qquad i = 1, \ldots, c, \tag{88}$$

where again $\mathbf{x}$ is assigned to ω_i if $g_i(\mathbf{x}) > g_j(\mathbf{x})$ for all $j \neq i$.

The generalization of our procedures from a two-category linear classifier to a multicategory linear machine is simplest in the linearly-separable case. Suppose that we have a set of labelled samples $\mathbf{y}_1, \mathbf{y}_2, \ldots, \mathbf{y}_n$, with n_1 in the subset $\mathcal{Y}_1$ labelled ω_1, n_2 in the subset $\mathcal{Y}_2$ labelled $\omega_2, \ldots$, and n_c in the subset $\mathcal{Y}_c$ labelled ω_c. We say that this set is linearly separable if there exists a linear machine that classifies all of them correctly. That is, if these samples are linearly separable, then there exists a set of weight vectors $\hat{\mathbf{a}}_1, \ldots, \hat{\mathbf{a}}_c$ such that if $\mathbf{y}_k \in \mathcal{Y}_i$, then

$$\hat{\mathbf{a}}_i^t \mathbf{y}_k > \hat{\mathbf{a}}_j^t \mathbf{y}_k \tag{89}$$

for all $j \neq i$.

One of the pleasant things about this definition is that it is possible to manipulate these inequalities and reduce the multicategory problem to the two-category case. Suppose for the moment that $\mathbf{y} \in \mathcal{Y}_1$, so that Eq. (89) becomes

$$\hat{\mathbf{a}}_1^t \mathbf{y} - \hat{\mathbf{a}}_j^t \mathbf{y} > 0, \qquad j = 2, \ldots, c. \tag{90}$$

This set of $c - 1$ inequalities can be thought of as requiring that the $c\hat{d}$-dimensional weight vector

$$\hat{\boldsymbol{\alpha}} = \begin{bmatrix} \mathbf{a}_1 \\ \mathbf{a}_2 \\ \cdot \\ \cdot \\ \cdot \\ \mathbf{a}_c \end{bmatrix}$$

correctly classifies all $c - 1$ of the $c\hat{d}$-dimensional samples

$$\boldsymbol{\eta}_{12} = \begin{bmatrix} \mathbf{y} \\ -\mathbf{y} \\ \mathbf{0} \\ \cdot \\ \cdot \\ \cdot \\ \mathbf{0} \end{bmatrix} \quad \boldsymbol{\eta}_{13} = \begin{bmatrix} \mathbf{y} \\ \mathbf{0} \\ -\mathbf{y} \\ \cdot \\ \cdot \\ \cdot \\ \mathbf{0} \end{bmatrix} \quad \cdots \quad \boldsymbol{\eta}_{1c} = \begin{bmatrix} \mathbf{y} \\ \mathbf{0} \\ \mathbf{0} \\ \cdot \\ \cdot \\ \cdot \\ -\mathbf{y} \end{bmatrix}.$$

More generally, if $\mathbf{y} \in \mathscr{Y}_i$, we construct $(c - 1)$ $c\hat{d}$-dimensional samples $\boldsymbol{\eta}_{ij}$ by partitioning $\boldsymbol{\eta}_{ij}$ into $c\hat{d}$-dimensional subvectors, with the ith subvector being $\mathbf{y}$, the jth being $-\mathbf{y}$, and all others being zero. Clearly, if $\hat{\boldsymbol{\alpha}}^t \boldsymbol{\eta}_{ij} > 0$ for all $j \neq i$, then the linear machine corresponding to the components of $\hat{\boldsymbol{\alpha}}$ classifies $\mathbf{y}$ correctly.

This construction, due to Carl Kesler, multiplies the dimensionality of the data by c and the number of samples by $c - 1$, which does not make its direct use attractive. Its importance resides in the fact that it allows us to convert many multicategory error-correction procedures to two-category procedures for the purpose of obtaining a convergence proof.

5.12.2   The Fixed-Increment Rule

In this section we shall use Kesler's construction to obtain a convergence proof for a generalization of the fixed-increment rule for a linear machine. Suppose that we have a set of n linearly-separable samples $\mathbf{y}_1, \ldots, \mathbf{y}_n$, and we use them to form an infinite sequence in which every sample appears infinitely often. Let L_k denote the linear machine whose weight vectors are $\mathbf{a}_1(k), \ldots, \mathbf{a}_c(k)$. Starting with an arbitrary initial linear machine L_1, we want to use the sequence of samples to construct a sequence of linear machines that converges to a solution machine, one that classifies all of the samples correctly. We shall propose an error-correction rule, in which weight changes are made if and only if the present linear machine misclassifies a sample. Let $\mathbf{y}^k$ denote the kth sample requiring correction, and suppose that $\mathbf{y}^k \in \mathscr{Y}_i$. Since $\mathbf{y}^k$ requires correction, there must be at least one $j \neq i$ for which

$$\cdot \mathbf{a}_i(k)^t \mathbf{y}^k \leq \mathbf{a}_j(k)^t \mathbf{y}^k. \tag{91}$$

Then, the fixed-increment rule for correcting L_k is

$$\left. \begin{aligned} \mathbf{a}_i(k + 1) &= \mathbf{a}_i(k) + \mathbf{y}^k \\ \mathbf{a}_j(k + 1) &= \mathbf{a}_j(k) - \mathbf{y}^k \\ \mathbf{a}_l(k + 1) &= \mathbf{a}_l(k), \quad l \neq i \text{ and } l \neq j. \end{aligned} \right\} \tag{92}$$

We shall now show that this rule must lead to a solution machine after a finite number of corrections. The proof is simple. For each linear machine L_k there corresponds a weight vector

$$\boldsymbol{\alpha}_k = \begin{bmatrix} \mathbf{a}_1(k) \\ \cdot \\ \cdot \\ \cdot \\ \mathbf{a}_c(k) \end{bmatrix}. \tag{93}$$

For each sample $\mathbf{y} \in \mathcal{Y}_i$ there are $c - 1$ samples $\boldsymbol{\eta}_{ij}$ formed as described in the previous section. In particular, corresponding to the vector $\mathbf{y}^k$ satisfying Eq. (91) there is a vector

$$
\boldsymbol{\eta}_{ij}^k = \begin{bmatrix} \vdots \\ \mathbf{y}^k \\ \vdots \\ -\mathbf{y}^k \\ \vdots \end{bmatrix} \begin{matrix} \\ \leftarrow i \\ \\ \leftarrow j \\ \end{matrix}
$$

satisfying

$$
\boldsymbol{\alpha}_k^t \boldsymbol{\eta}_{ij}^k \leq 0.
$$

Furthermore, the fixed-increment rule for correcting L_k is exactly the same as the fixed-increment rule for correcting $\boldsymbol{\alpha}_k$, viz.,

$$
\boldsymbol{\alpha}_{k+1} = \boldsymbol{\alpha}_k + \boldsymbol{\eta}_{ij}^k.
$$

Thus, we have obtained a complete correspondence between the multi-category case and the two-category case, in which the multicategory procedure produces a sequence of samples $\boldsymbol{\eta}^1, \boldsymbol{\eta}^2, \ldots, \boldsymbol{\eta}^k, \ldots$ and a sequence of weight vectors $\boldsymbol{\alpha}_1, \boldsymbol{\alpha}_2, \ldots, \boldsymbol{\alpha}_k, \ldots$. By our results for the two-category case, this latter sequence can not be infinite, but must terminate in a solution vector. Hence, the sequence $L_1, L_2, \ldots, L_k, \ldots$ must terminate in a solution machine after a finite number of corrections.

This use of Kesler's construction to establish equivalences between multi-category and two-category procedures is a powerful theoretical tool. It can be used to extend all of our results for the perceptron and relaxation procedures to the multicategory case, and applies as well to the error-correction rules for the method of potential functions. Unfortunately, it is not as directly useful in generalizing the MSE or the linear programming approaches.

5.12.3   Generalizations for MSE Procedures

Perhaps the simplest way to obtain a natural generalization of the MSE procedures to the multiclass case is to consider the problem as a set of c two-class problems. The ith problem is to obtain a weight vector $\mathbf{a}_i$ that is a minimum-squared-error solution to the equations

$$\left. \begin{array}{ll} \mathbf{a}_i^t \mathbf{y} = 1 & \text{for all } \mathbf{y} \in \mathcal{Y}_i \\ \mathbf{a}_i^t \mathbf{y} = -1 & \text{for all } \mathbf{y} \notin \mathcal{Y}_i. \end{array} \right\}$$

In view of the results of Section 5.8.3, we can say that when the number of samples is very large we will obtain a minimum mean-squared-error approximation to the Bayes discriminant function

$$P(\omega_i \mid \mathbf{x}) - P(\text{not } \omega_i \mid \mathbf{x}) = 2P(\omega_i \mid \mathbf{x}) - 1.$$

This observation has two immediate consequences. First, it suggests a modification in which we seek a weight vector $\mathbf{a}_i$ that is a minimum-squared-error solution to the equations

$$\left. \begin{array}{ll} \mathbf{a}_i^t \mathbf{y} = 1 & \text{for all } \mathbf{y} \in \mathcal{Y}_i \\ \mathbf{a}_i^t \mathbf{y} = 0 & \text{for all } \mathbf{y} \notin \mathcal{Y}_i, \end{array} \right\} \tag{94}$$

so that $\mathbf{a}^t \mathbf{y}$ will be a minimum mean-squared-error approximation to $P(\omega_i \mid \mathbf{x})$. Second, it justifies the use of the resulting discriminant functions in a linear machine, in which we assign $\mathbf{y}$ to ω_i if $\mathbf{a}_i^t \mathbf{y} > \mathbf{a}_j^t \mathbf{y}$ for all $j \neq i$.

The pseudoinverse solution to the multiclass MSE problem can be written in a form analogous to the form for the two-class case. Let Y be the n-by-$\hat{d}$ matrix of samples, which we assume to be partitioned as

$$Y = \begin{bmatrix} Y_1 \\ Y_2 \\ \cdot \\ \cdot \\ \bullet \\ Y_c \end{bmatrix}, \tag{95}$$

with the samples labelled ω_i comprising the rows of Y_i. Similarly, let A be the $\hat{d}$-by-c matrix of weight vectors

$$A = [\mathbf{a}_1 \mathbf{a}_2 \cdots \mathbf{a}_c], \tag{96}$$

and let B be the n-by-c matrix

$$B = \begin{bmatrix} B_1 \\ B_2 \\ \cdot \\ \cdot \\ \cdot \\ B_c \end{bmatrix}, \tag{97}$$

where all of the elements of B_i are zero except for those in the ith column, which are unity. Then the trace of the "squared" error matrix $(YA - B)^t \times (YA - B)$ is minimized by the solution*

$$A = Y^\dagger B, \tag{98}$$

where, as usual, $Y^\dagger$ is the pseudoinverse of Y.

This result can be generalized in a theoretically interesting fashion. Let λ_{ij} be the loss incurred for deciding ω_i when the true state of nature is ω_j, and let the jth submatrix of B be given by

$$B_j = - \begin{bmatrix} \lambda_{1j} & \lambda_{2j} & \cdots & \lambda_{cj} \\ \lambda_{1j} & \lambda_{2j} & \cdots & \lambda_{cj} \\ \cdot & & & \\ \cdot & & & \\ \cdot & & & \\ \lambda_{1j} & \lambda_{2j} & \cdots & \lambda_{cj} \end{bmatrix} \updownarrow n_j \qquad j = 1, \ldots, c. \tag{99}$$

Then, as the number of samples approaches infinity, the solution $A = Y^\dagger B$ yields discriminant functions $\mathbf{a}_i\mathbf{y}$ which provide a minimum-mean-square-error approximation to the Bayes discriminant function

$$g_{0i}(\mathbf{x}) = - \sum_{j=1}^c \lambda_{ij} P(\omega_j \mid \mathbf{x}). \tag{100}$$

The proof of this result is a direct extension of the proof given in Section 5.8.3, and, following time-honored tradition, we leave it as an exercise for the reader.

5.13 BIBLIOGRAPHICAL AND HISTORICAL REMARKS

Because linear discriminant functions are so amenable to analysis, far more papers have been written about them than the subject deserves. Thus, the following list of references, long as it is, is by no means exhaustive. Historically, all of this work begins with the classic paper by R. A. Fisher (1936). The application of linear discriminant functions to pattern classification was well described by Highleyman (1962), who posed the problem of finding the

* If we let $\mathbf{b}_i$ denote the ith column of B, the trace of $(YA - B)^t(YA - B)$ is equal to the sum of the squared lengths of the error vectors $Y\mathbf{a}_i - \mathbf{b}_i$. The solution $A = Y^\dagger B$ not only minimizes this sum, but it also minimizes each term in the sum.

optimal (minimum-risk) linear discriminant, and proposed plausible gradient descent procedures* to determine a solution from samples. Unfortunately, little can be said about such procedures without knowing the underlying distributions, and even then the situation is analytically complex (cf., Anderson and Bahadur, 1962).

While this work was statistically oriented, many of the pattern recognition papers that appeared in the late 1950's and early 1960's adopted other viewpoints. One viewpoint was that of neural-net brain models, in which individual neurons were modelled as threshold elements, two-category linear machines. This work had its origins in a famous paper by McCulloch and Pitts (1943), and tended to emphasize the goal of error-free performance and the feature of adaptivity or learning. Rosenblatt's perceptron (Rosenblatt, 1957, 1962; Block, 1962) employed various reinforcement rules for changing the neural weight values to improve performance. The best known of these was the fixed-increment rule, which guaranteed error-free performance whenever it could be achieved. Nilsson (1965) presents two proofs of the Perceptron Convergence Theorem and references several others, including the elegant and generalizable proof by Novikoff (1962). Our proof is based on the one given by Ridgway (1962). The behavior of the fixed-increment rule on nonseparable problems was analyzed by Efron (1964); Minsky and Papert (1969) and Block and Levin (1970) provide more accessible analyses. Simple modifications designed to improve performance on nonseparable problems were suggested by Duda and Singleton (1964) and Butz (1967).

A frequently proposed alternative for nonseparable problems was the use of more complicated discriminant functions, or the use of more complicated, sometimes random networks of threshold elements. The more general class of perceptrons as well as various piecewise linear classifiers (Nilsson, 1965; Duda and Fossum, 1966; Mangasarian, 1968) can be described in these terms. Unfortunately, the analysis of such networks is very difficult. Hawkins (1961) gives a good summary of various approaches to learning in threshold element networks, and Minsky and Selfridge (1961) give a critique of this work.

Another viewpoint for much of the early pattern recognition work was that of switching theory. Here again the basic emphasis was on obtaining error-free performance. The switching circuit most frequently proposed for pattern recognition applications was a single threshold element, which has also been called a threshold logic unit, a linear-input element, a majority gate, and, when adaptive, an adaline. Winder (1963) provides a good survey of pertinent work in this area. The standard procedures for realizing threshold functions are basically methods for solving simultaneous linear inequalities. Many of these are algebraic, however, and are not suitable for pattern

---

* Our presentation of iterative procedures as gradient-descent methods for minimizing criterion functions was inspired by a report by Blaydon (1967).

recognition applications. The relaxation procedure for solving linear inequalities was developed by Agmon (1954) and Motzkin and Schoenberg (1954); the use of a margin to obtain a solution in a finite number of steps was suggested by Mays (1964).

The fact that systems of linear inequalities could be solved by linear programming* was noted by Charnes (1953). Minnick showed how linear programming could be used to determine the weights for a threshold element (Minnick, 1961), and Mangasarian suggested its use in pattern classification (Mangasarian, 1965). All of these methods provided either a solution, or proof of nonseparability without a useful solution. In an important paper, Smith (1968) showed that the perceptron error criterion could be minimized by linear programming. Grinold (1969) pointed out that the computational advantages of the dual formulation could be extended to Smith's approach by using the revised simplex method with upper-bounded variables.

Not all of the papers with a switching theory orientation were concerned solely with error-free performance. In fact, one of the first papers to suggest the use of an adaptive threshold element for pattern classification posed the problem and its solution in statistical terms (Mattson, 1959). Similarly, the Widrow-Hoff procedure for minimizing the mean-square error was originally described as a stochastic descent procedure (Widrow and Hoff, 1960), and had its origins in Wiener filtering problems in communication and control theory. Koford and Groner (1966) pointed out the relation between the MSE solution and Fisher's linear discriminant, and Patterson and Womack (1966) showed that the MSE solution also gave a minimum-squared-error approximation to the Bayes discriminant. The fact that the pseudoinverse provided a closed-form solution was noted by Ho and Kashyap (1965), who linked the MSE solution to classical switching theory with their iterative procedures (Ho and Kashyap, 1965, 1966). The theory of the pseudoinverse (also known as the general reciprocal, generalized inverse, or Moore-Penrose inverse) is treated thoroughly by Rao and Mitra (1971).

The pattern recognition applications of stochastic approximation and the method of potential functions have an intertwined history. The method of potential functions was originally proposed by Bashkirov, Braverman, and Muchnik (1964), and its theoretical properties were developed in a series of papers by Aizerman, Braverman, and Rozonoer. The first of these linked the potential function correction rule to the fixed-increment rule (Aizerman, et al., 1964a), and shortly thereafter the method was modified to provide a minimum-squared-error approximation to the Bayes discriminant function (Aizerman, et al., 1964b). The relation of the method of potential functions to stochastic

---

* There are many fine books on linear programming, including the standard texts by Dantzig (1963) and Gass (1969). An exceptionally clear, elementary treatment is given by Glicksman (1963).

approximation was pointed out by Tsypkin and by Aizerman, et al., (1965), and independently by Blaydon (1966). As Aizerman points out, the method of potential functions is a rather general approach to pattern classification that can be specialized in a variety of ways (Aizerman 1969), although the specialization that has received most attention is the one involving stochastic approximation. The subject of stochastic approximation is treated thoroughly by Wasan (1969); a briefer treatment by Wilde (1964) is also highly recommended. Pattern classification applications can be found in Blaydon and Ho (1966), Fu (1968), Yau and Schumpert (1968), and in the many references they cite.

The problem of handling multiclass problems has been more vexing for some procedures than for others. The linear-machine structure is naturally suggested by the multivariate-normal solution, or by even simpler classifiers that use the nearest-mean or maximum-correlation criteria. This type of classifier was used in the early magnetic-ink character readers (Eldredge, Kamphoefner, and Wendt, 1956), and adaptive versions were investigated long before convergence proofs were known (e.g., Roberts, 1960, and the well known lernmatrix of Steinbuch, 1963). Kesler's construction and the convergence proof for the fixed-increment rule are attributed to Carl Kesler by Nilsson (1965). Chaplin and Levadi (1967) suggested a multiclass version of the MSE procedure in which the goal was to map vectors y in a given class into one of the vertices of a $(c - 1)$-dimensional simplex. Our treatment of multicategory MSE procedures is based on the generalized inverse approach of Wee (1968). Yau and Shumpert (1968) give multiclass versions of the stochastic approximation approach, and Smith (1969) suggests a procedure for extending the linear programming approach to the multiclass case.

REFERENCES

1. Agmon, S., "The relaxation method for linear inequalities," *Canadian Journal of Mathematics*, **6**, 382–392 (1954).

2. Aizerman, M. A., E. M. Braverman, and L. I. Rozonoer, "Theoretical foundations of the potential function method in pattern recognition learning," *Automation and Remote Control*, **25**, 821–837 (June 1964a).

3. Aizerman, M. A., E. M. Braverman, and L. I. Rozonoer, "The probability problem of pattern recognition learning and the method of potential functions," *Automation and Remote Control*, **25**, 1175–1193 (September 1964b).

4. Aizerman, M. A., E. M. Braverman, and L. I. Rozonoer, "The Robbins-Monro process and the method of potential functions," *Automation and Remote Control*, **26**, 1882–1885 (November 1965).

5. Aizerman, M. A., "Remarks on two problems connected with pattern recognition," in *Methodologies of Pattern Recognition*, pp. 1–10, S. Watanabe, ed. (Academic Press, New York, 1969).

6. Anderson, T. W. and R. R. Bahadur, "Classification into two multivariate normal distributions with different covariance matrices," *Ann. Math. Stat.*, **33**, 420–431 (June 1962).

7. Bashkirov, O. A., E. M. Braverman, and I. B. Muchnik, "Potential function algorithms for pattern recognition learning machines," *Automation and Remote Control*, **25**, 629–631 (May 1964).

8. Blaydon, C. C., "On a pattern classification result of Aizerman, Braverman, and Rozonoer," *IEEE Trans. Info. Theory* (Correspondence), **IT-12**, 82 83 (January 1966).

9. Blaydon, C. C., "Recursive algorithms for pattern classification," Technical Report No. 520, Division of Engineering and Applied Physics, Harvard University, Cambridge, Massachusetts (March 1967).

10. Blaydon, C. C. and Y-C. Ho, "On the abstraction problem in pattern classification," *Proc. NEC*, **22**, 857–862 (October 1966).

11. Block, H. D., "The perceptron: a model for brain functioning. I," *Rev. Mod. Phys.*, **34**, 123–135 (January, 1962).

12. Block, H. D. and S. A. Levin, "On the boundedness of an iterative procedure for solving a system of linear inequalities," *Proc. American Mathematical Society*, **26**, 229–235 (October 1970).

13. Braverman, E. M., "On the potential function method," *Automation and Remote Control*, **26**, 2130–2138 (December 1965).

14. Butz, A. R., "Perceptron type learning algorithms in nonseparable situations," *J. Math. Anal. and Appl.*, **17**, 560–576 (March 1967).

15. Chaplin, W. G. and V. S. Levadi, "A generalization of the linear threshold decision algorithm to multiple classes," in *Computer and Information Sciences—II*, pp. 337–354, J. T. Tou, ed. (Academic Press, New York, 1967).

16. Charnes, A., W. W. Cooper, and A. Henderson, *An Introduction to Linear Programming* (John Wiley, New York, 1953).

17. Courant, R. and D. Hilbert, *Methods of Mathematical Physics* (Interscience Publishers, New York, 1953).

18. Dantzig, G. B., *Linear Programming and Extensions* (Princeton University Press, Princeton, N.J., 1963).

19. Duda, R. O. and R. C. Singleton, "Training a threshold logic unit with imperfectly classified patterns," *WESCON* Paper 3.2 (August 1964).

20. Duda, R. O. and H. Fossum, "Pattern classification by iteratively determined linear and piecewise linear discriminant functions," *IEEE Trans. Elec. Comp.*, **EC-15**, 220–232 (April 1966).

21. Eldgredge, K. R., F. J. Kamphoefner, and P. H. Wendt, "Automatic input for business data processing systems," *Proc. EJCC*, 69–73 (December 1956).

22. Fisher, R. A., "The use of multiple measurements in taxonomic problems," *Ann. Eugenics*, **7**, Part II, 179–188 (1936); also in *Contributions to Mathematical Statistics* (John Wiley, New York, 1950).

23. Fu, K. S., *Sequential Methods in Pattern Recognition and Machine Learning* (Academic Press, New York, 1968).

24. Gass, S. I., *Linear Programming* (Third Edition, McGraw-Hill, New York, 1969).

25. Glicksman, A. M., *Linear Programming and the Theory of Games* (John Wiley, New York, 1963).

26. Grinold, R. C., "Comment on 'Pattern classification design by linear programming,' " *IEEE Trans. Comp.* (Correspondence), **C-18**, 378–379 (April 1969).

27. Hawkins, J. K., "Self-organizing systems—a review and commentary," *Proc. IRE*, **49**, 31–48 (January 1961).

28. Highleyman, W. H., "Linear decision functions, with application to pattern recognition," *Proc. IRE*, **50**, 1501–1514 (June 1962).

29. Ho, Y-C. and R. L. Kashyap, "An algorithm for linear inequalities and its applications," *IEEE Trans. Elec. Comp.*, **EC-14**, 683–688 (October 1965).

30. Ho, Y-C. and R. L. Kashyap, "A class of iterative procedures for linear inequalities," *J. SIAM Control*, **4**, 112–115 (1966).

31. Koford, J. S. and G. F. Groner, "The use of an adaptive threshold element to design a linear optimal pattern classifier," *IEEE Trans. Info. Theory*, **IT-12**, 42–50 (January 1966).

32. Mangasarian, O. L., "Linear and nonlinear separation of patterns by linear programming," *Operations Research*, **13**, 444–452 (May–June 1965).

33. Mangasarian, O. L., "Multisurface method of pattern separation," *IEEE Trans. Info. Theory*, **IT-14**, 801–807 (November 1968).

34. Mattson, R. L., "A self-organizing binary system," *Proc. EJCC*, 212–217 (December 1959).

35. Mays, C. H., "Effects of adaptation parameters on convergence time and tolerance for adaptive threshold elements," *IEEE Trans. Elec. Comp.*, **EC-13**, 465–468 (August 1964).

36. McCulloch, W. S. and W. H. Pitts, "A logical calculus of the ideas immanent in nervous activity," *Bulletin of Math. Biophysics*, **5**, 115–133 (1943); reprinted in W. S. McCulloch, *Embodiments of Mind*, pp. 19–39 (MIT Press, Cambridge, Mass., 1965).

37. Minnick, R. C., "Linear-input logic," *IRE Trans. Elec. Comp.*, **EC-10**, 6–16 (March 1961).

38. Minsky, M. and O. G. Selfridge, "Learning in random nets," in *Information Theory* (Fourth London Symposium), pp. 335–347, C. Cherry, ed. (Butterworths, London, 1961).

39. Minsky, M. and S. Papert, *Perceptrons: An Introduction to Computational Geometry* (MIT Press, Cambridge, Mass., 1969).

40. Motzkin, T. S. and I. J. Schoenberg, "The relaxation method for linear inequalities," *Canadian Journal of Mathematics*, **6**, 393–404 (1954).

41. Nilsson, N. J., *Learning Machines: Foundations of Trainable Pattern-Classifying Systems* (McGraw-Hill, New York, 1965).

42. Novikoff, A. B. J., "On convergence proofs for perceptrons," *Proc. Symp. on Math. Theory of Automata*, pp. 615–622 (Polytechnic Institute of Brooklyn, Brooklyn, N.Y., 1962).

43. Patterson, J. D. and B. F. Womack, "An adaptive pattern classification system," *IEEE Trans. Sys. Sci. Cyb.*, **SSC-2**, 62–67 (August 1966).

44. Ridgway, W. C., "An adaptive logic system with generalizing properties," Technical Report 1556-1, Stanford Electronics Laboratories, Stanford University, Stanford, Calif., (April 1962).

45. Rao, C. R. and S. K. Mitra, *Generalized Inverse of Matrices and its Applications* (John Wiley, New York, 1971).

46. Roberts, L. G., "Pattern recognition with an adaptive network," *IRE International Conv. Rec.*, Part 2, 66–70 (1960).

47. Rosenblatt, F., "The perceptron—a perceiving and recognizing automaton," Report 85-460-1, Cornell Aeronautical Laboratory, Ithaca, N.Y. (January 1957).

48. Rosenblatt, F., *Principles of Neurodynamics: Perceptrons and the theory of brain mechanisms* (Spartan Books, Washington, D.C., 1962).

49. Smith, F. W., "Pattern classifier design by linear programming," *IEEE Trans. on Comp.*, **C-17**, 367–372 (April 1968).

50. Smith, F. W., "Design of multicategory pattern classifiers with two-category classifier design procedures," *IEEE Trans. Comp.*, **C-18**, 548–551 (June 1969).

51. Steinbuch, K. and U. A. W. Piske, "Learning matrices and their applications," *IEEE Trans. Elec. Comp.*, **EC-12**, 846–862 (December 1963).

52. Tsypkin, Ya. Z., "Establishing characteristics of a function transformer from randomly observed points," *Automation and Remote Control*, **26**, 1878–1881 (November 1965).

53. Wasan, M. T., *Stochastic Approximation* (Cambridge University Press, New York, 1969).

54. Wee, W. G., "Generalized inverse approach to adaptive multiclass pattern classification," *IEEE Trans. Comp.*, **C-17**, 1157–1164 (December 1968).

55. Widrow, B. and M. E. Hoff, "Adaptive switching circuits," *1960 IRE WESCON Conv. Record*, Part 4, 96–104 (August 1960).

56. Wilde, D. G., *Optimum Seeking Methods* (Prentice-Hall, Englewood Cliffs, N.J., 1964).

57. Winder, R. O., "Threshold logic in artificial intelligence," *Artificial Intelligence* (A combined preprint of papers presented at the IEEE Winter General Meeting), pp. 108–128 (January 1963).

58. Yau, S. S. and J. M. Schumpert, "Design of pattern classifiers with the updating property using stochastic approximation techniques," *IEEE Trans. Comp.*, **C-17**, 861–872 (September 1968).

PROBLEMS

1. (a) Show that the distance from the hyperplane $g(\mathbf{x}) = \mathbf{w}^t\mathbf{x} + w_0 = 0$ to the point $\mathbf{x}$ is $|g(\mathbf{x})|/\|\mathbf{w}\|$ by minimizing $\|\mathbf{x} - \mathbf{x}_a\|^2$ subject to the constraint $g(\mathbf{x}_a) = 0$.
    (b) Show that the projection of $\mathbf{x}$ onto the hyperlane is given by

$$\mathbf{x}_p = \mathbf{x} - \frac{g(\mathbf{x})}{\|\mathbf{w}\|^2} \mathbf{w}.$$

2. Consider the three-category linear machine with discriminant functions $g_i(\mathbf{x}) = \mathbf{w}_i\mathbf{x} + w_{i0}$, $i = 1, 2, 3$. For the special case where $\mathbf{x}$ is two dimensional and the threshold weights w_{i0} are zero, sketch the weight vectors with their tails at the origin, the three lines joining their heads, and the decision boundaries. How does this sketch change when a constant vector is added to the three weight vectors?

3. In the multicategory case, a set of samples is said to be linearly separable if there exists a linear machine that can classify them all correctly. If for any ω_i samples labelled ω_i can be separated from all others by a single hyperplane, we shall say the samples are *totally linearly separable*. Show that totally linearly separable samples must be linearly separable, but that the converse need not be true. (Hint: for the converse, consider a case in which a linear machine like the one in Problem 2 separates the samples.)

4. A set of samples is said to be *pairwise linearly separable* if there exist $c(c - 1)/2$ hyperplanes H_{ij} such that H_{ij} separates samples labelled ω_i from samples ω_j. Show that a pairwise-linearly-separable set of patterns may not be linearly separable. (Hint: find a configuration of samples that requires decision boundaries like those shown in Figure 5-2b.)

5. Consider a linear machine with discriminant functions $g_i(\mathbf{x}) = \mathbf{w}_i^t\mathbf{x} + w_{i0}$, $i = 1, \ldots, c$. Show that the decision regions are convex by showing that if $\mathbf{x}_1 \in \mathcal{R}_i$ and $\mathbf{x}_2 \in \mathcal{R}_i$ then $\lambda\mathbf{x}_1 + (1 - \lambda)\mathbf{x}_2 \in \mathcal{R}_i$ if $0 \leq \lambda \leq 1$.

6. Let $\{\mathbf{y}_1, \ldots, \mathbf{y}_n\}$ be a finite set of linearly separable samples, and let $\mathbf{a}$ be called a solution vector if $\mathbf{a}^t\mathbf{y}_i \geq b$ for all i. Show that the minimum-length solution vector is unique. (Hint: consider the effect of averaging two solution vectors.)

7. The *convex hull* of a set of vectors $\mathbf{x}_1, \ldots, \mathbf{x}_n$ is the set of all vectors of the form

$$\mathbf{x} = \sum_{i=1}^{n} \alpha_i\mathbf{x}_i$$

where the coefficients α_i are nonnegative and sum to one. Given two sets of vectors, show that either they are linearly separable or their convex hulls intersect. (Hint: suppose that both statements are true, and consider the classification of a point in the intersection of the convex hulls.)

8. A classifier is said to be a *piecewise linear machine* if its discriminant functions have the form

$$g_i(\mathbf{x}) = \max_{j=1,\ldots,n_i} g_{ij}(\mathbf{x}),$$

where

$$g_{ij}(\mathbf{x}) = \mathbf{w}_{ij}^t\mathbf{x} + w_{ij0}, \qquad \begin{aligned} i &= 1,\ldots,c \\ j &= 1,\ldots,n_i. \end{aligned}$$

(a) Indicate how a piecewise linear machine can be viewed in terms of a linear machine for classifying subclasses of patterns.

(b) Show that the decision regions of a piecewise linear machine can be nonconvex; multiply connected.

9. Let the d components of $\mathbf{x}$ be either 0 or 1. Suppose we assign $\mathbf{x}$ to ω_1 if the number of nonzero components of $\mathbf{x}$ is odd, and to ω_2 otherwise. (In switching theory, this is called the *parity* function.)

(a) Show that this dichotomy is not linearly separable if $d > 1$.

(b) Show that this problem can be solved by a piecewise linear machine with $d + 1$ weight vectors $\mathbf{w}_{ij}$ (see Problem 8). (Hint: consider vectors of the form $\mathbf{w}_{ij} = \alpha_{ij}(1, 1, \ldots, 1)^t$.)

10. In the convergence proof for the perceptron procedure the scale factor α was taken to be β^2/γ. Using the notation in Section 5.5.2, show that if α is greater than $\beta^2/2\gamma$ the maximum number of corrections is given by

$$k_0 = \frac{\|\mathbf{a}_1 - \alpha\mathbf{a}\|^2}{2\alpha\gamma - \beta^2}.$$

If $\mathbf{a}_1 = \mathbf{0}$, what value of α minimizes k_0?

11. Modify the convergence proof given in Section 5.5.2 to prove the convergence of the following correction procedure: starting with an arbitrary initial weight vector $\mathbf{a}_1$, correct $\mathbf{a}_k$ according to

$$\mathbf{a}_{k+1} = \mathbf{a}_k + \rho_k\mathbf{y}^k$$

if and only if $\mathbf{a}_k^t\mathbf{y}^k$ fails to exceed the margin b, where ρ_k is bounded by $0 < \rho_a \le \rho_k \le \rho_b < \infty$. What happens if b is negative?

12. Let $\{\mathbf{y}_1, \ldots, \mathbf{y}_n\}$ be a finite set of linearly separable samples. Suggest an exhaustive procedure that will find a separating vector in a finite number of steps. (Hint: consider weight vectors whose components are integer valued.)

13. Consider the criterion function

$$J_q(\mathbf{a}) = \sum_{\mathbf{y}\in\mathcal{Y}} (\mathbf{a}^t\mathbf{y} - b)^2$$

where $\mathcal{Y}(\mathbf{a})$ is the set of samples for which $\mathbf{a}^t\mathbf{y} \le b$. Suppose that $\mathbf{y}_1$ is the only sample in $\mathcal{Y}(\mathbf{a}_k)$. Show that $\nabla J_q(\mathbf{a}_k) = 2(\mathbf{a}_k^t\mathbf{y}_1 - b)\mathbf{y}_1$ and that the matrix of second partial derivatives is given by $D = 2\mathbf{y}_1\mathbf{y}_1^t$. Use this to show that when the optimal

ρ_k is used in Eq. (8) the gradient descent algorithm yields

$$\mathbf{a}_{k+1} = \mathbf{a}_k + \frac{b - \mathbf{a}^t\mathbf{y}_1}{\|\mathbf{y}_1\|^2}\,\mathbf{y}_1.$$

14. Show that the scale factor α in the MSE solution corresponding to Fisher's linear discriminant (Section 5.8.2) is given by

$$\alpha = \frac{1}{1 + \dfrac{n_1 n_2}{n}\,(\mathbf{m}_1 - \mathbf{m}_2)^t S_W^{-1}(\mathbf{m}_1 - \mathbf{m}_2)}$$

15. Generalize the results of Section 5.8.3 to show that the vector **a** that minimizes the criterion function

$$J_s'(\mathbf{a}) = \sum_{\mathbf{y}\in\mathcal{Y}_1} (\mathbf{a}^t\mathbf{y} - (\lambda_{21} - \lambda_{11}))^2 + \sum_{\mathbf{y}\in\mathcal{Y}_2} (\mathbf{a}^t\mathbf{y} - (\lambda_{12} - \lambda_{22}))^2$$

provides asymptotically a minimum-mean-squared-error approximation to the Bayes discriminant function $(\lambda_{21} - \lambda_{11})P(\omega_1 \mid \mathbf{x}) - (\lambda_{12} - \lambda_{22})P(\omega_2 \mid \mathbf{x})$.

16. Consider the criterion function $J_m(\mathbf{a}) = E[(\mathbf{a}^t\mathbf{y}(\mathbf{x}) - z)^2]$ and the Bayes discriminant function $g_0(\mathbf{x})$.
(a) Show that

$$J_m = E[(\mathbf{a}^t\mathbf{y} - g_0)^2] - 2E[(\mathbf{a}^t\mathbf{y} - g_0)(z - g_0)] + E[(z - g_0)^2]$$

(b) Use the fact that the conditional mean of z is $g_0(\mathbf{x})$ in showing that the $\hat{\mathbf{a}}$ that minimizes J_m also minimizes $E[(\mathbf{a}^t\mathbf{y} - g_0)^2]$

17. A scalar analog of the relation $R_{k+1}^{-1} = R_k^{-1} + \mathbf{y}_k\mathbf{y}_k^t$ used in stochastic approximation is $\rho_{k+1}^{-1} = \rho_k^{-1} + y_k^2$. Show that this has the closed-form solution

$$\rho_k = \frac{\rho_1}{1 + \rho_1 \sum_{i=1}^{k-1} y_i^2}.$$

Assuming that $\rho_1 > 0$ and $0 < a \le y_i^2 \le b < \infty$, indicate why this sequence of coefficients will satisfy $\sum \rho_k \to +\infty$ and $\sum \rho_k^2 \to L < \infty$.

18. The linear programming problem formulated in Section 5.10.2 involved minimizing a single artificial variable t under the constraints $\mathbf{a}^t\mathbf{y}_i + t > b_i$ and $t \ge 0$. Show that the resulting weight vector minimizes the criterion function

$$J_t(\mathbf{a}) = \max_{\mathbf{a}^t\mathbf{y}_i \le b_i} [b_i - \mathbf{a}^t\mathbf{y}_i].$$

19. Suggest a multiclass generalization of the method of potential functions involving c discriminant functions, and suggest an error-correction procedure for determining the discriminant functions iteratively.

Chapter 6

UNSUPERVISED LEARNING AND CLUSTERING

6.1 INTRODUCTION

Until now we have assumed that the training samples used to design a classifier were labelled to show their category membership. Procedures that use labelled samples are said to be supervised. Now we shall investigate a number of *unsupervised* procedures that use unlabelled samples. That is, we shall see what can be done when all one has is a collection of samples without being told their classification.

One might wonder why anyone is interested in such an unpromising problem, and whether or not it is even possible in principle to learn anything of value from unlabelled samples. There are three basic reasons for interest in unsupervised procedures. First, the collection and labelling of a large set of sample patterns can be surprisingly costly and time consuming. If a classifier can be crudely designed on a small, labelled set of samples, and then "tuned up" by allowing it to run without supervision on a large, unlabelled set, much time and trouble can be saved. Second, in many applications the characteristics of the patterns can change slowly with time. If these changes can be tracked by a classifier running in an unsupervised mode, improved performance can be achieved. Finally, in the early stages of an investigation it may be valuable to gain some insight into the nature or structure of the data. The discovery of distinct subclasses or major departures from expected characteristics may significantly alter the approach taken to designing the classifier.

The answer to the question of whether or not it is possible in principle to learn anything from unlabelled data depends upon the assumptions one is willing to accept—theorems can not be proved without premises. We shall begin with the very restrictive assumption that the functional forms for the underlying probability densities are known, and that the only thing that must be learned is the value of an unknown parameter vector. Interestingly enough, the formal solution to this problem will turn out to be almost identical to the solution for the problem of supervised learning given in Chapter 3. Unfortunately, in the unsupervised case the solution suffers from the usual problems associated with parametric assumptions without providing any of the benefits of computational simplicity. This will lead us to various attempts to reformulate the problem as one of partitioning the data into subgroups or clusters. While some of the resulting clustering procedures have no known significant theoretical properties, they are still among the more useful tools for pattern recognition problems.

6.2 MIXTURE DENSITIES AND IDENTIFIABILITY

We begin by assuming that we know the complete probability structure for the problem with the sole exception of the values of some parameters. To be more specific, we make the following assumptions:

(1) The samples come from a known number c of classes.
(2) The a priori probabilities $P(\omega_j)$ for each class are known, $j = 1, \ldots, c$.
(3) The forms for the class-conditional probability densities $p(\mathbf{x} \mid \omega_j, \boldsymbol{\theta}_j)$ are known, $j = 1, \ldots, c$.
(4) All that is unknown are the values for the c parameter vectors $\boldsymbol{\theta}_1, \ldots, \boldsymbol{\theta}_c$.

Samples are assumed to be obtained by selecting a state of nature ω_j with probability $P(\omega_j)$ and then selecting an $\mathbf{x}$ according to the probability law $p(\mathbf{x} \mid \omega_j, \boldsymbol{\theta}_j)$. Thus, the probability density function for the samples is given by

$$p(\mathbf{x} \mid \boldsymbol{\theta}) = \sum_{j=1}^{c} p(\mathbf{x} \mid \omega_j, \boldsymbol{\theta}_j) P(\omega_j), \tag{1}$$

where $\boldsymbol{\theta} = (\boldsymbol{\theta}_1, \ldots, \boldsymbol{\theta}_c)$. A density function of this form is called a *mixture density*. The conditional densities $p(\mathbf{x} \mid \omega_j, \boldsymbol{\theta}_j)$ are called the *component densities*, and the a priori probabilities $P(\omega_j)$ are called the *mixing parameters*. The mixing parameters can also be included among the unknown parameters, but for the moment we shall assume that only $\boldsymbol{\theta}$ is unknown.

Our basic goal will be to use samples drawn from this mixture density to estimate the unknown parameter vector $\boldsymbol{\theta}$. Once we know $\boldsymbol{\theta}$ we can decompose the mixture into its components, and the problem is solved. Before seeking explicit solutions to this problem, however, let us ask whether or not it is possible in principle to recover θ from the mixture. Suppose that we had an unlimited number of samples, and that we used one of the nonparametric methods of Chapter 4 to determine the value of $p(\mathbf{x} \mid \theta)$ for every $\mathbf{x}$. If there is only one value of θ that will produce the observed values for $p(\mathbf{x} \mid \theta)$, then a solution is at least possible in principle. However, if several different values of θ can produce the same values for $p(\mathbf{x} \mid \theta)$, then there is no hope of obtaining a unique solution.

These considerations lead us to the following definition: a density $p(\mathbf{x} \mid \theta)$ is said to be *identifiable* if $\theta \neq \theta'$ implies that there exists an $\mathbf{x}$ such that $p(\mathbf{x} \mid \theta) \neq p(\mathbf{x} \mid \theta')$. As one might expect, the study of unsupervised learning is greatly simplified if we restrict ourselves to identifiable mixtures. Fortunately, most mixtures of commonly encountered density functions are identifiable. Mixtures of discrete distributions are not always so obliging. For a simple example, consider the case where x is binary and $P(x \mid \theta)$ is the mixture

$$P(x \mid \theta) = \tfrac{1}{2}\theta_1^x(1 - \theta_1)^{1-x} + \tfrac{1}{2}\theta_2^x(1 - \theta_2)^{1-x}$$

$$= \begin{cases} \tfrac{1}{2}(\theta_1 + \theta_2) & \text{if } x = 1 \\ 1 - \tfrac{1}{2}(\theta_1 + \theta_2) & \text{if } x = 0. \end{cases}$$

If we know, for example, that $P(x = 1 \mid \theta) = 0.6$, and hence that $P(x = 0 \mid \theta) = 0.4$, then we know the function $P(x \mid \theta)$, but we cannot determine θ, and hence cannot extract the component distributions. The most we can say is that $\theta_1 + \theta_2 = 1.2$. Thus, here we have a case in which the mixture distribution is not identifiable, and hence a case for which unsupervised learning is impossible in principle.

This kind of problem commonly occurs with discrete distributions. If there are too many components in the mixture, there may be more unknowns than independent equations, and identifiability can be a real problem. For the continuous case, the problems are less severe, although certain minor difficulties can arise due to the possibility of special cases. Thus, while it can be shown that mixtures of normal densities are usually identifiable, the parameters in the simple mixture density

$$p(x \mid \theta) = \frac{P(\omega_1)}{\sqrt{2\pi}} \exp[-\tfrac{1}{2}(x - \theta_1)^2] + \frac{P(\omega_2)}{\sqrt{2\pi}} \exp[-\tfrac{1}{2}(x - \theta_2)^2]$$

can not be uniquely identified if $P(\omega_1) = P(\omega_2)$, for then θ_1 and θ_2 can be interchanged without affecting $p(x \mid \theta)$. To avoid such irritations, we shall acknowledge that identifiability can be a problem, but shall henceforth assume that the mixture densities we are working with are identifiable.

6.3   MAXIMUM LIKELIHOOD ESTIMATES

Suppose now that we are given a set $\mathcal{X} = \{\mathbf{x}_1, \ldots, \mathbf{x}_n\}$ of n unlabelled samples drawn independently from the mixture density

$$p(\mathbf{x} \mid \boldsymbol{\theta}) = \sum_{j=1}^{c} p(\mathbf{x} \mid \omega_j, \boldsymbol{\theta}_j)P(\omega_j), \tag{1}$$

where the parameter vector $\boldsymbol{\theta}$ is fixed but unknown. The likelihood of the observed samples is by definition the joint density

$$p(\mathcal{X} \mid \boldsymbol{\theta}) = \prod_{k=1}^{n} p(\mathbf{x}_k \mid \boldsymbol{\theta}). \tag{2}$$

The maximum likelihood estimate $\hat{\boldsymbol{\theta}}$ is that value of $\boldsymbol{\theta}$ that maximizes $p(\mathcal{X} \mid \boldsymbol{\theta})$.

If we assume that $p(\mathcal{X} \mid \boldsymbol{\theta})$ is a differentiable function of $\boldsymbol{\theta}$, then we can derive some interesting necessary conditions for $\hat{\boldsymbol{\theta}}$. Let l be the logarithm of the likelihood, and let $\nabla_{\boldsymbol{\theta}_i} l$ be the gradient of l with respect to $\boldsymbol{\theta}_i$. Then

$$l = \sum_{k=1}^{n} \log p(\mathbf{x}_k \mid \boldsymbol{\theta}) \tag{3}$$

and

$$\nabla_{\boldsymbol{\theta}_i} l = \sum_{k=1}^{n} \frac{1}{p(\mathbf{x}_k \mid \boldsymbol{\theta})} \nabla_{\boldsymbol{\theta}_i} \left[\sum_{j=1}^{c} p(\mathbf{x}_k \mid \omega_j, \boldsymbol{\theta}_j)P(\omega_j) \right].$$

If we assume that the elements of $\boldsymbol{\theta}_i$ and $\boldsymbol{\theta}_j$ are functionally independent if $i \neq j$, and if we introduce the a posteriori probability

$$P(\omega_i \mid \mathbf{x}_k, \boldsymbol{\theta}_i) = \frac{p(\mathbf{x}_k \mid \omega_i, \boldsymbol{\theta}_i)P(\omega_i)}{p(\mathbf{x}_k \mid \boldsymbol{\theta})} \tag{4}$$

we see that the gradient of the log-likelihood can be written in the interesting form

$$\nabla_{\boldsymbol{\theta}_i} l = \sum_{k=1}^{n} P(\omega_i \mid \mathbf{x}_k, \boldsymbol{\theta}_i)\nabla_{\boldsymbol{\theta}_i} \log p(\mathbf{x}_k \mid \omega_i, \boldsymbol{\theta}_i). \tag{5}$$

Since the gradient must vanish at the $\boldsymbol{\theta}_i$ that maximizes l, the maximum-likelihood estimate $\hat{\boldsymbol{\theta}}_i$ must satisfy the conditions

$$\sum_{k=1}^{n} P(\omega_i \mid \mathbf{x}_k, \hat{\boldsymbol{\theta}}_i)\nabla_{\boldsymbol{\theta}_i} \log p(\mathbf{x}_k \mid \omega_i, \hat{\boldsymbol{\theta}}_i) = 0, \qquad i = 1, \ldots, c. \tag{6}$$

Conversely, among the solutions to these equations for $\hat{\boldsymbol{\theta}}_i$ we will find the maximum-likelihood solution.

It is not hard to generalize these results to include the a priori probabilities $P(\omega_i)$ among the unknown quantities. In this case the search for the maximum value of $p(\mathcal{X} \mid \theta)$ extends over θ and $P(\omega_i)$, subject to the constraints

$$P(\omega_i) \geq 0 \qquad i = 1, \ldots, c \tag{7}$$

and

$$\sum_{i=1}^{c} P(\omega_i) = 1. \tag{8}$$

Let $\hat{P}(\omega_i)$ be the maximum likelihood estimate for $P(\omega_i)$, and let $\hat{\theta}_i$ be the maximum likelihood estimate for θ_i. The diligent reader will be able to show that if the likelihood function is differentiable and if $\hat{P}(\omega_i) \neq 0$ for any i, then $\hat{P}(\omega_i)$ and $\hat{\theta}_i$ must satisfy

$$\hat{P}(\omega_i) = \frac{1}{n} \sum_{k=1}^{n} \hat{P}(\omega_i \mid \mathbf{x}_k, \hat{\theta}_i) \tag{9}$$

and

$$\sum_{k=1}^{n} \hat{P}(\omega_i \mid \mathbf{x}_k, \hat{\theta}_i) \nabla_{\theta_i} \log p(\mathbf{x}_k \mid \omega_i, \hat{\theta}_i) = 0, \tag{10}$$

where

$$\hat{P}(\omega_i \mid \mathbf{x}_k, \hat{\theta}_i) = \frac{p(\mathbf{x}_k \mid \omega_i, \hat{\theta}_i) \hat{P}(\omega_i)}{\sum_{j=1}^{c} p(\mathbf{x}_k \mid \omega_j, \hat{\theta}_j) \hat{P}(\omega_j)}. \tag{11}$$

6.4 APPLICATION TO NORMAL MIXTURES

It is enlightening to see how these general results apply to the case where the component densities are multivariate normal, $p(\mathbf{x} \mid \omega_i, \theta_i) \sim N(\mu_i, \Sigma_i)$. The following table illustrates a few of the different cases that can arise depending upon which parameters are known ($\sqrt{}$) and which are unknown (?):

Case	μ_i	Σ_i	$P(\omega_i)$	c
1	?	$\sqrt{}$	$\sqrt{}$	$\sqrt{}$
2	?	?	?	$\sqrt{}$
3	?	?	?	?

Case 1 is the simplest, and will be considered in detail because of its pedagogic value. Case 2 is more realistic, though somewhat more involved.

Case 3 represents the problem we face on encountering a completely unknown set of data. Unfortunately, it can not be solved by maximum-likelihood methods. We shall postpone discussion of what can be done when the number of classes is unknown until later in this chapter.

6.4.1 Case 1: Unknown Mean Vectors

If the only unknown quantities are the mean vectors $\boldsymbol{\mu}_i$, then $\boldsymbol{\theta}_i$ can be identified with $\boldsymbol{\mu}_i$ and Eq. (6) can be used to obtain necessary conditions on the maximum likelihood estimate for $\boldsymbol{\mu}_i$. Since

$$\log p(\mathbf{x} \mid \omega_i, \boldsymbol{\mu}_i) = -\log[(2\pi)^{d/2}|\Sigma_i|^{1/2}] - \tfrac{1}{2}(\mathbf{x} - \boldsymbol{\mu}_i)^t\Sigma_i^{-1}(\mathbf{x} - \boldsymbol{\mu}_i),$$

$$\nabla_{\boldsymbol{\mu}_i} \log p(\mathbf{x} \mid \omega_i, \boldsymbol{\mu}_i) = \Sigma_i^{-1}(\mathbf{x} - \boldsymbol{\mu}_i).$$

Thus, Eq. (6) for the maximum-likelihood estimate $\hat{\boldsymbol{\mu}}_i$ yields

$$\sum_{k=1}^{n} P(\omega_i \mid \mathbf{x}_k, \hat{\boldsymbol{\mu}}_i)\Sigma_i^{-1}(\mathbf{x}_k - \hat{\boldsymbol{\mu}}_i) = 0.$$

After multiplying by Σ_i and rearranging terms, we obtain

$$\hat{\boldsymbol{\mu}}_i = \frac{\sum_{k=1}^{n} P(\omega_i \mid \mathbf{x}_k, \hat{\boldsymbol{\mu}}_i)\mathbf{x}_k}{\sum_{k=1}^{n} P(\omega_i \mid \mathbf{x}_k, \hat{\boldsymbol{\mu}}_i)}. \tag{12}$$

This equation is intuitively very satisfying. It shows that the estimate for $\boldsymbol{\mu}_i$ is merely a weighted average of the samples. The weight for the kth sample is an estimate of how likely it is that $\mathbf{x}_k$ belongs to the ith class. If $P(\omega_i \mid \mathbf{x}_k, \hat{\boldsymbol{\mu}}_i)$ happened to be one for some of the samples and zero for the rest, then $\hat{\boldsymbol{\mu}}_i$ would be the mean of those samples estimated to belong to the ith class. More generally, suppose that $\hat{\boldsymbol{\mu}}_i$ is sufficiently close to the true value of $\boldsymbol{\mu}_i$ that $P(\omega_i \mid \mathbf{x}_k, \hat{\boldsymbol{\mu}}_i)$ is essentially the true a posteriori probability for ω_i. If we think of $P(\omega_i \mid \mathbf{x}_k, \hat{\boldsymbol{\mu}}_i)$ as the fraction of those samples having value $\mathbf{x}_k$ that come from the ith class, then we see that Eq. (12) essentially gives $\hat{\boldsymbol{\mu}}_i$ as the average of the samples coming from the ith class.

Unfortunately, Eq. (12) does not give $\hat{\boldsymbol{\mu}}_i$ explicitly, and if we substitute

$$P(\omega_i \mid \mathbf{x}_k, \hat{\boldsymbol{\mu}}_i) = \frac{p(\mathbf{x}_k \mid \omega_i, \hat{\boldsymbol{\mu}}_i)P(\omega_i)}{\sum_{j=1}^{c} p(\mathbf{x}_k \mid \omega_j, \hat{\boldsymbol{\mu}}_j)P(\omega_j)}$$

with $p(\mathbf{x} \mid \omega_i, \hat{\boldsymbol{\mu}}_i) \sim N(\hat{\boldsymbol{\mu}}_i, \Sigma_i)$, we obtain a tangled snarl of coupled simultaneous nonlinear equations. These equations usually do not have a unique solution, and we must test the solutions we get to find the one that actually maximizes the likelihood.

If we have some way of obtaining fairly good initial estimates $\hat{\mu}_i(0)$ for the unknown means, Eq. (12) suggests the following iterative scheme for improving the estimates:

$$\hat{\mu}_i(j+1) = \frac{\sum\limits_{k=1}^{n} P(\omega_i \mid x_k, \hat{\mu}_i(j))x_k}{\sum\limits_{k=1}^{n} P(\omega_i \mid x_k, \hat{\mu}_i(j))}. \tag{13}$$

This is basically a gradient ascent or hill-climbing procedure for maximizing the log-likelihood function. If the overlap between component densities is small, then the coupling between classes will be small and convergence will be fast. However, when convergence does occur, all that we can be sure of is that the gradient is zero. Like all hill-climbing procedures, this one carries no guarantee of yielding the global maximum.

6.4.2 An Example

To illustrate the kind of behavior that can occur, consider the simple one-dimensional, two-component normal mixture

$$p(x \mid \mu_1, \mu_2) = \frac{1}{3\sqrt{2\pi}} \exp[-\tfrac{1}{2}(x - \mu_1)^2] + \frac{2}{3\sqrt{2\pi}} \exp[-\tfrac{1}{2}(x - \mu_2)^2].$$

The 25 samples shown in Table 6-1 were drawn from this mixture with

TABLE 6-1. Twenty-five Samples from a Normal Mixture

k	x_k	(Class)	k	x_k	(Class)
1	0.608	2	13	3.240	2
2	−1.590	1	14	2.400	2
3	0.235	2	15	−2.499	1
4	3.949	2	16	2.608	2
5	−2.249	1	17	−3.458	1
6	2.704	2	18	0.257	2
7	−2.473	1	19	2.569	2
8	0.672	2	20	1.415	2
9	0.262	2	21	1.410	2
10	1.072	2	22	−2.653	1
11	−1.773	1	23	1.396	2
12	0.537	2	24	3.286	2
			25	−0.712	1

$\mu_1 = -2$ and $\mu_2 = 2$. Let us use these samples to compute the log-likelihood function

$$l(\mu_1, \mu_2) = \sum_{k=1}^{n} \log p(x_k \mid \mu_1, \mu_2)$$

for various values of μ_1 and μ_2. Figure 6.1 is a contour plot that shows how l varies with μ_1 and μ_2. The maximum value of l occurs at $\hat{\mu}_1 = -2.130$ and $\hat{\mu}_2 = 1.668$, which is in the rough vicinity of the true values $\mu_1 = -2$ and $\mu_2 = 2$.* However, l reaches another peak of comparable height at $\hat{\mu}_1 = 2.085$ and $\hat{\mu}_2 = -1.257$. Roughly speaking, this solution corresponds to interchanging μ_1 and μ_2. Note that had the a priori probabilities been equal,

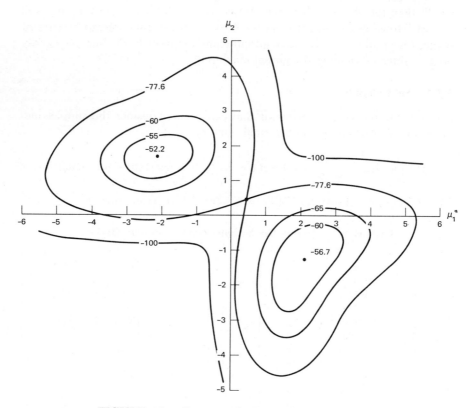

FIGURE 6.1.   Contours of a log-likelihood function.

* If the data in Table 6-1 are separated by class, the resulting sample means are $m_1 = -2.176$ and $m_2 = 1.684$. Thus, the maximum likelihood estimates for the unsupervised case are close to the maximum likelihood estimates for the supervised case.

interchanging μ_1 and μ_2 would have produced no change in the log-likelihood function. Thus, when the mixture density is not identifiable, the maximum likelihood solution is not unique.

Additional insight into the nature of these multiple solutions can be obtained by examining the resulting estimates for the mixture density. Figure 6.2 shows the true mixture density and the estimates obtained by using the maximum likelihood estimates as if they were the true parameter

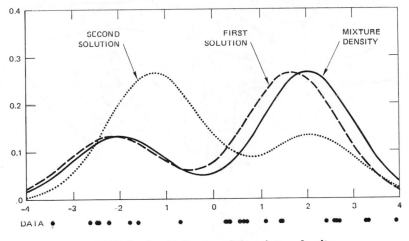

FIGURE 6.2.   Estimates of the mixture density.

values. The 25 sample values are shown as a scatter of points along the abscissa. Note that the peaks of both the true mixture density and the maximum likelihood solution are located so as to encompass two major groups of data points. The estimate corresponding to the smaller local maximum of the log-likelihood function has a mirror-image shape, but its peaks also encompass reasonable groups of data points. To the eye, neither of these solutions is clearly superior, and both are interesting.

If Eq. (13) is used to determine solutions to Eq. (12) iteratively, the results depend on the starting values $\hat{\mu}_1(0)$ and $\hat{\mu}_2(0)$. Figure 6.3 shows how different starting points lead to different solutions, and gives some indication of rates of convergence. Note that if $\hat{\mu}_1(0) = \hat{\mu}_2(0)$, convergence to a saddle point occurs in one step. This is not a coincidence. It happens for the simple reason that for this starting point $P(\omega_1 \mid x_k, \hat{\mu}_1(0)) = P(\omega_2 \mid x_k, \hat{\mu}_2(0))$. Thus, Eq. (13) yields the mean of all of the samples for $\hat{\mu}_1$ and $\hat{\mu}_2$ for all successive iterations. Clearly, this is a general phenomenon, and such saddle-point solutions can

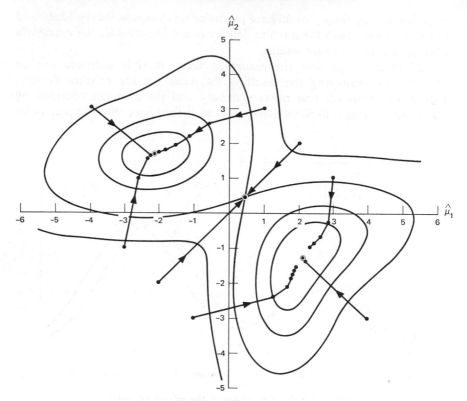

FIGURE 6.3. Trajectories for the iterative procedure.

be expected if the starting point does not bias the search away from a symmetric answer.

6.4.3 Case 2: All Parameters Unknown

If $\boldsymbol{\mu}_i$, Σ_i, and $P(\omega_i)$ are all unknown, and if no constraints are placed on the covariance matrix, then the maximum likelihood principle yields useless singular solutions. The reason for this can be appreciated from the following simple example. Let $p(x \mid \mu, \sigma^2)$ be the two-component normal mixture

$$ p(x \mid \mu, \sigma^2) = \frac{1}{2\sqrt{2\pi}\sigma} \exp\left[-\frac{1}{2}\left(\frac{x-\mu}{\sigma}\right)^2 \right] + \frac{1}{2\sqrt{2\pi}} \exp[-\tfrac{1}{2}x^2]. $$

The likelihood function for n samples drawn according to this probability law is merely the product of the n densities $p(x_k \mid \mu, \sigma^2)$. Suppose that we let $\mu = x_1$, so that

$$p(x_1 \mid \mu, \sigma^2) = \frac{1}{2\sqrt{2\pi}\sigma} + \frac{1}{2\sqrt{2\pi}} \exp[-\tfrac{1}{2}x_1^2].$$

Clearly, for the rest of the samples

$$p(x_k \mid \mu, \sigma^2) \geq \frac{1}{2\sqrt{2\pi}} \exp[-\tfrac{1}{2}x_k^2],$$

so that

$$p(x_1, \ldots, x_n \mid \mu, \sigma^2) \geq \left\{ \frac{1}{\sigma} + \exp[-\tfrac{1}{2}x_1^2] \right\} \frac{1}{(2\sqrt{2\pi})^n} \exp\left[-\tfrac{1}{2} \sum_{k=2}^{n} x_k^2 \right].$$

Thus, by letting σ approach zero we can make the likelihood arbitrarily large, and the maximum likelihood solution is singular.

Ordinarily, singular solutions are of no interest, and we are forced to conclude that the maximum likelihood principle fails for this class of normal mixtures. However, it is an empirical fact that meaningful solutions can still be obtained if we restrict our attention to the largest of the finite local maxima of the likelihood function. Assuming that the likelihood function is well behaved at such maxima, we can use Eqs. (9)–(11) to obtain estimates for μ_i, Σ_i, and $P(\omega_i)$. When we include the elements of Σ_i in the elements of the parameter vector θ_i, we must remember that only half of the off-diagonal elements are independent. In addition, it turns out to be much more convenient to let the independent elements of Σ_i^{-1} rather than Σ_i be the unknown parameters. With these observations, the actual differentiation of

$$\log p(x_k \mid \omega_i, \theta_i) = \log \frac{|\Sigma_i^{-1}|^{1/2}}{(2\pi)^{d/2}} - \tfrac{1}{2}(x_k - \mu_i)^t \Sigma_i^{-1}(x_k - \mu_i)$$

with respect to the elements of μ_i and Σ_i^{-1} is relatively routine. Let $x_p(k)$ be the pth element of x_k, $\mu_p(i)$ be the pth element of μ_i, $\sigma_{pq}(i)$ be the pqth element of Σ_i, and $\sigma^{pq}(i)$ be the pqth element of Σ_i^{-1}. Then

$$\nabla_{\mu_i} \log p(x_k \mid \omega_i, \theta_i) = \Sigma_i^{-1}(x_k - \mu_i)$$

and

$$\frac{\partial \log p(x_k \mid \omega_i, \theta_i)}{\partial \sigma^{pq}(i)} = \left(1 - \frac{\delta_{pq}}{2} \right) [\sigma_{pq}(i) - (x_p(k) - \mu_p(i))(x_q(k) - \mu_q(i))],$$

where δ_{pq} is the Kronecker delta. Substituting these results in Eq. (10) and doing a small amount of algebraic manipulation, we obtain the following equations for the local-maximum-likelihood estimates $\hat{\mu}_i$, $\hat{\Sigma}_i$, and $\hat{P}(\omega_i)$:

$$\hat{P}(\omega_i) = \frac{1}{n}\sum_{k=1}^{n}\hat{P}(\omega_i \mid \mathbf{x}_k, \hat{\theta}_i) \tag{14}$$

$$\hat{\mu}_i = \frac{\displaystyle\sum_{k=1}^{n}\hat{P}(\omega_i \mid \mathbf{x}_k, \hat{\theta}_i)\mathbf{x}_k}{\displaystyle\sum_{k=1}^{n}\hat{P}(\omega_i \mid \mathbf{x}_k, \hat{\theta}_i)} \tag{15}$$

$$\Sigma_i = \frac{\displaystyle\sum_{k=1}^{n}\hat{P}(\omega_i \mid \mathbf{x}_k, \hat{\theta}_i)(\mathbf{x}_k - \hat{\mu}_i)(\mathbf{x}_k - \mu_i)^t}{\displaystyle\sum_{k=1}^{n}\hat{P}(\omega_i \mid \mathbf{x}_k, \hat{\theta}_i)} \tag{16}$$

where

$$\hat{P}(\omega_i \mid \mathbf{x}_k, \hat{\theta}_i) = \frac{p(\mathbf{x}_k \mid \omega_i, \hat{\theta}_i)\hat{P}(\omega_i)}{\displaystyle\sum_{j=1}^{c}p(\mathbf{x}_k \mid \omega_j, \hat{\theta}_j)\hat{P}(\omega_j)}$$

$$= \frac{|\hat{\Sigma}_i|^{-1/2}\exp[-\frac{1}{2}(\mathbf{x}_k - \hat{\mu}_i)^t\hat{\Sigma}_i^{-1}(\mathbf{x}_k - \hat{\mu}_i)]\hat{P}(\omega_i)}{\displaystyle\sum_{j=1}^{c}|\hat{\Sigma}_j|^{-1/2}\exp[-\frac{1}{2}(\mathbf{x}_k - \hat{\mu}_j)^t\hat{\Sigma}_j^{-1}(\mathbf{x}_k - \hat{\mu}_j)]\hat{P}(\omega_j)}. \tag{17}$$

While the notation may make these equations appear to be rather formidable, their interpretation is actually quite simple. In the extreme case where $\hat{P}(\omega_i \mid \mathbf{x}_k, \hat{\theta}_i)$ is one when $\mathbf{x}_k$ is from Class ω_i and zero otherwise, $\hat{P}(\omega_i)$ is the fraction of samples from ω_i, $\hat{\mu}_i$ is the mean of those samples, and $\hat{\Sigma}_i$ is the corresponding sample covariance matrix. More generally, $\hat{P}(\omega_i \mid \mathbf{x}_k, \hat{\theta}_i)$ is between zero and one, and all of the samples play some role in the estimates. However, the estimates are basically still frequency ratios, sample means, and sample covariance matrices.

The problems involved in solving these implicit equations are similar to the problems discussed in Section 6.4.1, with the additional complication of having to avoid singular solutions. Of the various techniques that can be used to obtain a solution, the most obvious approach is to use initial estimates to evaluate Eq. (17) for $\hat{P}(\omega_i \mid \mathbf{x}_k, \hat{\theta}_i)$ and then to use Eqs. (14)–(16) to update these estimates. If the initial estimates are very good, having perhaps been obtained from a fairly large set of labelled samples, convergence can be quite rapid. However, the results do depend upon the starting point, and the problem of multiple solutions is always present. Furthermore, the repeated computation and inversion of the sample covariance matrices can be quite time consuming.

Considerable simplification can be obtained it it is possible to assume that the covariance matrices are diagonal. This has the added virtue of reducing the number of unknown parameters, which is very important when the number of samples is not large. If this assumption is too strong, it still may be possible to obtain some simplification by assuming that the c covariance matrices are equal, which also eliminates the problem of singular solutions. The derivation of the appropriate maximum likelihood equations for this case is treated in Problems 5 and 6.

6.4.4 A Simple Approximate Procedure

Of the various techniques that can be used to simplify the computation and accelerate convergence, we shall briefly consider one elementary, approximate method. From Eq. (17), it is clear that the probability $\hat{P}(\omega_i \mid \mathbf{x}_k, \hat{\boldsymbol{\theta}}_i)$ is large when the squared Mahalanobis distance $(\mathbf{x}_k - \hat{\boldsymbol{\mu}}_i)^t \hat{\Sigma}_i^{-1} (\mathbf{x}_k - \hat{\boldsymbol{\mu}}_i)$ is small. Suppose that we merely compute the squared Euclidean distance $\|\mathbf{x}_k - \hat{\boldsymbol{\mu}}_i\|^2$, find the mean $\hat{\boldsymbol{\mu}}_m$ nearest to $\mathbf{x}_k$, and approximate $\hat{P}(\omega_i \mid \mathbf{x}_k, \hat{\boldsymbol{\theta}}_i)$ as

$$\hat{P}(\omega_i \mid \mathbf{x}_k, \hat{\boldsymbol{\theta}}_i) \approx \begin{cases} 1 & i = m \\ 0 & \text{otherwise.} \end{cases}$$

Then the iterative application of Eq. (15) leads to the following procedure* for finding $\hat{\boldsymbol{\mu}}_1, \ldots, \hat{\boldsymbol{\mu}}_c$:

Procedure: Basic Isodata

1. Choose some initial values for the means $\hat{\boldsymbol{\mu}}_1, \ldots, \hat{\boldsymbol{\mu}}_c$.
Loop: 2. Classify the n samples by assigning them to the class of the closest mean.
3. Recompute the means as the average of the samples in their class.
4. If any mean changed value, go to Loop; otherwise, stop.

This is typical of a class of procedures that are known as *clustering* procedures. Later on we shall place it in the class of iterative optimization procedures, since the means tend to move so as to minimize a squared-error

---

* Throughout this chapter we shall name and describe various iterative procedures as if they were computer programs. All of these procedures have in fact been programmed, often with much more elaborate provisions for doing such things as breaking ties, avoiding trap states, and allowing more sophisticated terminating conditions. Thus, we occasionally include the word "basic" in their names to emphasize the fact that our interest is limited to explaining essential concepts.

criterion function. At the moment we view it merely as an approximate way to obtain maximum likelihood estimates for the means. The values obtained can be accepted as the answer, or can be used as starting points for the more exact computations.

It is interesting to see how this procedure behaves on the example data in Table 6-1. Figure 6.4 shows the sequence of values for $\hat{\mu}_1$ and $\hat{\mu}_2$ obtained

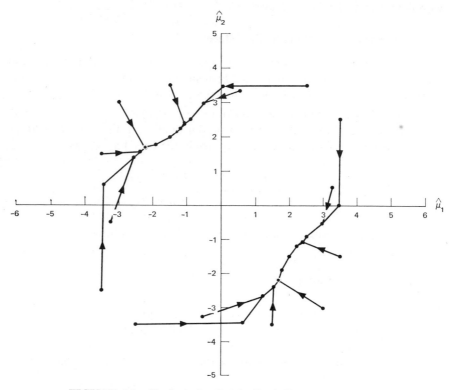

FIGURE 6.4.   Trajectories for the Basic Isodata Procedure.

for several different starting points. Since interchanging $\hat{\mu}_1$ and $\hat{\mu}_2$ merely interchanges the labels assigned to the data, the trajectories are symmetric about the line $\hat{\mu}_1 = \hat{\mu}_2$. The trajectories lead either to the point $\hat{\mu}_1 = -2.176$, $\hat{\mu}_2 = 1.684$ or to its image. This is close to the solution found by the maximum likelihood method (viz., $\hat{\mu}_1 = -2.130$ and $\hat{\mu}_2 = 1.668$), and the trajectories show a general resemblance to those shown in Figure 6.3 In general, when the overlap between the component densities is small the maximum likelihood approach and the Isodata procedure can be expected to give similar results.

6.5 UNSUPERVISED BAYESIAN LEARNING

6.5.1 The Bayes Classifier

Maximum likelihood methods do not consider the parameter vector θ to be random—it is just unknown. Prior knowledge about likely values for θ is irrelevant, although in practice such knowledge may be used in choosing good starting points for hill-climbing procedures. In this section we shall take a Bayesian approach to unsupervised learning. We shall assume that θ is a random variable with a known a priori distribution $p(\theta)$, and we shall use the samples to compute the a posteriori density $p(\theta \mid \mathscr{X})$. Interestingly enough, the analysis will virtually parallel the analysis of supervised Bayesian learning, showing that the two problems are formally very similar.

We begin with an explicit statement of our basic assumptions. We assume that:

1. The number of classes is known.
2. The a priori probabilities $P(\omega_j)$ for each class are known, $j = 1, \ldots, c$.
3. The forms for the class-conditional probability densities $p(\mathbf{x} \mid \omega_j, \theta_j)$ are known, $j = 1, \ldots, c$, but the parameter vector $\theta = (\theta_1, \ldots, \theta_c)$ is not known.
4. Part of our knowledge about θ is contained in a known a priori density $p(\theta)$.
5. The rest of our knowledge about θ is contained in a set $\mathscr{X}$ of n samples $\mathbf{x}_1, \ldots, \mathbf{x}_n$ drawn independently from the mixture density

$$p(\mathbf{x} \mid \theta) = \sum_{j=1}^{c} p(\mathbf{x} \mid \omega_j, \theta_j) P(\omega_j). \tag{1}$$

At this point we could go directly to the calculation of $p(\theta \mid \mathscr{X})$. However, let us first see how this density is used to determine the Bayes classifier. Suppose that a state of nature is selected with probability $P(\omega_i)$ and a feature vector $\mathbf{x}$ is selected according to the probability law $p(\mathbf{x} \mid \omega_i, \theta_i)$. To derive the Bayes classifier we must use all of the information at our disposal to compute the a posteriori probability $P(\omega_i \mid \mathbf{x})$. We exhibit the role of the samples explicitly by writing this as $P(\omega_i \mid \mathbf{x}, \mathscr{X})$. By Bayes rule,

$$P(\omega_i \mid \mathbf{x}, \mathscr{X}) = \frac{p(\mathbf{x} \mid \omega_i, \mathscr{X}) P(\omega_i \mid \mathscr{X})}{\displaystyle\sum_{j=1}^{c} p(\mathbf{x} \mid \omega_j, \mathscr{X}) P(\omega_j \mid \mathscr{X})}.$$

Since the selection of the state of nature ω_i was done independently of the previously drawn samples, $P(\omega_i \mid \mathscr{X}) = P(\omega_i)$, and we obtain

$$P(\omega_i \mid \mathbf{x}, \mathscr{X}) = \frac{p(\mathbf{x} \mid \omega_i, \mathscr{X})P(\omega_i)}{\sum\limits_{j=1}^{c} p(\mathbf{x} \mid \omega_j, \mathscr{X})P(\omega_j)}. \tag{18}$$

We introduce the unknown parameter vector by writing

$$p(\mathbf{x} \mid \omega_i, \mathscr{X}) = \int p(\mathbf{x}, \boldsymbol{\theta} \mid \omega_i, \mathscr{X}) \, d\boldsymbol{\theta}$$

$$= \int p(\mathbf{x} \mid \boldsymbol{\theta}, \omega_i, \mathscr{X})p(\boldsymbol{\theta} \mid \omega_i, \mathscr{X}) \, d\boldsymbol{\theta}.$$

Since the selection of $\mathbf{x}$ is independent of the samples, $p(\mathbf{x} \mid \boldsymbol{\theta}, \omega_i, \mathscr{X}) = p(\mathbf{x} \mid \omega_i, \boldsymbol{\theta}_i)$. Similarly, since knowledge of the state of nature when $\mathbf{x}$ is selected tells us nothing about the distribution of $\boldsymbol{\theta}$, $p(\boldsymbol{\theta} \mid \omega_i, \mathscr{X}) = p(\boldsymbol{\theta} \mid \mathscr{X})$. Thus we obtain

$$p(\mathbf{x} \mid \omega_i, \mathscr{X}) = \int p(\mathbf{x} \mid \omega_i, \boldsymbol{\theta}_i)p(\boldsymbol{\theta} \mid \mathscr{X}) \, d\boldsymbol{\theta}. \tag{19}$$

That is, our best estimate of $p(\mathbf{x} \mid \omega_i)$ is obtained by averaging $p(\mathbf{x} \mid \omega_i, \boldsymbol{\theta}_i)$ over $\boldsymbol{\theta}_i$. Whether or not this is a good estimate depends on the nature of $p(\boldsymbol{\theta} \mid \mathscr{X})$, and thus our attention turns at last to that density.

6.5.2 Learning the Parameter Vector

Using Bayes rule, we can write

$$p(\boldsymbol{\theta} \mid \mathscr{X}) = \frac{p(\mathscr{X} \mid \boldsymbol{\theta})p(\boldsymbol{\theta})}{\int p(\mathscr{X} \mid \boldsymbol{\theta})p(\boldsymbol{\theta}) \, d\boldsymbol{\theta}} \tag{20}$$

where the independence of the samples yields

$$p(\mathscr{X} \mid \boldsymbol{\theta}) = \prod_{k=1}^{n} p(\mathbf{x}_k \mid \boldsymbol{\theta}). \tag{21}$$

Alternatively, letting $\mathscr{X}^n$ denote the set of n samples, we can write Eq. (20) in the recursive form

$$p(\boldsymbol{\theta} \mid \mathscr{X}^n) = \frac{p(\mathbf{x}_n \mid \boldsymbol{\theta})p(\boldsymbol{\theta} \mid \mathscr{X}^{n-1})}{\int p(\mathbf{x}_n \mid \boldsymbol{\theta})p(\boldsymbol{\theta} \mid \mathscr{X}^{n-1}) \, d\boldsymbol{\theta}}. \tag{22}$$

These are the basic equations for unsupervised Bayesian learning. Eq. (20) emphasizes the relation between the Bayesian and the maximum likelihood solutions. If $p(\boldsymbol{\theta})$ is essentially uniform over the region where $p(\mathscr{X} \mid \boldsymbol{\theta})$ peaks, then $p(\boldsymbol{\theta} \mid \mathscr{X})$ peaks at the same place. If the only significant peak occurs at $\boldsymbol{\theta} = \hat{\boldsymbol{\theta}}$ and if the peak is very sharp, then Eqs. (19) and (18) yield

$$p(\mathbf{x} \mid \omega_i, \mathscr{X}) \approx p(\mathbf{x} \mid \omega_i, \hat{\boldsymbol{\theta}}_i)$$

and

$$P(\omega_i \mid \mathbf{x}, \mathscr{X}) \approx \frac{p(\mathbf{x} \mid \omega_i, \hat{\boldsymbol{\theta}}_i)P(\omega_i)}{\sum\limits_{j=1}^{c} p(\mathbf{x} \mid \omega_j, \hat{\boldsymbol{\theta}}_j)P(\omega_j)}.$$

That is, these conditions justify the use of the maximum likelihood estimate as if it were the true value of $\boldsymbol{\theta}$ in designing the Bayes classifier.

Of course, if $p(\boldsymbol{\theta})$ has been obtained by supervised learning using a large set of labelled samples, it will be far from uniform, and it will have a dominant influence on $p(\boldsymbol{\theta} \mid \mathscr{X}^n)$, when n is small. Eq. (22) shows how the observation of an additional unlabelled sample modifies our opinion about the true value of $\boldsymbol{\theta}$, and emphasizes the ideas of updating and learning. If the mixture density $p(\mathbf{x} \mid \boldsymbol{\theta})$ is identifiable, then each additional sample tends to sharpen $p(\boldsymbol{\theta} \mid \mathscr{X}^n)$, and under fairly general conditions $p(\boldsymbol{\theta} \mid \mathscr{X}^n)$ can be shown to converge (in probability) to a Dirac delta function centered at the true value of $\boldsymbol{\theta}$. Thus, even though we do not know the categories of the samples, identifiability assures us that we can learn the unknown parameter vector $\boldsymbol{\theta}$, and thereby learn the component densities $p(\mathbf{x} \mid \omega_i, \boldsymbol{\theta})$.

This, then, is the formal Bayesian solution to the problem of unsupervised learning. In retrospect, the fact that unsupervised learning of the parameters of a mixture density is so similar to supervised learning of the parameters of a component density is not at all surprising. Indeed, if the component density is itself a mixture, there would appear to be no essential difference between the two problems.

However, there are some significant differences between supervised and unsupervised learning. One of the major differences concerns the problem of identifiability. With supervised learning, lack of identifiability merely means that instead of obtaining a unique parameter vector we obtain an equivalence class of parameter vectors. However, since all of these yield the same component density, lack of identifiability presents no theoretical difficulty. With unsupervised learning, lack of identifiability is much more serious. When $\boldsymbol{\theta}$ can not be determined uniquely, the mixture can not be decomposed into its true components. Thus, while $p(\mathbf{x} \mid \mathscr{X}^n)$ may still converge to $p(\mathbf{x})$, $p(\mathbf{x} \mid \omega_i, \mathscr{X}^n)$ given by Eq. (19) will not in general converge to $p(\mathbf{x} \mid \omega_i)$, and a theoretical barrier to learning exists.

Another serious problem for unsupervised learning is computational complexity. With supervised learning, the possibility of finding sufficient statistics allows solutions that are analytically pleasing and computationally feasible. With unsupervised learning, there is no way to avoid the fact that the samples are obtained from a mixture density,

$$p(\mathbf{x} \mid \boldsymbol{\theta}) = \sum_{j=1}^{c} p(\mathbf{x} \mid \omega_j, \boldsymbol{\theta}_j) P(\omega_j), \tag{1}$$

and this gives us little hope of ever finding simple exact solutions for $p(\boldsymbol{\theta} \mid \mathcal{X})$. Such solutions are tied to the existence of a simple sufficient statistic, and the factorization theorem requires the ability to factor $p(\mathcal{X} \mid \boldsymbol{\theta})$ as

$$p(\mathcal{X} \mid \boldsymbol{\theta}) = g(\mathbf{s}, \boldsymbol{\theta}) h(\mathcal{X}).$$

But from Eqs. (21) and (1),

$$p(\mathcal{X} \mid \boldsymbol{\theta}) = \prod_{k=1}^{n} \left[\sum_{j=1}^{c} p(\mathbf{x}_k \mid \omega_j, \boldsymbol{\theta}_j) P(\omega_j) \right].$$

Thus, $p(\mathcal{X} \mid \boldsymbol{\theta})$ is the sum of c^n products of component densities. Each term in this sum can be interpreted as the joint probability of obtaining the samples $\mathbf{x}_1, \ldots, \mathbf{x}_n$ bearing a particular labelling, with the sum extending over all of the ways that the samples could be labelled. Clearly, this results in a thorough mixture of $\boldsymbol{\theta}$ and the $\mathbf{x}$'s, and no simple factoring should be expected. An exception to this statement arises if the component densities do not overlap, so that as $\boldsymbol{\theta}$ varies only one term the mixture density is non-zero. In that case, $p(\mathcal{X} \mid \boldsymbol{\theta})$ is the product of the n nonzero terms, and may possess a simple sufficient statistic. However, since that case allows the class of any sample to be determined, it actually reduces the problem to one of supervised learning, and thus is not a significant exception.

Another way to compare supervised and unsupervised learning is to substitute the mixture density for $p(\mathbf{x}_n \mid \boldsymbol{\theta})$ in Eq. (22) and obtain

$$p(\boldsymbol{\theta} \mid \mathcal{X}^n) = \frac{\sum\limits_{j=1}^{c} p(\mathbf{x}_n \mid \omega_j, \boldsymbol{\theta}_j) P(\omega_j)}{\sum\limits_{j=1}^{c} \int p(\mathbf{x}_n \mid \omega_j, \boldsymbol{\theta}_j) P(\omega_j) p(\boldsymbol{\theta} \mid \mathcal{X}^{n-1}) \, d\boldsymbol{\theta}} \, p(\boldsymbol{\theta} \mid \mathcal{X}^{n-1}). \tag{23}$$

If we consider the special case where $P(\omega_1) = 1$ and all the other a priori probabilities are zero, corresponding to the supervised case in which all samples come from Class 1, then Eq. (23) simplifies to

$$p(\boldsymbol{\theta} \mid \mathcal{X}^n) = \frac{p(\mathbf{x}_n \mid \omega_1, \boldsymbol{\theta}_1)}{\int p(\mathbf{x}_n \mid \omega_1, \boldsymbol{\theta}_1) p(\boldsymbol{\theta} \mid \mathcal{X}^{n-1}) \, d\boldsymbol{\theta}} \, p(\boldsymbol{\theta} \mid \mathcal{X}^{n-1}). \tag{24}$$

Let us compare Eqs. (23) and (24) to see how observing an additional sample changes our estimate of $\boldsymbol{\theta}$. In each case we can ignore the denominator, which is independent of $\boldsymbol{\theta}$. Thus, the only significant difference is that in the supervised case we multiply the "a priori" density for $\boldsymbol{\theta}$ by the component density $p(\mathbf{x}_n \mid \omega_1, \boldsymbol{\theta}_1)$, while in the unsupervised case we multiply it by the mixture density $\sum_{j=1}^{c} p(\mathbf{x}_n \mid \omega_j, \boldsymbol{\theta}_j)P(\omega_j)$. Assuming that the sample really did come from Class 1, we see that the effect of not knowing this category membership in the unsupervised case is to diminish the influence of $\mathbf{x}_n$ on changing $\boldsymbol{\theta}$. Since $\mathbf{x}_n$ could have come from any of the c classes, we cannot use it with full effectiveness in changing the component(s) of $\boldsymbol{\theta}$ associated with any one category. Rather, we must distribute its effect over the various categories in accordance with the probability that it arose from each category.

6.5.3 An Example

Consider the one-dimensional, two-component mixture with $p(x \mid \omega_1) \sim N(\mu, 1)$, $p(x \mid \omega_2, \theta) \sim N(\theta, 1)$, where μ, $P(\omega_1)$ and $P(\omega_2)$ are known. Here

$$p(x \mid \theta) = \frac{P(\omega_1)}{\sqrt{2\pi}} \exp[-\tfrac{1}{2}(x - \mu)^2] + \frac{P(\omega_2)}{\sqrt{2\pi}} \exp[-\tfrac{1}{2}(x - \theta)^2].$$

Viewed as a function of x, this mixture density is a superposition of two normal densities, one peaking at $x = \mu$ and the other peaking at $x = \theta$. Viewed as a function of θ, $p(x \mid \theta)$ has a single peak at $\theta = x$. Suppose that the a priori density $p(\theta)$ is uniform from a to b. Then after one observation

$$p(\theta \mid x_1) = \alpha p(x_1 \mid \theta) p(\theta)$$

$$= \begin{cases} \alpha' [P(\omega_1) \exp[-\tfrac{1}{2}(x_1 - \mu)^2] \\ \qquad + P(\omega_2) \exp[-\tfrac{1}{2}(x_1 - \theta)^2]] & a \le \theta \le b \\ 0 & \text{otherwise,} \end{cases}$$

where α and α' are normalizing constants, independent of θ. If the sample x_1 is in the range $a \le x_1 \le b$, then $p(\theta \mid x_1)$ peaks at $\theta = x_1$. Otherwise it peaks either at $\theta = a$ if $x_1 < a$ or at $\theta = b$ if $x_1 > b$. Note that the additive constant $\exp[-(1/2)(x_1 - \mu)^2]$ is large if x_1 is near μ, and thus the peak of $p(\theta \mid x_1)$ is less pronounced if x_1 is near μ. This corresponds to the fact that if x_1 is near μ, it is more likely to have come from the $p(x \mid \omega_1)$ component, and hence its influence on our estimate for θ is diminished.

With the addition of a second sample x_2, $p(\theta \mid x_1)$ changes to

$$p(\theta \mid x_1, x_2) = \beta p(x_2 \mid \theta) p(\theta \mid x_1)$$

$$= \begin{cases} \beta' [P(\omega_1)P(\omega_1) \exp[-\tfrac{1}{2}(x_1 - \mu)^2 - \tfrac{1}{2}(x_2 - \mu)^2] \\ + P(\omega_1)P(\omega_2) \exp[-\tfrac{1}{2}(x_1 - \mu)^2 - \tfrac{1}{2}(x_2 - \theta)^2] \\ + P(\omega_2)P(\omega_1) \exp[-\tfrac{1}{2}(x_1 - \theta)^2 - \tfrac{1}{2}(x_2 - \mu)^2] \\ + P(\omega_2)P(\omega_2) \exp[-\tfrac{1}{2}(x_1 - \theta)^2 - \tfrac{1}{2}(x_2 - \theta)^2]] \\ \qquad\qquad\qquad\qquad\qquad\qquad a \le \theta \le b \\ 0 \qquad\qquad\qquad\qquad\qquad\qquad\qquad \text{otherwise.} \end{cases}$$

Unfortunately, the primary thing we learn from this expression is that $p(\theta \mid \mathcal{X}^n)$ is already complicated when $n = 2$. The four terms in the sum correspond to the four ways in which the samples could have been drawn from the two component populations. With n samples there will be 2^n terms,

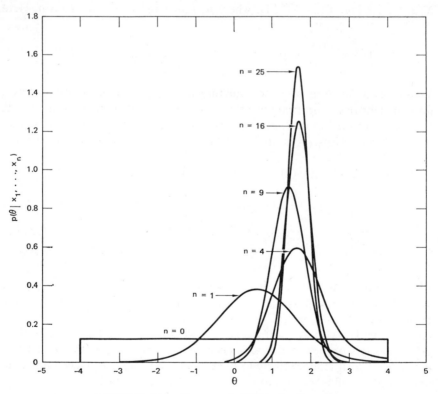

FIGURE 6.5. **Unsupervised Bayesian learning.**

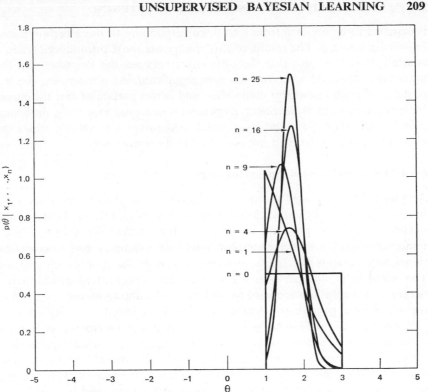

FIGURE 6.6.   The effect of narrowing the a priori density.

and no simple sufficient statistics can be found to facilitate understanding or to simplify computations.

It is possible to use the relation

$$p(\theta \mid \mathcal{X}^n) = \frac{p(x_n \mid \theta)p(\theta \mid \mathcal{X}^{n-1})}{\displaystyle\int p(x_n \mid \theta)p(\theta \mid \mathcal{X}^{n-1}) \, d\theta}$$

and numerical integration to obtain an approximate numerical solution for $p(\theta \mid \mathcal{X}^n)$. This was done for the data in Table 6-1 using the values $\mu = 2$, $P(\omega_1) = 1/3$, and $P(\omega_2) = 2/3$. An a priori density $p(\theta)$ uniform from -4 to 4 encompasses the data in that table. When this was used to start the recursive computation of $p(\theta \mid \mathcal{X}^n)$, the results shown in Figure 6.5 were obtained. As n goes to infinity we can confidently expect $p(\theta \mid \mathcal{X}^n)$ to approach an impulse centered at $\theta = 2$. This graph gives some idea of the rate of convergence.

One of the main differences between the Bayesian and the maximum likelihood approaches to unsupervised learning appears in the presence of the a priori density $p(\theta)$. Figure 6.6 shows how $p(\theta \mid \mathcal{X}^n)$ changes when $p(\theta)$

is assumed to be uniform from 1 to 3, corresponding to more certain initial knowledge about θ. The results of this change are most pronounced when n is small. It is here also that the differences between the Bayesian and the maximum likelihood solutions are most significant. As n increases, the importance of prior knowledge diminishes, and in this particular case the curves for $n = 25$ are virtually identical. In general, one would expect the difference to be small when the number of unlabelled samples is several times the effective number of labelled samples used to determine $p(\theta)$.

6.5.4 Decision-Directed Approximations

Although the problem of unsupervised learning can be stated as merely the problem of estimating parameters of a mixture density, neither the maximum likelihood nor the Bayesian approach yields analytically simple results. Exact solutions for even the simplest nontrivial examples lead to computational requirements that grow exponentially with the number of samples. The problem of unsupervised learning is too important to abandon just because exact solutions are hard to find, however, and numerous procedures for obtaining approximate solutions have been suggested.

Since the basic difference between supervised and unsupervised learning is the presence or absence of labels for the samples, an obvious approach to unsupervised learning is to use the a priori information to design a classifier and to use the decisions of this classifier to label the samples. This is called the *decision-directed* approach to unsupervised learning, and it is subject to many variations. It can be applied sequentially by updating the classifier each time an unlabelled sample is classified. Alternatively, it can be applied in parallel by waiting until all n samples are classified before updating the classifier. If desired, this process can be repeated until no changes occur in the way the samples are labelled.* Various heuristics can be introduced to make the extent of any corrections depend upon the confidence of the classification decision.

There are some obvious dangers associated with the decision-directed approach. If the initial classifier is not reasonably good, or if an unfortunate sequence of samples is encountered, the errors in classifying the unlabelled samples can drive the classifier the wrong way, resulting in a solution corresponding roughly to one of the lesser peaks of the likelihood function. Even if the initial classifier is optimal, the resulting labelling will not in general be the same as the true class membership; the act of classification will exclude samples from the tails of the desired distribution, and will include samples from the tails of the other distributions. Thus, if there is significant

---

* The Basic Isodata procedure described in Section 6.4.4 is essentially a decision-directed procedure of this type.

overlap between the component densities, one can expect biased estimates and less than optimal results.

Despite these drawbacks, the simplicity of decision-directed procedures makes the Bayesian approach computationally feasible, and a flawed solution is often better than none. If conditions are favorable, performance that is nearly optimal can be achieved at far less computational expense. The literature contains a few rather complicated analyses of particular decision-directed procedures, and numerous reports of experimental results. The basic conclusions are that most of these procedures work well if the parametric assumptions are valid, if there is little overlap between the component densities, and if the initial classifier design is at least roughly correct.

6.6 DATA DESCRIPTION AND CLUSTERING

Let us reconsider our original problem of learning something of use from a set of unlabelled samples. Viewed geometrically, these samples form clouds of points in a d-dimensional space. Suppose that we knew that these points came from a single normal distribution. Then the most we could learn from the data would be contained in the sufficient statistics—the sample mean and the sample covariance matrix. In essence, these statistics constitute a compact description of the data. The sample mean locates the center of gravity of the cloud. It can be thought of as the single point x that best represents all of the data in the sense of minimizing the sum of squared distances from x to the samples. The sample covariance matrix tells us how well the sample mean describes the data in terms of the amount of scatter that exists in various directions. If the data points are actually normally distributed, then the cloud has a simple hyperellipsoidal shape, and the sample mean tends to fall in the region where the samples are most densely concentrated.

Of course, if the samples are not normally distributed, these statistics can give a very misleading description of the data. Figure 6.7 shows four different data sets that all have the same mean and covariance matrix. Obviously, second-order statistics are incapable of revealing all of the structure in an arbitrary set of data.

By assuming that the samples come from a mixture of c normal distributions, we can approximate a greater variety of situations. In essence, this corresponds to assuming that the samples fall in hyperellipsoidally-shaped clouds of various sizes and orientations. If the number of component densities is not limited, we can approximate virtually any density function in this way, and use the parameters of the mixture to describe the data. Unfortunately, we have seen that the problem of estimating the parameters of a mixture

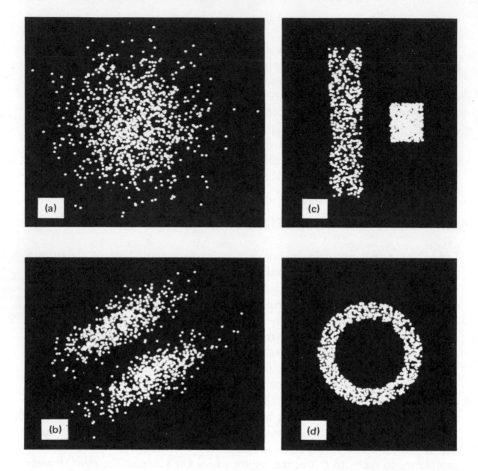

FIGURE 6.7.   Data sets having identical second-order statistics.

density is not trivial. Furthermore, in situations where we have relatively little a priori knowledge about the nature of the data, the assumption of particular parametric forms may lead to poor or meaningless results. Instead of finding structure in the data, we would be imposing structure on it.

One alternative is to use one of the nonparametric methods described in Chapter 4 to estimate the unknown mixture density. If accurate, the resulting estimate is certainly a complete description of what we can learn from the data. Regions of high local density, which might correspond to significant subclasses in the population, can be found from the peaks or modes of the estimated density.

If the goal is to find subclasses, a more direct alternative is to use a *clustering procedure*. Roughly speaking, clustering procedures yield a data description in terms of clusters or groups of data points that possess strong internal similarities. The more formal procedures use a criterion function, such as the sum of the squared distances from the cluster centers, and seek the grouping that extremizes the criterion function. Because even this can lead to unmanageable computational problems, other procedures have been proposed that are intuitively appealing but that lead to solutions having no established properties. Their use is usually justified on the ground that they are easy to apply and often yield interesting results that may guide the application of more rigorous procedures.

6.7 SIMILARITY MEASURES

Once we describe the clustering problem as one of finding natural groupings in a set of data, we are obliged to define what we mean by a natural grouping. In what sense are we to say that the samples in one cluster are more like one another than like samples in other clusters? This question actually involves two separate issues—how should one measure the similarity between samples, and how should one evaluate a partitioning of a set of samples into clusters? In this section we address the first of these issues.

The most obvious measure of the similarity (or dissimilarity) between two samples is the distance between them. One way to begin a clustering investigation is to define a suitable distance function and compute the matrix of distances between all pairs of samples. If distance is a good measure of dissimilarity, then one would expect the distance between samples in the same cluster to be significantly less than the distance between samples in the different clusters.

Suppose for the moment that we say that two samples belong to the same cluster if the Euclidean distance between them is less than some threshold distance d_0. It is immediately obvious that the choice of d_0 is very important. If d_0 is very large, all of the samples will be assigned to one cluster. If d_0 is very small, each sample will form an isolated cluster. To obtain "natural" clusters, d_0 will have to be greater than typical within-cluster distances and less than typical between-cluster distances (see Figure 6.8).

Less obvious perhaps is the fact that the results of clustering depend on the choice of Euclidean distance as a measure of dissimilarity. This choice implies that the feature space is isotropic. Consequently, clusters defined by Euclidean distance will be invariant to translations or rotations—rigid-body motions of the data points. However, they will not be invariant to linear transformations in general, or to other transformations that distort the

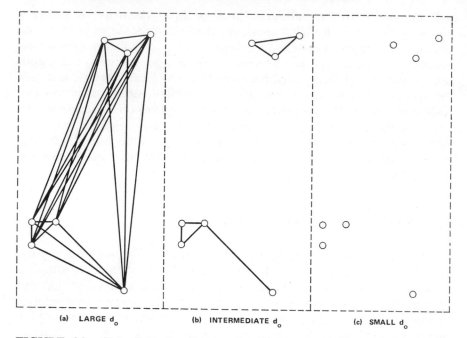

(a)   LARGE d_0 (b) INTERMEDIATE d_0 (c) SMALL d_0

FIGURE 6.8. The effect of a distance threshold on clustering (Lines are drawn between points closer than a distance d_0 apart).

distance relationships. Thus, as Figure 6.9 illustrates, a simple scaling of the coordinate axes can result in a different grouping of the data into clusters. Of course, this is of no concern for problems in which arbitrary rescaling is an unnatural or meaningless transformation. However, if clusters are to mean anything, they should be invariant to transformations natural to the problem.

One way to achieve invariance is to normalize the data prior to clustering. For example, to obtain invariance to displacement and scale changes, one might translate and scale the axes so that all of the features have zero mean and unit variance. To obtain invariance to rotation, one might rotate the axes so that they coincide with the eigenvectors of the sample covariance matrix. This transformation to *principal components* can be preceded and/or followed by normalization for scale.

However, the reader should not conclude that this kind of normalization is necessarily desirable. Consider, for example, the matter of translating and scaling the axes so that each feature has zero mean and unit variance. The rationale usually given for this normalization is that it prevents certain features from dominating distance calculations merely because they have large numerical values. Subtracting the mean and dividing by the standard deviation is an appropriate normalization if this spread of values is due to normal random variation; however, it can be quite inappropriate if the spread is due to the presence of subclasses (see Figure 6.10). Thus, this routine normalization may be less than helpful in the cases of greatest interest. Section 6.8.3 describes some better ways to obtain invariance to scaling.

An alternative to normalizing the data and using Euclidean distance is to use some kind of normalized distance, such as the Mahalanobis distance. More generally, one can abandon the use of distance altogether and introduce a nonmetric *similarity function* $s(\mathbf{x}, \mathbf{x}')$ to compare two vectors $\mathbf{x}$ and $\mathbf{x}'$. Conventionally, this is a symmetric function whose value is large when $\mathbf{x}$ and $\mathbf{x}'$ are similar. For example, when the angle between two vectors is a

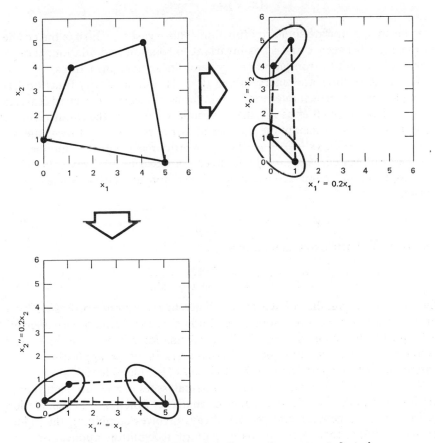

FIGURE 6.9.   The effect of scaling on the apparent clustering.

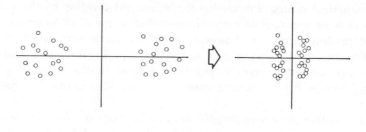

(a) UNNORMALIZED   (b) NORMALIZED

FIGURE 6.10.   Undesirable effects of normalization.

meaningful measure of their similarity, then the normalized inner product

$$s(\mathbf{x}, \mathbf{x}') = \frac{\mathbf{x}^t \mathbf{x}'}{\|\mathbf{x}\| \, \|\mathbf{x}'\|}$$

may be an appropriate similarity function. This measure, which is the cosine of the angle between $\mathbf{x}$ and $\mathbf{x}'$, is invariant to rotation and dilation, though it is not invariant to translation and general linear transformations.

When the features are binary valued (0 or 1), this similarity function has a simple nongeometrical interpretation in terms of measuring shared features or shared attributes. Let us say that a sample $\mathbf{x}$ *possesses* the ith attribute if $x_i = 1$. Then $\mathbf{x}^t\mathbf{x}'$ is merely the number of attributes possessed by $\mathbf{x}$ and $\mathbf{x}'$, and $\|\mathbf{x}\| \, \|\mathbf{x}'\| = (\mathbf{x}^t\mathbf{x}\mathbf{x}'^t\mathbf{x}')^{1/2}$ is the geometric mean of the number of attributes possessed by $\mathbf{x}$ and the number possessed by $\mathbf{x}'$. Thus, $s(\mathbf{x}, \mathbf{x}')$ is a measure of the relative possession of common attributes. Some simple variations are

$$s(\mathbf{x}, \mathbf{x}') = \frac{\mathbf{x}^t \mathbf{x}'}{d},$$

the fraction of attributes shared, and

$$s(\mathbf{x}, \mathbf{x}') = \frac{\mathbf{x}^t \mathbf{x}'}{\mathbf{x}^t\mathbf{x} + \mathbf{x}'^t\mathbf{x}' - \mathbf{x}^t\mathbf{x}'},$$

the ratio of the number of shared attributes to the number possessed by $\mathbf{x}$ or $\mathbf{x}'$. This latter measure (sometimes known as the Tanimoto coefficient) is frequently encountered in the fields of information retrieval and biological taxonomy. Other measures of similarity arise in other applications, the variety of measures testifying to the diversity of problem domains.

We feel obliged to mention that fundamental issues in measurement theory are involved in the use of any distance or similarity function. The calculation of the similarity between two vectors always involves combining the values of their components. Yet, in many pattern recognition applications the components of the feature vector measure seemingly noncomparable quantities. Using our early example of classifying lumber, how can one compare the brightness to the straightness-of-grain? Should the comparison depend on whether the brightness is measured in candles/m^2 or in foot-lamberts? How does one treat vectors whose components have a mixture of nominal, ordinal, interval, and ratio scales?* Ultimately, there is no methodological answer to these questions. When a user selects a particular similarity function or normalizes his data in a particular way, he introduces information that gives the procedure meaning. We have given examples of some alternatives that have proved to be useful. Beyond that we can do little more than alert the unwary to these pitfalls of clustering.

6.8 CRITERION FUNCTIONS FOR CLUSTERING

Suppose that we have a set $\mathcal{X}$ of n samples $x_1, \ldots, x_n$ that we want to partition into exactly c disjoint subsets $\mathcal{X}_1, \ldots, \mathcal{X}_c$. Each subset is to represent a cluster, with samples in the same cluster being somehow more similar than samples in different clusters. One way to make this into a well-defined problem is to define a criterion function that measures the clustering quality of any partition of the data. Then the problem is one of finding the partition that extremizes the criterion function. In this section we examine the characteristics of several basically similar criterion functions, postponing until later the question of how to find an optimal partition.

6.8.1 The Sum-of-Squared-Error Criterion

The simplest and most widely used criterion function for clustering is the sum-of-squared-error criterion. Let n_i be the number of samples in $\mathcal{X}_i$ and let m_i be the mean of those samples,

$$m_i = \frac{1}{n_i} \sum_{x \in \mathcal{X}_i} x. \tag{25}$$

Then the sum of squared errors is defined by

$$J_e = \sum_{i=1}^{c} \sum_{x \in \mathcal{X}_i} \|x - m_i\|^2. \tag{26}$$

This criterion function has a simple interpretation. For a given cluster $\mathcal{X}_i$, the mean vector m_i is the best representative of the samples in $\mathcal{X}_i$ in the sense that it minimizes the sum of the squared lengths of the "error" vectors $x - m_i$. Thus, J_e measures the total squared error incurred in representing the n samples $x_1, \ldots, x_n$ by the c cluster centers $m_1, \ldots, m_c$. The value of

* These fundamental considerations are by no means unique to clustering. They appear, for example, whenever one chooses a parametric form for an unknown probability density function. Clustering problems merely expose them more clearly.

J_e depends on how the samples are grouped into clusters, and an optimal partitioning is defined as one that minimizes J_e. Clusterings of this type are often called *minimum variance* partitions.

What kind of clustering problems are well suited to a sum-of-squared-error criterion? Basically, J_e is an appropriate criterion when the clusters form essentially compact clouds that are rather well separated from one another. It should work well for the two or three clusters in Figure 6.11, but one would not expect reasonable results for the data in Figure 6.12.* A less obvious problem arises when there are great differences in the number of samples in

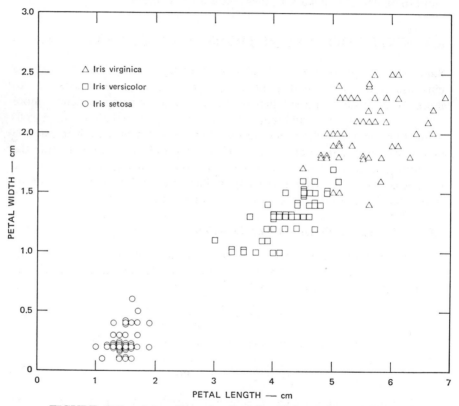

FIGURE 6.11.   A two-dimensional section of the Anderson iris data.

* These two data sets are well known for quite different reasons. Figure 6.11 shows two of four measurements made by E. Anderson on 150 samples of three species of iris. These data were listed and used by R. A. Fisher in his classic paper on discriminant analysis (Fisher 1936), and have since become a favorite example for illustrating clustering procedures. Figure 6.12 is well known in astronomy as the Hertzsprung and Russell (or spectrum-luminosity) diagram, which led to the subdivision of stars into such categories as giants, supergiants, main sequence stars, and dwarfs. It was used by E. W. Forgey and again by D. Wishart (1969) to illustrate the limitations of simple clustering procedures.

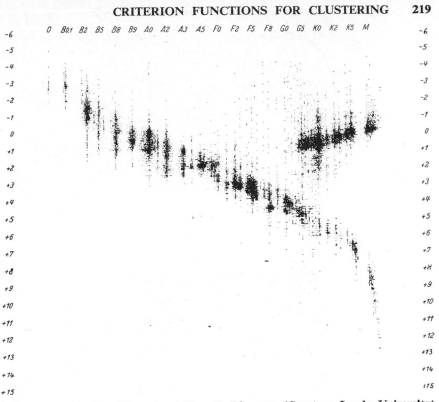

FIGURE 6.12.   The Herzsprung-Russell Diagram (Courtesy Lunds Universitet Institutionen für Astronomi).

different clusters. In that case it can happen that a partition that splits a large cluster is favored over one that maintains the integrity of the clusters merely because the slight reduction in squared error achieved is multiplied by many terms in the sum (see Figure 6.13). This situation frequently arises because of the presence of "outliers" or "wild shots," and brings up the problem of interpreting and evaluating the results of clustering. Since little can be said about that problem, we shall merely observe that if additional considerations render the results of minimizing J_e unsatisfactory, then these considerations should be used, if possible, in formulating a better criterion function.

6.8.2   Related Minimum Variance Criteria

By some simple algebraic manipulation we can eliminate the mean vectors from the expression for J_e and obtain the equivalent expression

$$J_e = \tfrac{1}{2} \sum_{i=1}^{c} n_i \bar{s}_i, \tag{27}$$

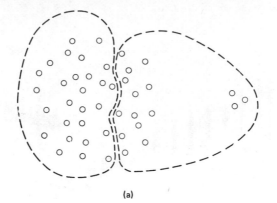

(a)

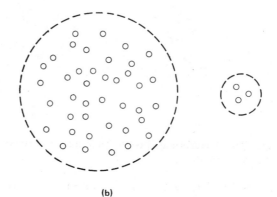

(b)

FIGURE 6.13. The problem of splitting large clusters: the sum of squared error is smaller for (a) than
for (b).

where

$$\bar{s}_i = \frac{1}{n_i^2} \sum_{\mathbf{x} \in \mathscr{X}_i} \sum_{\mathbf{x}' \in \mathscr{X}_i} \|\mathbf{x} - \mathbf{x}'\|^2. \tag{28}$$

Eq. (28) leads us to interpret $\bar{s}_i$ as the average squared distance between
points in the ith cluster, and emphasizes the fact that the sum-of-squared-error
criterion uses Euclidean distance as the measure of similarity. It also suggests
an obvious way of obtaining other criterion functions. For example, one can
replace $\bar{s}_i$ by the average, the median, or perhaps the maximum distance
between points in a cluster. More generally, one can introduce an appropriate

similarity function $s(\mathbf{x}, \mathbf{x}')$ and replace $\bar{s}_i$ by functions such as

$$\bar{s}_i = \frac{1}{n_i^2} \sum_{\mathbf{x} \in \mathscr{X}_i} \sum_{\mathbf{x}' \in \mathscr{X}_i} s(\mathbf{x}, \mathbf{x}') \tag{29}$$

or

$$\bar{s}_i = \min_{\mathbf{x}, \mathbf{x}' \in \mathscr{X}_i} s(\mathbf{x}, \mathbf{x}'). \tag{30}$$

As before, we define an optimal partitioning as one that extremizes the criterion function. This creates a well-defined problem, and the hope is that its solution discloses the intrinsic structure of the data.

6.8.3 Scattering Criteria

6.8.3.1 THE SCATTER MATRICES

Another interesting class of criterion functions can be derived from the scatter matrices used in multiple discriminant analysis. The following definitions directly parallel the definitions given in Section 4.11.

Mean vector for ith cluster:

$$\mathbf{m}_i = \frac{1}{n_i} \sum_{\mathbf{x} \in \mathscr{X}_i} \mathbf{x}. \tag{31}$$

Total mean vector:

$$\mathbf{m} = \frac{1}{n} \sum_{\mathscr{X}} \mathbf{x} = \frac{1}{n} \sum_{i=1}^{c} n_i \mathbf{m}_i. \tag{32}$$

Scatter matrix for ith cluster:

$$S_i = \sum_{\mathbf{x} \in \mathscr{X}_i} (\mathbf{x} - \mathbf{m}_i)(\mathbf{x} - \mathbf{m}_i)^t. \tag{33}$$

Within-cluster scatter matrix:

$$S_W = \sum_{i=1}^{c} S_i. \tag{34}$$

Between-cluster scatter matrix:

$$S_B = \sum_{i=1}^{c} n_i (\mathbf{m}_i - \mathbf{m})(\mathbf{m}_i - \mathbf{m})^t. \tag{35}$$

Total scatter matrix:

$$S_T = \sum_{\mathbf{x} \in \mathscr{X}} (\mathbf{x} - \mathbf{m})(\mathbf{x} - \mathbf{m})^t. \tag{36}$$

As before, it follows from these definitions that the total scatter matrix is the sum of the within-cluster scatter matrix and the between-cluster scatter matrix:

$$S_T = S_W + S_B. \tag{37}$$

Note that the total scatter matrix does not depend on how the set of samples is partitioned into clusters. It depends only on the total set of samples. The within-cluster and between-cluster scatter matrices do depend on the partitioning, however. Roughly speaking, there is an exchange between these two matrices, the between-cluster scatter going up as the within-cluster scatter goes down. This is fortunate, since by trying to minimize the within-cluster scatter we will also tend to maximize the between-cluster scatter.

To be more precise in talking about the amount of within-cluster or between-cluster scatter, we need a scalar measure of the "size" of a scatter matrix. The two measures that we shall consider are the *trace* and the *determinant*. In the univariate case, these two measures are equivalent, and we can define an optimal partition as one that minimizes S_W or maximizes S_B. In the multivariate case things are somewhat more complicated, and a number of related but distinct optimality criteria have been suggested.

6.8.3.2 THE TRACE CRITERION

Perhaps the simplest scalar measure of a scatter matrix is its trace, the sum of its diagonal elements. Roughly speaking, the trace measures the square of the scattering radius, since it is proportional to the sum of the variances in the coordinate directions. Thus, an obvious criterion function to minimize is the trace of S_W. In fact, this criterion is nothing more or less than the sum-of-squared-error criterion, since Eqs. (33) and (34) yield

$$\operatorname{tr} S_W = \sum_{i=1}^{c} \operatorname{tr} S_i = \sum_{i=1}^{c} \sum_{\mathbf{x} \in \mathcal{X}_i} \|\mathbf{x} - \mathbf{m}_i\|^2 = J_e. \tag{38}$$

Since $\operatorname{tr} S_T = \operatorname{tr} S_W + \operatorname{tr} S_B$ and $\operatorname{tr} S_T$ is independent of how the samples are partitioned, we see that no new results are obtained by trying to maximize $\operatorname{tr} S_B$. However, it is comforting to know that in trying to minimize the within-cluster criterion $J_e = \operatorname{tr} S_W$ we are also maximizing the between-cluster criterion

$$\operatorname{tr} S_B = \sum_{i=1}^{c} n_i \|\mathbf{m}_i - \mathbf{m}\|^2. \tag{39}$$

6.8.3.3 THE DETERMINANT CRITERION

In Section 4.11 we used the determinant of the scatter matrix to obtain a scalar measure of scatter. Roughly speaking, this measures the square of the scattering volume, since it is proportional to the product of the variances in the directions of the principal axes. Since S_B will be singular if the number of clusters is less than or equal to the dimensionality, $|S_B|$ is obviously a poor choice for a criterion function. S_W can also become singular, and will certainly be so if $n - c$ is less than the dimensionality d.* However, if we assume that S_W is nonsingular, we are led to consider the criterion function

$$J_d = |S_W| = \left| \sum_{i=1}^{c} S_i \right|. \tag{40}$$

The partition that minimizes J_d is often similar to the one that minimizes J_e, but the two need not be the same. We observed before that the minimum-squared-error partition might change if the axes are scaled. This does not happen with J_d. To see why, let T be a nonsingular matrix and consider the change of variables $\mathbf{x}' = T\mathbf{x}$. Keeping the partitioning fixed, we obtain new mean vectors $\mathbf{m}'_i = T\mathbf{m}_i$ and new scatter matrices $S'_i = TS_iT^t$. Thus, J_d changes to

$$J'_d = |S'_W| = |TS_WT^t| = |T|^2 J_d.$$

Since the scale factor $|T|^2$ is the same for all partitions, it follows that J_d and J'_d rank the partitions in the same way, and hence that the optimal clustering based on J_d is invariant to nonsingular linear transformations of the data.

6.8.3.4 INVARIANT CRITERIA

It is not hard to show that the eigenvalues $\lambda_1, \ldots, \lambda_d$ of $S_W^{-1}S_B$ are invariant under nonsingular linear transformations of the data. Indeed, these eigenvalues are the basic linear invariants of the scatter matrices. Their numerical values measure the ratio of between-cluster to within-cluster scatter in the direction of the eigenvectors, and partitions that yield large values are usually desirable. Of course, as we pointed out in Section 4.11, the fact that the rank of S_B can not exceed $c - 1$ means that no more than $c - 1$ of these eigenvalues can be nonzero. Nevertheless, good partitions are ones for which the nonzero eigenvalues are large.

One can invent a great variety of invariant clustering criteria by composing appropriate functions of these eigenvalues. Some of these follow naturally from standard matrix operations. For example, since the trace of a matrix is the sum of its eigenvalues, one might elect to maximize the criterion function†

$$\text{tr } S_W^{-1}S_B = \sum_{i=1}^{d} \lambda_i. \tag{41}$$

---

* This follows from the fact that the rank of S_i can not exceed $n_i - 1$, and thus the rank of S_W can not exceed $\Sigma(n_i - 1) = n - c$. Of course, if the samples are confined to a lower dimensional subspace it is possible to have S_W be singular even though $n - c \geq d$. In such cases, some kind of dimensionality-reduction procedure must be used before the determinant criterion can be applied (see Section 6.14).

† Another invariant criterion is

$$|S_W^{-1}S_B| = \prod_{i=1}^{d} \lambda_i.$$

However, since its value is usually zero it is not very useful.

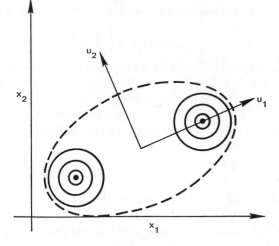

(a) UNNORMALIZED

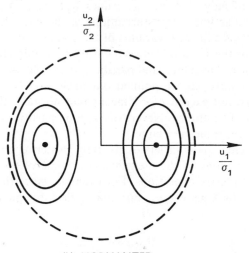

(b) NORMALIZED

FIGURE 6.14. The effect of transforming to normalized principal components (Note: the partition that minimizes $S_T^{-1} S_W$ in (a) minimizes the sum of squared errors in (b).).

By using the relation $S_T = S_W + S_B$, one can derive the following invariant relatives of $\text{tr } S_W$ and $|S_W|$:

$$\text{tr } S_T^{-1} S_W = \sum_{i=1}^{d} \frac{1}{1 + \lambda_i} \tag{42}$$

$$\frac{|S_W|}{|S_T|} = \prod_{i=1}^{d} \frac{1}{1 + \lambda_i}. \tag{43}$$

Since all of these criterion functions are invariant to linear transformations, the same is true of the partitions that extremize them. In the special case of two clusters, only one eigenvalue is nonzero, and all of these criteria yield the same clustering. However, when the samples are partitioned into more than two clusters, the optimal partitions, though often similar, need not be the same.

With regard to the criterion functions involving S_T, note that S_T does not depend on how the samples are partitioned into clusters. Thus, the clusterings that minimize $|S_W|/|S_T|$ are exactly the same as the ones that minimize $|S_W|$. If we rotate and scale the axes so that S_T becomes the identity matrix, we see that minimizing $\text{tr } S_T^{-1} S_W$ is equivalent to minimizing the sum-of-squared-error criterion $\text{tr } S_W$ after performing this normalization. Figure 6.14 illustrates the effects of this transformation graphically. Clearly, this criterion suffers from the very defects that we warned about in Section 6.7, and it is probably the least desirable of these criteria.

One final warning about invariant criteria is in order. If different apparent groupings can be obtained by scaling the axes or by applying any other linear transformation, then all of these groupings will be exposed by invariant procedures. Thus, invariant criterion functions are more likely to possess multiple local extrema, and are correspondingly more difficult to extremize.

The variety of the criterion functions we have discussed and the somewhat subtle differences between them should not be allowed to obscure their essential similarity. In every case the underlying model is that the samples form c fairly well separated clouds of points. The within-cluster scatter matrix S_W is used to measure the compactness of these clouds, and the basic goal is to find the most compact grouping. While this approach has proved useful for many problems, it is not universally applicable. For example, it will not extract a very dense cluster embedded in the center of a diffuse cluster, or separate intertwined line-like clusters. For such cases one must devise other criterion functions that are better matched to the structure present or being sought.

6.9 ITERATIVE OPTIMIZATION

Once a criterion function has been selected, clustering becomes a well-defined problem in discrete optimization: find those partitions of the set of samples that extremize the criterion function. Since the sample set is finite, there are only a finite number of possible partitions. Thus, in theory the clustering problem can always be solved by exhaustive enumeration. However, in practice such an approach is unthinkable for all but the simplest problems. There are approximately $c^n/c!$ ways of partitioning a set of n elements into c subsets,† and this exponential growth with n is overwhelming. For example, an exhaustive search for the best set of 5 clusters in 100 samples would require considering more than 10^{67} partitionings. Thus, in most applications an exhaustive search is completely infeasible.

The approach most frequently used in seeking optimal partitions is iterative optimization. The basic idea is to find some reasonable initial partition and to "move" samples from one group to another if such a move will improve the value of the criterion function. Like hill-climbing procedures in general, these approaches guarantee local but not global optimization. Different starting points can lead to different solutions, and one never knows whether or not the best solution has been found. Despite these limitations, the fact that the computational requirements are bearable makes this approach significant.

Let us consider the use of iterative improvement to minimize the sum-of-squared-error criterion J_e, written as

$$J_e = \sum_{i=1}^{c} J_i,$$

where

$$J_i = \sum_{\mathbf{x} \in \mathcal{X}_i} \|\mathbf{x} - \mathbf{m}_i\|^2$$

and

$$\mathbf{m}_i = \frac{1}{n_i} \sum_{\mathbf{x} \in \mathcal{X}_i} \mathbf{x}.$$

Suppose that a sample $\hat{\mathbf{x}}$ currently in cluster $\mathcal{X}_i$ is tentatively moved to $\mathcal{X}_j$. Then $\mathbf{m}_j$ changes to

$$\mathbf{m}_j^* = \mathbf{m}_j + \frac{\hat{\mathbf{x}} - \mathbf{m}_j}{n_j + 1}$$

---

† The reader who likes combinatorial problems will enjoy showing that there are exactly

$$\frac{1}{c!} \sum_{i=1}^{c} \binom{c}{i} (-1)^{c-i} i^n$$

partitions of n items into c nonempty subsets. (see W. Feller, *An Introduction to Probability Theory and Its Applications*, Vol. I, p. 58 (John Wiley, New York, Second Edition, 1959)). If $n \gg c$, the last term is the most significant.

and J_j increases to

$$J_j^* = \sum_{x \in \mathcal{X}_j} \|x - m_j^*\|^2 + \|\hat{x} - m_j^*\|^2$$

$$= \sum_{x \in \mathcal{X}_j} \left\|x - m_j - \frac{\hat{x} - m_j}{n_j + 1}\right\|^2 + \left\|\frac{n_j}{n_j + 1}(\hat{x} - m_j)\right\|^2$$

$$= J_j + \frac{n_j}{n_j + 1}\|\hat{x} - m_j\|^2.$$

Under the assumption that $n_i \neq 1$ (singleton clusters should not be destroyed), a similar calculation shows that m_i changes to

$$m_i^* = m_i - \frac{\hat{x} - m_i}{n_i - 1}$$

and J_i decreases to

$$J_i^* = J_i - \frac{n_i}{n_i - 1}\|\hat{x} - m_i\|^2.$$

These equations greatly simplify the computation of the change in the criterion function. The transfer of $\hat{x}$ from $\mathcal{X}_i$ to $\mathcal{X}_j$ is advantageous if the decrease in J_i is greater than the increase in J_j. This is the case if

$$n_i/(n_i - 1)\|\hat{x} - m_i\|^2 > n_j/(n_j + 1)\|\hat{x} - m_j\|^2,$$

which typically happens whenever $\hat{x}$ is closer to m_j than m_i. If reassignment is profitable, the greatest decrease in sum of squared error is obtained by selecting the cluster for which $n_j/(n_j + 1)\|\hat{x} - m_j\|^2$ is minimum. This leads to the following clustering procedure:

Procedure: Basic Minimum Squared Error
 1. Select an initial partition of the n samples into clusters and compute J_e and the means $m_1, \ldots, m_c$.

Loop: 2. Select the next candidate sample $\hat{x}$. Suppose that $\hat{x}$ is currently in $\mathcal{X}_i$.

 3. If $n_i = 1$ go to Next; otherwise compute

$$\rho_j = \begin{cases} \dfrac{n_j}{n_j + 1}\|\hat{x} - m_j\|^2 & j \neq i \\[3mm] \dfrac{n_i}{n_i - 1}\|\hat{x} - m_i\|^2 & j = i. \end{cases}$$

 4. Transfer $\hat{x}$ to $\mathcal{X}_k$ if $\rho_k \leq \rho_j$ for all j.
 5. Update J_e, m_i, and m_k.

Next: 6. If J_e has not changed in n attempts, stop; otherwise go to Loop.

If this procedure is compared to the Basic Isodata procedure described in Section 6.4.4, it is clear that the former is essentially a sequential version of the latter. Where the Basic Isodata procedure waits until all n samples have been reclassified before updating, the Basic Minimum Squared Error procedure updates after each sample is reclassified. It has been experimentally observed that this procedure is more susceptible to being trapped at a local minimum, and it has the further disadvantage of making the results depend on the order in which the candidates are selected. However, it is at least a stepwise optimal procedure, and it can be easily modified to apply to problems in which samples are acquired sequentially and clustering must be done in real time.

One question that plagues all hill-climbing procedures is the choice of the starting point. Unfortunately, there is no simple, universally good solution to this problem. One approach is to select c samples randomly for the initial cluster centers, using them to partition the data on a minimum-distance basis. Repetition with different random selections can give some indication of the sensitivity of the solution to the starting point. Another approach is to find the c-cluster starting point from the solution to the $(c-1)$-cluster problem. The solution for the one-cluster problem is the total sample mean; the starting point for the c-cluster problem can be the final means for the $(c-1)$-cluster problem plus the sample that is furthest from the nearest cluster center. This approach leads us directly to the so-called hierarchical clustering procedures, which are simple methods that can provide very good starting points for iterative optimization.

6.10   HIERARCHICAL CLUSTERING

6.10.1   Definitions

Let us consider a sequence of partitions of the n samples into c clusters. The first of these is a partition into n clusters, each cluster containing exactly one sample. The next is a partition into $n-1$ clusters, the next a partition into $n-2$, and so on until the nth, in which all the samples form one cluster. We shall say that we are at level k in the sequence when $c = n - k + 1$. Thus, level one corresponds to n clusters and level n to one. Given any two samples $\mathbf{x}$ and $\mathbf{x}'$, at some level they will be grouped together in the same cluster. If the sequence has the property that whenever two samples are in the same cluster at level k they remain together at all higher levels, then the sequence is said to be a *hierarchical clustering*. The classical examples of hierarchical clustering appear in biological taxonomy, where individuals are grouped into species, species into genera, genera into families, and so on.

In fact, this kind of clustering permeates classificatory activities in the sciences.

For every hierarchical clustering there is a corresponding tree, called a *dendrogram*, that shows how the samples are grouped. Figure 6.15 shows a dendrogram for a hypothetical problem involving six samples. Level 1 shows the six samples as singleton clusters. At level 2, samples x_3 and x_5 have been grouped to form a cluster, and they stay together at all subsequent levels. If it is possible to measure the similarity between clusters, then the dendrogram is usually drawn to scale to show the similarity between the clusters that are grouped. In Figure 6.15, for example, the similarity between the two groups of samples that are merged at level 6 has a value of 30. The similarity values are often used to help determine whether the groupings are natural or forced. For our hypothetical example, one would be inclined to say that the groupings at levels 4 or 5 are natural, but that the large reduction in similarity needed to go to level 6 makes that grouping forced. We shall see shortly how such similarity values can be obtained.

Because of their conceptual simplicity, hierarchical clustering procedures are among the best-known methods. The procedures themselves can be divided into two distinct classes, agglomerative and divisive. *Agglomerative* (bottom-up, clumping) procedures start with c singleton clusters and form

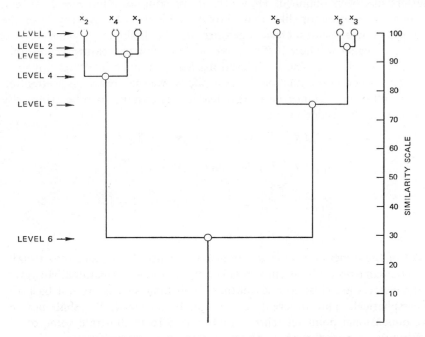

FIGURE 6.15.   A dendrogram for hierarchical clustering.

the sequence by successively merging clusters. *Divisive* (top-down, splitting) procedures start with all of the samples in one cluster and form the sequence by successively splitting clusters. The computation needed to go from one level to another is usually simpler for the agglomerative procedures. However, when there are many samples and one is interested in only a small number of clusters, this computation will have to be repeated many times. For simplicity, we shall limit our attention to the agglomerative procedures, referring the reader to the literature for divisive methods.

6.10.2 Agglomerative Hierarchical Clustering

The major steps in agglomerative clustering are contained in the following procedure:

Procedure: Basic Agglomerative Clustering

    1. Let $\hat{c} = n$ and $\mathscr{X}_i = \{\mathbf{x}_i\}$, $i = 1, \ldots, n$.
Loop: 2. If $\hat{c} \leq c$, stop.
    3. Find the nearest pair of distinct clusters, say $\mathscr{X}_i$ and $\mathscr{X}_j$.
    4. Merge $\mathscr{X}_i$ and $\mathscr{X}_j$, delete $\mathscr{X}_j$, and decrement $\hat{c}$ by one.
    5. Go to Loop.

As described, this procedure terminates when the specified number of clusters has been obtained. However, if we continue until $c = 1$ we can produce a dendrogram like that shown in Figure 6.15. At any level the distance between nearest clusters can provide the dissimilarity value for that level. The reader will note that we have not said how to measure the distance between two clusters. The considerations here are much like those involved in selecting a criterion function. For simplicity, we shall restrict our attention to the following distance measures, leaving extensions to other similarity measures to the reader's imagination:

$$d_{\min}(\mathscr{X}_i, \mathscr{X}_j) = \min_{\mathbf{x} \in \mathscr{X}_i, \mathbf{x}' \in \mathscr{X}_j} \|\mathbf{x} - \mathbf{x}'\|$$

$$d_{\max}(\mathscr{X}_i, \mathscr{X}_j) = \max_{\mathbf{x} \in \mathscr{X}_i, \mathbf{x}' \in \mathscr{X}_j} \|\mathbf{x} - \mathbf{x}'\|$$

$$d_{\mathrm{avg}}(\mathscr{X}_i, \mathscr{X}_j) = \frac{1}{n_i n_j} \sum_{\mathbf{x} \in \mathscr{X}_i} \sum_{\mathbf{x}' \in \mathscr{X}_j} \|\mathbf{x} - \mathbf{x}'\|$$

$$d_{\mathrm{mean}}(\mathscr{X}_i, \mathscr{X}_j) = \|\mathbf{m}_i - \mathbf{m}_j\|.$$

All of these measures have a minimum-variance flavor, and they usually yield the same results if the clusters are compact and well separated. However, if the clusters are close to one another, or if their shapes are not basically hyperspherical, quite different results can be obtained. We shall use the two-dimensional point sets shown in Figure 6.16 to illustrate some of the differences.

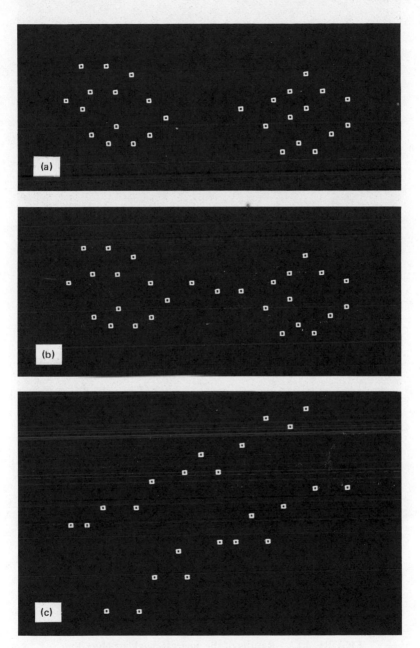

FIGURE 6.16. Three illustrative examples.

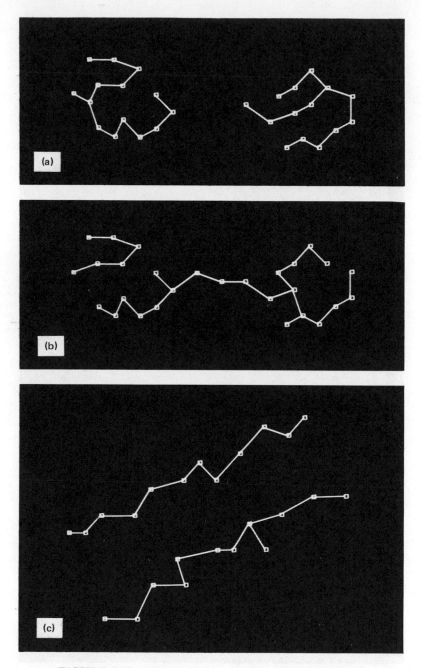

FIGURE 6.17. Results of the nearest-neighbor algorithm.

6.10.2.1 THE NEAREST-NEIGHBOR ALGORITHM

Consider first the behavior when d_{min} is used.* Suppose that we think of the data points as being nodes of a graph, with edges forming a path between nodes in the same subset $\mathscr{X}_i$.† When d_{min} is used to measure the distance between subsets, the nearest neighbors determine the nearest subsets. The merging of $\mathscr{X}_i$ and $\mathscr{X}_j$ corresponds to adding an edge between the nearest pair of nodes in $\mathscr{X}_i$ and $\mathscr{X}_j$. Since edges linking clusters always go between distinct clusters, the resulting graph never has any closed loops or circuits; in the terminology of graph theory, this procedure generates a *tree*. If it is allowed to continue until all of the subsets are linked, the result is a *spanning tree*, a tree with a path from any node to any other node. Moreover, it can be shown that the sum of the edge lengths of the resulting tree will not exceed the sum of the edge lengths for any other spanning tree for that set of samples. Thus, with the use of d_{min} as the distance measure, the agglomerative clustering procedure becomes an algorithm for generating a *minimal spanning tree*.

Figure 6.17 shows the results of applying this procedure to the data of Figure 6.16. In all cases the procedure was stopped at $c = 2$; a minimal spanning tree can be obtained by adding the shortest possible edge between the two clusters. In the first case where the clusters are compact and well separated, the obvious clusters are found. In the second case, the presence of a few points located so as to produce a bridge between the clusters results in a rather unexpected grouping into one large, elongated cluster, and one small, compact cluster. This behavior is often called the "chaining effect," and is sometimes considered to be a defect of this distance measure. To the extent that the results are very sensitive to noise or to slight changes in position of the data points, this is certainly a valid criticism. However, as the third case illustrates, this very tendency to form chains can be advantageous if the clusters are elongated or possess elongated limbs.

6.10.2.2 THE FURTHEST-NEIGHBOR ALGORITHM

When d_{max} is used to measure the distance between subsets, the growth of elongated clusters is discouraged.‡ Application of the procedure can be thought of as producing a graph in which edges connect all of the nodes in

---

* In the literature, the resulting procedure is often called the *nearest-neighbor* or the *minimum* algorithm. If it is terminated when the distance between nearest clusters exceeds an arbitrary threshold, it is called the *single-linkage* algorithm.

† Although we will not make deep use of graph theory, we assume that the reader has a general familiarity with the subject. A clear, rigorous treatment is given by O. Ore, *Theory of Graphs* (American Math. Soc. Colloquium Publ., Vol. 38, 1962).

‡ In the literature, the resulting procedure is often called the *furthest neighbor* or the *maximum* algorithm. If it is terminated when the distance between nearest clusters exceeds an arbitrary threshold, it is called the *complete-linkage* algorithm.

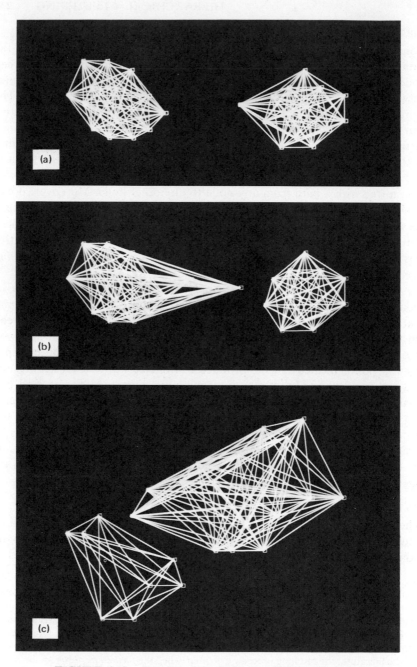

FIGURE 6.18.   Results of the furthest-neighbor algorithm.

a cluster. In the terminology of graph theory, every cluster constitutes a *complete* subgraph. The distance between two clusters is determined by the most distant nodes in the two clusters. When the nearest clusters are merged, the graph is changed by adding edges between every pair of nodes in the two clusters. If we define the *diameter* of a cluster as the largest distance between points in the cluster, then the distance between two clusters is merely the diameter of their union. If we define the diameter of a partition as the largest diameter for clusters in the partition, then each iteration increases the diameter of the partition as little as possible. As Figure 6.18 illustrates, this is advantageous when the true clusters are compact and roughly equal in size. However, when this is not the case, as happens with the two elongated clusters, the resulting groupings can be meaningless. This is another example of imposing structure on data rather than finding structure in it.

6.10.2.3 COMPROMISES

The minimum and maximum measures represent two extremes in measuring the distance between clusters. Like all procedures that involve minima or maxima, they tend to be overly sensitive to "mavericks" or "sports" or "outliers" or "wildshots." The use of averaging is an obvious way to ameliorate these problems, and d_{avg} and d_{mean} are natural compromises between d_{min} and d_{max}. Computationally, d_{mean} is the simplest of all of these measures, since the others require computing all $n_i n_j$ pairs of distances $\|\mathbf{x} - \mathbf{x}'\|$. However, a measure such as d_{avg} can be used when the distances $\|\mathbf{x} - \mathbf{x}'\|$ are replaced by similarity measures, where the similarity between mean vectors may be difficult or impossible to define. We leave it to the reader to decide how the use of d_{avg} or d_{mean} might change the way that the points in Figure 6.16 are grouped.

6.10.3 Stepwise-Optimal Hierarchical Clustering

We observed earlier that if clusters are grown by merging the nearest pair of clusters, then the results have a minimum variance flavor. However, when the measure of distance between clusters is chosen arbitrarily, one can rarely assert that the resulting partition extremizes any particular criterion function. In effect, hierarchical clustering defines a cluster as whatever results from applying the clustering procedure. However, with a simple modification it is possible to obtain a stepwise-optimal procedure for extremizing a criterion function. This is done merely by replacing Step 3 of the Basic Agglomerative Clustering Procedure (Section 6.10.2) by

3'.   Find the pair of distinct clusters $\mathcal{X}_i$ and $\mathcal{X}_j$ whose merger would increase (or decrease) the criterion function as little as possible.

This assures us that at each iteration we have done the best possible thing, even if it does not guarantee that the final partition is optimal.

We saw earlier that the use of $d_{\max}$ causes the smallest possible stepwise increase in the diameter of the partition. Another simple example is provided by the sum-of-squared-error criterion function J_e. By an analysis very similar to that used in Section 6.9, we find that the pair of clusters whose merger increases J_e as little as possible is the pair for which the "distance"

$$d_e(\mathcal{X}_i, \mathcal{X}_j) = \sqrt{\frac{n_i n_j}{n_i + n_j}} \, \|\mathbf{m}_i - \mathbf{m}_j\|$$

is minimum. Thus, in selecting clusters to be merged, this criterion takes into account the number of samples in each cluster as well as the distance between clusters. In general, the use of d_e tends to favor growth by adding singletons or small clusters to large clusters over merging medium-sized clusters. While the final partition may not minimize J_e, it usually provides a very good starting point for further iterative optimization.

6.10.4 Hierarchical Clustering and Induced Metrics

Suppose that we are unable to supply a metric for our data, but that we can measure a *dissimilarity* value $\delta(\mathbf{x}, \mathbf{x}')$ for every pair of samples, where $\delta(\mathbf{x}, \mathbf{x}') \geq 0$, equality holding if and only if $\mathbf{x} = \mathbf{x}'$. Then agglomerative clustering can still be used, with the understanding that the nearest pair of clusters is the least dissimilar pair. Interestingly enough, if we define the dissimilarity between two clusters by

$$\delta_{\min}(\mathcal{X}_i, \mathcal{X}_j) = \min_{\mathbf{x} \in \mathcal{X}_i, \mathbf{x}' \in \mathcal{X}_j} \delta(\mathbf{x}, \mathbf{x}')$$

or

$$\delta_{\max}(\mathcal{X}_i, \mathcal{X}_j) = \max_{\mathbf{x} \in \mathcal{X}_i, \mathbf{x}' \in \mathcal{X}_j} \delta(\mathbf{x}, \mathbf{x}'),$$

then the hierarchical clustering procedure will induce a distance function for the given set of n samples. Furthermore, the ranking of the distances between samples will be invariant to any monotonic transformation of the dissimilarity values.

To see how this comes about, we begin by defining the *value* v_k for the clustering at level k. For level 1, $v_1 = 0$. For all higher levels, v_k is the minimum dissimilarity between pairs of distinct clusters at level $k - 1$. A moment's reflection will make it clear that with both $\delta_{\min}$ and $\delta_{\max}$ the value v_k either stays the same or increases as k increases. Moreover, we shall assume that no two of the n samples are identical, so that $v_2 > 0$. Thus, $0 = v_1 < v_2 \leq v_3 \leq \cdots \leq v_n$.

We can now define the *distance* $d(\mathbf{x}, \mathbf{x}')$ between $\mathbf{x}$ and $\mathbf{x}'$ as the value of the lowest level clustering for which $\mathbf{x}$ and $\mathbf{x}'$ are in the same cluster. To show that this is a legitimate distance function, or *metric*, we need to show three things:

(1) $d(\mathbf{x}, \mathbf{x}') = 0 \Leftrightarrow \mathbf{x} = \mathbf{x}'$
(2) $d(\mathbf{x}, \mathbf{x}') = d(\mathbf{x}', \mathbf{x})$
(3) $d(\mathbf{x}, \mathbf{x}'') \leq d(\mathbf{x}, \mathbf{x}') + d(\mathbf{x}', \mathbf{x}'')$.

It is easy to see that the first requirement is satisfied. The lowest level for which $\mathbf{x}$ and $\mathbf{x}$ are in the same cluster is level 1, so that $d(\mathbf{x}, \mathbf{x}) = v_1 = 0$. Conversely, if $d(\mathbf{x}, \mathbf{x}') = 0$, the fact that $v_2 > 0$ implies that $\mathbf{x}$ and $\mathbf{x}'$ must be in the same cluster at level 1, and hence that $\mathbf{x} = \mathbf{x}'$. The truth of the second requirement follows immediately from the definition of $d(\mathbf{x}, \mathbf{x}')$. This leaves the third requirement, the triangle inequality. Let $d(\mathbf{x}, \mathbf{x}') = v_i$ and $d(\mathbf{x}', \mathbf{x}'') = v_j$, so that $\mathbf{x}$ and $\mathbf{x}'$ are in the same cluster at level i and $\mathbf{x}'$ and $\mathbf{x}''$ are in the same cluster at level j. Because of the hierarchical nesting of clusters, one of these clusters includes the other. If $k = \max(i, j)$, it is clear that at level k $\mathbf{x}$, $\mathbf{x}'$, and $\mathbf{x}''$ are all in the same cluster, and hence that

$$d(\mathbf{x}, \mathbf{x}'') \leq v_k.$$

But since the values v_k are monotonically nondecreasing, it follows that $v_k = \max(v_i, v_j)$ and hence that

$$d(\mathbf{x}, \mathbf{x}'') \leq \max(d(\mathbf{x}, \mathbf{x}'), d(\mathbf{x}', \mathbf{x}'')).$$

This is known as the *ultrametric inequality*. It is even stronger than the triangle inequality, since $\max(d(\mathbf{x}, \mathbf{x}'), d(\mathbf{x}', \mathbf{x}'')) \leq d(\mathbf{x}, \mathbf{x}') + d(\mathbf{x}', \mathbf{x}'')$. Thus, all the conditions are satisfied, and we have created a bona fide metric for comparing the n samples.

6.11   GRAPH THEORETIC METHODS

In two or three instances we have used linear graphs to add insight into the nature of certain clustering procedures. Where the mathematics of normal mixtures and minimum-variance partitions seems to keep returning us to the picture of clusters as isolated clumps of points, the language and concepts of graph theory lead us to consider much more intricate structures. Unfortunately, few of these possibilities have been systematically explored, and there is no uniform way of posing clustering problems as problems in graph theory. Thus, the effective use of these ideas is still largely an art, and the reader who wants to explore the possibilities should be prepared to be creative.

We begin our brief look into graph-theoretic methods by reconsidering the simple procedure that produced the graphs shown in Figure 6.8. Here a threshold distance d_0 was selected, and two points were said to be in the same cluster if the distance between them was less than d_0. This procedure can easily be generalized to apply to arbitrary similarity measures. Suppose that we pick a threshold value s_0 and say that $\mathbf{x}$ is similar to $\mathbf{x}'$ if $s(\mathbf{x}, \mathbf{x}') > s_0$. This defines an n-by-n *similarity matrix* $S = [s_{ij}]$, where

$$s_{ij} = \begin{cases} 1 & \text{if } s(\mathbf{x}_i, \mathbf{x}_j) > s_0 \\ 0 & \text{otherwise} \end{cases} \qquad i, j = 1, \ldots, n$$

This matrix defines a *similarity graph* in which nodes correspond to points and an edge joins node i and node j if and only if $s_{ij} = 1$.

The clusterings produced by the single-linkage algorithm and by a modified version of the complete-linkage algorithm are readily described in terms of this graph. With the single-linkage algorithm, two samples $\mathbf{x}$ and $\mathbf{x}'$ are in the same cluster if and only if there exists a chain $\mathbf{x}_1, \mathbf{x}_2, \ldots, \mathbf{x}_k$ such that $\mathbf{x}$ is similar to $\mathbf{x}_1$, $\mathbf{x}_1$ is similar to $\mathbf{x}_2$, and so on for the whole chain. Thus, this clustering corresponds to the *connected components* of the similarity graph. With the complete-linkage algorithm, all samples in a given cluster must be similar to one another, and no sample can be in more than one cluster. If we drop this second requirement, then this clustering corresponds to the *maximal complete subgraphs* of the similarity graph, the "largest" subgraphs with edges joining all pairs of nodes. (In general, the clusters of the complete-linkage algorithm will be found among the maximal complete subgraphs, but they cannot be determined without knowing the unquantized similarity values.)

In the preceding section we noted that the nearest-neighbor algorithm could be viewed as an algorithm for finding a minimal spanning tree. Conversely, given a minimal spanning tree we can find the clusterings produced by the nearest-neighbor algorithm. Removal of the longest edge produces the two-cluster grouping, removal of the next longest edge produces the three-cluster grouping, and so on. This amounts to an inverted way of obtaining a divisive hierarchical procedure, and suggests other ways of dividing the graph into subgraphs. For example, in selecting an edge to remove, we can compare its length to the lengths of other edges incident upon its nodes. Let us say that an edge is *inconsistent* if its length l is significantly larger than $\bar{l}$, the average length of all other edges incident on its nodes. Figure 6.19 shows a minimal spanning tree for a two-dimensional point set and the clusters obtained by systematically removing all edges for which $l > 2\bar{l}$. Note how the sensitivity of this criterion to local conditions gives results that are quite different from merely removing the two longest edges.

When the data points are strung out into long chains, a minimal spanning tree forms a natural skeleton for the chain. If we define the *diameter path* as

(a) POINT SET   (b) MINIMAL SPANNING TREE   (c) CLUSTERS

**FIGURE 6.19.   Clusters formed by removing inconsistent edges (From
C. T. Zahn, 1971. Copyright 1971, Institute of Electrical and Electronics
Engineers, reprinted by permission.)**

the longest path through the tree, then a chain will be characterized by the
shallow depth of branching off the diameter path. In contrast, for a large,
uniform cloud of data points, the tree will usually not have an obvious
diameter path, but rather several distinct, near-diameter paths. For any of
these, an appreciable number of nodes will be off the path. While slight
changes in the locations of the data points can cause major rerouting of a
minimal spanning tree, they typically have little effect on such statistics.

One of the useful statistics that can be obtained from a minimal spanning
tree is the edge length distribution. Figure 6.20 shows a situation in which a
dense cluster is embedded in a sparse one. The lengths of the edges of the
minimal spanning tree exhibit two distinct clusters which would easily be
detected by a minimum-variance procedure. By deleting all edges longer
than some intermediate value, we can extract the dense cluster as the largest
connected component of the remaining graph. While more complicated configurations can not be disposed of this easily, the flexibility of the graph-
theoretic approach suggests that it is applicable to a wide variety of clustering
problems.

6.12   THE PROBLEM OF VALIDITY

With almost all of the procedures we have considered thus far we have
assumed that the number of clusters is known. That is a reasonable assumption if we are upgrading a classifier that has been designed on a small sample
set, or if we are tracking slowly time-varying patterns. However, it is a very

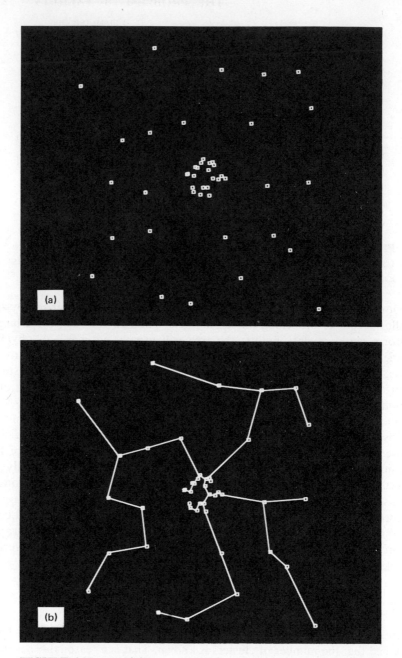

FIGURE 6.20. A minimum spanning tree with a bimodal edge length distribution.

unnatural assumption if we are exploring an essentially unknown set of data. Thus, a constantly recurring problem in cluster analysis is that of deciding just how many clusters are present.

When clustering is done by extremizing a criterion function, a common approach is to repeat the clustering procedure for $c = 1$, $c = 2$, $c = 3$, etc., and to see how the criterion function changes with c. For example, it is clear that the sum-of-squared-error criterion J_e must decrease monotonically with c, since the squared error can be reduced each time c is increased merely by transferring a single sample to the new cluster. If the n samples are really grouped into $\hat{c}$ compact, well separated clusters, one would expect to see J_e decrease rapidly until $c = \hat{c}$, decreasing much more slowly thereafter until it reaches zero at $c = n$. Similar arguments have been advanced for hierarchical clustering procedures, the usual assumption being that large disparities in the levels at which clusters merge indicate the presence of natural groupings.

A more formal approach to this problem is to devise some measure of goodness of fit that expresses how well a given c-cluster description matches the data. The chi-square and Kolmogorov-Smirnov statistics are the traditional measures of goodness of fit, but the curse of dimensionality usually demands the use of simpler measures, such as a criterion function $J(c)$. Since we expect a description in terms of $c + 1$ clusters to give a better fit than a description in terms of c clusters, we would like to know what constitutes a statistically significant improvement in $J(c)$.

A formal way to proceed is to advance the *null hypothesis* that there are exactly c clusters present, and to compute the sampling distribution for $J(c + 1)$ under this hypothesis. This distribution tells us what kind of apparent improvement to expect when a c-cluster description is actually correct. The decision procedure would be to accept the null hypothesis if the observed value of $J(c + 1)$ falls within limits corresponding to an acceptable probability of false rejection.

Unfortunately, it is usually very difficult to do anything more than crudely estimate the sampling distribution of $J(c + 1)$. The resulting solutions are not above suspicion, and the statistical problem of testing cluster validity is still essentially unsolved. However, under the assumption that a suspicious test is better than none, we include the following approximate analysis for the simple sum-of-squared-error criterion.

Suppose that we have a set $\mathscr{X}$ of n samples and we want to decide whether or not there is any justification for assuming that they form more than one cluster. Let us advance the null hypothesis that all n samples come from a normal population with mean μ and covariance matrix $\sigma^2 I$. If this hypothesis were true, any clusters found would have to have been formed by chance, and any observed decrease in the sum of squared error obtained by clustering would have no significance.

The sum of squared error $J_e(1)$ is a random variable, since it depends on the particular set of samples:

$$J_e(1) = \sum_{x \in \mathscr{X}} \|x - m\|^2,$$

where m is the mean of the n samples. Under the null hypothesis, the distribution for $J_e(1)$ is approximately normal with mean $nd\sigma^2$ and variance $2nd\sigma^4$.

Suppose now that we partition the set of samples into two subsets $\mathscr{X}_1$ and $\mathscr{X}_2$ so as to minimize $J_e(2)$, where

$$J_e(2) = \sum_{i=1}^{2} \sum_{x \in \mathscr{X}_i} \|x - m_i\|^2,$$

m_i being the mean of the samples in $\mathscr{X}_i$. Under the null hypothesis, this partitioning is spurious, but it nevertheless results in a value for $J_e(2)$ that is smaller than $J_e(1)$. If we knew the sampling distribution for $J_e(2)$, we could determine how small $J_e(2)$ would have to be before we were forced to abandon a one-cluster null hypothesis. Lacking an analytical solution for the optimal partitioning, we cannot derive an exact solution for the sampling distribution. However, we can obtain a rough estimate by considering the suboptimal partition provided by a hyperplane through the sample mean. For large n, it can be shown that the sum of squared error for this partition is approximately normal with mean $n(d - 2/\pi)\sigma^2$ and variance $2n(d - 8/\pi^2)\sigma^4$.

This result agrees with our statement that $J_e(2)$ is smaller than $J_e(1)$, since the mean of $J_e(2)$ for the suboptimal partition—$n(d - 2/\pi)\sigma^2$—is less than the mean for $J_e(1)$—$nd\sigma^2$. To be considered significant, the reduction in the sum of squared error must certainly be greater than this. We can obtain an approximate critical value for $J_e(2)$ by assuming that the suboptimal partition is nearly optimal, by using the normal approximation for the sampling distribution, and by estimating σ^2 by

$$\hat{\sigma}^2 = \frac{1}{nd} \sum_{x \in \mathscr{X}} \|x - m\|^2 = \frac{1}{nd} J_e(1).$$

The final result can be stated as follows: Reject the null hypothesis at the p-percent significance level if

$$\frac{J_e(2)}{J_e(1)} < 1 - \frac{2}{\pi d} - \alpha \sqrt{\frac{2(1 - 8/\pi^2 d)}{nd}}, \tag{44}$$

where α is determined by

$$p = 100 \int_{\alpha}^{\infty} \frac{1}{\sqrt{2\pi}} e^{-1/2u^2} \, du.$$

Thus, this provides us with a test for deciding whether or not the splitting of a cluster is justified. Clearly, the c-cluster problem can be treated by applying the same test to all clusters found.

6.13 LOW-DIMENSIONAL REPRESENTATIONS AND MULTIDIMENSIONAL SCALING

Part of the problem of deciding whether or not a given clustering means anything stems from our inability to visualize the structure of multidimensional data. This problem is further aggravated when similarity or dissimilarity measures are used that lack the familiar properties of distance. One way to attack this problem is to try to represent the data points as points in some lower-dimensional space in such a way that the distances between points in the lower-dimensional space correspond to the dissimilarities between points in the original space. If acceptably accurate representations can be found in two or perhaps three dimensions, this can be an extremely valuable way to gain insight into the structure of the data. The general process of finding a configuration of points whose interpoint distances correspond to dissimilarities is often called *multidimensional scaling*.

Let us begin with the simpler case where it is meaningful to talk about the distances between the n samples $\mathbf{x}_1, \ldots, \mathbf{x}_n$. Let $\mathbf{y}_i$ be the lower-dimensional *image* of $\mathbf{x}_i$, δ_{ij} be the distance between $\mathbf{x}_i$ and $\mathbf{x}_j$, and d_{ij} be the distance between $\mathbf{y}_i$ and $\mathbf{y}_j$. Then we are looking for a *configuration* of image points $\mathbf{y}_1, \ldots, \mathbf{y}_n$ for which the $n(n-1)/2$ distances d_{ij} between image points are as close as possible to the corresponding original distances δ_{ij}. Since it will usually not be possible to find a configuration for which $d_{ij} = \delta_{ij}$ for all i and j, we need some criterion for deciding whether or not one configuration is better than another. The following sum-of-squared-error functions are all reasonable candidates:

$$J_{ee} = \frac{1}{\sum\limits_{i<j} \delta_{ij}^2} \sum_{i<j} (d_{ij} - \delta_{ij})^2 \tag{45}$$

$$J_{ff} = \sum_{i<j} \left(\frac{d_{ij} - \delta_{ij}}{\delta_{ij}} \right)^2 \tag{46}$$

$$J_{ef} = \frac{1}{\sum\limits_{i<j} \delta_{ij}} \sum_{i<j} \frac{(d_{ij} - \delta_{ij})^2}{\delta_{ij}}. \tag{47}$$

Since these criterion functions involve only the distances between points, they are invariant to rigid-body motions of the configurations. Moreover, they have all been normalized so that their minimum values are invariant to dilations of the sample points. J_{ee} emphasizes the largest errors, regardless whether the distances δ_{ij} are large or small. J_{ff} emphasizes the largest fractional errors, regardless whether the errors $|d_{ij} - \delta_{ij}|$ are large or small. J_{ef} is a useful compromise, emphasizing the largest product of error and fractional error.

Once a criterion function has been selected, an optimal configuration $\mathbf{y}_1, \ldots, \mathbf{y}_n$ is defined as one that minimizes that criterion function. An optimal configuration can be sought by a standard gradient-descent procedure, starting with some initial configuration and changing the $\mathbf{y}_i$'s in the direction of greatest rate of decrease in the criterion function. Since

$$d_{ij} = \|\mathbf{y}_i - \mathbf{y}_j\|,$$

the gradient of d_{ij} with respect to $\mathbf{y}_i$ is merely a unit vector in the direction of $\mathbf{y}_i - \mathbf{y}_j$. Thus, the gradients of the criterion functions are easy to compute:*

$$\nabla_{\mathbf{y}_k} J_{ee} = \frac{2}{\sum_{i<j} \delta_{ij}^2} \sum_{j \neq k} (d_{kj} - \delta_{kj}) \frac{\mathbf{y}_k - \mathbf{y}_j}{d_{kj}}$$

$$\nabla_{\mathbf{y}_k} J_{ff} = 2 \sum_{j \neq k} \frac{d_{kj} - \delta_{kj}}{\delta_{kj}^2} \frac{\mathbf{y}_k - \mathbf{y}_j}{d_{kj}}$$

$$\nabla_{\mathbf{y}_k} J_{ef} = \frac{2}{\sum_{i<j} \delta_{ij}} \sum_{j \neq k} \frac{d_{kj} - \delta_{kj}}{\delta_{kj}} \frac{\mathbf{y}_k - \mathbf{y}_j}{d_{kj}}.$$

The starting configuration can be chosen randomly, or in any convenient way that spreads the image points about. If the image points lie in a $\hat{d}$-dimensional space, then a simple and effective starting configuration can be found by selecting those $\hat{d}$ coordinates of the samples that have the largest variance.

The following example illustrates the kind of results than can be obtained by these techniques.† The data consist of thirty points spaced at unit intervals along a three-dimensional helix:

$$x_1(k) = \cos x_3$$
$$x_2(k) = \sin x_3$$
$$x_3(k) = k/\sqrt{2}, \qquad k = 0, 1, \ldots, 29.$$

---

* Second partial derivatives can also be computed easily, so that Newton's algorithm can be used. Note that if $\mathbf{y}_i = \mathbf{y}_j$, the unit vector from $\mathbf{y}_i$ to $\mathbf{y}_j$ is undefined. Should that situation arise, $(\mathbf{y}_i - \mathbf{y}_j)/d_{ij}$ can be replaced by an arbitrary unit vector.

† This example was taken from J. W. Sammon, Jr., "A nonlinear mapping for data structure analysis," *IEEE Trans. Comp.*, C-**18**, 401–409 (May 1969).

Figure 6.21(a) shows a perspective representation of the three-dimensional data. When the J_{ef} criterion was used, twenty iterations of a gradient descent procedure produced the two-dimensional configuration shown in Figure 6.21(b). Of course, translations, rotations, and reflections of this configuration would be equally good solutions.

In nonmetric multidimensional scaling problems, the quantities δ_{ij} are dissimilarities whose numerical values are not as important as their rank order. An ideal configuration would be one for which the rank order of the distances d_{ij} is the same as the rank order of the dissimilarities δ_{ij}. Let us order the $m = n(n-1)/2$ dissimilarities so that $\delta_{i_1 j_1} \le \cdots \le \delta_{i_m j_m}$, and let $\hat{d}_{ij}$ be *any* m numbers satisfying the *monotonicity constraint*

$$\hat{d}_{i_1 j_1} \le \hat{d}_{i_2 j_2} \le \cdots \le \hat{d}_{i_m j_m}.$$

In general, the distances d_{ij} will not satisfy this constraint, and the numbers $\hat{d}_{ij}$ will not be distances. However, the degree to which the d_{ij} satisfy this constraint is measured by

$$\hat{J}_{\mathrm{mon}} = \min_{\hat{d}_{ij}} \sum_{i<j} (d_{ij} - \hat{d}_{ij})^2,$$

where it is always to be understood that the $\hat{d}_{ij}$ must satisfy the monotonicity constraint. Thus, $\hat{J}_{\mathrm{mon}}$ measures the degree to which the configuration of

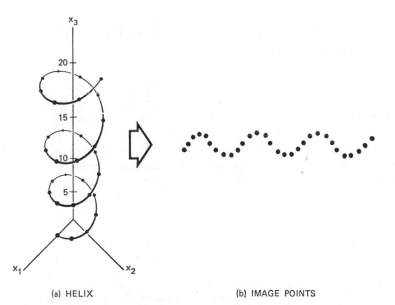

(a) HELIX   (b) IMAGE POINTS

FIGURE 6.21.   A two-dimensional representation of data points in three dimensions (Adapted from J. W. Sammon, 1969).

points $y_1, \ldots, y_n$ represents the original data. Unfortunately, $\hat{J}_{mon}$ can not be used to define an optimal configuration because it can be made to vanish by collapsing the configuration to a single point. However, this defect is easily removed by a normalization such as the following:

$$J_{mon} = \frac{\hat{J}_{mon}}{\sum_{i<j} d_{ij}^2}. \tag{48}$$

Thus, J_{mon} is invariant to translations, rotations, and dilations of the configuration, and an optimal configuration can be defined as one that minimizes this criterion function. It has been observed experimentally that when the number of points is larger than dimensionality of the image space, the monotonicity constraint is actually quite confining. This might be expected from the fact that the number of constraints grows as the square of the number of points, and it is the basis for the frequently encountered statement that this procedure allows the recovery of metric information from nonmetric data. The quality of the representation generally improves as the dimensionality of the image space is increased, and it may be necessary to go beyond three dimensions to obtain an acceptably small value of J_{mon}. However, this may be a small price to pay to allow the use of the many clustering procedures available for data points in metric spaces.

6.14   CLUSTERING AND DIMENSIONALITY REDUCTION

Because the curse of dimensionality plagues so many pattern recognition procedures, a variety of methods for dimensionality reduction have been proposed. Unlike the procedures that we have just examined, most of these methods provide a functional mapping, so that one can determine the image of an arbitrary feature vector. The classical procedures of statistics are *principal components analysis* and *factor analysis*, both of which reduce dimensionality by forming linear combinations of the features.* If we think of the problem as one of removing or combining (i.e., grouping) highly correlated features, then it becomes clear that the techniques of clustering

---

* The object of principal components analysis (known in the communication theory literature as the Karhunen-Loéve expansion) is to find a lower-dimensional representation that accounts for the variance of the features. The object of factor analysis is to find a lower-dimensional representation that accounts for the correlations among the features. For more information, see M. G. Kendall and A. Stuart, *The Advanced Theory of Statistics*, *Vol. 3*, Chapter 43 (Hafner, New York, 1966) or H. H. Harman, *Modern Factor Analysis* (University of Chicago Press, Chicago and London, Second Edition, 1967).

are applicable to this problem. In terms of the *data matrix*, whose n rows are the d-dimensional samples, ordinary clustering can be thought of as a grouping of the rows, with a smaller number of cluster centers being used to represent the data, whereas dimensionality reduction can be though of as a grouping the columns, with combined features being used to represent the data.

Let us consider a simple modification of hierarchical clustering to reduce dimensionality. In place of an n-by-n matrix of distances between samples, we consider a d-by-d *correlation matrix* $R = [\rho_{ij}]$, where the correlation coefficient ρ_{ij} is related to the covariances (or sample covariances) by

$$\rho_{ij} = \frac{\sigma_{ij}}{\sqrt{\sigma_{ii}\sigma_{jj}}}.$$

Since $0 \leq \rho_{ij}^2 \leq 1$, with $\rho_{ij}^2 = 0$ for uncorrelated features and $\rho_{ij}^2 = 1$ for completely correlated features, ρ_{ij}^2 plays the role of a similarity function for features. Two features for which ρ_{ij}^2 is large are clearly good candidates to be merged into one feature, thereby reducing the dimensionality by one. Repetition of this process leads to the following hierarchical procedure:

Procedure: Hierarchical Dimensionality Reduction
        1. Let $\hat{d} = d$ and $\mathscr{F}_i = \{x_i\}$, $i = 1, \ldots, d$.
Loop: 2. If $\hat{d} = d'$, stop.
        3. Compute the correlation matrix and find the most correlated pair of distinct clusters of features, say $\mathscr{F}_i$ and $\mathscr{F}_j$.
        4. Merge $\mathscr{F}_i$ and $\mathscr{F}_j$, delete $\mathscr{F}_j$, and decrement $\hat{d}$ by one.
        5. Go to Loop.

Probably the simplest way to merge two groups of features is just to average them. (This tacitly assumes that the features have been scaled so that their numerical ranges are comparable.) With this definition of a new feature, there is no problem in defining the correlation matrix for groups of features. It is not hard to think of variations on this general theme, but we shall not pursue this topic further.

For the purposes of pattern *classification*, the most serious criticism of all of the approaches to dimensionality reduction that we have mentioned is that they are overly concerned with faithful *representation* of the data. Greatest emphasis is usually placed on those features or groups of features that have the greatest variability. But for classification, we are interested in *discrimination*, not representation. Roughly speaking, the most interesting features are the ones for which the difference in the class means is large relative to the standard deviations, not the ones for which the standard deviations are large. In short, we are interested in something more like the method of multiple discriminant analysis described in Chapter 4.

There is a growing body of theory on methods of dimensionality reduction for pattern classification. Some of these methods seek to form new features out of linear combinations of old ones. Others seek merely a smaller subset of the original features. A major problem confronting this theory is that the division of pattern recognition into feature extraction followed by classification is theoretically artificial. A completely optimal feature extractor can never be anything but an optimal classifier. It is only when constraints are placed on the classifier or limitations are placed on the size of the set of samples that one can formulate nontrivial (and very complicated) problems. Various ways of circumventing this problem that may be useful under the proper circumstances can be found in the literature, and we have included a few entry points to this literature. When it is possible to exploit knowledge of the problem domain to obtain more informative features, that is usually a more profitable course of action. In the second half of this book we shall devote ourselves to a systematic examination of ways of extracting features from visual data, and with the larger problem of visual scene analysis.

6.15 BIBLIOGRAPHICAL AND HISTORICAL REMARKS

The literature on unsupervised learning and clustering is so large and is scattered across so many disciplines that the following references must be viewed as little more than a selective random sampling. Fortunately, several of the references we cite contain extensive bibliographies, relieving us of many scholarly burdens. Historically, the literature dates back at least to 1894 when Karl Pearson used sample moments to determine the parameters in a mixture of two univariate normal densities. Assuming exact knowledge of values of the mixture density, Doetsch (1936) used Fourier transforms to decompose univariate normal mixtures. Medgyessy (1961) extended this approach to other classes of mixtures, in the process exposing the problem of identifiability. Teicher (1961, 1963) and later Yakowitz and Spragins (1968) demonstrated the identifiability of several families of mixtures, the latter authors showing the equivalence of identifiability and linear independence of the component densities.

The phrases "unsupervised learning" or "learning without a teacher" usually refer to estimation of parameters of the component densities from samples drawn from the mixture density. Spragins (1966) and Cooper (1969) give valuable surveys of this work, and its relation to compound sequential Bayes learning is clarified by Cover (1969). Some of this work is quite general, being primarily concerned with theoretical possibilities. Thus, Stanat (1968) shows how Doetsch's method can be applied to learn multivariate normal and multivariate Bernoulli mixtures, and Yakowitz (1970) demonstrates the possibility of learning virtually any identifiable mixture.

Surprisingly few papers treat maximum-likelihood estimates. Hasselblad (1966) derived maximum-likelihood formulas for estimating the parameters of univariate normal mixtures. Day (1969) derived the formulas for the multivariate, equal covariance matrix case, and pointed out the existence of singular solutions with general normal mixtures. Our treatment of the multivariate case is based directly on the exceptionally clear paper by Wolfe (1970), who also derived formulas for multivariate Bernoulli mixtures. The formulation of the Bayesian approach to unsupervised learning is usually attributed to Daly (1962); more general formulations have since been given by several authors (cf., Hilborn and Lainiotis 1968). Daly pointed out the exponential growth of the optimum system and the need for approximate solutions. Spragins' survey provides references to the literature on decision-directed approximations prior to 1966, with subsequent work being referenced by Patrick, Costello, and Monds (1970). Approximate solutions have also been obtained by the use of histograms (Patrick and Hancock 1966), quantized parameters (Fralick 1967), and randomized decisions (Agrawala 1970).

We have not mentioned all the ways that one might use to estimate unknown parameters. In particular, we have neglected the time-honored and robust method of sample moments, primarily because the situation becomes very complicated when there are more than two components in the mixture. However, some interesting solutions for special cases have been derived by David and Paul Cooper (1964) and elaborated further by Paul Cooper (1967). Because of its slow convergence, we have also omitted mention of the use of stochastic approximation; for the interested reader, the article by Young and Coraluppi (1970) can be recommended.

Much of the early work in clustering was done in the biological sciences, where it appears in studies of numerical taxonomy. Here the major concern is with hierarchical clustering. The influential book by Sokal and Sneath (1963) is an excellent source of references to this literature. Psychologists and sociologists have also contributed to clustering, although they are usually more concerned with clustering features than with clustering samples (Tryon 1939; Tryon and Bailey 1970). The advent of the digital computer made cluster analysis practical, and caused the literature on clustering to spread over many disciplines. The well known survey by Ball (1965) gives a comprehensive overview of this work and is highly recommended; Ball's insights have had a major influence on our treatment of the subject. We have also benefited from the dissertation by Ling (1971), which includes a list of 140 references. The surveys by Bolshev (1969) and Dorofeyuk (1971) give extensive references to the Russian literature on clustering.

Sokal and Sneath (1963) and Ball (1965) list many of the similarity measures and criterion functions that have seen use. The matters of measurement scales, invariance criteria, and appropriate statistical operations are illuminated by Stevens (1968), and related fundamental philosophical issues concerning clustering are treated by Watanabe (1969). The critique of clustering given by Fleiss and Zubin (1969) points out the unhappy consequences of being careless about such matters.

Jones (1968) credits Thorndike (1953) with being the first to use the sum-of-squared-error criterion, which appears so frequently in the literature. The invariant criteria we presented were derived from Friedman and Rubin (1967), who pointed out that these criteria are related to Hotelling's Trace Criterion and the F-ratio of classical statistics. The observation that all these criteria give the same optimal partitions in the two-cluster case is due to Fukunaga and Koontz (1970). Of the various criteria we did not mention, the "cohesion" criterion of Watanabe (1969, Chapter 8) is of particular interest since it involves more than pairwise similarity.

In the text we outlined the basic steps in a number of standard optimization and clustering programs. These descriptions were intentionally simplified, and even the more complete descriptions found in the literature do not always mention such matters as how ties are broken or how "wild shots" are rejected. The Isodata algorithm of Ball and Hall (1967) differs from our simplified description in several ways, most notably in the splitting of clusters that have too much within-cluster variability, and the merging of clusters that have too little between-cluster variability. Our description of the basic minimum-squared-error procedure is derived from an unpublished computer program developed by R. C. Singleton and W. H. Kautz at Stanford Research Institute in 1965. This procedure is also closely related to the adaptive sequential procedure of Sebestyen (1962), and to the so-called k-means procedure, whose convergence properties were studied by MacQueen (1967). Interesting applications of such procedures to character recognition are described by Andrews, Atrubin, and Hu (1968) and by Casey and Nagy (1968).

Sokal and Sneath (1963) reference much of the early work on hierarchical clustering, and Wishart (1969) gives explicit references to the original sources for the single-linkage, nearest-neighbor, complete-linkage, furthest-neighbor, minimum-squared-error, and several other procedures. Lance and Williams (1967) show how most of these procedures can be obtained by specializing a general distance function in different ways; in addition, they reference the major papers on divisive hierarchical clustering. The relation between single-linkage procedures and minimal spanning trees was shown by Gower and Ross (1969), who recommended a simple, efficient algorithm for finding minimal spanning trees given by Prim (1957). The equivalence between hierarchical clustering and a distance function satisfying the ultrametric inequality was shown by Johnson (1967).

The great majority of papers on clustering have either explicitly or implicitly accepted some form of minimum-variance criterion. Wishart (1969) pointed out the serious limitations inherent in this approach, and as an alternative suggested a procedure resembling k_n-nearest-neighbor estimation of modes of the mixture density. Critiques of minimum-variance methods have also been given by Ling (1971) and Zahn (1971), both of whom favored graph-theoretic approaches to clustering. Zahn's work, though intended for data of any dimensionality, was motivated by a desire to find mathematical procedures that group sets of points in two dimensions in a way that seems visually natural. (Haralick and Kelly (1969) and Haralick and Dinstein (1971) also treat certain picture processing operations as clustering procedures, a viewpoint that applies to many of the procedures described in Part II of this book.)

Most of the early work on graph-theoretic methods was done for information retrieval purposes. Auguston and Minker (1970) credit Kuhns (1959) with the first application of graph theory to clustering. They give an experimental comparison of several graph-theoretic techniques intended for information retrieval applications, and give many references to work in this domain. It is interesting that among papers with a graph-theoretic orientation we find three that are concerned with statistical tests for cluster validity, viz., those by Bonner (1964), Hartigan (1967), and Ling (1971). Hall, Tepping, and Ball (1971) computed how the sum of squared error varies with the dimensionality of the data and the assumed number of clusters for both uniform and simplex data, and suggested these distributions as useful standards for comparison. Wolfe (1970) suggests a test for cluster validity based on an assumed chi-square distribution for the log-likelihood function.

Green and Carmone (1970), whose valuable monograph on multidimensional scaling contains an extensive bibliography, trace the origins of multidimensional scaling to a paper by Richardson (1938). Recent interest in the topic was stimulated by two developments, nonmetric multidimensional scaling and computer graphics applications. The nonmetric approach originated by Shepard (1962) and extended by Kruskal (1964a) is well suited to many problems in psychology and sociology. The computational aspects of minimizing the criterion J_{mon} subject to a monotonicity constraint are described in detail by Kruskal (1964b). Calvert (1968) used a variation of Shepard's criterion to provide a two-dimensional computer display of multivariate data. The computationally simpler J_{ef} criterion was proposed and used by Sammon (1969) to display data for interactive analysis.

The interest in man-machine systems stems partly from the difficulty of specifying criterion functions and clustering procedures that do what we really want them to do. Mattson and Dammann (1965) were one of the first to suggest a man-machine solution to this problem. The great potential of interactive systems is well described by Ball and Hall (1970) in a paper on their PROMENADE system. Other well-known systems include BC TRY (Tryon and Bailey 1966; 1970), SARF (Stanley, Lendaris, and Nienow 1967), INTERSPACE (Patrick 1969), and OLPARS (Sammon 1970).

Neither automatic nor man-machine systems for pattern recognition can escape the fundamental problems of high-dimensional data. Various procedures have been proposed for reducing the dimensionality, either by selecting the best subset of the available features or by combining the features, usually in a linear fashion. To avoid enormous computational problems, most of these procedures use some criterion other than probability of error in making the selection. For example, Miller (1962) used a tr $S_W^{-1}S_B$ criterion, Lewis (1962) used an entropy criterion, and Marill and Green (1963) used a divergence criterion. In some cases one can bound the probability of error by more easily computed criterion functions, but the final test is always one of actual performance. In the text we restricted our attention to a simple procedure due to King (1967), selecting it primarily because of its close relation to clustering. An excellent presentation of mathematical methods for dimensionality reduction is given by Meisel (1972).

REFERENCES

1. Agrawala, A. K., "Learning with a probabilistic teacher," *IEEE Trans. Info: Theory*, **IT-16,** 373–379 (July 1970).

2. Andrews, D. R., A. J. Atrubin, and K. C. Hu, "The IBM 1975 Optical Page Reader. Part 3: Recognition logic development," *IBM Journal*, **12,** 334–371 (September 1968).

3. Augustson, J. G. and J. Minker, "An analysis of some graph theoretical cluster techniques," *J. ACM*, **17,** 571–588 (October 1970).

4. Ball, G. H., "Data analysis in the social sciences: what about the details?", *Proc. FJCC*, pp. 533–560 (Spartan Books, Washington, D.C., 1965).

5. Ball, G. H. and D. J. Hall, "A clustering technique for summarizing multivariate data," *Behavioral Science*, **12,** 153–155 (March 1967).

6. Ball, G. H. and D. J. Hall, "Some implications of interactive graphic computer systems for data analysis and statistics," *Technometrics*, **12,** 17–31 (February 1970).

7. Bolshev, L. N., "Cluster analysis," *Bulletin, International Statistical Institute*, **43,** 411–425 (1969).

8. Bonner, R. E. "On some clustering techniques," *IBM Journal*, **8,** 22–32 (January 1964).

9. Calvert, T. W., "Projections of multidimensional data for use in man computer graphics," *Proc. FJCC*, pp. 227–231 (Thompson Book Co., Washington, D.C., 1968).

10. Casey, R. G. and G. Nagy, "An autonomous reading machine," *IEEE Trans. Comp.*, **C-17**, 492–503 (May 1968).

11. Cooper, D. B. and P. W. Cooper, "Nonsupervised adaptive signal detection and pattern recognition," *Information and Control*, **7**, 416–444 (September 1964).

12. Cooper, P. W., "Some topics on nonsupervised adaptive detection for multivariate normal distributions," in *Computer and Information Sciences—II*, pp. 123–146, J. T. Tou, ed. (Academic Press, New York, 1967).

13. Cooper, P. W., "Nonsupervised learning in statistical pattern recognition," in *Methodologies of Pattern Recognition*, pp. 97–109, S. Watanabe, ed. (Academic Press, New York, 1969).

14. Cover, T. M., "Learning in pattern recognition," in *Methodologies of Pattern Recognition*, pp. 111–132, S. Watanabe, ed. (Academic Press, New York, 1969).

15. Daly, R. F., "The adaptive binary-detection problem on the real line," Technical Report 2003-3, Stanford University, Stanford, Calif. (February 1962).

16. Day, N. E., "Estimating the components of a mixture of normal distributions," *Biometrika*, **56**, 463–474 (December 1969).

17. Doetsch, G., "Zerlegung einer Funktion in Gausche Fehlerkurven und zeitliche Zuruckverfolgung eines Temperaturzustandes," *Mathematische Zeitschrift*, **41**, 283–318 (1936).

18. Dorofeyuk, A. A., "Automatic classification algorithms (review)," *Automation and Remote Control*, **32**, 1928–1958 (December 1971).

19. Fleiss, J. L. and J. Zubin, "On the methods and theory of clustering," *Multivariate Behavioral Research*, **4**, 235–250 (April 1969).

20. Fralick, S. C., "Learning to recognize patterns without a teacher," *IEEE Trans. Info. Theory*, **IT-13**, 57–64 (January 1967).

21. Friedman, H. P. and J. Rubin, "On some invariant criteria for grouping data," *J. American Statistical Assn.*, **62**, 1159–1178 (December 1967).

22. Fukunaga, K. and W. L. G. Koontz, "A criterion and an algorithm for grouping data," *IEEE Trans. Comp.*, **C-19**, 917–923 (October 1970).

23. Gower, J. C. and G. J. S. Ross, "Minimum spanning trees and single linkage cluster analysis," *Appl. Statistics*, **18**, No. 1, 54–64 (1969).

24. Green, P. E. and F. J. Carmone, *Multidimensional Scaling and Related Techniques in Marketing Analysis* (Allyn and Bacon, Boston, Mass., 1970).

25. Hall, D. J., B. Tepping, and G. H. Ball, "Theoretical and experimental clustering characteristics for multivariate random and structured data," in "Applications of cluster analysis to Bureau of the Census data," Final Report, Contract Cco-9312, SRI Project 7600, Stanford Research Institute, Menlo Park, Calif. (1970).

26. Haralick, R. M. and G. L. Kelly, "Pattern recognition with measurement space and spatial clustering for multiple images," *Proc. IEEE*, **57**, 654–665 (April 1969).

27. Haralick, R. M. and I. Dinstein, "An iterative clustering procedure," *IEEE Transactions on Sys., Man, and Cyb.*, **SMC-1**, 275–289 (July 1971).

28. Hartigan, J. A., "Representation of similarity matrices by trees," *J. American Statistical Assn.*, **62**, 1140–1158 (December 1967).

29. Hasselblad, V., "Estimation of parameters for a mixture of normal distributions," *Technometrics*, **8**, 431–444 (August 1966).

30. Hillborn, C. G., Jr. and D. G. Lainiotis, "Optimal unsupervised learning multicategory dependent hypotheses pattern recognition," *IEEE Trans. Info. Theory*, **IT-14**, 468–470 (May 1968).

31. Johnson, S. C., "Hierarchical clustering schemes," *Psychometrika*, **32**, 241–254 (September 1967).

32. Jones, K. L., "Problems of grouping individuals and the method of modality," *Behavioral Science*, **13**, 496–511 (November 1968).

33. King, B. F., "Stepwise clustering procedures," *J. American Statistical Assn.*, **62**, 86–101 (March 1967).

34. Kruskal, J. B., "Multidimensional scaling by optimizing goodness of fit to a nonmetric hypothesis," *Psychometrika*, **29**, 1–27 (March 1964a).

35. Kruskal, J. B., "Nonmetric multidimensional scaling: a numerical method," *Psychometrika*, **29**, 115–129 (June 1964b).

36. Kuhns, J. L., "Mathematical analysis of correlation clusters," in "Word correlation and automatic indexing," Progress Report No. 2, C 82-OU1, Ramo-Wooldridge Corporation, Canoga Park, Calif. (December 1959).

37. Lance, G. N. and W. T. Williams, "A general theory of classificatory sorting strategies. 1. Hierarchical systems," *Computer Journal*, **9**, 373–380 (February 1967).

38. Lewis, P. M., "The characteristic selection problem in recognition systems," *IRE Trans. Info. Theory*, **IT-8**, 171–178 (February 1962).

39. Ling, R. F., "Cluster Analysis," Technical Report No. 18, Department of Statistics, Yale University, New Haven, Conn. (January 1971).

40. MacQueen, J., "Some methods for classification and analysis of multivariate observations," in *Proc. Fifth Berkeley Symposium on Math. Stat. and Prob.*, **I**, 281–297, L. M. LeCam and J. Neyman, eds. (University of California Press, Berkeley and Los Angeles, Calif., 1967).

41. Marill, T. and D. M. Green, "On the effectiveness of receptors in recognition systems," *IEEE Trans. Info. Theory*, **IT-9**, 11–17 (January 1963).

42. Mattson, R. L. and J. E. Dammann, "A technique for detecting and coding subclasses in pattern recognition problems," *IBM Journal*, **9**, 294–302 (July 1965).

43. Medgyessy, P., *Decomposition of Superpositions of Distribution Functions* (Plenum Press, New York, 1961).

44. Meisel, W. S., *Computer-Oriented Approaches to Pattern Recognition* (Academic Press, New York and London, 1972).

45. Miller, R. G., "Statistical prediction by discriminant analysis," *Meteorological Monographs*, **4**, 25 (October 1962).

46. Patrick, E. A. and J. C. Hancock, "Nonsupervised sequential classification and recognition of patterns," *IEEE Trans. Info. Theory*, **IT-12**, 362–372 (July 1966).

47. Patrick, E. A., "(Interspace) Interactive system for pattern analysis, classification, and enhancement," paper presented at the Computers and Communications Conference, Rome, N.Y. (September 1969).

48. Patrick, E. A., J. P. Costello, and F. C. Monds, "Decision directed estimation of a two class decision boundary," *IEEE Trans. Comp.*, **C-19**, 197–205 (March 1970).

49. Pearson, K., "Contributions to the mathematical theory of evolution," *Philosophical Transactions of the Royal Society of London*, **185**, 71–110 (1894).

50. Prim, R. C., "Shortest connection networks and some generalizations," *Bell System Technical Journal*, **36**, 1389–1401 (November 1957).

51. Richardson, M. W., "Multidimensional psychophysics," *Psychological Bulletin*, **35**, 659–660 (1938).

52. Sammon, J. W., Jr., "A nonlinear mapping for data structure analysis," *IEEE Trans. Comp.*, **C-18**, 401–409 (May 1969).

53. Sammon, J. W., Jr., "Interactive pattern analysis and classification," *IEEE Trans. Comp.*, **C-19**, 594–616 (July 1970).

54. Sebestyen, G. S., "Pattern recognition by an adaptive process of sample set construction," *IRE Trans. Info. Theory*, **IT-8**, S82–S91 (September 1962).

55. Shepard, R. N., "The analysis of proximities: multidimensional scaling with an unknown distance function," *Psychometrika*, **27**, 125–139, 219–246 (1962).

56. Sokal, R. R. and P. H. A. Sneath, *Principles of Numerical Taxonomy* (W. H. Freeman, San Francisco, Calif., 1963).

57. Spragins, J., "Learning without a teacher," *IEEE Trans. Info. Theory*, **IT-12**, 223–230 (April 1966).

58. Stanat, D. F., "Unsupervised learning of mixtures of probability functions," in *Pattern Recognition*, pp. 357–389, L. Kanal, ed. (Thompson Book Co., Washington, D.C., 1968).

59. Stanley, G. L., G. G. Lendaris, and W. C. Nienow, "Pattern Recognition Program," Technical Report 567-16, AC Electronics Defense Research Laboratories, Santa Barbara, Calif. (1967).

60. Stevens, S. S., "Measurement, statistics, and the schemapiric view," *Science*, **161**, 849–856 (30 August 1968).

61. Teicher, H., "Identifiability of mixtures," *Ann. Math. Stat.*, **32**, 244–248 (March 1961).

62. Teicher, H., "Identifiability of finite mixtures," *Ann. Math. Stat.*, **34**, 1265–1269 (December 1963).

63. Thorndike, R. L., "Who belongs in the family?" *Psychometrika*, **18**, 267–276 (1953).

64. Tryon, R. C., *Cluster Analysis* (Edwards Brothers, Ann Arbor, Mich., 1939).

65. Tryon, R. C. and D. E. Bailey, "The BC TRY computer system of cluster and factor analysis," *Multivariate Behavioral Research*, **1**, 95–111 (January 1966).

66. Tryon, R. C. and D. E. Bailey, *Cluster Analysis* (McGraw-Hill, New York, 1970).

67. M. S. Watanabe, *Knowing and Guessing* (John Wiley, New York, 1969).

68. Wishart, D., "Mode analysis: a generalization of nearest neighbor which reduces chaining effects," in *Numerical Taxonomy*, pp. 282–308, A. J. Cole, ed. (Academic Press, London and New York, 1969).

69. Wolfe, J. H., "Pattern clustering by multivariate mixture analysis," *Multivariate Behavioral Research*, **5**, 329–350 (July 1970).

70. Yakowitz, S. J. and J. D. Spragins, "On the identifiability of finite mixtures," *Ann. Math. Stat.*, **39**, 209–214 (February 1968).

71. Yakowitz, S. J., "Unsupervised learning and the identification of finite mixtures," *IEEE Trans. Info. Theory*, **IT-16**, 330–338 (May 1970).

72. Young, T. Y. and G. Coraluppi, "Stochastic estimation of a mixture of normal density functions using an information criterion," *IEEE Trans. Info. Theory*, **IT-16**, 258–263 (May 1970).

73. Zahn, C. T., "Graph-theoretical methods for detecting and describing gestalt clusters," *IEEE Trans. Comp.*, **C-20**, 68–86 (January 1971).

PROBLEMS

1. Suppose that x can assume the values $0, 1, \ldots, m$ and that $P(x \mid \theta)$ is a mixture of c binomial distributions

$$P(x \mid \theta) = \sum_{j=1}^{c} \binom{m}{x} \theta_j^m (1 - \theta_j)^{m-x} P(\omega_j).$$

Assuming that the a priori probabilities are known, explain why this mixture is not identifiable if $m < c$. How does this answer change if the a priori probabilities are also unknown?

2. Let $\mathbf{x}$ be a binary vector and $P(\mathbf{x} \mid \theta)$ be a mixture of c multivariate Bernoulli distributions,

$$P(\mathbf{x} \mid \theta) = \sum_{i=1}^{c} P(\mathbf{x} \mid \omega_i, \theta_i) P(\omega_i)$$

where

$$P(\mathbf{x} \mid \omega_i, \theta_i) = \prod_{j=1}^{d} \theta_{ij}^{x_j} (1 - \theta_{ij})^{1-x_j}.$$

(a) Show that

$$\frac{\partial \log P(\mathbf{x} \mid \omega_i, \boldsymbol{\theta}_i)}{\partial \theta_{ij}} = \frac{x_i - \theta_{ij}}{\theta_{ij}(1 - \theta_{ij})}.$$

(b) Using the general equations for maximum likelihood estimates, show that the maximum likelihood estimate $\hat{\boldsymbol{\theta}}_i$ for $\boldsymbol{\theta}_i$ must satisfy

$$\hat{\boldsymbol{\theta}}_i = \frac{\sum\limits_{k=1}^{n} \hat{P}(\omega_i \mid \mathbf{x}_k, \hat{\boldsymbol{\theta}}_i)\mathbf{x}_k}{\sum\limits_{k=1}^{n} \hat{P}(\omega_i \mid \mathbf{x}_k, \hat{\boldsymbol{\theta}}_i)}.$$

3. Consider the univariate normal mixture

$$p(\mathbf{x} \mid \boldsymbol{\theta}) = \frac{P(\omega_1)}{\sqrt{2\pi}\,\sigma_1} \exp\left[-\frac{1}{2}\left(\frac{x - \mu_1}{\sigma_1}\right)^2\right] + \frac{P(\omega_2)}{\sqrt{2\pi}\,\sigma_2} \exp\left[-\frac{1}{2}\left(\frac{x - \mu_2}{\sigma_2}\right)^2\right].$$

Write a computer program that uses the general maximum likelihood equations of Section 6.4.3 iteratively to estimate the unknown means, variances, and a priori probabilities. Use this program to find maximum likelihood estimates of these parameters for the data in Table 6-1. (Answer: $\hat{\mu}_1 = -2.404$, $\hat{\mu}_2 = 1.491$, $\hat{\sigma}_1 = 0.577$, $\hat{\sigma}_2 = 1.338$, $\hat{P}(\omega_1) = 0.268$, $\hat{P}(\omega_2) = 0.732$.)

4. Let $p(\mathbf{x} \mid \boldsymbol{\theta})$ be a c-component normal mixture with $p(\mathbf{x} \mid \omega_i, \boldsymbol{\theta}_i) \sim N(\boldsymbol{\mu}_i, \sigma_i^2 I)$. Using the results of Section 6.3, show that the maximum likelihood estimate for σ_i^2 must satisfy

$$\hat{\sigma}_i^2 = \frac{\frac{1}{d}\sum\limits_{k=1}^{n} \hat{P}(\omega_i \mid \mathbf{x}_k, \hat{\boldsymbol{\theta}}_i)\, \|\mathbf{x}_k - \hat{\boldsymbol{\mu}}_i\|^2}{\sum\limits_{k=1}^{m} \hat{P}(\omega_i \mid \mathbf{x}_k, \hat{\boldsymbol{\theta}}_i)}$$

where $\hat{\boldsymbol{\mu}}_i$ and $\hat{P}(\omega_i \mid \mathbf{x}_k, \hat{\boldsymbol{\theta}}_i)$ are given by Eqs. (15) and (17), respectively.

5. The derivation of the equations for maximum likelihood estimation of parameters of a mixture density was made under the assumption that the parameters in each component density are functionally independent. Suppose instead that

$$p(\mathbf{x} \mid \alpha) = \sum_{j=1}^{c} p(\mathbf{x} \mid \omega_j, \alpha)P(\omega_j),$$

where α is a parameter that appears in a number of the component densities. Let l be the n-sample log-likelihood function, and show that

$$\frac{\partial l}{\partial \alpha} = \sum_{k=1}^{n} \sum_{j=1}^{c} P(\omega_j \mid \mathbf{x}_k, \alpha) \frac{\partial \log p(\mathbf{x}_k \mid \omega_j, \alpha)}{\partial \alpha}$$

where

$$P(\omega_j \mid \mathbf{x}_k, \alpha) = \frac{p(\mathbf{x}_k \mid \omega_j, \alpha)P(\omega_j)}{p(\mathbf{x}_k \mid \alpha)}.$$

6. Let $p(\mathbf{x} \mid \omega_i, \boldsymbol{\theta}_i) \sim N(\boldsymbol{\mu}_i, \Sigma)$, where Σ is a common covariance matrix for the c component densities. Let σ_{pq} be the pqth element of Σ, σ^{pq} be the pqth element of Σ^{-1}, $x_p(k)$ be the pth element of $\mathbf{x}_k$, and $\mu_p(i)$ be the pth element of $\boldsymbol{\mu}_i$.

(a) Show that

$$\frac{\partial \log p(\mathbf{x}_k \mid \omega_i, \boldsymbol{\theta}_i)}{\partial \sigma^{pq}} = \left(1 - \frac{\delta_{pq}}{2}\right) [\sigma_{pq} - (x_p(k) - \mu_p(i))(x_q(k) - \mu_q(i))].$$

(b) Use this result and the results of Problem 5 to show that the maximum likelihood estimate for Σ must satisfy

$$\hat{\Sigma} = \frac{1}{n} \sum_{k=1}^{n} \mathbf{x}_k \mathbf{x}_k^t - \sum_{i=1}^{c} \hat{P}(\omega_i)\hat{\boldsymbol{\mu}}_i\hat{\boldsymbol{\mu}}_i^t,$$

where $\hat{P}(\omega_i)$ and $\hat{\boldsymbol{\mu}}_i$ are the maximum likelihood estimates given by Eqs. (14) and (15) in the text.

7. Show that the maximum likelihood estimate of an a priori probability can be zero by considering the following special case. Let $p(x \mid \omega_1) \sim N(0, 1)$ and $p(x \mid \omega_2) \sim N(0, (1/2))$, so that $P(\omega_1)$ is the only unknown parameter in the mixture

$$p(x) = \frac{P(\omega_1)}{\sqrt{2\pi}} e^{-(1/2)x^2} + \frac{(1 - P(\omega_1))}{\sqrt{\pi}} e^{-x^2}.$$

Show that the maximum likelihood estimate $\hat{P}(\omega_1)$ of $P(\omega_1)$ is zero if one sample x_1 is observed and if $x_1^2 < \log 2$. What is the value of $\hat{P}(\omega_1)$ if $x_1^2 > \log 2$?

8. Consider the univariate normal mixture

$$p(x \mid \mu_1, \ldots, \mu_c) = \sum_{j=1}^{c} \frac{P(\omega_j)}{\sqrt{2\pi}\,\sigma} \exp\left[-\frac{1}{2}\left(\frac{x - \mu_j}{\sigma}\right)^2\right]$$

in which all the components have the same, known variance, σ^2. Suppose that the means are so far apart compared to σ that for any observed x all but one of the terms in this sum are negligible. Use a heuristic argument to show that the value of

$$\max_{\mu_1,\ldots,\mu_c} \left\{\frac{1}{n} \log p(x_1, \ldots, x_n \mid \mu_1, \ldots, \mu_c)\right\}$$

ought to be approximately

$$\sum_{j=1}^{c} P(\omega_j) \log P(\omega_j) - \tfrac{1}{2} \log 2\pi\sigma e$$

when the number n of independently drawn samples is large. Compare this with the value shown on Figure 6.1.

9. Let θ_1 and θ_2 be unknown parameters for the component densities $p(x \mid \omega_1, \theta_1)$ and $p(x \mid \omega_2, \theta_2)$, respectively. Assume that θ_1 and θ_2 are initially statistically independent, so that $p(\theta_1, \theta_2) = p_1(\theta_1)p_2(\theta_2)$. Show that after one sample x_1 from the mixture density is observed, $p(\theta_1, \theta_2 \mid x_1)$ can no longer be factored as

$$p(\theta_1 \mid x_1)p_2(\theta_2 \mid x_1)$$

if

$$\frac{\partial p(x \mid \omega_i, \theta_i)}{\partial \theta_i} \neq 0, \quad i = 1, 2.$$

What does this imply in general about the statistical dependence of parameters in unsupervised learning?

10. Let $\mathbf{x}_1, \ldots, \mathbf{x}_n$ be n d-dimensional samples and Σ be any nonsingular d-by-d matrix. Show that the vector $\mathbf{x}$ that minimizes

$$\sum_{k=1}^{m} (\mathbf{x}_k - \mathbf{x})^t \Sigma^{-1}(\mathbf{x}_k - \mathbf{x})$$

is the sample mean, $\dfrac{1}{n}\sum_{k=1}^{n}\mathbf{x}_k$.

11. Let $s(\mathbf{x}, \mathbf{x}') = \mathbf{x}^t\mathbf{x}'/(\|\mathbf{x}\| \cdot \|\mathbf{x}'\|)$. Interpret this similarity measure if the d features have binary values, where $x_i = 1$ if $\mathbf{x}$ possesses the ith feature and $x_i = -1$ if it does not. Show that for this case

$$\|\mathbf{x} - \mathbf{x}'\|^2 = 2d^2(1 - s(\mathbf{x}, \mathbf{x}')).$$

12. If a set of n samples $\mathcal{X}$ is partitioned into c disjoint subsets $\mathcal{X}_1, \ldots, \mathcal{X}_c$, the sample mean $\mathbf{m}_i$ for samples in $\mathcal{X}_i$ is undefined if $\mathcal{X}_i$ is empty. In such a case, the sum of squared errors involves only the nonempty subsets:

$$J_e = \sum_{\substack{\text{nonempty} \\ \mathcal{X}_i}} \sum_{\mathbf{x}\in\mathcal{X}_i} \|\mathbf{x} - \mathbf{m}_i\|^2.$$

Assuming that $n \geq c$, show that there are no empty subsets in a partition that minimizes J_e.

13. Consider a set of $n = 2k + 1$ samples, k of which coincide at $x = -2$, k at $x = 0$, and one at $x = a > 0$. Show that the two-cluster partitioning that minimizes J_e groups the k samples at $x = 0$ with the one at $x = a$ if $a^2 < 2(k + 1)$. What is the optimal grouping if $a^2 > 2(k + 1)$?

14. Let $\mathbf{x}_1 = (4\ 5)^t$, $\mathbf{x}_2 = (1\ 4)^t$, $\mathbf{x}_3 = (0\ 1)^t$ and $\mathbf{x}_4 = (5\ 0)^t$, and consider the following three partitions:

1. $\mathcal{X}_1 = \{\mathbf{x}_1, \mathbf{x}_2\}, \mathcal{X}_2 = \{\mathbf{x}_3, \mathbf{x}_4\}$
2. $\mathcal{X}_1 = \{\mathbf{x}_1, \mathbf{x}_4\}, \mathcal{X}_2 = \{\mathbf{x}_2, \mathbf{x}_3\}$
3. $\mathcal{X}_1 = \{\mathbf{x}_1, \mathbf{x}_2, \mathbf{x}_3\}, \mathcal{X}_2 = \{\mathbf{x}_4\}$.

Show that by the sum-of-squared error (or tr S_W) criterion, the third partition is favored, whereas by the invariant $|S_W|$ criterion the first two partitions are favored. (Numerical answers for the three partitions: (1) and (2), tr $S_W = 18$, $|S_W| = 16$; (3), tr $S_W = 52/3$, $|S_W| = 64/3$.)

15. Show the eigenvalues $\lambda_1, \ldots, \lambda_d$ of $S_W^{-1}S_B$ are invariant to nonsingular linear transformations of the data. Show that the eigenvalues $\nu_1, \ldots, \nu_d$ of $S_T^{-1}S_W$ are related to those of $S_W^{-1}S_B$ by $\nu_i = 1/(1 + \lambda_i)$. How does this show that $J_d = |S_W|/|S_T|$ is invariant to nonsingular linear transformations of the data?

16. One way to generalize the basic-minimum-squared-error procedure is to define the criterion function

$$J_T = \sum_{i=1}^{c} \sum_{\mathbf{x}\in\mathcal{X}_i} (\mathbf{x}_i - \mathbf{m}_i)^t S_T^{-1}(\mathbf{x}_i - \mathbf{m}_i),$$

where $\mathbf{m}_i$ is the mean of the n_i samples in $\mathcal{X}_i$ and S_T is the total scatter matrix.
(a) Show that J_T is invariant to nonsingular linear transformations of the data.

(b) Show that the transfer of a sample $\hat{\mathbf{x}}$ from $\mathcal{X}_i$ to $\mathcal{X}_j$ causes J_T to change to

$$J_T^* = J_T - \left[\frac{n_j}{n_j + 1} (\hat{\mathbf{x}} - \mathbf{m}_j)^t S_T^{-1} (\hat{\mathbf{x}} - \mathbf{m}_j) - \frac{n_i}{n_i - 1} (\hat{\mathbf{x}} - \mathbf{m}_i)^t S_T^{-1} (\hat{\mathbf{x}} - \mathbf{m}_i) \right].$$

(c) Suggest an iterative procedure for minimizing J_T.

17.   Use the facts that $S_T = S_W + S_B$, $J_e = \text{tr } S_W$, and $\text{tr } S_B = \sum n_i \| \mathbf{m}_i - \mathbf{m} \|^2$ to derive the equations given in Section 6.9 for the change in J_e resulting from transferring a sample $\hat{\mathbf{x}}$ from cluster $\mathcal{X}_i$ to cluster $\mathcal{X}_j$.

18.   Let cluster $\mathcal{X}_i$ contain n_i samples, and let d_{ij} be some measure of the distance between two clusters $\mathcal{X}_i$ and $\mathcal{X}_j$. In general, one might expect that if $\mathcal{X}_i$ and $\mathcal{X}_j$ are merged to form a new cluster $\mathcal{X}_k$, then the distance from $\mathcal{X}_k$ to some other cluster $\mathcal{X}_h$ is not simply related to d_{hi} and d_{hj}. However, consider the equation

$$d_{hk} = \alpha_i d_{hi} + \alpha_j d_{hj} + \beta d_{ij} + \gamma |d_{hi} - d_{hj}|.$$

Show that the following choices for the coefficients α_i, α_j, β, and γ lead to the distance functions indicated. (For other cases, see Lance and Williams, 1967.)

(a) $d_{\min}$: $\alpha_i = \alpha_j = 0.5$, $\beta = 0$, $\gamma = -0.5$.
(b) $d_{\max}$: $\alpha_i = \alpha_j = 0.5$, $\beta = 0$, $\gamma = 0.5$.
(c) d_{avg}: $\alpha_i = \dfrac{n_i}{n_i + n_j}$, $\alpha_j = \dfrac{n_j}{n_i + n_j}$, $\beta = \gamma = 0$.
(d) d_{mean}^2: $\alpha_i = \dfrac{n_i}{n_i + n_j}$, $\alpha_j = \dfrac{n_j}{n_i + n_j}$, $\beta = -\alpha_i \alpha_j$, $\gamma = 0$.

19.   Consider a hierarchical clustering procedure in which clusters are merged so as to produce the smallest increase in the sum-of-squared error at each step. If the ith cluster contains n_i samples with sample mean $\mathbf{m}_i$, show that the smallest increase results from merging the pair of clusters for which

$$\frac{n_i n_j}{n_i + n_j} \| \mathbf{m}_i - \mathbf{m}_j \|^2$$

is minimum.

20.   Consider the representation of the points $\mathbf{x}_1 = (1\ 0)^t$, $\mathbf{x}_2 = (0\ 0)^t$ and $\mathbf{x}_3 = (0\ 1)^t$ by a one-dimensional configuration. To obtain a unique solution, assume that the image points satisfy $0 = y_1 < y_2 < y_3$.
(a) Show that the criterion function J_{ee} is minimized by the configuration with $y_2 = (1 + \sqrt{2})/3$ and $y_3 = 2y_2$.
(b) Show that the criterion function J_{ff} is minimized by the configuration with $y_2 = (2 + \sqrt{2})/4$ and $y_3 = 2y_2$.

Part II

SCENE ANALYSIS

Chapter 7

REPRESENTATION
AND INITIAL
SIMPLIFICATIONS

7.1 INTRODUCTION

Our purpose in the second part of this book is to present the fundamentals of automatic scene analysis. We will be interested in computer-based methods for simplifying and describing pictures in order to answer such questions as "Does the picture show a chair?," "Name all the objects in the picture," "Do two pictures show the same object?" or, more generally, "Describe the scene." Let us catalog several of the many applications of scene analysis just to convey a feeling for the range of the field.

Optical character recognition was the focus of interest in early work and remains an important commercial application. The problem here is one of classification, rather than description, so the mathematical tools discussed in Part I are appropriate. In this application, and in classification problems generally, the function of the scene analysis techniques we will be concerned with is to provide a set of features to a pattern classifier. Interest in a quite different problem domain is motivated by the work of particle physicists, who take many pictures of interactions in bubble and spark chambers. Their problem is usually to discover the occurrence of certain events by analyzing tracks in the photograph. A third important problem domain arises from the biomedical sciences. The large number of microscope slides examined visually, for both clinical and research purposes, is a natural motivation for work on automated procedures. As a final example, there exist robot manipulators and vehicles whose versatility and power are greatly enhanced when they are provided with sensory, and especially visual, abilities.

It is important to note that merely naming a problem domain says little about the difficulty of the scene analysis problems encountered therein. As an example, consider for a moment optical character recognition, which is in·some ways a rather simple problem domain. The difficulty of a character recognition problem depends upon many things: whether the characters are made by hand or machine; if by machine then whether a single font or many fonts are used; if by hand then whether one author or many will be encountered, and so on through a long list of specifications. Hence, scene analysis is concerned not only with a wide variety of problem domains but with enormous variability of problems within a single domain. It would be naive, of course, to expect that a single technique or even a small number of techniques would be applicable across such a broad spectrum of problems. Indeed, this variability makes it difficult to characterize scene analysis as a whole, except to note that the process is essentially one of simplification. The general problem is to transform a picture, represented perhaps by tens of thousands of bits, to a "description" or "classification" represented by only tens of bits. We will be interested, then, in methods for simplifying pictures—for suppressing irrelevant detail, characterizing shapes and sizes of objects in a picture, integrating parts of a picture into meaningful entities and in general reducing the complexity of the data.

7.2 REPRESENTATIONS

Suppose we have an ordinary photographic transparency, and want to analyze it using a digital computer. One of our first problems, obviously, is to select a representation of the picture that is suitable for the machine. There are many means for doing this, but we can put them in perspective by recognizing that a black-and-white picture can be thought of as a real-valued function of two variables. To be specific, suppose that the picture occupies a plane coordinatized by x and y. We will define a *picture function** $g(x, y)$ to be proportional to the light intensity impinging on the picture at the point (x, y). The intensity of a picture at a point is also called the *gray level* or the *brightness*. In any event, from a mathematical point of view a picture is defined by specifying its picture function.

Once we have agreed to consider pictures as functions, it is obvious that any means for representing a function in a digital computer can be used to represent a picture. Some methods can be dismissed immediately as being inappropriate. Polynomials, for example, are generally represented by storing

---

* The reader should not confuse our use of $g(x, y)$ here with the discriminant functions of Part I.

their coefficients, but few interesting picture functions are merely low degree polynomials. More generally, an interesting picture function seldom has a simple analytic form, so its representation is usually accomplished by sampling the picture function at a discrete number of points in the X–Y plane and storing the sample values. This process is called *sampling* or *quantization*. In order to define a quantization algorithm, we must first specify where the samples are to be taken. The simplest specification is to partition the picture plane by a quadruled grid and to sample the picture function at the center of each cell. Now in general the picture function can assume any value between some minimum (black) and maximum (white), while the digital computer can represent only a finite number of values. We must therefore also partition the range of amplitudes of the picture function into a finite number of cells. If this is done, we will have specified an algorithm for representing the original picture function as an array of integers where each element of the array specifies the approximate gray level of the picture in the corresponding cell.

Let us consider in a little more detail the problem of partitioning the gray scale into a set of discrete cells. The simplest way to accomplish this is merely to divide the range of picture intensities, from black to white, into uniform intervals. If we decide to do this, we have only to specify the number of cells, or, in other words, the fineness of the partition. Unfortunately, there is no theoretical guidance on this question, and one usually makes some compromise between the desire for accurate representation and the need to keep computational requirements within reasonable bounds. We are not, however, constrained to make the quantization cells uniform in size. Suppose, for example, we had reason to believe that most of the detail in the picture occurred in generally dark regions. If we were constrained to use at most a given number of cells, it would surely make sense to quantize non-uniformly. We would quantize the dark portion of the gray scale into relatively fine cells, and quantize the light portion into relatively coarse ones. If we had no special prior knowledge about the picture, we might take as our guide the construction of the human eye-brain combination, which seems to be approximately logarithmic in its response to light. In other words, logarithmic changes in the physical intensity of a visual stimulus are perceived by a human observer as being equally spaces "apparent" changes. This phenomenon (which also seems to hold for auditory and tactile stimuli) suggests that we first take the logarithm of the picture function and quantize $\log g(x, y)$ uniformly.

Let us now turn our attention to the question of grid size. This question is analogous to the problem of quantizing the gray scale, but here some theoretical guidance is available in the form of the well-known Shannon sampling theorem. A discussion of this theorem requires some knowledge of two-dimensional Fourier transforms, so it will be deferred until the next

FIGURE 7.1.   A television monitor picture.

chapter. We may note that the picture plane can be partitioned by some means other than a quadruled grid. In a quadruled grid, two cells having a common corner need not have a common side, a property that has mildly unpleasant consequences in certain picture processing operations that will be discussed later. To remedy this, a partition of the picture plane into hexagons is occasionally suggested, but for many purposes the benefit obtained is not worth the additional complexity. For the remainder of the book, then, we will assume wherever convenient that a picture can be represented by an ordinary matrix whose real entries define the (approximate) values of the picture function in the corresponding region of the picture plane. When there is no danger of confusion, we will call the (i, j) element of this matrix $g(i, j)$ and in this case speak of g as a *digital picture function*. The unquantized picture function $g(x, y)$ will be referred to as the *analog* picture function. For convenience, we will also establish the convention that low and high values of the quantized picture function mean, respectively, dark and light levels of intensity.

As an example of the foregoing, consider Figures 7.1 and 7.2. Figure 7.1 shows a simple three-dimensional scene containing elementary geometrical objects. The picture was photographed directly from an ordinary television monitor, but for our immediate purpose it is immaterial whether we use television pictures, photographic transparencies, or any other kind of picture. Figure 7.2 shows a quantized representation of Figure 7.1. We have

FIGURE 7.2.   A digital picture.

used a quadruled quantization grid 120 cells on a side and have quantized the gray scale into 16 uniformly spaced levels. The quantized picture itself is of course a matrix, but we have displayed the numerical array pictorially as an array of discrete points. Each point in the displayed array has one of 16 gray levels, where the gray level is specified by the corresponding number in the matrix. We might note here that the back edge of the wedge is just distinguishable in the quantized picture from the wall behind it. There is, in fact, a difference of one gray level between these regions. Unfortunately, there are many one-level differences in the middle of the floor and wall caused by shading in the original picture. Hence, in a simplified view of the world a one-level difference in gray scale might be considered "insignificant." We will not dwell on the subject now, but we might anticipate that the problem of determining what gray level transitions are "significant" is an important one that is not likely to be generally susceptible to quick and easy solutions.

7.3   SPATIAL DIFFERENTIATION

As we remarked earlier, the process of scene analysis is generally a process of simplification—a complicated object, the original picture, is converted into a simpler form by some sequence of steps. In such a sequence, one natural step is to convert the given picture into an outline drawing. We would hope that this step would preserve the important features of the original picture, but would reduce the computational requirements imposed on subsequent steps. There are also psychological grounds for considering outline drawings of the picture. Experiments have shown that humans concentrate most of their attention on the borders between more or less homogeneous regions. Of course, we recognize that in reducing a picture to a line drawing we face certain hazards. The reduced picture generally contains less information than the original, and there is no guarantee that the information lost is irrelevant. For the time being, however, we will proceed under the assumption that the reduction of a picture to an outline drawing is useful in some circumstances, and turn our attention to means for accomplishing this.

An outline drawing of a picture can be produced by emphasizing regions containing abrupt dark-light transitions, and de-emphasizing regions of approximately homogeneous intensity. Another way of putting this is to say that outlines are edges, and edges are by definition transitions between two markedly dissimilar intensities. In terms of the picture function, an edge is a region of the $X–Y$ plane where $g(x, y)$ has a gradient with a large magnitude. The problem of producing an outline drawing thus requires estimating the magnitude of the gradient of a function. Now the gradient can be estimated if we know the directional derivatives of the function along any two orthogonal directions. Hence we need only select a pair of orthogonal directions and an approximation to a (one-dimensional) derivative in order to have on hand the essential ingredients of an algorithm for producing outline drawings.

As an example of both historical and practical interest, let us approximate the magnitude of the gradient at picture point (i, j) by

$$\|\nabla g(i, j)\| \approx R(i, j)$$
$$= \sqrt{[g(i, j) - g(i + 1, j + 1)]^2 + [g(i, j + 1) - g(i + 1, j)]^2}.$$

Notice that this corresponds to selecting for our orthogonal directions the lines whose slopes are plus and minus one. Diagrammatically, we consider at cell (i, j) a 2×2 window whose diagonal elements are associated by subtraction:

i, j	$i, j + 1$
$i + 1, j$	$i + 1, j + 1$

The directional derivative in each direction is approximated by simply subtracting adjacent elements. The operator $R(i, j)$ is sometimes called the *Roberts cross operator*. Consider for a moment its qualitative behavior. If the point (i, j) is in a region of uniform intensity, the value of $R(i, j)$ is zero, as one would hope. If there is a discontinuity in intensity between column j and column $(j + 1)$, then $R(i, j)$ has a large value, and similarly if there is a discontinuity between row i and row $(i + 1)$. The Roberts cross operator is often simplified for computational efficiency by using absolute magnitudes rather than squares and square roots. We define $F(i, j)$ by

$$F(i,j) = |g(i,j) - g(i + 1, j + 1)| + |g(i, j + 1) - g(i + 1, j)|.$$

Clearly, $R(i, j) \leq F(i, j) \leq \sqrt{2} R(i, j)$ and $F(i, j)$ behaves qualitatively very much like $R(i, j)$.

In Figure 7.3 we have shown the result of applying F to the digital picture of Figure 7.2 and displaying the (i, j) cell if $F(i, j) > 2$. The most obvious shortcoming is that the back edge of the wedge has been lost. As we remarked earlier, there is only one gray level difference between the intensities on each side of the lost line. If such a difference were considered significant and the threshold of 2 lowered we would discover unacceptably large numbers of "spurious" lines in the floor and wall. On the whole, however, much of the "essential" information of Figure 7.2 has been retained.

Let us digress for a moment for a word on terminology. The picture shown in Figure 7.3 is usually called a *gradient picture*. The process of obtaining the gradient picture is variously known as *spatial differentiation*, *edge enhancement*, *sharpening*, or simply taking the gradient. Strictly speaking, Figure 7.3 shows a thresholded gradient picture. Since thresholding a gradient picture is fairly common, the unthresholded gradient picture is loosely called

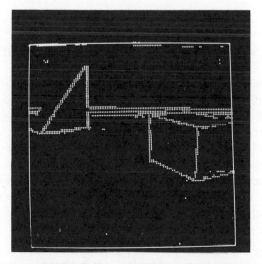

FIGURE 7.3.   A gradient picture.

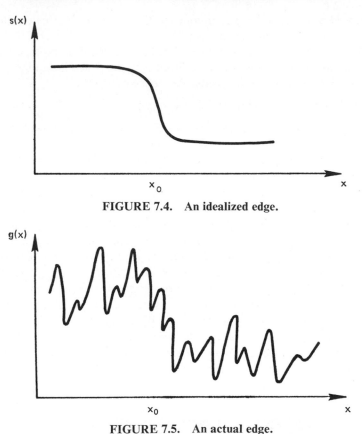

FIGURE 7.4.   An idealized edge.

FIGURE 7.5.   An actual edge.

the analog gradient picture, which of course it is not. That's enough confusion for now.

We now examine in a little more detail the problem of taking the gradient.
The root of the difficulty is the existence of noise. In the language of communication theory, we might say that the digital picture function $g(i,j)$ is the sum
of two picture functions: an "ideal" picture, or signal, $s(i,j)$ and a pure
noise picture $n(i,j)$. Our problem is that we really want to estimate the gradient
not of g but of the ideal picture s. To illustrate this let us restrict our attention
to the one-dimensional case and, for simplicity, let us only consider the
analog case. In Figure 7.4 we have shown a one-dimensional ideal picture
function* $s(x)$ that undergoes an abrupt change in the vicinity of x_0. Unfortunately, we only have $g(x) = s(x) + n(x)$ available to us (Figure 7.5).

---

* We can interpret a one-dimensional picture as being the intensity function of the two-
dimensional picture along some one-dimensional cut in the picture plane.

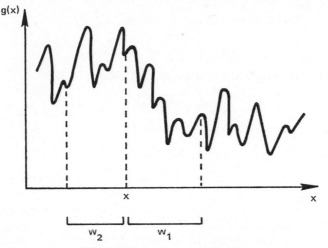

FIGURE 7.6.   Averaging windows.

What would be a reasonable procedure for estimating from $g(x)$ the location of x_0? Intuitively, the answer must involve some kind of averaging. We would like to smooth the function g enough to average out the worst of the noise, but not smooth it so much that we blur the jump in s completely. If we were empirically inclined, we might define a derivative estimation operator $D(x)$ by

$$D(x) = \frac{1}{w_1} \int_x^{x+w_1} g(u)\, du - \frac{1}{w_2} \int_{x-w_2}^x g(u)\, du.$$

As shown in Figure 7.6, this operator places windows of length w_2 and w_1 just before and after x, averages the function g over each of these windows, and takes the difference of the averages. For an appropriate choice of window sizes, such an operator might work very well. Analogously, the estimation of the gradient in the two-dimensional case requires some combination of averaging and differencing. This fact has led to the development of a number of gradient estimators using windows of various sizes.

As an example of a gradient operator using a 3×3 window* consider the following, where for notational simplicity we will let the picture elements in the window be as shown below:

a	b	c
d	e	f
g	h	i

* Suggested by I. Sobel.

We define S_x by

$$S_x = (c + 2f + i) - (a + 2d + g)$$

and S_y by

$$S_y = (g + 2h + i) - (a + 2b + c).$$

Then we define the gradient at the point e by either

$$S = \sqrt{S_x^2 + S_y^2}$$

or, if we want a computationally more efficient definition,

$$S = |S_x| + |S_y|.$$

Consider for a moment the definition of S_x. This definition is an attempt to estimate the partial derivative of the picture function in the X direction. First, two weighted averages are formed to estimate the picture at f and d (normalizing constants are ignored). The two weighted averages are then subtracted in order to obtain an estimate of the partial derivative. An analogous operation is performed to obtain S_y. The weighting constants $1, 2, 1$ are based on only intuitive grounds. In the next chapter we will approach the problem from a more mathematical point of view and discuss the requirements on an "optimal" gradient estimator.

7.4 SPATIAL SMOOTHING

In the last section we introduced the classical technique of combating noise by means of averaging. Although our immediate purpose was to estimate the gradient of a function, it is clear that the technique can be used more generally to "clean up" noisy pictures. As before, the basic idea is to replace the gray scale value at a point by the average value of the picture function in the immediate vicinity. The danger, of course, is that the averaging process blurs details. For simplicity, let us first examine the case of a one-dimensional analog picture function $g(x)$. We define a smoothed version $g_w(x)$ by

$$g_w(x) = \frac{1}{w} \int_{x-w/2}^{x+w/2} g(u)\, du.$$

This process is called *regularization* of functions. It is not a very difficult calculus exercise to prove that regularization smooths functions in a precise sense: if $g(x)$ is discontinuous, then $g_w(x)$ is continuous, and if $g(x)$ is continuous, then $g_w(x)$ has a continuous derivative. These properties are illustrated in Figure 7.7a and b. Notice that the width of the "transition region" of $g_w(x)$ depends upon the window size. Increasing w results in more pronounced blurring of the picture. Conversely, the smaller the window w

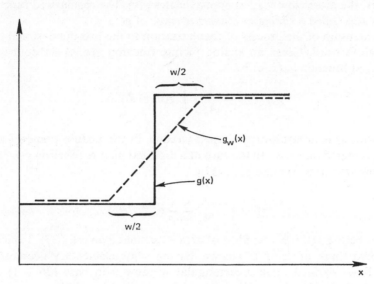

FIGURE 7.7a. Example of regularization in one dimension.

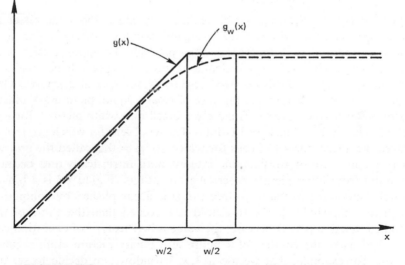

FIGURE 7.7b. Another example of regularization in one dimension.

becomes, the more closely $g_w(x)$ approximates $g(x)$. The regularized function $g_w(x)$ is also called a *sliding* or *moving average* of $g(x)$.

The extension of the process of regularization to the two-dimensional case is straightforward. Given an analog picture function $g(x, y)$ we define the regularized function $g_w(x, y)$ by

$$ g_w(x, y) = \frac{1}{A_w} \int\int_{w(x,y)} g(u, v) \, du \, dv, $$

where $w(x, y)$ is an arbitrarily shaped window in the picture plane of area A_w and centered on (x, y). In the case of a digitized picture function $g(i, j)$ we define the smoothed version $g_w(i, j)$ by

$$ g_w(i, j) = \frac{1}{A_w} \sum\sum_{w(i,j)} g(m, n), $$

where as before $w(i, j)$ is a window of area A_w centered on cell (i, j). Typically one would think of using a window having some elementary geometrical shape. If we decided upon a rectangular window with base $(2b + 1)$ and height $(2h + 1)$, then the regularized version of $g(i, j)$ would be

$$ g_w(i, j) = \frac{1}{(2b + 1)(2h + 1)} \sum_{-b \le m \le b} \sum_{-h \le n \le h} g(i + m, j + n). $$

Qualitatively, regularizing a picture has very much the same effect as defocusing a camera, with a large averaging window corresponding to a camera severely out of focus. This is often precisely the opposite effect that is wanted—we prefer as sharp and clear a picture as can possibly be obtained. Consequently, regularization is used selectively for special purposes. One situation in which it is useful is the case of *binary* digital pictures. A binary picture, as one would expect, is merely a black and white picture; for any (i, j), $g(i, j)$ is either 0 (black) or 1 (white). The set of cells for which $g(i, j) = 1$ is called the *figure;* the set of cells for which $g(i, j) = 0$ is called the *ground*. Binary pictures are of considerable interest both intrinsically and because they result from other picture processing operations (Figure 7.3 is a binary picture). Smoothing a binary picture $g(i, j)$ is accomplished by comparing $g_w(i, j)$ to a threshold. If the threshold is exceeded then the value of the smoothed function is 1. Otherwise, the value is 0. This type of operation can be used to make the contour of a figure in a binary picture more regular. Suppose, for example, that we use a 3 × 3 window and decide to set the threshold at 0.4. This operator would set a cell (i, j) in the smoothed picture to 1 if and only if at least 4 cells in the window surrounding (i, j) were 1. When we smooth the simple binary picture shown in Figure 7.8 the result depicted in Figure 7.9 is obtained, where we see that the spur on the upper

	1					
		1	1	1		
		1	1	1		
		1	1	1		

		1	1	1		
		1	1	1		
		1	1	1		

FIGURE 7.8 (left), 7.9 (right). Example of regularization in two dimensions.

		1	1	1		
		1	1	1		
		1	1	1		
		1	1	1		

		1	1	1		
		1	1	1		
		1	1	1		
		1	1	1		
		1	1	1		

FIGURE 7.10 (left), 7.11 (right). Another example of regularization in two dimensions.

left of the figure has been removed. (Blank cells are 0's.) On the other hand, when the same smoothing operation is applied to the disconnected figure shown in Figure 7.10, the results shown in Figure 7.11 are obtained, where we observe that the gap separating the two halves of the picture has been completely filled in. If we considered one cell gaps in the figure to be significant we would be a bit disappointed in the performance of this particular smoothing operator. In other words, even these very simple examples demonstrate that regularization is a two-edged sword that must be used with caution.

If we are dealing with binary pictures there is an alternative smoothing technique that often allows us to exercise more precise control than does regularization. This technique is called *logical averaging* or *logical smoothing*. It is based on the observation that the picture elements appearing within the averaging window can be treated as boolean or logical variables, and the value of the smoothed picture function at a point can be defined by any boolean function of these variables. As an example, suppose we wanted to construct a logical smoothing operator with the following specifications:

(a) A "0" cell is changed to a "1" cell if and only if all its neighbors are "1".
(b) A "1" cell is changed to a "0" cell if and only if all its neighbors are "0".

This specification asks for an operator that will complement isolated 0's and 1's, but leave the picture otherwise unchanged. It would be a reasonable operator to apply if one were confronted with so-called "salt-and-pepper" noise, which is the occasional random complementing of binary picture values. A logical smoothing operator using a 3×3 window and having the required properties is the following, where for notational simplicity we will let the picture elements in the window be as shown below:

a	b	c
d	e	f
g	h	i

We define e', the new picture value at the center cell of the window, by

$$e' = \bar{e}(abcdfghi) \lor e(a \lor b \lor c \lor d \lor f \lor g \lor h \lor i),$$

where $a \lor b$ means "a or b", $\bar{a}$ means "not a", and ab means "a and b". It is easy to see that this logical function has the desired properties. The new value e' is 1 if and only if e is 0 and all its neighbors are 1, or if e itself is 1 and at least one of its neighbors is 1. The advantage of logical smoothing over regularization, then, is that it allows us to specify more elaborate conditions under which a cell value is to be changed. In fact, regularization (of binary pictures) is a special case of logical smoothing, since the numerical operations of regularization can be defined by a boolean expression. Other boolean operators can be constructed to combat special noise idiosyncracies or to take advantage of prior knowledge about the figures likely to be encountered.

7.5   TEMPLATE MATCHING

7.5.1   Template Matching—Metric Interpretation

In a great variety of scene analysis problems the analyzer is confronted with one variation or another of a single simple question: Does the scene contain within it a picture of a previously specified object? The technique classically employed to answer this class of questions is called *template matching*. Let us consider template matching first within the simple context of binary pictures, and then extend our discussion to the general case. We proceed by means of an example.

Suppose we have a gradient picture, such as Figure 7.3, that shows elementary geometrical solids in outline form, and we would like to ascertain whether or not a triangle appears. (A triangle indicates the presence of a wedge.) A very simple approach to the problem might involve making a template, or mask, like the one shown in Figure 7.12 and scanning it systematically across the entire picture. If we found a position for which the "hole"

FIGURE 7.12. A simple template.

in the template was filled with white, we would declare that a triangle had been found at that position. An immediate objection to this procedure is that any sufficiently large region of solid white would result in our erroneously declaring that a triangle had been found.

This objection could be overcome if we were to look not merely for a white region that filled the template, but for a white triangular region surrounded by black regions. In Figure 7.13 we have shown diagrammatically how this can be done with a template. Using the new template, we announce that a triangle has been found only if each template region covers an area of the picture whose gray values corresponds to the template label. In other words, the 0 regions of the template must "show" only gray values of 0, and the 1 region must show only gray values of 1. Notice that the template in Figure 7.13 is itself a binary picture. (For simplicity, we have not shown the quantization of the template onto a quadruled grid.) The size of the template, however, is typically smaller than the size of the original picture, since our aim is to discover the presence of a "sub-picture" within the given picture. Mathematically, we say that the domain of definition of the template is smaller than the domain of definition of the original picture.

In most practical applications, one would not expect to find the perfect template match contemplated above. A more realistic approach would be to define some measure of how well a portion of a picture matched a template.

One such definition is the following:

Let $g(i,j)$ be our digital picture, let
      $t(i,j)$ be the template, and let
      D be the domain of definition of the template.

(D, for example, might be a 20 × 20 square, whereas the domain of definition of the picture might be a 500 × 500 square.) Then a measure of how well a portion of the picture matches the template can be defined as

$$M(m, n) = \sum\sum_{\substack{i,j \text{ such} \\ \text{that} \\ (i-m, j-n) \\ \text{is in } D.}} |g(i, j) - t(i - m, j - n)|. \tag{1}$$

Notice that this definition amounts to translating the template $t(i,j)$ to position (m, n) in the picture and setting $M(m, n)$ equal to the number of cells for which the picture and the translated template differ in gray value. Since we are presumably interested in finding a match to the template anywhere in the picture, we would have to compute $M(m, n)$ for all template translations (m, n) and note those translations for which $M(m, n)$ is small.

Let us abstract from the previous discussion the essential elements of template matching. In terms of picture functions, we are looking for a region

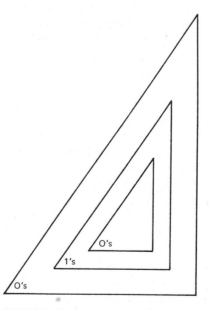

FIGURE 7.13.   A more refined template.

of the picture plane such that the picture function in that region is similar to
a previously specified picture function called the template. Hence, we need
in general a means for measuring the similarity, or distance, between two
picture functions, and the notion of a metric becomes useful. For the moment
we need not be concerned with the formal definition of the class of functions
called metrics, except to note that is is the standard abstraction of the notion
of Euclidean distance. Our definition of $M(m, n)$ given in (1) satisfies the
definition and is sometimes called the metric based on the L^1 norm. Two
other metrics are

$$E(m, n) = \left\{ \sum_i \sum_j [g(i, j) - t(i - m, j - n)]^2 \right\}^{1/2} \tag{2}$$

and

$$S(m, n) = \max_{i, j} |g(i, j) - t(i - m, j - n)|, \tag{3}$$

where in each case the range of i and j is the same as in (1). The definition in
(2) is the standard Euclidean distance between two vectors. The definition
in (3) is sometimes called the metric based on the L^∞ norm. Note that these
definitions are not restricted to binary pictures although, as we saw above, a
definition may have a particularly simple interpretation when restricted to
binary pictures.

Let us examine definition (2) in a little more detail. It is often convenient
to remove the square root by considering the measure of distance to be
$E^2(m, n)$. If we do this, and multiply out, we obtain

$$E^2(m, n) = \sum_i \sum_j [g^2(i, j) - 2g(i, j)t(i - m, j - n) + t^2(i - m, j - n)],$$

where, as usual we sum over all (i, j) such that the arguments of t remain
within its domain of definition. Now as we move the template around the
picture by varying m and n the summation of the last term is unchanged,
since for any m and n the range of the arguments of t^2 is the domain of
definition of t. The summation of the first term—the *picture energy* in the
window—in general varies with (m, n), since the range of i and j vary with
m and n. Suppose for a moment that this variation in picture energy is small
enough to be ignored. Then $E^2(m, n)$ is small when $\sum_i \sum_j g(i, j)t(i - m, j - n)$
is large. Accordingly, we define $R_{gt}(m, n)$, the *cross-correlation* between the
two functions g and t, by

$$R_{gt}(m, n) = \sum_i \sum_j g(i, j)t(i - m, j - n), \tag{4}$$

where, as always, we sum over all i and j within the domain of the translated
template. We can use this definition as a measure of the similarity between
the template and the region of the picture in the vicinity of (m, n); the template and the picture are declared similar when the cross-correlation is

large. Of course, if we translated the template to a region of the picture that was all white then the cross-correlation would have a high value. This is just another way of saying that our initial supposition (that $\sum_i \sum_j g^2(i, j)$ is independent of (m, n)) is grossly unjustified. One alternative to computing E^2 is to compute the *normalized cross-correlation* $N_{gt}(m, n)$ given by

$$N_{gt}(m, n) = \frac{1}{\left[\sum_i \sum_j g(i, j)^2\right]^{1/2}} R_{gt}(m, n),$$

where we place the usual restriction on the range of i and j. By the Cauchy-Schwarz inequality, we have

$$N_{gt}(m, n) \leq \left[\sum_i \sum_j t(i - m, j - n)^2\right]^{1/2} \tag{5}$$

with equality if and only if the picture function in the region of interest is a multiple of the template function. Hence, the normalized cross-correlation has a maximum value when the match with the picture function is perfect (up to a scale factor). On the other hand, in some circumstances our supposition about $\sum \sum g^2$ is satisfied precisely. For example, suppose we have a binary picture and we let white be 1 but let black be -1 instead of the usual zero. Then the sum of the squares of the picture function values over any domain of fixed size is constant, and the cross-correlation has a maximum exactly when E^2 has a minimum. The use of cross-correlation as a measure of similarity has its roots in certain analogous, but not identical, problems in pattern classification and signal detection. It is still often used, partly because there exist a number of efficient implementations. As we have seen, however, using cross-correlation in template matching involves a tacit assumption that the picture energy in every window is roughly the same.

Let us reconsider our introductory example: the problem of locating a triangle in Figure 7.3. Assuming that we had settled upon one of the distance measures as our measure of similarity, we still must design the template itself. A little reflection will lead us to the conclusion that the problem as stated can only be solved by having a whole family of templates. The wedge, in the absence of any explicit constraints, can appear anywhere in the scene and can be viewed from any angle. Its triangular face, then, can appear in a wide range of sizes and can have a wide range of apparent interior angles. For each such wedge orientation we evidently need a separate template and, since each template must be scanned across the scene, the computational burden is likely to be large. In such situations a common approach is to replace the *global* template by a set of *local* templates. The local templates are designed to match various parts of the object of interest, the rationale being that the individual parts vary in appearance less than the entire object.

In our triangle example, we might first look for three separate lines and then worry about devising a method for recognizing when three lines form a triangle. This approach is reasonable in a large class of problems whose hallmark is wide variability in the appearance of the object of interest. On the other hand, there are some pattern classification problems that can be sufficiently constrained or stylized to insure that each pattern will always appear in isolation and at the same size and orientation. In these simple problems it is sometimes practical to construct a single template matched to the pattern as a whole. In other words, the choice of whether to use local or global templates is primarily dictated by the anticipated variability in the pictures to be processed.

Template matching appears in a variety of superficially different, but essentially equivalent, forms. The choice of forms ultimately becomes one of convenience and efficiency. As a simple example, suppose we wanted to detect the presence of a vertical edge. We could use a "binary" template (like the one in Figure 7.13, but shaped like a single vertical line) and apply it to a gradient picture. Alternatively, we could easily devise a template matched to the shape of a vertical line in the original picture. (Actually, if we operated on the original picture we would probably want to use a pair of templates, one for dark-light transitions and one for light-dark transitions. This symmetry problem is avoided if we use the gradient picture because we usually take the magnitude of the gradient.) Figure 7.14 shows a template that will detect a left to right transition of dark to light along a vertical line if it is used with the similarity definition in (1). The template region labelled "low" would have values near the dark end of the gray scale, and conversely for the region labelled "high." A possible problem with this template is that it is not invariant to the absolute values of the gray scale; adding a constant to the gray scale will change the degree of match. This consideration might lead us

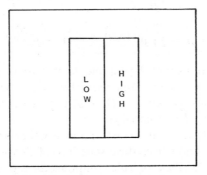

FIGURE 7.14.   A template for vertical edges.

to a procedure in which the template regions labelled "low" and "high" were respectively given values of -1 and $+1$, and we used correlation as our definition of similarity (4). This procedure is equivalent to subtracting adjacent columns and adding up the differences. In other words, the procedure looks for differences in gray scale along a vertical line, and is therefore almost the same thing as using a binary template on a gradient picture.

We should note that an important aspect of template matching, whether performed on the original picture or a processed version of the original picture, is that the operation makes use of only local information. If we are trying to decide, say, whether a vertical line is present in a given region of the picture, the only thing that affects our decision is the set of intensity values in that region. This local aspect is both the reason for the appealing simplicity of template matching and the source of its most stringent limitations.

7.5.2 Template Matching—Statistical Interpretation

Certain forms of template matching can be interpreted within the framework of statistical decision theory developed in Part I. Let us illustrate this interpretation with a simple example.

Suppose we have a binary picture $g(i, j)$ and suppose further that the picture is known to depict one of two possible ideal scenes, say $r(i, j)$ or $s(i, j)$. The actual picture g, however, is only an imperfect representation of an ideal scene. Let us assume that with probability $p > 1/2$ a given picture cell in g has the value specified by the ideal scene that g represents. If these cell probabilities are independent then we can easily write the probabilities of observing a picture g conditioned on either r or s being the ideal scene. Specifically, if we let ω_r and ω_s be respectively the events that $r(i, j)$ and $s(i, j)$ are the ideal scenes, we have

$$P(g \mid \omega_r) = \prod_{i,j} p^{1-|g(i,j)-r(i,j)|}(1-p)^{|g(i,j)-r(i,j)|} \tag{6}$$

and

$$P(g \mid \omega_s) = \prod_{i,j} p^{1-|g(i,j)-s(i,j)|}(1-p)^{|g(i,j)-s(i,j)|}. \tag{7}$$

Notice in these equations that the exponents of p are one if the ideal picture and the actual picture have the same value for a given (i, j), and zero otherwise; conversely, the exponents of $(1 - p)$ are one if the ideal and actual pictures are different for a given (i, j).

Suppose now that we want to determine whether the picture g depicts scene r or scene s. We know from the discussions of Chapter 2 that a minimum probability of error classification rule computes the a posteriori probabilities $P(\omega_r \mid g)$ and $P(\omega_s \mid g)$ and selects either ω_r or ω_s according to which probability is larger. If we assume for simplicity that the a priori probabilities of the two scenes are equal, then we know that this rule is equivalent to a rule that selects the class for which the conditional probability is larger. As in previous chapters, we can simplify things by selecting the class for which the logarithm of the conditional probability is maximized. Thus, from (6) and (7), it suffices to compute

$$\log P(g \mid \omega_r) = \left[\log\left(\frac{1-p}{p}\right) \right] \sum_{i,j} |g(i,j) - r(i,j)| + \sum_{i,j} \log p \qquad (8)$$

and

$$\log P(g \mid \omega_s) = \left[\log\left(\frac{1-p}{p}\right) \right] \sum_{i,j} |g(i,j) - s(i,j)| + \sum_{i,j} \log p. \qquad (9)$$

Now notice that $\log[(1-p)/p]$ is negative, since we have specified $p > 1/2$; furthermore, the last terms of (8) and (9) are the same. Hence, the minimum probability of error rule for classifying picture g selects ω_r if

$$\sum_{i,j} |g(i,j) - r(i,j)| < \sum_{i,j} |g(i,j) - s(i,j)| \qquad (10)$$

and selects ω_s otherwise. Thus, we see that in this example our statistical assumptions lead to a minimum probability of error rule that is a template match using the similarity measure defined by Eq. (1); the ideal pictures r and s, as we would anticipate on intuitive grounds, are the templates.

There are several points about the preceding example worth noting. First, suppose we know that the picture g may in fact show neither r nor s; hence we want to allow the alternative of rejecting g in addition to the alternatives of classifying it as scene r or scene s. This refinement can also be analyzed in statistical terms. As a matter of practice, however, it is more common to set a threshold on the template similarity measure. If the best match achieved fails to satisfy the threshold, then g is rejected; that is, g is declared not to depict any of the ideal scenes.

A different typical situation was discussed earlier. Often the ideal scene of interest is only a subpart of g. In this case, the templates are defined on domains smaller than the domain of g and are scanned across the picture. Each template position provides us with a new classification problem that, in principle at least, can be analyzed along the lines of our illustrative problem.

The application of formal statistical classification methods to problems of detecting objects in pictures has proved to be difficult in practice. One of the chief difficulties has been in establishing useful statistical assumptions. As an example of this difficulty, consider the problem just mentioned of scanning a template across a picture to detect an object. Suppose good template matches occurred at two template locations only a single picture cell apart. Certainly, we would not want to say that two separate objects had been detected; much more probably, the same object in the picture is responsible for both matches. Formally, this would be represented statistically by nonindependent probabilities. In practice, however, it is usually far easier to develop ad hoc procedures for circumventing such difficulties than it is to overcome them by a formal analytical assault. Nevertheless, the statistical viewpoint provides worthwhile guidance, if not universal prescriptions, for the design of template-matching procedures.

7.6   REGION ANALYSIS

7.6.1   Basic Concepts

In a previous section we discussed means for simplifying a picture by enhancing or extracting edges. We now turn our attention to a technique that is in a sense complementary. This technique, called *region analysis*, attempts to simplify a digital picture by partitioning it into a set of disjoint regions. In the simplest case, each region is composed of picture cells having the same gray value and connected to each other. Before proceeding any further, therefore, we must make precise the notion of when two picture cells are connected. In particular, we must define whether a cell is connected to all eight surrounding cells (8-connected), or whether it is connected only to those four cells sharing a common edge (4-connected).

To illustrate the subtleties of this question, consider the simple binary picture in Figure 7.15, where the unmarked cells are background 0's. Suppose we initially define connectedness to be 8-connectedness. Then, since cells sharing only a common vertex are connected, the figure is connected. However, by the same token the background is also connected—the "hole" in the figure is not separated from the "surrounding" background. Hence, we are in the uncomfortable position of having on our hands a connected, shell-like figure with no inside. Suppose, therefore, that we use 4-connectedness as our definition. Then the figure is not connected. Neither, however, is the background. Hence, we are in the equally embarrassing position of having a disconnected figure that has a distinct interior. This state of affairs reflects a

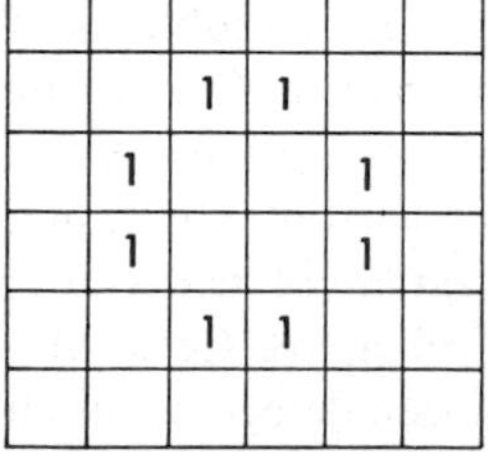

FIGURE 7.15.   Connectivity on a quadruled grid.

basic property of the quadruled grid. We will arbitrarily use 4-connectedness as our definition. In the following, then, when we speak of connected or adjacent cells we specifically mean 4-connected. (We note in passing that a hexagonal grid does not suffer from this malady, since any two hexagonal cells with a common vertex also share a common side.)

With the definition of connectedness settled, let us return to the question of analyzing a picture by partitioning it into regions. We will call a set of picture cells R an *elementary connected region* if:

(1) All the cells in R have the same gray value.
(2) Any two cells in R are connected by a chain of adjacent cells each of which is in R.
(3) Any set of cells that properly contains R fails to satisfy these two conditions.

The second condition can be taken as the definition of a *connected region*. The third condition insures that the elementary regions are as large as possible. Figure 7.16 shows the elementary connected regions of the digital picture Figure 7.2. The algorithm that produced the boundaries between these regions merely placed a line between every pair of adjacent cells having different gray values. (For clarity, we have coarsened the original 120 × 120 quantization to 60 × 60.) Notice that the elementary regions show the slight, typically unwanted, changes of shadows and shading as well as the "significant"

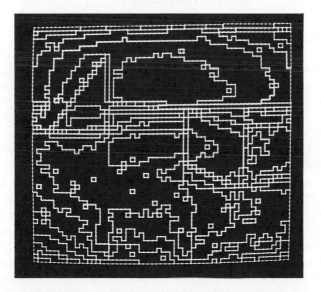

FIGURE 7.16.   The elementary connected regions of
Fig. 7.2. (Reproduced courtesy of Claude Fennema.)

1	1	1	1	1	1	1	1	1	1	1
1	1	1	1	1	1	1	1	1	1	1
1	1	4	4	4	5	6	6	6	1	1
1	1	4	4	4	5	6	6	6	1	1
1	1	4	4	4	5	7	7	7	1	1
1	1	8	8	8	8	7	7	7	1	1
1	1	1	1	1	1	1	1	1	1	1
1	1	1	1	1	1	1	1	1	1	1

FIGURE 7.17.   Example of region definition using a tolerance of one.

1	1	1	1	1	1	1	1	1	1	1
1	1	1	1	1	1	1	1	1	1	1
1	1	4	4	4	5	6	6	6	1	1
1	1	4	4	4	5	6	6	6	1	1
1	1	4	4	4	5	7	7	7	1	1
1	1	8	8	8	8	7	7	7	1	1
1	1	1	1	1	1	1	1	1	1	1
1	1	1	1	1	1	1	1	1	1	1

FIGURE 7.18   Example of elementary connected regions.

regions associated with the faces of the geometrical objects. There are at least two ways of combating this: by relaxing the first condition, or by merging regions. With the first alternative, we permit two adjacent cells to be put into the same elementary region if the difference in gray levels is less than a specified threshold. Figure 7.17 shows a simple example in which we allow a tolerance of 1 gray level. A line is placed between adjacent cells only if the difference in their gray levels is strictly greater than one. This results in a boundary spur within one of the regions. More seriously, we have adjacent 4's and 8's in the same region. In general, this procedure allows the possibility of adjacent cells of arbitrarily different gray values to be put into the same region. Alternatively, we could form the elementary connected regions as originally defined, and use some criterion to decide when to merge two regions sharing a common boundary. As an example of this, suppose we decide to merge two adjacent regions if the average difference in the gray levels of the cells on each side of the common boundary is less than or equal to one. As can be seen from Figure 7.18, this will result in the 4's and 5's being merged, and in the 7's and 8's being merged. The region of 6's will be merged

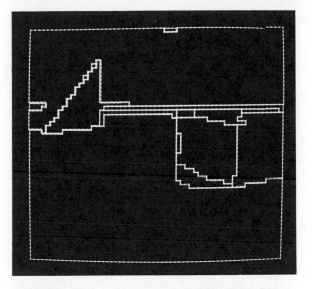

FIGURE 7.19.   A merged version of Fig. 7.16. (Reproduced courtesy of Claude Fennema.)

with either the 5's or the 7's, depending upon the order in which the region boundaries are considered. Additionally, either the 4's or the 8's (depending on the order in which regions are considered) will not be merged with anything. Hence the outcome is dependent upon the particular implementation of the algorithm, but in any event the 8's will not be merged with the 4's and 5's.

It is not difficult to construct other criteria for both defining and merging regions. As an example, consider the following merging algorithm. Let R_1 and R_2 be two regions with a common boundary, and let the length of the perimeters of the regions be P_1 and P_2. Let L be the length of that portion of the common boundary separating cells whose gray levels differ by less than d. We merge the two regions if, for a given threshold t,

$$\max\left\{\frac{L}{P_1}, \frac{L}{P_2}\right\} \geq t.$$

One interpretation of this algorithm is the following: we might think of L as the dubious portion of the common boundary. If one of the regions, say R_2, is more or less surrounded by R_1, then the common boundary will be a large fraction of P_2. Furthermore, if this common boundary is dubious, then L will be a large fraction of P_2 and the regions will be merged. Hence, the algorithm will tend to make R_1 more regular if this can be done without ignoring well-defined boundaries. Figure 7.19 shows the result of processing Figure 7.16 using this algorithm with $d = 2$ and $t = 0.45$.

7.6.2 Extensions

The basic ideas of region analysis can be extended to incorporate other properties of pictures in addition to intensity. One of the most interesting possibilities is to partition the picture into regions according to color. Before we can consider this possibility we must extend our definition of a picture function to include color information. We do this by taking advantage of the fact that the space of all possible colors can be spanned by a three-dimensional vector space. This fact, which rests on physiological rather than physical evidence, motivates us to define a picture function as a vector-valued function $\mathbf{g}(x, y) = [g_1(x, y), g_2(x, y), g_3(x, y)]$ where g_1, g_2, and g_3 give the coordinates of the color of the picture at the point (x, y).* The parametrization of the color space is not unique, so to define the picture function completely we must specify the basis vectors. One basis is the set of the three "primary" colors, red, green, and blue. Physically, using this basis corresponds to taking three (scalar) pictures of a single scene using, successively, red, green, and blue filters. The three component picture functions in this basis are called the red, green, and blue *color separations*, and will be denoted by $g_R(x, y)$, $g_G(x, y)$, and $g_B(x, y)$.

A region analysis might begin by forming elementary connected regions composed of picture cells having identical red, green, and blue coordinates. Regions could then be merged according to some criterion analogous to those described for black and white pictures. For example, we might merge two regions whose g_R, g_G, and g_B values were close. A particularly interesting criterion would allow merges between adjacent regions that had different intensities but the same hue. This criterion would be appropriate if we wanted the analysis to be unaffected by changes of illumination or the presence of shadows. Accordingly, we define the *normalized color coordinates* at a picture point by (suppressing the dependence on x and y)

$$g_r = \frac{g_R}{g_R + g_G + g_B},$$

$$g_g = \frac{g_G}{g_R + g_G + g_B},$$

$$g_b = \frac{g_B}{g_R + g_G + g_B}.$$

Since these three numbers (also called the chromaticity coordinates or trichromatic coefficients) sum to unity, we can take any two of them, say g_r

---

* This idea can be extended to a general vector-valued picture function that includes range, texture, and so on.

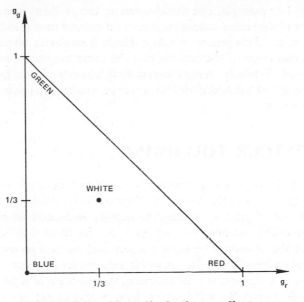

FIGURE 7.20.   Normalized color coordinates.

and g_g, to define the normalized color coordinates at a point in the picture. Figure 7.20 shows a representation of the 2-dimensional normalized color space. Any normalized color we measure will fall within the triangle; "pure" red, green, and blue will fall near the vertices. Notice that normalizing colors amounts to changing the basis of the 3 dimensional color space from the original red, green, and blue coordinates to normalized red, normalized green, and total intensity.

A region analysis based on the normalized colors will (ideally) be insensitive to changes of intensity, but will be sensitive to changes in what we loosely speak of as "color." For example, suppose we have a picture containing among other things a yellow surface, but suppose the surface is partially in shadow. Ideally,* a region analysis using as data the 2-dimensional normalized color picture function $[g_r(x, y), g_g(x, y)]$ would be able to isolate the entire yellow surface as a single region, whereas an analysis based only on a black and white scalar picture function would presumably separate the surface at the shadow line into two regions.

We should point out here that although we have introduced color as a tool in region analysis it is clearly relevant to other techniques that we have been

* The study of color is a subtle one, because color is ultimately a physiological or perceptual phenomenon rather than a purely physical one involving only the energy and frequency of electromagnetic waves. In addition, there are technical problems involved in computations based on small differences of measured values.

discussing. For example, one could estimate the gradient separately in each component of the vector-valued picture function and then sum the magnitude of the estimates. This process would enhance boundaries between regions of different colors even if the regions had the same brightness in a black and white picture. Similarly, template-matching algorithms can be extended to take advantage of the additional information available from a vector-valued picture function.

7.7   CONTOUR FOLLOWING

A recurring theme in scene analysis is that a picture may be simplified by representing objects in the picture by their outlines. We have previously discussed the use of gradient operators; another technique developed for the purpose is called *contour following* and, as the name implies, it involves tracing out the boundary between a figure and its background. Let us first assume that we have analog pictures with only two levels of gray. This assumption allows us to ignore, for the moment, the problem of separating a figure from its background. We will describe, by way of example, one of the simplest contour following algorithms. Imagine a contour following bug that scans across a picture until it enters a dark region (that is, the figure). It then curves to the left until it leaves the figure, at which point it immediately begins to curve to the right. Repeating this process, the bug will follow the figure boundary in a clockwise direction until it returns to the neighborhood of the starting point. The set of transition points between figure and background can be taken to represent the contour. This process is illustrated in Figure 7.21. We can make several observations about this algorithm immediately.

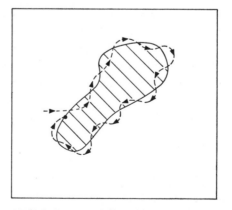

FIGURE 7.21.   Example of contour following on an analog figure.

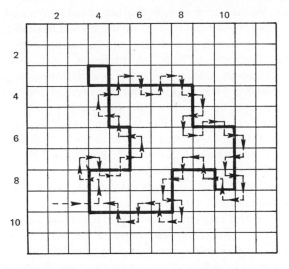

FIGURE 7.22.   Example of contour following on a digital figure.

First, the radius of curvature employed by the bug determines the "resolution" of the contour follower. The bug will obviously not detect curves that are sharp compared to this radius of curvature. Similarly, if there are holes in the figure just inside the boundary the bug can wander into a hole and produce erroneous transition points. Finally, the algorithm as stated is not well-defined, since the centers of each curved section of the trace have not been specified.

One of the objections noted above disappears when we are dealing with binary digital pictures. In particular, a digitized version of the algorithm can be simply and precisely defined as follows:

Scan the picture until a figure cell is encountered.

Then:

   If you are in a figure cell turn left and take a step.

   If you are in a ground cell turn right and take a step.

Terminate when you are within one cell of the starting point.

Figure 7.22 illustrates the operation of this algorithm on a simple binary picture. Notice that the bug never enters the top figure cell, which is 8-connected to the rest of the figure. It would be pleasant if we could state that the algorithm "knows" about 4- and 8-connectedness, and employs 4-connectedness in defining the set of figure cells connected to the cell it initially enters.

Unfortunately, this is not the case. The bug would have entered the 8 connected cell if it had entered cell (4, 5) from the bottom instead of from the side. Thus the set of transition points determined by the algorithm depends upon the initial scan. Similarly, a "hole" in the figure that is 8-connected to the background creates an ambiguity in the set of transition points that the algorithm determines. This shortcoming is the result of the extreme simplicity of the algorithm. Specifically, only three bits are being used at each point to decide which way to turn: two bits tell from which direction the cell was entered and the third bit indicates whether the cell is figure or background. Other contour following algorithms can be constructed that avoid problems in asymmetry and ambiguity inherent in the one described. These more elaborate algorithms examine the cells surrounding the current location of the bug and thus require more computation time.

There are two major conditions that must be fulfilled if a contour following algorithm is to be successfully employed. First, since a picture function generally has many gray levels, there must be some way of defining the figure whose contour is to be followed. In simple cases the figure can be extracted from the background by the simple expedient of thresholding the picture. We merely declare that everything in the picture darker (or lighter) than a fixed value is figure. This reduces the picture to the binary case described above. When this cannot be done, it is sometimes possible to follow a contour based on a sufficiently large change in gray value, locally, between the figure and the background. Some algorithms accomplish this by combining a gradient operator with a contour follower. The gradient operator finds the local direction of the contour (assuming a point on the contour has been found to begin with) by finding the direction of the most prominent edge near a contour point. A small step taken in this direction is assumed to result in a new point near the figure boundary. The gradient operator is called to find a prominent edge near this point, and the process is repeated.

The second major prerequisite for successful contour following is that the figure have no spurious gaps in it. Even in the simple case of binary digital pictures a contour follower may accidently get "inside" a figure. This presents a serious problem when contour following techniques are used in the recognition of hand-printed alphanumeric characters. If, for example, the loop of a "6" is not completely closed, the contour follower produces an output markedly different from the desired one. These difficulties can sometimes be overcome by first smoothing the picture in order to fill small gaps.

We should observe that contour following is intrinsically a serial operation. An error made at any step in the process makes it more likely that succeeding steps will also be in error. This is to be contrasted with operations, like template matching, that can be performed in parallel. In the latter case, the failure to find a match in one part of the picture doesn't directly affect the outcome in another part. For this reason, the applicability of contour following seems restricted to pictures with low noise levels.

7.8 BIBLIOGRAPHICAL AND HISTORICAL REMARKS

There are very few general references on the subject of automatic scene analysis. The only text specifically on the subject is the scholarly work of Rosenfeld (1969). Some useful volumes of collected papers have been assembled by Fischer, et al. (1962), Tippett, et al. (1965), Uhr (1966), Kanal (1968), Cheng, et al. (1968), Kolers and Eden (1968), Grasselli (1969), Watanabe (1969), and Lipkin and Rosenfeld (1970). Another useful collection of papers is the *IEEE Transactions on Computers* "Special Issue on Feature Extraction and Selection in Pattern Recognition."*

We shall emphasize neither the problem of enhancing images for subsequent interpretation by humans, nor the problem of encoding images for efficient transmission and storage. A survey of these areas has been written by Huang, et al. (1971), and contains an extensive bibliography.

Most of the ideas discussed in this chapter were introduced in the early days of scene analysis, when "scene analysis" consisted almost exclusively of optical character recognition. In the following paragraphs we cite some representative sources of these ideas, with the understanding that the references have been selected on the basis of clarity and variety and not on the basis of priority.

The problem of representing pictures in a digital computer has two parts: both an amplitude and a spatial quantization scheme must be chosen. The problem of amplitude quantization has generally been resolved by appealing to physiological precedents. Gregory (1966) contains a very readable popularized account of these matters; a more comprehensive reference source is provided by Graham et al. (1965). The text by Cornsweet (1970) gives a broad introduction to human visual perception. The problem of spatial quantization has been resolved, almost universely, by digitizing the picture onto a quad-ruled grid. Cheng and Ledley (1968) and Simon and Guiho (1971) discuss this process analytically by treating it as a problem in approximation theory. (A different analytic approach, the Fourier transform, will be discussed in the next chapter.) The topological advantages of a hexagonal grid over a square grid have been observed by a number of workers, but few have actually used one. Golay (1969) has proposed an organization for a parallel computer capable of performing interesting operations on pictures quantized

---

* *IEEE Trans. Comp.*, Vol. 20, No. 9 (September 1971).

onto a hexagonal array. Ingram and Preston (1970) subsequently used his methods for processing pictures of blood cells.

The complementary operations of spatial differentiation and spatial smoothing appeared in the character recognition literature at least as early as the paper by Dinneen (1955). Doyle (1960) introduced logical averaging in the same context. Gradient operators have been used as a preliminary step in the processing of pictures of three dimensional scenes by Roberts (1965) and Forsen (1968). Kanal and Randall (1964) used an approximation to the Laplacian of the picture function to enhance transitions in gray level. Yarbus (1967) has provided interesting psychophysical evidence of the importance of edges by tracking eye movements as a human examines a picture.

Template matching appears, in one form or another, in a great many papers concerned with the analysis of visual scenes. Highleyman (1961) used global templates to recognize handprinted alphanumeric characters. Munson (1968) used local templates for the same purpose. Kanal and Randall (1964) used templates to detect the presence of features of objects in aerial photographs. Roberts (1965) used local templates to detect the presence of short segments of straight lines. Griffith (1971) used a probabilistic model as a basis for the design of a line detector. Rosenfeld and Thurston (1971) used a family of templates to detect texture edges. Barnea and Silverman (1972) discuss a family of efficient template-matching algorithms. Finally, the classic work of Hubel and Wiesel, summarized by Hubel (1963), showed that the cat evidently does the equivalent of local template matching to detect the presence of straight line segments.

Scene decomposition by region analysis seems to be a more recent suggestion than the other techniques discussed in this chapter. Guzmán (1968) analyzed ideal line drawings by grouping together regions belonging to the same three-dimensional object. Brice and Fennema (1970) developed techniques to extract meaningful regions directly from a digital picture, and Section 7.5 is based largely on their work. Haralick and Kelly (1969) used clustering techniques to decompose a picture into regions. We can mention here that textural properties of pictures have also been suggested as a means for defining regions. Gibson (1950) has explored the textural cues that humans use, particularly in judging depth. Brodatz (1966) assembled an interesting photographic album of textures to challenge those who would design algorithms for texture recognition.

Contour following has been applied to both analog and digital pictures, primarily because it is easily implemented with the aid of a flying-spot scanner. Greanias et al. (1963) used a flying-spot scanner to extract contour information directly from hand-printed numbers. Mason and Clemens (1968) used a slight variation of the contour follower described earlier on digitized machine printing. Rosenfeld (1970) discussed a more sophisticated contour follower and proved that it works correctly by first proving some theorems about connectivity in digital pictures. Ledley (1964) used contour following in his analysis of digitized pictures of chromosomes. An ingenious combination of contour following and smoothing was developed by Zahn (1969), while Pingle (1969) developed an operator combining contour following with edge detection. Kelly (1971) reported a novel "planning contour follower" that first obtains a rough approximation to the contour from a reduced-resolution version of the picture.

REFERENCES

1. Barnea, D. I. and H. F. Silverman, "A Class of Algorithms for Fast Digital Image Registration," *IEEE Trans. Comp.*, **C-21**, 179–186 (February 1972).

2. Brice, C. R. and C. L. Fennema, "Scene Analysis Using Regions," *Artificial Intelligence*, **1**, 205–226 (Fall 1970).

3. Brodatz, P., *Textures* (Dover Publications, New York, 1966).

4. Cheng, G. C., R. S. Ledley, D. K. Pollock, and A. Rosenfeld, eds., *Pictorial Pattern Recognition* (Proc. Symp. Automatic Photointerpretation) (Thompson, Washington, D.C., 1968).

5. Cheng, G. C. and R. S. Ledley, "A Theory of Picture Digitization and Applications," in *Pictorial Pattern Recognition*, pp. 329–352, G. C. Chang et al., eds. (Thompson, Washington, D.C., 1968).

6. Cornsweet, T. N., *Visual Perception* (Academic Press, New York, 1970).

7. Dinneen, G. P., "Programming Pattern Recognition," *Proc. WJCC*, 94–100 (March 1955).

8. Doyle, W., "Recognition of Sloppy, Hand-Printed Characters," *Proc. WJCC*, 133–142 (May 1960).

9. Fischer, Jr., G. L., D. K. Pollock, B. Radack, and M. E. Stevens, eds., *Optical Character Recognition* (Spartan, Washington, D.C., 1962).

10. Forsen, G. E., "Processing Visual Data with an Automaton Eye," in *Pictorial Pattern Recognition*, pp. 471–502, G. C. Cheng et al., eds. (Thompson, Washington, D.C., 1968).

11. Gibson, J. J., *The Perception of the Visual World* (Houghton Mifflin, Boston, Mass., 1950).

12. Golay, M. J. E., "Hexagonal Parallel Pattern Transformations," *IEEE Trans. Elec. Comp.*, **C-18**, 733–740 (August 1969).

13. Graham, C. H., et al., eds., *Vision and Visual Perception* (John Wiley, New York, 1965).

14. Grasselli, A., ed., *Automatic Interpretation and Classification of Images* (Academic Press, New York, 1969).

15. Greanias, E. C., P. F. Meagher, R. J. Norman, and P. Essinger, "The

Recognition of Handwritten Numerals by Contour Analysis," *IBM Journal*, **7**, 14–21 (January 1963).

16. Gregory, R. L., *Eye and Brain* (World University Library, McGraw-Hill, New York, 1966).

17. Griffith, A. K., "Mathematical Models for Automatic Line Detection," *Proc. Second Int. Joint Conf. on Art. Int.*, 17–26 (London 1971).

18. Guzmán, A., "Decomposition of a Visual Scene into Three-Dimensional Bodies," *Proc. FJCC*, **33**, 291–304 (1968).

19. Haralick, R. M. and G. L. Kelly, "Pattern Recognition with Measurement Space and Spatial Clustering for Multiple Images," *Proc. IEEE*, **57**, 654–665 (April 1969).

20. Highleyman, W. H., "An Analog Method for Character Recognition," *IRE Trans. Elec. Comp.*, **EC-10**, 502–512 (September 1961).

21. Huang, T. S., W. F. Schreiber, and O. J. Tretiak, "Image Processing," *Proc. IEEE*, **59**, 1586–1609 (November 1971).

22. Hubel, D. H., "The Visual Cortex of the Brain," *Scientific American*, **209**, 54–62 (November 1963).

23. Ingram, M. and K. Preston, "Automatic Analysis of Blood Cells," *Scientific American*, **223**, 72–83 (November 1970).

24. Kanal, L. N., ed., *Pattern Recognition* (Thompson Book Company, Washington, D.C., 1968).

25. Kanal, L. N. and Randall, N. C., "Recognition System Design by Statistical Analysis," *Proc. ACM National Conference* (1964).

26. Kelly, M. D., "Edge Detection in Pictures by Computer Using Planning," in *Machine Intelligence 6*, pp. 397–409, B. Meltzer and D. Michie, eds. (American Elsevier Publishing Co., New York, 1971).

27. Kolers, P. A. and M. Eden, eds., *Recognizing Patterns* (MIT Press, Cambridge, Mass., 1968).

28. Ledley, R. S., "High-Speed Automatic Analysis of Biomedical Pictures," *Science*, **146**, 216–223 (October 9, 1964).

29. Lipkin, B. S. and A. Rosenfeld, eds., *Picture Processing and Psychopictorics* (Academic Press, New York, 1970).

30. Mason, S. J. and J. K. Clemens, "Character Recognition in an Experimental Reading Machine for the Blind," in *Recognizing Patterns*, pp. 156–167, P. A. Kolers and M. Eden, eds. (MIT Press, Cambridge, Mass., 1968).

31. Munson, J. H., "Experiments in the Recognition of Hand-Printed Text: Part I—Character Recognition," *Proc. FJCC*, 1125–1138 (December 1968).

32. Pingle, K. K., "Visual Perception by a Computer," in *Automatic Interpretation and Classification of Images*, pp. 277–284, A. Grasselli, ed. (Academic Press, New York, 1969).

33. Roberts, L. G., "Machine Perception of Three-Dimensional Solids," in *Optical and Electro-Optical Information Processing*, pp. 159–197, J. T. Tippett, et al., eds. (MIT Press, Cambridge, Mass., 1965).

34. Rosenfeld, A., *Picture Processing by Computer* (Academic Press, New York, 1969).

35. Rosenfeld, A., "Connectivity in Digital Pictures," *J. ACM*, **17**, 146–160 (January 1970).

36. Rosenfeld, A. and M. Thurston, "Edge and Curve Detection for Visual Scene Analysis," *IEEE Trans. Comp.*, **C-20**, 562–569 (May 1971).

37. Simon, J. C. and G. Guiho, "Picture Representation and Transformations by Computer," *Pattern Recognition*, **3**, 169–178 (July 1971).

38. Tippett, J. T., D. A. Berkowitz, L. C. Clapp, C. J. Koester, and A. Vanderburgh, eds., *Optical and Electro-Optical Information Processing* (MIT Press, Cambridge, Mass., 1965).

39. Uhr, L., ed., *Pattern Recognition* (John Wiley, New York, 1966).

40. Watanabe, S., ed., *Methodologies of Pattern Recognition* (Academic Press, New York, 1969).

41. Yarbus, A. L., *Eye Movements and Vision*, Translation Editor: Lorrin A. Riggs (Russian) (Plenum Press, New York, 1967).

42. Zahn, C. T., "A Formal Description for Two-Dimensional Patterns," *Proc. Int. Joint Conf. on Art. Int.*, pp. 621–628, D. E. Walker and L. M. Norton, eds. (May 1969).

PROBLEMS

1. In an earth-resources study an airplane takes a picture with a camera aimed at an arbitrary but known angle to the (assumed planar) ground. Devise a scheme (but don't necessarily work out algebraic details) for spatially quantizing the picture plane so that each picture cell corresponds to an equal amount of land area.

2. The *Laplacian* of a function is the sum of its second (unmixed) partial derivatives. Define an algorithm that computes an approximation to the Laplacian of a digital picture function and use some examples to examine qualitatively its behavior.

3. Construct a smoothing operator that fills gaps in lines of figure cells if the gaps are no longer than a single cell.

4. Design a family of local templates that might be used for classifying neatly hand-printed block letters.

5. Define an operator capable of detecting textures composed of more-or-less parallel straight lines, such as might be found in pictures of corduroy. Define another operator for detecting the texture of herring-bone tweed.

6. Specify a criterion for merging two regions that favors the creation or maintenance of regions with straight line boundaries.

7. Specify a contour-following algorithm for finding the contour of an 8-connected digitized figure.

Chapter 8

THE SPATIAL
FREQUENCY DOMAIN

8.1   INTRODUCTION

Our purpose in this chapter is to introduce the two-dimensional Fourier transform and to discuss some of its applications to scene analysis. Our interest in transforms stems from two sources: it provides both a natural setting in which to investigate certain theoretical aspects of picture processing, and a convenient means for implementing such operations as smoothing, sharpening, and template matching.

Before proceeding with the details we have two side remarks for the reader. First, we assume that the reader has at least a little familiarity with the one-dimensional Fourier transform widely used in communication theory. Second, we hasten to assure the digitally inclined onlooker that, although our discussion will be entirely in terms of analog picture functions, there are extremely efficient digital methods for computing the Fourier transform of a digital picture. For that matter, there are both good analog and good digital techniques for transforming pictures. The twin developments of Fourier optics for analog pictures and the so-called fast Fourier transform for digital pictures have doubled the incentive to look closely at the utility of transform techniques in scene analysis.

We begin our discussion with some fundamental definitions. Given an analog picture function $g(x, y)$, which we assume to be defined over the infinite plane, we define its *Fourier transform* $G(f_x, f_y)$ by

$$G(f_x, f_y) = \mathscr{F}\{g(x, y)\}$$

$$= \iint\limits_{-\infty}^{\infty} g(x, y) \exp[-2\pi i(f_x x + f_y y)] \, dx \, dy. \tag{1}$$

Similarly, given a function $G(f_x, f_y)$, we define its *inverse Fourier transform* $g(x, y)$ by

$$g(x, y) = \mathscr{F}^{-1}\{G(f_x, f_y)\}$$

$$= \int\!\!\!\int_{-\infty}^{\infty} G(f_x, f_y) \exp[2\pi i(f_x x + f_y y)]\, df_x\, df_y. \qquad (2)$$

Brushing aside for the moment any mathematical questions about the existence of the defining integrals, our intuitive view of the definitions will be the following. We will view (2) as being an expansion of the picture function $g(x, y)$ in terms of a "generalized sum" of complex exponentials. For each pair of values of the *spatial frequencies* f_x and f_y we have one exponential in the generalized sum, this exponential being multiplied by the weighting coefficient $G(f_x, f_y)$. How are these weighting coefficients obtained? By a fundamental result of Fourier analysis called the inversion theorem, the weighting coefficients are given by the definition (1). Hence, the Fourier transform of $g(x, y)$ can be looked upon as being merely the weighting coefficients of the expansion of g in a (generalized) sum of exponentials.

Let us return briefly to the question of the existence of the Fourier transform pair (1) and (2). The answer to this question is not as elegant as one might hope, but the following set of sufficient conditions is commonly quoted:

1. g must be absolutely integrable over the entire picture plane.
2. g must have only a finite number of discontinuities and a finite number of maxima and minima in any finite rectangle.
3. g must have no infinite discontinuities.

While the question of the existence of a Fourier transform is interesting mathematically it will not concern us further here, because practical difficulties are rarely if ever caused by problems involving the existence of the defining integrals.

We would like to consider in a little more detail the intuitive consequences of the definition of the Fourier transform pair. In particular, we will develop the interpretation that high spatial frequencies correspond to the presence of sharp changes in the intensity of the picture. Now the transform of a picture function defines the weighting coefficients of its expansion in a sum of complex exponentials; hence, to understand the transform we need a feeling for what the exponential

$$\exp[2\pi i(f_x x + f_y y)]$$

looks like pictorially for a given value of f_x and f_y. Unfortunately, this function is a complex-valued function of the two variables x and y, and drawing it is difficult. An idea of what it looks like can be obtained by noting

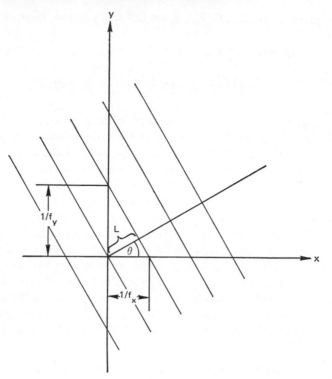

FIGURE 8.1. A zero phase locus (From *Introduction to Fourier Optics* by Joseph Goodman. Copyright 1968 by McGraw-Hill, Inc. Used with permission of McGraw-Hill Book Company.)

the locus of points in the X–Y plane for which the function is real and positive. This so-called zero phase locus is found by setting the exponent equal to $2\pi in$ for all integers n. Thus,

$$2\pi i(f_x x + f_y y) = 2\pi in,$$

or

$$y = -\frac{f_x}{f_y}\,x + \frac{n}{f_y}\,.$$

Hence, as shown in Figure 8.1,* the locus of zero phase is a series of parallel straight lines. The slope of each line is $-(f_x/f_y)$, and the normal to all of them is a line oriented at an angle $\theta = \tan^{-1}(f_y/f_x)$. The distance L between

* From Goodman (1968).

the lines is called the *spatial period* and is easily found to be

$$L = \frac{1}{\sqrt{f_x^2 + f_y^2}}.$$

Hence, the higher the spatial frequencies are, the closer together are the lines of zero phase. There are thus two geometrical aspects associated with a given point (f_x, f_y) in the spatial frequency plane: an orientation θ and a spacing L.

We would like now to consider the intuitive implications of the Fourier transform of a picture having a large magnitude at some particular spatial frequency. Suppose, therefore, that we have a picture $g(x, y)$ whose transform $G(f_x, f_y)$ has a large magnitude at, say, (u, v). Since $G(u, v)$ has a large magnitude, the term $G(u, v) \exp[2\pi i(ux + vy)]$ will be an important contribution to the generalized sum of exponentials of Eq. (2). Now it is quite easy to show that a consequence of $g(x, y)$ being real-valued is that $G(f_x, f_y) = G^*(-f_x, -f_y)$, where the asterisk signifies complex conjugate. Recalling that complex conjugates have the same magnitude, we see that $G(-u, -v)$ must have the same magnitude as $G(u, v)$; hence, the term

$$G(-u, -v) \exp[2\pi i(-ux, -vy)]$$

will also be an important contribution to the sum of exponentials of Eq. (2). Suppose now that $G(f_x, f_y)$ has a small magnitude except at (u, v) and $(-u, -v)$. Then the picture will look very much like

$$G(u, v) \exp[2\pi i(ux + vy)] + G(-u, -v) \exp[2\pi i(-ux - vy)],$$

since this term dominates the sum of exponentials of Eq. (2). It is easy to show that this term is purely real; if it is plotted, it looks like a sinusoidally undulating surface whose crests are a set of parallel lines like those shown in Figure 8.1. Hence, each symmetric pair (u, v) and $(-u, -v)$ of spatial frequencies contributes to the generalized sum (2) one picture consisting of parallel stripes of sinusoidally varying intensity. The greater the magnitude of the transform is at (u, v), the more important is this contribution.

By way of example, suppose we have a picture function $g(x, y)$ consisting of vertically oriented dark and light stripes. If the intensity transitions between dark and light stripes are all sinusoidal, then the Fourier transform $G(f_x, f_y)$ is nonzero at only two points in the spatial frequency plane, both of which lie on the f_x axis. If the transitions between stripes are abrupt, then the Fourier transform will be nonzero at more than just two points; however, the transform will remain zero off the f_x axis, since the stripes are vertical in the picture. By analogy with the one-dimensional Fourier transform, the more abrupt the transitions are, the greater will be the magnitude of $G(f_x, 0)$ for large values of f_x.

In general, edges in a picture introduce spatial frequencies along a line in the complex frequency plane orthogonal to the edge. The sharper the edge is, the further out from the origin we must go along this line before the weighting coefficients become negligible. Our intuitive view then, is that high spatial frequencies correspond to sharp edges, low spatial frequencies correspond to the absence of edges (and therefore regions of approximately uniform gray level), and the orientation of a spatial frequency corresponds to the orientation of an edge in the picture.

8.2   THE SAMPLING THEOREM

In the previous chapter we left unanswered the question of how finely a picture must be quantized in order to preserve all its information. We now present the primary theoretical result bearing on the question, the celebrated Shannon sampling theorem.

The basic idea behind the sampling theorem rests on the correspondence between abrupt changes in the intensity of a picture and high spatial frequencies in its transform. If a picture's transform contained no high frequencies then the picture itself could not contain abrupt gray level transitions, so we might suspect that such a picture need not be quantized very finely. Accordingly, we call a picture function $g(x, y)$ *bandlimited* if its Fourier transform $G(f_x, f_y)$ is zero whenever either $|f_x|$ or $|f_y|$ is greater than some number W. The Shannon sampling theorem states that a bandlimited function can be reconstructed *exactly* from picture samples taken a nonzero distance apart, and specifies how the reconstruction is done.

The mathematical details of the sampling theorem are a little clearer if we restrict our attention to the one-dimensional case. In the case of one-dimensional picture functions* the Fourier transform pair (1) and (2) simplify to

$$G(f_x) = \mathcal{F}\{g(x)\}$$

$$= \int_{-\infty}^{\infty} g(x) \exp[-2\pi i f_x x] \, dx \tag{3}$$

and

$$g(x) = \mathcal{F}^{-1}\{G(f_x)\}$$

$$= \int_{-\infty}^{\infty} G(f_x) \exp[2\pi i f_x x] \, df_x. \tag{4}$$

---

* As before, we can think of a one-dimensional picture function as being the value of a two-dimensional picture function along a cut in the picture plane.

A one-dimensional picture function $g(x)$ is bandlimited if its Fourier transform $G(f_x)$ is zero whenever $|f_x|$ is greater than some number W called the *bandwidth*.

We need one further preliminary definition in order to simplify the statement of the sampling theorem. Since the theorem will involve functions of the form $\sin(\pi u)/\pi u$ we define a new function called the *sinc* by

$$\operatorname{sinc} u = \frac{\sin(\pi u)}{\pi u}.$$

Figure 8.2 illustrates this definition.

Let us suppose, then, that we have a (one-dimensional) picture function g whose Fourier transform G is bandlimited to bandwidth W. We expand $G(f_x)$ in the region $-W < f_x < W$ by a Fourier series

$$G(f_x) = \sum_{m=-\infty}^{\infty} c_m \exp\left[-2\pi i f_x\left(\frac{m}{2W}\right)\right], \tag{5}$$

where the coefficients c_m of the expansion are given by

$$c_m = \frac{1}{2W}\int_{-W}^{W} G(f_x)\exp\left[2\pi i f_x\left(\frac{m}{2W}\right)\right] df_x. \tag{6}$$

Now G is identically zero outside its bandwidth, so in the inverse transform (4) we can replace the infinite limits with $\pm W$. Hence, the integral in (6) is precisely the inverse transform $g(x)$ evaluated at the point $x = m/2W$. Therefore (6) becomes

$$c_m = \frac{1}{2W}\, g\left(\frac{m}{2W}\right). \tag{7}$$

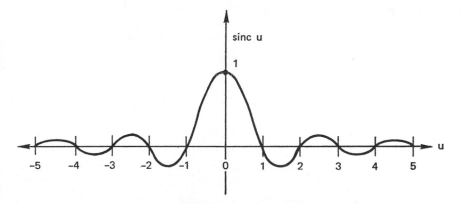

FIGURE 8.2.   The sinc function.

Substituting (7) into (5) we obtain

$$G(f_x) = \frac{1}{2W} \sum_{m=-\infty}^{\infty} g\left(\frac{m}{2W}\right) \exp\left[-2\pi i f_x\left(\frac{m}{2W}\right)\right] \qquad -W < f_x < W, \quad (8)$$

$$G(f_x) = 0 \qquad\qquad\qquad\qquad\qquad\qquad\qquad\qquad \text{otherwise.}$$

From (8) we can already see that the picture function g is completely determined by samples taken finitely far apart, since its transform depends only on values of g taken at intervals of $\frac{1}{2}W$. Finally, the sampling theorem is obtained by taking the inverse transform of (8). This is not difficult since it only involves integrating the exponential between the limits $\pm W$, but we shall omit the details and present the result,

$$g(x) = \sum_{m=-\infty}^{\infty} g\left(\frac{m}{2W}\right) \text{sinc}\left[2W\left(x - \frac{m}{2W}\right)\right]. \qquad (9)$$

The result in (9) is one statement of the Shannon sampling theorem. In words, it prescribes reproducing g by centering a sinc function every $\frac{1}{2}W$ units along the X axis, scaling each sinc by multiplying it by the value of g at its center point, and adding up all the scaled sincs. The greater the bandwidth W is, the smaller the sampling interval $\frac{1}{2}W$ must be. This, it should be obvious, is merely another way of saying that a larger bandwidth means that the picture function can wiggle faster, so it must be sampled more finely in order to capture all the wiggles. A further theoretical result that bears out this interpretation is known as Bernstein's inequality. This inequality, which we present without proof, can be stated as follows. Suppose the picture function, in addition to being bandlimited, has a maximum magnitude of M. Then its derivative has a maximum magnitude of $2\pi WM$. Formally, if g is bandlimited to W and $|g(x)| < M$ for all x, then $|g'(x)| \leq 2\pi WM$. Since any physically possible picture will have some maximum intensity, Bernstein's inequality states that the maximum rate of change of the picture function is proportional to its bandwidth.

The situation for two-dimensional picture functions is analogous mathematically and intuitively to the one-dimensional case just discussed. A two-dimensional picture function can be completely defined by samples of it taken on a quadruled grid with spacing $\frac{1}{2}W$. A minor complication is introduced by the fact that a picture function can have different bandwidths in the f_x and f_y directions—we can have $G(f_x, f_y) = 0$ whenever either $|f_x| > W_x$ or $|f_y| > W_y$. If this happens we can sample on a rectangular grid rather than on a square one, with spacing $1/2W_x$ and $1/2W_y$ in the X and Y direction respectively. With this slight generalization the two-dimensional analog of

(9) becomes

$$g(x, y) = \sum_{m=-\infty}^{\infty} \sum_{n=-\infty}^{\infty} g\left(\frac{m}{2W_x}, \frac{n}{2W_y}\right)$$

$$\times \operatorname{sinc}\left[2W_x\left(x - \frac{m}{2W_x}\right)\right] \operatorname{sinc}\left[2W_y\left(x - \frac{n}{2W_y}\right)\right], \quad (10)$$

which is again a sum of (products of) sincs, with each sinc scaled by the appropriate sample value of the original picture function.

To summarize, we have been interested in the sampling theorem from two complementary points of view. From a practical standpoint, it prescribes how finely a picture function must be quantized in order to retain all the original information. From an intuitive point of view, it provides additional insight into the meaning of high spatial frequencies.

8.3 TEMPLATE MATCHING AND THE CONVOLUTION THEOREM

In the previous chapter we pointed out that template matching, in any of a variety of forms, is a fundamental operation in analyzing pictures. We would now like to develop the close connection between one form of template matching and Fourier transforms. For our present purpose, we will define template matching to be cross-correlation. This definition, which was presented in digital form in (7.5), has the following analog form: Given an analog picture function $g(x, y)$ and an analog template $t(x, y)$, the cross-correlation $R_{gt}(x, y)$ between them is defined by*

$$R_{gt}(x, y) = \iint_{-\infty}^{\infty} g(\alpha, \beta)t(\alpha - x, \beta - y) \, d\alpha \, d\beta. \quad (11)$$

For no immediately obvious reason, we now define the *convolution* of two picture functions g and t, denoted $g * t$, by

$$g * t(x, y) = \iint_{-\infty}^{\infty} g(\alpha, \beta)t(x - \alpha, y - \beta) \, d\alpha \, d\beta. \quad (12)$$

Note the interpretation of the commutative convolution operation: for fixed (x, y) the function t is translated to (x, y) and flipped about the translated

---

* In (7.5) the limits of summation were such that the arguments of t were in the domain of the translated template. For the present purpose, it is more convenient to use infinite limits and consider the template function to be zero outside of its "domain."

axes. The flipped function is then correlated with the original picture function
g. Accordingly, given a template function $t(x, y)$, we define its flipped version
$\hat{t}(x, y)$ by

$$\hat{t}(x, y) = t(-x, -y).$$

Clearly,

$$g * \hat{t}(x, y) = R_{gt}(x, y), \tag{13}$$

since

$$g * \hat{t}(x, y) = \int\!\!\int_{-\infty}^{\infty} g(\alpha, \beta)\hat{t}(x - \alpha, y - \beta)\, d\alpha\, d\beta$$

$$= \int\!\!\int_{-\infty}^{\infty} g(\alpha, \beta)t(\alpha - x, \beta - y)\, d\alpha\, d\beta$$

$$= R_{gt}(x, y).$$

Thus, convolution is essentially equivalent to correlation. We shall shortly
see, by means of the convolution theorem, that convolution is also equivalent
to multiplication of transforms. Hence, we will be able to derive a method
for performing cross-correlation by multiplication.

The derivation of the convolution theorem is made a little easier if we first
establish an elementary result usually referred to as the shifting theorem:

SHIFTING THEOREM: If $\mathcal{F}\{g(x, y)\} = G(f_x, f_y)$, then

$$\mathcal{F}\{g(x - \alpha, y - \beta)\} = \exp[-2\pi i(f_x\alpha + f_y\beta)]G(f_x, f_y).$$

Proof: Writing the definition of the transform and substituting $x' = x - \alpha$
and $y' = y - \beta$ we have

$$\mathcal{F}\{g(x - \alpha, y - \beta)\}$$

$$= \int\!\!\int_{-\infty}^{\infty} g(x - \alpha, y - \beta)\exp[-2\pi i(f_x x + f_y y)]\, dx\, dy$$

$$= \int\!\!\int_{-\infty}^{\infty} g(x', y')\exp[-2\pi i(f_x(x' + \alpha) + f_y(y' + \beta))]\, dx'\, dy'$$

$$= \exp[-2\pi i(f_x\alpha + f_y\beta)]G(f_x, f_y),$$

which completes the proof.

With these preliminary remarks, we can state the convolution theorem
and prove it in a few lines.

CONVOLUTION THEOREM.   Given two functions g and t with Fourier transforms G and T,

$$\mathcal{F}\{g * t(x, y)\} = \mathcal{F}\{g(x, y)\}\mathcal{F}\{t(x, y)\} = G(f_x, f_y)T(f_x, f_y).$$

Proof: By definition

$$\mathcal{F}\{g * t(x, y)\}$$

$$= \int\int_{-\infty}^{\infty}\left\{\int\int_{-\infty}^{\infty} g(\alpha, \beta)t(x - \alpha, y - \beta)\, d\alpha\, d\beta\right\} \exp[-2\pi i(f_x x + f_y y)]\, dx\, dy.$$

Interchanging the order of integration

$$\mathcal{F}\{g * t(x, y)\}$$

$$= \int\int_{-\infty}^{\infty} g(\alpha, \beta)\left(\int\int_{-\infty}^{\infty} t(x - \alpha, y - \beta) \exp[-2\pi i(f_x x + f_y y)]\, dx\, dy\right) d\alpha\, d\beta$$

$$= \int\int_{-\infty}^{\infty} g(\alpha, \beta)[\mathcal{F}\{t(x - \alpha, y - \beta)\}]\, d\alpha\, d\beta.$$

By the shifting theorem,

$$\mathcal{F}\{g * t(x, y)\} = \int\int_{-\infty}^{\infty} g(\alpha, \beta)T(f_x, f_y) \exp[-2\pi i(f_x\alpha + f_y\beta)]\, d\alpha\, d\beta$$

$$= G(f_x, f_y)T(f_x, f_y),$$

which completes the proof.

By combining (13) with the convolution theorem, we obtain the following formula for the cross-correlation function of a picture g with a template t:

$$R_{gt}(x, y) = g * \hat{t}(x, y)$$

$$= \mathcal{F}^{-1}\{G(f_x, f_y)\hat{T}(f_x, f_y)\}. \tag{14}$$

Eq. (14) is the standard statement about the use of Fourier transforms in template matching. Although the formula requires going through the transform operation three times, it is sometimes easier to do this rather than carry out the correlation directly. This is especially true in dealing with analog pictures in the form of transparencies, since Fourier transformation and multiplication are both natural operations in Fourier optics. Notice that the result of the operations prescribed in (14) gives the value of the cross-correlation everywhere. In other words, the value of the cross-correlation for all translations of the template is obtained in a single operation. We could, therefore, think of $R_{gt}(x, y)$ as another "picture function" whose intensity gives the degree of match of the picture function with a template translated to location (x, y). Hence, this operation is often suggested as a means for discovering whether the "shape" t occurs anywhere within the picture g.

8.4 SPATIAL FILTERING

In the last section we saw that cross-correlation can be performed in the frequency plane by merely multiplying transforms. In this section we would like to consider the implications of transform multiplication in a little more detail and point out some further applications.

Let us first establish some terminology. Suppose we have an initial input picture function $g_i(x, y)$ with Fourier transform $G_i(f_x, f_y)$, and we multiply G_i by another function $H(f_x, f_y)$. The function H defines a *linear spatial filter* and is called the *transfer function* of the filter. The product

$$G_o(f_x, f_y) = G_i(f_x, f_y)H(f_x, f_y)$$

is the Fourier transform of the output of the filter. The output picture function $g_o(x, y)$ is the inverse Fourier transform of G_o. By the convolution theorem, we have

$$\begin{aligned}
g_o(x, y) &= \mathscr{F}^{-1}\{G_o(f_x, f_y)\} \\
&= \mathscr{F}^{-1}\{G_i(f_x, f_y)H(f_x, f_y)\} \\
&= g_i * h(x, y),
\end{aligned} \tag{15}$$

where

$$h(x, y) = \mathscr{F}^{-1}\{H(f_x, f_y)\}.$$

The function $h(x, y)$ is called the *impulse response* or *point spread function*. Clearly, by virtue of the convolution theorem, a filter can be defined either by its transfer function H or its impulse response h. Let us given one interpretation of $h(x, y)$. Suppose we have for our input function $g_i(x, y)$ a Dirac delta function $\delta(x, y)$. By direct application of (15) we have

$$\begin{aligned}
g_o(x, y) &= \delta(x, y) * h(x, y) \\
&= \iint h(\alpha, \beta)\, \delta(x - \alpha, y - \beta)\, d\alpha\, d\beta \\
&= h(x, y).
\end{aligned}$$

Thus, the function $h(x, y)$ is the response of the filter to an intense point source of light.

The convolution theorem allows us to interpret spatial filtering from two points of view: the output of the filter can be thought of as either the convolution of the input picture with the impulse response of the filter, or as the inverse transform of the product of the filter transfer function and the transform of the input picture. Each of these points of view is valuable in certain situations. In the previous section, when we were concerned with template matching, it was convenient to use the convolution (or picture domain) interpretation; the impulse response was identified with a flipped template, and the filtering operation was seen to be equivalent to cross-correlation. In the present section we will emphasize the frequency domain interpretation of spatial filtering.

Before proceeding further, we should comment on the "linear" part of linear spatial filtering. Suppose we have an arbitrary filtering operation $\mathcal{T}$, which transforms an input picture g to an output picture $\mathcal{T}(g)$. The operation is said to be linear if, for any constant α and any two picture functions g_1 and g_2, we have $\mathcal{T}(\alpha g_1 + g_2) = \alpha \mathcal{T}(g_1) + \mathcal{T}(g_2)$. Now the Fourier transformation is itself linear; it is easy to show that

$$\mathcal{F}\{\alpha g_1 + g_2\} = \alpha \mathcal{F}\{g_1\} + \mathcal{F}\{g_2\}.$$

Using this property and the second line of (15), it is a simple exercise to show that filtering of the type we have been considering is in fact linear. We shall continue to restrict our attention to linear filters.

An intuitive understanding of linear spatial filtering is probably best gained through the medium of a few examples. Accordingly, let us discuss and illustrate the operations of *low-pass* and *high-pass* spatial filtering. A low-pass filter is characterized by a transfer function $H(f_x, f_y)$ having a relatively small magnitude for frequency pairs (f_x, f_y) far from the origin of the frequency plane and a relatively large magnitude for frequencies near the origin. In other words, a low-pass filter attenuates high spatial frequencies and passes low spatial frequencies. Since we have already noted that high spatial frequencies are introduced by the occurrence of sharp edges in the original picture, we would expect low-pass filtering to remove sharp edges and hence produce blurred pictures. Low-pass filtering operations, as a class, are analogous to the spatial smoothing operations discussed in the previous chapter. In a complementary fashion, a high-pass spatial filter is characterized by a transfer function having a relatively large magnitude for spatial frequencies far from the origin, and a relatively low magnitude for frequencies near the origin. In other words, a high-pass filter attenuates low frequencies and passes high frequencies. Since high spatial frequencies correspond to sharp edges, high-pass filtering enhances edges and is therefore analogous to spatial differentiation.

As an illustrative example, consider the sequence of pictures shown in Figures 8.3a–8.3f. Figure 8.3a shows the same television monitor picture that was used for illustrative purposes in the previous chapter; Figure 8.3b is again a 120 × 120 digitization of this picture, with the intensity quantized to one of 16 levels going from black (zero) to white (15). In Figure 8.3c we have shown the Fourier transform of the digitized picture. To bring out the

FIGURE 8.3a.   Television monitor picture.

FIGURE 8.3b.   Digitized picture.

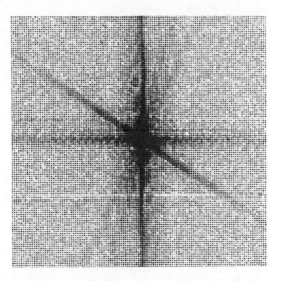

FIGURE 8.3c. Log-magnitude of Fourier transform.

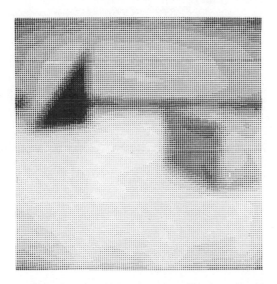

FIGURE 8.3d. Result of low-pass filtering operation.

Figure 8.3e.   Result of high-pass filtering operation.

FIGURE 8.3f.   Result of high-frequency emphasis filtering operation.

detail, we have displayed the logarithm of the magnitude of the transform; fortuitously, a high magnitude is represented by black. Notice that the transform has a large magnitude along both the f_x and f_y axes. This is caused, respectively, by the prominent vertical and horizontal edges in the original picture. Similarly, the slanting edges in the original picture give rise to the dark diagonal regions in the transform, each region being orthogonal to at least one slanting edge. Finally, notice that the original picture contains large regions of approximately uniform intensity; thus, the transform has large magnitude near the origin.

We digress here briefly to say a word about the scales on the f_x and f_y axes in Figure 8.3c. The unit of frequency is always the inverse of the unit of distance used in the picture plane. We have been unconcerned with measuring distances in the picture plane and have not yet fixed any particular unit. Since we are dealing with quantized pictures, let us now fix the unit of distance in the picture plane as one "picture-cell." The unit of spatial frequency is therefore (picture-cell)$^{-1}$ or, more commonly, cycles per picture-cell. Now the original analog picture of Figure 8.3a was sampled, by definition, at intervals of 1 picture-cell in order to produce the quantized picture of Figure 8.3b. From the Shannon sampling theorem, we know that this sampling interval allows perfect reconstruction of the analog picture only if the analog picture is bandlimited to spatial frequencies less than $\frac{1}{2}$ cycles per picture-cell. Notice that this is in harmony with intuition; the highest representable spatial frequency in a quantized picture is an alternating sequence of black and white picture cells, and this pattern has a spatial frequency of precisely $\frac{1}{2}$ cycles per picture-cell. From either the mathematical or intuitive point of view, then, the highest spatial frequency represented in Figure 8.3c is $\frac{1}{2}$ cycles per picture-cell, and thus the scales on both the f_x and f_y axes run from $-\frac{1}{2}$ to $+\frac{1}{2}$ cycles per picture-cell.

Let us now subject the Fourier transform already obtained to a low-pass filtering operation. In view of the preceding discussion, the transfer function $H(f_x, f_y)$ of the filter need only be specified for spatial frequencies of magnitude less than $\frac{1}{2}$. For illustrative purposes, we have used the transfer function

$$H(f_x, f_y) = [(\cos \pi f_x)(\cos \pi f_y)]^{16}. \tag{16}$$

Notice that $H(0, 0) = 1$, so that the spatial frequency $(0, 0)$ is "passed" without alteration. At high frequencies—in particular, whenever either f_x or f_y is $\frac{1}{2}$—we have $H(f_x, f_y) = 0$. Thus high frequencies are severely attenuated. We have arbitrarily raised the product of cosines to the 16th power in order to make the transfer function fall off quite rapidly from its maximum value of 1 to its minimum value of 0. To apply this low-pass filter, we simply follow the prescription given by the second line of Eq. (15); the Fourier transform of the digitized picture (Figure 8.3c) is multiplied by the transfer function given by Eq. (16) and the product inverted by the inverse Fourier transform. The result is given in Figure 8.3d. As expected, we have produced a severely blurred version of the original picture, too blurred in fact to be likely to be useful. We have deliberately done this in order to make the qualitative effect of low-pass filtering evident; nevertheless, it is clear that low-pass filtering, like spatial smoothing, must be employed cautiously. A less severe blurring could have been produced by using a smaller exponent in (16).

Let us now consider two examples of high-pass filtering. For the first example, we will use the transfer function

$$H(f_x, f_y) = 1.5 - [(\cos \pi f_x)(\cos \pi f_y)]^4. \tag{17}$$

This transfer function has a value of 0.5 at the origin of the frequency plane, and a value of 1.5 whenever either $|f_x|$ or $|f_y|$ is $\frac{1}{2}$. In other words, it attenuates low frequencies (but not as sharply as possible), and boosts high frequencies. The product of cosines is raised to the fourth power, which means that the transition from low frequency behavior to high frequency behavior is not as sharp as the transition in the previous example. The result of applying this filter to our illustrative example is given in Figure 8.3e. Here we see that some of the blurred edges in Figure 8.3b are just a little more sharply defined; concomitantly, the noise in the floor is a bit more pronounced. Because the low frequencies have been suppressed, the dark triangle of the wedge is now lighter and less uniform.

As a second example of high-pass filtering, we will use a filter whose transfer function is

$$H(f_x, f_y) = 2.0 - [(\cos \pi f_x)(\cos \pi f_y)]^4. \tag{18}$$

This transfer function differs from the previous one only by an additive constant of 0.5; its value varies from 1.0 at the origin to 2.0 at high frequencies, so it might better be termed a "high-frequency-emphasis" filter rather than a high-pass filter. The result of applying it to our illustrative example is given in Figure 8.3f. This picture looks more like the original digitized picture than Figure 8.3e because the low frequencies have not been attenuated and the general balance of light and dark regions therefore is unaffected. The emphasis has resulted in the edges being a little more prominent, but not dramatically so.

Figures 8.4a–f present a parallel series of examples showing the results of applying the sequence of operations just discussed to a different initial picture. Figure 8.4a shows a television monitor picture of an open office doorway. The black rectangles on the left are pieces of black paper pasted on the wall so that we can compare "real" objects like the chair with "idealized" straight line, black-white objects. Figure 8.4b is a 120 × 120 quantization of the

FIGURE 8.4a. Television monitor picture.

FIGURE 8.4b. Digitized picture.

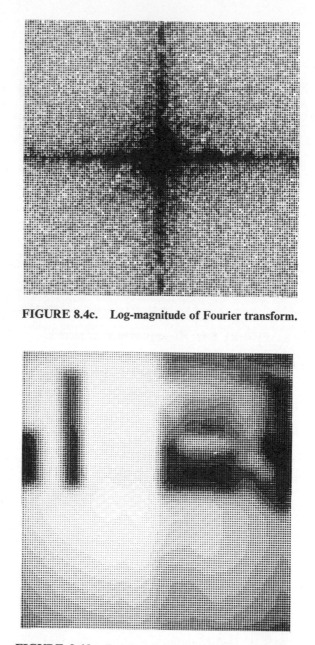

FIGURE 8.4c. Log-magnitude of Fourier transform.

FIGURE 8.4d. Result of low-pass filtering operation.

FIGURE 8.4e.   Result of high-pass filtering operation.

FIGURE 8.4f.   Result of high-frequency emphasis filtering operation.

picture, and Figure 8.4c shows the logarithm of the magnitude of its Fourier transform. The digitized picture has prominent edges only in the horizontal and vertical directions, so the Fourier transform has prominent high frequency components only along the f_x and f_y axes. Figure 8.4d shows the effect of low-pass filtering the digitized picture using the transfer function of (16). Figure 8.4e shows the effect of applying the high-pass filter defined by (17). Some of the detail, such as the bookcase, is a little more understandable in the high-pass version. Notice that the long black rectangle has a very dark border surrounded by a very light border. This phenomenon is usually referred to as overshoot, and occurs whenever the filtered picture has a sharp discontinuity. Finally, Figure 8.4f shows the result of applying the high frequency emphasis filter defined by (18).

We have presented the two previous series of examples for illustrative purposes, and have not tried to optimize these filters in any sense. Nevertheless, we should point out that Fourier filtering operations are not a panacea that can always be relied upon to produce ideal pictures, but are instead a tool that must be used selectively. In the opinion of some researchers, they are best suited to application domains that give rise to repetitive or periodic pictures, since Fourier transforms involve expansions of pictures in terms of exponentials which are themselves periodic.

8.5 MEAN SQUARE ESTIMATION
(This section can be omitted at first reading.)

We have thus far discussed some heuristic methods for performing sharpening and smoothing operations on pictures. In this section we will formalize the problem of developing these techniques in order to present the classical results of Wiener and Kolmogoroff on optimal estimation. The basic problem will be to specify the requirements of a spatial filter that cleans up noisy pictures in an "optimal" fashion. Our treatment will be of necessity brief; for a more detailed exposition we refer the reader to the literature, and especially the texts, cited at the end of the chapter.

We begin by assuming that a picture function $g(x, y)$ can be written as

$$g(x, y) = s(x, y) + n(x, y),$$

where s is an ideal picture, or signal, and n is a pure noise picture. The problem is to estimate the signal s given only the actual picture g. In order to have a well-defined estimation problem, we assume that both s and g are random picture functions. Formally, for any set of m points in the picture plane, we assume that the vector $(s(x_1, y_1), \ldots, s(x_m, y_m))$ is a vector-valued random variable obeying its own probability law, and similarly for the pure noise picture. We will assume that the noise picture has zero mean; that is, $E[n(x, y)] = 0$ for all (x, y). We want to find a spatial filter with impulse response $h(x, y)$ (or, equivalently, with transfer function $H(f_x, f_y)$) that accepts $g(x, y)$ as its input and produces an output, say $\hat{s}(x, y)$, that is an "optimal" approximation to the ideal picture $s(x, y)$. We will use mean-square-error as our optimality criterion, so that the problem becomes one of finding the filter H minimizing

$$E[(s(x, y) - \hat{s}(x, y))^2].$$

Before we solve this minimization problem, we must establish a few preliminary definitions and results. Given two random picture functions s and $\hat{s}$, we define their *cross-correlation* $C_{s\hat{s}}(x, y)$ by

$$C_{s\hat{s}}(x, y) = E[s(u, v)\hat{s}(u - x, v - y)].$$

Notice the similarity between this definition of cross-correlation and the previous one introduced in connection with template matching. In each case one function is translated with respect to the other, and the product of corresponding values "averaged:" in the previous case by summing over the picture plane, in this case by formally taking expectations. If the two functions are identical—if $\hat{s} = s$—then the function C_{ss} is called the *autocorrelation function*. The Fourier transform of the autocorrelation function of a random picture function s is called the *power spectral density* of s, and will be denoted by $P_{ss}(f_x, f_y)$. This terminology is appropriate because it can be shown that the integral of P_{ss} over any subset of the spatial frequency plane is precisely the amount of power in the random picture contributed by those spatial frequencies. By definition,

$$P_{ss}(f_x, f_y) = \iint_{-\infty}^{\infty} C_{ss}(x, y) \exp[-2\pi i(f_x x + f_y y)] \, dx \, dy.$$

Similarly, the *cross spectral density* of two random picture functions s and $\hat{s}$ is the Fourier transform of the cross-correlation:

$$P_{s\hat{s}}(f_x, f_y) = \iint_{-\infty}^{\infty} C_{s\hat{s}}(x, y) \exp[-2\pi i(f_x x + f_y y)] \, dx \, dy.$$

By the inversion theorem,

$$C_{s\hat{s}}(x, y) = \iint_{-\infty}^{\infty} P_{s\hat{s}}(f_x, f_y) \exp[2\pi i(f_x x + f_y y)] \, df_x \, df_y.$$

Therefore

$$C_{s\hat{s}}(0, 0) \triangleq E[s(u, v)\hat{s}(u, v)]$$

$$= \iint\limits_{-\infty}^{\infty} P_{s\hat{s}}(f_x, f_y) \, df_x \, df_y.$$

Similarly,

$$C_{ss}(0, 0) \triangleq E[s^2(u, v)]$$

$$= \iint\limits_{-\infty}^{\infty} P_{ss}(f_x, f_y) \, df_x \, df_y$$

and

$$C_{\hat{s}\hat{s}}(0, 0) \triangleq E[\hat{s}^2(u, v)]$$

$$= \iint\limits_{-\infty}^{\infty} P_{\hat{s}\hat{s}}(f_x, f_y) \, df_x \, df_y.$$

We need one further set of results before we can solve our minimization problem. This set of results establishes the relations between the cross spectral densities of filter input and output; in other words, they are the relations we will need to account for the effect of the filtering operation. We state them without proof, but they can easily be derived by direct application of the definitions (the asterisk signifies the complex conjugate).

$$P_{s\hat{s}}(f_x, f_y) = H^*(f_x, f_y)P_{sg}(f_x, f_y)$$

$$P_{\hat{s}s}(f_x, f_y) := H(f_x, f_y)P_{sg}^*(f_x, f_y)$$

$$P_{\hat{s}\hat{s}}(f_x, f_y) = H(f_x, f_y)H^*(f_x, f_y)P_{gg}(f_x, f_y).$$

With these preliminary definitions and results available, we can now derive the filter H that produces the best estimate of the original signal s. Since we want to minimize the expected squared error, we write

$$E[(s(x, y) - \hat{s}(x, y))^2]$$

$$= E[s^2(x, y)] - E[s(x, y)\hat{s}(x, y)] - E[\hat{s}(x, y)s(x, y)] + E[\hat{s}^2(x, y)]$$

$$= C_{ss}(0, 0) - C_{s\hat{s}}(0, 0) - C_{\hat{s}s}(0, 0) + C_{\hat{s}\hat{s}}(0, 0)$$

$$= \iint\limits_{-\infty}^{\infty} [P_{ss}(f_x, f_y) - P_{s\hat{s}}(f_x, f_y) - P_{\hat{s}s}(f_x, f_y) + P_{\hat{s}\hat{s}}(f_x, f_y)] \, df_x \, df_y.$$

Now using our relations for the cross spectral densities, we have (suppressing the dependency on f_x and f_y)

$$E[(s(x, y) - \hat{s}(x, y))^2] = \int\int_{-\infty}^{\infty} [P_{ss} - H^*P_{sg} - HP_{sg}^* + HH^*P_{gg}]\, df_x\, df_y.$$

We factor the integrand to obtain

$$E[(s(x, y) - \hat{s}(x, y))^2]$$

$$= \int\int_{-\infty}^{\infty} \left[P_{gg}\left(H - \frac{P_{sg}}{P_{gg}}\right)\left(H - \frac{P_{sg}}{P_{gg}}\right)^* - \frac{P_{sg}P_{sg}^*}{P_{gg}} + P_{ss} \right] df_x\, df_y.$$

This form of the integrand makes it obvious that the mean square error is minimized by taking the transfer function H of the filter to be

$$H(f_x, f_y) = \frac{P_{sg}(f_x, f_y)}{P_{gg}(f_x, f_y)},$$

which is the renowned Wiener filter.

It is a little difficult to interpret the general Wiener filter intuitively, primarily because there seems to be no simple intuitive interpretation of the cross spectral density. The situation becomes much more agreeable if we make the assumption that the zero mean noise is not correlated with the signal, so that

$$E[s(t)n(t - \tau)] = E[s(t)]E[n(t - \tau)] = 0.$$

In this case it is easy to verify that

$$P_{sg}(f_x, f_y) = P_{ss}(f_x, f_y)$$

and

$$P_{gg}(f_x, f_y) = P_{ss}(f_x, f_y) + P_{nn}(f_x, f_y).$$

Hence,

$$H(f_x, f_y) = \frac{P_{ss}(f_x, f_y)}{P_{ss}(f_x, f_y) + P_{nn}(f_x, f_y)}.$$

This equation has an intuitively appealing interpretation. The spectral density of a random picture, as we mentioned earlier, specifies the amount of power in the picture contributed by each spatial frequency.* Hence, the transfer function of the filter has a large magnitude at those spatial frequencies for which the signal power is large compared to the noise power. It achieves its maximum magnitude of unity at frequencies containing no noise power, and conversely suppresses completely frequencies containing no signal power. This intuitive interpretation is perhaps the most worthwhile thing to remember about Wiener filtering. Every spatial frequency is multiplied by a number

* Strictly speaking, the power contributed by all frequencies lying in a small rectangle of dimensions Δf_x and Δf_y is $P(f_x, f_y)\Delta f_x\Delta f_y$.

between zero and one. The weight given to any single frequency is exactly equal to the fractional amount of signal power at that spatial frequency compared to the total signal plus noise power at that frequency. As a simple illustration, suppose we know that the signal is bandlimited to spatial frequencies lower, say, than W. If the noise is known to contain only spatial frequencies above W then, in accordance with both mathematical and intuitive considerations the signal is best extracted from the noise by a low pass filter that passes only frequencies below W.

A related question of interest is to ask for the filter that forms the best estimate of the derivative of the picture function. The question has an easy answer if by "derivative" we mean the directional derivative of the signal s along any direction in the picture plane. (This of course includes the partial derivatives with respect to X and Y as special cases.) The best estimate of the directional derivative of the signal can be shown to be the directional derivative of the best estimate of the signal. In other words, the best estimate is formed by first processing the given picture function g with the Wiener filter derived above, and then differentiating the output. Essentially, this simplicity comes about because the operation of taking the directional derivative is a linear one, and the class of filters we have been considering perform linear operations on their inputs.

Suppose, by way of contrast, that we want to estimate the magnitude of the gradient of the signal. It would be pleasant to report that this estimate is optimally formed by merely taking the magnitude of the gradient of the Wiener estimate of the signal. Unfortunately this is not the case, essentially because the operation of taking the magnitude is not a linear one. However, the procedure is likely to be a "good," if not optimal, method for estimating the magnitude of the gradient.

8.6   BIBLIOGRAPHICAL AND HISTORICAL REMARKS

Spatial filtering is the natural extension to two dimensions of the traditional one-dimensional, or temporal, filtering processes employed in communication networks. In both one and two-dimensional settings the Fourier transform is a tool of fundamental importance; readers interested in developing their acquaintance with it can consult the standard texts of Aseltine (1958), Papoulis (1962) and Bracewell (1965). Our introduction to the two-dimensional transform follows the very readable development of Goodman (1968). The text by Andrews (1970) is the only one we know of specifically on the subject of transform techniques in image processing, and contains many good pictorial examples.

As we mentioned earlier, there are both good analog methods and good digital methods for carrying out the transform operation. The analog methods are based on certain Fourier-transforming properties of optical systems employing coherent light. An excellent introduction to these methods can be found in the text by Goodman cited above. Another good source of information on optical methods is the volume of collected papers edited by Tippett et al. (1965). Rosenfeld (1969) discusses a number of methods for processing a picture optically and contains a wealth of references. Poppelbaum (1968) describes an optical method obviating the usual requirement that the picture be available on a transparency.

Digital implementation of the Fourier transform became feasible for large problems with the development by Cooley and Tukey (1965) of what is now called the fast Fourier transform (FFT). The degree of interest in the FFT is attested to by the fact that within a space of three years two special issues on the FFT were published by *IEEE Trans. on Audio and Electroacoustics.**
The second of these issues contains an extensive bibliography. Introductions to the FFT were written by Gentleman and Sande (1966) and by Bringham and Morrow (1967). Singleton (June 1967, October 1967) discusses the problem of computing large transforms for which the size of the transform exceeds core storage. Singleton (1968, 1968a) also gives ALGOL procedures for the FFT. Pease (1968) discusses an adaptation of the FFT for parallel processing.

Fourier methods in picture processing have been applied primarily to either template matching problems, as discussed in Section 8.3, or to image enhancement problems, as discussed in Section 8.4. A particularly good description of the application of Fourier optics to template matching is given by Vander Lugt et al. (1965). Most researchers interested in picture enhancement have confined their attention to the problem of improving images for the benefit of human interpreters. Nathan (1968) was concerned with removing various specific kinds of noise from television pictures transmitted from spacecraft. Selzer (1968) used a variety of spatial filters to improve the quality of X-ray photographs. Oppenheim et al. (1968) were interested in (among other things) the application of non-linear filtering to image enhancement. Their approach was to take the logarithm of the picture function, process that with a linear filter, and then take the inverse logarithm of the result. Andrews (1969) discusses a family of filters for object detection. A special issue devoted to image enhancement was published by the journal *Pattern Recognition.*†

---

* *IEEE Trans. on Audio and Electroacoustics*, AU-15, No. 2 (June 1967) and AU-17, No. 2 (June 1969).
† *Pattern Recognition*, **2**, No. 2 (May 1970).

A few workers have been interested in the direct analysis of the Fourier transform of an image. Holmes et al. (1965) detected the presence of roughly parallel straight lines by finding prominent peaks in the magnitude of the transform. Lendaris and Stanley (1965, 1970) were interested in recognizing patterns by analyzing their transforms.

Mean square estimation, discussed in Section 8.5, is but one topic in statistical communication theory. This theory is concerned with such problems as detecting or estimating signals in the presence of noise and is therefore applicable, at least in principle, to the problem of extracting "ideal" pictures from noisy ones. In spite of this potential utility, very little work has in fact been done in this area, probably because of the difficulty of establishing useful statistical assumptions. Readers interested in investigating this area further may want to consult the standard texts of Papoulis (1965), Wozencraft and Jacobs (1967) and Sakrison (1968).

REFERENCES

1. Andrews, H. C., "Automatic Interpretation and Classification of Images by Use of the Fourier Domain," in *Automatic Interpretation and Classification of Images*, pp. 187–198, A. Grasselli, ed. (Academic Press, New York, 1969).

2. Andrews, H. C., *Computer Techniques in Image Processing* (Academic Press, New York and London, 1970).

3. Aseltine, J. A., *Transform Methods in Linear System Analysis* (McGraw-Hill, New York, 1958).

4. Bracewell, R. N., *The Fourier Transform and Its Applications* (McGraw-Hill, New York, 1965).

5. Bringham, E. O. and R. E. Morrow, "The Fast Fourier Transform," *IEEE Spectrum*, **4**, 63–70 (December 1967).

6. Cooley, J. W. and J. W. Tukey, "An Algorithm for Machine Calculation of Complex Fourier Series," *Mathematics of Computation*, **19**, 297–301 (April 1965).

7. Gentleman, W. M. and G. Sande, "Fast Fourier Transforms—for Fun and Profit," *Proc. FJCC*, pp. 568–578 (Spartan, Washington, D.C., 1966).

8. Goodman, J. W., *Introduction to Fourier Optics* (McGraw-Hill, New York, 1968).

9. Holmes, W. S., et al., "Optical-Electronic Spatial Filtering for Pattern Recognition," in *Optical and Electro-Optical Information Processing*, pp. 199–207, J. T. Tippett et al., eds. (MIT Press, Cambridge, Mass., 1965).

10. Lendaris, G. G. and G. L. Stanley, "An Opticalogical Self-Organizing Recognition System," in *Optical and Electro-Optical Information Processing*, pp. 535–550, J. T. Tippett et al., eds. (MIT Press, Cambridge, Mass., 1965).

11. Lendaris, G. G. and S. L. Stanley, "Diffraction-Pattern Sampling for Automatic Pattern Recognition," *Proc. IEEE*, **58**, 198–216 (February 1970).

12. Nathan, R., "Picture Enhancement for the Moon, Mars, and Man," in *Pictorial Pattern Recognition*, pp. 239–266, G. C. Cheng et al., eds. (Thompson Book Company, Washington, D.C., 1968).

13. Oppenheim, A. V., et al., "Nonlinear Filtering of Multiplied and Convolved Signals," *Proc. IEEE*, **56**, 1264–1291 (August 1968).

14. Papoulis, A., *The Fourier Integral and Its Applications* (McGraw-Hill, New York, 1962).

15. Papoulis, A., *Probability, Random Variables, and Stochastic Processes* (McGraw-Hill, New York, 1965).

16. Pease, M. C., "An Adaptation of the Fast Fourier Transform for Parallel Processing," *J. ACM*, **15**, 252–264 (April 1968).

17. Poppelbaum, W. J., "Adaptive On-Line Fourier Transform," in *Pictorial Pattern Recognition*, pp. 387–394, G. C. Cheng et al., eds. (Thompson Book Company, Washington, D.C., 1968).

18. Rosenfeld, A., *Picture Processing by Computer* (Academic Press, New York, 1969).

19. Sakrison, D. J., *Communication Theory: Transmission of Waveforms and Digital Information* (John Wiley, New York, 1968).

20. Selzer, Robert H., "The Use of Computers to Improve Biomedical Image Quality," *Proc. FJCC*, pp. 817–834 (December 1968).

21. Singleton, R. C., "A Method for Computing the Fast Fourier Transform with Auxiliary Memory and Limited High-Speed Storage," *IEEE Trans. on Audio and Electroacoustics*, **AU-15**, 91–98 (June 1967).

22. Singleton, R. C., "On Computing the Fast Fourier Transform," *Comm. ACM*, **10**, 647–654 (October 1967).

23. Singleton, R. C., "Algol Procedures for the Fast Fourier Transform," Algorithm 338, *Comm. ACM*, **11**, 773–776 (November 1968).

24. Singleton, R. C., "An Algol Procedure for the Fast Fourier Transform with Arbitrary Factors," Algorithm 339, *Comm. ACM*, **11**, 776–779 (November 1968).

25. Tippett, J. T., D. A. Berkowitz, L. C. Clapp, C. J. Koester, and A. Vanderburgh, eds., *Optical and Electro-Optical Information Processing* (MIT Press, Cambridge, Mass., 1965).

26. Vander Lugt, A., et al., "Character-Reading by Optical Spatial Filtering," in *Optical and Electro-Optical Information Processing*, pp. 125–141, J. T. Tippett et al., eds. (MIT Press, Cambridge, Mass., 1965).

27. Wozencraft, J. M. and I. M. Jacobs, *Principles of Communication Engineering* (John Wiley, New York, 1967).

PROBLEMS

1. Derive the following fundamental properties of the two-dimensional Fourier transform:

(a) **Linearity Theorem:**

$$\mathcal{F}\{ag_1 + bg_2\} = a\mathcal{F}\{g_1\} + b\mathcal{F}\{g_2\}$$

for any transformable functions g_1 and g_2 and any constants a and b.

(b) **Stretching Theorem:**

If $\mathcal{F}\{g(x,y)\} = G(f_x, f_y)$, then

$$\mathcal{F}\{g(ax, by)\} = \frac{1}{|ab|}\, G\left(\frac{f_x}{a}, \frac{f_y}{b}\right).$$

(c) **Parseval's Theorem:**

If $\mathcal{F}\{g(x,y)\} = G(f_x, f_y)$, then

$$\int\limits_{-\infty}^{\infty}\!\!\int \|g(x,y)\|^2\, dx\, dy = \int\limits_{-\infty}^{\infty}\!\!\int \|G(f_x, f_y)\|^2\, df_x df_y,$$

where $\|\cdot\|^2$ means the squared magnitude of a complex number. Give a physical interpretation for this theorem.

2. Give an intuitive explanation of why the output picture of a linear spatial filter should be the convolution of the input picture with the impulse response.

3. Suggest a method based on Fourier methods for automatically focusing a camera.

4. Prove that

$$P_{\hat{s}\hat{s}}(f_x, f_y) = \|H(f_x, f_y)\|^2 P_{gg}(f_x, f_y).$$

5. (a) Write the transfer function of the best linear filter for estimating the value of a signal whose power spectral density does not overlap the power spectral density of the noise. (Consider only the one-dimensional case.) Write an expression for the output of the filter in terms of its impulse response.

   (b) Under the conditions of (a), write an expression for the best estimate of the derivative of the signal. Explain qualitatively why this estimate is in harmony with the intuitively appealing estimate, discussed in the previous chapter, formed by differencing average values of the picture function.

6. (a) An arbitrary picture $g(x,y)$ is sometimes written as $g(x,y) = I(x,y) \cdot r(x,y)$, where $I(x,y)$ is the illumination intensity falling on the three-dimensional object point corresponding to the picture point (x,y) and $r(x,y)$ is the reflectance of that point. We may assume that the illumination varies slowly with (x,y) but that the reflectance, which is a property of objects and textures, varies rapidly with (x,y). Invent a generic form for a nonlinear spatial filter that separates the illumination and reflectance components.

   (b) Suppose now that we want to emphasize picture discontinuities due to reflectance and suppress picture variations due to illumination. Using the filter form obtained in (a), suggest a specific filter for accomplishing this.

Chapter 9

DESCRIPTIONS OF LINE AND SHAPE

9.1 INTRODUCTION

Our purpose in this chapter is to discuss the problem of describing lines and shapes in pictures. For this purpose, we will assume that parts of the picture have been isolated as meaningful entities. The goal will be to develop a body of techniques enabling us to characterize these entities in a natural manner. Before we begin the discussion of specific techniques, we have some preliminary remarks to make about the general problem.

In a sense, the entire subject of automatic scene analysis might be defined as the problem of describing lines and shapes in pictures. The most important simplification in the present chapter is the assumption that an "entity" has been isolated in the picture. More precisely, our assumption is that some subset of the picture plane, called the *figure*, has already been defined as a result of previous processing. During the course of our discussion, we will be talking about various kinds of figures: figures composed of discrete points, figures composed of lines, and figures composed of areas. The kind of figure under discussion at any point should be clear from context. In any event, the subject of the chapter is really the characterization of subsets of the plane.

Since we will be concerned in this chapter with the problem of figure description, we should first say a word about the problem of extracting a figure from an arbitrary picture. The question of how humans solve this *figure-ground problem* has intrigued psychologists, particularly the Gestaltists, for many years. No clear, comprehensive theory seems to have emerged from their efforts; moreover, there are optical illusions in which figure and background appear to alternate. We should not, therefore, anticipate the discovery of a universally applicable algorithm for figure extraction. On the other hand, there are a variety of techniques which are useful in particular situations. Many of the simpler ones are based on the methods discussed in Chapter 7. Probably the simplest figure extraction method of all is merely to threshold the original picture: any picture point whose intensity exceeds (or fails to exceed) some threshold is declared to be part of the figure. A generalization of this is to partition the range of gray values into intervals, and to declare all picture points with intensities in a given interval to be part of the same figure. A second method of figure extraction is to threshold the gradient picture and thereby obtain a line-like drawing. A third method is to perform a region analysis and treat each region (at least tentatively) as a distinct figure. Finally, we note that any of these operations can be combined with spatial filtering operations of the type described in the previous chapter. In any event, we shall proceed with our discussion under the assumption that a figure has in fact been extracted from the picture. For convenience, we will discuss under separate headings descriptions of lines and descriptions of more general "shapes," although it should be obvious that the two will overlap when we talk about thick lines (or line-like shapes).

9.2 LINE DESCRIPTION

In this section we will present a number of ways of describing lines or line-like figures. The general approach will be to fit the figure by one or more straight lines (or perhaps polynomial curves), so we have two problems: where to break the original figure into segments, and how to fit a line to each segment. We will be discussing methods for solving both classes of problems, but must forewarn the reader that most of the methods are heuristic—they are not dignified by much supporting theory, and must be used judiciously. We begin our discussion with the second, and simpler, problem, and therefore assume that we have on hand a set of discrete points in the X–Y plane to which we want to fit a single line. The following subsections present two analytical approaches to this problem.

9.2.1 Minimum-Squared-Error Line Fitting

The classical approach to line fitting is to find the single line that achieves the minimum-squared-error (MSE). More precisely, given a set of points $\{(x_i, y_i)\}$, $i = 1, \ldots, n$, in the plane, we seek two numbers c_0 and c_1 such that the error function

$$\sum_{=1}^{n} [(c_0 + c_1 x_i) - y_i]^2$$

is minimum. In other words, we want to find the straight line such that the sum of squares of the vertical distances from each point to the line is minimum. This problem, and indeed a generalization of this problem, can be elegantly solved by the use of the pseudoinverse of a matrix. In Chapter 5 the pseudoinverse was derived by purely analytic methods. For variety, let us take a moment to reach the same result by a geometric argument.

Suppose we have the matrix equation

$$A\mathbf{u} = \mathbf{b}.$$

If we let $\mathbf{a}^i$, $i = 1, \ldots, k$, be the columns of A and u_i be the components of $\mathbf{u}$, then a standard interpretation of the equation is that the u_i are the weighting coefficients used to make a linear combination of the columns of A add up to the given vector $\mathbf{b}$:

$$\sum_{i=1}^{k} u_i \mathbf{a}^i = \mathbf{b}.$$

If $\mathbf{b}$ lies in the space spanned by the columns of A, then of course the equation has a solution. Suppose, though, that $\mathbf{b}$ lies outside the span of $\{\mathbf{a}^i\}$. In that case we might still want to find the "best approximation" to $\mathbf{b}$ that can be found within the span of the $\mathbf{a}^i$ vectors. Specifically, we still can ask for coefficients u_i, or a vector $\mathbf{u}$, such that $\|A\mathbf{u} - \mathbf{b}\|^2$ is minimum. Clearly, this best estimate is obtained when the error vector $(\mathbf{b} - A\mathbf{u})$ is orthogonal to the span of $\{\mathbf{a}^i\}$. Figure 9.1 illustrates this situation for the case where A contains only two three-dimensional columns and $\mathbf{b}$ lies outside

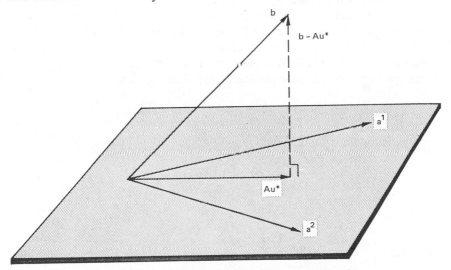

FIGURE 9.1.   Minimum-square-error approximation.

their span. We will let $\mathbf{u}^*$ be the optimal weighting vector and $A\mathbf{u}^*$ be the best approximation to $\mathbf{b}$ that can be found within the span of $\{\mathbf{a}^i\}$. We write the condition that $(\mathbf{b} - A\mathbf{u}^*)$ is orthogonal to the columns of A as

$$A^t(\mathbf{b} - A\mathbf{u}^*) = 0,$$

or

$$A^t\mathbf{b} = A^tA\mathbf{u}^*.$$

Now if the matrix A^tA has an inverse, we can solve for $\mathbf{u}^*$ and obtain

$$\mathbf{u}^* = (A^tA)^{-1}A^t\mathbf{b} = A^\dagger\mathbf{b},$$

where the matrix $A^\dagger = (A^tA)^{-1}A^t$ is called the *pseudoinverse* of A. Notice that if A is invertible then $A^\dagger = A^{-1}$. Before we leave the pseudoinverse we must show that the matrix (A^tA) is invertible. In general, this matrix is invertible if the columns of A are linearly independent, as can be seen from the following simple demonstration. Any matrix is invertible if its null set is zero or, in our case, if $(A^tA)\mathbf{v} = 0$ implies that $\mathbf{v}$ itself is the zero vector. So suppose on the contrary that $\mathbf{v} \neq 0$. Since the columns of A are assumed to be linearly independent, $A\mathbf{v} \neq 0$. Now the matrix product $A^t(A\mathbf{v})$ can be interpreted as the dot products of the columns of A with the vector $A\mathbf{v}$. Since $A\mathbf{v}$ is a nonzero vector lying in the span of the columns of A it cannot be orthogonal to all the columns; hence all the dot products cannot be zero so $A^tA\mathbf{v} \neq 0$. Thus, by contraposition, the null set of A^tA is the zero vector so the matrix is invertible.

Let us summarize the discussion of the pseudoinverse. Under the assumption that the columns of A are linearly independent, we have found that $\|A\mathbf{u} - \mathbf{b}\|^2$ has minimum value if we take $\mathbf{u} = A^\dagger\mathbf{b}$. Let us now return to our original line-fitting problem. Suppose we take our set of points $\{(x_i, y_i)\}$ and write the following matrix equation of the form $A\mathbf{u} = \mathbf{b}$:

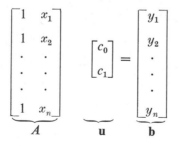

If we take $\begin{bmatrix} c_0 \\ c_1 \end{bmatrix}$ to be $A^\dagger\mathbf{b}$, then we are assured that $\|A\mathbf{u} - \mathbf{b}\|^2$ is minimum.*

---

* Note that the columns of A are linearly dependent if and only if $x_1 = x_2 \cdots = x_n$.

But

$$\|A\mathbf{u} - \mathbf{b}\|^2 = \left\| \begin{bmatrix} c_0 + c_1 x_1 \\ c_0 + c_1 x_2 \\ \cdot \\ \cdot \\ \cdot \\ c_0 + c_1 x_n \end{bmatrix} - \begin{bmatrix} y_1 \\ y_2 \\ \cdot \\ \cdot \\ \cdot \\ y_n \end{bmatrix} \right\|^2$$

$$= \sum_{i=1}^{n} [(c_0 + c_1 x_i) - y_i]^2,$$

which is precisely the MSE criterion for the coefficients c_0 and c_1 of the best line. Hence, the MSE solution is obtained by multiplying the vector $\mathbf{b}$ of Y-values by the pseudoinverse of A, the matrix of X-values:

$$\begin{bmatrix} c_0 \\ c_1 \end{bmatrix} = A^\dagger \mathbf{b}.$$

The pseudoinverse approach can easily be extended to find the MSE polynomial fit to a set of points. Suppose we want to find coefficients $c_0, c_1, \ldots, c_d$ such that

$$\sum_{i=1}^{n} [(c_0 + c_1 x_i + c_2 x_i^2 + \cdots + c_d x_i^d) - y_i]^2$$

is minimum. We proceed as in the linear case, but this time we let the matrix A of X-values be

$$A = \begin{bmatrix} 1 & x_1 & x_1^2 & \cdots & x_1^d \\ & & \cdot & & \\ & & \cdot & & \\ & & \cdot & & \\ 1 & x_n & x_n^2 & \cdots & x_n^d \end{bmatrix}$$

and let $\mathbf{u}$ be

$$\mathbf{u} = \begin{bmatrix} c_0 \\ c_1 \\ \cdot \\ \cdot \\ \cdot \\ c_d \end{bmatrix}.$$

Setting $\mathbf{u} = A^\dagger \mathbf{b}$, we immediately have the coefficients $c_0, c_1, \ldots, c_d$ such that

$$\|A\mathbf{u} - \mathbf{b}\|^2 = \sum_{i=1}^{n} [(c_0 + \cdots + c_d x_i^d) - y_i]^2$$

is minimum.

9.2.2   Eigenvector Line Fitting

An interesting analytic method for fitting a straight line to a set of points can be derived if we alter slightly the definition of "best" fit used in the MSE approach. In particular, we will define a line to be the best fit to a set of points if it minimizes the sum of squares of the perpendicular distances from the points to the line. For reasons that will presently become apparent, we will call this line the best *eigenvector fit*. To illustrate the distinction, in Figure 9.2 the MSE method would select the line minimizing the sum of squared lengths of the vertical solid lines, whereas the method to be discussed in the present section would minimize the sum of squared lengths of the dotted lines. Thus the eigenvector fit, unlike the MSE fit, is not a function of the choice of axes.

Let us establish some notation. As usual, we will assume that we have a set of n points $\{(x_i, y_i)\}$, $i = 1, \ldots, n$, to which we want to fit a straight line. We will denote the ith point (x_i, y_i) as the vector $\mathbf{v}_i$, and let d_i be the perpendicular distance from $\mathbf{v}_i$ to the line. (Thus, for a given set of points, d_i is a function of the line. For the time being we will not explicitly denote this dependence.) Our task is to find the line minimizing $d^2 = \sum_{i=1}^{n} d_i^2$.

The derivation of the best line is considerably simplified if we first establish

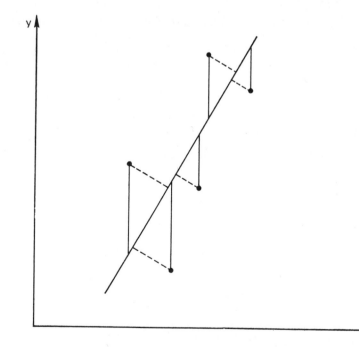

FIGURE 9.2.   Two best-fit criteria.

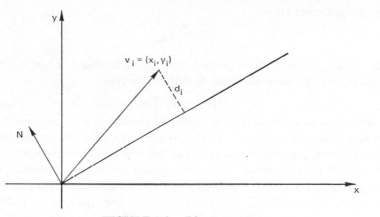

FIGURE 9.3.   Line geometry.

the fact that any line minimizing d^2 must pass through the mean (or center of gravity) of the points $\{(x_i, y_i)\}$. This can be easily demonstrated by the following argument. Suppose we have found the line minimizing d^2. We set up a new coordinate system, the U-W system, such that the W-axis is parallel to the best line. Let (u_i, w_i) be the U-W coordinates of (x_i, y_i). In the U-W system, the equation of the best line is $u = u_0$, for some u_0, and the squared distance from the ith point to the best line is $(u_i - u_0)^2$. An elementary calculus argument shows that d^2 is minimum if u_0 is the U-coordinate of the mean of the n points. The best line therefore passes through the mean and, since the mean does not depend on coordinate systems, our initial assertion is proven.

In view of the preceding argument, we may as well assume that the set of n given points has zero mean. Our problem then becomes the following: given a set of n points with zero mean, find the best line passing through the origin such that d^2 is minimized. Suppose (as shown in Figure 9.3) we characterize a line through the origin by its unit normal vector $\mathbf{N}$. Then, explicitly denoting the dependence on $\mathbf{N}$, we have

$$d_i^2(\mathbf{N}) = (\mathbf{N} \cdot \mathbf{v}_i)^2 = (\mathbf{N}^t \mathbf{v}_i)^2$$

and

$$
\begin{aligned}
d^2(\mathbf{N}) &= \sum_{i=1}^{n} d_i^2(\mathbf{N}) \\
&= \sum_{i=1}^{n} (\mathbf{N}^t \mathbf{v}_i)^2 \\
&= \sum_{i=1}^{n} (\mathbf{N}^t \mathbf{v}_i)(\mathbf{v}_i^t \mathbf{N}) \\
&= \mathbf{N}^t \sum_{i=1}^{n} (\mathbf{v}_i \mathbf{v}_i^t) \mathbf{N}.
\end{aligned}
$$

The symmetric matrix

$$S \triangleq \sum_{i=1}^{n} \mathbf{v}_i \mathbf{v}_i^t$$

is the scatter matrix of the n given points. The best line is therefore characterized by the unit normal vector $\mathbf{N}$ that minimizes

$$d^2(\mathbf{N}) = \mathbf{N}^t S \mathbf{N}.$$

We leave it as an exercise for the reader to show that this quadratic form is minimized, subject to $\|\mathbf{N}\| = 1$, by taking $\mathbf{N}$ to be the eigenvector of S associated with the smallest eigenvalue. Since distinct eigenvectors of symmetric matrices are orthogonal, the best fitting line is in the direction of the principal eigenvector of S, that is, the eigenvector associated with the largest eigenvalue. Our prescription for the best-fitting line, then, is the following:

(1) Standardize the points by subtracting the mean of the set from each point.
(2) Find the principal eigenvector of the scatter matrix of the set of standardized points.
(3) The best-fitting line is the unique line through the mean of the set of points and parallel to this eigenvector.

An interesting example of how different an MSE fit and an eigenvector fit can be is shown in Figure 9.4. The eigenvector fit is presumably the straight

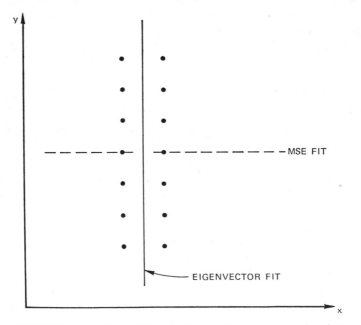

FIGURE 9.4. Two different fits to the same set of points.

line wanted, while the MSE fit is as "wrong" as could be. The poor result is caused entirely by an accident of the coordinate system. If the X and Y axes were interchanged, then the eigenvector fit and the MSE fit would be identical.

As an epilogue to our discussion of MSE and eigenvector fits, we observe that both methods are analytic solutions to the problem of minimizing a best-fit criterion. When dealing with digital pictures it is often desirable to use other criteria that are intractable analytically.* One can often minimize such criteria by a search, provided of course that a reasonable starting point for the search can easily be found. As an example, suppose we determine an approximate fit to a set of points by merely connecting the left-most and right-most points in the set. In a digital picture, we could perturb these end-points over a small range of neighboring picture cells in order to minimize our criterion. This perturbation could be exhaustive or could be guided by a hill-climbing algorithm. Thus, the basic strategy of minimizing a best-fit criterion can be used even when analytic solutions are infeasible.

9.2.3 Line Fitting by Clustering

In the preceding discussions we assumed that all the figure points were to be fitted by a single line. We now turn our attention to the more general problem of describing a figure by means of a set of lines. This means, specifically, that we must be able to partition a figure into subsets such that each subset can be reasonably represented by a single line. There are a number of methods for accomplishing this. The following paragraphs describe two methods based on clustering. The idea behind each technique is to transform the original figure into a new domain in which colinear subsets of the figure fall into clusters. These clusters, in principle, can then be found by applying clustering techniques such as the one described in Chapter 6.

9.2.3.1 A POINT-TO-CURVE TRANSFORMATION

Suppose, as usual, that we have a set of n figure points $\{(x_i, y_i)\}, i = 1, \ldots, n$, to which we want to fit some yet-to-be determined number of straight lines. One class of methods involves mapping each point (x_i, y_i) into a curve in a new *parameter space* in such a way as to make colinear points map into concurrent curves. If several curves are concurrent, their common point specifies, in some parametrization, the equation of the straight line in the $X-Y$ plane containing the colinear points.

A particular example of this class of methods is fixed if we specify a parametrization for the family of straight lines. For reasons explained later, we prefer the so-called *normal parametrization* of a straight line. As illustrated

* One such criterion specifies zero loss for a point within ϵ of the fitted line and unit loss otherwise.

in Figure 9.5, this parametrization defines a straight line by the angle θ of its normal and its distance ρ from the origin. It is not hard to verify that the equation of the straight line corresponding to this geometry is

$$x \cos \theta + y \sin \theta = \rho.$$

Accordingly, we map each point (x_i, y_i) into the curve in the θ–ρ plane defined by

$$\rho = x_i \cos \theta + y_i \sin \theta.$$

Notice that this transformation amounts to little more than a change in our viewpoint; we are treating (x_i, y_i) as fixed and (θ, ρ) as variables. If we have several points (x_i, y_i) in the X–Y plane all lying on the line $x \cos \theta_0 + y \sin \theta_0 = \rho_0$, then their corresponding curves in the $\theta - \rho$ plane must pass through the point (θ_0, ρ_0). Formally, under our transformation the image of (x_i, y_i) is the curve

$$\rho = x_i \cos \theta + y_i \sin \theta$$

or, since (x_i, y_i) lies on the line defined by (θ_0, ρ_0)

$$\rho = x_i \cos \theta + \left[\frac{\rho_0 - x_i \cos \theta_0}{\sin \theta_0} \right] \sin \theta.$$

But this last equation is satisfied by $\theta = \theta_0$ and $\rho = \rho_0$, so the images of all the colinear (x_i, y_i) pass through the point (θ_0, ρ_0).

In principle, the method outlined solves the problem of fitting the given points by a number of straight lines. In practice, however, two difficulties

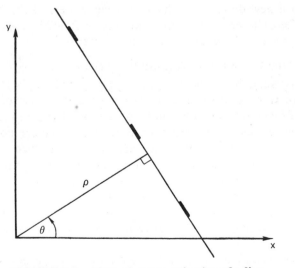

FIGURE 9.5. Normal parametrization of a line.

occur. First, if we have n points to begin with we must solve approximately $n^2/2$ equations to find all the intersections. Second, the presence of noise assures us that subsets of points will be only roughly colinear, and hence the images of the points will be only roughly concurrent. Both these difficulties can be eased if we quantize θ and ρ and carry out the process using a two-dimensional array of counters in the θ–ρ plane. For each point in the original figure, the corresponding (quantized) curve is entered in the array by incrementing the count in each cell along the curve. Colinear points then result in certain counters containing large numbers. Approximately colinear points result in modes of the two-dimensional histogram represented by the array. Notice, incidently, that we need only consider values of θ between 0 and 2π, and values of ρ between 0 and the maximum diameter of the retina. Furthermore, the method is isotropic in that it is not sensitive to the orientation of the coordinate axes. These last observations are an important consequence of the normal parametrization of a straight line and they make this parametrization more convenient than, say, the familiar slope-intercept parametrization. We shall see more of the normal form of a line when we discuss integral geometric methods later.

9.2.3.2 CLUSTERING SEGMENTS

We will temporarily broaden the ground rules of line fitting to include the problem of fitting lines to a collection of (typically) short line segments. Our motivation is that occasionally a picture is reduced to a collection of short line segments by means of a template matching operation. In such a situation, a next obvious step would be to fit colinear segments by straight lines. A clue as to how this might be done is offered by the particular coordinatization of the segments shown in Figure 9.5. We will represent a given segment by the coordinates (θ, ρ), where ρ is the length of a vector from the origin normal to the line containing the segment and θ is the angle of the normal with respect to the X-axis. We notice immediately that this coordinatization of the segments is not one-to-one. In fact, all colinear segments have the same (θ, ρ) coordinates. This suggests that nearly colinear segments can be found by representing each segment as a point in the (θ, ρ) plane and clustering these points. One drawback of this method is that it, too, is sensitive to the choice of coordinate axes in the picture plane. If a segment is far from the origin, then a small error in its orientation results in a large error in its ρ coordinate.

9.2.4 Line Segmentation

In some situations the problem of partitioning the figure into subsets can be thought of as a segmentation problem. We might, for example, have reason to expect the figure points to lie on some (possibly complex) curve, rather than lie on random line segments. In these situations it is natural to look for techniques that partition the figure points, or the curve, into a number of consecutive line segments such that each segment can be reasonably approximated by a straight line. The following paragraphs discuss two methods, both extremely simple, for accomplishing this.

9.2.4.1 ITERATIVE END-POINT FITS

The method of iterative end-point fit, in its simplest form, proceeds as follows. Given our usual set of n points, we fit an initial line, call it AB, by merely connecting the end-points of the set.* The distances from each point to this line are computed, and if all the distances are less than some pre-set threshold the process is finished. If not, we find the point furthest from AB, call it C, and break the initial line into the two new lines AC and CB. This process is then repeated separately on the two new lines, possibly with different thresholds. Figure 9.6 illustrates this technique. The initial line AB has been broken into AC and CB, and CB has been broken into CD and DB. The final result is the sequence of connected segments AC, CD, and DB.

The method has two drawbacks, both of which can be traced to the fact that it can be strongly influenced by single points. The first, and minor drawback, is that a segment finally selected may not be a particularly good fit to the points in its immediate vicinity. This problem can be alleviated by a post-fit process that uses a more sophisticated algorithm to adjust the position of the line segments. In other words, the iterative algorithm can be used to determine an approximate fit and approximate positions of the break points, and these approximations can be improved during a second pass. The more serious drawback of the iterative process is that a single "wild" point can drastically change the final result. While this problem can also be alleviated, for example, by a preliminary smoothing process, the same basic problem is encountered by many other picture processing

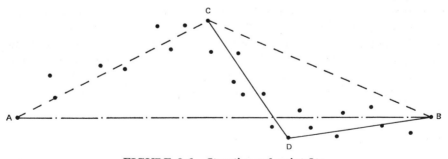

FIGURE 9.6.   Iterative end-point fits.

* The end-points might be the left- and right-most points in the set, the top- and bottom-most points, or some other pair of distinguished points.

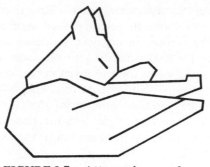

**FIGURE 9.7.   Attneave's example
(From Attneave, 1954).**

algorithms. Simplicity is often obtained at the price of basing decisions on purely local picture information. The applicability of simple algorithms, therefore, is generally restricted to data that is initially largely noise-free.

9.2.4.2 POINTS OF MAXIMUM CURVATURE

We would like to consider here a little different kind of segmentation problem. Given a smooth contour (that might be obtained, for example, from a contour follower), what is a reasonable way to segment the curve into a series of straight lines? One suggestion, based on psychological experiments, is to break the curve at points of high curvature and connect the breakpoints by straight lines. The validity of this approach is attested to by a famous example due to Attneave,* shown in Figure 9.7, constructed according to this rule. Few people have difficulty in recognizing it as a sleeping cat. Mathematically, this approach is related to the so-called *intrinsic equation* of a curve. The intrinsic equation of a curve is defined to be its curvature as a function of its arc length. Hence, the method under discussion is essentially equivalent to representing the intrinsic equation by its extreme points. (We are glossing over some mathematical difficulties in defining curvature at the intersection of two straight lines.)

9.2.5 Chain-Encoding

A very convenient method for representing an arbitrary curve is known as *chain-encoding*. For purposes of simplicity, we will assume that initially the curve is represented as a black-white picture on the unquantized plane, and that we want to represent it digitally in some manner. Rather than digitize the entire picture in the conventional way, we place a mesh over the analog picture and identify those points where the curve crosses some line of the

---

* F. Attneave, "Some informational aspects of visual perception," *Psychol. Rev.*, **61**, pp. 183–193 (1954).

mesh. The vertices of the mesh nearest each intersection are taken to represent the curve. Figure 9.8a shows the distinguished vertices for the given curve. We then encode the vertices in an octal sequence by giving the direction from one vertex to the next according to the code shown in Figure 9.8b. For example, the chain code for the given curve, starting from the lower end point, is 1, 1, 2, 1, 0. Notice that this scheme can be described as a discrete version of the intrinsic equation of the curve: The code specifies angle (as opposed to change of angle) as a function of line length, with the understanding that the diagonal lines are longer than vertical and horizontal ones by a factor of $\sqrt{2}$.

Chain encoding is particularly convenient for comparing the shape of two curves. For simplicity, suppose we want to measure the similarity between two curves having the same length and orientation. Let the chains be $a = a_1, \ldots, a_n$ and $b = b_1, \ldots, b_n$. We define the *chain cross-correlation* C_{ab} between the two curves by

$$C_{ab} = \frac{1}{n} \sum_{i=1}^{n} \overline{a_i b_i}$$

where we define

$$\overline{a_i b_i} \triangleq \cos(\angle a_i - \angle b_i).$$

Notice that if the two curves are identical then the chain cross-correlation achieves its maximum value of 1. More generally, the two chains will be of different length and we will want to slide one chain along the other in order

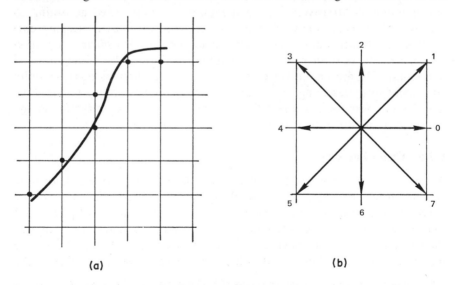

(a)   (b)

FIGURE 9.8.   Chain encoding.

to find the best fit. Accordingly, we generalize the definition of chain cross-correlation to

$$C_{ab}(j) = \frac{1}{k} \sum_{i=1}^{n} \overline{a_i b_{i+j}},$$

where k is the length of the intersection of the two sequences. Thus, the best match is obtained by computing $C_{ab}(j)$ for all values of the displacement j and picking the maximum. The primary limitation on the effectiveness of chain cross-correlations is that the two curves must be of the same scale and orientation. If either of these conditions is not met, then either the method must be abandoned or one of the sequences must be geometrically rotated and/or scaled with respect to the other.

9.3   SHAPE DESCRIPTION

Let us now turn our attention to the problem of describing the shape of a figure. As usual, we will assume that a figure has been abstracted from the background; hence, as with line description, we are really dealing with the problem of characterizing subsets of the plane (possibly quantized onto a rectangular grid). Before launching into a discussion of specific methods, let us digress briefly and consider a little more carefully the notion of a "description."

Suppose we are given an arbitrary subset of the plane and are asked to describe it. A mathematically complete description would specify, for every point in the plane, whether or not that point was a member of the subset. If we are dealing with digital pictures, and hence a quantized plane, the situation is a little simpler: we would list all the picture cells belonging to the figure. In either case, completely specifying the points in the figure does violence to our intuitive notion that a description of a complex thing should be simpler in some sense than the thing being described. An alternative method of describing a figure depends upon recognizing it as a member of some well-known or previously described class. We could, for example, describe a given figure as a parallelogram. If the figures of interest are in fact members of simple, easily-recognizable classes, then this approach can be usefully employed. More generally, however, it begs the question, since one of the goals in analyzing a scene is often to recognize figures. Hence, our primary interest is in methods that lead to simpler characterizations of figures than enumeration of points, but that do not presuppose the recognition of a figure as a member of some class.

Even after we exclude very explicit descriptions of the type referred to above, we still have wide latitude in our choice of characterizations. Broadly speaking, our choice depends upon how "informative" we want the description to be. The more informative the description, the fewer sets there are that satisfy that description. If we want to take the trouble, we can easily formalize the notion of what it means for one description to be *more informative* than another. We will say that a description D_1 is more informative than another description D_2 if the set of figures described by D_1 is included in the set of figures described by D_2. If the opposite inclusion holds, then D_2 is the more informative description. If neither inclusion holds, then the information contents of the two descriptions are not comparable. Under this definition, obviously, no description of a set can be more informative than the set itself. In the language of information theory, the more informative description reduces our initial ignorance of the figure to a greater extent.

While very informative descriptions have the advantage of precision, they also have several significant disadvantages. Perhaps the most important revolves around the fact that it is often convenient to think of certain families of figures as being equivalent; for example, we may want to think of all translations of a given figure as being indistinguishable from the figure itself. If we restricted ourselves to very informative descriptions, the descriptions of a given figure and one of its translations would be different. Other often-used equivalence classes of a given figure are the sets of its rotations and dilations. In general, we speak of descriptions that are *invariant* under certain sets of transformations. The challenge is to find descriptions that are invariant to transformations leaving figures unaltered in "unimportant" ways, yet sensitive to transformations that change figures in "important" ways.

9.3.1   Topological Properties

A fundamental way of characterizing a subset of the plane is to specify some of the *topological properties* of the set. A topological property is a property that is invariant to so-called rubber-sheet distortions. Put graphically, if the picture plane were represented by a rubber sheet then a topological property of a subset of the sheet would be unchanged by any stretching deformation of the sheet. (But a topological property will in general be changed by ripping the sheet or fastening part of the sheet to itself.) A rubber-sheet distortion of the plane is called a *topological mapping*, or *homeomorphism*, of the plane onto itself. Formally, it is defined as a one-to-one continuous mapping whose inverse is also continuous. Notice that topological properties of sets cannot involve any notions of distance, since distances are distorted by topological mappings. Similarly, they cannot involve any properties that ultimately depend upon the notion of distance, such as the area of a set, parallelism between two curves, perpendicularity of two lines, and so forth. Obviously, topological descriptions of sets will be very general indeed, and thus will not be very informative in the sense discussed above.

One of the commonly used topological descriptions of a set is the number of its *connected components*. A connected component of a set is a subset of maximal size such that any two of its points can be joined by a connected curve lying entirely within the subset. Figure 9.9 shows a set with two connected components. Clearly, the definition of a connected component just given is merely a formalization of the intuitive concept of connectedness. The reader may recall (from our discussion of 4- and 8-connectedness on a quadruled grid) that even this simple topological property is subject to ambiguity if the picture plane is quantized. As before, we will use 4-connectedness for figure points and 8-connectedness for ground points whenever we are dealing with digital pictures quantized onto a quadruled grid.

A second topological property of interest is the number of *holes* in the figure. Formally, the number of holes in a figure is one less than the number of connected components in the complement of the figure. Figure 9.10 shows a figure with two holes. Letting C be the number of connected components of a figure and H the number of holes, we define the *Euler* number E by $E = C - H$. Obviously, the Euler number of a figure is also a topological property.

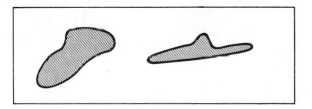

FIGURE 9.9. A figure with two connected components.

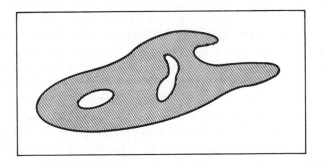

FIGURE 9.10. A figure with two holes.

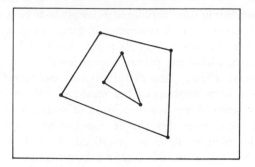

FIGURE 9.11a.   A polygonal network.

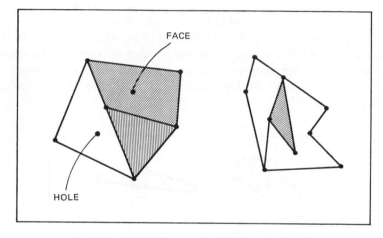

FIGURE 9.11b.   A polygonal network.

Suppose for a moment that we restrict our attention to figures made up of only straight lines. We will consider the figure to consist of the straight lines themselves, so the stick figure shown in Figure 9.11a has two connected components (the quadrilateral and the triangle). Stick figures of this sort are known as *polygonal networks*. Sometimes it is convenient arbitrarily to distinguish between two types of interior regions of such a network, and call some of them *faces* and some of them *holes*. Figure 9.11b shows a polygonal network with two connected components, three faces, and three holes. The Euler number of a polygonal network can be written in a particularly simple form. If we let V be the number of vertices, S be the number of sides (or edges), and F be the number of faces, then the famed *Euler formula* relating these quantities is

$$V - S + F = C - H = E.$$

In Figure 9.11b, for example, we have

$$15 - 19 + 3 = 2 - 3 = -1.$$

Topological descriptions of figures find application in scene analysis as a preliminary sorting parameter, as a check on the accuracy of other descriptions, and as an adjunct to other descriptions. Some character recognition methods, for example, use the number of holes as one of the features describing the character shape. In general, a problem in which topological descriptions alone suffice is unusual.

9.3.2   Linear Properties

For simplicity, let us restrict our attention temporarily to figures quantized onto a quadruled grid. We will be interested in characterizing properties of such figures according to whether or not they can be computed by a "simple" machine. In particular, we will discuss properties of quantized figures that can be recognized by the linear machines treated in Part I.

Suppose, then, that we have the situation shown in Figure 9.12. We begin with a binary digital picture in which the "1" cells are the figure points. We assume we have a family of *predicate functions* f_i which accept the values in some picture cells as their input and produce either a zero (false) or a one (true) as their output. The f_i can be thought of as features of the figure—a figure either has the ith feature or not. The features are the input to a linear machine, which forms the linear combination $T = \sum_{i=1}^{n} w_i f_i$ and compares it to a threshold t. Finally, we say the figure has the property P if the linear combination exceeds t, and does not have property P otherwise. The question is, what class of figure properties can this device compute?

It is immediately clear that the question has no interesting answer unless we place restrictions on the predicate functions f_i. If we assume that a single predicate can compute any desired property of a figure (that is, whether the figure has the property or not), then we use that single predicate and throw away the rest of the machine. Accordingly, we will place restrictions on the

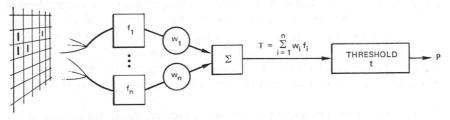

FIGURE 9.12.   A linear property-computing machine.

manner in which the predicate functions obtain information from the retina of picture points. Two interesting kinds of restrictions are *diameter limitation* and *order limitation*. We say that a predicate is diameter-limited to diameter d if the set of picture cells on which it depends all lie within a circle of diameter d. Analogously, a predicate is order-limited to order n if it depends on no more than n picture cells.* Similarly, a diameter (or order) limited linear machine is one in which all the predicates are diameter (or order) limited. Note that we are not restricting either the number or the logical form of the predicates—we are only restricting the choice of input cells of any single predicate. We say that a *linear property* of a figure is one computable by a linear machine (with an announced limitation on the predicates).

With these definitions, we can present some quite remarkable results on linear properties of figures. In some cases we will prove the result; in others we will merely state it. The reader interested in further discussion of these matters is referred to the excellent book by the originators of this theory, Minsky and Papert (1969). We begin with an easily proved property of diameter-limited linear machines.

Result 1: No diameter-limited linear machine can tell whether an arbitrary figure is connected.

This result is established by means of an example. Given a maximum diameter d, we can construct figures contradicting the hypothesis that there exists a diameter-limited linear machine capable of telling the connected figures from the disconnected ones. The figures we need are shown in Figures 9.13a–d, with the quadruled grid suppressed for clarity. In each case, we are assuming that the diameter limitation d is smaller than the width of the figure, so that no predicate can "see" both ends. For convenience, we have grouped the predicates as shown in Figure 9.13a: Group 1 predicates depend on the left end of the figure, Group 2 the right, and Group 3 predicates depend on the remainder of the retina. Without any loss of generality, let us suppose that the linear sum T is to exceed the threshold t for connected figures. Since Figure 9.13a is not connected, we have the sum, say T_a, less than t. Since Figure 9.13b is connected, we must have $T_b > t$ and, moreover, this increase $T_b - T_a$ must be due entirely to the contribution of the predicates in Group 2. Similarly, in Figure 9.13c we have $T_c > t$, and the increase $T_c - T_a$ must be due only to the predicates of Group 1. Finally, in Figure 9.13d the contribution to the sum from both groups of predicates must increase, because each group "sees" the same change as they saw previously. Thus the sum T_d for the last picture would be even more positive than either

---

* Of course we intend that these limitations not be vacuous; that is, the diameter of the retina is assumed to be greater than d and assumed to have more than n cells.

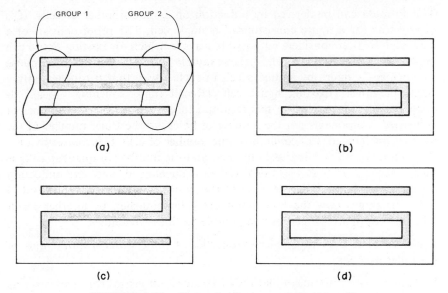

FIGURE 9.13. Examples for connectedness result.

T_c or T_b, so the threshold would be exceeded and the linear machine would erroneously declare Figure 9.13d to be connected.

An analogous result for order-limited linear machines is given by

Result 2: The order of a linear machine capable of computing connectedness grows without bound as the number of cells in the retina goes to infinity.

In particular, it can be shown that the minimum order of a linear machine capable of computing connectedness is proportional to the square root of the number of cells in the retina. Together, the first two results indicate that connectivity, an elementary topological property, is in fact quite complicated from the point of view of linear machines.

Our third result concerns the ability of diameter and order-limited linear machines to compute predicates involving the Euler number.

Result 3: The property "A figure has an Euler number greater than k" can be computed by a linear machine of order 4 and diameter 2.

This result stems from the fact that the Euler number of a figure can be computed by a linear sum each term of which involves only a few cells. Specifically, let U be the number of cells in the figure, P the number of horizontally or vertically adjacent pairs of cells, and Q the number of 2×2 quadruples of cells in the figure. Then it is not too hard to show that the Euler number is given by

$$E = C - H = U - P + Q.$$

This formula can be derived by induction on U, the number of cells. It is clearly true for a figure consisting of a single cell. The proof consists of a case analysis that considers all possible ways in which an existing figure can be augmented by a single cell. As an example of the case analysis, suppose we augment a figure by adding a cell in such a way that it touches only a single previously existing figure cell. (Recall that "touching" means 4-connected.) Adding a cell in this fashion can change neither the number of connected components nor the number of holes, so the Euler number of the figure is unchanged. Concomitantly, the number of cells U increases by one, the number of pairs P increases by one, and the number of quadruples Q is unchanged so $U - P + Q$ also remains unchanged and the induction argument holds for this case. One of the points of interest about Result 3 is that it shows how the Euler number is distinguished by another result relating it to figure properties computable by linear machines.

Result 4: The only topological properties of finite order are functions of the Euler number.

By "finite order," we mean that the order does not grow arbitrarily large as the number of cells in the retina grows arbitrarily large. It is interesting to note that although a finite order linear machine can compute the Euler number of a figure, it cannot tell whether the figure is connected.

The last result we present on linear properties concerns *convexity*. A figure is said to be convex if every straight line segment whose endpoints are in the figure is contained by the figure. From this definition it can be argued that a figure is convex if the midpoint of a straight line lies in the figure whenever the endpoints of the line are in the figure. Intuitively, then, we might guess that a machine for computing convexity need only consider points in the retina taken three at a time, and indeed this is so. Specifically, we have

Result 5: Convexity can be computed by a linear machine of order 3.

The results on linear properties that we have presented can be interpreted from two points of view. From a practical point of view they are only moderately interesting, because the constraint of using only linear threshold functions is severe compared to the ease with which more general types of functions can be implemented. More generally, however, the results illuminate the connection between a classic decision-making device in pattern recognition and simple properties of figures.

9.3.3 Metric Properties

For the remainder of this chapter we will be concerned with figure properties that depend ultimately upon the notion of a *metric*. Conceptually, metrics are generalizations of Euclidean distance, so a metric property will in general be changed if the picture plane undergoes any distortion. This being the case, we might anticipate that metric properties will often lead to more informative figure descriptions than the topological properties discussed earlier.

Let us begin by restating the formal definition of a metric given in Chapter 6. A metric d is a real-valued function of two points in the picture plane such that for all points x, y, and z in the picture plane the following properties are satisfied:

i) $d(x, y) \geq 0$ and $d(x, y) = 0$ if and only if $x = y$ (positivity).
ii) $d(x, y) = d(y, x)$ (symmetry).
iii) $d(x, y) + d(y, z) \geq d(x, z)$ (triangle inequality).

The most common metric is of course Euclidean distance. Given the points $x = (x_1, x_2)$ and $y = (y_1, y_2)$, it is not hard to verify that the function

$$d_E(x, y) = [(x_1 - y_1)^2 + (x_2 - y_2)^2]^{1/2}$$

satisfies conditions (i)–(iii). Two other metrics that are useful in scene analysis are the *absolute value metric*

$$d_A(x, y) = |x_1 - y_1| + |x_2 - y_2|$$

and the *maximum value metric*

$$d_M(x, y) = \max\{|x_1 - y_1|, |x_2 - y_2|\}.$$

Readers familiar with real analysis will recognize d_A as the metric based on the L^1 norm and d_M as the metric based on the L^∞ norm. One way to get an intuitive feeling for these definitions is to examine, for each metric, the locus of points in the picture plane unit distance from the origin. These loci are plotted in Figure 9.14. The metric d_A is sometimes called the city block

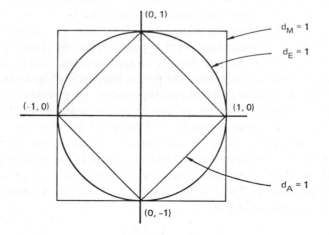

FIGURE 9.14. Unit-distance loci in several metrics.

metric (although the locus is diamond shaped) because "distances" are measured parallel to the coordinate axes. As an exercise, let us show that the function d_A does in fact satisfy conditions (i)–(iii). It is immediately obvious that d_A is positive and symmetric. To verify the triangle inequality, we write

$$d_A(x, y) + d_A(y, z) = |x_1 - y_1| + |x_2 - y_2| + |y_1 - z_1| + |y_2 - z_2|.$$

But

$$|x_1 - y_1| + |y_1 - z_1| \geq |x_1 - z_1|$$

by the triangle inequality for real numbers, and similarly for the second component, so

$$d_A(x, y) + d_A(y, z) \geq |x_1 - z_1| + |x_2 - z_2| = d_A(x, z)$$

and (iii) is verified. Before leaving the formal definitions, we should point out some appealing-looking functions that are *not* metrics. The function d_E^2 is not a metric, as can be seen by taking $x = (1, 0)$, $y = (2, 0)$, and $z = (3, 0)$, thereby violating the triangle inequality. Some additional subtleties are introduced if we are dealing with quantized pictures. The picture points will have integer coordinates, but if we compute, say the Euclidean distance between a pair of picture points the result will not in general be an integer. If we insisted upon having integer distances we might be tempted to round off the true Euclidean distance. This rounded-Euclidean-distance function, unfortunately, violates the triangle inequality, as can be seen by taking $x = (0, 0)$, $y = (1, 1)$, and $z = (2, 2)$, thereby obtaining $d(x, y) = 1$, $d(y, z) = 1$, and $d(x, z) = 3$. Alternatively, we might try to truncate the Euclidean distance rather than round it, but this also violates the triangle inequality as can be seen by taking $x = (0, 0)$, $y = (1, 1)$, and $z = (3, 4)$. In practice, these difficulties are often bypassed either by simply overlooking them or by using the computationally simpler absolute value metric which yields integer distances whenever the points have integer coordinates.

With these preliminary formalities disposed of, let us catalog some of the more obvious metric properties that can be used in shape description. Among the simplest metric figure properties are *area* and *length of perimeter*. They are easily computable from digital figures, and are often used either as components of more complete descriptions or as initial sorting parameters for deciding which of several figures in a scene should be processed first. Together, they are used to compute the *thinness ratio* T, defined for a figure of area A and perimeter P by

$$T = 4\pi \left(\frac{A}{P^2} \right).$$

A famous theorem of great antiquity is that T has a maximum value of 1, which it achieves if the figure in question is a circle. Analogously, of all triangles the equilateral triangle has maximum T(of $T = \pi\sqrt{3}/9$), and of all quadrilaterals the square has maximum T(of $T = \pi/4$). More generally, the thinness ratio of a regular n-gon is

$$\frac{\pi}{n}\cot\left(\frac{\pi}{n}\right),$$

which increases monotonically to one as the number of sides increases. Loosely speaking, then, the fatter a figure is the greater will be the associated thinness ratio; conversely, line-like figures will have a thinness ratio close to zero. Moreover, the thinness ratio is dimensionless and hence depends only on the shape (but not the scale) of the figure.

A second property that can be used to measure the elongatedness of a figure is the *aspect ratio*. The aspect ratio of a rectangle is the ratio of its length to its width, so that an aspect ratio near one indicates a "fat" rectangle. In order to extend the concept to arbitrary figures, we enclose the figure in some rectangle and take the aspect ratio of the figure to be the aspect ratio of the circumscribed rectangle. Several different definitions are possible, corresponding to the various ways in which a rectangle can be placed around the figure. The simplest definition specifies that the sides of the rectangle be parallel to the coordinate axes of the picture plane. However, as Figure 9.15 illustrates, an accident of coordinate systems can sometimes lead to a situation in which a very thin figure has an aspect ratio near one. A more

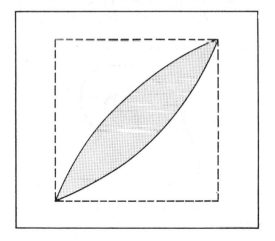

FIGURE 9.15.   A thin figure with an aspect ratio of one.

sophisticated definition specifies that the sides of the rectangle be parallel to the eigenvectors of the scatter matrix* of the figure points. As we saw in the line-fitting case, a line parallel to the principal eigenvector is a good fit to the figure points themselves if the figure is line-like. For any figure, the eigenvectors correspond physically to the directions about which the figure has maximum and minimum moments of inertia; thus, they agree closely with our intuitive notion of the direction in which the figure is fattest and thinnest. Furthermore, the eigenvalues themselves are the two moments of inertia about these axes, so a third alternative definition of aspect ratio is the ratio of the eigenvalues of the scatter matrix. In practice, the computation required by this refined definition must be balanced against the amount of information obtained.

9.3.4   Descriptions Based on Irregularities

We continue our discussion of metric properties with two descriptive methods designed to make explicit the significant "irregularities" of figures. The first method exploits deviations from convexity; the second capitalizes on local extrema of the perimeter.

9.3.4.1   CONVEX HULL AND CONVEX DEFICIENCY

We earlier defined a convex set as a set containing every line segment that connects two of its points. The *convex hull* H of an arbitrary set S is the smallest convex set containing S. If S is convex to begin with then of course $H = S$. If S happens to have only one connected component, then H can be visualized as the set enclosed by a rubber band stretched around the perimeter of S. The set difference $H - S$ is called the *convex deficiency* D of the set S.

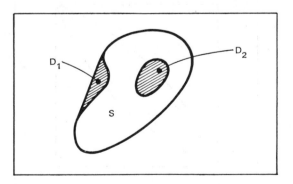

FIGURE 9.16.   Convex deficiency of a figure.

* Recall that the scatter matrix of n points is proportional to the sample covariance matrix of the points.

In Figure 9.16 the convex deficiency of S is shown as the shaded area. Obviously, any set is completely defined by its convex hull and convex deficiency. Our motivation for considering these sets in figure description is that they often provide a natural way of partitioning a complicated figure into several less complicated figures. For example, if the reader undertook the task of describing in English the set of S of Figure 9.16, he might well describe first the convex hull and then the two parts of the convex deficiency. A further partitioning of a figure is obtained in a natural way by noting that the components of any convex deficiency come in two different varieties: those components lying on the boundary of the convex hull and those components completely encircled by S. For want of a better name, these two types are sometimes called bays and lakes. In Figure 9.16 D_1 is a bay and D_2 a lake. The bays and lakes of a figure can be described by their number, approximate position with respect to the figure, and in general by any means available for figure description. Thus a figure can be described by describing its convex hull, which is typically simpler than the figure itself, and its lakes and bays.

We should mention here that extending the concept of convexity to digitized figures requires some care. The difficulty stems from the fact that the quantized image of a convex analog figure is in general not convex. A digitized circle, for example, has a staircase-like boundary and thus fails to be convex. One conceptually simple approach to this problem is the following: stretch a rubber band around the quantized figure, and define the convex deficiency to consist of only those ground cells lying entirely within the rubber band. If the convex deficiency is empty, then of course the (quantized) figure is defined to be convex. Loosely speaking, these definitions amount to a tolerance allowance that must be used up before a digitized figure is declared non-convex.

9.3.4.2 LOCAL EXTREMA OF FIGURE BOUNDARY

In a previous section we discussed the description of a curve by means of its points of high curvature. The motivation there was that informative points are those points at which an abrupt change of some kind takes place. In the same vein, we can describe the boundary of a figure by the points at which it achieves a local extremum in either the X or Y directions. In Figure 9.17, for example, points 1, 2, 3, and 5 are alternating local minima and maxima in the X direction, and points 4 and 6 are the (unique) maximum and minimum in the Y direction. As it happens, these points are also near points of high curvature of the boundary, a common but not universal situation.

If figure description by extreme points is to be feasible, it is clearly necessary to smooth out minor fluctuations in the figure boundary. One way of doing

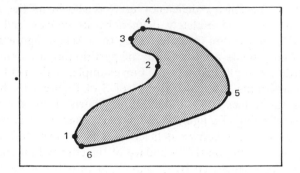

FIGURE 9.17.   Local extrema of a figure.

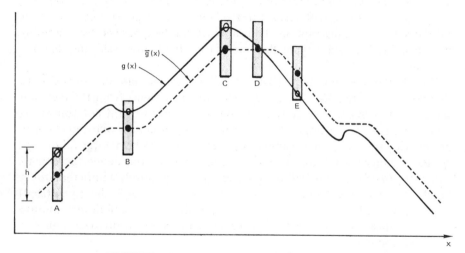

FIGURE 9.18.   Hysteresis smoothing mechanism.

this is to regularize the figure by forming a moving average, but this results in an effective loss of resolution as well. A more powerful method is called *hysteresis smoothing*. Hysteresis smoothing is actually a nonlinear process for finding the "significant" extrema of a real-valued function; for figure description purposes, it is merely applied separately to the X and Y coordinates of the boundary points. This being the case, we will illustrate its operation using as an example a function of a single variable.

Suppose, as shown in Figure 9.18, we have a function $g(x)$ whose significant extrema we seek. Imagine that a vertical wire rectangle is pulled along by a cursor that follows g precisely. The wire rectangle is defined to have the property that it does not move up unless it is pulled up by the cursor and, conversely, it does not move down unless pulled down. Otherwise, the rectangle merely is pulled along sideways without changing its vertical orientation. At A in the figure the cursor is pulling the rectangle upward as it moves along. At B the cursor has just passed the small local maximum, and the rectangle, because it has been pulled neither up nor down, is merely translated sideways at the same height. At C another local maximum has been reached (the fact that it is also a global maximum is irrelevant). At D the rectangle has been translated without moving up or down, and at E the cursor begins to pull the rectangle down. The function $\bar{g}(x)$ traced out by the center of the wire rectangle as it follows the cursor is the hysteresis-smoothed version of $g(x)$. The height h of the rectangle is called the *hysteresis gap*, and is an independent parameter analogous to the window width of the moving average process. The local extrema of the smoothed function determine the significant local extrema of the original function. Typically, as Figure 9.18 illustrates, the smoothed function achieves a local extreme nonuniquely.* When this occurs, a reasonable choice is the extreme point having smallest X-coordinate, as at C. (Note that the region of $\bar{g}(x)$ near B is a "region of inflection," not an extreme region.)

It is instructive to compare the general characteristics of hysteresis smoothing with regularization, since they are the two most prominent candidate solutions to the recurring problem of finding extrema of functions. The basic problem with regularization as a method for finding extrema is that a relatively wide averaging window must be used if minor fluctuations are to be smoothed out completely; a wide averaging window is also likely to blur significant extrema. An example of this is shown in Figure 9.19, where we have depicted a function $g(x)$ having two pronounced peaks and several minor noise ripples. We have regularized $g(x)$ to obtain $g_w(x)$, using in the process an averaging window wide enough to suppress the noise ripples completely. Unfortunately, we have also succeeded in eliminating any hint of the fact that $g(x)$ has two prominent peaks. Of course, we could use a narrower averaging window. Then $g_w(x)$ would retain something of a two-peaked nature, but it would also contain some noise. We would therefore be compelled to formulate some rule to decide which of its local extrema are significant. In all likelihood, we would choose a rule very similar to hysteresis smoothing; hence, we might well decide to use hysteresis smoothing exclusively, and omit preliminary averaging.

Returning to our original topic—the description of a figure by the extrema of its boundary—we note some examples that give a little of the flavor of the method. The reader can satisfy himself that a plus sign and a circle have identical descriptions in terms of extrema, although their convex deficiencies are vastly different. On the other hand, a plus sign at the usual orientation

---

* The extreme point of $\bar{g}$ is unique if g has a sufficiently large jump discontinuity.

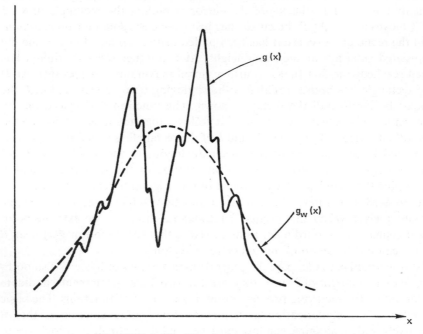

FIGURE 9.19.   Regularization of a function.

and a plus sign turned at 45 degrees have much different extrema descriptions. If the plus sign is turned at 45 degrees, then an extrema description coincides quite closely with a description in terms of points of high curvature. This is not the case if the plus sign is at its usual orientation. Clearly, in general an extrema description is sensitive to the orientation of the figure with respect to the coordinate axes.

9.3.5   The Skeleton of a Figure

A most intriguing way of characterizing a figure is provided by the *medial axis* or *prairie fire* transformation. Its purpose is to extract from the original figure a stick-figure-like representation aptly called a *skeleton*. Moreover, the transformation also extracts supplementary information that, together with the skeleton, permits the original figure to be reconstructed. For simplicity, we will confine our discussion of the medial axis transformation to single-component analog figures.

There are many equivalent definitions of the skeleton of a figure. Perhaps the most intuitive is the following. Imagine that the interior of the figure is composed of dry grass and that the exterior, or background, of the figure is composed of unburnable wet grass. Suppose a fire is set simultaneously at all points along the figure boundary. The fire will propagate, at uniform speed, toward the middle of the figure. At some points, however, the advancing line of fire from one region of the boundary will intersect the fire front from some other region and the two fronts will extinguish each other. These points are called *quench* points of the fire; the set of quench points defines the skeleton of the figure. Let us consider two very simple examples. If the figure is a circle, then the advancing fire line will describe concentric circles of continuously decreasing radius until the fire is extinguished at the center of the circle. In this simplest possible case, the skeleton therefore consists of a single point: the center of the circle. As a second example, consider the rectangle of Figure 9.20. The advancing fire line, initially, is also rectangular and adjacent sides extinguish each other, forming branches *a*, *b*, *c* and *d* of the skeleton. At the instant that these branches are complete the short sides of the fire-line rectangle have zero length, and the two remaining long sides extinguish each other to form branch *e* of the skeleton.

It is often convenient to define a skeleton in terms of distances rather than in terms of extinguishing fire fronts. To do this, we need to make precise the notion of the distance from a given point to a set of points. Accordingly, we define the distance of a point $\mathbf{x}$ to a set A as the distance from $\mathbf{x}$ to the closest point of A. Formally, for a given metric d we define $d(\mathbf{x}, A)$ by

$$d(\mathbf{x}, A) = \inf\{d(\mathbf{x}, \mathbf{y}) : \mathbf{y} \subset A\}$$

where the symbol inf means the infimum or greatest lower bound. Given an arbitrary figure with boundary B, we can associate with every point of the figure its distance to B. For some points, however, we notice that the distance is not achieved uniquely. For such a point $\mathbf{x}$ we find at least two boundary points, say $\mathbf{y}$ and $\mathbf{z}$, such that $d(\mathbf{x}, B) = d(\mathbf{x}, \mathbf{y}) = d(\mathbf{x}, \mathbf{z})$. These "singular"

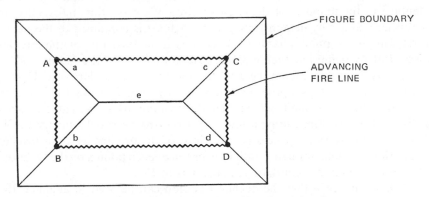

FIGURE 9.20.   The skeleton of a rectangle.

points **x** define the skeleton. It is intuitively clear that this definition of the skeleton is equivalent to the previous one. Since the fire propagates at uniform speed, a quench point must be equidistant from at least two separate boundary points which, in turn, must be nearer to the quench point than all other boundary points. Clearly, for a circular figure only the center satisfies this condition. In Figure 9.20 branches *a*, *b*, *c* and *d* are equidistant from one long and one short side of the rectangle, whereas branch *e* is equidistant from the two long sides. This definition makes explicit the dependence of the skeleton on the choice of metric *d*. We have been tacitly assuming, and will continue to assume, the use of the Euclidean metric.

The metric interpretation of the skeleton provides a natural foundation for building a more complete description of the figure. With every point **x** on the skeleton of a figure having boundary *B*, we associate a value $q(\mathbf{x})$ defined by

$$q(\mathbf{x}) = d(\mathbf{x}, B).$$

The function $q(\mathbf{x})$ is called the *quench function* of the skeleton. Obviously, it is merely the distance from a given skeletal point to the boundary of the figure. (We may also note that $q(\mathbf{x})$ is proportional to the time at which the fire reaches **x**.) For any figure with skeleton *S* and quench function *q*, we call the pair (S, q) the *skeletal pair* of the figure. It is a fact of major interest that the original figure can be reconstructed from its skeletal pair. The reconstruction is simple: at every point **x** on the skeletal figure, we center a circular disc of radius $q(\mathbf{x})$. The union of all such discs is precisely the original figure. Thus, in a sense the skeletal pair is the natural extension of the description of a circle to arbitrary sets.

Let us examine in a little more detail the assertion that the skeletal pair contains all the information needed to reconstruct the original figure. To establish the assertion, we need to show that the set *F* of figure points is identical to the union *U* of the circular discs. We show this, informally, in the usual manner by demonstrating that each set is contained in the other. First, suppose a point **y** is in *U*. Then **y** is in at least one of the circular discs. But by definition each circular disc is in *F*, since the radius $q(\mathbf{x})$ of any disc is the distance from the disc's center **x** to the boundary of *F*. Hence, **y** is in *F*. Conversely, suppose we have a point **y** in *F*. To show that **y** is also in *U*, it suffices to exhibit one circular disc containing **y**. We can find such a disc as follows. First, draw a line to **y** from the nearest boundary point. This line establishes the successive positions of the fire line as it approaches **y**. Continue the line through **y** until it reaches a quench point **x** on the skeleton. The disc centered at **x** contains **y**; hence **y** is in *U*.

We have just seen that the quench function can be used to augment the skeleton *S* in order to obtain a complete description of the figure. It can also be used to obtain a less informative, and therefore simpler, figure description. The basic idea is to discard portions of the skeleton along which the fire propagates slowly. Let us explore this idea with respect to Figure 9.20. First, suppose that the fire propagates normal to the fire line with unit velocity. Now each of the branches a, b, c, and d bisect their respective right angles, as can be seen immediately from either of the definitions of the skeleton. Finally, an elementary argument shows that each of the points A, B, C, and D propagate along their respective branches with velocity $\sqrt{2}$. The fire along branch e, on the other hand, propagates with infinite velocity since the entire branch is formed at the same instant. We might, then, decide to eliminate from the skeleton all branches along which the propagation velocity is less than 1.5. This would reduce the skeleton to the single branch e. If we recreated the figure using only this branch together with its associated values $q(\mathbf{x})$ we obtain Figure 9.21.

In the simple example of Figure 9.20 the propagation velocity along any one branch is constant. More generally, the propagation velocity at any point $\mathbf{x}$ on the skeleton is $(dq/ds)^{-1}$, where s is the distance to $\mathbf{x}$ along the skeleton. This can most easily be seen by considering $q(\mathbf{x})$ to be the time at which the fire reaches quench point $\mathbf{x}$, rather than the distance from $\mathbf{x}$ to the boundary. (Since the fire velocity is constant in the direction normal to the fire line, the two differ only by a constant multiple.) Thus, $(dq/ds)^{-1}$ is the distance ds along the skeleton divided by the time dq required for the fire-line to traverse this distance. The reader familiar with propagation of plane waves will recognize all this as being merely the phase velocity of a plane wave along the tangent to the skeleton at point $\mathbf{x}$.

Let us develop a little more insight into the meaning of the propagation velocity along a branch. Suppose, as shown in Figure 9.22, we have a portion of a figure boundary where two straight lines meet at an angle of 2θ. The

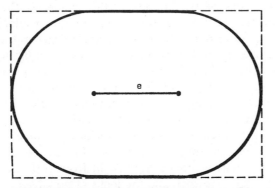

FIGURE 9.21.   Reconstruction of a figure from a one-branch skeleton.

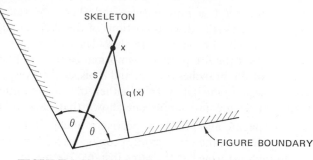

FIGURE 9.22.   A skeleton near an angular boundary.

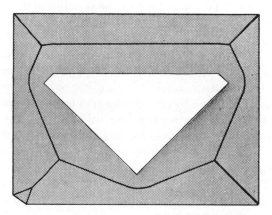

FIGURE 9.23.   Example of a skeleton.

skeleton in this region of the figure bisects the angle. Since $q(\mathbf{x}) = s(\sin \theta)$ we immediately have $(dq/ds)^{-1} = 1/(\sin \theta)$. Thus, the larger the angle is between the two sides of the boundary, the smaller is the propagation velocity along that segment of skeleton. The two limiting velocities are unity and infinity, achieved respectively when the angle degenerates to a straight line or when it closes up to form two parallel lines (as in branch e of Figure 9.20). Thus, ignoring skeletal branches with low propagation velocity amounts roughly to ignoring bends in "almost straight" lines.

A more complicated example is shown in Figures 9.23–25,* which depict a polygonal figure with one hole. Figure 9.23 shows the complete skeleton. It is an interesting theorem that the skeleton of any polygon is composed of segments that are either straight lines or arcs of parabolas. Fundamentally, this is because the locus of points equidistant from two straight lines is a straight line (the angle bisector), and the locus of points equidistant from a

* Reproduced by permission of Ugo Montanari.

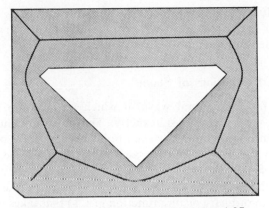

FIGURE 9.24.   Skeleton thresholded at 1.25.

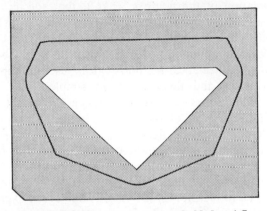

FIGURE 9.25.   Skeleton thresholded at 1.5.

point and a straight line is a parabola. Figure 9.24 shows the skeleton in which all portions having propagation velocity less than 1.25 are deleted. The only change is in the bottom left, where branches associated with the obtuse angles of the boundary are deleted. If the figure were reconstructed from this skeleton, its bottom left corner would be a quadrant of a circle. In Figure 9.25 the threshold has been raised to 1.5. The skeleton alone (that is without considering the quench function) corresponds quite closely to what we might think of as an "internal" line fit of the figure.

Our discussion thus far has been entirely in terms of analog figures. The situation in the digital case is essentially similar, except that it is difficult to use the Euclidean metric. Typically, approximations to the Euclidean metric of varying sophistication are employed. Additionally, different (but equivalent) definitions of the skeleton may lead to more efficient serial realizations of the essentially parallel transformation. Such considerations lead us a little astray from our primary interest in descriptions of shape, and we refer the reader to the literature cited at the end of the chapter.

9.3.6   Analytic Descriptions of Shape

We have thus far seen several ways in which an arbitrary figure can be represented, in principle at least, exactly. The most straightforward such representation merely specifies, for each point in the picture plane, whether that point is in the figure. This representation is called the *characteristic* function of the figure; the characteristic function is zero for points outside the figure and one for points inside the figure. Obviously, the characteristic function is just an ordinary picture function $g(x, y)$ that takes on only values of zero and one. A second exact representation of a figure can be based on the intrinsic equation of the figure $k = k(s)$, that specifies the boundary curvature k as a function of the arc length s measured from some arbitrary boundary point. These complete figure descriptions run counter to our notion that a description should be simpler than the object being described. However, various mathematical methods can be used to approximate these complete descriptions and thereby obtain simpler ones. The standard approach is to form a series expansion of an exact representation, and then use only the first few terms of the series. The coefficients of these terms constitute the description of the figure.

Let us note immediately one candidate description that does *not* work. We can, naively, expand the figure characteristic function $g(x, y)$ in a Taylor series about some point (x_0, y_0). Unfortunately, the expansion does not converge to $g(x, y)$. In fact, for all (x, y) the value of the expansion is either zero or one, depending upon whether (x_0, y_0) is outside the figure or inside. The trouble is that the characteristic function is highly discontinuous at the figure boundary. In the following paragraphs we will discuss two methods that circumvent this difficulty. The first is based on an expansion of the intrinsic function of the figure; the second is closely related to its Fourier transform.

9.3.6.1   EXPANSION OF THE INTRINSIC FUNCTION

In dealing with the intrinsic function of a figure we implicitly assume a figure having no holes and only one connected component. If the figure has more than one component then we use as many intrinsic functions as there are components. Any holes in the figure are ignored (although we could use the intrinsic function of the boundary of a hole). For our immediate purpose, an important property of the intrinsic function $k(s)$ of a figure is its periodicity. Starting from an arbitrary boundary point, $k(s)$ specifies boundary curvature as a function of arc length.* If the boundary of a figure has length L, then clearly $k(s) = k(s + L)$ independent of the choice of starting point. Hence, a natural expansion of the intrinsic function is the Fourier series. Specifically, we write $k(s)$ as

$$k(s) = \sum_{n=-\infty}^{\infty} c_n \exp\left\{n \frac{2\pi i}{L} s\right\},$$

where the coefficients c_n are given by

$$c_n = \frac{1}{L} \int_0^L k(s) \exp\left\{-n \frac{2\pi i}{L} s\right\} ds.$$

Given a figure, the first few coefficients of the expansion can be computed. These coefficients constitute the figure description. If the boundary does not contain sharp discontinuities of curvature then even a few terms of the Fourier series yields a good approximation and hence the coefficients are quite informative.

Let us consider for a moment a potential difficulty with the intrinsic function. If the boundary changes direction instantaneously at a point, then the curvature at that point is not defined. A rectangle, for example, has an intrinsic function that is identically zero everywhere except at four points; at these points the function is infinite. To remedy this, we can define a new "intrinsic function" as the integral of the old one; that is, we describe the figure by a function that specifies the tangent angle of the boundary as a function of arc length. Formally, we define a new function $\theta(s)$ by

$$\theta(s) = \int_0^s k(\zeta) \, d\zeta.$$

This, however, introduces a new difficulty; $\theta(s)$ is not periodic, since $\theta(s + L) = \theta(s) + 2\pi$. However, it is not hard to show that $\theta(s) - 2\pi s/L$ is periodic with period L, and can therefore be expanded in a Fourier series. We can make one further modification to our function. Notice that the mean value of $\theta(s) - 2\pi s/L$ is affected by the choice of boundary reference point. Hence, it is natural to remove this dependence by subtracting out the mean. Accordingly, we define the *slope intrinsic function* $\hat{\theta}(s)$ by

$$\hat{\theta}(s) = \theta(s) - \frac{2\pi s}{L} - \mu,$$

where

$$\mu = \frac{1}{L} \int_0^L \left[\theta(s) - \frac{2\pi s}{L}\right] ds.$$

* Curvature, we recall, is the rate of change of angle with respect to arc length.

The effect of approximating the slope intrinsic function by a truncated Fourier series is illustrated in Figure 9.26a–d.* Figure 9.26a shows a set of five numerals. Figures 9.26b–d shows the boundaries obtained after approximating the slope intrinsic function by, respectively, five, ten, and fifteen terms of the Fourier series. Clearly, even a few terms are sufficient to describe the boundaries with considerable accuracy.

9.3.6.2 APPROXIMATION BY MOMENTS

Given an arbitrary picture function $g(x, y)$, the (p, q)th *moment* m_{pq} of the function g is defined as

$$m_{pq} = \int_{-\infty}^{\infty} \int_{-\infty}^{\infty} x^p y^q g(x, y) \, dx \, dy \qquad p, q = 0, 1, 2, \ldots.$$

(Since we are defining moments for arbitrary picture functions, then *a fortiori* all of the following will hold for a figure characteristic function.) If the picture function g is sufficiently well behaved mathematically, which all physically

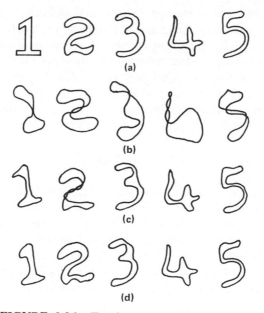

(a)

(b)

(c)

(d)

FIGURE 9.26. Fourier approximations. (a) Original, (b) Five harmonics, (c) Ten harmonics, (d) Fifteen harmonics (From E. L. Brill, 1969; reproduced by permission).

* From Brill, E. L., "Character Recognition Via Fourier Descriptors," WESCON, Paper 25/3 (1968).

realizable picture functions are, then the set of moments m_{pq} have a property of fundamental importance: they uniquely determine, and are uniquely determined by, the picture function g. Thus, the double sequence of moments constitutes a complete figure description, and a partial figure description can be obtained by using some subset of them.

The reader likely suspects by now that the set of moments are the coefficients in a series expansion of some complete description of the figure. This is, in fact, the case. We define the *moment generating function* $M(u, v)$ of a picture function $g(x, y)$ by

$$M(u, v) = \int_{-\infty}^{\infty} \int_{-\infty}^{\infty} \exp\{ux + vy\} g(x, y) \, dx \, dy.$$

Notice that this definition is reminiscent of the definition of the Fourier transform of g. Under our assumption that g is well-behaved, the moment generating function can be expanded in a power series as

$$M(u, v) = \sum_{p=0}^{\infty} \sum_{q=0}^{\infty} a_{pq} \frac{u^p v^q}{p! \, q!}.$$

We assert that the coefficients a_{pq} are precisely the moments of g. To see this, we evaluate at the point $(0, 0)$ the (p, q)th partial derivative of the series expansion and obtain

$$\frac{\partial^{p+q} M(0, 0)}{\partial u^p \, \partial v^q} = a_{pq}.$$

On the other hand, using the definition of the moment generating function, the (p, q)th partial derivative of M is

$$\frac{\partial^{p+q} M(u, v)}{\partial u^p \, \partial v^q} = \int_{-\infty}^{\infty} \int_{-\infty}^{\infty} x^p y^q \exp\{ux + vy\} g(x, y) \, dx \, dy,$$

so

$$a_{pq} = \frac{\partial^{p+q} M(0, 0)}{\partial u^p \, \partial v^q} = \int_{-\infty}^{\infty} \int_{-\infty}^{\infty} x^p y^q g(x, y) \, dx \, dy = m_{pq}.$$

The moment generating function plays a prominent role in statistics, where the function $g(x, y)$ has the interpretation of a probability density function. Notice, in our case, that the zeroth order moment m_{00} is simply the volume under the surface $g(x, y)$. Since we are interpreting g as being the characteristic function of a figure, m_{00} is the figure's area. In the statistical case, the two first order moments m_{10} and m_{01} are the X and Y values of the means of the probability density function. In our case almost the same thing is true.

Dividing m_{10} and m_{01} by m_{00} normalizes out the area of the figure and yields the X and Y values of the centroid of the figure.

A related set of moments are the *central moments* of the function $g(x, y)$, defined by

$$\mu_{pq} = \int_{-\infty}^{\infty} \int_{-\infty}^{\infty} \left(x - \frac{m_{10}}{m_{00}}\right)^p \left(y - \frac{m_{01}}{m_{00}}\right)^q g(x, y) \, dx \, dy.$$

This merely amounts to a change of coordinate systems that centers the X and Y axes at the centroid of the figure. The first central moments μ_{10} and μ_{01} of a figure are obviously zero. The second moments μ_{20}, μ_{02}, and μ_{11} are moments of inertia and are analogous to the variances and covariance of a bivariate probability function. The eigenvectors of the matrix of second central moments are the directions about which the figure has maximum and minimum moments of inertia. The eigenvalues are the principal moments, whose ratio describes in some sense the fatness or thinness of the figure.

As a sidelight, we can interpret the method of moments as a subterfuge for accomplishing what could not be accomplished by means of a simple Taylor series expansion of a figure characteristic function. The Taylor series did not work because the characteristic function of a set is not well-behaved; it has a jump discontinuity everywhere along the set boundary. Roughly speaking, however, a function with jump discontinuities has a smooth Fourier transform which, being well-behaved, can be expanded in a power series. The moment generating function plays a role analogous to the Fourier transform and allows us to construct as informative a figure description as we want by using more and more coefficients of its expansion.

At this point it may be instructive to summarize the aspect of figure description we have been exploring. We have seen at least four different methods for obtaining a complete description: the figure itself (mathematically, the characteristic function of the figure), the Fourier transform of a figure (or a picture function), the skeletal pair of a figure, and the moment generating function of the figure. As a general rule, it is not especially useful merely to replace one complete description by another. After all, the information is exactly equivalent and the form of the information is often less intuitive than the original figure. The primary value of transforming one description domain into another is that certain simplifying operations may be especially natural or easy to implement in the second domain. Probably the best example of this is the Fourier transform domain, in which filtering and template matching operations have elegant interpretations. In the case of the skeletal pair, the quench function can be used in a natural way to simplify the skeleton. However, as we consider domains in which geometric intuition and insight become more difficult, the domain becomes less generally useful in scene analysis.

9.3.7   Integral Geometric Descriptions

Integral geometry is an established mathematical discipline concerned with calculating the probabilities of various kinds of random geometrical events. Its application to the problem of describing figures has the following general flavor. Suppose we are given a single-component, simply-connected figure. Imagine an experiment in which random lines are tossed at the retina on which the figure is displayed. For the sake of specificity, suppose that we are interested in two different aspects of the experiment: first, in the proportion of random lines that intersect the figure, and second, the average length of the chord cut off by the figure on those lines that do intersect. These properties, and many others like them, are strongly dependent on the given figure and hence may be used for descriptive purposes. To illustrate what we have in mind, Figure 9.27a shows a circular figure with a few random lines superimposed. The distribution of chord lengths u intercepted by the circle is given in Figure 9.27b. It is reasonable to suppose that this distribution is a characteristic of the circular shape of the figure. Consequently, properties of the distribution, such as its mean and variance, should be useful for figure description purposes.

A traditional way of warning the unwary about the subtleties of the subject of integral geometry is the famous *Bertrand paradox*. Suppose we take as our figure a circle of unit radius and ask for the probability that a random chord of the circle has a length greater than the side of an inscribed equilateral triangle. This is equivalent to tossing random (infinite) lines at the retina and asking for the conditional probability, given that a line

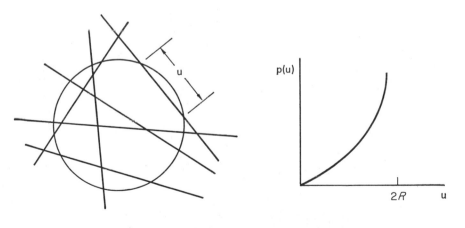

(a) RANDOM LINES
    INTERSECTING A CIRCLE

(b) PROBABILITY DENSITY
    FUNCTION FOR CHORD LENGTHS

FIGURE 9.27.   Intersecting a figure with random lines.

intersects the circle, that the length of the chord is greater than $\sqrt{3}$. We offer the reader the following solutions.

First, by reason of symmetry we may, with no loss of generality, assume that a triangle can be constructed so that one end of the chord passes through a vertex of the triangle. Clearly, as can be seen from Figure 9.28, the only way the chord can be longer than a side of the triangle is if its other end lies somewhere on the arc subtended by the opposite side. Hence, the probability we seek is precisely 1/3.

Second, again by symmetry, we may as well assume that the orientation of the chord is fixed—say it is horizontal in Figure 9.27. Then, if it is to be longer than a side of the triangle, it must cross the vertical diameter somewhere between A and B. Since any crossing point of the vertical diameter is equally likely, the answer must be 1/2.

Finally, let us note that any chord is uniquely determined by the foot of a perpendicular from the center of the circle. Hence, there is a unique chord corresponding to each point in the circle. If we choose a point lying within a concentric circle of radius 1/2 then, as Figure 9.28 suggests, the corresponding chord will be longer than a side of the triangle; otherwise it will be shorter. Therefore the probability we seek is the ratio of areas of the two concentric circles, or 1/4. In summary, we have three straightforward methods for computing the desired probability yielding answers of 1/3, 1/2, and 1/4.

The source of the confusion is the ambiguous term "toss a line at random." To make this term precise, we must first specify a parametrization of the set of all lines, and then specify a probability distribution over these

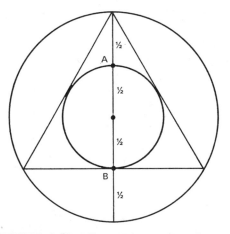

FIGURE 9.28. Geometric construction for Bertrand's paradox.

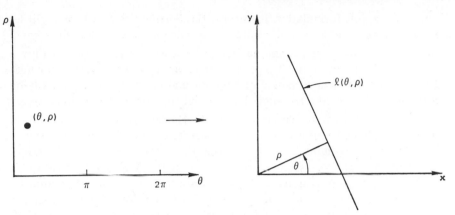

FIGURE 9.29.   Mapping from the θ–ρ plane to a line in the X–Y plane.

parameters. The various answers arrived at above all correspond to the different ways in which this specification can be carried out. Without any further principles, we cannot say that any one of the answers is correct—only that they are different. The principle appealed to at this juncture is called *invariance*. A full explanation of invariance requires an excursion into measure theory, which we can do without, but the basic idea is very simple. We demand that all of our results be invariant to a translation or rotation of figures. This narrows down the possibilities considerably. In fact, it can be shown that there is a unique parametrization of the set of lines that accomplishes this, namely the (θ, ρ) coordinates discussed earlier. Specifically, as shown in Figure 9.29, an arbitrary line in the X–Y plane is described by constructing a perpendicular from the origin of coordinates to the line. The length of the perpendicular is ρ and the angle it makes with the X axis is θ. Thus, to each point in the θ–ρ plane there corresponds a line $l(\theta, \rho)$ in the X–Y plane. We now have to specify a distribution on the parameters θ and ρ in order to complete our description of "at random." Here we are faced with a little awkwardness. If the picture plane is assumed to be infinite, then ρ must have arbitrarily large values and a uniform distribution cannot be defined.* Fortunately, this is easily circumvented by agreeing initially that we will consider only those lines passing through a previously defined retina. This means that we can restrict our attention to that subset of the θ–ρ plane corresponding to the lines $l(\theta, \rho)$ passing through the retina. We then define "at random" to mean a uniform distribution on this set.

* The problem is exactly the same as trying to make precise "choose a number at random from among all the real numbers." The unmodified phrase "at random" is usually taken to mean "with a uniform distribution," and we are confronted with the mythical "uniform distribution on all the real numbers."

Let us use this formulation to resolve the Bertrand paradox. We will let our retina be a circle of unit radius, and calculate the probability that a random line through the retina has length at least $\sqrt{3}$. As shown in Figure 9.30, the set of points in the θ–ρ plane corresponding to lines passing through the circular retina is a rectangle of height 1 and width 2π. The points lying in the lower half of the rectangle correspond to chords of the circle longer than $\sqrt{3}$, as we saw in the earlier arguments. Hence, because the distribution on the θ–ρ plane is uniform on the big rectangle, the answer is 1/2.

Let us catalog without proof some properties of the intersection of random lines with figures. We assume throughout that the θ–ρ parametrization is used, so the properties quoted will be invariant to any translation or rotation that leaves the figure completely within the retina. We should anticipate before we begin that some of the properties will depend on the retina itself. For example, if the retina is very large compared to the figure then only a small fraction of the random lines thrown on the retina will even intersect the figure. In the following we will let R be the length of the perimeter of the retina, and we will assume that the figure consists of one simply-connected component with boundary B. Our first result is concerned with whether or not a random line is likely to intersect the figure.

Result 1: The probability that a random line intersects the figure is H/R, where H is the length of the perimeter of the convex hull of the boundary B.

The reader should have little difficulty in seeing why the probability in question depends on the convex hull of the boundary; a line intersects the figure if and only if it intersects its convex hull. Thus, Result 1 is an elegant statement of the intuitively obvious fact that the bigger the figure is (compared to the size of the retina) the more likely it is for a random line to intersect it.

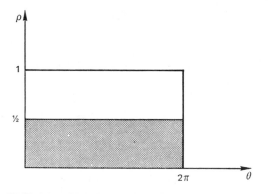

FIGURE 9.30.   Resolution of Bertrand's paradox.

The second result is concerned with the number of times a random line intersects the figure.

Result 2:   The expected number of times that a single line intersects B is $(2 |B|)/R$ where $|B|$ is the length of the boundary.

Of course this expectation must depend on B itself rather than H, because if B is very wiggly then a line crossing B once is likely to cross B many times.

The last result we want to list is concerned with the area of the figure.

Result 3:   The expected length of the intersection of a random line with an arbitrary figure is proportional to the area of the figure.

The previous results are typical of the integral geometric approach. However, it is clear that these results are not by themselves especially useful for figure description. For example, if we wanted to measure the length of the boundary of the figure there is surely a more straightforward method than tossing random lines and using Result 2.* We obtain a little more useful view of integral geometry if we broaden our horizons and explicitly recognize that the result of a line-tossing experiment is an observation on a random variable. Our interest stems from the fact that the distribution of this random variable depends upon the figure. So far we have been concerned with only the mean value of such a random variable. To make clear the implications of this distinction, consider the following example.

Suppose we want to decide which of two equally likely figures is presented on a retina. For simplicity, let us assume that this decision can be made merely on the basis of the area of the figure, and that someone suggests the area be computed using Result 3. The straightforward application of Result 3 presumably entails tossing a fairly large number of lines in order to estimate accurately the expected length of an intercepted chord. On the other hand, suppose we treat the length of an intercepted chord as a random variable, and suppose we are so fortunate as to know in advance the probability density function governing this random variable for each of the two figures. The stage is thus set for classical Bayesian decision theory. Tossing a single random line provides an observation that is assigned, in the usual manner, to the figure achieving the minimum posterior probability of error. Of course, it may be the case that tossing a single line results in an unacceptably high Bayes probability of error. This is analogous to describing a pattern by a not-very-informative set of features. One possible remedy is to toss several lines, each of which casts an independent vote for one figure or the

* The integral geometry approach is often claimed to have the advantage of "robustness." A small break in B might pose a problem for a curve follower, but is unlikely to affect a line-tossing strategy very much.

other, and then tabulate the votes. A more sophisticated approach is to appeal to the principles of sequential decision theory. In the present setting, sequential decision theory specifies which of three actions are to be taken upon observing the result of a line toss: decide the figure is of type 1, decide it is of type 2, or decide to toss another line. Typically, this approach results in the minimum expected number of line tosses needed to achieve a given probability of error. In any event, the main point here is that the full distribution of an observed random variable can be used to characterize the figure; hence, we have much more flexibility than we would have if we confined our attention only to mean values.

Before leaving the subject of integral geometry, we briefly mention two extensions. First, we can use more elaborate observations on our line-tossing experiment. For example, suppose that all the figures of interest are smooth, so that it is meaningful to define the curvature of the boundary at each point. Then when we toss a line, we might observe the curvature of the boundary at an intersection point. These observations, as one would anticipate, are related to the total curvature of the figure boundary. A second extension is to toss other curves at the retina instead of straight lines. For example, we could toss line segments (instead of infinite lines); the outcome of this experiment can be related to the angle between two long straight lines on the retina. We leave further extensions to the literature and the reader's imagination.

9.4 BIBLIOGRAPHICAL AND HISTORICAL REMARKS

9.4.1 Line Description

The earliest work on fitting a line to a set of points was probably motivated by the work of experimental scientists; the easiest way to "explain" a set of observations is to relate the dependent and independent variables by means of the equation of a straight line. Minimum-squared-error line fitting and eigenvector line fitting are two classical solutions to this classical problem. We might remark that the MSE line fit also arises in a branch of statistics called regression analysis. Without going into details, under appropriate assumptions the MSE fit minimizes the expected squared error between a random variable and a so-called linear estimate of the random variable. The relation between the purely numerical MSE approach and the statistical approach is often referred to as the Gauss-Markov theorem (which gives an idea of just how old MSE fits are), and is detailed in standard statistical texts such as Wilks (1962).

The other line-fitting methods discussed in this chapter have all been developed for the purpose of analyzing pictures. The point-to-curve transformation of Section 9.1.3 was suggested by Duda and Hart (1972). It is based on an earlier point-to-line transformation presented as a U.S. Patent by Hough (1962) and introduced into the more standard technical literature by Rosenfeld (1969). Some of the methods discussed in this chapter have not, to our knowledge, appeared in the literature. The line segment clustering method of Section 9.1.3 was communicated to us by N. J. Nilsson; the iterative end-point fit method of Section 9.1.4 was suggested to us by G. E. Forsen. The suggestion that boundaries of figures be segmented at points of high curvature rests on the apparent importance to humans of these points, as demonstrated by psychologists such as Attneave (1954). Zahn (1969) has used this approach to simplify the description of curves. The very useful method of chain encoding was developed by Freeman (1961, 1961a), and was applied by him and his colleagues to such problems as "apictorial jigsaw puzzles" (Freeman and Garder (1964)) and automatic map-matching (Feder and Freeman (1966)). Freeman and Glass (1969) used spline functions to investigate the effect of quantization on chain encoded curves. Montanari (1970) gave an iterative method for computing a relatively smooth, polygonal approximation to an arbitrary chain encoded curve. Montanari (1970a) examined curve digitization in a general setting and established some interesting limit properties. Finally, we should mention the worthwhile survey prepared by Levine (1969) that reviews the general problem of extracting descriptions of figures.

9.4.2 Shape Description

The very simple topological properties discussed early in Section 9.3 have been used by a large number of workers. As one example, Greanias (1963) used topological properties as a partial description of handprinted alphanumeric characters. Fischler (1969) used Euler's formula to check whether a figure description obtained by other means was legal. Munson (1968) also used topological properties as a partial description of handprinted alphanumeric characters.

The theory of linear properties was developed by Minsky and Papert (1969) in an attempt to answer questions about (among other things) the pattern recognition capabilities of linear machines. This general problem of characterizing the pattern classification capabilities of a given class of abstract machines has also been investigated by Blum and Hewitt (1967), who approached it from the point of view of automata theory. Gray (1971) showed that a number of figure properties can be computed by appropriately defined local operations, and described a special-purpose image processing computer for implementing these operations. Hodes (1970) measured the complexity of a figure property in terms of the size of the logical formula needed to define it.

The simple metric properties of area, perimeter, extent in a given direction and the like are so fundamental that they have been employed in one form or another by virtually every worker in the field. The problem of approximating the Euclidean metric on a quantized plane has been investigated by Rosenfeld and Pfaltz (1968). Pólya and Szegö (1951) were interested in the family of physical consequences that stem from the fact that the thinness ratio achieves its maximum value for the circle.

Figure descriptions based on the convex hull and convex deficiency are to some extent topological in nature, and we have already cited some representative examples of their use. Munson (1968) describes an efficient implementation of essentially the suggestion of Section 9.3.4 for finding the convex hull of a digitized figure. Sklansky (1969) is concerned with an alternative definition of convexity in the quantized picture plane. His definition asserts that a quantized figure F is convex if there exists at least one convex unquantized figure whose quantized representation F is. Hysteresis smoothing, which is useful in many types of picture processing operations, was used by Mason and Clemens (1968) for purposes of character recognition.

The prairie fire, or medial axis, transformation was originally developed by Blum (1967). Calabi and Hartnett (1968) were concerned with mathematical details about its use in characterizing subsets of the two-dimensional plane. Montanari (1968) developed an efficient method for computing the skeleton of a quantized figure by converting the problem into one of finding the minimum cost path through a graph. Montanari (1969) developed a method for computing the skeleton of a polygonal figure by simulating the propagation analytically.

The analytic approach to figure description has been followed by relatively few workers, possibly because the expansion coefficients obtained do not always have a clear geometrical interpretation. Brill (1968) and Brill et al., (1969) used a Fourier expansion of the slope intrinsic function of the figure boundary. A more detailed and accessible treatment is given by Zahn and Roskies (1972). Moment approximations have been considered by Hu (1962) and Alt (1962).

The application of integral geometry to figure description was first pointed out in a delightfully readable paper by Novikoff (1962). Some of these ideas are expanded upon by Ball (1962a, 1962b). Wong and Steppe (1969) combined sequential decision theory with integral geometry, thereby substantially reducing the number of line tosses required for certain descriptive purposes. A readable mathematical introduction to the subject of integral geometry was written by Kendall and Moran (1963), and contains a large bibliography.

REFERENCES

1. Alt, F. L., "Digital Pattern Recognition by Moments," *J. ACM,* **9,** 240–258 (April 1962).

2. Attneave, F., "Some Informational Aspects of Visual Perception," *Psychol. Rev.,* **61,** 183–193 (1954).

3. Ball, G. H., "An Invariant Input for a Pattern-Recognition Machine," Ph.D. Thesis, Department of Electrical Engineering, Stanford University, Stanford, Calif. (1962).

4. Ball, G. H., "The Application of Integral Geometry to Machine Recognition of Visual Patterns," WESCON Paper 6.3 (August 1962).

5. Blum, H., "A Transformation for Extracting New Descriptors of Shape," in *Symp. Models for Perception of Speech and Visual Form,* pp. 362–380, Weiant Whaten-Dunn, ed. (MIT Press, Cambridge, Mass., 1967).

6. Blum, M. and C. Hewitt, "Automata on a 2-Dimensional Tape," *IEEE Conf. Record Eighth Ann. Symp. Switching and Automata Theory* (IEEE, New York, 1967).

7. Brill, E. L., "Character Recognition Via Fourier Descriptors," WESCON, Paper 25/3, Los Angeles (1968).

8. Brill, E. L., R. P. Heydorn, and J. D. Hill, "Some Approaches to Character Recognition for Postal Address Reader Applications," *Proc. Auto. Pattern Recog.,* pp. 19–40 (Nat. Security Industrial Assn., Washington, D.C., May 1969).

9. Calabi, L. and W. E. Hartnett, "Shape Recognition, Prairie Fires, Convex Deficiencies and Skeletons," *Amer. Math. Monthly,* **75,** 335–342 (April 1968).

10. Duda, R. O. and P. E. Hart, "Use of the Hough Transformation to Detect Lines and Curves in Pictures," *Comm. ACM,* **15,** 11–15 (January 1972).

11. Feder, J. and H. Freeman, "Digital Curve Matching Using a Contour Correlation Algorithm," *IEEE Intl. Conv. Rec.,* Pt. 3 (March 1966).

12. Fischler, M. A., "Machine Perception and Description of Pictorial Data," *Proc. Int. Joint Conf. on Art. Int.,* pp. 629–639, D. E. Walker and L. M. Norton, eds. (May 1969).

13. Freeman, H., "On the Encoding of Arbitrary Geometric Configurations," *IRE Trans. Elec. Comp.,* **EC-10,** 260–268 (June 1961).

14. Freeman, H., "Techniques for the Digital Computer Analysis of Chain-Encoded Arbitrary Plane Curves," *1961 Proc. Natl. Elec. Conf.,* **18,** 312–324 (1961).

15. Freeman, H. and L. Garder, "Apictorial Jigsaw Puzzles: The Computer Solution of a Problem in Pattern Recognition," *IEEE Trans. Elec. Comp.,* **EC-13,** 118–127 (April 1964).

16. Freeman, H. and J. M. Glass, "On the Quantization of Line-Drawing Data," *IEEE Trans. Sys. Sci. Cyb.,* **SSC-5,** 70–78 (January 1969).

17. Gray, S. B., "Local Properties of Binary Images in Two Dimensions," *IEEE Trans. Comp.,* **C-20,** 551–561 (May 1971).

18. Greanias, E. C., P. F. Meagher, R. J. Norman, and P. Essinger, "The Recognition of Handwritten Numerals by Contour Analysis," *IBM Journal*, **7**, 14–21 (January 1963).

19. Hodes, L., "The Logical Complexity of Geometric Properties in the Plane," *J. ACM*, **17**, 339–347 (April 1970).

20. Hough, P. V. C., "Method and Means for Recognizing Complex Patterns," U.S. Patent 3069654 (December 18, 1962).

21. Hu, M. K., "Visual Pattern Recognition by Moment Invariants," *IRE Trans. Info. Thy.*, **IT-8**, 179–187 (February 1962).

22. Kendall, M. G. and P. A. P. Moran, *Geometrical Probability* (Charles Griffin & Company, London, 1963).

23. Levine, M. D., "Feature Extraction: A Survey," *Proc. IEEE*, **57**, 1391–1407 (August 1969).

24. Mason, S. J. and J. K. Clemens, "Character Recognition in an Experimental Reading Machine for the Blind," in *Recognizing Patterns*, pp. 156–167, P. A. Kolers and M. Eden, eds. (MIT Press, Cambridge, Mass., 1968).

25. Minsky, M. and S. Papert, *Perceptrons* (MIT Press, Cambridge, Mass., 1969).

26. Montanari, U., "A Method for Obtaining Skeletons Using a Quasi-Euclidean Distance," *J. ACM*, **15**, 600–624 (October 1968).

27. Montanari, U., "Continuous Skeletons from Digitized Images," *J. ACM*, **16**, 534–549 (October 1969).

28. Montanari, U., "A Note on Minimal Length Polygonal Approximations to a Digitized Contour," *Comm. ACM*, **13**, 41–47 (January 1970).

29. Montanari, U., "On Limit Properties in Digitization Schemes," *J. ACM*, **17**, 348–360 (April 1970).

30. Munson, J. H., "Experiments in the Recognition of Hand-Printed Text: Part I—Character Recognition," *Proc. FJCC*, pp. 1125–1138 (December 1968).

31. Novikoff, A. B. J., "Integral Geometry as a Tool in Pattern Perception," in *Principles of Self-Organization*, pp. 347–368, Von Foerster and Zopf, eds. (Pergamon Press, New York, 1962).

32. Pólya, G. and G. Szegö, *Isoperimetric Inequalities in Mathematical Physics* (Princeton University Press, Princeton, N.J., 1951).

33. Rosenfeld, A., *Picture Processing by Computer* (Academic Press, New York, 1969).

34. Rosenfeld, A. and J. L. Pflatz, "Distance Functions on Digital Pictures," *Pattern Recognition*, **1**, 33–62 (July 1968).

35. Sklansky, J., "Recognizing Convex Blobs," *Proc. Int. Joint Conf. on Art. Int.*, pp. 107–116, D. E. Walker and L. M. Norton, eds. (May 1969).

36. Wilks, S. S., *Mathematical Statistics* (John Wiley, New York, 1962).

37. Wong, E. and J. A. Steppe, "Invariant Recognition of Geometric Shapes," in *Methodologies of Pattern Recognition*, pp. 535–546, S. Watanabe, ed. (Academic Press, New York, 1969).

38. Zahn, C. T., "A Formal Description for Two-Dimensional Patterns," *Proc. Int. Joint Conf. on Art. Int.*, pp. 621–628, D. E. Walker and L. M. Norton, eds. (May 1969).

39. Zahn, C. T. and R. Z. Roskies, "Fourier Descriptors for Plane Closed Curves," *IEEE Trans. Comp.*, C-21, 269–281 (March 1972).

PROBLEMS

1. Given a set of n points $\{(x_i, y_i)\}$, $i = 1, \ldots, n$, in the X–Y plane, suppose we want to fit the points by a curve of the form $\sum_{j=1}^{d} a_j \varphi_j(x)$, where the functions $\varphi_j(x)$, $j = 1, \ldots, d$ are arbitrary given functions and the coefficients a_j, $j = 1, \ldots, d$ are to be determined. Derive a general solution for the coefficients that minimizes the squared error (in a direction parallel to the Y axis) between the set of points and the curve.

2. (a) Given a real symmetric matrix S, show that the function $v^t S v / v^t v$ of a vector v is minimized (maximized) by taking v to be the eigenvector associated with the smallest (largest) eigenvalue of S.

    (b) Show for the two-dimensional case that the locus of points x satisfying $x^t S x = c$, for a positive constant c, is an ellipse whose axes coincide with the eigenvectors of S.

3. (a) Show that the point-curve transformation that takes a point (x, y) in the picture plane into the curve $\rho = x \cos \theta + y \sin \theta$ in the parameter plane has the property that points lying on the same curve in the parameter plane correspond to lines through the same point in the picture plane.

    (b) Show that the two-dimensional histogram technique described in the text is equivalent to the following technique: For each quantized value of θ, project all the figure points onto a line of slope angle θ and form a histogram of the projections using histogram cells of the same size as the quantization cells on ρ.

    (c) Show that a transformation taking a picture point into a right circular cone in a three-dimensional parameter space can be used to find circular configurations of points in the picture plane.

4. Specify an algorithm extending (in an unambiguous fashion) the method of iterative end-point fits to simple closed curves.

5. (a) Sketch a curve on a grid and write its chain code. Define an operation on the code that produces a new code representing the same curve magnified by a factor of two. Sketch the piecewise linear curve corresponding to the scaled code.

    (b) Now define an operation on a chain code that rotates the encoded curve through an angle of 45°. Apply this operation to the code representing the magnified version of the original curve. On a separate piece of paper, sketch the piecewise linear curve corresponding to the "rotated chain code," and visually compare the two piecewise linear curves.

6. (a) Prove Euler's formula for polygonal networks consisting of a single connected component with no holes. (Hint: Use induction on the number of lines.)

(b) Extend the result of Part (a) to networks with an arbitrary number of connected components.

(c) Extend the result of Part (b) to include networks with holes.

7. Show that the area of an arbitrary polygon is given by

$$A = \tfrac{1}{2} \sum_j (x_{j+1} y_j - x_j y_{j+1}),$$

where (x_j, y_j) are the coordinates of the jth vertex of the polygon and the summation begins with any vertex and continues in a clockwise sense around the polygon until the initial vertex is reached again.

8. Invent an algorithm for finding the convex hull of a digitized figure.

9. Invent an algorithm for performing hysteresis smoothing on an arbitrary closed contour.

10. (a) Draw a nonconvex pentagon and sketch its skeleton.

(b) Suppose now that we want to simplify the skeleton by discarding portions along which the fire propagates at a rate lower than some threshold. Sketch a series of pictures showing successive simplifications that are obtained as the threshold on propagation velocity is raised.

(c) Sketch the figure corresponding to each skeleton in (b).

11. Show that the slope intrinsic function $\hat{\theta}(s)$ defined in the text is a zero-mean, periodic function with period L.

12. Show that the probability that a random line crosses a curve C is the ratio of the perimeter of the convex hull of C to the perimeter of the retina on which it is displayed.

Chapter 10

PERSPECTIVE TRANSFORMATIONS

10.1 INTRODUCTION

We have been interested thus far in what might be called, for want of a better name, two-dimensional scene analysis. By this we mean that we have not considered any of the three-dimensional relations either between the camera and the objects of the scene or among the objects themselves. In some situations, such as optical character recognition, this strictly two-dimensional approach is adequate. In many interesting applications, however, the three-dimensional nature of the object in the scene and/or the picture-taking process is of critical importance. For example, the fundamental problem of locating the position of an object with respect to the camera lies within the province of what we will call (again for want of a better term) three-dimensional scene analysis. As a second example, an algorithm that intelligently processes pictures containing occluded, or partially hidden, objects needs at least a rudimentary concept of three-dimensional relations. Finally, the capability of a scene analyzer can often be enhanced by capitalizing on certain mathematical properties of the picture-taking process. In the remainder of the book we will be primarily concerned with three-dimensional scene analysis. We will be interested both in methods for answering questions that intrinsically require three-dimensional information, and also in methods that exploit three-dimensional information to aid the two-dimensional techniques that are part of any scene analysis. As one would expect, both problems are served by the same mathematical model, to which we now turn our attention.

10.2   MODELLING PICTURE-TAKING

Our purpose in the present chapter is to discuss the *perspective transformation*, which is the natural first-order approximation to the process of taking a picture. Ultimately, we will derive and illustrate some useful general relations between points in three-dimensional space and their images in a picture. For the moment, let us introduce the topic in the simplest possible setting. Our basic model is shown in Figure 10.1. The camera is represented by a pinhole lens together with an image plane lying a distance of f behind the lens.* The image of a point $\mathbf{v}$ in three-dimensional space is determined by the intersection of the image plane with the projecting ray defined by $\mathbf{v}$ and the lens center. We will consistently refer to this intersection $\mathbf{v}_p$ as the *picture* or *image point* corresponding to the *object point* $\mathbf{v}$.

While the model of Figure 10.1 is adequate, it suffers from the minor annoyance that images are inverted left to right and top to bottom. To avoid this, we will intercept the projecting ray with a front image plane as shown in Figure 10.2. This front image plane can be thought of as a plane containing a transparent slide, whereas the back image plane contains the original film. The process illustrated in Figure 10.2 is called *central projection*, the lens point being the *center of projection*.

We will sometimes refer to the image $\mathbf{v}_p$ as being the *projection* of $\mathbf{v}$ onto the picture plane. Figure 10.2 also shows a useful coordinatization of the

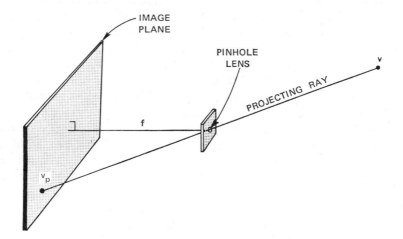

FIGURE 10.1.   Elementary camera model.

---

* The actual lens on a real photographic or television camera can always be replaced by a mathematically equivalent pinhole lens at an appropriate distance from the image plane.

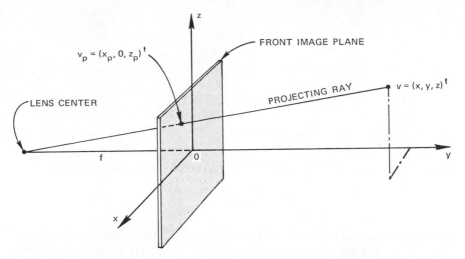

FIGURE 10.2.   Camera model with front image plane.

process of central projection. We have aligned the Y axis with the *optical axis*, or *principal ray*, of the camera, the principal ray being the ray from the lens perpendicular to the image plane. The center of coordinates is the intersection of the principal ray with the image plane.

The process of central projection is many-to-one. As illustrated in Figure 10.2, although every object point has a single, well-defined image point, all object points lying on a line through the lens center have the same image. Thus, for each image point there is a line in space, defined by the image point and the lens center, along which the corresponding object point must lie. We have, therefore, two questions of fundamental importance associated with the picture-taking process: given an arbitrary object point, what is the location of its image, and given an arbitrary image point, what is the straight line along which the corresponding object point must lie. The answers to these questions are provided by the direct and inverse perspective transformations.

Let us intuitively derive the direct perspective transformation for the simple case depicted in Figure 10.2. By inspection, the answer involves only similar triangles. If we let $\mathbf{v} = (x, y, z)^t$ and let $\mathbf{v}_p = (x_p, y_p, z_p)^t$, then clearly

$$\frac{x_p}{f} = \frac{x}{f + y}$$

$$y_p = 0$$

and

$$\frac{z_p}{f} = \frac{z}{f + y},$$

or

$$x_p = \frac{fx}{f + y}$$

$$y_p = 0 \tag{1}$$

$$z_p = \frac{fz}{f + y} \,.$$

These equations are particularly obvious if we choose an object point on either the X–Y plane or the Y–Z plane, in which cases the similar triangles are easily visualized. We note also that (1) can be recast into the form

$$x = \frac{x_p}{f} (y + f) = \frac{x_p}{z_p} z, \tag{2}$$

which are the equations of a straight line passing through the lens point $(0, -f, 0)^t$ and the picture point $(x_p, 0, z_p)^t$. Thus, (2) is one form of the inverse perspective transformation, since for a given image point $(x_p, 0, z_p)^t$ it gives the equations of the corresponding line in space. In the remainder of this chapter we will elaborate these simple equations and derive some results of general utility in scene analysis.

10.3   THE PERSPECTIVE TRANSFORMATION IN HOMOGENEOUS COORDINATES

10.3.1   The Direct Perspective Transformation

The mathematics of perspective transformations can be put into another useful form if we first go to the trouble of representing vectors in *homogeneous coordinates*. The basic idea is to convert the non-linear transformations of Eqs. (1) and (2) into linear transformations in a different coordinate system. Notice that (1) fails to be linear because the Y coordinate of the object point appears in the denominator. With this in mind, we define the homogeneous coordinates $\tilde{\mathbf{v}}$ of a point $\mathbf{v} = (x, y, z)^t$ by $\tilde{\mathbf{v}} = (wx, wy, wz, w)^t$, where w is an arbitrary constant. Clearly, the actual Cartesian coordinates of a point $\mathbf{v}$ are obtained from its homogeneous coordinates by dividing each of the first three components of the homogeneous vector by the fourth component. Homogeneous coordinates are evidently an artifact for performing a division at the price of augmenting the dimensionality of the space by one. Notice that homogeneous vectors differing only by a scale factor represent the same physical point. Thus, the two homogeneous vectors $\tilde{\mathbf{v}} = (wx, wy, wz, w)^t$ and $k\tilde{\mathbf{v}} = (kwx, kwy, kwz, kw)^t$ both represent the same physical point $\mathbf{v} = (x, y, z)^t$. We will consistently use the tilde ($\sim$) to indicate the representation of an arbitrary vector in homogeneous coordinates.

We suggested above that the direct perspective transformation given in Eq. (1) is linear when expressed in terms of homogeneous coordinates. We now assert that, under a suitable interpretation, the matrix

$$P = \begin{bmatrix} 1 & 0 & 0 & 0 \\ 0 & 1 & 0 & 0 \\ 0 & 0 & 1 & 0 \\ 0 & \dfrac{1}{f} & 0 & 1 \end{bmatrix} \tag{3}$$

is in fact the linear transformation that takes an object point (expressed in homogeneous coordinates) to its image point (also expressed in homogeneous coordinates); in other words, we assert that $\tilde{\mathbf{v}}_p = P\tilde{\mathbf{v}}$. To explore this assertion, let us carry out the indicated calculation. Given an object point $\tilde{\mathbf{v}} = (wx, wy, wz, w)^t$, we compute that the corresponding image point (in homogeneous coordinates) is given by

$$\tilde{\mathbf{v}}_n = P\tilde{\mathbf{v}} = \begin{bmatrix} wx \\ wy \\ wz \\ \dfrac{wy}{f} + w \end{bmatrix}. \tag{4}$$

Dividing each of the first three components by the fourth, we obtain the Cartesian coordinates of the picture point as

$$\mathbf{v}_p = \begin{bmatrix} \dfrac{fx}{f + y} \\ \dfrac{fy}{f + y} \\ \dfrac{fz}{f + y} \end{bmatrix}. \tag{5}$$

Notice that the second component of (5) is nonzero whenever the Y component of the object point is nonzero, which does not agree with the physical situation shown in Figure 10.2. We will shortly see that the second component of the picture point mathematically is a free variable in the inverse perspective transformation. For the moment, we will postpone a discussion of this role and emphasize that the first and third components of (5) agree with the similar triangle results of Eq. (1).

10.3.2   The Inverse Perspective Transformation

Let us now turn our attention to the inverse perspective transformation. Recall that the inverse transformation is supposed to specify the straight line upon which the object point corresponding to a given image point must lie. Since we have asserted that the direct transformation is given by the matrix P, the inverse transformation is formally given by P^{-1}; that is, from Eq. (4)

$$\tilde{\mathbf{v}} = P^{-1}\tilde{\mathbf{v}}_p \qquad (6)$$

where P^{-1} is easily found to be

$$P^{-1} = \begin{bmatrix} 1 & 0 & 0 & 0 \\ 0 & 1 & 0 & 0 \\ 0 & 0 & 1 & 0 \\ 0 & -\dfrac{1}{f} & 0 & 1 \end{bmatrix}. \qquad (7)$$

Suppose we carry out the calculation of Eq. (6). What should we use for the image point $\mathbf{v}_p$ (and hence for $\tilde{\mathbf{v}}_p$)? From the basic model of Figure 10.2 we know that the Y component of any image point is zero. However, if we take $y_p = 0$ and substitute $(wx_p, 0, wz_p, w)^t$ into (6) we find (after converting to ordinary Cartesian coordinates) that $\mathbf{v} = (x_p, 0, z_p)^t$. This will hardly do, since we want a transformation that maps a picture point into a straight line and not into a single point. A way out of this difficulty is suggested by (5); it shows that the second component of the picture point, although physically zero, is mathematically related to the distance along the optical axis from image plane to object point. Using this observation as a hint, let us take y_p as a free variable, take $\mathbf{v}_p = (x_p, y_p, z_p)^t$, and use in Eq. (6) the corresponding homogeneous representation $\tilde{\mathbf{v}}_p = (wx_p, wy_p, wz_p, w)^t$. Upon evaluating (6) and changing from homogeneous to ordinary coordinates by the usual division process, we find that

$$\mathbf{v} = \begin{bmatrix} \dfrac{fx_p}{f - y_p} \\[2ex] \dfrac{fy_p}{f - y_p} \\[2ex] \dfrac{fz_p}{f - y_p} \end{bmatrix}. \qquad (8)$$

Because y_p is a free variable, we know that for given picture coordinates x_p and z_p the object point $\mathbf{v}$ traces out some curve in space as y_p varies. The form of this curve is most easily found by eliminating the parameter y_p from the three equations of (8)

$$x = \frac{fx_p}{f - y_p} \; ; \qquad y = \frac{fy_p}{f - y_p} \; ; \qquad z = \frac{fz_p}{f - y_p} . \tag{9}$$

Upon doing this we obtain

$$x = \frac{x_p}{f}(y + f) = \frac{x_p}{z_p} z \tag{2}$$

which is exactly the Eq. (2) derived previously. Hence, we know that, treating y_p as a free variable, the inverse perspective transformation of Eq. (6) does in fact take an image point into the corresponding straight line. From an inspection of Eq. (9) we see that for y_p negative the object point is between the lens and the image plane; when $y_p = 0$ the object point coincides with the image point; finally, as y_p approaches f the object point recedes along the projecting ray to infinity.

As an aside, notice that the homogeneous coordinate representation of the perspective transformation has disadvantages as well as advantages. On the one hand, it allows us to express a nonlinear transformation in a linear form, a fact that has some pleasant consequences in subsequent analysis. On the other hand, it results in a lack of mathematical purity; the matrix P^{-1} certainly maps a picture point into the corresponding straight line (using y_p as a free variable), but the matrix P maps an object point into a picture point only under an interpretation that requires us to ignore the second component of a vector. We could, of course, delete the second row of P and have a more straight-forward direct transformation, but then P^{-1} would not even exist. The underlying reason is that P maps an object point into a three-dimensional vector (after converting to ordinary coordinates), one of whose components has nothing to do with the physical picture point, but which is related to the distance from camera to object point. The general conclusion is that the homogeneous representation is useful, but must be used thoughtfully.

The inverse perspective transformation can be cast in another useful form by means of the following simple analysis. Let v_l be the location of the lens center; that is, $v_l = (0, -f, 0)^t$. Then directly from Figure 10.2 we see that any point v on the projecting ray can be written as

$$v = v_l + \lambda(v_p - v_l) \tag{10}$$

where λ is a free parameter ranging over the non-negative real numbers and v_p is the actual picture point $(x_p, 0, z_p)^t$. We can express the relation between λ and y_p by equating any of the components of the vector equation (10) with the corresponding component of (8) to obtain

$$\lambda = \frac{f}{f - y_p} \qquad (11)$$

or

$$y_p = \frac{f(\lambda - 1)}{\lambda}.$$

Thus, if we follow the ray from the lens center ($\lambda = 0$) through the picture plane ($\lambda = 1$) and on out into space, y_p increases monotonically from minus infinity to f, being negative for points behind the picture plane, zero for points on the picture plane, and positive for points in front of the picture plane.

Let us recapitulate our introductory discussion of perspective transformations. The matrix P of Eq. (3) maps an object point into its corresponding image point, both points being expressed in homogeneous coordinates. The actual picture coordinates are given by the first and third components of Eq. (5). The matrix P^{-1} maps an image point (expressed in homogeneous coordinates) into an object point (also expressed in homogeneous coordinates) that traces out the projecting ray as the free variable y_p varies. The equation of this ray is given in parametric form by Eq. (9) and explicitly by Eq. (2). An alternative parametrization that is sometimes more convenient is given in Eq. (10).

In the next section we will extend these results to a setting of much greater practical interest.

10.4   PERSPECTIVE TRANSFORMATIONS WITH TWO REFERENCE FRAMES

In practice the transformations given in the previous section are hard to use because of an awkwardness of coordinate systems. It is true that the single reference frame of Figure 10.2 is very convenient for locating picture points; after all, it is centered at the center of the image plane. By the same token, however, it is notably inconvenient for locating object points, since it constrains us to measure distances to a set of axes whose position is determined by the camera.* In other words, the system used in the last section is "camera-centric," and this is often unnatural and bothersome. In order to rectify this situation we ideally need two coordinate systems: a *picture coordinate*

---

* Note that although the previous discussion used homogeneous coordinates to simplify the mathematics, all points were physically expressed in a single Cartesian coordinate system.

system in which to locate picture points, and a *global* or *world coordinate system* in which to locate everything else. Figure 10.3 illustrates one version of the coordinate systems we have in mind. The global reference system, which in the figure has unprimed coordinates, is used to locate both the camera and the object point **v**. The camera is translated from the origin, panned through an angle θ, and tilted through an angle φ. The image point is measured with respect to an image coordinate system, primed in Figure 10.3, that is identical to the single reference frame used in the last section. In this section we will use a change of coordinates to generalize the previous results to the two-reference-frame situation depicted in Figure 10.3. Our final result will be a pair of transformations in which all quantities are expressed in the co-ordinate system most appropriate for their representation.

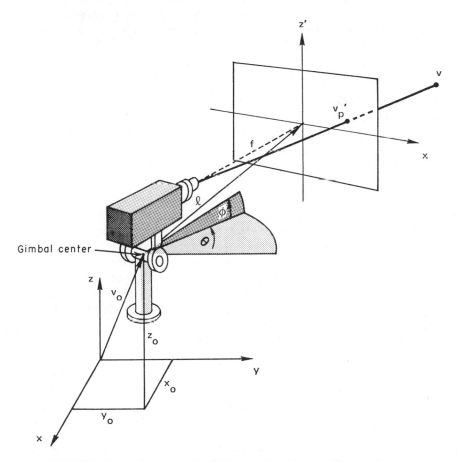

FIGURE 10.3. Perspective transformation with two reference frames.

Before proceeding with the formal manipulations we have a side comment to make. A change of coordinates is one of those things that everyone knows can be done, but that few like to do themselves. Accordingly, the impatient reader may want to skip to the results of Eqs. (18) and (26), after first making sure that he understands the meaning of the geometrical parameters described in the following paragraph. For those interested in the details, we will try to minimize confusion by adhering faithfully to the following conventions. We will let primed and unprimed symbols represent the same physical point expressed in the primed (picture) and unprimed (global) coordinate systems. Thus, v and v' both refer to the identical point. Now with each Cartesian reference frame there is an associated homogeneous coordinate representation obtained in the standard way described previously. We will continue to use the tilde ($\sim$) to indicate this, so that $\tilde{v}$ and $\tilde{v}'$ both refer ultimately to the same physical point: namely the point whose Cartesian coordinates are v in the unprimed global system and v' in the image coordinate system.

10.4.1 Direct Perspective Transformation: Two Reference Frames

The overall transformation of coordinates that we want is the mapping between the unprimed global coordinate system and the primed image coordinate system. In order to define this mapping, we must define the position and orientation of the image reference frame with respect to the global frame. This can be done in the following three steps. First, we translate the global system to the center of rotation of the camera (which might be called the gimbal center). Then we pan and tilt the axes so that the Y axis is aligned with the optical axis of the camera. (The resulting reference frame will be called the gimbal coordinate system.) Finally, we translate the gimbal reference frame from the gimbal center to the center of the image plane. Let us set down some notation. We will let $v_0 = (x_0, y_0, z_0)^t$ be the vector from the origin of the global frame to the gimbal center. Let θ be the pan angle of the camera, measured counterclockwise from the Y axis; let φ be the tilt angle of the camera, measured positive in an upward direction. Let the vector l be the constant offset between gimbal center and image plane center, where l is measured in the gimbal coordinate system.* It is convenient to write the offset l as $l = (l_1, l_2 + f, l_3)^t$, so that if the gimbal center were at the lens center we would have $l_1 = l_2 = l_3 = 0$ and a constant offset of f along the optical axis. To illustrate this notation, Figure 10.3 shows schematically a translation vector v_0 with all positive components, a positive pan and tilt angle, and an offset vector that has a zero-valued first component.

---

* Strictly speaking, we should use something like double primes to indicate that the offset vector is measured with respect to the gimbal reference system.

The actual transformation of coordinates can be performed in a routine fashion to obtain the result we need. However, the transformation is especially elegant if we resort to homogeneous coordinates; in this setting pure translation, which is a non-linear operation in ordinary Cartesian coordinates, becomes linear. In particular, it is easily verified that the matrix

$$T = \begin{bmatrix} 1 & 0 & 0 & -x_0 \\ 0 & 1 & 0 & -y_0 \\ 0 & 0 & 1 & -z_0 \\ 0 & 0 & 0 & 1 \end{bmatrix} \tag{12}$$

maps the homogeneous representation of the vector $(x, y, z)^t$ into the homogeneous representation of the vector $(x - x_0, y - y_0, z - z_0)^t$. Moreover, a pure rotation operation, which is a linear transformation in three-dimensional Cartesian coordinates, remains linear in homogeneous coordinates. It is not hard to verify that the matrix

$$R = \begin{bmatrix} \cos\theta & \sin\theta & 0 & 0 \\ -\cos\varphi\sin\theta & \cos\varphi\cos\theta & \sin\varphi & 0 \\ \sin\varphi\sin\theta & -\sin\varphi\cos\theta & \cos\varphi & 0 \\ 0 & 0 & 0 & 1 \end{bmatrix} \tag{13}$$

is in fact the rotation operator that pans through an angle θ and tilts through an angle φ. In other words, given the homogeneous coordinates $\tilde{v}$ of a point with respect to the global reference frame, $R\tilde{v}$ gives the homogeneous coordinates of the same point with respect to a picture reference frame panned through θ and tilted through φ. Finally, the matrix G for performing the gimbal offset is, analogously to Eq. (12), given by

$$G = \begin{bmatrix} 1 & 0 & 0 & -l_1 \\ 0 & 1 & 0 & -(l_2 + f) \\ 0 & 0 & 1 & -l_3 \\ 0 & 0 & 0 & 1 \end{bmatrix}. \tag{14}$$

Hence, the complete change of reference systems, expressed in homogeneous coordinates, is given by the matrix product GRT. Adhering to the conventions about tildes and primes, we write

$$\tilde{v}' = GRT\tilde{v}. \tag{15}$$

At this point we are almost finished. The perspective transformation itself is clearest when all points are expressed in image coordinates, as we saw in the previous section. Rewriting Eq. (4) with primes to denote image coordinates, we have

$$\tilde{\mathbf{v}}'_p = P\tilde{\mathbf{v}}'. \tag{16}$$

Combining the change of coordinates (15) with the perspective transformation (16) we have

$$\tilde{\mathbf{v}}'_p = PGRT\tilde{\mathbf{v}}. \tag{17}$$

Eq. (17) is the formal solution to our problem. It maps an object point expressed in homogeneous global coordinates into an image point expressed in homogeneous picture coordinates, with all the geometrical descriptors of the camera as parameters.

While Eq. (17) is a convenient form for certain applications, we will be able to derive a number of interesting and useful facts if we carry out the actual calculation and then convert the results to ordinary Cartesian coordinates. Specifically, suppose we have an object point $\mathbf{v} = (x, y, z)$, and want to find its image point (x'_p, z'_p) (recall from the previous section that only the first and third components of the image point are meaningful). Substituting the homogeneous representation $\tilde{\mathbf{v}} = (wx, wy, wz, w)^t$ in Eq. (17) and dividing the first and third component of the resulting vector by the fourth component, we obtain a result of major importance:

$$
\begin{aligned}
x'_p &= f\frac{(x - x_0)\cos\theta + (y - y_0)\sin\theta - l_1}{-(x - x_0)\cos\varphi\sin\theta + (y - y_0)\cos\varphi\cos\theta + (z - z_0)\sin\varphi - l_2} \\
z'_p &= f\frac{(x - x_0)\sin\varphi\sin\theta - (y - y_0)\sin\varphi\cos\theta + (z - z_0)\cos\varphi - l_3}{-(x - x_0)\cos\varphi\sin\theta + (y - y_0)\cos\varphi\cos\theta + (z - z_0)\sin\varphi - l_2}.
\end{aligned}
\tag{18}
$$

A discussion of these formidable-looking expressions will be postponed until we have on hand the analogous equations for the inverse transformation.

10.4.2   Inverse Perspective Transformation: Two Reference Frames

The general inverse perspective transformation in homogeneous coordinates can be obtained most easily from the direct transformation (17). Since each of the four matrices has an inverse,

$$\tilde{\mathbf{v}} = T^{-1}R^{-1}G^{-1}P^{-1}\tilde{\mathbf{v}}'_p. \tag{19}$$

It is easily verified that

$$T^{-1} = \begin{bmatrix} 1 & 0 & 0 & x_0 \\ 0 & 1 & 0 & y_0 \\ 0 & 0 & 1 & z_0 \\ 0 & 0 & 0 & 1 \end{bmatrix}, \tag{20}$$

$$G^{-1} = \begin{bmatrix} 1 & 0 & 0 & l_1 \\ 0 & 1 & 0 & l_2 + f \\ 0 & 0 & 1 & l_3 \\ 0 & 0 & 0 & 1 \end{bmatrix}, \tag{21}$$

and

$$R^{-1} = R^t. \tag{22}$$

As we did for the direct transformation, it is useful to evaluate (19) and convert the results to ordinary Cartesian coordinates by dividing each of the first three components of $\tilde{\mathbf{v}}$ by the fourth. As usual, we will let $\tilde{\mathbf{v}}'_p = (wx'_p, wy'_p, wz'_p, w)^t$ where y'_p is the free parameter. After a boring calculation, we obtain the object point $\mathbf{v}$ as

$$\mathbf{v} = \frac{1}{f - y'_p} \begin{bmatrix} (fx'_p - l_1 y'_p + l_1 f)\cos\theta + (l_2 y'_p - l_2 f - f^2)\cos\varphi\sin\theta \\ \quad - (l_3 y'_p - fz'_p - l_3 f)\sin\varphi\sin\theta \\ (fx'_p - l_1 y'_p + l_1 f)\sin\theta - (l_2 y'_p - l_2 f - f^2)\cos\varphi\cos\theta \\ \quad + (l_3 y'_p - fz'_p - l_3 f)\sin\varphi\cos\theta \\ -(l_2 y'_p - l_2 f - f^2)\sin\varphi - (l_3 y'_p - fz'_p - l_3 f)\cos\varphi \end{bmatrix} + \begin{bmatrix} x_0 \\ y_0 \\ z_0 \end{bmatrix}. \tag{23}$$

Once again, the inverse transformation can be cast into a more useful form by writing the object point $\mathbf{v}$ as

$$\mathbf{v} = \mathbf{v}_l + \lambda(\mathbf{v}_p - \mathbf{v}_l), \tag{10}$$

where the lens point $\mathbf{v}_l$ is found by letting y'_p approach minus infinity in (23), and the picture point $\mathbf{v}_p$ (expressed in global coordinates) is found by letting y'_p be zero. Upon evaluating (23) for these quantities, we find that

$$\mathbf{v}_p = \begin{bmatrix} x_0 \\ y_0 \\ z_0 \end{bmatrix} + \begin{bmatrix} (x'_p + l_1)\cos\theta - (f + l_2)\cos\varphi\sin\theta + (z'_p + l_3)\sin\varphi\sin\theta \\ (x'_p + l_1)\sin\theta + (f + l_2)\cos\varphi\cos\theta - (z'_p + l_3)\sin\varphi\cos\theta \\ (f + l_2)\sin\varphi \qquad + (z'_p + l_3)\cos\varphi \end{bmatrix} \tag{24}$$

and

$$
\mathbf{v}_l = \begin{bmatrix} x_0 \\ y_0 \\ z_0 \end{bmatrix} + \begin{bmatrix} l_1 \cos\theta - l_2 \cos\varphi \sin\theta + l_3 \sin\varphi \sin\theta \\ l_1 \sin\theta + l_2 \cos\varphi \cos\theta - l_3 \sin\varphi \cos\theta \\ l_2 \sin\varphi \quad + l_3 \cos\varphi \end{bmatrix}. \tag{25}
$$

Combining Eqs. (10), (24), and (25), we arrive at our final expression giving the projecting ray in terms of the picture point (x_p', z_p'), a free non-negative parameter λ, and all of the camera geometry parameters:

$$
\mathbf{v} = \begin{bmatrix} x \\ y \\ z \end{bmatrix} = \begin{bmatrix} x_0 + l_1 \cos\theta - l_2 \cos\varphi \sin\theta + l_3 \sin\varphi \sin\theta \\ y_0 + l_1 \sin\theta + l_2 \cos\varphi \cos\theta - l_3 \sin\varphi \cos\theta \\ z_0 + l_2 \sin\varphi + l_3 \cos\varphi \end{bmatrix}
$$
$$
+ \lambda \begin{bmatrix} x_p' \cos\theta - f \cos\varphi \sin\theta + z_p' \sin\varphi \sin\theta \\ x_p' \sin\theta + f \cos\varphi \cos\theta - z_p' \sin\varphi \cos\theta \\ f \sin\varphi + z_p' \cos\varphi \end{bmatrix}. \tag{26}
$$

Let us summarize the results of this section. We have generalized the simple projective model to a two-coordinate-systems model, so that all quantities can be measured in a natural way. Equations (17) and (19) give the direct and inverse perspective transformations in homogeneous coordinates, where the homogeneous coordinates of image and object points are referred, respectively, to image and global Cartesian coordinates. Equations (18) and (26) express the transformations in terms of the picture and global Cartesian coordinates themselves. In the next section we will illustrate these results by applying them in a number of different situations.

10.5   ILLUSTRATIVE APPLICATIONS

10.5.1   Camera Calibration

The perspective transformations derived in the preceding sections all embody certain geometrical parameters. Even in the simplest case, the distance f from image plane to pinhole lens must be known in order to define the transformation completely. In the more general case we need to know the translation, rotation, and offset parameters as well. While in principle these parameters can be directly measured, in practice it is usually more convenient to determine at least some of the parameters using the camera itself as the measuring instrument. The basic idea is to set the parameters to values that minimize the deviation between measured and computed positions of image points.

Suppose, then, that we have on hand a photograph showing images of several points whose global coordinates are known. Let $\{\mathbf{v}_i\}$, $i = 1, \ldots, n$ be the set of n object points and let $\{\mathbf{v}'_{pi}\}$, $i = 1, \ldots, n$ be their corresponding images. Now Eq. (18) gives the coordinates of an image point in terms of an object point and the geometrical parameters. Let us write the functional form of (18) as

$$\mathbf{v}'_p = \mathbf{h}(\mathbf{v}, \boldsymbol{\pi}),$$

where $\mathbf{h}$ is a vector-valued function giving the computed picture coordinates of the image of $\mathbf{v}$, and $\boldsymbol{\pi}$ is a parameter vector whose components are the geometrical parameters to be determined. One obvious way to determine these parameters is to choose $\boldsymbol{\pi}$ so that the computed positions $\mathbf{h}(\mathbf{v}_i, \boldsymbol{\pi})$ of the images are near their actual positions $\mathbf{v}'_{pi}$—for example, so that

$$\sum_{i=1}^{n} \| \mathbf{v}'_{pi} - \mathbf{h}(\mathbf{v}_i, \boldsymbol{\pi}) \|^2$$

is minimized. The minimization can be carried out in various ways. Suppose, as a very simple example, that the only unspecified parameter is f, the distance from pinhole lens to image plane. This number merely sets the scale of the final picture; doubling f doubles the picture size, as both the basic proportional triangle argument and Eq. (18) demonstrate. Hence, f can be found by analytically minimizing the error function, using any number of object and image points as input data. More generally, when there are a large number of unspecified parameters, the error function is minimized numerically by gradient-following search methods. (In Sec. 12.3 we outline a method for determining a reasonable starting point for a gradient search.)

10.5.2 Object Location

We have seen that, in general, the location of an object point is not determined uniquely by its photographic image. All that can be said is that the object point lies somewhere along the projecting ray defined by lens center and picture point. Occasionally, however, we may have some additional prior knowledge about the object point corresponding to a given image point. For example, we may know the distance from camera to object point, or we may know that the object point lies on some wall, floor, or other specified surface. Since the projecting ray is a one-parameter system, any such prior information can be used in conjunction with the image point to specify uniquely the location of the object point.

As an example of the foregoing, suppose we want to find the location of an object point known a priori to lie on the floor. For simplicity we will assume that the global coordinate system has been set up with the X–Y plane coincident with the floor, so that our prior information consists of the single fact that the Z-coordinate of the object point is zero. Again for simplicity, let us assume that the center of rotation of the camera is at the lens center, so that the offset vector l is zero. Since the object point lies on the floor, the third component of Eq. (26) must be zero; hence we can first solve for λ by setting $z = 0$ and then substitute back in (26) to find the unknown X and Y coordinates of $\mathbf{v}$.* If we do this, we find that

$$x = x_0 - \frac{z_0 x_p' \cos \theta + (z_p' \sin \varphi - f \cos \varphi)(z_0 \sin \theta)}{z_p' \cos \varphi + f \sin \varphi}$$

$$y = y_0 - \frac{z_0 x_p' \sin \theta - (z_p' \sin \varphi - f \cos \varphi)(z_0 \cos \theta)}{z_p' \cos \varphi + f \sin \varphi}.$$

10.5.3 Vertical Lines: Perspective Distortion

There are several interesting properties of pictures that can be derived by applying the direct transformation (18) to simple physical situations. For our present purpose, we don't need the full generality of Eq. (18); the effects we want to show can be demonstrated even if all the camera location parameters are zero with the single exception of the tilt angle φ. Accordingly, we will take $x_0 = y_0 = z_0 = l_1 = l_2 = l_3 = \theta = 0$, and reduce (18) to the much simpler form

$$x_p' = \frac{fx}{y \cos \varphi + z \sin \varphi}$$

$$z_p' = \frac{-fy \sin \varphi + fz \cos \varphi}{y \cos \varphi + z \sin \varphi}.$$

(27)

Let us investigate the properties of the image of a vertical line. The vertical object line is traced out by an object point

$$\mathbf{v} = \begin{bmatrix} x \\ y \\ z \end{bmatrix} = \begin{bmatrix} x_1 \\ y_1 \\ z \end{bmatrix},$$

where x_1 and y_1 are the coordinates of the point where the line pierces the floor plane and z is a free parameter ranging over all the real numbers. If we substitute $\mathbf{v}$ into (27) and eliminate the free parameter z between the two

---

* The idea of using a point on the floor for establishing object location was developed by Roberts (1965), who called the underlying assumption the *support hypothesis*.

equations we obtain the equation of a straight line in the image plane:*

$$z'_p = \left(\frac{-y_1}{x_1 \sin \varphi}\right)x'_p + \frac{f}{\tan \varphi}.$$

(28)

An inspection of this simple equation yields a number of interesting observations. Most important of these is that the Z' intercept does not depend upon the location of the vertical line itself; it only depends upon the line being in fact vertical. Thus, for given camera geometry, the images of all vertical lines pass through the unique *vertical vanishing point* whose picture coordinates are $(0, f/\tan \varphi)$. Figure 10.4 illustrates this effect with a picture of a single

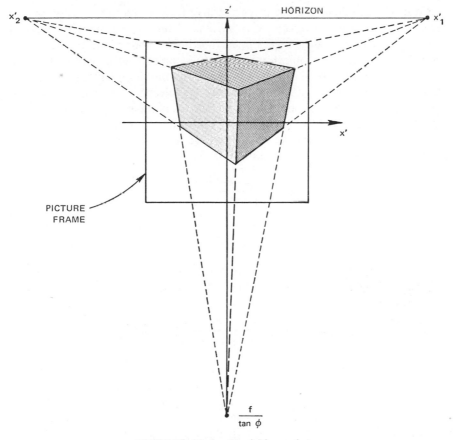

FIGURE 10.4.   Vanishing points.

* An elementary argument shows that the projective transformation carries straight lines into straight lines, so the form of the result could have been anticipated.

rectangular parallelepiped taken by a camera tilted sharply downward ($\varphi < 0$). The reader can verify other properties of Eq. (28) that conform with intuition. For example, as $|\varphi|$ increases from zero to 90 degrees the vertical vanishing point moves towards the center of the picture plane and the slope becomes flatter. Similarly, for a given tilt angle this effect becomes more pronounced as the vertical object lines moves towards the periphery of the field of view (that is, as $|x_1|$ becomes large compared to y_1). In summary, the vertical vanishing point can be computed from the camera parameters alone, and yields a simple necessary condition on the images of vertical lines.

10.5.4   Horizontal Lines and Vanishing Points

As a final example of the use of perspective transformations, let us explore some properties of the image of a horizontal line. For simplicity, we will consider the image of an object line lying in the floor plane of the global coordinate system. Any object point $\mathbf{v} = (x, y, z)^t$ on such a line has the form $(x, mx + b, 0)^t$, where m and b are respectively the slope and Y-intercept of the line. Since we want to take a picture of an object on the floor, the camera had better be raised above the floor and perhaps pointed downward. Accordingly, we will take the geometrical camera parameters as $x_0 = y_0 = l_1 = l_2 = l_3 = \theta = 0$, and let z_0 be positive and φ be negative. For these parameters the direct transformation (18) simplifies to

$$x'_p = \frac{fx}{y \cos \varphi + (z - z_0) \sin \varphi}$$

$$z'_p = \frac{-fy \sin \varphi + f(z - z_0) \cos \varphi}{y \cos \varphi + (z - z_0) \sin \varphi}. \tag{29}$$

Upon substituting $(x, mx + b, 0)^t$ in (29) and eliminating the free parameter x between the two equations, we obtain the equation of a straight line in the image plane:

$$z'_p = \frac{-mz_0 x'_p + f(b \sin \varphi + z_0 \cos \varphi)}{z_0 \sin \varphi - b \cos \varphi}. \tag{30}$$

There is nothing particularly simple about either the slope or the intercept of this image line; however, let us consider the intersection of the image line with the *horizon line* of the picture. The horizon line of any picture is defined to be the intersection of the picture plane with a plane through the lens center parallel to the floor. As illustrated in the end-on view of Figure 10.5, the equation (in picture coordinates) of the horizon line is $z' = -f \tan \varphi$. Evidently, the X'-intercept of the image line (30) with the horizon line is found by equating (30) to $-f(\tan \varphi)$. Upon solving for the horizon intercept

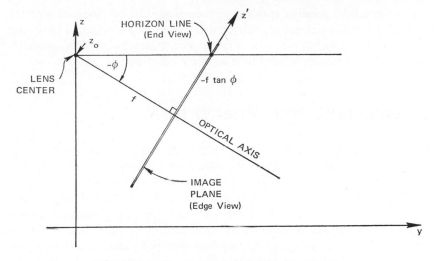

FIGURE 10.5.   Computation of the horizon line.

x'_h we find that

$$x'_h = \frac{f}{m \cos \varphi}.\tag{31}$$

This result could also have been obtained by substituting $(x, mx + b, 0)$ in the first equation of (29) and letting x become infinite. Hence, the horizon intercept well deserves being called the horizontal or *horizon vanishing point* of the image of the line; it is the limit of the image point as the object point recedes to infinity along the straight line $y = mx + b$.

We can make a number of interesting observations about Eq. (31). First, notice that the vanishing point does not depend upon the distance z_0 of the camera above the plane containing the object line. Further, it does not depend upon the translation parameter b of the object line. Hence, we can draw the important conclusion that any two lines parallel to the floor plane have the same vanishing point if and only if they are parallel to each other. As a final note, suppose we have two orthogonal object lines lying in a plane parallel to the floor. Let their slopes be m_1 and m_2 and their horizon vanishing points have intercepts x'_1 and x'_2. Since the lines are orthogonal, $m_1 m_2 = -1$. Hence, directly from Eq. (31) we have

$$x'_1 x'_2 = \frac{-f^2}{\cos^2 \varphi}.\tag{32}$$

The two vanishing points x'_1 and x'_2 are sometimes called *conjugate vanishing* *points.** Since their product is negative they always lie on opposite sides of the center line of the picture, as illustrated in Figure 10.4. Conjugate vanishing points are one example of how a given constraint on objects (namely, orthogonality) can be translated into a simple constraint on images.

10.6 STEREOSCOPIC PERCEPTION

We have emphasized several times that the perspective transformation is many-to-one, so that a given image point does not uniquely determine the location of its corresponding object point. The standard method for supplying the additional information needed to achieve uniqueness is called *stereoscopy*, and is based upon the use of two pictures. The basic arrangement for stereoscopy, or stereoscopic perception, is illustrated in Figure 10.6. We have shown two image planes I_1 and I_2, two lens centers $\mathbf{L}_1$ and $\mathbf{L}_2$, and two projecting rays r_1 and r_2 between respective lens centers and an object point $\mathbf{v}$. The

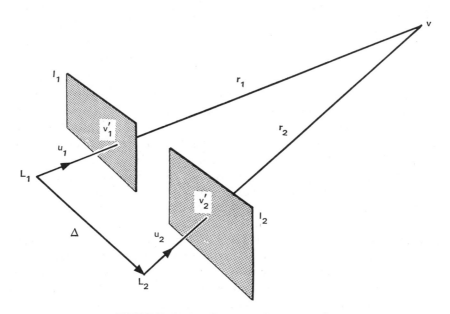

FIGURE 10.6.   Geometry for stereopsis.

* Strictly speaking, x_1' and x_2' are only the X' coordinates of the vanishing points. We ignore this distinction because for a given picture the horizon line, and hence the Z' coordinate, is fixed.

vectors $\mathbf{u}_1$ and $\mathbf{u}_2$ are taken to be unit vectors in the direction of the projecting rays. The vector $\mathbf{\Delta} = \mathbf{L}_2 - \mathbf{L}_1$ is called the *baseline vector;* its magnitude is called simply the baseline. For clarity, both global and local coordinate systems have been omitted from Figure 10.6.

Evidently, a stereoscopic calculation involves two separate parts. First, the two image points $\mathbf{v}_1'$ and $\mathbf{v}_2'$ corresponding to the object point $\mathbf{v}$ must be located. Second, a trigonometric calculation must be performed to determine the intersection of the two projecting rays. Let us briefly consider the first requirement, often referred to as the *correspondence problem.* It is usually satisfied in one of two ways. The most straightforward way is simply to identify, using one means or another, the location of the image of $\mathbf{v}$ in each of the pictures. Often, however, it is easier to locate the image of $\mathbf{v}$ in one of the pictures and then use a template matching procedure to locate the corresponding image in the other picture. Specifically, suppose the point $\mathbf{v}_1'$ is located first. Then, since we seek a point (or small region) of I_2 that matches $\mathbf{v}_1'$, we use as the template a small region of I_1 centered on $\mathbf{v}_1'$. The template so constructed is scanned across I_2 until a match is found. Notice, however, that Figure 10.6 suggests an important simplification; $\mathbf{v}_2'$ always lies on the plane defined by $\mathbf{L}_1$, $\mathbf{L}_2$, and $\mathbf{v}_1'$. Hence, the template need be scanned only along the line defined by the intersection of this plane with the image plane. Further, the X' coordinate of $\mathbf{v}_2'$ must always be algebraically smaller than that of $\mathbf{v}_1'$; otherwise, the projecting rays would converge behind the image planes (which would mean that the object point is behind the cameras). Thus, the template need be scanned over only a small region of I_2, and this accounts for the convenience of the method in many problems.

Let us now turn our attention to the trigonometric problem of determining the intersection of the two projecting rays. Ideally, there exist two numbers, say a and b, such that $a\mathbf{u}_1 = \mathbf{\Delta} + b\mathbf{u}_2$. Upon finding such numbers one would merely set $\mathbf{v} = \mathbf{L}_1 + a\mathbf{u}_1$. In practice, however, we can take it for granted that the two projecting rays will fail to intersect because of various errors. A reasonable recourse in this case is to place $\mathbf{v}$ midway between the two projecting rays at their point of closest approach. Formally, we set

$$\mathbf{v} = \frac{a_0\mathbf{u}_1 + (\mathbf{\Delta} + b_0\mathbf{u}_2)}{2} + \mathbf{L}_1 \tag{33}$$

where a_0 and b_0 are the values of a and b that minimize

$$J(a, b) = \|a\mathbf{u}_1 - (\mathbf{\Delta} + b\mathbf{u}_2)\|^2. \tag{34}$$

As a special case, notice that if the projecting rays do in fact intersect then the minimum value of $J(a, b)$ is zero, $a_0\mathbf{u}_1 = \mathbf{\Delta} + b_0\mathbf{u}_2$, and $\mathbf{v} = a_0\mathbf{u}_1 + \mathbf{L}_1$. One can easily verify by elementary calculus methods that $J(a, b)$ is minimized by setting

$$a_0 = \frac{\mathbf{u}_1 \cdot \mathbf{\Delta} - (\mathbf{u}_1 \cdot \mathbf{u}_2)(\mathbf{u}_2 \cdot \mathbf{\Delta})}{1 - (\mathbf{u}_1 \cdot \mathbf{u}_2)^2}$$

$$b_0 = \frac{(\mathbf{u}_1 \cdot \mathbf{u}_2)(\mathbf{u}_1 \cdot \mathbf{\Delta}) - (\mathbf{u}_2 \cdot \mathbf{\Delta})}{1 - (\mathbf{u}_1 \cdot \mathbf{u}_2)^2}.$$

(35)

It remains to specify $\mathbf{L}_1$ (the location of the first lens center) and the two unit vectors $\mathbf{u}_1$ and $\mathbf{u}_2$ in the direction of the projecting rays. These quantities are available from our discussion of the inverse perspective transformation. The lens location of an arbitrary camera is given by Eq. (25). A vector in the direction of the projecting ray is defined by $\mathbf{v}_p - \mathbf{L}$, where the global coordinates of the picture point $\mathbf{v}_p$ are given by (24). Hence, in (33) and (35) we set

$$\mathbf{u}_i = \frac{\mathbf{v}_{p_i} - \mathbf{L}_i}{\|\mathbf{v}_{p_i} - \mathbf{L}_i\|}$$

(36)

where of course the i subscripts the picture and lens points of the two cameras.

Summarizing, the location of the object point $\mathbf{v}$ corresponding to two given picture points $\mathbf{v}'_{p_1}$ and $\mathbf{v}'_{p_2}$ is given by Eq. (33), where a_0 and b_0 are given by Eq. (35). The two unit vectors $\mathbf{u}_1$ and $\mathbf{u}_2$ are obtained by substituting Eqs. (24) and (25) into Eq. (36).

Equation (33), which we might call the stereopsis or triangulation equation, is typically employed simply to establish the location of the object point corresponding to a specified pair of image points. However, it can also be used to gain some insight into the nature of the picture-taking process. As an illustration of this, let us use Eq. (33) to investigate the effect of picture quantization on triangulation accuracy. Imagine an experiment in which two pictures of a single object point $\mathbf{v}$ are taken with two different cameras. Let each of the pictures be quantized, so that the true image points are replaced by the center points of the grid cells in which they fall. If the object point corresponding to the quantized image points is computed using Eq. (33), in general the resulting vector will be different from the original object point $\mathbf{v}$. One measure of this difference is the percentage range error, where range is defined as the distance from an object point to the midpoint of the baseline. It is intuitively clear that the percentage range error will typically increase as the true range increases, for as the true range increases the projecting rays become more nearly parallel and small errors are likely to have severe consequences. Accordingly, consider an experiment in which an object point is moved further and further from the cameras; for simplicity, we can always maintain the object point on the optical axis of the first camera, which amounts to insuring that quantization error will occur only in the second picture. A top view of this arrangement is shown in Figure 10.7. In an actual

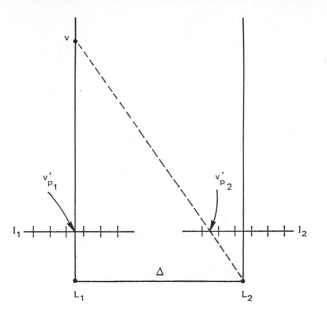

FIGURE 10.7.   **Diagram for stereopsis experiment.**

implementation of this experiment, the picture plane was arbitrarily quantized onto a grid whose cell size was $f/200$, and the results of the experiment plotted in Figure 10.8. The curious serrated nature of the error curve is easily interpreted with the aid of Figure 10.7. As the object point v recedes along the principal ray of the first camera, its image moves from left to right across the second picture plane. The quantized image, therefore, is first to the right and then to the left of the true image, making the projecting rays first too nearly parallel and then too convergent. Consequently, the computed location of the object point is first too far away (positive range error) and then too near (negative range error). Finally, as the object point recedes the image point enters the next quantization cell and the process repeats, but with increasingly larger swings because the projecting rays are more nearly parallel.

10.7 BIBLIOGRAPHICAL AND HISTORICAL REMARKS

Our purpose in this chapter has been to introduce perspective transformations in a form appropriate to scene analysis applications. The topic is properly a part of projective geometry, a subject whose foundations go back

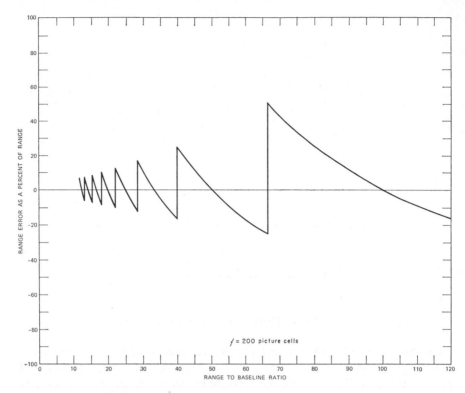

FIGURE 10.8.   Result of stereopsis experiment.

at least to 1639 and the time of Desargues, and that was systematically developed in the 19th century by such famous geometers as Poncelet, Möbius, Plücker, Steiner, and von Staudt. Although there are many modern introductions to projective geometry—for example, the standard texts by Coxeter (1961) and Graustein (1963)—the point of view is quite different from ours and the material a bit diffuse for the reader interested in scene analysis. In a similar vein, photogrammetrists have a proprietary interest in perspective transformations, but the central problems confronting them motivate methods that are not typically of immediate interest to us. Readers interested in a comprehensive overview of photogrammetry are referred to the monumental *Manual of Photogrammetry*;* Ghosh (1968) gives a mathematical discussion of stereophotogrammetry.

Having bypassed the extensive literature on projective geometry and photogrammetry, we can offer only a very few references treating perspective

---

* *Manual of Photogrammetry*, Third Edition (2 vols.), published by the American Society of Photogrammetry, Washington, D.C., (1966). (No author or editor named.)

transformations from the viewpoint of scene analysis. Roberts (1965) introduced these transformations to the pattern recognition community in his classic paper on three-dimensional machine perception, and our development follows his in its essential features. An unpublished report by Hart (1969) on stereoscopic calculations discusses the sensitivity of the triangulation process to pan, tilt and quantization errors. Sobel (1970) was concerned with the problem of camera calibration.

Interest in perspective transformations and allied topics is also motivated by the desire to depict three-dimensional objects on computer-driven displays. Ahuja and Coons (1968) give an exposition of the use of perspective transformations for display purposes. Warnock (1968), Loutrel (1970), and Bouknight (1970) all give algorithms for solving the so-called "hidden line problem" associated with the display of three-dimensional objects.

For many years psychologists have studied how humans perceive pictorial representations of three-dimensional scenes. Although this work has not often led directly to techniques for automatically analyzing pictures, it provides interesting background material. We cite three particularly readable books in this area. Gregory (1970) presents evidence for the importance of depth information for human visual perception, and illustrates his points with three-dimensional pictures. Pirenne (1970) gives an entirely non-mathematical discussion of the perspective transformation, and uses many photographs taken with a pinhole camera to illustrate its properties. Finally, Julesz (1971) describes many remarkable phenomena disclosed by his random-dot stereograms that vividly illustrate the perceptual processes at work in the deeper centers of the brain.

REFERENCES

1. Ahuja, D. V. and S. A. Coons, "Geometry for Construction and Display," *IBM Systems Journal*, **7**, Nos. 3 and 4, 188–205 (1968).

2. Bouknight, W. J., "A Procedure for Generation of Three-Dimensional Half-Toned Computer Graphics Presentations," *Comm. ACM*, **13**, 527–536 (September 1970).

3. Coxeter, H. S. M., *The Real Projective Plane* (Cambridge University Press, Cambridge, 1961).

4. Ghosh, S. K., *Theory of Stereophotogrammetry* (Ohio State University, Department of Geodetic Science, Columbus, Ohio, 1968).

5. Graustein, W. C., *Introduction to Higher Geometry* (Macmillan, New York, 1963).

6. Gregory, R. L., *The Intelligent Eye* (McGraw-Hill, New York, 1970).

7. Hart, P. E., "Stereographic Perception of 3-dimensional Scenes," Final Report, SRI Project 7642, Stanford Research Institute, Menlo Park, California (August 1969).

8. Julez, B., *Foundations of Cyclopean Perception* (University of Chicago Press, Chicago and London, 1971).

9. Loutrel, P. P., "A Solution to the Hidden-Line Problem for Computer-Drawn Polyhedra," *IEEE Trans. Comp.*, **C-19**, 205–213 (March 1970).

10. Pirenne, M. H., *Optics, Painting, and Photography* (Cambridge University Press, New York, 1970).

11. Roberts, L. G., "Machine Perception of Three-Dimensional Solids," in *Optical and Electro-Optical Information Processing*, pp. 159–197, J. T. Tippett, et al., eds. (MIT Press, Cambridge, Massachusetts, 1965).

12. Sobel, Irwin, "Camera Models and Machine Perception," Stanford Artificial Intelligence Project, Memo AIM-121, Computer Science Department, Stanford University (May 1970).

13. Warnock, J. E., "A Hidden-Line Algorithm for Halftone Picture Representations," Tech. Rept. 4–5, Department of Computer Science, University of Utah, Salt Lake City, Utah (May 1968).

PROBLEMS

1.   Show that the general bilinear function of three variables x, y, and z can be written as a linear transformation of x, y, z, and w if homogeneous coordinates are used.

2.   Show analytically that an arbitrary line in space projects onto a line in a given picture plane.

3.   Generalize Eq. (18) to allow the camera to rotate on its own optical axis.

4.   Suppose the camera translation parameters x_0 and y_0 and the pan angle θ are unknown. Show how these parameters can be determined analytically (i.e., without search) from a picture showing an arbitrary line and point lying in the floor plane and whose locations are known.

5.   Assess, by either computational or analytic means, the range error that occurs when two stereo cameras with nominally parallel optical axes are in fact misaligned by one degree.

6.   Suppose an object point in 3-space is illuminated by a point source of light so that its shadow falls on some surface (wall, floor, etc.). Assuming that the locations of light source and surface are known, show how the 3-space location of the point can be determined from a single picture showing both the point and its shadow.

Chapter 11

PROJECTIVE
INVARIANTS

11.1 INTRODUCTION

One of the fundamental problems of scene analysis is the problem of recognizing when two given pictures show the same object. The problem is broad enough to admit the possibility of many different kinds of solutions, depending upon exactly what is assumed known at the outset. If the three-dimensional structure of the object is known, then the problem becomes one of verifying that each picture does in fact show the known object. If the three-dimensional structure is not known in advance, then we may have to depend upon properties of objects that remain unchanged from picture to picture. Such properties are called *projective*, or *projective invariants*, and are the primary concern of this chapter.

In order to make our introductory discussion of projective invariants concrete, we will proceed by means of an example. Suppose we have two photographs, both of which show an automobile. (See Figure 11.1.) Our problem is to decide whether the same car is depicted in both pictures. Now it may be the case that there are obvious differences in the two pictures. For example, one car may have four doors and the other two. We will be interested in more subtle distinctions, and will dismiss such obvious cases from the discussion. Instead, we will be interested in cases where the problem can be solved only by explicit consideration of the picture-taking process. In order to have a mathematically tractable problem, we will make the important assumption that each of the pictures is represented by a selected finite set of distinguished points. For the illustrative automobile example the selected points might be the (images of) tips of the fenders, tips of the bumpers, center of the wheels, and so forth. Similarly, we will assume that the object itself can be represented by the corresponding distinguished points. In other

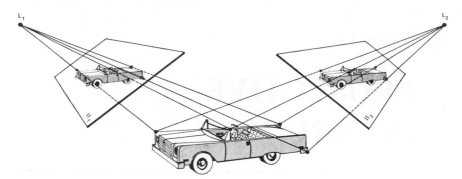

FIGURE 11.1.   Two images of the same object.

words, we are assuming that a picture consists of a finite set of labelled points in a two-dimensional space, and that an object is a finite set of labelled points in a three-dimensional space.

Before proceeding with a discussion of specific methods, we should point out the fundamental ambiguity inherent in the problem of determining whether two pictures show the same object. Even if two photographs are identical, we cannot deduce that they are photographs of the same physical object. One, for example, might be a photograph of a picture of the object while the other might be a photograph of the object itself. On the other hand, it is certainly possible to assert on occasion that two photographs show different objects. The ambiguity stems from the many-to-one nature of the perspective transformation. As we saw in the last chapter, there are infinitely many objects all of which map into the same picture under central projection. Hence, the most we can hope to do is to establish when two given pictures show different objects. If for a given pair of pictures this cannot be established, then we can conclude only that the same object *may* be shown in each picture. Formally, we can hope to derive necessary, but not sufficient, conditions for two pictures to show the same object.

In summary, our principal interest in this chapter is in the following abstract problem: Given two pictures, derive necessary conditions for the pictures to be two central projections of the same object, where both pictures and objects are defined to consist of a finite set of labelled points. We will refer to this problem as the *second view problem*. Throughout the chapter, it will be assumed that the relative positions and orientations of the cameras are unknown.* Hence, the problem is to find object properties that do not vary from picture to picture—in other words, to find projective invariants.

---

* Notice that if the camera locations were known, then, as suggested by Fig. 11.1, the problem would merely be one of determining whether corresponding rays intersect each other in space.

The second view problem has received relatively little attention from researchers in scene analysis, and we know of no universally applicable solutions. Nevertheless, the problem leads us to investigate fundamental mathematical properties of the projective model, so it seems worthwhile to present some techniques that have been put forth.

11.2 THE CROSS RATIO

A projective invariant of fundamental importance is called variously the *cross*, *double*, or *anharmonic ratio*. As we will shortly see, the cross ratio itself involves "one-dimensional pictures." However, it can be embedded in a two-dimensional setting, and is therefore of major interest to us. We begin by introducing some basic terminology.

Any set of lines passing through a single point is called a *pencil of lines*, or more simply, a *pencil*. Figure 11.2 shows a pencil consisting of the four coplanar lines ①, ②, ③, ④; the common point L is called the *center of the pencil*. In a dual fashion, any set of points lying on a single line is called a *range of points*, or more simply, a *range*. Figure 11.2 shows two ranges of points x_1, x_2, x_3, x_4 and y_1, y_2, y_3, y_4, lying respectively on lines X and Y.

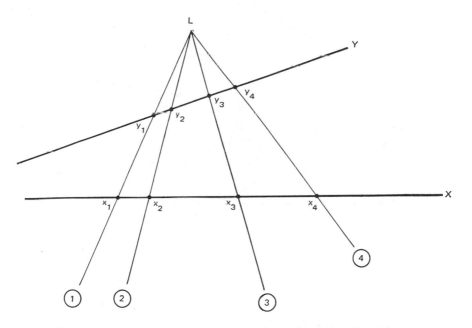

FIGURE 11.2.   A pencil of four lines intersecting two ranges of points.

Usually, we won't distinguish between the name of the line and the name of the range of points, and in the case of Figure 11.2 we speak of the two ranges X and Y. Ranges X and Y are two *sections* of the pencil centered on L and are said to be in *perspective correspondence* (or simply *perspective*). Notice that Figure 11.2 can be interpreted as a model for the process of taking a one-dimensional picture of a one-dimensional object, X being the object, Y the picture, and L the lens center. Consider now Figure 11.3. Ranges X and Y are in perspective correspondence, as are ranges Y and Z. The two ranges X and Z are therefore said to be in *projective correspondence* (or simply *projective*). In general, any two ranges are projective if they can be connected by a chain of perspective correspondences. Now it is an interesting theorem of projective geometry that any two projective ranges can be connected by a chain of at most two perspective correspondences. In other words, given two projective ranges there exists a third range in perspective correspondence to both. Hence, it is always possible for two projective ranges to be pictures of the same (one-dimensional) object. In terms of Figure 11.3, if we were given

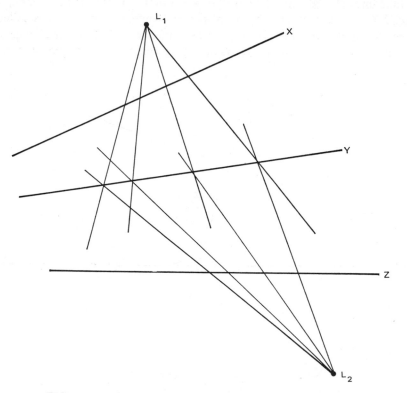

FIGURE 11.3.   Projective and perspective correspondences.

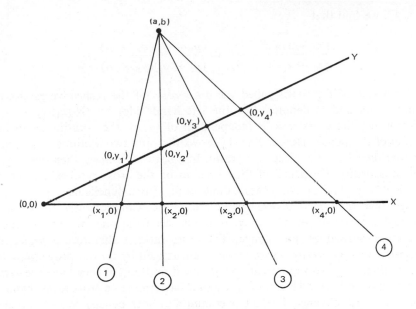

FIGURE 11.4. Illustration for derivation of the cross-ratio.

two pictures consisting of ranges X and Z, a necessary condition that they show the same object is that X and Z be in projective correspondence. The cross ratio is a quantitative measure of whether two given ranges are projective, and therefore provides a solution to the second view problem for the case of one-dimensional objects and pictures.

Consider now Figure 11.4, in which we have shown two perspective ranges X and Y cutting a pencil of four lines. Suppose we take X and Y as the axes of a skewed Cartesian coordinate system. In this system let (a, b) be the coordinates of the center of the pencil, let $(x_i, 0)$, $i = 1, \ldots, 4$, be the coordinates of the range of points on X, and let $(0, y_i)$, $i = 1, \ldots, 4$, be the coordinates of the range of points on Y. It is easy to verify, for the ith line of the pencil, that the condition

$$\frac{a}{x_i} + \frac{b}{y_i} = 1 \qquad i = 1, \ldots, 4$$

must hold. Subtracting the corresponding condition for the jth line from that of the ith, we have

$$a\left(\frac{x_j - x_i}{x_i x_j}\right) = -b\left(\frac{y_j - y_i}{y_j y_i}\right) \qquad i, j = 1, \ldots, 4, \text{ and } i \neq j.$$

Let us temporarily refer to this equation as "j, i". Upon dividing the product of equations "3, 1" and "2, 4" by the product of equations "2, 1" and

"3, 4", we find that

$$\frac{(x_3 - x_1)(x_2 - x_4)}{(x_2 - x_1)(x_3 - x_4)} = \frac{(y_3 - y_1)(y_2 - y_4)}{(y_2 - y_1)(y_3 - y_4)}. \tag{1}$$

Each side of Eq. (1) is called the *cross ratio* of the respective ranges of four points and is denoted (for the left hand side) by $CR(x_1, x_2, x_3, x_4)$. Notice that the cross ratio is independent of (a, b), the coordinates of the center of the pencil. Hence, Eq. (1) shows that any two sections of a pencil of four lines have the same cross ratio. In a natural fashion, then, we define the cross ratio of a pencil of four lines to be the cross ratio of any of its sections. Eq. (1) also establishes a dual result: if two pencils have a common range, then they must have the same cross ratio. Consequently, if we chain through a series of perspective correspondences from one range to another, the cross ratio does not change. The cross ratio is therefore a *projective property*, or a *projective invariant*—it is unchanged by central projection. To put it differently, two ranges are projective if and only if they have the same cross ratio. In Figure 11.3, ranges X and Z have the same cross ratio; namely the cross ratio of range Y which is common to both pencils. We have therefore arrived at a solution to the one-dimensional version of the second view problem: a necessary condition that two (one-dimensional) pictures show the same object is that any two sets of four corresponding picture points have the same cross ratio.*

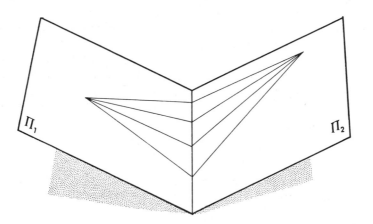

FIGURE 11.5.   Two non-coplanar pencils.

* We are of course ignoring here problems of noise.

Before leaving the cross ratio we have a few further comments. First, since the cross ratio depends only on differences it is independent of the origin of coordinates. Thus, it is not necessary to perform a construction similar to that shown in Figure 11.4 in order to compute the cross ratio of a pencil. Second, two pencils lying in different planes can have the same cross ratio; for example, in Figure 11.5 the two pencils have a common range on the intersection of the two planes, and thus have the same cross ratio. Finally, we observe that there are several possible definitions of the cross ratio, depending upon the order in which the points are labelled. If the labels of four points of a range are permuted, then a different cross ratio results. It can be shown that, of the 24 different labelling possibilities, only 6 yield distinct definitions of the cross ratio. (Interestingly enough, these six form a group under an appropriate composition operation.) For purposes of this chapter we will adopt as standard the cross ratio given by each side of Eq. (1), and note that the labels on points must be observed to preserve consistency.

11.3 TWO-DIMENSIONAL PROJECTIVE COORDINATES

In the last section we saw that the cross ratio is a one-dimensional projective invariant. In this section we will embed the cross ratio in the plane in order to handle the case of two-dimensional objects and two-dimensional pictures. Of course, ultimately we will be interested in the general case of three-dimensional objects and two-dimensional pictures. However, the general case involves additional difficulties; the present case is the most complicated situation for which we have a solution involving neither additional assumptions nor excessive computation. It depends on the invariance of two-dimensional projective coordinates, which we now define.

Suppose, as shown in Figure 11.6, that we have four given points A, B, C, U in the plane, and suppose that no three of them are collinear. We can take these four points as the *base* of a two-dimensional projective coordinate system; the triangle ABC is called the *reference triangle*, and U is called, for reasons that shortly will become obvious, the *unit point*. Given a new point P in the plane (not necessarily within the reference triangle), we define its *projective coordinate* on the AC axis to be $CR(A, X, Y, C)$, the cross ratio of the four named points on the AC axis. Since*

$$CR(A, X, Y, C) = \frac{|Y - A| \cdot |X - C|}{|X - A| \cdot |Y - C|},$$

* Motivated by Eq. (1), we will use the symbol $|Y - A|$ to denote the signed distance between A and Y.

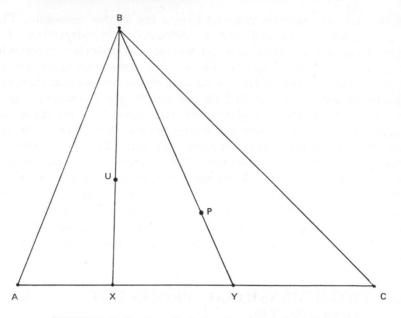

FIGURE 11.6.   Two-dimensional projective coordinates.

we observe immediately that if P lies in AB its projective coordinate is zero; if P lies on BU its projective coordinate is unity; and if P lies on BC its projective coordinate is infinity. The projective coordinates of P on the AB and BC axes are defined, in a similar fashion, by constructing lines from the opposite vertices through U and P. Thus, given the four base points, the projective coordinates of P are established. Conversely, suppose we are given the projective coordinate of P on, say, the AC axis. Since A, X, and C are fixed, the position of Y is also fixed. Hence, we know that P itself must be located somewhere along line BY. Its precise location is fixed if we know either of the two remaining projective coordinates, since either will specify a line whose intersection with BY determines P. Typically, then, any two of the three projective coordinates of a point suffice to specify the point uniquely. The sole exception occurs if P lies on a side of the reference triangle, in which case the projective coordinate of the point on that axis must be used.

We now want to show that the projective coordinates of a point P in a plane (with respect to some base) are invariant under central projection. The general situation is shown in Figure 11.7, where we can think of ABC as the object plane, L as an arbitrary lens center, and $A'B'C'$ as an arbitrary image plane. Our method will be to show that the projective coordinates of P' with respect to the base A', B', C', U' are the same as the projective coordinates of P with respect to the base A, B, C, U. If we do this we are finished, since we will have shown that the projective coordinates of P in every projection are the same as the projective coordinates of P in the original object plane. We begin by observing that the projective coordinate of P on the AC axis is $CR(A, X, Y, C)$. Concentrating our attention now on the plane ALC, we note that $CR(A, X, Y, C) = CR(A', X', Y', C')$, since both ranges are sections of the same pencil centered on L. But $CR(A', X', Y', C')$ is the definition of the piojective coordinate of P' with respect to the base A', B', C', U' in the image plane. An identical argument holds for the other two axes, so we have shown that the projective coordinates of the point P in

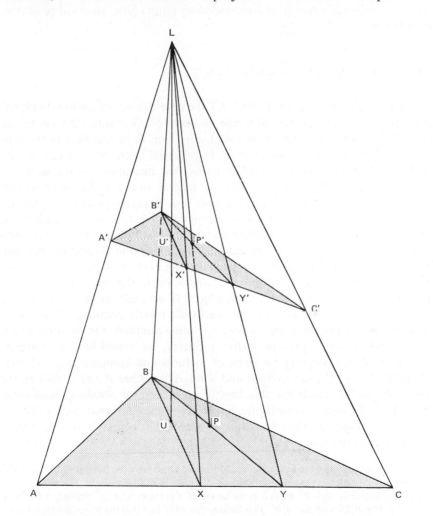

FIGURE 11.7.   Demonstration of invariance of projective coordinates.

the object plane with respect to any base are identical to the projective co-ordinates of an image of P with respect to the image of the base.* Thus, projective coordinates are aptly named; they are in fact invariant under central projection.

The preceding demonstration provides the basis for a solution to the two-dimensional second view problem. Assuming that the object plane contains at least five distinguished points, we designate any four points as the base of a projective coordinate system and compute the coordinates of the remaining points with respect to this base. A necessary condition that two images show the same object is merely that corresponding points have identical projective coordinates.

11.4   THE   INTER-LENS   LINE

In the preceding section we showed, for the case of two-dimensional objects, that projective coordinates are true projective invariants; the projective coordinates of every image of an object were seen to be identical to the pro-jective coordinates of the object itself. In practical situations, we can usually make do with less elegant results. In particular, one often has on hand two pictures, and merely wants to solve the second view problem with respect to these specific pictures. Thus we need not demand properties that are common simultaneously to all possible images, but merely to these two images. We will call such properties *quasi-projective* and will devote our attention to them for the remainder of this chapter. To make the distinction between projective and quasi-projective properties more explicit, suppose we have on hand three pictures, say A, B, and C, and want to determine if it could be the case that they all depict the same object. If we could use a true projective property like projective coordinates, we would merely compute this property in all three pictures and compare corresponding numbers. On the other hand, if we were to use a quasi-projective property, we would have to compute the value of this property for pairs of pictures and compare, say, whether A and B showed the same object and similarly whether B and C showed the same object. In return for this loss of elegance, we obtain a substantial benefit; we are able to describe quasi-projective methods that make either no special assumptions (like two-dimensionality of objects), or, at worst, fairly mild assumptions.

---

* To make the argument rigorous we would have to show that the diagram of Figure 11.7 is correct—in particular, that lines shown as straight are in fact straight. For example, we would have to show that X' defined as the image of X is the same as X' defined as the inter-section of line $B'U'$ with line $A'B'$. This follows from the fact that the projective transforma-tion takes straight lines into straight lines; we leave further details to the reader.

The first quasi-projective property we want to discuss capitalizes on an important property of the line connecting the lens points of two given cameras. A sketch of the general situation is given by Figure 11.8, in which L_1 and L_2 are the lens points of two cameras, π_1 and π_2 their corresponding image planes, and P_1 and P_2 corresponding images of an arbitrary object point P lying somewhere in the three-dimensional space. As shown, let C_1 and C_2 be the points where the inter-lens line L_1L_2 pierces the respective image planes. For ease of exposition, we will assume that the image planes are not parallel. We assert that line P_1C_1 intersects line P_2C_2 somewhere along XZ, the intersection of the two image planes. To see this, concentrate attention on the triangular plane PL_1L_2. Clearly, P_1C_1 lies in this plane, as does P_2C_2; hence, either the lines intersect or they are parallel. Now P_1C_1 and P_2C_2 also lie in their respective image planes. If the image planes are parallel, so are the lines; since we have assumed otherwise, the lines intersect and, furthermore, intersect somewhere on the line of intersection of the image planes. So we have shown that the piercing points of the inter-lens line have a special property: lines from corresponding image points through respective piercing points intersect on the line of intersection of the image planes.

Consider now a situation in which we have four object points, P, Q, R, and S, and respective images P_i, Q_i, R_i, and S_i, $i = 1, 2$. Again, we can construct

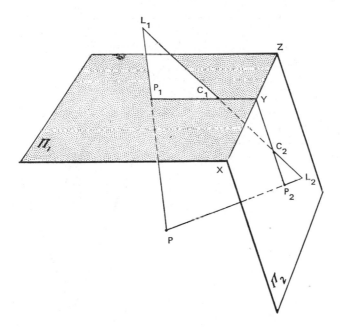

FIGURE 11.8.   Geometry of the inter-lens line.

points C_1 and C_2 where the inter-lens line pierces the image planes. This situation is depicted in Figure 11.9, where for clarity we have left out the object points, lens points, and inter-lens line. As we have just seen, lines from corresponding image points through respective piercing points must intersect, as shown on XZ. Thus we have two pencils C_1 and C_2, of four lines each, intersecting on a common range $P'Q'R'S'$ of four points. Hence, the cross ratios of the two pencils must be equal. We have arrived, then, at an important quasi-projective property: given two images of the same object, there exists a point in each—namely, the piercing point of the inter-lens line—such that the cross ratios of corresponding pencils centered on these points are equal. (Although we have not proved it, this quasi-projective property holds even when the two image planes are parallel. However, if the inter-lens line is parallel to either (or both) of the image planes, the piercing point(s) move to infinity and the method is unattractive on purely computational grounds.) Note, incidentally, that the quasi-projective nature of this property figured heavily in its derivation, since we used the inter-lens line defined by two cameras.

Let us consider for a moment how the inter-lens line property might be used in practice. First, assume that we know the relative positions of the two

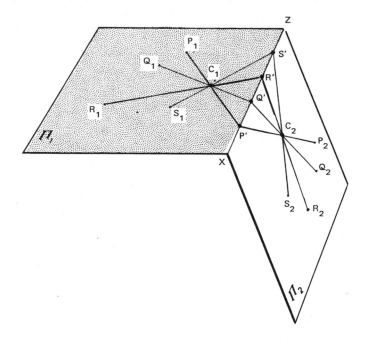

FIGURE 11.9.   Two pencils with a common range

cameras at the time they took their respective pictures. In this case, the piercing points of the inter-lens line can be computed directly, and the cross ratios defined by sets of four corresponding image points computed from this. By the same token, however, if the relative camera positions are known we could perform the standard stereo calculations and see whether or not the rays from respective lenses through corresponding image points in fact intersected. On the other hand, suppose that the relative camera positions are not known in advance. Then we can, in principle at least, perform a search over each image plane in order to find points C_1 and C_2 such that corresponding pencils of lines with these centers have the same cross ratio. If such points can be found, then the necessary condition for the two pictures to show the same object is fulfilled; otherwise, it is not. Notice, however, that if we perform a search we must have available more than four image points per picture. As a matter of fact, the search clearly takes place in a four dimensional space, since there are two coordinates for each of the two sought-for piercing points. Thus, we must be able to form at least four independent cross ratios in each picture in order to avoid degenerate solutions.

For the sake of specificity, let us set up the second view problem as a four-dimensional search problem, using the method described above. We assume to begin with that we have two pictures each showing n corresponding points, say $P_i^1, \ldots, P_i^n$, $i = 1, 2$. For the ith picture, and for any given pencil center C_i, we can always form n-3 independent pencils of four lines each; we need insure only that each subset of four picture points defining a given pencil contains at least one picture point shared by no other subset. Thus, we can always form at least n-3 independent cross ratios. Call the n-3 cross ratios of the ith picture $R_i^1, \ldots, R_i^{n-3}$. Obviously, all of the cross ratios of the ith picture are functions of C_i, the vector whose coordinates specify the pencil center. Now ideally, if the two pictures in fact show the same object, there exists a point in each picture, say C_i^*, such that

$$R_1^j(C_1^*) = R_2^j(C_2^*)$$

for all $j = 1, \ldots, n$-3. In practice, this is rarely the case. Instead, we expect that corresponding cross ratios would be only approximately equal. Accordingly, we can set up the search problem as the minimization of a form such as

$$J(C_1^*, C_2^*) = \min_{C_1, C_2} \sum_{j=1}^{n-3} \| R_1^j(C_1) - R_2^j(C_2) \|.$$

If values C_1^* and C_2^* are found, say by a gradient search process, that make the sum acceptably small, then we decide that the necessary condition for the two pictures to show the same object is satisfied; otherwise it is not.

Thus, the second view problem has been converted into a gradient minimization problem followed by a decision problem.

11.5 AN ORTHOGONAL PROJECTION APPROXIMATION

An especially simple quasi-projective invariant can be derived from the assumption that the picture-taking process is modelled by orthogonal, rather than central, projection. Orthogonal projection, as the name implies, involves forming an image point by projecting an object point orthogonally onto the picture plane. If there are several object points, then the projecting rays form a parallel bundle of lines; it is this parallelism that is exploited by the method described below. Notice, by the way, that if the distance from lens point to a set of object points is large compared to the distance between pairs of object points, then the projecting rays will be approximately parallel. Hence, the method is of interest in practical situations since cameras are often placed relatively far from objects in order to avoid severe perspective distortions. (For example, portrait photographers usually place their cameras at least nine feet from the subject so that the resulting picture does not come out all nose.)

The basic geometry of the orthogonal approximation is illustrated in Figure 11.10. We have shown two image planes, π_1 and π_2, an object line PQ, and two image lines P_1Q_1 and P_2Q_2 lying in respective image planes. The lens centers of the two cameras are not shown, and can be assumed to be at infinity at the intersection of the respective pairs of projecting rays. An important role in the present method is played by XZ, the line of intersection of the two image planes. In particular, we assert that the components in the XZ direction of lines PQ, P_1Q_1, and P_2Q_2 all have the same length. If the assertion is true, then the length of the components of corresponding image lines in the XZ direction is a quasi-projective invariant; they are the same in any two pictures of a single object line.

Although it is probably obvious, let us sketch a proof of the assertion stated above. The proof rests on two properties of orthogonal projections: first, an orthogonal projection is a linear transformation and, second, the orthogonal projection of any line parallel to the image plane has the same length as the line itself. To capitalize on the linearity property, imagine that line PQ is the sum of two components, one of which is in the XZ direction. By linearity, the orthogonal projection (say in the first image plane) of the sum is the sum of the orthogonal projections. Hence, P_1Q_1 is the sum of two vectors, one of which is the projection of the XZ component of PQ. But, by the second property, the XZ component of PQ is unchanged in length by orthogonal

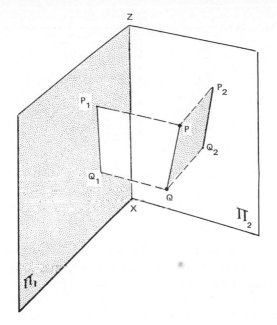

FIGURE 11.10.   Geometry for an orthogonal approximation.

projection; so the length of the XZ components of both image and object lines are the same. Since an identical argument holds for the second image plane, a complete proof can be constructed.

When it comes to practical use of this quasi-projective property, we find that arguments very much like those employed in the previous section apply. As before, if the relative positions of the two cameras are known, it is easy to compute the projections of all image lines on XZ; but, of course, if the relative camera positions are known there are better ways of solving the second view problem. When the relative camera positions are not known, then, as before, we can use search methods for solving the second view problem. Figure 11.11 gives a hint as to how the search problem can be formulated. In the figure, we have shown the image planes of Figure 11.10 unfolded with respect to XZ until the two images are coplanar. Since the XZ components of both image lines are equal, lines P_1P_2 and Q_1Q_2 are parallel. Thus, if we are given two pictures of the same object, the pictures can be placed on a plane in such a relative orientation as to make lines connecting corresponding picture points parallel. Alternatively, there is evidently a preferred direction in each image plane such that the components of corresponding image lines in these directions are equal. In either case, a little

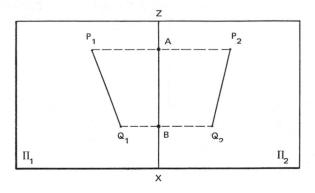

FIGURE 11.11. The picture planes of Fig. 11.10 unfolded with respect to XZ.

thought indicates that the search problem is a two-dimensional one in which
both coordinates of the search space represent angular rotations. In practice,
then, one would search for relative picture orientations such that the
parallelism criterion is most nearly satisfied (or, alternatively, for preferred
directions such that the equal-component criterion is most nearly satisfied).
In either case, one would need at least three picture points to avoid degenerate
solutions. Finally, there would remain the problem of deciding whether the
criterion was sufficiently well-satisfied to warrant a declaration that this
particular necessary condition on the "sameness" of the two pictures is
satisfied. Thus, as in the previous section, the second view problem has been
converted into a search problem followed by a decision problem.

Having dwelt at some length on the similarities between this method and
the one described previously, it would be well to point out some important
differences. In the previous case, the search was carried out over a four-
dimensional search space. Moreover, the search space was unbounded since
physically we were looking for piercing points that could be located anywhere
in each infinite picture plane. On the other hand, the present method involves
a search over only a two-dimensional bounded search space—bounded
because physically we are searching for orientations that can range only
between zero and 360 degrees. Thus the present method enjoys the advantage
that the associated search problem is substantially easier. With this computational advantage, however, goes a drawback. A little reflection leads to
the conclusion that the present method employs only one-dimensional
object information; in particular, the method depends exclusively on the XZ
component of distances between pairs of object points. Hence, although
the method does in fact lead to a necessary condition that two pictures show
the same object, the condition is weaker than would be obtained by the computationally more difficult method.

11.6   OBJECT RECONSTRUCTION

We have alluded several times to the fact that the second view problem has a straightforward solution when the relative positions of the two cameras are known in advance. The solution involves performing the calculations needed for evaluation of the stereopsis triangulation equation. Referring back to the previous chapter, we see from Eqs. (34) and (35) that $J(a_0, b_0)$ is the minimum distance between rays through a pair of corresponding picture points. Thus, an obvious solution to the second view problem (when the relative camera positions are known) is to compute the minimum distance between the members of every pair of corresponding rays and then to note whether all of these distances are zero. If this is the case—that is, if rays through corresponding picture points intersect each other—then a necessary condition that the two pictures show the same object will have been satisfied. Furthermore, under the assumption that both pictures do in fact show the same object, the method reconstructs the three-dimensional object itself. Obviously, the object is defined by the intersections of the corresponding rays.*

The preceding method can be generalized in an obvious way to cover the case of unknown camera positions. The basic idea is to carry out a search over all possible camera positions in order to find a pair of camera positions that results in the intersection of corresponding projecting rays. If such camera positions can be found, then a necessary condition that both pictures show the same object will have been satisfied. Moreover, under the assumption that both pictures do in fact show the same object, the solution reconstructs both the three-dimensional object and the relative positions of the cameras.

Let us consider a little more closely how the search problem could be set up. First, it is obvious that only the relative positions of the two cameras are important; nothing can be said about the absolute camera positions. This being the case, we may as well assume that, in some global coordinate system, the position of the first camera is fixed; for convenience, we will assume that the first camera is at the origin of the coordinate system and that it has zero pan and tilt angles. The position of the second camera with respect to the first is defined by three translation parameters and three rotation parameters. For simplicity, let us assume that cameras are never rotated about their own optical axis, so that the general formulation used in the preceding chapter

---

* In practice, of course, we would not expect corresponding rays to intersect even when both pictures do show the same object. We would, because of noise, expect only that the minimum distance between rays be small, in which case the object would be defined by the "almost intersections" of pairs of rays.

applies. Under this assumption, the position of the second camera is defined by three translation parameters and only two angles. Now we remarked earlier that Eqs. (34) and (35) of the previous chapter give the minimum distance between rays through a pair of corresponding picture points. However, the unit vectors u_1 and u_2 in the direction of the projecting rays are functions of the camera positions as well as the picture point coordinates. Hence, for every pair of corresponding picture points and for all possible (relative) camera positions we can in principle compute how nearly corresponding rays intersect. In principle, then, we can conduct a search over the space of all (relative) camera positions in order to find positions which result in the corresponding rays most nearly intersecting. If the two pictures do in fact show the same object, then relative camera positions exist for which corresponding rays do intersect; specifically, the positions are just the ones the cameras occupied at the time they took the pictures. Thus, the method of object reconstruction computes a quasi-projective property in a manner analogous to the two previous methods.

We should comment here on the relative merits of this method compared with the last two. In a sense, the method of object reconstruction is the strongest of the methods we have discussed, since it makes use of all possible information inherent in the pictures. Loosely speaking, the method of object reconstruction asks the question "Does an object exist such that two of its projections *are* the two given pictures." By comparison, the two preceding methods ask questions of the form "Does an object exist such that two of its projections have certain properties in common with the two given pictures." In other words, the preceding methods compare functions of the given pictures, while the present method compares the pictures themselves. On the other hand, the method of object reconstruction involves a search over the space of all (relative) camera positions. Under our assumptions, this is a five-dimensional space parametrized by three translation and two rotation variables; so the search space is not only of high dimensionality, but it is unbounded along three coordinate axes. Since the difficulty of implementing any of the quasi-projective methods depends largely on the difficulty of the associated search problem, it is apparent that object reconstruction generally presents the greatest implementation difficulty of any of the methods we have discussed.

11.7   BIBLIOGRAPHICAL AND HISTORICAL REMARKS

As we mentioned in the introduction to this chapter, the second view problem (in the form stated here) has received very little attention from researchers in scene analysis. This is partly because the problem itself is a rather special one. Indeed, our motivation in presenting the various methods has stemmed more from a desire to provide insight into the properties of perspective transformations than from a belief in the intrinsic importance of the second view problem. Another reason for the lack of attention is that the methods we have discussed are in a sense methods of last resort; they are appealed to only when the pictures to be compared are so similar that some kind of fine-grained mensuration technique must be used. Research effort in the young field of scene analys s is presently directed at less subtle (but still difficult) distinctions. In any event, we know of only three references that specifically treat the second view problem as defined in this chapter. All three appear in an obscure collection of Russian papers edited by Kudryavtsev (1968). Rastrigin (1968) developed the method, discussed in Section 5, based on the orthogonal projection approximation to central projection. Yurans (1968) developed the method based on inter-lens line piercing points discussed in Section 4. The application of projective coordinates to the two-dimensional second view problem was noted by El'bur (1968). The method of object reconstruction was developed independently by Bledsoe and Hart* and by Hodges*.

Since the subject of projective geometry is concerned with projective invariants, one might expect to find in standard texts projective properties that lead to a variety of solutions to the second view problem. To a certain extent this is true; two-dimensional projective coordinates are an elementary topic and are discussed, for example, by Graustein (1963). However, as we saw in Section 3, two-dimensional projective coordinates are applicable only when the objects of interest are themselves two-dimensional. In general, it seems to be the case that classical projective geometry restricts its attention to one-to-one projective transformations—that is, to transformations that map a d-dimensional space into another d-dimensional space. In scene analysis, to the contrary, we are most interested in transformations that map a three-dimensional space into a two-dimensional space. Such a transformation is emphatically not one-to-one, and as a result we were forced to direct our attention to quasi-projective invariants rather than more elegant true projective invariants.

REFERENCES

1. El'bur, R. E., "Utilization of the Apparatus of Projective Geometry in the Process of the Identification of Individuals by their Photographs," in *Problems of Cybernetics and Law*, pp. 321–348, V. N. Kudryavtsev, ed. (1968).

2. Graustein, W. C., *Introduction to Higher Geometry* (Macmillan, New York, 1963).

* Unpublished communication.

3. Kudryavtsev, V. N., ed., *Problems of Cybernetics and Law*, U.S. Department of Commerce, Clearinghouse for Federal Scientific and Technical Information, Joint Publications Research Service JPRS: 43,954, (January 10, 1968).

4. Rastrigin, L. A., "About the Identification of Images of Spatial Objects," in *Problems of Cybernetics and Law*, pp. 361–368, V. N. Kudryavtsev, ed. (1968).

5. Yurans, V., "Certain Questions Concerning the Theory of Identification of Objects with the Use of the Apparatus of Projective Geometry," in *Problems of Cybernetics and Law*, pp. 349–360, V. N. Kudryavtsev, ed. (1968).

PROBLEMS

1. (a) Show that, of the twenty-four possible cross ratios of four points, only six are distinct.

(b) Show that the six distinct cross ratios of four points form a group under the operation of composition of functions.

2. Given a pencil P of four co-planar lines, let $v_1, \ldots, v_4$ be four vectors whose tails lie at the center of the pencil and whose heads point, respectively, in the direction of the lines of the pencil. Let v_i^* be a vector orthogonal to v_i, obtained in the usual way by interchanging the components of v_i and taking the negative of the new first component. Show that the cross ratio of the pencil is given by

$$\frac{(v_1^* \cdot v_2)(v_3^* \cdot v_4)}{(v_1^* \cdot v_4)(v_3^* \cdot v_2)}.$$

(Hint: Compute the cross ratio of the pencil by computing the cross ratio of a section taken parallel to the fourth line of the pencil.)

3. Referring to Figure 11.6, characterize the subsets of the infinite line AC for which the projective coordinate of P on AC is

(a) between 0 and 1

(b) between 1 and ∞

(c) between $-\infty$ and $-\left\|\left|\dfrac{X-C}{X-A}\right|\right\|$

(d) between $-\left\|\left|\dfrac{X-C}{X-A}\right|\right\|$ and 0.

4. Specify a simple gradient search procedure for finding a local minimum of an arbitrary function.

5. Set up formally the gradient search problem associated with the quasi-invariant based on approximating the perspective transformation by an orthogonal transformation. Suppose now that the two given pictures are of unknown relative scale. (For example, one of the pictures may, unknown to you, be an enlargement.) Incorporate a scale factor in the formal search problem, and find its minimizing value analytically.

6. Set up formally the search problem associated with the method of object reconstruction. Devise a computer experiment for exploring whether the form to be minimized has many or few relative minima.

Chapter 12

DESCRIPTIVE METHODS IN SCENE ANALYSIS

12.1 INTRODUCTION

Thus far in Part II of this book we have discussed a wide variety of methods for extracting various kinds of information from pictorial data. We now turn our attention to a family of methods that use such information to describe, in one sense or another, entire scenes.

As the reader may recall from our earlier discussion of figure description, there are many ways in which the notion of "description" can be interpreted. In traditional pattern recognition problems, describing a scene is taken to mean assigning it to one of a predetermined number of classes. Although this viewpoint is useful in many practical situations, there are other important and interesting problem domains in which it is not the natural one. In these other domains, we are interested in a discursive description, in an explication of the structure of the scene, rather than in a classification. For this class of problems, the classification methods of Part I are by themselves inadequate and other methods that deal explicitly with structural relations must be used.

The methods discussed in this chapter all depend on two assumptions: First, we assume that certain pieces of information have already been extracted from the scene and are available in symbolic form. For example, by using some of the techniques described in previous chapters we may have extracted information about lines and shapes in the picture. Second, we assume the existence of some prior structural information about the class of scenes to be analyzed. For example, we may know in advance that all scenes show only polyhedral objects. The general task of the methods to be discussed, then, is to combine prior knowledge of a class of scenes with specific symbolic knowledge of a given scene in order to produce some type of structural description of the given scene. We remark here that the development of such techniques is still in its infancy; nevertheless, the succeeding discussions present methods of some generality and considerable ingenuity.

12.2   DESCRIPTIVE FORMALISMS

We begin our discussion of descriptive methods by presenting some formalisms within which descriptions can be generated and expressed. These formalisms can be thought of as general frameworks that are not specialized to any particular class of scenes or environments. Later, we will discuss some methods that make more explicit assumptions about the visual world that they analyze.

12.2.1   Syntactic Descriptions

Let us introduce this topic with an elementary example. Figure 12.1 shows a simple scene depicting a box and a cylinder. At a very crude level of description, the scene might be characterized merely as "box and cylinder." Since we are interested in scene structure, we might elaborate this a little and describe the scene as "box to left of cylinder." Proceeding to finer descriptions, the box in turn can be described as a collection of three quadrilaterals, and so on to any desired level of detail.

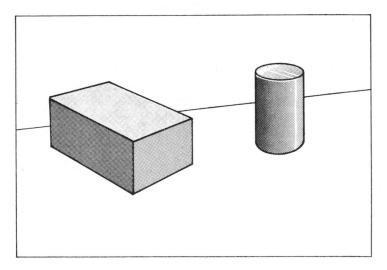

FIGURE 12.1.   A simple scene.

This process of successively refining the structural description of a scene bears a marked resemblance to a process of obtaining a structural description of an English sentence. Accordingly, it is natural to consider the notion of a *grammar* as a formalism within which a picture can be described. This formalism has been closely studied because of its relevance to programming languages and automatic language translation; hence, the *syntactic approach* has the attraction of an established body of theory potentially useful in scene analysis problems. For simplicity, let us begin our discussion of syntactic methods by restricting our attention to one-dimensional strings of symbols. Such symbol strings are of course the raw material of traditional syntactic analysis. We will later consider ways in which traditional ideas can be extended to the two-dimensional picture plane.

A *grammar* is a formal construct consisting of three types of entities: *terminal* or *primitive* symbols, *nonterminal* symbols, and *re-writing rules* or *productions*. A grammar can be used in either a *generative* or *analytic* mode. When a grammar is used in the generative mode, it allows the construction of a string of terminal symbols by means of successive applications of the re-writing rules. A string of terminal symbols constructed using a given grammar in the generative mode is called a *sentence*. The set of all sentences that can be constructed using a given grammar is called the *language* of the grammar.

Before considering the analytic use of a grammar, let us illustrate these abstract ideas by means of a very simple grammar. Let the set of terminal symbols be $T = \{a, b\}$ and the set of non-terminal symbols be $N = \{S, B\}$. The symbol S stands for "sentence" and is thus distinguished from the other non-terminal symbols. Our illustrative grammar has the following five re-writing rules:

1. $S ::- a$
2. $S ::= aS$
3. $S ::= aB$
4. $B ::= b$
5. $B ::= bS$

When the grammar is used in the generative mode, the symbol "$::=$" has the meaning "replace the symbol on the left with the string of symbols on the right." Let us use the grammar to construct a simple sentence. We begin by setting the sentence symbol equal to itself:

$$S = S.$$

Arbitrarily applying Rule 2 to the right side of the equation, we obtain

$$S = aS.$$

Applying Rule 2 again we obtain

$$S = aaS.$$

Now using Rule 3 we have

$$S = aaaB.$$

Applying Rule 5 we obtain

$$S = aaabS.$$

Finally, applying Rule 1 we reach

$$S = aaaba,$$

and no further substitutions are possible. Thus, when the production rules are applied in the sequence 2, 2, 3, 5, 1 to the initial sentence symbol S we generate the sequence of terminal symbols *aaaba*. Obviously, applying the rules in a different sequence results in a different sentence.

Let us now turn our attention to the problem of using a grammar to analyze a string of primitive symbols. We have two questions to answer: first, is the string a sentence of the language defined by the grammar and, second, what is the structure of the string if it is a sentence? The process of answering these questions through analytical use of a grammar is called *parsing*. One method of parsing a string, called top-down parsing, involves constructing a tree of all possible ways in which the rewrite rules might have been applied in order to produce the string in the first place. If no sequence of rules can be found then the string is not a sentence; if there is a unique sequence, then the completed path through the tree defines the structure of the string. If there is more than one sequence of rules, then the structure of the string is *syntactically ambiguous*.

Parsing is most easily understood by means of an example. Suppose, therefore, that we parse the string *aaaba* previously constructed (which of course is a sentence). The basic idea is to scan the set of productions to see which of them are applicable to the initial string. Since the string begins with an "*a*," only the first three productions are applicable. Therefore the string either has the form "*a*," "*aS*," or "*aB*." Obviously, the string is not simply "*a*." Initially, it might be thought to have the form "*aB*," except we see from the productions that anything of the form "*B*" must begin with "*b*"; so our string doesn't have the form "*aB*." Hence, the string must have the form "*aS*," where now $S = aaba$. At this point, the process begins all over again with the string *aaba*. Figure 12.2 illustrates this repetitive process in the form of a *parsing tree*. The numbers on the branches of the tree are rule numbers. A node is crossed out when there are no applicable rewrite rules. Notice that the completed tree specifies the sequence 2, 2, 3, 5, 1 of rewrite rules that was used to generate the string originally. Furthermore, in this example there is

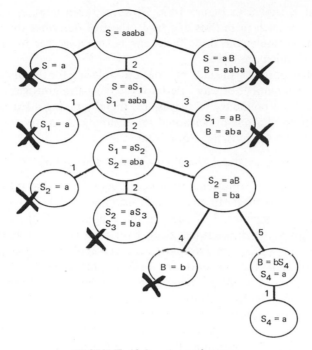

FIGURE 12.2.   A parsing tree.

only one path through the tree; hence, the sentence *aaaba* is generated by the grammar in a unique fashion.

The reader may have already noticed that the language of our very simple grammar is easily characterized; it consists of all sequences of *a*'s and *b*'s, starting with an "*a*" and having no adjacent *b*'s. More generally, it is not so simple to characterize either the language of a grammar or the grammar that generates a given set of sentences. These questions, and related questions of parsing efficiency and ambiguity, lie within the province of the theory of formal languages. Interesting as these topics are, we will forgo them and concentrate on the basic problem of applying syntactic techniques to two-dimensional scenes.

The principal conceptual difficulty encountered in extending a formal syntax to two dimensions stems from a fundamental fact: the one-dimensional line has a natural ordering, whereas the two-dimensional plane does not. Hence, the natural operation with one-dimensional strings of symbols is concatenation—placing one symbol next to another. No natural analog exists in two dimensions. To make this distinction more graphic, consider again the simple scene of Figure 12.1. One (self-explanatory) parsing tree of this scene is shown in Figure 12.3. However, even if we specify precise descriptions for such primitives as "face" the tree describes the scene only vaguely. For example, the three faces can be put together in many ways, only a few of which are boxes.

The problem posed by the lack of a natural ordering for the plane has been approached in a number of ways. Perhaps the most straightforward is to rely exclusively on the boundary of the figure, thereby taking advantage of the natural ordering of a one-dimensional set of points. As a trivial instance of this approach, we might define "quadrilateral" as

$$\text{quadrilateral} ::= \text{line} + \text{line} + \text{line} + \text{line},$$

where the "+" means concatenation and it is understood that the concatenation must close on itself. In this simple example the choice of primitives (straight lines) is obvious. For more general figures having, say, smooth curve boundaries, the choice is less clear. Even after we do settle on some set of primitive curves, it is often not easy to decide where on the figure boundary one primitive ends and the next one begins. This problem of identifying primitives in a scene is not peculiar to the boundary-description approach; it is an inherent difficulty of syntactic methods.

The boundary-description approach has obvious limitations. Suppose, for example, that we wanted to describe the box in Figure 12.1 using straight line segments as primitives. Assuming that the (non-terminal) quadrilateral faces have already been described in terms of straight lines, we still need to specify the relations among the three quadrilaterals. One way in which this might be done is to specify "hooks" or attachment points on each quadrilateral. Such

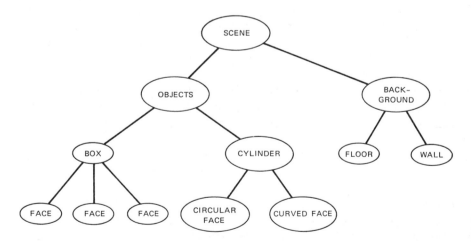

FIGURE 12.3.   One possible parsing tree for the scene of Fig. 12.1.

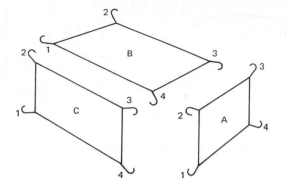

FIGURE 12.4. Decomposition of a box into quadrilaterals.

an arrangement is shown in Figure 12.4, where for clarity we have depicted the quadrilaterals as having the same appearance as the sides of the box in Figure 12.1. A syntactic description of the box would, with appropriate notation, specify "quad A, hook 1 attached to quad C, hook 4" and so on through all the vertices.

A related approach to specifying relations among primitives is based on standardized attachment points. Suppose we insist ahead of time that every primitive have two distinguished points, a *head* and a *tail*. Concatenation of two terminal symbols is taken to mean "vector addition"—that is, head-to-tail concatenation of the pictorial primitives associated with the terminal symbols.* Extending this idea, each nonterminal pictorial construction also has a head and a tail. Its tail is the tail of the first primitive in its definition, and its head is the head of the last primitive. Thus, if the terminal symbols a, b, and c represent three pictorial primitives, then the nonterminal concatenation A defined by $A = a + b + c$ would have the tail of "a" as its tail and the head of "c" as its head. Thus, the formalism that deals with concatenating (or analyzing) terminal symbols also works for non-terminals. As an example of this approach, suppose we describe the cylinder of Figure 12.1 using the primitives shown in Figure 12.5. We denote the head-to-tail concatenation operation by "$+$" and define the symbol "$\sim$" to mean "reverse the head and tail of the primitive." We then write, in an obvious but certainly not unique fashion,

$$\text{cylinder} = \tilde{v} + b + v + \tilde{t} + b.$$

---

* We are tacitly assuming that pictorial primitives can be translated in the picture plane. but not rotated.

FIGURE 12.5.   A set of pictorial primitives.

Using self-explanatory non-terminal symbols, this sentence can be parsed as

$$\tilde{v} + b + v + \tilde{t} + b.$$

side   top

cylinder

We need not limit ourselves to only the "+" and "$\sim$" operators defined above. To indicate just one other possibility, we will define "$p * q$" to mean "head of p touching head of q and tail of p touching tail of q." Using this additional operator, we can describe a picture of a cylinder by, for example, the productions

1. Cylinder ::= Side $*$ Top
2. Side   ::= $\tilde{v} + b + v$
3. Top   ::= $t * b$.

Let us use this example to illustrate how a picture might be syntactically analyzed to detect the presence of a cylinder. The important thing to emphasize is that the analytic use of any grammar assumes the availability of *primitive recognizers*—processes or mechanisms for detecting primitives in the picture. In our example, we need recognizers for detecting vertical lines and two types of curved lines regardless of the choice of productions. Notice also that we have not said anything about the representation of the picture to be analyzed; it might be an analog picture, a gradient picture, a line drawing, or have any other form. We assume that the primitive recognizers are appropriate for the particular pictorial representation.

Suppose now that we are given a picture and want to determine whether it contains a cylinder. Using a top-down parsing procedure, we see from Productions 1 and 2 that a cylinder must have a Side and that a Side must have a vertical line. We therefore scan the picture for the occurrence of a vertical line. (Note that if we were parsing a one-dimensional symbol string we would simply examine the first element.) Having found a vertical line, we consider its lower end to be the head and its upper end to be the tail, since we are seeking a "*ṽ*" rather than a "*v*". From Production 2 we see that a "*b*" primitive must be attached to the head of the vertical, so the region surrounding the lower end of the vertical line is examined. If no "*b*" is found, then we must search again for a different vertical line. Suppose, to the contrary, that a "*b*" is found. As prescribed by Production 2, the vicinity of the end of the "*b*" curve is inspected for the occurrence of a second vertical. If one is found, we can declare that a Side has been found. Attention then centers on finding a Top attached to the Side as prescribed by Production 1. If such a Top is in fact found, then the parsing process terminates successfully; moreover, we have an explicit description that allows us to identify parts of the picture with specific parts of an abstract "Cylinder."

It is worth observing that the top-down parsing process directs the application of the primitive recognizers. Each recognizer, with the exception in our example of the first, does not have to be applied to the entire scene; instead, a recognizer is applied only to a localized region of the picture. This *goal-directed* aspect of top-down parsing not only reduces the computational burden on the primitive recognizers, but also reduces the probability of erroneously detecting a primitive.

Our discussion of syntactic methods has been brief. Before leaving the topic, however, there are a few general remarks that can be made. One of the most serious problems in using a grammar has already been alluded to: the problem of detecting primitives in a scene. The nature of the parsing process itself makes it important to find the primitives accurately, since misrecognition of a single primitive can drastically alter the final result. As a loose analogy, we can imagine the difficulty that would be encountered by, say, a FORTRAN compiler that occasionally is given misread alphanumeric characters. A second comment concerns the appropriateness of syntactic analysis for various classes of pictures. Again, by analogy, let us consider the use of a grammar for programming languages. One of the most attractive aspects of this use stems from the recursive nature of a grammar. A rewriting rule can be applied an indefinite number of times, so it is possible to express in a very compact way some basic characteristics of an infinite set of sentences. In the scene analysis case, a grammar is most appropriate when the scene of interest is built up from a small set of primitives by recursive application of a small set of rewriting rules. When this is not the case—when the power of recursion cannot be applied—then the grammar becomes a formal way for exhaustively describing "in words" the entire content of a picture, and the advantages of compactness of description are lost. Thus, the formal syntactic approach to scene description has non-trivial difficulties associated with it, as well as some very powerful already-existing tools.

12.2.2   Relational Graphs

In many scene analysis problems we are interested in describing "in words"—
that is, symbolically—the structure of a particular scene. We have just seen
that formal syntactic methods can be applied in such situations; a second
means for specifying symbolic descriptions is provided by *relational graphs*.

Rather than introduce this topic with a formal definition, let us proceed
by means of an example. In Figure 12.3 we have shown a parsing tree for the
scene of Figure 12.1. The *nodes* of the tree are labelled with parts of the scene;
the *arcs* of the tree (arcs are just the connections between the nodes) are
unlabelled. Although the arcs have no explicit labels, we can note that their
implicit meaning is that the node at the bottom of the arc is "part-of" the
node at the top of the arc.* In other words, the arcs of the parsing tree
specify a particular relation between the nodes that they connect.

The basic idea of using an arc to symbolize a relation can be generalized
in several obvious ways. First, we can broaden the class of allowed relations
to include any relation that can be conveniently determined from the picture.
We can also consider relational graphs, rather than trees, so that relations
between two arbitrary nodes can be specified. (A graph in general contains
closed loops whereas a tree does not.) With these generalizations, we can
express much richer descriptions than we can with simple parsing trees.

As an illustration, suppose we elaborate the parsing tree of Figure 12.3
into a more complete relational graph description of the scene of Figure 12.1.
Arbitrarily, we will settle upon using the relations "part-of," "a-type-of,"
"adjacent-to," "left-of," "right-of," "above," and "below". One relational
graph description of the scene is given in Figure 12.6. As a notational convenience we have placed arrows on each of the arcs to indicate the sense of
the relation, thus making the relational graph a *directed graph*. The directions
of the arrows have been chosen so that a rough "English translation" is
obtained by reading first the node label at the tail of an arrow, then the arrow
label, and finally the node label at the head of the arrow. Notice that the
relational graph shown can be made more informative even without defining
additional relations; for example, the circular face and curved face of the
cylinder are related by the symmetric pair "above" and "below" as well as by
"adjacent-to." This is just one more example of the wide latitude we have in
choosing the amount of information we want to incorporate in any given
description.

---

* To be precise, we should say that the part of the scene represented by the node at the
bottom of an arc is "part-of" the part of the scene represented by the node at the top of
the arc. This is too cumbersome to be worth saying more than once.

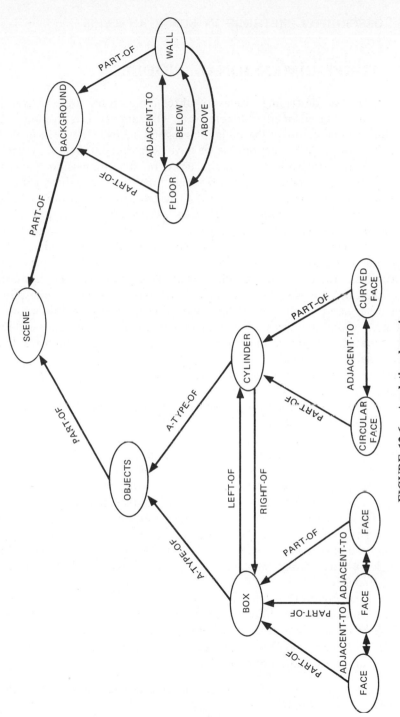

FIGURE 12.6. A relational graph.

12.3   THREE-DIMENSIONAL MODELS

The problem of describing scenes of three-dimensional objects can be approached in two distinctly different ways. One approach is to ignore the three-dimensional nature of the actual objects and describe the scene in terms of two-dimensional constructions, as we have been doing. Often, however, it is most useful to interpret the scene in terms of three-dimensional objects. Thus, the second approach is to describe the three-dimensional environment from which the scene was taken, rather than describe the picture *per se*. Let us refer to these two alternative approaches as *two-dimensional* and *three-dimensional scene description*. To illustrate the distinction between them, consider again the very simple scene shown in Figure 12.1. A two-dimensional description of this scene might specify, in some formalism and to some degree of precision, "three adjacent quadrilaterals, three collinear line segments, one ellipse, and one distorted rectangle." A three-dimensional description, on the other hand, might specify "box and cylinder resting on a floor and in front of a wall." In terms of human understanding, at least, the three-dimensional description is much clearer and more intuitive than the two-dimensional description.*

A moment's thought will indicate that a three-dimensional description can be extracted from a single picture only with the aid of prior information about the objects that populate the environment of interest. Fundamentally, this is because of the many-to-one nature of perspective transformations; there are an infinite number of three-dimensional objects that can correspond to any single view. In order to produce a three-dimensional description of a scene, then, we need both a set of three-dimensional models of objects in the environment and a well-defined procedure for interpreting a given scene in terms of these models. If the environment is sufficiently simple, then the set of models need not be specified in great detail and the model-matching procedure can be trivial. Suppose, to continue with the example of Figure 12.1, that the only objects in the environment are boxes and cylinders. Then our model of the environment can be as crude as "a box has all straight edges and a cylinder has some curved edges." Even this crude model would enable us to interpret Figure 12.1 in terms of three-dimensional objects, rather than in terms of plane figures. Although this example is elementary, the underlying idea is an important one; prior knowledge can take the form of information about three-dimensional objects, as well as information about only the two-dimensional representation of objects.

* In fact, interpreting a two-dimensional scene in terms of three-dimensional objects is one definition of *perceiving* the scene.

As we consider more complicated environments, we in general will be forced to use more accurate and complete models. Often however, it is possible to translate critical facts about models into simple facts about their images. As an illustration of this sort of situation, suppose we know that the environment contains only two types of objects: boxes and truncated four-sided pyramids. Suppose further, for simplicity, that objects always rest with one of their faces on the plane of the floor (so that they are in a stable attitude). From our previous study of perspective transformations we know that the images of vertical lines pass through the vertical vanishing point of the picture, and that the images of orthogonal horizontal lines pass through conjugate vanishing points on the horizon line. These properties let us translate the central facts about boxes and pyramids into simple constraints about their pictures.

In the general case, we are not likely to be so fortunate as to be able to incorporate all the necessary model information into a few simple tests. Instead, we will have to make a more thorough comparison between each one of the three-dimensional models and the pictures at hand. To introduce the basic approach, imagine the following thought experiment. Suppose we have, to begin with, a finite number of models of three-dimensional objects and suppose we are given a picture showing one of these objects in its entirety. As in the past, we will define an object (or more precisely its model) to consist of a selected finite number of points in three-space (for example, the vertices of a polyhedron), and define a picture to be a finite number of points in the plane. The problem is to determine which object appears in the picture. Conceptually, we can take each model in turn and place it in all possible positions with respect to the camera. For each position, the projection of the model onto the image plane is computed and compared to the actual image. The model that achieves, for some position, the best match between its projection and the actual image is declared to be the model shown in the picture. Notice, incidentally, the analogy between this model-matching paradigm and template matching. Each model in effect generates a family of two-dimensional templates, one template for each relative position of model and camera.

The problem of computing the best match between a model and an image can be split into two sub-problems: the problem of identifying corresponding points in the model and the image, and the problem of computing the degree of match between these two sets of corresponding points.* In our informal introductory thought experiment we suppressed the issue of finding corresponding points, and, unfortunately, nothing very profound can be said in

---

* Strictly speaking, we should speak of the match between projections of model points and image points.

general about the problem. We can notice that the problem is a more difficult version of the correspondence problem encountered earlier in connection with stereoscopic perception, but this doesn't help very much in suggesting general solutions. On the other hand, in a given application we are certainly free to make use of any special properties of the models involved. For example, if we are dealing with pictures of polyhedra, it may be that elementary geometric properties are sufficient to establish the correspondence between model and picture points, or at least to reduce substantially the number of ambiguous correspondences. In any event, for purposes of discussion, let us assume that we have in fact made the necessary correspondence between the points in a given model and the points of an image, and now consider how we might compute the best match between the image and the set of all possible projections of the model.

The problem of computing the best match between a model and a picture is very similar to the problem of calibrating a camera that we discussed in Chapter 10. In each case, we are seeking the geometrical parameters of the perspective transformation that result in the closest match between computed image points and observed image points. To review the mathematical formulation, suppose the model consists of the set $\{\mathbf{v}_i\}$, $i = 1, \ldots, n$, of n three-dimensional points, and suppose the (presumed) corresponding image points are $\{\mathbf{v}'_{pi}\}$, $i = 1, \ldots, n$. The direct perspective transformation gives the picture coordinates of an image point in terms of an object point and the geometrical parameters of the transformation. For simplicity, let us assume that a camera is never rotated about its optical axis, so that the transformation is given by Eq. (18) of Chapter 10. The functional form of that equation is

$$\mathbf{v}'_p = \mathbf{h}(\mathbf{v}, \boldsymbol{\pi}),$$

where $\mathbf{h}$ is a vector-valued function giving the computed picture coordinates of the image of $\mathbf{v}$, and $\boldsymbol{\pi}$ is a vector composed of the geometrical parameters specifying the translation and rotation of the camera with respect to the model. In the following discussion, we will assume that the second components of both $\mathbf{v}'_p$ and its homogeneous representation $\tilde{\mathbf{v}}'_p$ have been deleted, since we have seen that this component is related to the distance from object to lens, and is not related to any actual picture coordinate. Now $\mathbf{h}$ is sufficiently complicated to make it difficult to solve directly for the components of $\boldsymbol{\pi}$, given a set of corresponding model and image points. Further, it may be the case that n is large enough to result in $\boldsymbol{\pi}$ being over-determined. In such situations it is common to use a gradient search procedure to minimize an appropriate error function—for example, to minimize

$$J(\boldsymbol{\pi}) = \sum_{i=1}^{n} \|\mathbf{v}'_{pi} - \mathbf{h}(\mathbf{v}_i, \boldsymbol{\pi})\|^2.$$

In this case, however, we can manipulate the homogeneous coordinate form of the perspective transformation to obtain an approximate solution for π. If this solution is not sufficiently accurate, then at least we would expect it to serve as a reasonable starting point for a search procedure.

Let us sketch an approximate analytic solution to the problem of solving for the geometrical parameters, given corresponding sets of n image points and n object points. We begin by copying Eq. (17) of Chapter 10, which gives the homogeneous form of the general perspective transformation

$$\tilde{\mathbf{v}}'_p = PGRT\tilde{\mathbf{v}}.$$

Next, we define the $4 \times n$ matrix V to have as its columns the n vectors $\tilde{\mathbf{v}}_i$, $i = 1, \ldots, n$, and we define the $3 \times n$ matrix V' to have as its columns the n vectors $\tilde{\mathbf{v}}'_{pi}$. In other words, V is composed of the set of n model points (in homogeneous coordinates) and V' of the set of n observed image points. Let us define the 3×4 matrix H to be the matrix product $PGRT$ with the second row deleted. We would like now to be able to state our problem as one of finding the matrix H such that $HV = V'$. In words, given the model and image points, we seek the perspective transformation H (which includes the relative position of model and camera) such that each model point is projected into its corresponding image point. Unfortunately, the situation is a little more complicated than this. First, although H has 12 components, there are only five independent parameters; namely, the three translation and two rotation parameters of the camera. Each of the twelve components of H is a function of these parameters. Thus, in principle, we are not free to choose an arbitrary matrix H. We will ignore this difficulty for the sake of tractability, but in doing so we must emphasize that the resulting analysis is only approximate. The second complication results from the fact that we cannot simultaneously specify the scale of both an object point (in homogeneous coordinates) and its image point (again, of course, in homogeneous coordinates). In particular, if we have an object point $\mathbf{v} = (x, y, z)^t$ and an image point $\mathbf{v}'_p = (x'_p, z'_p)^t$ we cannot freely write their homogeneous representations as $\tilde{\mathbf{v}} = (x, y, z, w)^t$ and $\tilde{\mathbf{v}}'_p = (x'_p, z'_p, w)^t$, since this would force the perspective transformation H to produce the same number w for the last homogeneous coordinate of both an object point and its corresponding image point. To avoid this pitfall we introduce a diagonal scale matrix D, which will allow us to scale each of the homogeneous image vectors by an arbitrary factor. Accordingly, we now state our original problem as follows: Find the 3×4 matrix H and the $n \times n$ diagonal matrix D such that

$$HV = V'D.$$

There are $n + 12$ unknowns in this matrix equation, n contributed by D and 12 by H, and there are $3n$ equations. Accordingly, we can hope to find a solution if n is at least six. In practice, we would probably try to have more than six model points, so it is natural to solve this equation by a mean squares method. Specifically, we would like to find matrices H and D such that the sum of the squared differences between the components of HV and $V'D$ is minimized. This minimization problem involves straightforward manipulations so we will merely state the result, which unfortunately is a bit on the messy side. Let

$$A = V^t(VV^t)^{-1}V - I,$$

let

$$Q = (V')^t V',$$

and let S be a matrix whose (i, j)th element $s_{ij} = a_{ij}q_{ji}$. (In words, the matrix S is formed by the element-by-element multiplication of A and Q^t.) Let the n-dimensional vector $\mathbf{d}$ have as components the diagonal elements of D. Then the solution to the minimization problem is to use as the diagonal elements of D the solution to the homogeneous equation

$$S\mathbf{d} = 0 \tag{1}$$

and to set

$$H = V'DV^t(VV^t)^{-1}. \tag{2}$$

Before proceeding further, we can pause for a moment and comment on the form of the solution. First, notice that the homogeneous form of the perspective transformation, although useful, cannot hide the essentially non-linear nature of the transformation. Introduction of the diagonal matrix D amounts to being an artifice to compensate for the artifice of homogeneous coordinates. In a similar vein, the definition of S involves a distinctly non-linear operation on matrices.

Once H has been determined, we can find the values of the geometrical parameters by equating corresponding components of H with the components of $PGRT$. For example, by directly multiplying out we find that the $(1, 1)$ component of $PGRT$ is $\cos \theta$, so we can immediately find the value of the camera pan angle.* After the best values of the geometrical parameters have been found, the model can be projected onto the picture plane and compared with the image. The degree of match achieved (as measured, say, by a sum of squared errors) is the final numerical result of the procedure, and is used as the basis for deciding whether this particular model fits the pictorial data.

---

* By the same token, equating corresponding elements also can reveal the roughness of our approximate analysis. For example, the $(1, 2)$ element of $PGRT$ happens to be $\sin \theta$, but there is no assurance that an angle θ exists whose cosine and sine are given respectively by the $(1, 1)$ and $(1, 2)$ elements of the H we compute.

Elements of the model-matching approach appear in many different forms. We mentioned earlier the possibility that, on occasion, critical facts about models can be translated into simple facts about their images. On a different note, suppose our problem is to ascertain whether a given picture shows any important new features of a three-dimensional environment—for example, whether an object has been moved, or whether a new object has been introduced. A basic approach to this problem is to compare the new picture with the projection of the old model of the environment. In the simplest case of a stationary camera, this comparison can be performed by subtracting successive pictures on an element-by-element basis and noting significant changes. If the camera can move between pictures simple subtraction is inadequate; instead we may want to store a three-dimensional model of the environment and compare the new picture with a computed projection of the model.

Before closing our discussion, we should note the close connection between model matching and certain topics in computer graphics. Problems in both areas, for example, often involve the computation of the two-dimensional image of a three-dimensional scene. This computation in turn often requires a solution of the so-called *hidden-line problem*—the problem of determining which parts of three-dimensional objects are occluded in a given projection. We leave discussion of these and related topics to the literature cited at the end of the chapter.

12.4   THE ANALYSIS OF POLYHEDRA

In the last section we discussed some methods for making use of very explicit knowledge of a three-dimensional environment—in the extreme case, of complete knowledge of the structure of objects. Very often, however, such complete knowledge is unavailable; in fact, the object of a scene analysis may be to extract exactly this sort of information. On the other hand, if we have no prior knowledge at all of the three-dimensional world we are obviously restricted to very limited types of analyses. The most typical problem lies between these extremes; we may have prior knowledge of the general family of objects in the environment, but have no prior knowledge of detailed structure. Among this class of problems, the analysis of pictures of polyhedra (plane-bounded solids) occupies a prominent position. In the following, we present some general methods for extracting three different types of information from pictures of polyhedra. These methods are of considerable interest not only because polyhedra are basic geometrical building blocks, but also because we must thoroughly understand these simple solids before we can hope to understand more complicated ones.

12.4.1 Line Semantics

Our interest here is in the seemingly curious problem of assigning "meanings" to lines in a picture. This problem deserves attention only if, first of all, we can be precise about what it means for a line to have a meaning and, second, if we can find reasonable methods for ascertaining such meanings. As it happens, both these conditions are satisfied; we can very easily make precise the notion of the meaning of a line in a picture of a polyhedron and, more-over, there is a simple and ingenious way to determine it. If we can success-fully assign a meaning to each line in the picture then, in one sense, the scene analysis is complete. Before we begin, we make two assumptions: we will assume that the environment contains only polyhedra of degree three— that is, exactly three plane surfaces come together at each of the vertices of the polyhedra. (Such polyhedra are sometimes called *trihedral solids*.) We further assume that the camera is in a *general position* with respect to the objects in the environment. This means that a small perturbation in the camera position results in an essentially similar picture—the number of lines and the configurations in which they come together remain unchanged.

Our first important observation is that a single line in a picture (under our assumptions) can have exactly four meanings: it can represent a concave edge of a polyhedron, a non-occluding convex edge, or an occluding (hiding) convex edge that occludes more distant parts of the scene either on one side or the other. For simplicity, we will refer to non-occluding convex edges as convex edges, and occluding convex edges as occluding edges. All of these edge types are present in the scene of Figure 12.7, which shows a fireplace

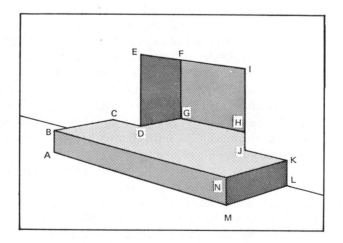

FIGURE 12.7. Fireplace with hearth.

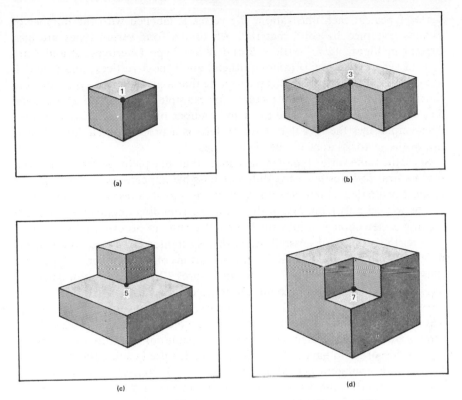

FIGURE 12.8. The four vertex types of trihedral solids.

with a raised hearth. As examples, lines AM and FG are concave edges, lines BN and DE are convex edges, and lines AB, BC, and EI are occluding edges. It is important to note that, because we are dealing with plane-bounded objects, the meaning of a line must remain the same over its full length. As a notation, we will label convex lines with "$+$", concave lines with "$-$", and occluding lines with an arrow. The sense of the arrow is chosen such that, if you imagine standing on the picture plane and looking down the line in the direction of the arrow, the *un*occluded plane lies to the right of the line.

The second important observation is that the vertices of a trihedral solid are of only four generic types. If the planes defining a vertex are thought of as partitioning the surrounding space into, loosely speaking, octants, then the polyhedron itself can occupy either one, three, five, or seven of these octants.* The basic idea of assigning a type to a vertex becomes much clearer with the aid of an illustration. Figure 12.8 shows the four possible

---

* Strictly speaking, we should use the term "octants" only if the planes are mutually orthogonal; nevertheless, the general remarks apply for planes meeting at arbitrary angles.

vertex types; in each illustration, the vertex is labelled with the number of octants occupied by solid material. All of the four vertex types are also present in Figure 12.7. Vertices B and N are Type 1 vertices; E and I are Type 3 vertices; A and D (among others) are Type 5 vertices; and G and L are Type 7 vertices. It is important to note that a given vertex type can have different representations in a picture; for example, both A and D are Type 5's, but they don't even have the same number of lines radiating outward. This emphasizes the fact that a vertex type is a property of a solid object, not of the pictorial appearance of the object.

Since the same vertex type can have more than one pictorial representation, it is natural to investigate the different possible appearances of the various types. Fortunately, there are not very many possibilities; each vertex type can be viewed only from one of the empty surrounding octants and, because moving a viewpoint within a single octant results in no essentially different picture, the number of possibilities is sharply limited. It is therefore feasible to list explicitly all of the possible representations of the four vertex types and thus to produce the "catalog" shown in Figures 12.9a–l. Each configuration has been labelled according to our announced convention "+" and "−" for lines representing convex and concave edges, and arrows for occluding edges whose associated planes are to the right in the picture as one looks along the arrow. We have deliberately shown the 12 possible configurations in standard positions in order to have a "neutral" catalog for use in subsequent analyses. Many of the configurations appear in Figure 12.7. Vertex N, for example is easily visualized as the Type 1 vertex shown in Figure 12.9l; vertex D is the Type 5 vertex of Figure 12.9h; vertex I is the Type 3 vertex shown in Figure 12.9b; and vertex L, a Type 7 vertex, can be recognized as the vertex of Figure 12.9k. We can be assured that the catalog of vertex types is complete by appealing to the fact that a vertex can be viewed only from one of the empty surrounding octants. Thus, the catalog shows one Type 7 vertex, three Type 5 vertices, and five Type 3 vertices. It shows only three Type 1 vertices (instead of seven) because of certain symmetry considerations. Figure 12.9m shows a "T" configuration; a "T" always corresponds to an edge (the crossbar) that occludes a more distant part of the object, and not to a vertex of the actual trihedral solid. A moment of thought indicates that the crossbar of the "T" must always be labelled with arrows from right to left, but that the stem of the "T" can in general have any label.

An inspection of Figure 12.9 makes it clear that the type of a vertex in a picture cannot be determined by inspecting solely that vertex; after all, the catalog shows six "V" vertices (Figures 12.9a–f), three "W" vertices (Figures 12.9g–i), and three "Y" vertices (Figures 12.9j–l). Additionally, the "T" vertex of Figure 12.9m really has four different possible meanings corresponding to the four different possible labels on its stem. If we want ultimately

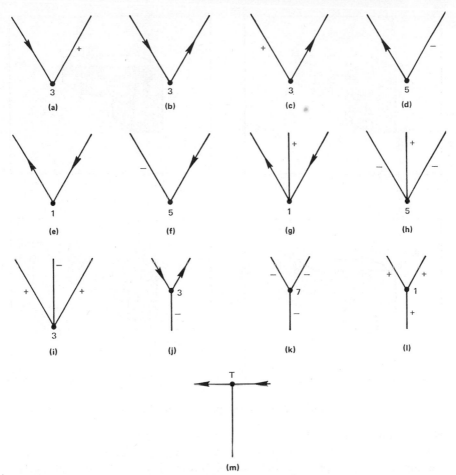

FIGURE 12.9.   Catalog of all possible representations of the vertices of trihedral solids.

to label the vertices (and therefore the lines) in a given picture, we can evidently do so only by making use of some sort of contextual information. To illustrate the basic approach, consider the following example. Figure 12.10a shows a simple trihedral solid—an inverted block letter *L*. To begin the line-labelling process, notice that the exterior boundary of the *L* can be labelled with a clockwise sequence of arrows, as shown in Figure 12.10b.*

---

* This is a direct consequence of the fact that if we follow clockwise the exterior boundary of a picture of an object, all the planes of the object always lie to our right. Thus, the boundary of an arbitrary picture can always be labelled with a sequence of clockwise arrows.

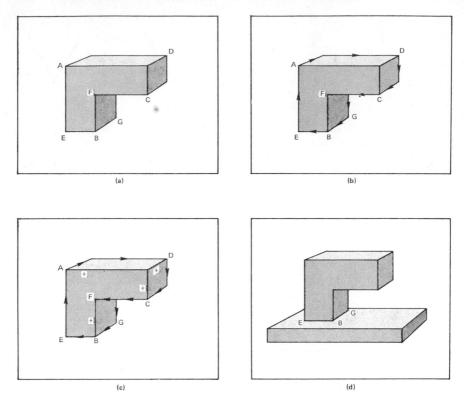

FIGURE 12.10.   Example of vertex labelling.

Now examine vertices A, B, C, and D of Figure 12.10b; each of these is a "W" type of vertex with arrows on the outside legs. Upon inspecting the catalog of vertex types, we find that only Figure 12.9g has this property; hence, the middle legs of vertices A, B, C, and D can be labelled with "$+$," as shown in Figure 12.10c. In Figure 12.10c we have also placed an arrow near the single "T" vertex, since we know that the crossbar of a "T" always has the arrow labels shown in Figure 12.9m. Thus, in this example we have easily been able to assign a unique label to each of the lines. On the other hand Figure 12.10d, although only a little more complicated, presents more of a problem; vertices B, E, and G cannot be assigned a unique legal label. There is a good reason for this: it is impossible to tell from the picture whether the inverted L rests on the slab or floats above it. However, the only legal labellings—labellings not leading to contradictions at other vertices— reveal these two situations as the only possibilities.

Let us abstract from the preceding example a formal vertex-labelling procedure. To motivate the formalism, first notice that the essence of the method is to assign a tentative catalog type to one vertex, and from this assignment to infer a constraint on the catalog entries applicable to adjacent vertices. This process is repeated until (or unless) we arrive at a vertex whose tentative line labels are satisfied by no catalog entry, at which point some other tentative labels must be tried. Evidently, the process involves a systematic search of a tree of possible vertex labels. Accordingly, we associate with a given picture of a trihedral solid a search tree. The nodes of the search tree correspond to the vertices of the picture, and the arcs descending from a given node correspond to the possible catalog labels that can be placed on the vertex. To illustrate the procedure, consider the box-with-square-hole of Figure 12.11; the initial portion of its associated search tree is given in Figure 12.12. We have arbitrarily decided to examine vertices in the order in which they are numbered. Vertex 1, part of the square hole, might be any of the three "W" type vertices in the catalog of Figure 12.9. The arcs emanating from node 1 have therefore been labelled with the letters of these three catalog entries. As an aid to visualization, we have also sketched near each arc the lines comprising the square hole, and have labelled them according to the dictates of the respective vertex types. We now have three different alternative constraints on vertex 2, corresponding to the three possible labels of vertex 1, and each of these must be examined. If vertex 1 corresponds to catalog entry g, then vertex 2 must satisfy the constraint "V-vertex-with-out-arrow-on-left." Upon inspecting the catalog, we find that only entries d and e satisfy this condition, and hence there are two arcs descending from the leftmost node 2 in Figure 12.12. In a similar fashion, the other alternative constraints on vertex 2 are used to complete the second

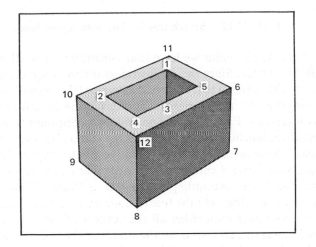

FIGURE 12.11.   Box with a square hole.

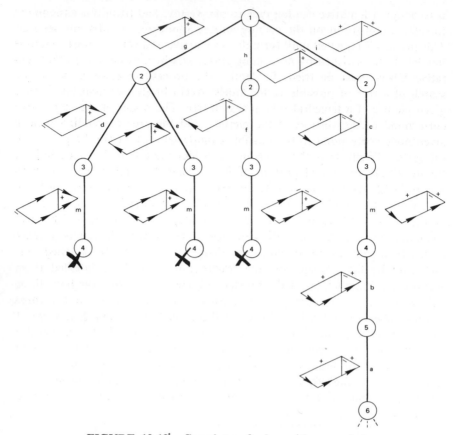

FIGURE 12.12. Search tree for box with square hole.

layer of the tree. At this point we have four constraints (not all distinct) on vertex 3, the "*T*" vertex. Since these constraints involve only the stem of the "*T*," we see from the catalog that the crossbar can be labelled with right-to-left arrows (viewing the "*T*" in an upright position). We now have four alternative constraints on vertex 4. Each of these constraints corresponds to a complete, although tentative, labelling of the lines into the vertex, because the adjacent vertices 2 and 3 have already received tentative catalog types. Three of the four constraints on vertex 4 cannot be satisfied; that is, no catalog entry fits the tentative line labels. Accordingly, the tree is "pruned" at the appropriate three nodes, leaving only the fourth node as a viable alternative. This search process continues until either all the vertices of the polyhedron have been assigned consistent labels, or all the nodes at the tips of the tree have been pruned so that no further search is possible. In the latter case, we can be assured that there exists no trihedral solid corresponding to the given picture—that is, the line drawing contains an error. In the former case, we may find that there is more than one way in which the vertices can be consistently labelled. The reader can easily verify that the tree of Figure 12.12 can be completed in a unique fashion, yielding a unique interpretation for each line in Figure 12.11.

Before leaving the subject we have some final observations. First, notice that the procedure allows us to infer something about the meaning of one part of the scene from information in other parts. This procedure is therefore a particularly clear, if elementary, example of the exploitation of *context* in picture analysis. Notice also that the process of exploring the search tree can be guided in various ways. We pointed out above that the external boundary of a figure can always be labelled with clockwise arrows, thereby limiting the number of catalog types assignable to a vertex on the boundary. The reader can verify that, while this information is irrelevant to the labelling of the first five vertices of Figure 12.11, it is of considerable help in labelling the remaining vertices. Finally, notice that the catalog of vertex types contains no duplication or ambiguities; the precise vertex type is uniquely determined once its lines have been labelled. Thus, we can conclude in general that the process of labelling lines with their meanings allows us to interpret some parts of a scene unambiguously, and may reveal well-posed ambiguities that can be resolved only by more elaborate analyses.

12.4.2   Grouping Regions into Objects

A fundamental problem in the analysis of pictures of polyhedra is the problem of partitioning a picture into separate objects. In the following, we will discuss a heuristic approach to this class of problems—an approach guided by insight and intuition, but not resting on any complete theoretical analysis. Before presenting any specific method, however, there are some preliminary remarks to be made.

Suppose we have a line drawing showing several polyhedra, possibly occluding one another, and want to partition the picture into separate bodies. To be a little more precise, we can consider the line drawing to be a collection of disjoint regions; the problem is to group the regions together so that each group forms the pictorial representation of a single polyhedron. Now if we had prior knowledge of the particular polyhedra in the environment we could use some variation of the model-matching approach to solve the problem; here, we are assuming only that we know the objects to be polyhedra. Under this assumption, the first thing to notice is that the problem does not have an unambiguous solution. To illustrate this, consider again Figure 12.10d. We pointed out earlier the possibility that the inverted "*L*" could either be resting on the slab or floating above it. If the latter, the "L" and the slab are surely separate objects; if the former, then either the "L" is attached to the slab (in which case they jointly form a single non-convex polyhedron) or the "L" is a separate body. There is, additionally, a more profound type of ambiguity to be considered: each of the regions in the scene can be interpreted as the bases of pyramidal objects. The tips of the pyramids are occluded by the bases, and the pyramids themselves are positioned in space in such a way that the bases just line up to form the regions in the picture. (Note that we are not assuming any kind of support hypothesis for the objects; we are not assuming a camera in general position; and we are not assuming that the polyhedra are of degree three.) In view of these remarks, it is evident that the stated problem of partitioning a picture into objects is not a well-posed one, since there is no test for the validity of a proposed solution. The most we can hope for, then, is a partitioning method that provides "reasonable" answers for most pictures—for solutions that most humans would accept as straightforward and plausible.

To motivate the heuristic approach we will be following, consider the simple polyhedron shown in Figure 12.13a. In this simplest of examples we certainly expect any reasonable partitioning method to place regions 1, 2, and 3 in one group and to place region 4 (the background) in another. If we examine the seven visible vertices of the polyhedron, we see that three are V's (as defined in the previous section), three are W's, and one is a Y. This inspection, together with the fact that regions 1, 2, and 3 belong together, suggests the following heuristic rules:

(1) A Y vertex gives evidence that the three regions meeting at the Y should be grouped together, and
(2) A W vertex gives evidence that the two regions included between the narrow angles of the W should be grouped together.

By this reasoning, we might also suggest the rule that a V vertex gives evidence that the two regions meeting at the V should not be grouped together, but we will confine ourselves in this discussion to "positive" evidence only. Figure 12.13b, showing two stacked boxes with a triangular prism behind them, suggests some more heuristic rules for inferring region groupings from vertex evidence. Vertex A, which we will call an "X" type vertex, suggests the following heuristic rule:

(3) An X vertex gives evidence for grouping together the regions on each side of the "straight-through" line of the X. (In Figure 12.13b vertex A gives evidence for grouping together regions 5 and 6 and regions 7 and 8.)

Finally, now, consider the T vertices C and D. We saw in a previous discussion that the crossbar of a T always occludes a more distant part of the

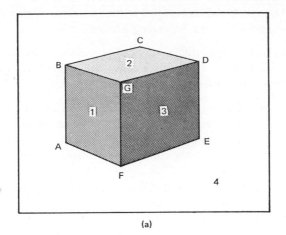

(a)

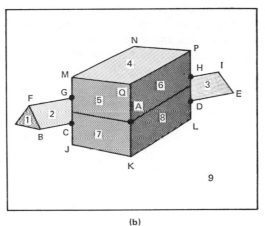

(b)

FIGURE 12.13.   Two simple scenes.

scene (this is true whether the polyhedra are of degree three or not). The fact that the stems of the T's are collinear, however, suggests more than just occlusion; it suggests that the regions lying on the same side of each of the stems are part of the same object. Now it may be the case that a single region lies on the same side of each of the stems; if this is the case, the evidence for grouping regions is valid but superfluous. As an illustration, vertices C and D of Figure 12.13b give evidence that regions 2 and 3 belong to the same group; they also give the superfluous evidence that region 9 in the vicinity of

C belongs to the same group as region 9 in the vicinity of region D. Motivated by this example, we adopt the following heuristic rule:

(4) Two collinear T vertices give evidence for grouping together the regions on the same side of the stem of T's; if a single region lies on the same side of both stems, the evidence is disregarded.

The four heuristic rules are illustrated in Figure 12.14a–d, where we have used dotted lines to link together regions according to the evidence provided by the vertices. For purposes of subsequent discussion we define a *link* to be a piece of evidence, provided by a vertex, for grouping together two regions as part of the same object.

We have just seen that the vertices in a picture (of polyhedra) suggest evidence for grouping regions together as parts of objects. The heuristic rules we formulated are reasonable and plausible, but it would certainly be surprising if they proved to be infallible; they were, after all, formulated only on the basis of some simple examples. It seems clear that a single link should not by itself be considered strong enough evidence for irrevocably grouping together the two linked regions as part of the same object. Instead, we may want to analyze the relations among the links in order to amass stronger evidence for grouping regions together. To illustrate one approach, we proceed by means of an example. Figure 12.15a shows a simple scene consisting of a truncated pyramid resting on a slab. An inspection of the vertices

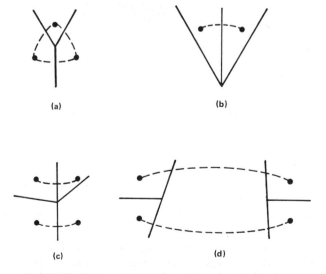

(a)

(b)

(c)

(d)

FIGURE 12.14.   Illustration of four heuristic rules.

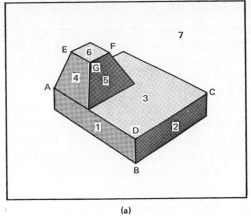

(a)

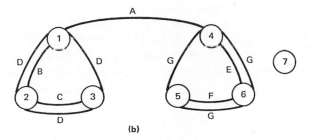

(b)

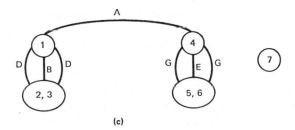

(c)

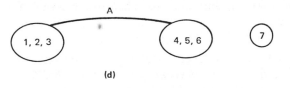

(d)

FIGURE 12.15. Example of grouping regions together.

results in the link information given in Figure 12.15b, where we have represented the regions of the picture by the nodes of a graph and the links between regions as arcs connecting the nodes. For clarity each of the arcs (links) has been labelled with the vertex it is derived from; for example, the link between nodes (regions) 1 and 3 results from the fact that vertex D has the Y configuration and concommitant links of Figure 12.14a. An examination of Figure 12.15b confirms the suspicion that single links are insufficient evidence by themselves for grouping regions; regions 1 and 4, which are "clearly" part of separate objects, are linked. To avoid this difficulty, we will adopt the following heuristic rule for grouping together nodes (and therefore regions):

Two nodes are to be grouped together if there are at least two links between them. Any links from these two nodes to other nodes remain connected to the newly formed "group node."

Figure 12.15c illustrates the application of this rule to the graph of Figure 12.15b. There are several pairs of double-linked nodes in Figure 12.15b; we have arbitrarily applied the rule to nodes 2 and 3 and to nodes 5 and 6. Notice how, in accordance with the second part of the rule, the links from the remaining nodes are attached to the new group nodes. Since the graph of Figure 12.15c contains nodes linked by at least two arcs, the same heuristic rule can be applied again. Figure 12.15d gives the result of this application; there are now no nodes connected by at least two arcs so the process terminates. The final grouping of regions is defined by the nodes of the final graph. In this case regions 1, 2, and 3 are grouped together as one object; regions 4, 5, and 6 form another object; and region 7, the background, forms a third object. In this example, then, the process of first finding links and then merging nodes yields a satisfactory result. The reader can also verify that the same procedure yields satisfactory results for the scenes of Figure 12.13a, b, and, in fact, for many other more complicated scenes.

While the method presented above works satisfactorily for many scenes, it is also not very difficult to trick it. In the scene of Figure 12.16a, vertices A and B introduce enough links to cause all the regions, including the background, to be grouped together as one object. To combat failures of this sort, we may want to introduce new heuristic rules of modify some of the original rules. One simple modification that suffices in the present case is to replace Rule (1) by the following heuristic rule:

(1′) A Y vertex gives evidence that the three regions meeting at the Y should be grouped together *unless one of the regions is background, in which case none of the regions should be grouped together.*

The reader can verify that this rule (which tacitly assumes that we know in advance which regions represent background) leads to satisfactory results

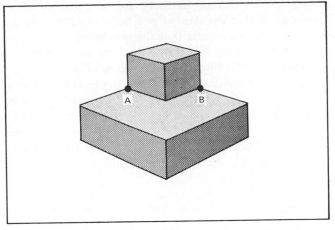

(a)

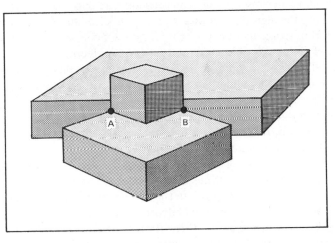

(b)

FIGURE 12.16.   Two troublesome scenes for region grouping.

for the scene of Figure 12.16a. We should not, however, expect this single modification to leave us with an infallible set of rules. The reasoning that led us to Rule (1′) fails in Figure 12.16b; here, vertices A and B produce enough links to cause all regions except the background to be grouped together as one object.

Let us close this discussion with a few final remarks. We have seen that the apparently difficult problem of partitioning a picture of polyhedra into separate bodies can in fact be partially solved by a remarkably simple family of methods. Within the class of polyhedral pictures, the methods are quite general. They do not require that the polyhedra be of degree three, be convex, or be in general position; and they certainly do not require any information about specific objects in the scene. On the other hand, the methods presented here are not perfect; even moderately elaborate forms of these methods will fail on some scenes. Unfortunately, it is not easy to characterize the class of scenes for which a particular member of this family of methods produces adequate results. Perhaps the most useful general statement is to note that experience has shown that methods in this family often work very well on a wide variety of quite complicated pictures, but may fail on some simple scenes.

12.4.3   Monocular Determination of Three-Dimensional Structure

An important problem in scene analysis is the problem of determining from a picture (or pictures) the three-dimensional structure of the visible part of an object. In an earlier discussion of stereoscopy we showed how this problem can be solved through the use of a stereo pair of pictures; here our interest is in a solution requiring only a single picture. Of course, if we know nothing whatsoever about the object of interest it is perfectly clear that its three-dimensional structure cannot be determined from one picture.* In the subsequent discussion, the underlying assumption will be that the object of interest is a polyhedron. Our first goal is to develop a general method for determining three-dimensional structure from the information provided by a single picture and a "few" additional facts. We will then refine this method under the further restriction that the polyhedral objects are of degree three.

Let us begin by reviewing some basic properties of perspective transformations. To fix ideas, we will relate these properties to the simple polyhedron shown in Figure 12.17. Each point in that scene, and in particular each of the images of the vertices of the polyhedron, specifies the position of a ray in space. Each vertex of the actual three-dimensional solid must lie on the ray that extends from the camera lens center, passes through its image and continues out into space; the precise position of the vertex is fixed if we know its distance from the lens center. Thus, given the (monocular) picture, the problem of determining the three-dimensional structure of the polyhedron is equivalent to the problem of determining the distances from the lens center to each of its seven vertices. It should be clear that the picture, together with the additional fact that the object shown is a polyhedron, does not provide

---

* Although one picture does not suffice, a single camera position may. If the camera can be finely focussed on a part of the object, the distance from camera to object part can be read from the focus setting. We leave an exploration of this approach to the references cited at the end of this chapter.

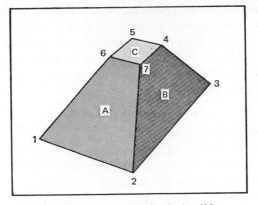

FIGURE 12.17.   A trihedral solid.

enough information to solve this problem. Suppose, however, that we also know the three-space locations of vertices 1, 2, 3, and 7. Since three points fix the position of a plane, we can use the known three-space coordinates of vertices 1, 2, and 7 to determine the three-space position of plane A. Now vertex 6 lies on plane A; hence its position is fixed by the intersection of its corresponding ray with this plane. In a similar fashion, the three-space location of vertex 4 can be determined from the known locations of vertices 2, 3, and 7. At this juncture the three-space positions of vertices 4, 6, and 7 are known, so plane C is fixed and the location of vertex 5 can be found. For this example, then, the given picture, the information that the object shown in the picture is a polyhedron, and the three-space locations of vertices 1, 2, 3, and 7 are sufficient to determine the three-space locations of the remaining vertices and therefore the three-dimensional structure of the visible portion of the polyhedron.

In view of the preceding example, it is natural to ask whether any four "known" vertices suffice in general to determine the three-dimensional structure. The answer to this question is no: If the four points are not independent—that is, if any three of them lie on an edge or if they all lie on a face—then it is easy to show that they do not suffice. Suppose, however, that we know four independent points on the polyhedron, but suppose that it is not possible to chain themtogether in the previous manner. For example, in Figure 12.17 we may know pairs of opposite vertices such as 1, 2, 4, and 5; do they suffice to determine the structure? For this example, the answer is yes. Designating the unknown distance from the lens to vertex 7 as d, it is possible to specify vertex 6 in terms of d and then to specify vertex 5 in terms of d; but vertex 5 is already known, so d can be solved for and the position of all vertices established.

The approach illustrated above turns on the observation that certain distinguished points of the solid lie on more than one plane. Accordingly, the approach can be formalized by expressing this observation in analytic form. We will, for simplicity, refer all equations to a coordinate system whose origin is at the lens center. To begin with, note that any plane of the polyhedron has an equation of the form

$$\mathbf{x} \cdot \mathbf{v} = 1,$$

where $\mathbf{x}$ is a three-dimensional vector lying on the plane and $\mathbf{v}$ is a three-dimensional vector whose direction is normal to the plane and whose length is the reciprocal of the distance from the origin to the plane. Let P be any point lying on the plane; its image, say P', specifies a ray in space. Because we have taken the origin of coordinates to coincide with the lens center, any point on the ray has the form $a\mathbf{u}$, where $\mathbf{u}$ is a three-dimensional unit vector in the direction of the ray and a is the distance from the point to the origin. Thus the condition that P lies on the ray specified by its image and simultaneously on the plane defined by v can be written as

$$a\mathbf{u} \cdot \mathbf{v} = 1$$

or

$$\mathbf{u} \cdot \mathbf{v} = \frac{1}{a} = b.$$

Let us apply this elementary analysis to the scene of Figure 12.17. We will subscript variables with letters and numbers to indicate the plane or point to which they apply. Because vertices 1, 2, 6, and 7 are on plane A we write

$$\mathbf{u}_1 \cdot \mathbf{v}_A = b_1$$
$$\mathbf{u}_2 \cdot \mathbf{v}_A = b_2$$
$$\mathbf{u}_6 \cdot \mathbf{v}_A = b_6$$
$$\mathbf{u}_7 \cdot \mathbf{v}_A = b_7.$$

Similarly, for planes B and C we write

$$\mathbf{u}_2 \cdot \mathbf{v}_B = b_2$$
$$\mathbf{u}_3 \cdot \mathbf{v}_B = b_3$$
$$\mathbf{u}_4 \cdot \mathbf{v}_B = b_4$$
$$\mathbf{u}_7 \cdot \mathbf{v}_B = b_7$$

and

$$\mathbf{u}_4 \cdot \mathbf{v}_C = b_4$$
$$\mathbf{u}_5 \cdot \mathbf{v}_C = b_5$$
$$\mathbf{u}_6 \cdot \mathbf{v}_C = b_6$$
$$\mathbf{u}_7 \cdot \mathbf{v}_C = b_7.$$

This system of linear equations expresses the fact that various distinguished points, all vertices in this example, lie on certain planes of the polyhedron. The $\mathbf{u}_i$ vectors are given directly by the picture and hence are known quantities. Each of the three planes is specified by one three-dimensional vector, and each of the seven points by a scalar. Hence we have a system consisting of 12 equations and 16 unknowns. If the equations are linearly independent, then a unique solution can be found if any four of the unknown variables are fixed, provided, as we saw earlier, that the variables fixed are independent.

It is instructive to establish for the case of an arbitrary picture (of a poly-hedron) the number of equations and variables involved in expressing the incidence of points and planes. Each plane requires three numbers for its specification and each distinguished point one, so

(Number of variables)
$$= 3(\text{Number of planes}) + (\text{Number of distinguished points}).$$

On the other hand, one equation can be written for each distinguished point on each plane, so

(Number of equations) $= \sum_{\substack{\text{all} \\ \text{planes}}}$ (Number of distinguished points on the plane).

The difference between the number of variables and the number of equations places a lower bound on the number of variables that must be known in order to fix the three-dimensional structure of the polyhedron. The lower bound is achieved when the resulting system of linear equations has full rank.

So far the approach developed has been completely general. Given an arbitrary picture, the incidence of points and planes can be expressed as a linear system, the rank of the system found by standard techniques, and the number of free parameters established. If the locations of the necessary number of (independent) points can be found by some other means, then the equations can be solved uniquely and the problem of determining the three-dimensional structure solved.

We would like now to give a different interpretation of the procedure described above. The interpretation is restricted to pictures of trihedral solids, but it is of interest because it makes precise the loose notion of "chaining" from one face of a polyhedron to the next. The interpretation rests on a certain kind of *dual graph* of a picture of a polyhedron. The nodes of the dual graph correspond to the visible planes of the polyhedron; two nodes of the dual graph are connected by an arc if they share a common (and visible) edge.* However, if two planes share more than one edge (all of

---

* Note that the line-labelling procedure discussed earlier allows us to deduce from a picture whether two faces of a polyhedron share an edge. Two faces share an edge if the line separating them is labelled with either a plus or a minus; if the line separating them is labelled with an arrow it represents an occluding edge and not a shared edge.

which are necessarily collinear), only one arc is placed between the corresponding nodes. Figure 12.18a shows a step-like trihedral solid; the corresponding dual graph is given in Figure 12.18b. To illustrate how the dual graph can be used to interpret the sequential process of chaining from one face of a polyhedron to another, suppose that the location of vertices A, C, D, and E are known; then the locations of faces 1 and 5 are known. To indicate that these faces are known we will merge the corresponding nodes together, as shown in Figure 12.18d; other arcs attached to nodes 1 and 5 remain attached after merging, just as in the node-merging process discussed previously. To maintain consistency with later steps, Figure 12.18c shows a preliminary arc inserted between nodes 1 and 5. We will follow the rule that nodes can be merged if they are connected by at least two arcs. Continuing with Figure 12.18d, we interpret the merged node "1, 5" to mean that the three-space locations of faces 1 and 5 are known. Now node "1, 5" is connected by two arcs to node 2. This means that face 2 shares two noncollinear edges with faces whose locations are known; since the face locations are known, the edge locations are also known. Because a plane is fixed by any two collinear lines lying in it, the location of face 2 is also known. To reflect this fact, node 2 is merged with node "1, 5" to form node "1, 5, 2" as shown in Figure 12.18e. This process can be repeated, in our example, until all the original nodes have been merged into one.

The process illustrated above is really nothing more than a way of keeping track, at any stage of analysis, of the faces of the polyhedron whose locations in three-space have been determined. The basic rule of merging two nodes if they are connected by at least two arcs is a restatement of the conditions under which the location of one face can be inferred from the known locations of adjacent other faces. The initial step of adding an arc can be viewed as an artifice for initiating the process. It amounts to an assertion that the two faces share two non-collinear edges; this is patently impossible, but the additional edge is the fictitious equivalent of specifying the positions of the two planes. In the example, it was the case that adding a single edge allowed us to merge all the nodes into one. When this happens—that is, when we can add a single arc in such a fashion that all the nodes can subsequently be merged together—we say that the graph is 1-*mergeable*. We have shown, informally, that the structure of the visible portion of a trihedral solid can be determined from four known points if the dual graph is 1-mergeable. More generally, a dual graph is k-*mergeable* if no fewer than k arcs must be added in order to reduce the graph to a single node by a sequence of merges. It is not hard to show that the structure of the visible part of a trihedral solid is determined by $k + 3$ independent points whenever the dual graph is k-mergeable. As an example, the polyhedron of Figure 12.10a has a 2-mergeable dual graph, and it is easy to verify that the positions of five points must be known in order to determine the visible structure.

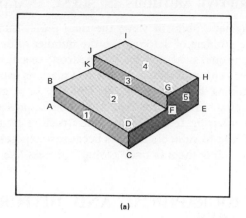

(a)

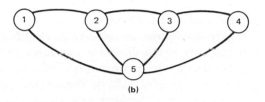

(b)

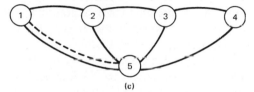

(c)

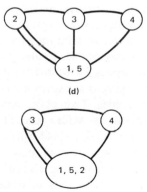

(d)

(e)

FIGURE 12.18.   Merging the dual graph of a trihedral solid.

From a pragmatic point of view, the dual graph leads to an alternative solution to the problem of determining the number of degrees of freedom in the three-dimensional structure of a polyhedron; specifically, the problem of determining the rank of a system of linear equations can be replaced by the problem of finding the degree of mergeability of a graph. Moreover, a particular merging sequence corresponds to the sequence of steps a human might take in inferring three-dimensional structure by a chaining process. This can itself lead to valuable insights because it exposes the steps of a process rather than hiding them in one "global" process like matrix inversion.

12.5 BIBLIOGRAPHICAL AND HISTORICAL REMARKS

Researchers in scene analysis have recognized for some time a large body of problems that require descriptive, as opposed to classificatory, methods for their solution. Initial work in this direction was based on syntactic analysis, perhaps the first example of the decomposition of a picture into primitives being reported by Grimsdale, et al. (1959). The syntactic approach was given additional impetus as a result of the work of Kirsch (1964) and Narasimham (1964, 1969), both of whom presented formal grammars for picture-processing purposes. An application of syntactic methods to the problem of automatic chromosome analysis was reported by Ledley (1964), who was able to use the boundary-description approach exclusively. Shaw (1969, 1970) developed an extensive "picture description language," a fragment of which we have presented as the method of standardized attachment points. Grenander (1969) analyzed abstractly the mathematics underlying the mechanism for transforming ideal, or noiseless, figures into real ones. Pfaltz and Rosenfeld (1969) have defined *web grammars* in an attempt to find a natural generalization of syntactic methods to two dimensions. Evans (1970) was especially interested in inferring from a set of scenes a grammar that can produce them. Winston (1970) exploited relational graphs in a study aimed at deducing abstract models of objects from a set of scenes. Two good surveys of syntactic methods in scene analysis were written by Miller and Shaw (1968) and by Fu and Swain (1971). Feldman and Gries (1968) provide probably the best entry into the extensive literature on syntactic analysis and parsing; Earley (1970) describes a particularly efficient parsing algorithm.

The use of three-dimensional models in scene analysis, perhaps in retrospect a straightforward approach, was not reported until the influential paper by Roberts (1965). Duda and Hart (1970) used partial three-dimensional models to direct the scene analyses performed by a mobile robot. Barrow and Popplestone (1971) stored model information in the form of relational graphs describing pictures of objects, rather than the objects themselves. Model-matching methods often require the solution of the hidden-line problem—the problem of determining which portions of a three-dimensional object are visible in a given projection. Algorithms for the solution of this problem have been described by Warnock (1968), Loutrel (1970), and Bouknight (1970).

The apparent simplicity of polyhedral objects has attracted the attention of a number of workers. Huffman (1971) was primarily interested in characterizing the properties of pictures of real trihedral solids in order to determine whether or not a picture shows an impossible, or nonsense, object; our line-labelling procedure is based directly on his work. An alternative procedure is given by Clowes (1971). The simple heuristic rules we discussed for grouping picture regions into objects were invented by Guzmán (1968); he elaborated these simple methods to a high degree, and produced an algorithm capable of analyzing idealized pictures complicated enough to give at least momentary pause to a human. Brice and Fennema (1970) incorporated a simple version of these rules in a program using regions as a basic data type throughout a complete scene analysis. The determination of three-dimensional structure by augmented monocular information was explored by Falk (1970), who developed the dual graph method for analyzing the amount of additional information required. An unpublished report by Horn (1968) discusses the use of focussing data to determine depth information.

The reader has likely noticed by now that several of the methods discussed in this chapter ultimately involve some kind of combinatorial search. Parsing is essentially a search process; the line-labelling procedure involves a tree search; and, although we have not made the point explicitly, the dual graph method of analyzing the degrees of freedom in the three-dimensional structure of a trihedral solid also involves a search process. Combinatorial search problems of this sort occur frequently in the field of artificial intelligence and general methods for their efficient solution have been investigated. An excellent introduction to this class of methods is provided in the text by Nilsson (1971).

REFERENCES

1. Barrow, H. G. and R. J. Popplestone, "Relational Descriptions in Picture Processing," in *Machine Intelligence* 6, pp. 377–396, B. Meltzer and D. Michie, eds. (American Elsevier Publishing Co., New York, 1971).

2. Bouknight, W. J., "A Procedure for Generation of Three-Dimensional Half-toned Computer Graphics Presentations," *Comm. ACM*, **13**, 527–536 (September 1970).

3. Brice, C. R. and C. L. Fennema, "Scene Analysis Using Regions," *Artificial Intelligence*, **1**, No. 3, 205–226 (Fall 1970).

4. Clowes, M. B., "On Seeing Things," *Artificial Intelligence*, **2**, No. 1, pp. 79–116 (Spring 1971).

5. Duda, R. O. and P. E. Hart, "Experiments in Scene Analysis," *Proc. First Natl. Symp. Industrial Robots*, pp. 119–130 (April 1970).

6. Earley, J., "An Efficient Context-Free Parsing Algorithm," *Comm. ACM*, **13**, 94–102 (February 1970).

7. Evans, T. G., "Grammatical Inference Techniques in Pattern Analysis," in *Software Engineering*, Vol. 2, pp. 183–202, J. T. Tou, ed. (Academic Press, New York, 1971).

8. Falk, G., "Computer Interpretation of Imperfect Line Data as a Three-Dimensional Scene," Stanford Artificial Intelligence Project, Memo AIM-132, Computer Science Department, Stanford University, Stanford, Calif. (August 1970).

9. Feldman, J. and D. Gries, "Translator Writing Systems," *Comm. ACM*, **11**, 77–113 (February 1968).

10. Fu, K. S. and P. H. Swain, "On Syntactic Pattern Recognition," in *Software Engineering*, Vol. 2, pp. 155–182, J. T. Tou, ed. (Academic Press, New York, 1971).

11. Grenander, U., "Foundations of Pattern Analysis," *Quarterly of Applied Math.*, **27**, 2–55 (April 1969).

12. Grimsdale, R. L., "Automatic Pattern Recognition—New Morphological System Using a Digital Computer," *Wireless World*, **65**, 499–501 (November 1959).

13. Guzmán, A., "Decomposition of a Visual Scene into Three-Dimensional Bodies," *Proc. FJCC*, **33**, 291–304 (1968).

14. Horn, B., "Focusing," Artificial Intelligence Memo No. 160, Project MAC, Massachusetts Institute of Technology, Cambridge, Massachusetts (May 1968).

15. Huffman, D. A., "Impossible Objects as Nonsense Sentences," in *Machine Intelligence 6*, pp. 295–323, B. Meltzer and D. Michie, eds. (American Elsevier Publishing Co., New York 1971).

16. Kirsch, R. A., "Computer Interpretation of English Text and Picture Patterns," *IEEE Trans. Elec. Comp.*, **EC-13**, 363–376 (August 1964).

17. Ledley, R. S., "High-Speed Automatic Analysis of Biomedical Pictures," *Science*, **146**, 216–223 (October 9, 1964).

18. Loutrel, P. P., "A Solution to the Hidden-Line Problem for Computer-Drawn Polyhedra," *IEEE Trans. Comp.*, **C-19**, 205–213 (March 1970).

19. Miller, W. F. and A. C. Shaw, "Linguistic Methods in Picture Processing—A Survey," *Proc. FJCC*, pp. 279–290 (December 1968).

20. Narasimhan, R., "Labelling Schemata and Syntactic Description of Pictures," *Information and Control*, **7**, 151–179 (June 1964).

21. Narasimham, R., "On the Description, Generation, and Recognition of Classes of Pictures," in *Automatic Interpretation and Classification of Images*, pp. 1–42, A. Grasselli, ed. (Academic Press, New York, 1969).

22. Nilsson, N. J., *Problem-Solving Methods in Artificial Intelligence* (McGraw-Hill, New York, 1971).

23. Pfaltz, J. L. and A. Rosenfeld, "Web Grammars," *Proc. Int. Joint Conf. on Art. Int.*, pp. 609–619, D. E. Walker and L. M. Norton, eds. (May 1969).

24. Roberts, L. G., "Machine Perception of Three-Dimensional Solids," in *Optical and Electro-Optical Information Processing*, pp. 159–197, J. T. Tippet, et al., eds. (MIT Press, Cambridge, Mass., 1965).

25. Shaw, A. C., "A Formal Picture Description Scheme as a Basis for Picture Processing Systems," *Information and Control*, **14**, 9–52 (1969).

26. Shaw, Alan C., "Parsing of Graph-Representable Pictures," *J. ACM*, **17**, 453–481 (July 1970).

27. Warnock, J. E., "A Hidden-Line Algorithm for Halftone Picture Representation," Technical Report 4-5, Department of Computer Science, University of Utah, Salt Lake City, Utah (May 1968).

28. Winston, P., "Learning Structural Descriptions from Examples," Technical Report MAC TR-76, Project MAC, Massachusetts Institute of Technology, Cambridge, (September 1970).

PROBLEMS

1. Show by constructing a parsing tree that aabba is not a sentence from the language of the grammar discussed in Section 12.2.

2. Using the approach based on standardized attachment points, construct a grammar whose language includes at least three different line drawings of a cube.

3. Devise a rule for deciding whether two arbitrary non-overlapping figures are in a left/right relation. The rule should produce decisions in harmony with human preferences and should not, for example, be so simple as to require one object being entirely to the left of the other for the relation to be satisfied. Devise another rule for deciding whether the figures are in an above/below relation. Are the rules identical except for a 90° change in orientation?

4. Design an algorithm for deciding from a picture whether two polyhedra are in a supporting/supported-by relation.

5. Find a 4 × 4 matrix S that scales each component of a three-dimensional vector v by an arbitrary amount. (We assume v is first converted to its homogeneous form $\tilde{v}$ and that $S\tilde{v}$ is converted back to ordinary coordinates.) Show how S can be used to enable a single model of a cube to serve as a model of an arbitrary rectangular parallelepiped.

6. Derive Eqs. 1 and 2, the solution to the least-mean-square model-matching problem.

7. Specify in outline form an algorithm for solving the hidden-line problem. Can the algorithm be substantially simplified if it is to be applied only to pictures of polyhedra? to pictures of rectangular solids?

8.   Sketch some trihedral solids to illustrate all the vertex types in the catalog of Figure 12.9. Label each vertex with its catalog type, and label each line with a plus, minus, or appropriately oriented arrow.

9.   Construct a search tree for each of the solids sketched in the preceding problem. Specify a good heuristic rule for deciding the order in which the vertices are to be examined.

10.   Why can there not be a Type 2, 4, 6, or 8 vertex?

11.   Sketch a scene showing at least four polyhedral objects, and that contains at least one "X" type vertex and at least one pair of matching "T" vertices. Group the regions of the scene into objects using the heuristic method described in the chapter. (Use either Rule 1 or Rule 1' as you choose.)

12.   Sketch a scene showing polyhedral objects for which the heuristic rules discussed in the chapter implausibly group the regions into objects. Suggest modifications and additions to the rules to improve their performance. You should consider modifying both the rules for placing links between regions and the rules for grouping regions together.

13.   Draw the dual graph for the polyhedron of Figure 12.10d and analyze its mergeability. (Assume that the figure shows a single polyhedron.)

14.   Sketch a trihedral solid containing at least one "hole." Analyze its mergeability. Construct the search tree needed to label the vertices of the solid and note whether there exists more than one consistent interpretation.

15.   How, if at all, can the dual graph interpretation be extended to polyhedra of degree greater than three?

AUTHOR INDEX

Abend, K., 37, 78, 123
Abramson, N., 76
Agmon, S., 181
Agrawala, A. K., 8, 249
Ahuja, D. V., 403
Aizerman, M. A., 181, 182
Albrecht, R., 36
Allais, D. C., 77
Alt, F. L., 374
Anderson, E., 218
Anderson, T. W., 36, 37, 49, 180
Andrews, D. R., 250
Andrews, H. C., 322, 323
Aoki, M., 77
Arkedev, A. G., 122
Aseltine, J. A., 322
Atrubin, A. J., 250
Attneave, F., 339, 373
Augustson, J. G., 251

Bahadur, R. R., 37, 123, 180
Bailey, D. E., 249, 252
Ball, G. H., 249, 250, 251, 252, 374
Barnea, D. I., 294
Barrow, H. G., 462
Barus, C., 122
Bashkirov, O. A., 181
Beisner, H. M., 77
Blackwell, D., 36
Blaydon, C. C., 123, 180, 182
Bledsoe, W. W., 423
Block, H. D., 180
Blum, H., 374
Blum, M., 373
Bolshev, L. N., 249

Bongard, M. M., 8
Bonner, R. E., 251
Bouknight, W. J., 403, 463
Bracewell, R. N., 322
Braverman, D., 76
Braverman, E. M., 122, 181
Brice, C. R., 294, 463
Brill, E. L., 364, 374
Bringham, E. O., 323
Brodatz, P., 294
Brown, D. T., 123
Bryan, J. G., 123
Butz, A. R., 180

Cacoullos, T., 122
Calabi, L., 374
Calvert, T. W., 251
Carmone, F. J., 251
Casey, R. G., 250
Chandrasekaran, B., 77, 78
Chaplin, W. G., 182
Charnes, A., 181
Chen, C. H., 77
Cheng, G. C., 293
Chernoff, H., 36
Chien, Y. T., 77
Chow, C. K., 36, 37, 123
Chu, J. T., 36
Chueh, J. C., 36
Clemens, J. K., 294, 374
Clowes, M. B., 463
Cooley, J. W., 323
Coons, S. A., 403
Cooper, D. B., 249
Cooper, P. W., 37, 248, 249

Coraluppi, G., 249
Cornsweet, T. N., 293
Costello, J. P., 249
Courant, R., 174
Cover, T. M., 77, 122, 248
Coxeter, H. S. M., 402

Daly, R. F., 249
Dammann, J. E., 252
Dantzig, G. B., 181
Day, N. E., 249
Dinneen, G. P., 294
Dinstein, I., 251
Doetsch, G., 248
Dorofeyuk, A. A., 249
Doyle, W., 294
Duda, R. O., 180, 373, 462
Dynkin, E. B., 77

Earley, J., 462
Eden, M., 293
Edie, J. L., 122
Efron, B., 180
Ehrich, R. W., 37
Eldredge, K. R., 182
El'Bur, R. E., 423
Evans, T. G., 462

Falk, G., 463
Feder, J., 373
Feldman, J., 462
Feller, W., 43, 226
Fennema, C. L., 285, 287, 294, 463
Ferguson, T. S., 36
Fischer, G. L., Jr., 293
Fischler, M. A., 373
Fisher, R. A., 36, 76, 77, 123,
    179, 218
Fisz, M., 121
Fix, E., 121, 122
Fleiss, J. L., 250
Forgey, E. W., 218
Forsen, G. E., 294
Fossum, H., 180
Fralick, S. C., 122, 249
Freeman, H., 373
Friedman, H. P., 250

Fu, K. S., 37, 77, 182, 462
Fukunaga, K., 78, 250

Garder, L., 373
Gass, S. I., 181
Gentleman, W. M., 323
Ghosh, S. K., 402
Gibbons, J. D., 121
Gibson, J. J., 294
Girschick, M. A., 36
Glass, J. M., 373
Glicksman, A. M., 181
Golay, M. J. E., 293
Goodman, J. W., 300, 322
Gose, E. E., 8
Gower, J. C., 250
Graham, C. H., 293
Grasselli, A., 293
Graustein, W. C., 402, 423
Gray, S. B., 373
Greanias, E. C., 294, 373
Green, D. M., 37, 252
Green, P. E., 251
Gregory, R. L., 293, 403
Grenander, U., 462
Gries, D., 462
Griffith, A. K., 294
Grimsdale, R. L., 462
Grinold, R. C., 181
Groner, G. F., 181
Guiho, G., 293
Guzmán, A., 294, 463

Hall, D. J., 250, 251, 252
Hancock, J. C., 249
Haralick, R. M., 251, 294
Harley, T. J., Jr., 32, 37, 77, 78, 123
Hart, P. E., 122, 373, 403, 423, 462
Hartigan, J. A., 251
Hartnett, W. E., 374
Hasselblad, V., 249
Hawkins, J. K., 8, 180
Hellman, M. E., 122
Hewitt, C., 373
Highleyman, W. H., 75, 78, 179, 294
Hilbert, D., 174
Hillborn, C. G., 249

Ho, Y. C., 8, 181, 182
Hodes, L., 373
Hodges, J. L., 121, 122
Hodges, R., 423
Hoel, P. G., 76
Hoff, M. E., 181
Holcomb, R. L., 122
Holmes, W. S., 324
Horn, B., 463
Hough, P. V. C., 373
Hu, K. C., 250
Hu, M. K., 374
Huang, T. S., 8, 293
Hubel, D. H., 294
Huffman, D. A., 463
Hughes, G. F., 72, 77, 78

Ingram, M., 294
Ito, T., 123

Jacobs, I. M., 324
Jaynes, E. T., 76
Johnson, S. C., 251
Jones, J. W., 37
Jones, K. L., 250
Julesz, B., 403

Kamphoefner, F. J., 182
Kanal, L. N., 37, 77, 78, 123,
    293, 294
Kashyap, R. L., 123, 181
Kautz, W. H., 250
Kazmierczak, H., 37
Keehn, D. G., 76
Kelly, G. L., 251, 294
Kelly, M. D., 295
Kendall, M. G., 374
Kesler, C., 176, 182
Kessell, D. L., 78
King, B. F., 252
Kirsch, R. A., 462
Koford, J. S., 181
Kolers, P. A., 8, 293
Koontz, W. L. G., 250
Kronmal, R. A., 122
Kruskal, J. B., 251
Kudryavtsev, V. N., 423

Kuhns, J. L., 251
Kullback, S., 123

Lachenbruch, P. A., 78
Lainiotis, D. G., 36, 77, 249
Lance, G. N., 250, 260
Leadbetter, M. R., 122
Ledley, R. S., 293, 295, 462
Lee, R. C. T., 37
Lehmann, E. L., 77
Lendaris, G. G., 252, 324
Levadi, V. S., 182
Levin, S. A., 180
Levine, M. D., 8, 373
Lewis, P. M., II, 123, 252
Ling, R. F., 249, 251
Liu, C. N., 123
Loftsgaarden, D. O., 122
Loutrel, P. P., 403, 463
Luce, R. D., 36

MacQueen, J., 250
Mangasarian, O. L., 180, 181
Marill, T., 37, 252
Mason, S. J., 294, 374
Mattson, R. L., 123, 181, 252
Mays, C. H., 181
McCulloch, W. S., 180
Medgyessy, P., 248
Meisel, W. S., 122, 252
Mickey, M. R., 78
Miller, R. G., 252
Miller, W. F., 462
Minker, J., 251
Minnick, R. C., 181
Minsky, M., 8, 37, 180, 346, 373
Mitra, S. K., 181
Monds, F. C., 249
Montanari, U., 360, 373, 374
Moran, P. A. P., 374
Morgenstern, O., 36
Morrow, R. E., 323
Moses, L. E., 36
Motzkin, T. S., 181
Muchnik, I. B., 181
Munson, J. H., 294, 373, 374
Murthy, V. K., 122

Nagy, G., 8, 250
Narasimhan, R., 462
Nathan, R., 323
Neyman, J., 36, 76
Nienow, W. C., 252
Nilsson, N. J., 8, 36, 37, 180,
    182, 463
Novikoff, A. B. J., 180, 374

Oppenheim, A. V., 323
Ore, O., 233

Papert, S., 180, 346, 373
Papoulis, A., 322, 324
Park, S. K., 36
Parzen, E., 89, 121
Patrick, E. A., 249, 252
Patterson, J. D., 181
Pearson, E. S., 36
Pearson, K., 248
Pease, M. C., 323
Peterson, D. W., 123
Pfaltz, J. L., 374, 462
Pingle, K. K., 295
Pirenne, M. H., 403
Pitts, W., 180
Pólya, G., 374
Poppelbaum, W. J., 323
Popplestone, R. J., 462
Preston, K., 294
Prim, R. C., 250

Quesenberry, C. P., 122

Raiffa, H., 36
Randall, N. C., 77, 294
Rao, C. R., 181
Rastrigin, L. A., 423
Raviv, J., 37
Richardson, M. W., 251
Ridgway, W. C., 180
Riseman, E. M., 37
Roberts, L. G., 182, 294, 403, 462
Rosenblatt, F., 180
Rosenblatt, M., 121
Rosenfeld, A., 8, 293, 294, 323, 374
Roskies, R. Z., 374

Ross, G. J. S., 250
Rozonoer, L. I., 181
Rubin, J., 250

Sakrison, D. J., 324
Sammon, J. W., Jr., 244, 245, 251, 252
Sande, G., 323
Savage, L. J., 76
Schoenberg, I. J., 181
Schreiber, W. F., 8
Schumpert, J. M., 182
Scott, R. W., 122
Sebestyen, G. S., 122, 250
Selfridge, O. G., 180
Selzer, R. H., 323
Shaw, A. C., 462
Shepard, R. N., 251
Silverman, H. F., 294
Simon, J. C., 293
Singleton, R. C., 180, 250, 323
Sklansky, J., 374
Slagle, J. R., 37
Smith, F. W., 181, 182
Sneath, P. H. A., 249, 250
Sobel, I., 403
Sokal, R. R., 249, 250
Specht, D. F., 122
Spragins, J. D., 77, 248, 249
Stanat, D. F., 248
Stanley, G. L., 252, 324
Steinbuch, K., 37, 182
Steppe, J. A., 374
Stevens, M. E., 8
Stevens, S. S., 250
Swain, P. H., 462
Szegö, G., 374

Tarter, M. E., 122
Tatsuoka, M. M., 123
Teicher, H., 248
Tepping, B., 251
Thomas, J. B., 121
Thorndike, R. L., 250
Thurston, M., 294
Tiedeman, D. V., 123
Tippett, J. T., 293, 323
Tretiak, O. J., 8

Tryon, R. C., 249, 252
Tsypkin, Ya., Z.,123, 182
Tukey, J. W., 323

Uhr, L., 293

Vander Lugt, A., 323
von Neumann, J., 36

Wagner, T. J., 122
Wald, A., 36, 37
Warnock, J. E., 403, 463
Wasan, M. T., 182
Watanabe, M. S. or S., 8, 250, 293
Watson, G. S., 122
Wee, W. G., 182
Wendt, P. H., 182
Werner, W., 36
Widrow, B., 181
Wilde, D. G., 182

Wilks, S. S., 76, 120, 372
Williams, W. T., 250, 260
Winder, R. O., 37, 180
Winston, P., 462
Wishart, D., 218, 250, 251
Wolfe, J. H., 249, 251
Womack, B. F., 181
Wong, E., 374
Wozencraft, J. M., 324

Yakowitz, S. J., 248, 249
Yarbus, A. L., 294
Yau, S. S., 182
Young, T. Y., 249
Yurans, V., 423

Zahn, C. T., 239, 251, 295,
    373, 374
Zubin, J., 250

SUBJECT INDEX

Abstraction. *See* Classifier design

Action, 13-15

Adaline, 180. *See also* Linear discriminant functions

Adaptive classifiers, 180

Adaptive learning. *See* Descent procedures

Agglomerative hierarchical clustering, 229, 230-237

Alpha perceptron. *See* Perceptron

Analytic descriptions of shape, 362-366
  characteristic function, 362
  intrinsic function, 362-364
  moment approximation, 364-366

Anharmonic ratio. *See* Cross ratio

Applications, 8

Area-to-perimeter ratio. *See* Thinness ratio

Artificial intelligence, 1, 8

Artificial variables, 167, 168

Aspect ratio, 351

Attribute detector. *See* Feature extractor

Attributes, 216. *See also* Features

Autocorrelation function, 319

Averaging, 271-276. *See also* Smoothing

Averaging window, 271

Bahadur-Lazarsfeld expansion, 111-113

Bandlimited picture function, 302

Bandwidth, 303

Bartlett's identity, 78, 82

Base (of projective coordinates), 411

Baseline vector, 399

Basic feasible solution, 167

Bayes
  classifier, 17-20, 22
  decision rule, 13, 15, 32, 35
  decision theory, 10-15, 31-32, 36
  rate, 16, 98
  risk, 15
  rule, 11, 14, 32, 50, 57

Bayesian learning, 45, 54, 57-59, 203-211

Bays, 353

Bernoulli distribution, 32-33, 37, 83

Bernstein's inequality, 304

Bertrand paradox, 367, 370

Bhattacharrya coefficient, 40

Binary features. *See* Discrete features

Binary pictures, 274

Border following, 290-293

Boundary spur, 286

Brightness quantization, 265

Camera calibration, 392-393, 438-439

Camera model, 380-381

Capacity of a hyperplane, 69-70

Cauchy distribution, 39

Cauchy-Schwarz inequality, 280

Central moments, 366

Central projection, 380-381

Chain cross-correlation, 340

Chain-encoding, 339-341

Change of coordinates, 386-392

Character recognition, 37

Characteristic function, 122, 362
Characteristics. *See* Features
Characterization. *See* Feature
    extractor
Chow expansion, 113-114
Chromaticity coordinates, 288
Classification, 4, 15-17
Classifier, 2, 4
    adaptive, 180
    Bayes, 17-20, 22
    design, 44, 130
    minimum distance, 26
Clumping, 229
Clustering, 190, 211-248
    and dimensionality reduction,
        246-248
    by iterative optimization, 225-228
    criterion functions for, 217-225
    graph theoretic, 237-239
    hierarchical, 228-237
        agglomerative, 229, 230-237
        divisive, 230, 250
    similarity measures for, 213-217
    validity of, 239-243
Cohesion, 250
Color, 288-289
Communication theory, 27, 77, 122
Complete-linkage clustering, 233
Component densities, 190
Compound
    conditional risk, 35
    decision theory, 34, 37
    risk, 34
Condensed nearest-neighbor rule, 122
Conjugate density, 77
Conjugate vanishing points. *See*
        Vanishing points
Connected
    region, 285
    region, elementary, 285
    4 versus 8, 284
Context, 34, 37
Contour following, 290-293
Convergence
    Bayesian, 58, 77
    modes of, 89
    of density estimates, 87

Convergence (*continued*)
    k_n-nearest neighbor, 95
    Parzen, 89-91
    of descent procedures, 140
    fixed-increment, 142-145,
        146-147
    Ho-Kashyap, 161-166
    relaxation, 148-149
    stochastic approximation, 158-159
    Widrow-Hoff, 156
    of nearest neighbor, 99-100, 122
Convex
    decision regions, 133
    deficiency, 352
    hull, 186, 352, 370
    set, 352
Convolution
    defined, 305
    theorem, 307
Coordinates, transformation of,
        386-392
Correction rule. *See* Descent
        procedures
Correlation
    coefficient, 112, 247
    cross-correlation, 279
        chain, 340
        normalized, 280
        of random pictures, 319
    detector, 27, 77
    matrix, 247
Correspondence
    perspective, 408
    projective, 408
Correspondence problem, 399
Covariance, 23
    matrix, 23
    sample, 49
Criterion function
    clustering, 217-225
    expected squared error, 157
    Fisher, 116, 120
    perceptron, 141, 168
    relaxation, 147
    sum of squared error, 151
Cross-correlation. *See* Correlation
Cross ratio, 407-411

Cross spectral density, 319
Curse of dimensionality, 95, 136
Curvature, 363

Data matrix, 247
Decision
  boundaries, 18, 133
  function, 15
  regions, 18, 133
  rule, 11, 14-15
    deterministic, 15
    randomized, 15, 41, 98
    see also Bayes decision rule
  surfaces, 18, 133
  theory, 10-15, 31-32, 36-37
    compound, 34, 37
    sequential, 37
    sequential compound, 34
  trees, 37
Decision-directed methods,
    210-211, 249
Degrees of freedom, 136. See also
    Dimensionality
Dendrogram, 229
Density, spectral, 319. See also
    Probability density
Dependence tree, 114
Depth
  error, 400-402
  perception, 398-401
Descent procedures, 140-141, 170-171
  Fixed increment, 143
  Ho-Kashyap, 160, 163
  LMS, 156
  relaxation, 148
  stochastic approximation, 158, 159
  variable increment, 146
  Widrow-Hoff, 156
Descriptive scene analysis, 425-462
  a priori information, 425
  of polyhedra, 441-462
  syntactic methods, 426-433
  using relational graphs, 434-435
  using three-dimensional models,
    436-441
Descriptive techniques. See
    Syntactic techniques

Design samples, 44
Detector, attribute. See Feature
    extractor
Deterministic decision rule, 15
Diameter
  limitation, 346
  limited perceptron, see Diameter
    limitation
  of a cluster, 235
  path, 238
Dichotomy, 69
Differentiation of picture, 268, 272
Dimensionality
  curse of, 95, 136
  problems of, 66-73, 95, 136
  reduction of, 115, 118, 123,
    246-248, 252
Direct perspective transformation.
    See Perspective transformation
Directed graph, 434-435, 454
Discrete features, 31-34, 37, 42, 83,
    108-114, 123
Discriminant analysis, 85,
    114-121, 123
  multiple, 118-121, 123
Discriminant functions, 17-20,
    24-31, 33, 36, 37, 116, 123,
    130-179
  Fisher, 114-118, 123
  generalized, 135
  linear, 26, 29, 33, 37, 131-134
  minimum-risk, 37
  polynomial, 37, 106, 135
  quadratic, 30, 37, 42, 134
Distance. See Metric
Divisive hierarchical clustering,
    230, 250
Dogmatism, 55, 82
Double ratio. See Cross ratio
Dual graph, 459
Dual problem, 169, 181

Edge detection, 268-272, 281,
    290-293
Eigenvector line fitting, 332-335
Elementary connected region. See
    Connected

End-point line fitting, 338-339
Enhancement of pictures, 267-272,
     308-318
Entropy, 76, 123
Error correction procedures, 150
Error rate. *See* Probability of error
Estimation of
  a posteriori probabilities, 97-98
  a priori probabilities, 80
  density functions, 44-45, 85-97
  error rate, 73-76, 78, 122
  parameters. *See* Parameter
     estimation
  pictures, 318-322
Euler formula, 344, 347
Euler number, 343, 347, 348
Exponential family, 62-66
Eye movements, 294
Eye tracking, 294

Factor analysis, 246
Factorization theorem, 60-61
Falk's method, 456-463
Fast Fourier transform, 323. *See
     also* Fourier transform
Feasible solution, 167
Feature
  extractor, 2, 4, 5
  ordering. *See* Dimensionality
     reduction
  selection. *See* Dimensionality
     reduction
  space, 3, 18, 20
  vector, 3
Features, 2
Figure, 274, 327
Figure-ground problem, 327
Filtering theory, 77, 122. *See
     also* Spatial filtering
Fisher's linear discriminant, 114-118,
     123, 152-154, 181
Fixed-increment rule, 143, 150,
     176-177, 180
Fourier transform
  defined, 298
  existence of, 299
  inverse, 299
  zero-phase locus of, 300

Fractional-correction rule. *See*
     Relaxation rule
Furthest-neighbor clustering, 233

Game theory, 15, 36
Game trees, 38
Gauss-Markov theorem, 372
Gaussian density. *See* Normal
     density
Generalization, 3, 68-70, 75-76, 77
Generalized discriminant function, 135
Generalized inverse. *See* Pseudo-
     inverse
Gimbal center, 387
Global coordinates, 387
Goal-directed search, 433
Gradient
  descent. *See* Descent procedures
  of picture function, 268
  operators, 267-272
  vector, 47
Grammar, 427-429. *See also*
     Syntactic descriptions
Grand mean vector. *See* Total mean
     vector
Grand scatter matrix. *See* Total
     scatter matrix
Graph
  directed, 434-435, 454
  dual, 459
Graph-theoretic clustering, 237-239
Gray level, 264-266
Grid
  hexagonal, 266, 293-294
  picture, 265
  quadruled, 264, 265
Ground, 274
Grouping regions into objects,
     449-456
  link, 452
  merging rules, 454
  vertex types, 450-452, 454
Guzmán's method, 449-456

H method, 74, 78
Head-to-tail concatenation, 431-432
Hexagonal grid, 266, 293-294
Hidden line problem, 441, 463

Hierarchical clustering, 228-237
  agglomerative, 229, 230-239
  divisive, 230, 250
High-curvature segmentation, 339
Hill climbing, 195. *See also* Descent
  procedures
Histogram, 2, 249
Ho-Kashyap procedures, 159-166
Holdout method, 74, 78
Homeomorphism, 342
Homogeneous coordinates, 382-386
Horizon line, 395-397
Hough transformation, 373. *See also*
  Point-to-curve-transformation
Huffman labelling, 442-449
Hypercube, 33, 88
Hyperellipsoid, 24, 27, 30
Hyperhyperboloid, 30, 135
Hyperparaboloid, 30
Hyperplane, 27, 29, 30, 33, 69-70,
  131-132
Hyperquadrics, 30, 134
Hypersphere, 24, 26, 30, 135
Hypothesis testing. *See* Decision
  theory
Hysteresis smoothing, 354-356

Identifiability, 58, 191, 205
Impossible object, 463
Impulse response, 308
Inconsistent
  edges, 238
  inequalities. *See* Nonseparability
Independent binary features, 32-34,
  37, 83, 108
Integral geometry, 367-372
Inter-lens line, 414-418
  geometry of, 415
  quasi-projective properties of,
    414-416
Intrinsic equation, 339-340, 362
Intrinsic function, expansion of,
  362-364
Invariance, 342, 369
Invariant clustering criteria, 223-225
Invariant descriptions, 342
Inverse Fourier transform. *See* Fourier
  transform

Inverse perspective transformation.
  See Perspective transformation
Irregularities of a figure, 352-356
  by convexity properties, 352-353
  by local extrema of boundary,
    353-356
Isodata, 201, 210, 228, 250
Items. *See* Features

k-means clustering procedure, 250
k-mergeable graph, 460
k-nearest neighbor rule, 103-105
k_n-nearest-neighbor estimation, 95-98
Kalman filtering, 77
Karhunen-Loéve expansion, 246
Kernel density, 61-62
Kesler's construction, 174-176, 182
Kiefer-Wolfowitz procedure, 159

Label, 45, 100, 157, 189, 210
Lakes, 353
Language of a grammar, 427
Laplacian, 297
Learning
  adaptive. *See* Descent procedures
  Bayesian, 45, 54, 57-59, 203-211
  supervised, 45
  the mean, 52-57
  unsupervised, 45, 189
  without a teacher, 248
Leaving one out, 75-76, 78
Lernmatrix, 182
Light intensity, 264
Likelihood, 13, 16, 46
  principle, 45-47, 198
  ratio, 16
Line description, 327-341
Line drawing. *See* Outline drawing
Line fitting, 328-339
  by clustering, 335-337
  by eigenvectors, 332-335
  minimum-squared-error, 328-331
Line following, 290-293
Line segmentation, 337-339
Line semantics, 442-449
  convex and concave edges, 442-443
  hole search example, 447-449

Line semantics (*continued*)
  octants, 443-444
  possible representations, 444-445
  vertex types, 443-449
Linear dichotomies, 69
Linear discriminant functions, 26,
    29, 33, 37, 131-134
Linear inequalities, 138, 151, 166,
    180-181
Linear-input element, 180. *See also*
    Linear discriminant functions
Linear machine, 27, 133, 174-179,
    182, 345-348
Linear operator, 309
Linear programming, 166-167, 181
Linear properties of pictures, 345-348
Linear separability, 69-70, 138,
    149-151, 159-161, 163,
    167-169, 180
  multicategory, 175, 186
Linear spatial filtering. *See* Spatial
    filtering
Linearity theorem, 326
LMS rule, 156
Logarithmic quantization, 265
Logical averaging, 275, 276
Loss, 13-16
  function or matrix, 13
    symmetrical, 16
    zero-one, 16

Machine perception, 1
Mahalanobis distance, 24
Majority gate, 180. *See also* Linear
    discriminant functions
Man-machine systems, 251-252
Margin, 138
  vector, 151-152, 153, 154
Markov dependence, 37, 113, 123
Matrix picture, 266-267
Maximum algorithm for clustering, 233
Maximum likelihood
  estimation, 45-47, 192-193
  singular solutions, 198
Mean, 22
  vector, 23
  sample, 48

Mean (*continued*)
  learning the, 52-57
Mean square estimation of pictures,
    318-322
Mean square line fit, 328-331
Measurements. *See* Features
Medial axis transformation. *See*
    Skeleton of a figure
Merging, 286-287, 450-455, 459-462
Metric
  absolute-value, 349
  city-block, 349
  defined, 237, 349
  Euclidean, 26, 349
  Mahalanobis, 24
  Manhatten. *See* City-block
  maximum-value, 349
  properties of pictures, 348-352
  unit-distance loci of, 349
Minimal spanning tree, 233, 238, 250
Minimum algorithm for clustering, 233
Minimum-distance classifier, 26, 29
Minimum-risk linear discriminant,
    37, 130
Minimum-squared-error
  approximation to Bayes
    discriminant, 154-155, 157,
    179, 181-182
  criterion function, 151, 179, 217
  descent procedures, 156, 158-159,
    160
  line fitting, 328-331
Minimum variance
  clustering, 218
  criteria, 219
  partitions, 218
Mixing parameters, 190
Mixture
  decomposition, 205
  density, 190
Mode, 85, 212
Model matching, 436-441
Models. *See* Model-Matching
Modes of convergence, 89
Moment generating function, 365
Moments, approximation by, 364-366
  central, 366

Moments (*continued*)
generating function, 366
Monocular determination of three-
dimensional structure, 456-462
dual graph, 459
merging nodes, 460-461
plane equations, 458-459
Moving average, 274
MSE. *See* Minimum squared error
Multicategory classification, 13-15,
17-20, 21, 97-98, 132-134,
174-179, 182
Multidimensional scaling,
243-246, 251
Multimodal, 85, 212
Multiple discriminant analysis,
118-121, 123
Multivariate Bernoulli distribution,
32-33, 37, 83
Multivariate normal density, 23-24

Natural conjugate density, 77
Nearest-mean classifier, 182
Nearest-neighbor clustering, 233
Nearest-neighbor rule, 98-103
condensed, 122
Nearest-vertex quantization. *See*
Chain-encoding
Networks of threshold elements, 180
Neural networks, 180
Newton's algorithm, 141
Nonlinear
discriminant functions. *See*
Discriminant functions
mapping, 244
Nonparametric techniques, 85-121
Nonseparability, 149-151, 163, 168
Norm
Euclidean, 26
Mahalanobis, 24
See also Metric
Normal density
discriminant functions for, 24-31
learning the mean of, 52-57
multivariate, 23-24
sufficient statistics for, 62-64
univariate, 22

Normal mixtures, 193-202
Normal parametrization, 335-336, 369
Normalized color coordinates, 288
Normalized cross-correlation, 280
Numerical taxonomy, 249

Object reconstruction, 421-422
Objective function, 166
Optical axis, 381
Optimal linear discriminant, 37,
130, 180
Order limitation, 346
Order-limited perceptron. *See* Order
limitation
Orthogonal projection approximation,
418-421
Outline drawing, 267-268
Overrelaxation, 148

Pairwise linear separability, 186
Parameter estimation, 45
Bayesian, 49-51
Bernoulli distribution, 81
exponential density, 80
maximum likelihood, 45-47
normal density, 47-49
normal mixture, 193-202
uniform density, 80
Parameter space, 325
Parameters, mixing, 190
Parity function, 187
Parseval's theorem, 326
Parsing, 428-430, 462
ambiguity, 428
one vs. two dimensions, 429
top down, 432
tree, 428-430
Partition, for clustering, 217
Parzen windows (or estimators),
88-95
Pattern recognition
applications, 8
classification model, 4-5
descriptive or linguistic model, 5-6
Pencil of lines, 407
Perception
animal, 1, 8

Perception (*continued*)
  depth, 398-401
  machine, 1, 436
Perceptron, 144, 180. *See also*
  Linear machine
Perceptron Convergence Theorem,
  143-145, 180
Perimeter, 370-371
Perimeter-squared-to-area ratio,
  350-351
Perspective correspondence, 408
Perspective distortion, 394-396
Perspective transformation, 379-404
  applications of, 392-401
  direct, 381-382
  in homogeneous coordinates,
    382-386
  inverse, 382, 384-386
  vanishing points of, 394-398
  with two reference frames, 386-392
φ-functions, 135
Photogrammetry, 402
Picture coding, 8, 293
Picture description language, 431-433,
  462. *See also* Syntactic
  descriptions
Picture energy, 279
Picture enhancement, 8, 267-272,
  293, 308-318
Picture function
  binary, 274
  defined, 264
  digital, 266
  gradient, 268
Picture grammars. *See* Syntactic
  descriptions
Piecewise-linear
  classifiers, 180
  machine, 187
Point
  image, 380
  object, 380
Point spread function, 308
Point-to-curve transformation,
  335-337
Polygonal network, 344
Polyhedra, analysis of, 441-463

Polyhedra (*continued*)
  See also Grouping regions into
    objects; Line semantics;
    Monocular determination of
    three-dimensional structure
Polynomial discriminant functions,
  37, 106, 135
Pooled data, 116
Potential functions, 172-174, 181-182
Power spectral density, 319
Prairie fire transformation. *See*
  Skeleton of a figure
Predicate functions, 345
Preprocessing, 267-295
Preprocessor. *See* Feature extractor
Primitive recognizer, 432. *See also*
  Syntactic descriptions
Primitive symbol, 427
Principal components, 214, 246
Principal ray. *See* Optical axis
Probability
  a posteriori, 11, 14
  a priori, 10, 14
  density, 11, 14, 44, 85
  of error, 12-13, 16, 20-22, 36, 40,
    43, 70-76, 78, 98-105
Problem-average error rate, 72
Productions, 427. *See also* Syntactic
  descriptions
Projecting ray, 381
Projection, central, 380
Projective coordinates, 411-414
Projective correspondence, 408
Projective invariants, 405-422
Property filter. *See* Feature extractor
Properties. *See* Features
Prototype, 26
Pseudoinverse, 152, 181, 329, 330

Quadratic discriminant function, 30,
  37, 42, 134
Quadruled grid, 264, 265
Quantization. *See* Sampling
Quantization error, 400-402
Quasi-projective, 414, 416, 422
Quench function, 358
Quench points, 357

Rademacher-Walsh
  expansion, 108-111
  polynomials, 109
Random line, 368, 369
Randomized decision rule, 15,
  41, 98
Range error, 400-402
Range of points, 407
Rayleigh quotient, 117
Receptor. *See* Feature extractor
Recursive Bayes procedures, 58, 204
Reduction of dimensionality, 115,
  118, 123, 246-248, 252
Reference frames for perspective
  transformations
  global, 387
  picture, 381
  stereo, 398
Reference triangle, 411
Reflectance, 326
Region analysis, 284-290
Region grouping, 449-456
Region merging, 286-287
Regression functions, 159
Regularization, 272-276
Reinforcement learning, 144
Reject, 14, 16, 36, 40
  rate, 36
Relational graphs, 434-435. *See
  also* Syntactic descriptions
Relaxation rule, 148, 181
Representation of a picture,
  264-267
Reproducing density, 53, 56, 77
Retina, 367
Risk, 14-15
Roberts cross operator, 268-272
Robbins-Monro procedure, 159
Rules of a grammar, 427-428

Sample, 44
  covariance matrix, 49
  mean, 48
  moments, 248, 249
  risk, 130
  size, 44, 67
  variance, 116

Samples, 2, 7, 22, 24, 44, 74
  design or training, 44
  test, 74
Sampling
  defined, 265
  theorem, 302-305
Scaling, multidimensional,
  243-246, 251
Scatter, 116
  between-class, 117
  within-class, 116
Scatter matrix, 116-119
  between-class, 117, 119
  total, 118
  within-class, 117, 118
Scatter diagram, 4, 25
Search, 38, 428-429, 447-448, 463.
  See also Descent procedures
Second view problem, 406
Segmentation
  of line, 337-339
  of picture, 327-328
Sentence of a grammar, 427-428
Separating vector, 138
Sequential decision theory, 37
Sequential compound decision
  theory, 34
Series expansions
  Bahadur-Lazarsfeld, 111-113
  Chow, 113-114
  discriminant functions, 157
  Fourier, 363-364
  Parzen, 106
  potential functions, 173
  power, 365
  Rademacher-Walsh, 108-111
Shannon sampling theorem,
  302-304, 313
Shape description, 341-374
  informativeness of, 342
  methods of, 342-374
Sharpening, 268-272
Shifting theorem, 306
Signal detection, 27
Similarity
  graph, 238
  matrix, 238

Similarity (*continued*)
  measures, 213-217
  See also Template matching
Simplex algorithm, 166
Sinc function, 303-305
Single-linkage clustering, 233
Skeletal pair, 358
Skeleton of a figure, 356-363
  of polygonal figure, 360-361
  quench function, 358
  quench points, 357
  skeletal pair, 358
Sliding average, 274
Slope intrinsic function, 363
Smoothing, 272-276, 354-356
Solution
  machine, 176
  region, 138
  vector, 138
Spanning tree
  definition, 233
  minimal, 233, 238, 250
Spatial differentiation, 268-272
Spatial filtering, 308-318
  defined, 308
  examples of, 310-318
  high-pass, 309
  low-pass, 309
Spatial frequency, 299
Spatial period, 301
Spectral density, 319
State-conditional probability
    density, 11, 14
State of nature, 10
Steepest descent. *See* Descent
    procedures
Step size, 140, 148, 164
Stereo. *See* Stereoscopic perception
Stereogram, 403
Stereophotogrammetry, 402
Stereopsis. *See* Stereoscopic perception
Stereoscopic perception, 398-403
Stick figure. *See* Skeleton of a figure
Stochastic approximation, 159,
    181-182, 249
Stretching theorem, 326
Substitution error, 40
Sufficient statistics, 59-62
Sum-of-squared error
  criterion function, 151, 179,
    217, 222

Sum-of-squared error (*continued*)
  descent procedures, 156,
    158-159, 160
Supervised learning, 45, 58
Support hypothesis, 393-394
Switching theory, 180
Symbols of a grammar, 427-428
Symmetrical loss function, 16
Syntactic descriptions, 426-433
  by boundary description, 430

Tanimoto coefficient, 216
Template, 26
Template matching, 26, 276-284
Template matching and convolution,
    305-308
Terminal symbol, 427
Ternary features, 31-32, 37, 42
Test samples, 74
Testing data. *See* Test samples
Testing on the training data, 74
Texture, 294
Thinness ratio, 350-351
Thinning. *See* Skeleton of a figure
Three-dimensional models. *See*
    Model matching
Threshold elements, 180. *See also*
    Linear discriminant functions
Threshold logic unit, 180. *See also*
    Linear discriminant functions
Threshold weight, 33, 131
Tie breaking, 15, 18, 20, 131, 133
Top-down parsing, 432-433
Topological mapping, 342
Topological property
  defined, 342
  examples of, 343-345
Total linear separability, 186
Total mean vector, 118
Total scatter matrix, 118
Tracking, 189
Training data. *See* Design samples
Training procedures. *See* Descent
    procedures
Training sequence, 142-143
Transducer, 4
Transfer function, 308

Tree
  dependence, 114
  game, 38
  search, 38, 428-429, 447-448, 463
Triangle inequality, 350
Triangulation equation, 400
Trichromatic coefficients, 288
Trihedral solids, 442-449

U Method, 75-76, 78
Ultrametric inequality, 237
Underrelaxation, 148
Unimodal, 66, 85, 134
Unit point, 411
Unsupervised learning, 45, 189
  Bayesian, 203-211

Vanishing points
  conjugate, 397-398
  horizon, 396-398

Vanishing points (*continued*)
  vertical, 394-396
Variable-increment rule, 146
Variance, 22
Vertex types of trihedral solids,
    443-449

Web grammars, 462
Weight space, 138
Weight vector, 131, 135
Widrow-Hoff procedure, 155-156, 181
Wiener filtering, 181, 318-322
Window
  function, 88
  width, 89

Zero-one loss function, 16
Zero-phase locus, 300